Microsoft® Virtualization

SECRETS

Microsoft® Virtualization
SECRETS

DO WHAT YOU NEVER THOUGHT POSSIBLE WITH MICROSOFT VIRTUALIZATION

John Savill

WILEY

John Wiley & Sons, Inc.

EXECUTIVE EDITOR: Carol Long
PROJECT EDITOR: Katherine Burt
TECHNICAL EDITOR: Michael Soul
PRODUCTION EDITOR: Daniel Scribner
COPY EDITOR: Luann Rouff
EDITORIAL MANAGER: Mary Beth Wakefield
FREELANCER EDITORIAL MANAGER: Rosemarie Graham
ASSOCIATE DIRECTOR OF MARKETING: David Mayhew
MARKETING MANAGER: Ashley Zurcher
BUSINESS MANAGER: Amy Knies
PRODUCTION MANAGER: Tim Tate
VICE PRESIDENT AND EXECUTIVE GROUP PUBLISHER: Richard Swadley
VICE PRESIDENT AND EXECUTIVE PUBLISHER: Neil Edde
ASSOCIATE PUBLISHER: Jim Minatel
PROJECT COORDINATOR, COVER: Katie Crocker
COMPOSITORS: Kate Kaminski, Craig Woods, Happenstance Type-O-Rama
PROOFREADER: Louise Watson, Word One
INDEXER: John Sleeva
COVER IMAGE: Ryan Sneed
COVER DESIGNER: © Chad Baker / Lifesize / Getty Images

Microsoft® Virtualization Secrets

Published by
John Wiley & Sons, Inc.
10475 Crosspoint Boulevard
Indianapolis, IN 46256
www.wiley.com

Copyright © 2012 by John Savill

Published by John Wiley & Sons, Inc., Indianapolis, Indiana

Published simultaneously in Canada

ISBN: 978-1-118-29316-4
ISBN: 9781118293171 (ebk)
ISBN: 9781118421352 (ebk)
ISBN: 9781118433799 (ebk)

Manufactured in the United States of America

10 9 8 7 6 5 4 3 2 1

This book is dedicated to my wife, Julie, and my children, Abigail, Benjamin, and Kevin. I love you all.

About the Author

 John Savill is a technical specialist who focuses on Microsoft core infrastructure technologies, including Windows, Hyper-V, System Center, and anything that does something cool. He has been working with Microsoft technologies for 18 years and is the creator of the highly popular NTFAQ.COM website and a senior contributing editor for *Windows IT Pro* magazine. He has written four previous books covering Windows and advanced Active Directory architecture. When he is not writing books, he creates technology videos, many of which are available on the web, and regularly presents online and at industry leading events.

Outside of technology John enjoys teaching Krav Maga, spending time with his family, and participating in any kind of event that involves running in mud, crawling under electrified barbed wire, and generally pushing limits. He is also planning to write a computer game that he's had in his head for a few years. Maybe after the next book. . . .

Acknowledgments

I have had the opportunity to work with very smart and talented people who are very generous in sharing their knowledge and have made this book possible. Even those who may not have directly worked with me on this book have still helped build my knowledge to make this possible, so thank you to everyone who has ever taken time to help me learn.

First, I want to thank Carol Long and the acquisitions team at Wiley Publishing for believing in this book and guiding me to the Secrets series, which has been the perfect fit for my vision of this book. Thank you to the project editors, initially Christy Parrish and then Katherine Burt, who really brought the whole book together and helped me through all the tough spots. Luann Rouff did an amazing job on the copy editing of the book, and my appreciation also goes to the technical editor, Michael Soul.

Writing this type of book is always a balancing act between making sure no assumptions are made about existing knowledge and providing useful information that can really provide value. A good friend and colleague, Rahul Jain, did a fantastic job of reading every chapter and providing feedback on its logical flow and clarity in explaining the technologies. A great deal of the material includes new technologies, and I consulted and got help from many people to ensure both the accuracy of the content and its relevance to organizations in order to provide real-world guidance. With that in mind, I want to thank the following people who directly helped on this book through technical input or support; A. J. Smith, Adam Carter, Ben Armstrong, David Trupkin, Doug Thompson, Elden Christensen, Eric Han, Gavriella Schuster, Jeff Woolsey, Jocelyn Berrendonner, Karri Alexion-Tiernan, Kevin Holman, Kiran Bangalore, Lane Sorgen, Mark Kornegay, Mark Russinovich, Michael Leworthy, Mike Schutz, Paul Kimbel, Robert Youngjohns, Ross Ortega, See-Mong Tan, Snesha Foss, Sophia Salim, Steve Silverberg, and Stuart Johnston.

I also want to thank my wife, Julie. I started writing this book when our twins were only nine months old, and I was only able to write because Julie pretty much single-handedly looked after the entire family and gave her endless support. Thank you. Thank you to my children, Abigail, Benjamin, and Kevin, for bringing so much happiness to my life and making everything I do worthwhile. I'm sorry Daddy spends so much time at the computer.

Finally, thank you to the readers of this book, my previous works, and hopefully future works. Without you I wouldn't be given these opportunities to share what I've learned over the years. With that, on with the show. . . .

Contents at a Glance

Contents

Introduction

Welcome to the far-reaching world of Microsoft virtualization technologies. With so many virtualization technologies available today, it can be difficult to understand and compare them all in order to determine what offers the most benefits. However, it's important to understand that finding a good solution is not a question of which technology should be used, but how different technologies can best work together. This book provides a foundation for understanding all the major Microsoft virtualization technologies, including how they work and when and how to get the most from them in your environment.

This book also provides guidance on creating the best architecture for your entire organization—both on the desktop and in the datacenter—using the current virtualization technologies that are available and with a view of what is coming in the near future. In addition, I cover many tips and best practices I have learned over many years of consulting and implementing the technologies at companies both large and small.

I have tried hard to keep each chapter self-contained so that you can focus on a specific virtualization technology that you may be considering without having to read all the other chapters; however, reading the entire book will give you the most complete understanding of the technologies. By the end of the book, I would be surprised if you didn't see a use for all the types of virtualization and how they could help, which is a reflection of the sheer number of challenges organizations face today and how rapidly technologies are being created to meet those challenges.

What You'll Learn from This Book

Microsoft Virtualization Secrets will not only introduce you to all the types of virtualization and the Microsoft-specific solutions, but also guide you through how to use the technologies—both in isolation and in partnership with other technologies. Many of the chapters deal with a specific virtualization solution, but some chapters serve to bring together many different technologies to help you architect the best and most complete solution for your organization. After reading this book you will understand all the types of virtualization that are available and when to use them.

Where possible, download the products, install them, and experiment with configurations. I have found that nothing helps me learn a technology as well as just installing it, finding problems, and solving them. This book will help you with all three of those stages, and present best practices related to architecture.

Who Should Read This Book

This book is aimed at anyone who needs to use, design, implement, or justify the use of Microsoft solutions, as well as those who are just curious about the various technologies. For those people who are highly experienced in a specific virtualization technology, I still hope to offer unique tips and information on new features in the latest generation of technology, in addition to providing information on virtualization technologies that you may not have experience with.

How This Book Is Structured

With so many virtualization technologies covered in this book, most chapters focus on a specific virtualization technology, providing an overview of the type of virtualization, the Microsoft solution, and key information on its design and implementation. There are a few exceptions.

Chapter 1 provides a high-level overview of the entire virtualization stack. Chapter 2 provides details about the Windows client, which is a key target for most of the virtualization technologies and is used for the management of Windows Server 2012, so a good understanding will benefit you in most aspects of your virtual endeavors. Chapters 3 through 7 focus on technologies that relate to the client desktop or desktop experience. Chapters 8 through 11 focus on server virtualization and management technologies, including implementing a virtual desktop infrastructure. Chapter 12 looks at technologies to enable connectivity to enterprise systems from remote clients, and Chapter 13 brings everything together, explaining how to architect the right desktop and datacenter solution using all the technologies discussed. Chapter 14 covers the Microsoft public cloud offerings, which are services that can be used by organizations without any on-premise infrastructure. Finally, Chapter 15 provides a bonus set of content that covers the major new features of Windows Server 2012 that are not directly virtualization-related but provide great capabilities to improve your environment.

Features and Icons Used in This Book

The following features and icons are used in this book to help draw your attention to some of the most important and useful information, including valuable tips, insights, and advice that can help you unlock the secrets of Microsoft virtualization.

> ► Watch for margin notes like this one that highlight some key piece of information or discuss some poorly documented or hard-to-find technique or approach.

SIDEBARS

Sidebars like this one feature additional information about topics related to the nearby text.

TIP The Tip icon indicates a helpful trick or technique.

NOTE The Note icon points out or expands on items of importance or interest.

CROSSREF The Cross-Reference icon points to chapters where additional information can be found.

WARNING The Warning icon warns you about possible negative side effects or precautions you should take before making a change.

CHAPTER 1

Understanding Virtualization

IN THIS CHAPTER

- ▶ Understanding the different categories of virtualization
- ▶ Understanding early session virtualization
- ▶ Changing focus in corporate datacenters
- ▶ Examining the cloud and cloud services
- ▶ Meeting the needs of mobile workers
- ▶ Using virtualization to address today's challenges

Virtualization is a somewhat broad term that has gotten even broader over time as users, organizations, and the technologies they use have evolved. This chapter starts at the beginning of the virtualization journey—my journey anyway. I share my personal experiences to not only highlight the dramatic changes that have taken place, but also to demonstrate the many features of today's technology that still echo the ideas from over three decades ago. I discuss the ways the technology has grown, shifted, and made its way into nearly every organization and almost every aspect of our digital world. This chapter describes the main trends in virtualization over the past 30 years and provides a good background for the rest of the book, which dives deeper into Microsoft's products in each area of virtualization.

WHAT IS VIRTUALIZATION?

It's important to start by defining the term virtualization. It means different things to different people when thinking about computing. For the purposes of this book, you can think of *virtualization* as breaking the bonds between different aspects of the computing environment, abstracting a certain feature or functionality from other parts. This abstraction and breaking of tight bonds provides great flexibility in system design and enables many of the current capabilities that are the focus of IT and this book.

Over time the "virtualization" tag was applied to many other technologies that had been around for some time, because they also broke those tight couplings and abstracted concepts. Over the next few pages I introduce the major types of virtualization, which are explored in detail throughout the book.

When the word *virtualization* is used without qualification, many people think of machine virtualization, which is the easiest to understand. With machine virtualization the abstraction occurs between the operating system and the hardware via a hypervisor. The *hypervisor* divides up the physical resources of the server, such as processor and memory, into *virtual machines*. These virtual (synthetic) machines have virtual hard disks, network adapters, and other system resources independent of the physical hardware. This means you can typically move a virtual machine fairly easily between different physical machines, as long as they use the same hypervisor. If you try to move a system drive from one physical computer and put it in another, it's unlikely to work well, if at all, because of differences in hardware configuration. In addition, by creating several virtual machines on one physical computer, you can run multiple instances of the operating system on a single server, gaining higher utilization as hardware is consolidated, an idea I expand on later in this chapter.

In *presentation virtualization*, also called *session virtualization*, the user session is abstracted from the local device and runs on a remote server with connections from multiple users. Only the screen updates are sent to each user's local device, while all the computing actually takes place on the remote server. In other words, the presentation of the session is abstracted from where the actual computation takes place. Terminal Services and Citrix XenApp are examples of session virtualization solutions.

Technologies that enable users to use many different devices but with the same data and environment configuration have also gained the virtualization stamp. Users of previous Windows operating systems will know of Folder Redirection and Roaming Profiles. Later in the book you learn about other, more advanced technologies, particularly for the virtualization of user settings. Here again, the user data and settings are abstracted from the underlying computer on which they are typically hard linked into the operating system.

One relatively new technology is *application virtualization*, which enables the decoupling of an application from the operating system. Traditionally, in order to use an application it typically had to be installed on the user's computer, adding components onto the operating system, updating settings containers, and writing data to the local disk. With application virtualization, application code is downloaded from a remote site and runs locally on a computer without requiring any changes to the operating system, so it has zero footprint. Note that this differs from session virtualization in that the computation is on the user's device, not on the remote server. The Microsoft application virtualization technology is App-V.

Throughout this book I describe the technologies that implement these and other categories of virtualization, including how they are used, when they should be used, and how to build the right IT infrastructure using the appropriate virtualization technology. To provide some context, the following section looks at changes in the industry over the last 30 years as I've experienced them. This is my personal view, not a traditional textbook history of computers, which you can find elsewhere. It reflects what I've seen in my years of consulting and acting as a trusted advisor for enterprises of various sizes and stripes, and provides some insight into what lies ahead.

The Dawn of Virtualization

When I was about eight years old I got my first computer, a ZX Spectrum with 48KB of memory, which connected to the television, and software (games mostly) on cassette tapes. I still have it on the wall in my office as a reminder of where my love of computers started. I played around with the BASIC language that came with it, creating epic code such as the following and feeling very proud when I would enter it on machines in stores:

```
10 PRINT "JOHN IS GREAT"
20 GOTO 10
```

▶ For American readers, the ZX Spectrum was similar to a Commodore 64. There were many schoolyard arguments over which one was better.

Over time I moved on to a Dragon 32 that used cartridges, a new Spectrum with 128KB of memory and built-in tape drive, called the ZX Spectrum 128 +2, and a Commodore Amiga. Then one day my dad brought home a PC—I think it was a 286 with MS-DOS and 5.25-inch disks. When the technology evolved to the point of 386 computers and acquired larger internal disks, we upgraded our machine, installed Windows, and I started to play around with the C programming language and later with Java.

When I was 18 years old I got a job at Logica, which at the time was a large systems house. I worked in the Financial Services division and was hired as the VAX/VMS systems administrator. I had no clue what that meant, but they said they would train me and pay some of my tuition while I worked toward my degree. The position sounded amazingly advanced, and as I walked into my first day at work I had visions of futuristic computing devices that would make my home machine look like junk. Unfortunately, instead of some mind-controlled holographic projection computer, I saw an old-looking console screen with green text on it.

As I would later find out, this device (a VT220) was just a dumb terminal that allowed keyboard entry to be sent to a VAX/VMS box that sat in the basement (where I spent a large part of my early "systems management" duties changing backup tapes and collecting printouts to deliver to developers on the team). The VAX/VMS server had all the actual computing power, memory, storage, and network connectivity. Everyone in the team shared the servers and had their own session on this shared computer, which used time-sharing of the computer's resources, specifically the CPU. This was very different from my experience up to that point, whereby all the computation was performed on my actual device. For these large enterprise applications, however, it made sense to share the computer power; so there were multiple instances of our application running on the same physical server, each in its own space. There were other mainframe devices from IBM that actually created virtual environments that could act as separate environments. Windows for Workgroups–based PCs were introduced into our team and certain types of workload, such as document creation, moved to the GUI-based Windows device.

▶ Session virtualization!

▶ machine virtualization!

I discovered Windows NT by accident one day when I pressed Ctrl+Alt+Del to reboot and a security dialog was displayed instead. This Windows NT box was used as a file server for data the team created on the machines. I started investigating and learning the Windows NT technology, which is when I started the SavillTech.com and ntfaq.com sites to answer frequently asked questions (FAQs).

In order to really test and investigate how to perform certain actions, I needed multiple Windows NT servers for different types of server role and workload, and I needed a client. As a result, at one point I had six desktop computers running either NT Server or NT Workstation, one for each role. I found some nice drive bays that enabled me to switch out the hard drives easily, so I could change the particular operating system a physical box was running. Sometimes I could dual boot (choose between two operating systems on one disk), but these servers were not very active. Most of the time the CPU was barely used, the memory wasn't doing that much, and the busiest part was the disk.

▶ This one physical box for each operating system instance is exactly the same process that organizations followed until a few years ago.

A turning point in my long relationship with computers occurred while watching a presenter at a conference. The exact date and conference elude me, but I'm pretty sure it was in fact a Microsoft conference, which strikes me as ironic now. I remember little from the session, but one thing stuck in my mind and eclipsed everything else that day. The presenter had one machine on which he was running multiple operating systems simultaneously. This was a foreign concept to me, and I remember getting very excited about the possibility of actually fitting my legs under my crowded desk. My electricity bill might become more manageable as well! I strained my eyes to see what was being used and discovered it was VMware Workstation.

The next day at work I researched this machine virtualization technology that enabled one physical box to be carved into multiple virtual environments. The VMware Workstation software was installed on top of Windows as an application that allocated resources from the actual Windows installation on the physical box. Known as a *type 2 hypervisor*, this solution did not directly sit on the actual hardware but rather worked through another operating system. The downside of this type 2 hypervisor was some performance loss, as all operations had to run through the host operating system, but for my testing purposes it worked great. At home, I quickly went from six boxes to three boxes, as shown in Figure 1-1. I then increased the actual number of operating system instances, as they were now easy to create and didn't cost me anything extra because I had capacity on my machines. I just threw in some extra memory (which I could afford by selling the other three computers) when I needed more VMs, as typically that was my limiting factor.

By this time I had changed jobs and now worked at Deutsche Bank, where I was an architect creating a new middleware system for connecting the various financial systems in the U.K. The system transformed messages from the native format of each system to a common generic format to enable easy routing. This was implemented on Sun Solaris using an Oracle database, and I wrote the front end in Java. Interestingly, there were some Windows-based financial applications that accessed huge amounts of data, which created heavy data traffic to and from the database. Such applications performed very poorly if they were run on a desktop outside of the datacenter because of network constraints. To solve this, the applications ran on a Windows Server that was located in the datacenter with Terminal Services installed. Users accessed an application from either a Remote Desktop Protocol (RDP) client on the Windows Server itself or a special thin RDP client. This was essentially a glorified version of my first VT220, but the green text was replaced with a color bitmap display; keyboard-only input was now keyboard and mouse; and communication was now via IP (Internet Protocol) instead of LAT (Local Area Transport). Nevertheless, it was exactly the same concept: a dumb client with all the computation performed on

▶ Remember that only the screen updates (bitmaps) and the keyboard/mouse commands are sent over the link, so the actual data never travels across the network.

a server that was shared by many users. It was back to session virtualization! I was also informed that because the data was sensitive, this session virtualization was preferred, because running the application in the datacenter meant the data never left there.

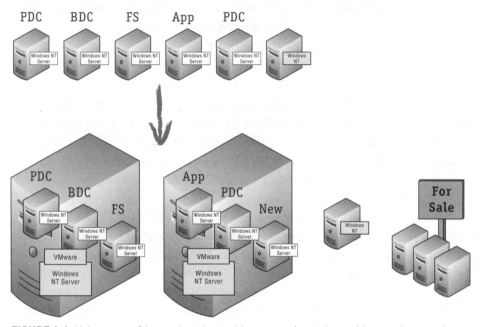

FIGURE 1-1: Using a type 2 hypervisor, I was able to move from six machines to three, and increased the number of operating system instances I could run. Note that the two PDCs reflect a second domain.

Time passed and Microsoft purchased Connectix, which made an alternative solution to VMware Workstation, Virtual PC, giving Microsoft its own machine virtualization solution. Virtual PC has both a desktop and a server version, Virtual Server, but both offerings are still type 2 hypervisors running on top of Windows. In the meantime, VMware released ESX, which is a *type 1 hypervisor*, meaning the hypervisor runs directly on the server hardware. The performance of a virtual machine running on such a hypervisor is nearly the same as running on the physical server. I actually used this technology for a while and it was very powerful; Microsoft didn't really have anything comparable. This all changed with the release of Windows Server 2008, which included Hyper-V, a type 1 hypervisor. What we think of as Windows Server actually sits on top of the hypervisor to act as a management partition. As you will see in Chapter 8, which focuses on Hyper-V, it has gone from strength to strength—to the point that it is now considered one of the top hypervisors in the industry.

My lab still consists of three servers but they are a lot bigger. They run a mix of Windows Server 2008 R2 and Windows Server 2012 Hyper-V, and I now have around 35 virtual machines running! One change I recently made was to my e-mail. For a period of time I experimented with hosting e-mail on Exchange in my lab, but I never took the time to ensure I was backing up the data regularly or to enable new services. I've now moved over to the Office 365–hosted Exchange, Lync, and SharePoint solution, as I am also working on some other projects for which I want SharePoint and improved messaging for collaboration. Quite honestly, I didn't want to maintain an internal SharePoint solution and worry about backing up important data.

In short, I have seen dramatic change over 30 years of working and playing with computers. As much as the technology has changed, however, many features still echo the ideas that were current when I first started, such as session virtualization and consolidation of workloads.

The Evolution of the Datacenter and the Cloud

A lot of what I've described so far mirrors the evolution of corporate datacenters and IT departments around the world. This journey for many companies starts with each operating system running on its own physical box—a number of servers for the domain controllers, a number of file servers, mail servers, you get the idea. To decide which server to buy for a new application, the highest possible peak load required for that application is used. For example, a Friday night batch might be used to decide the level of hardware needed. Also considered is the future growth of the server's load over its lifetime, typically 4–6 years, meaning a company usually purchases a server that will run at about 10 percent CPU capacity and maybe use only half the amount of memory available just to cover those few peak times and future growth *if* everything goes according to plan. This can be a large financial outlay that wastes rack space and power. The bigger, more powerful servers also generate more heat, which in turn requires more cooling and power, which also translates into greater cost. Strict processes are required to deploy anything new because of the associated costs to procure the hardware.

▶ Most datacenters use large cabinets that hold a number of servers that slot in horizontally. These servers typically take up 1, 2, or 4 units of space in the rack, so the bigger the servers the more space is occupied in the rack, therefore requiring more racks.

Backups are performed nightly to tape, which is either kept in a closet or, for organizations concerned about the loss of a site, sent offsite and rotated on a regular cycle (maybe every six weeks) to enable restoration from different days in case corruption or deletion is not immediately noticed. Storage is also very expensive, so applications are carefully designed in terms of data use.

Features such as clustering became more popular because they enabled certain services and applications to be *highly available*—a service can automatically move to another server that is part of the same cluster should a server fail, ensuring the service is always available to users. The cluster solutions rely on shared storage, which can be expensive, but the high availability gained for critical services justifies the external storage solutions, which also offer other capabilities, such as higher data integrity and easy duplication and backup of data.

Some organizations need the ability to continue operations even in the event of complete site loss—for example, a flood or other natural disaster. In these scenarios, organizations opt for a second datacenter in an alternate location that can run their critical systems. These disaster recovery (DR) datacenters are typically categorized as follows:

> **Hot:** A hot site is a second location that replicates almost exactly the primary datacenter and has near real-time replicas of the data. If the primary location fails, a hot DR site is up and running quickly. This option requires complex networking and expensive technologies, so it is typically reserved for the most critical systems, such as those used by government and financial organizations.

> **Warm:** A warm site also has alternate systems available, but they do not replicate in real time; so, there may be some lag in data transfer. Manual processes are required to get up and running on a warm site, making it much slower to start performing than a hot site, but costs are typically significantly less than those of a hot site.

> **Cold:** A cold site is a location that may have some servers but they typically don't match the production site hardware. Nor does this option provide data replication or easy access to backups. It provides an alternate location, but it requires a significant setup effort before it can actually be used, meaning there is a long lag time between a failure and when the organization is up and running again. The exact time depends on number of systems, size of backups to be restored, and complexity of the environment.

For the warm and cold options, I have seen many companies leverage third-party services that effectively rent out servers and facilities in the event of a disaster, based on a retainer fee. These services enable companies to avoid maintaining a second location and complete set of servers but still give them a disaster recovery service should it be needed—at significantly lower cost than running their own non-shared DR site.

MAKING SURE YOUR DISASTER RECOVERY IS USABLE IN A DISASTER

Failing to prepare is preparing to fail.

—JOHN WOODEN, HEAD COACH OF THE UCLA BRUINS,
10-TIME NATIONAL CHAMPIONSHIP WINNERS

For all the DR options, because the operating system backups are hardware specific, DR sites must have replica hardware of the primary site (unless virtualization is used), which is hard to maintain. Keep in mind, this is a huge expense for a scenario that might never occur. In addition, if DR locations are used, it's vital to test the failover process periodically. I've worked with a number of companies that invested in DR capabilities but rarely tested them; and when they actually had to use it or finally performed a test, they realized they had forgotten to add a replica of some key workload on which everything else depended, making the DR site basically useless.

A test every six months is a good middle ground. Many organizations test by running live on the DR site for an entire week before moving back to their primary location. This requires a lot of planning and work to reverse the replication from the DR to production. Another option is to have the capability at the DR location to run all required processes in a separate test network, enabling testing of the DR systems without affecting production. Even if a third-party service is used for the DR service, it's important to ensure that a periodic test is included in the service.

As IT systems become increasingly important to organizations and the number of IT systems grows, so does the complexity and amount of work required to maintain those systems. Many companies begin to suffer from *server sprawl,* where a disproportionate number of servers are available relative to the actual resources needed, which results in huge amounts of IT administration overhead. Organizations begin to adopt technologies to help manage all the physical servers and operating system instances, but it quickly becomes apparent that these organizations are spending huge amounts of money on hardware and power for servers that are greatly underutilized.

Power is also getting a lot more expensive and people are becoming concerned about the ecological costs of growth. When it became impossible to ignore that the planet was getting a little toasty, there was a large wave of interest in being more energy efficient. Virtualization is the main enabler for more efficient datacenters that better utilize the available resources, reducing the hardware footprint and saving money and power.

Efficiency has also improved through the use of energy-saving technological advancements, such as processors that require less power. Operating systems also made a huge leap forward with the ability to turn off idle cores on multi-core processors, condensing the need for 10 physical servers into one using virtualization for the operating systems. Today, many organizations are making this move from physical server to virtual server for many of their workloads. (Up to this point I have been the Ghost of IT Past; now I'm shifting to the Ghost of IT Present.)

The move from physical to virtual is a big endeavor. Careful analysis of all the existing servers must be performed to understand their actual resource usage in terms of memory, processor, disk, and network—including average resource utilization versus peak loads, and when those peaks occur. Only then can plans be made as to where to co-locate various existing systems when virtualized onto shared physical hosts. For example, suppose you have two physical servers, one peaking on a Friday night, in terms of resource utilization, and the other peaking on Monday morning. In this case, you could place those two systems on the same virtualization host because their peaks occur at different times. That way, you only need to plan out the actual resource of the virtualization host to handle the average load of one server and one peak. This same principle applies to the entire environment, in reality. Typically 10 to 20 operating system instances will end up on a single host. Hosts can then be clustered together to enable high availability for the virtual environment and even enable the movement of virtual machines around hosts based on resource requirement changes. In other words, if a virtual machine gets very busy and is causing resource contention with other virtual machines on a host, then the virtual machine can be moved to a different host that is less utilized.

Virtualization is not without its challenges, though. Yes, your hardware is better utilized. Yes, you save money on hardware, power, and even licensing. Yes, your DR is far simpler because now the operating systems are virtualized, meaning the actual hardware does not matter because the operating systems are running inside the VM. Therefore, you can use one type of server in your datacenter and something completely different at the DR location; you just need to use the same hypervisor. Yes, you can provision new operating systems in virtual machines very quickly because you don't have to wait for a physical server to arrive, and you can create a new operating system instance by deploying a template (a prepared operating system installation ready for duplication). Yes, it can even make applications that don't natively have any kind of

▶ The Microsoft Assessment and Planning (MAP) Toolkit helps perform this analysis and even identifies the best placement of operating system instances on physical hosts when virtualized. The best news is it's free!

high availability highly available, by making the VM highly available at the hypervisor level through clustering technologies. Yes, it sounds fantastic, and machine virtualization absolutely is a huge asset to organizations or it wouldn't have been adopted so readily, but nothing is ever perfect.

One common side effect of virtualization is *virtualization sprawl,* or the uncontrolled creation of virtual machines in an organization leading to an environment that's hard to manage or audit, similar to server sprawl. Suddenly there is no direct cost correlation between new operating system instances, which are now virtual machines and not physical servers that have a purchase price. It can become easy to just create new virtual machines and not track their usage, resulting in the maintenance of operating systems that are no longer used. There are technologies to help mitigate this issue, such as charging business units based on the number of virtual machines they have or perhaps computer hours used. Another option is to assign business units a quota of virtual instances and then implement tracking to identify unused virtual environments that can be archived.

Aside from the tendency to sprawl, there is a bigger challenge: Virtualization has not helped reduce the management of the IT infrastructure; it has actually made it harder. Where previously I had 1,000 physical servers, each running one operating system and an application, I now have 1,000 virtual machines, each with its own operating system that needs all the same patching and maintenance as the operating systems on those physical boxes needed. I have not cut down on the amount of management work required. Now, I also have to manage the virtualization environment, and because I've consolidated resources, I now have to carefully track the resource utilization of processors, memory, disks, and the network to ensure that the virtual machines are sufficiently allocated on the shared infrastructure. Additionally, before I had one egg in each basket, metaphorically speaking, so if I dropped one basket I lost one egg. With virtualization, I now have a lot of eggs in each basket, so dropping a basket has huge ramifications. Therefore, extra planning is required to ensure the resiliency and availability of the virtualization host environment, including networking and storage.

Some companies have shifted to management tools that enable automation because of the huge number of operating systems their IT departments have to manage. Remember, the more you can automate a process, the easier it will be to manage and the more consistent the result will be. There are a number of great Microsoft tools to better manage an infrastructure that uses virtualization. I have listed a few of them here, and I cover them in far greater detail in Chapters 9 and 10.

▶ System Center Configuration Manager (SCCM) can easily deploy patches to thousands of servers in a staged and controlled manner. It also provides the capability to easily set maintenance windows for different groups of servers.

▶ Virtualization management solutions, such as System Center Virtual Machine Manager (SCVMM), can simplify deployment in a virtual environment through the use of templates, which enable a company to define server operating system instances without the need for human intervention—other than giving the new VM a name.

▶ System Center Orchestrator, and other tools, use run books to automate manual tasks performed on many different systems.

▶ PowerShell enables the complete management of servers and applications from a command and scripting environment and remote management on many servers simultaneously. If you have never looked at PowerShell, start now. PowerShell is very much at the heart of Windows 8.

▶ A run book is a set of defined actions for tasks performed on one or more systems, such as regular maintenance activities or exception processes.

UNDERSTANDING THE TYPES OF CLOUD AND CLOUD SERVICES

Today's organizations want the freedom to focus on the application or service rather than all the individual operating system instances running inside virtual machines. Business units and users need to be able to provision their own virtual environment, or *private cloud*, within the structure predefined by the IT group, using simple self-service portals. This shift is the next step in the IT journey—from physical to virtual and now to private cloud.

> **CROSSREF** This shift to the private cloud is covered in detail in Chapter 10.

The private cloud builds on virtualization but focuses on providing services to businesses in a highly scalable but manageable manner with infrastructure components taking care of the creation and maintenance of the underlying virtual machines and operating systems. The private cloud enables a company to focus on the service being provided, which could be a multi-tiered service consisting of numerous web servers interacting with clients, then a middleware tier performing processing, then a back-end database tier. With a private cloud, a complete instance of the entire service can be deployed with the click of a button; and the actual servicing of the environment is transparent to the operation of the service.

If certain aspects of the service are becoming highly utilized, then that tier can easily be scaled out by merely requesting additional instances of that tier; the infrastructure handles all the work of creating additional virtual machines, installing the correct code, and adding to any load balancing.

To many business users and executives, the idea of the private cloud is fantastic. To their IT departments, the private cloud is terrifying. Many of my clients have expressed concern that business users can just create their own VMs—and even worse, *many* VMs as part of a single service deployment. In other words, they fear they will be overrun. However, it's important to realize that the private cloud is a complete solution comprised of many parts. It has the capabilities to model services, deploy virtual environments and install the needed applications, and maintain them. It has an easy-to-use, self-service, end user interface that relies on templates; but it also has powerful capabilities that enable IT departments to model a cloud of resources and features to which their business users are confined and to define quotas limiting the amount of resources each group or user consumes. *Show-back* and *chargeback* capabilities can be used to track and charge (respectively) business units for what they actually use, rather than creating huge numbers of virtual environments and services. The IT department is still involved, but it does its work up front, proactively defining groups of resources as clouds and then assigning them to groups of users.

The looming private cloud is needed. Traditional virtualization enables the quick creation of a virtual environment, but it's a manual exercise for the busy IT administrator; and fulfilling a user request for a virtual machine can actually take several weeks. Users won't wait this long if there is another option (which I'm getting to). As mentioned earlier, with the private cloud the IT work is done up front, so users can create new environments using self-service interfaces in minutes; and, if needed, workflows can still be used for manager approval or other sign-off actions. So what is this other option? The public cloud.

The *public cloud* is a huge factor for nearly every organization today. It offers various services that are hosted in the provider datacenters and accessed over the Internet by an organization. This means the organization requires no infrastructure, and typically just pays for what it uses. It would be incorrect to think of the public cloud as only appropriate for business users who are unhappy with their local IT departments. The public cloud has extensive capabilities and covers multiple scenarios for which an organization's IT infrastructure is not the right solution, and many organizations will make use of both private and public clouds.

CROSSREF   Chapter 14 covers public clouds and their services in greater detail.

The following material covers the three types of public cloud service that are typical today: Infrastructure as a Service (IaaS), Platform as a Service (PaaS), and Software as a Service (SaaS):

- **IaaS:** You can think of IaaS as a virtual machine in the cloud. The provider has a virtual environment and you purchase virtual machine instances, within which you manage the operating system, the patching, the data, and the applications. An example of IaaS is Amazon's Elastic Compute Cloud (EC2), which enables an organization to run operating systems inside Amazon's virtual environment.

- **PaaS:** PaaS provides a framework on which custom applications can be run. Organizations can focus on writing the best application possible within the guidelines of the platform's capabilities; everything else is taken care of. There are no worries about patching operating systems, updating frameworks, backing up SQL databases, or configuring high availability. After providing the application, the organization pays only for the resources used. Windows Azure is the classic example of a PaaS.

- **SaaS:** SaaS offers the ultimate public cloud service in terms of lowest maintenance. It is a complete solution provided by the vendor. Organizations don't need to write or maintain anything; their only responsibility is to configure who should be allowed to use the software. A commercial example of SaaS is Hotmail, the popular online messaging service. An enterprise example is Office 365, which provides a cloud-hosted Exchange, SharePoint, and Lync service—with everything accessed over the Internet. No application or operating system management is required by the customer.

Figure 1-2 clearly highlights the differences between these three services. The shaded areas depict the management areas for which the customer is responsible. The on-premise solution is self-explanatory; the organization must manage all aspects of its own environment.

Moving to IaaS basically provides the capability to host virtual machines. As shown in Figure 1-2, the IaaS provider is responsible for networking, storage, server, and the virtualization layer; you are responsible for all aspects of the operating system within the VM, the middleware, the runtime, data, and of course the application. While it may seem like the IaaS provides the most flexibility, the trade-off is the amount of management still required; however, many organizations test the water by first using IaaS before moving on to reduce their management efforts and gain the benefits offered with PaaS and SaaS.

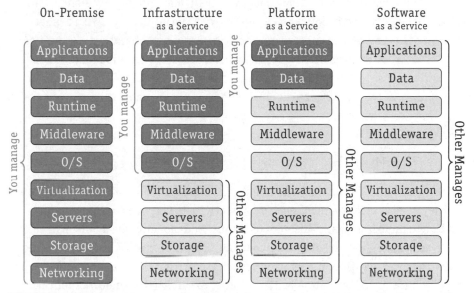

FIGURE 1-2: The nine main management areas—from the network to the application—and the parts you have to manage for each type of service.

Moving to Platform as a Service dramatically changes the amount of management your organization needs to perform. With PaaS, you only have to concern yourself with the application you manage and its data, leaving everything else to the PaaS provider. Note that although you manage the data, the provider typically still provides services to actually replicate and protect the data.

Finally, when you move to using Software as a Service you are no longer responsible for managing anything in terms of infrastructure—you just use the cloud-based software. Not every system can use SaaS, as organizations have their own custom code, but the goal for many organizations where software cannot be provided by SaaS is a combination of PaaS and IaaS; and there will always be some on-premise systems.

SHIFTING TECHNOLOGICAL PARADIGMS

Of course the emergence of the cloud wasn't driven solely by organizations needing more manageable virtualization solutions. The increasing desire of workers for flexibility in terms of where and how they perform their computing tasks has had a tremendous influence. The line between work life and personal life has blurred as

▶ Tethering a mobile device to a laptop enables the laptop to use the mobile device's data connection, thereby connecting the laptop to the Internet.

a natural consequence of the many different devices available to us now. Consider how quickly the cell phone morphed into a "smartphone," capable of handling many aspects of our busy lives, including checking e-mail, managing your calendar, linking to social media, and keeping you informed with the latest news. With a great computer at home with the latest operating system and broadband connectivity to the Internet, slate devices with Wi-Fi, and mobile devices with very fast data capabilities that can be tethered to laptops, users can work anywhere—at the office, at home, or even at the local Starbucks. Technology needs to enable this kind of flexibility that users demand.

Understanding the Needs of the Mobile Worker

▶ Notice "device," not PC! There was an earlier movement to Bring Your Own PC (BYOPC), but this has changed now to any kind of device (BYOD), including slates such as the iPad.

Just being connected is not enough for most mobile workers. In order to be productive, they need the right kind of secure connectivity to corporate resources and it must be available from many different locations. Additionally, the mobile user may need to access corporate resources using many different types of device, including some with newer or different operating systems than what they have at work, including those running iOS or Android with no ability to run native Windows applications. iPad owners, for example, want to be able to connect it to the corporate e-mail and use it at work. In the past, organizations could simply refuse to accommodate the few workers who wanted outside access; however, today it's the senior executives at organizations bringing in the new wave of slate devices and requiring the IT department to find a way to make them work. This shift in power, where consumers have the latest technologies and gradually force their workplaces to integrate them, is referred to as the *consumerization of IT*.

CROSSREF You can read more about enabling secure connections for mobile workers in Chapter 12.

What Consumerization Means to an Organization

The consumerization of IT is changing the way organizations manage their resources. In fact, instead of providing users with computers, many companies are allocating an annual computer budget for users to buy their own machines. But beyond changes in accounting, users utilizing their own devices for work presents a huge challenge from an IT perspective. Some devices may not be running corporate installations of Windows and may not even be capable of running some corporate applications. The iPad, for example, runs iOS, which is really a mobile device operating system with limited ability to run applications locally. Even when the device is capable, problems may still persist. Licensing would not work, users often don't want corporate applications installed on their devices, and many applications integrate with Active Directory, which wouldn't be present on a noncorporate device. Clearly, another solution is needed to enable corporate application and data access on these noncorporate assets.

One of the biggest concerns is security, because these devices may not have the latest anti-virus solutions or firewalls installed. A user's personal device is unlikely to have the necessary encryption to protect corporate data, so users are limited in terms of what they can store on noncorporate assets. If you look at the lack of security on the average home machine, you would likely not want to let it near your corporate network! Connectivity needs to be enabled for these mobile users while still maintaining the security and health of the corporate environment.

Users working on personal devices also present legal problems. When a corporate device is lost, the organization can often perform a remote wipe operation to delete everything. Such a solution isn't going to be very popular with a user if it means deleting baby's first steps. Policies need to be in place around using personal devices for corporate purposes. For example, such a policy could specify appropriate access to corporate e-mail on an Exchange server using a noncorporate mobile device. To enable access, the device could be required to accept the security policy set by Exchange ActiveSync, which might include requiring a PIN, and to have lockout and wipe settings.

The challenges presented by the consumerization of IT are significant and varied, but there are solutions and they require a bit of a return to our technology roots.

EMBRACING THE RETURN OF THE DUMB TERMINAL

Virtual Desktop Infrastructure (VDI)—the desktop equivalent of the cloud—and session virtualization can often provide the solution to some of the problems presented by mobile workers. VDI enables users to remotely connect to a client operating system running in a virtual environment within the corporate datacenter.

Session virtualization, on the other hand, is an often overlooked option that can be a better fit than VDI for many scenarios. While VDI provides each user with his own client operating system on a virtual machine, session virtualization provides the same user experience but provides a session on a shared server operating system. VDI is frequently seen as a cure-all for everything from poor desktop management to solving application compatibility problems. Although that isn't the case, it's still a great solution when used in the right ways.

> **CROSSREF** Chapter 11 describes the VDI in detail, and Chapter 7 covers session virtualization.

Regardless of which option you use, you can provide a Windows environment for outside users who are connected to the corporate infrastructure that can run corporate applications and access corporate data, all while running within the datacenter. The user accesses this Windows environment through remote desktop protocols using a client application that could be running on an iPad, a mobile phone, a home machine, or a laptop. The device doesn't matter because it is just serving as a dumb terminal (like my old VT220). The device displays the Windows desktop and applications, but the actual work is being done on a back-end server. Therefore, the user's device does not have to be part of the domain. It doesn't even have to be capable of running Windows applications; it just needs a client that can communicate the Windows environment in the datacenter using the remote protocol. The concerns related to data on a device are also resolved using VDI and session virtualization because no corporate data is stored locally on the client device—it's all in the datacenter with the user's session, which means there are no concerns about lost corporate data and wiping devices if a user loses his laptop.

While changes to the datacenter have been more revolutionary than evolutionary, the world of the desktop has not exactly stood still. Virtualization is also a critical aspect of the desktop today, especially in terms of meeting the new flexibility requirements governing how users want, and often need, to work, and as organizations replace older Windows versions with Windows 7 or Windows 8. The main areas of focus for the desktop relate to client virtualization, user data and settings virtualization, and application virtualization, all of which are discussed in the coming chapters, although many other types of virtualization can also come into play when architecting the best desktop infrastructure and supporting multiple client devices.

SUMMARY

The brief tour of virtualization you took in this chapter should have demonstrated that virtualization solves many problems and enables many new ways of working, but only if it is well architected and implemented. If not, it can cause more work and introduce new problems. Embracing the consumerization of IT and offering mobile users a productive environment is achieved through virtualization; there really is no other solution. Through technologies such as VDI, session virtualization, and even public cloud services, users on any device and in any connected location can have a functionally rich environment within which to work. I often find myself on a device that is acting as nothing more than a much better version of my VT220 dumb terminal, and if I were the average user, I would likely have no idea that the operating system environment within which I was working wasn't running on the device in my hand.

The rest of this book walks you through the major types of virtualization that are available, how they can be used, and how they *should* be used. Chapter 13 covers the different types of on-premise virtualization, putting them into context so you can architect the right infrastructure for your organization. Ultimately, most organizations will have a mix of on-premise solutions and public cloud solutions in order to make the best use of all the available technologies—and at a price they can afford.

CHAPTER 2

Understanding Windows 7 and 8 Client OS Key Technologies

IN THIS CHAPTER

▶ The evolution of Windows and its design goals

▶ Major interface changes from Windows 1 through Windows 8

▶ File system and registry virtualization

▶ User Access Control

▶ Booting from VHD

▶ Navigating Windows 8

▶ Windows To Go

Many of the features of Windows 7 and Windows 8 have evolved from features that can be traced back to the very first versions of Windows; so in order to understand the capabilities of a system, it can be helpful to look at how that system has evolved and why. This chapter takes a backward look at the first versions of Windows and how it has evolved to where we are today, including shifts in hardware and usage scenarios. I do not cover every feature and interim release of Windows, which would constitute a book in itself, but rather the key aspects that have shaped Windows and affect how we interact with it and virtualization-related features. Windows 8 reflects a major change in working with Windows, as you will see in this chapter. Reading this entire chapter is not essential to understanding virtualization, but, given that almost all the types of virtualization involve the Windows desktop and with Windows Server 2012 the management is done from a Windows 8 client, a good understanding of Windows interaction will definitely help in your day-to-day activities.

TRACING THE EVOLUTION OF THE WINDOWS CLIENT OPERATING SYSTEM

▶ Windows was not using multithreading but enabled the execution of multiple applications simultaneously using cooperative multitasking, where each application releases control of the CPU to allow others to run, hopefully!

Windows 1.0, introduced in late 1985, provided a very basic graphical interface that ran on top of the MS-DOS operating system, a hybrid approach that continued until Microsoft released its first 32-bit family of operating systems: Windows NT. Windows 1.0 provided the capability to run multiple applications at the same time and introduced many of the application window elements still used today, such as scroll bars, icons, dialog boxes, and even drop-down menus. It also included applications such as Paint, Calculator, and Notepad that are still present today, with some updates. Windows 2.0, which arrived two years later, took advantage of newer graphical technologies, 286 and 386 (Windows 2.1) processors, and more memory. Windows could now be overlapped and the control panel was introduced. Figure 2-1 shows the original Windows 2.0 interface with a few in-box applications running. Notice the icons at the bottom; this model returns to Windows much later in the form of the taskbar.

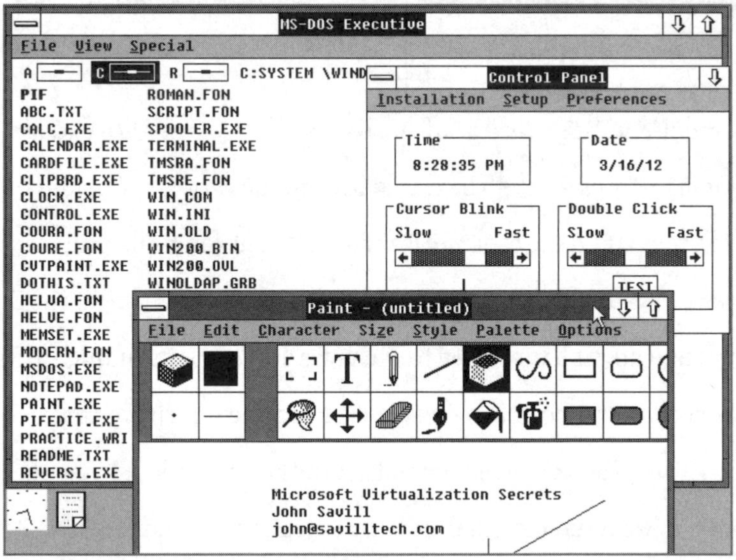

FIGURE 2-1: This screenshot of the Windows 2.0 interface shows some key elements that are still present in Windows today, such as the buttons to close, minimize, and maximize windows.

▶ The shell is the primary user interface for an operating system; it includes the key elements with which the user interacts.

The big leap for Windows was version 3, introduced in 1990, and its subsequent 3.1, 3.11, and Windows for Workgroups editions. The graphical interface was updated significantly with a new Program Manager that formed the shell of Windows. This version fully exploited the 386 processor's memory management capabilities, providing support for more memory and much higher-performing applications. In addition to Program Manager, both File Manager and Print Manager made their first appearance, along with an enhanced control panel. For many people, however, it was the inclusion of games such as Minesweeper, Hearts, and Solitaire that finally gave them a reason to love Windows. Windows for Workgroups was rapidly adopted by organizations because it enabled multiple machines to work collaboratively and share information, and those machines could access resources in domain networks. Figure 2-2 shows the Windows 3 interface, here with the Program Manager, Paintbrush, and Minesweeper application windows open and the File Manager and Control Panel minimized. This interface remained until Windows 95 for all the Windows operating systems.

▶ Prior to Windows NT, the Ctrl + Alt + Del sequence was used to force a reboot of a PC, but its usage changed to bringing up task lists and other functions.

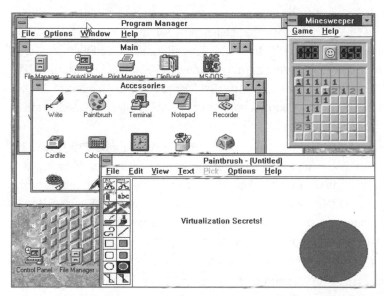

▶ The NT in Windows NT stands for New Technology, although many people noted that the acronym WNT is one letter up from VMS, the operating system David Cutler worked on at Digital before developing NT at Microsoft.

FIGURE 2-2: The Windows 3 shell was the foundation for Windows until the major Windows 95 update

While Windows 3 and Windows for Workgroups 3 were doing well with consumers in both the home environment and the enterprise, Microsoft released version 3.1 of Windows NT in 1993. Windows NT 3.1 was actually the first version of NT but its numbering reflected (matched) the associated operating systems. Windows NT was Microsoft's first true 32-bit operating system, unlike the Windows 3 16-bit counterparts, which meant it could take advantage of higher-end hardware and much more memory, making it ideal for more advanced desktop and server scenarios. Windows NT enabled preemptive multitasking, which gives the operating system more control over the slicing of compute time between applications. Windows NT also provided the Program Manager shell, File Manager, and Print Manager, and had many other elements in

▶ Windows 3.1 did offer some limited 32-bit support through Win32s, which was a subset of the Win32 application programming interface (API) available in Windows NT.

common with earlier versions; but rather than run on MS-DOS, it ran directly on a new NT kernel.

Additionally, whereas Windows 3 and Windows for Workgroups ran only on the x86 platforms, Windows NT 3.1 was available for x86-32, DEC Alpha, and MIPS. This capability to run on many different architectures was enabled through its *Hardware Abstraction Layer (HAL)*, which enabled a generic set of instructions to be converted to architecture-specific instructions. Windows NT also had its own file system, NTFS, which supported long filenames and file system security and audit capabilities. All versions of Windows NT had at least one desktop and one server version. Windows NT 3.5 was released in 1994, followed by version 3.51 in 1995, and both still used the Program Manager shell and could be used on the same architectures, with the addition of PowerPC for NT 3.51. The major enhancements in 3.5 and 3.51 were full TCP/IP implementation, support for VFAT, which enabled long filenames on a File Allocation Table (FAT) partition, plus support for running Windows 95 32-bit applications in NT 3.51. Windows NT 3.1 introduced the Ctrl + Alt + Del *Secure Attention Sequence (SAS)*, which ensured the security of the logon screen by only displaying it and asking for credentials after the SAS was pressed.

The first 10 years of Windows included a huge increase in the number of applications available for it, and, with improved hardware, more applications could be run at the same time. However, the Program Manager shell was not designed to handle a large number of applications installed and running on the operating system. Program Manager became very cumbersome because it occupied a significant amount of the screen's real estate. That meant if many applications were running, they had to be minimized before users could access Program Manager in order to start other applications.

Windows 95, released in 1995, radically changed the Windows interface and replaced the shell with Explorer, which introduced the Start button, the taskbar, and the system tray. Windows Explorer could also be used for file management, rather than File Manager. Figure 2-3 shows the Windows 95 interface, including the new cascading menu, which enabled easy access to applications, and the taskbar, which showed open applications, making it easy to switch between them. Windows 95 also moved to a 32-bit platform while still supporting 16-bit code through a technology called *thunking;* and it enabled preemptive multitasking and added plug-and-play support for hardware, which was a huge improvement over the painful previous experience of manually determining different interrupt request (IRQ) lines and I/O values for hardware devices. The Recycle Bin was introduced as a way for users to recover data that they deleted, providing it had been enabled, and Network Neighborhood was introduced, which gave users an easy way to browse the network. Windows 95 also included Internet Explorer, with versions 1 through 4 available for Windows 95 and its various updates. Windows 95 still

▶ As an interesting point of reference, the hardware requirements for Windows NT 3.51 Workstation were a 386 processor, 12 MB of memory, and 90 MB of disk space.

▶ An update available for Windows NT 3.51, the Shell Technology Preview, provided the Start menu and the taskbar. I remember trying it when it was released; it crashed consistently.

runs on MS-DOS and includes MS-DOS 7.0. Windows 95 was aimed at the consumer market while the business world used Windows NT.

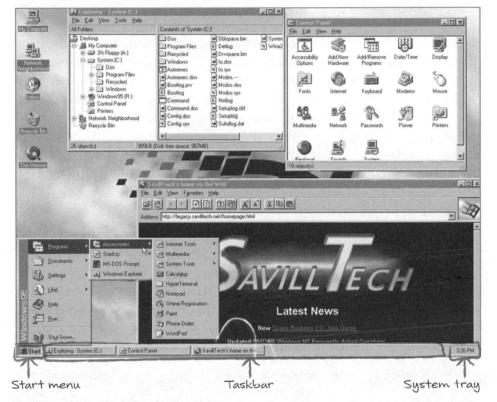

Start menu   Taskbar   System tray

FIGURE 2-3: Windows 95 introduced the Start button, cascading menus, and the taskbar, providing easy access to the shell while using minimal screen real estate.

Windows NT 4, released in 1996, adopted the new Explorer shell introduced with Windows 95. One major change in Windows NT 4.0 was the introduction of the *Graphics Device Interface,* which moved graphics rendering from user mode to kernel mode. This move resulted in better graphics performance but it meant that third-party graphics drivers were running in the kernel, so a bad graphics driver could cause the entire system to become unstable. Also included as part of Windows NT 4 was *DirectX,* which enabled advanced graphical capabilities and would evolve into the technology used by most graphical applications. The Windows Task Manager also made its first appearance, providing a way to identify processes running on the system and access basic performance information. Windows NT 4.0 holds the honor of having the most *service packs* of any operating system, with a final version of Service Pack 6a (a minor update to Service Pack 6 to fix some issues with the original Service

▶ This was a huge issue in Windows Vista, for which a single bad graphics driver caused more than half of all the Windows Vista crashes.

▶ While small enhancements have been made to Task Manager since NT 4.0, it has remained relatively unchanged through Windows 7. Task Manager is accessed by right-clicking the taskbar or pressing Ctrl + Alt + Del.

Pack 6 release). A service pack, of course, is a major collection of fixes and updates for a product. It occasionally includes new features, but that is not the norm. Figure 2-4 shows the Processes tab of Task Manager, and Figure 2-5 shows the Performance tab.

In 1998 Windows 98 was released, still running on top of MS-DOS, version 7.1. It included Active Desktop, which enabled web content to be integrated with the main desktop via Internet Explorer, and the Quick Launch toolbar, which could be enabled on the taskbar to provide easy access to frequently used applications. As a result of the enhanced integration with Internet Explorer, Windows 98 also featured back and forward navigation buttons in Windows Explorer, customizable folder views, thumbnails for viewing images, and an address bar. Windows 98 also introduced the *Windows Driver Model (WDM)*, which provided a better development experience for hardware vendors that wrote drivers for Windows. USB and ACPI both had good support in Windows 98, enabling users to employ a wide range of hardware to utilize all their machine's capabilities.

In February 2000, Microsoft released Windows 2000, which was a major update to the NT family of operating systems. It added a large number of features, including all the shell updates from Windows 98 and Windows 98 Second Edition, but also the new *Microsoft Management Console (MMC)*, which was the foundation for management tools in Windows, and Encrypted File System on the new NTFS version 3 file system. Windows 2000 was the first version of NT to include a disk defragmentation solution. Microsoft had previously maintained that NTFS did not need defragmenting,

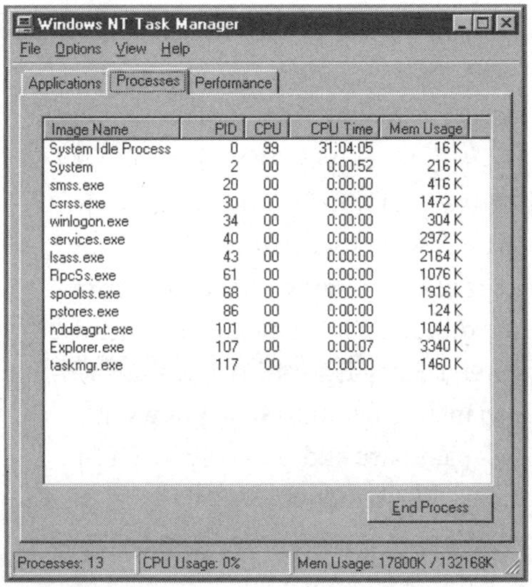

▶ Windows 2000 Server introduced Active Directory, a replacement for the old NT domain model. It offers a full-featured directory service and forms the foundation of most Microsoft services today.

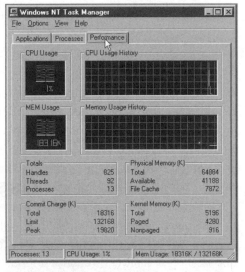

FIGURE 2-4: This tab of Task Manager provides information about each process running on a system.

FIGURE 2-5: This tab of Task Manager provides basic performance information about the processes running on a system.

but when third-party solutions began to fill this gap, its position changed. In fact, the Windows 2000 disk defragmenter was a licensed, limited version of a third-party product called Diskeeper, which had been on the market for a number of years providing defragmentation for NTFS and other file systems.

Windows 2000 also introduced *dynamic disk type*, which enabled software RAID capabilities such as disk striping (RAID 0), mirroring (RAID 1), and striping with parity (RAID 5). The various accessibility features of the home editions of Windows were integrated into Windows 2000. Windows 2000 also introduced the *Windows File Protection* feature, which was designed to stop applications or malware from replacing key operating system files, along with a *System File Checker* scan utility to ensure that key files were the authentic versions. To help fix broken installations, Windows 2000 featured the *Recovery Console*, which could be booted either from the Windows 2000 media or by pre-installing onto the Windows installation. It provided a command-line interface that administrators could use to try to resolve issues. Microsoft also released Windows Me in 2000, the last of the Windows versions that were not NT-based and still ran on top of MS-DOS, version 8.0. It limited access to many DOS functions, however, breaking several applications as Windows Me attempted to adopt some of the NT codebase features. Windows Me was not well received; it suffered from stability issues, and the release of Windows XP the following year also hurt its adoption. Windows 2000 was only available for x86 and Itanium architectures, dropping support for DEC Alpha, MIPS, and PowerPC.

In October 2001, Microsoft released Windows XP, which unified the professional and consumer versions of the Windows client and marked the complete retirement of MS-DOS. Windows XP runs on the NT kernel and originally supported 32-bit processors (and later 64-bit in a special version). Many people still use Windows XP today, which is a testament to its stability and quality. Windows XP was made available in a large number of editions, each of which has a different subset of features—from Starter through Home up to Professional Edition. Windows XP features a far richer graphical shell than previous versions, providing the machine has more than 64MB of memory. Third parties could create visual styles, and Microsoft included a new style dubbed Luna but officially known as *Windows XP style*. The new visual style featured bolder colors, rounded corners, and shadows on icons and menus, giving it a more modern look. Windows XP also includes the capability to group taskbar buttons in order to minimize space for multiple instances of a single application, and new applications added to the Start menu are highlighted, making them easier to find. Figure 2-6 shows the Windows XP interface and the category view of the control panel, which was designed to be less intimidating and more user friendly. Windows

▶ The Windows 2000 "classic" theme was still available in Windows XP for that retro feel.

▶ Windows XP also included Internet Explorer 6, which is still needed by some applications and a reason why many organizations need to retain access to Windows XP.

▶ The built-in support for RDP is used by most virtual desktop infrastructure architectures for access to hosted client operating systems.

XP also introduced fast user switching, which enables a second person to log on to a machine without having to log off an existing session. Remote Desktop and Remote Assistance are also core parts of the operating system, making remote access to the desktop simple using the Remote Desktop Protocol.

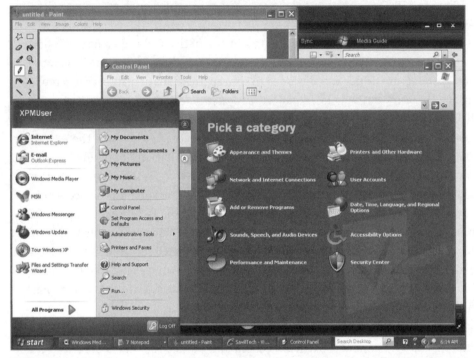

FIGURE 2-6: In the Windows XP interface, notice the Notepad taskbar icon at the bottom, which has a drop-down arrow and a count of 7, indicating taskbar grouping for Notepad.

▶ The R2 goal was to not change the operating system to minimize additional testing required but to provide additional features. This was abandoned with Windows Server 2008 R2, which is a new operating system.

Windows Server 2003 was released in 2003 with a minor kernel version increment over Windows XP (5.2 compared to XP's version 5.1), although Windows Server 2003 is often thought of as the server version of Windows XP, especially in terms of application compatibility. Windows 2003 still used the "classic" shell appearance but it featured many usability improvements to Explorer and the overall interface. Users who wanted the XP-style look could set the Themes service to Automatic to achieve the XP look and feel, but this was discouraged because it used extra system resources (a server's goal is to host services, not look pretty). Windows Server 2003 was the first operating system to have a Release 2 (R2), which is now the standard for server operating systems, providing organizations with a steady OS release schedule—a major server OS version every four years and an R2 release at the midpoint, so two years after the major release.

KEY FEATURES INTRODUCED IN WINDOWS VISTA AND WINDOWS 7

Windows Vista, code-named Longhorn, was talked about and tested for a long time before finally being released to manufacturing in November 2006, a five-year gap since the initial release of Windows XP. Windows Vista included a huge number of new features and a large number of security improvements. Many of the great Windows 7 features people often talk about were actually introduced in Windows Vista. Figure 2-7 is one of the slides I have used when talking about Windows Vista and even Windows 7. It gives you an idea of the sheer scale of changes made in Windows Vista. The server version of Longhorn, Windows Server 2008, was released in February 2008, more than a year past the Windows Vista release, and it included Service Pack 1 because Windows Server 2008 shares the same codebase as Windows Vista, and SP1 for Windows Vista had already been released. Both 32-bit and 64-bit editions of Windows Vista and Windows Server 2008 were released to support the shift to 64-bit-capable processors and systems.

▶ When considering a move to a 64-bit client OS, make sure that 64-bit drivers are available for all hardware and any software that uses drivers, such as antivirus. Any 32-bit applications should run fine on a 64-bit OS.

FIGURE 2-7: Some of the major Windows Vista features

In the autumn of 2009, Microsoft released Windows 7 and Windows Server 2008 R2, which built on many of the great features introduced in Windows Vista but made

▶ I don't expect to see 32-bit editions removed from the client version because of the wide range of devices and form factors needed for clients.

the operating system more user friendly by making features like User Access Control less aggressive in its interactions with the user and better optimized for hardware, providing better support for smaller form factor machines such as netbooks and slate devices. Windows Server 2008 R2 retired the 32-bit version, leaving only the 64-bit version and a special Itanium version. In the remainder of this section I want to examine key features and changes present in Windows Vista and Windows 7.

Graphical Changes

While still using the Explorer shell, Windows Vista introduced the Aero theme, and Aero Glass if the machine has a Windows Device Driver Model (WDDM) graphics driver, 64MB of graphical memory, and DirectX 9 support. The Windows 2000 theme is still included, named Windows Standard. Aero Glass introduced not only translucent Windows, as shown in Figure 2-8, but other rich graphical capabilities thanks to the inclusion of the new *Desktop Window Manager (DWM)*, which implements composition of the desktop (and behind the scenes actually enables Aero Glass).

Aero   Aero glass

FIGURE 2-8: The Aero and Aero Glass theme views

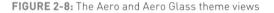

▶ UX stands for user experience.

The Desktop Window Manager runs as a service, the Desktop Window Manager Session Manager, with an internal name of UxSMS that is implemented in the dwm.exe image. This service is responsible for compositing the desktop display for the entire operating system when you run the Windows Aero theme.

In all previous operating systems, and Windows Vista when not running Windows Aero, each application writes directly to the screen buffer, which is written to the display. In the event that one application's window passes over another application's graphical area on-screen, the application is notified via a WM_PAINT message and told to redraw its window. If an application is busy, it may not process this WM_PAINT message, which results in trails left behind the moving window. Similarly, if you move a window across the screen and it can't be redrawn fast enough, the window is broken into pieces as you drag it.

▶ This is known as tearing.

This has changed with the Desktop Window Manager. Each application has its display output redirected to a dedicated area of system memory; from these the DWM creates a composite image that it copies to the display buffer. This means the DWM has access to the graphical output of each application, and for each refresh of the screen it does not need the application to redraw its content. Instead, it uses the snapshot of the last display update it received from the application to composite the latest buffer on-screen. Therefore, when an application is not responding it will not result in any trails; the DWM uses the application's off-screen buffer. This process is shown in Figure 2-9.

If you are running in any other graphical mode, including Vista Basic, DWM is not heavily used. The DWM process, while always running, is essentially idle, and the trail-type behavior of moving windows is still evident because the display is not composited. The DWM process is running even without Windows Aero, as it still handles *Windows Ghosting*, whereby a nonresponsive window takes on a frosted, whited-out appearance.

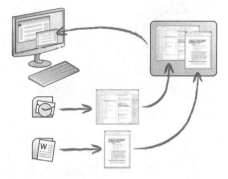

FIGURE 2-9: After each application writes to its own graphical display buffer, Desktop Window Manager can composite them on-screen.

This same capability of the DWM to maintain a separate graphical buffer for every running application also enables some other major graphical shell advances. Flip (Alt + Tab) and Flip 3D (⊞ + Tab) provide quick access to the windows of all running applications, displaying live thumbnails of applications, as shown in Figure 2-10. When the operating system needs a thumbnail, it can create one by shrinking the graphical buffer for the application that the DWM has available. This same capability is used for live thumbnails, shown in Figure 2-11, which are displayed when the mouse is hovered over the taskbar buttons. What cannot be seen in the screenshot is that the image of each application is actually live; for example, Media Player is actually playing the video, even in Flip 3D and Flip.

Windows Vista also introduced the sidebar, which contains *gadgets*, small elements displayed on-screen that have a single function: to present some information or provide quick access to functions. Examples of gadgets are the clock, picture viewer, news feed, and CPU information. The gadget concept remains in Windows 7 and Windows 8 but the sidebar itself was removed, enabling you to freely place gadgets anywhere you like on the desktop, rather than in a fixed bar area.

FIGURE 2-10: Flip 3D display of open applications

FIGURE 2-11: Live thumbnails provide easy access to an application's state without having to actually switch to the application, and stacked instances are supported as shown. The left view is from Windows Vista and the right view is from Windows 7.

The Aero Glass capability was extended further in Windows 7 with the introduction of Show Desktop, Aero Snap, Aero Shake, and Aero Peek:

▶ *Show Desktop* is an area on the far right of the system tray which, when hovered over, makes all application windows transparent so the desktop can be seen.

▶ *Aero Shake* minimizes all open applications other than the selected application. To use it, click the title bar of the desired application and shake it a few times. Shaking again restores the minimized applications back to the desktop.

▶ *Aero Snap* enables you to easily arrange applications on the desktop by dragging an application to the left or right side of the screen, where it automatically occupies 50% of the screen. Another option is to drag the application to the top of the screen to maximize it or off the top to restore it to normal size. For a detailed explanation, see http://www.windowsitpro.com/article/desktop-management/q-what-are-the-different-aero-snap-positions.

▶ *Aero Peek*, shown in Figure 2-12, makes all windows on the desktop invisible except for the application whose live thumbnail is being hovered over by the mouse. To activate Aero Peek, move the mouse to the taskbar icon. When the live thumbnail is displayed, move the mouse up over the live thumbnail.

FIGURE 2-12: Aero Peek shows the application window for the live thumbnail the mouse is hovered over.

Windows 7 introduced a fairly major change to the taskbar, which since Windows 95 had not really changed. The shift was designed to minimize the number of icons displayed on the screen. Over the evolution of Windows, the increasing number of icons representing applications created a messy desktop. A single application could display an icon on the desktop, on the Quick Launch toolbar, on the Start menu, and in the system tray, if running on the taskbar. In Windows 7, the taskbar is thicker, with an improved notification area. The Quick Launch toolbar and the taskbar are integrated, so selecting the Quick Launch icon opens the application, and that same icon now represents the running application, so hovering over it shows the live thumbnail. If the application is running, the icon on the taskbar becomes a button, and when the mouse hovers over it, the predominant color in the icon fills the button with a feature called color *hot-track*, as detailed at http://www.windowsitpro .com/article/desktop-management/q-what-is-hot-track-. All these features reduce the number of icons needed on the desktop.

The icons on the taskbar are now active—for example, overlays can be placed on taskbar icons showing information about the application, such as the status for a messenger application. Additionally, progress information for processes related to the application can be shown on the taskbar icon, such as file downloads and copy operations. Any application can be pinned to the taskbar, and actions can be added to the live thumbnails—for example, Media Player controls are available to control media playback. *Jump Lists* provide a way for application options and data to be available directly from the application icon through the right-click action. You can also access a Jump List by clicking the arrow next to the program in the Start menu. Figure 2-13 shows the four key taskbar capabilities just described.

Pop-ups now have a configuration option that shows the process generating the balloon and the option to never show pop-ups again for that process. The system tray has also been simplified, hiding infrequently used icons to prevent distraction and general clutter.

Windows 7 also introduced scalable icons, enabling devices with very high resolution displays to run Windows 7 while maintaining graphical fidelity and smoothness, and giving users a high degree of customization over the icon sizes.

Office 2007 introduced the use of a ribbon in its user interface, replacing the traditional drop-down menus and toolbars with a set of tabs exposing groups of command icons. This ribbon has been added into a couple of Windows 7 applications—namely, Paint and WordPad—but the key point is the ribbon is now an intrinsic part of the Windows platform. Microsoft supplies software developers with the Windows Ribbon framework, a set of application programming interfaces that provide a standard toolset to create application interfaces. The functionality will be expanded in subsequent Windows operating systems.

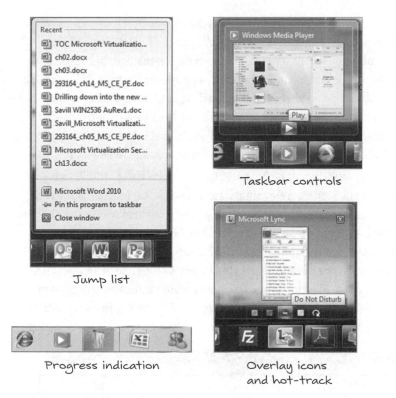

Jump list

Taskbar controls

Progress indication

Overlay icons and hot-track

FIGURE 2-13: Key taskbar enhancements in Windows 7

Windows Explorer Changes

One of the big changes made in Windows 7 was the organization of and access to data. Search had become widely available in Windows Vista, with not only Search integration on the Start menu but also in other operating system interfaces such as the control panel, which enables users to just type **display** and the correct control panel applets related to the display are automatically found. While these search capabilities help users find data on their computers, it can still be fairly cumbersome, which led to the introduction of *libraries* in Windows 7.

Windows Vista and many previous operating systems use particular folders for certain types of data in each user profile: one for documents, one for pictures, one for music, and so on. A parallel set of type-specific folders exists in a shared area, accessible by everyone. The folders directly reflect the hierarchical file structure on the storage medium.

Windows 7 still has folders in the user profile for documents, pictures, and so on, but they are not the focus of (Windows) Explorer, searching, or file dialogs. If you open a Windows 7 profile you will find personal folders for the major data collections: My Documents, My Pictures, and so on. There is also a public profile containing Public Documents, Public Music, and so on, equivalent to the shared folders. Libraries are essentially indexes into the file structure, providing a unified view of both the user's personal data and the public data. You can also add additional folders to a library for a complete single view and search targets with data spread across multiple locations.

By default there are four libraries—Documents, Music, Pictures, and Videos—each of which is linked by default to the relevant personal and public folders. However, users can add and remove folders from the library to locate them where the user's data actually resides. In Figure 2-14 you can see that I have customized my libraries to include only my own document areas, and I added some of my own custom libraries. To add folders to the library, select the library's properties and then click the Include a folder button. The tick in the leftmost column indicates the current default location for saving files added to the library; to change it, you select a different location and click the Set save location button.

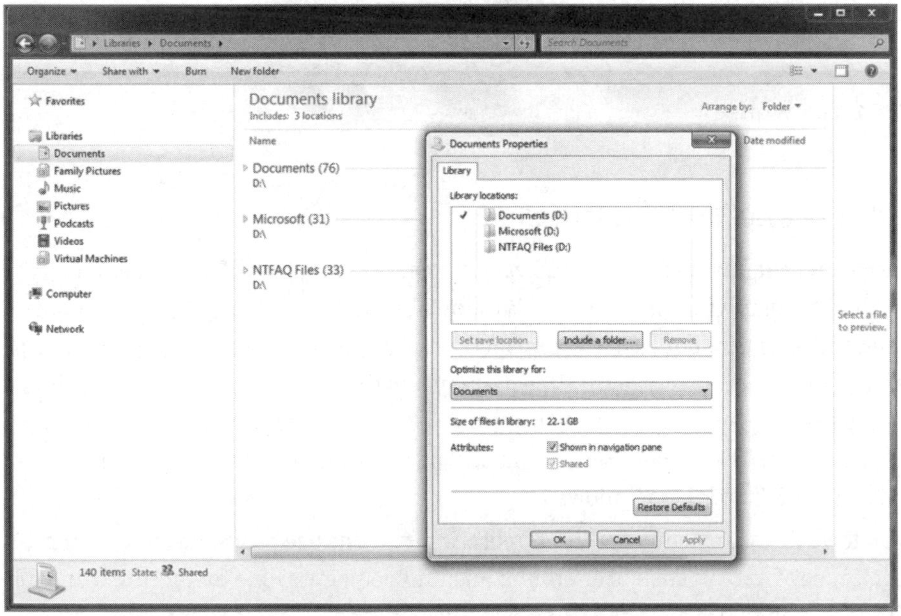

FIGURE 2-14: Customizing a library via its properties

Although you can use libraries as just a quick shortcut to the most popular areas for your data collections, their real power lies in searching and viewing types of data. For example, you can choose to arrange the library by data type instead of by folder, which will then group all the data by type regardless of which folder it actually resides in. When you select one of the data types, you will see only data of that type from anywhere in the library.

All of Windows 7 is based around the libraries, so programs like Media Player and Media Center access their content via your libraries instead of their own library mechanisms. This way, the operating system maintains only one library system.

The Windows 7 Explorer also features a preview window, which gives a peek into the content of the current file selected, including Office documents and many other types of application data, minimizing the need to launch an application to see what the content of a file is. Overall, Explorer has been made less cluttered and easier to navigate.

▶ By default, the normal menus of Explorer are hidden. Press the Alt key to unhide the full menus in Explorer and gain access to more advanced options and features.

Examining Touch Features in Windows 7

Windows has had touch capabilities through its various tablet editions for a long time, but that touch interaction was designed to be used with a pen, not a finger. The touch ecosystem experienced a sea change with the release of new devices such as the iPhone, iPad, and various Android devices that were either phone- or slate-based. Windows 7 added new capabilities that enabled hardware vendors to create devices running Windows 7 that supported multi-touch, which means detecting multiple finger gestures at the same time, thereby enabling more advanced interactions. The touch features work with existing Windows applications; for example, a single tap represents a left click, while holding the touch point in place represents a right click. Using multiple fingers enables options such as zooming out and zooming in, plus rotating content and scrolling through windows. A number of applications were designed to take advantage of touch, such as Windows Media Center and Internet Explorer 9. One difficulty with Windows 7 is that many applications were not designed with touch in mind, so although the operating system is fully touch-capable, the applications can be hard to use because some elements, such as very small icons and menus, cannot easily be navigated through touch alone.

User Access Control

User Access Control (UAC) is a major reason why people find Windows Vista hard to use and nagging, although this security feature is very useful and can be configured to reduce the number of interactions required. The goal of UAC is to protect both the user's data and computer. With Windows XP, nearly every user is a local administrator of his machine, which allows him to access all the required functions and capabilities; but it also means the user can do a lot of damage. In addition, any kind of malware could be running, as the user has full access to the system. Most of the daily tasks that users perform do not need elevated permissions. Windows Vista and Windows 7 were carefully designed to reduce the number of actions that require administrative privileges, thus minimizing the number of users who need to be local administrators.

User Access Control allocates an administrator with two security tokens—one is a fully privileged token and the other is a stripped-down token containing only basic permissions, which is what the user runs with by default. If an action requires the more privileged token, the User Account Control dialog is displayed, prompting the user to confirm that the action should be taken and then granting permission to use the higher-privilege token. Use of this higher-privilege token is known as *elevation*. The problem with UAC in Windows Vista is that it prompts for confirmation for many actions that are initiated directly by mouse click or command entry, behavior that earned UAC its "nagging" tag. This behavior drove many users to disable UAC through the User Accounts control panel applet.

Windows 7 made UAC more user friendly, reducing the number of times it prompts users and introducing four different levels of UAC interaction, selected through the User Accounts control panel applet. This allows more granular control of interactions, rather than the limited on or off offered in Windows Vista, which requires a policy for more granular options. Figure 2-15 shows the UAC controls in Windows Vista (above) and Windows 7 (below).

Virtualizing Client Files and the Registry

Another part of User Access Control is virtualization of key parts of the operating system file system and registry. Prior to Windows Vista, some applications would write user-specific configurations and even user data to areas of the operating system that were not designed to be used for user-specific information. In Windows Vista and later, where many users are not administrators, these legacy applications fail to function. File and registry virtualization is designed to capture write and read actions to particular parts of the operating system and redirect them to an area that is user specific. The following areas are protected by file system virtualization:

- \Program Files, \Program Files (x86) and subfolders
- \Windows and all subfolders
- %AllUsersProfile%
- \Documents and Settings (symbolic link)

► One configuration requires users to reenter their password at every UAC dialog, which is obviously very unpopular.

► A bad idea. If the prompts are an issue, use "User Account Control" to automatically elevate privileges when required.

► To force an application to run with the administrator privilege token, right-click on the program and select Run as Administrator. If you are not an administrator, you will be prompted for administrator credentials. This is known as over-the-shoulder elevation.

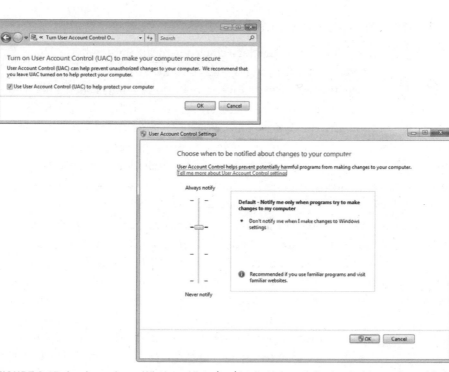

FIGURE 2-15: As shown here, Windows Vista (top) lacks the granular level of control provided by Windows 7 (bottom).

Any file system activity to the preceding locations is redirected to a subfolder of the %LOCALAPPDATA%\VirtualStore\ folder. LOCALAPPDATA is a variable that for my account equals C:\Users\john\AppData\Local, but it would be different for each user. Similar redirection is performed for any attempted registry writes to HKEY_LOCAL_MACHINE\SOFTWARE, which are redirected to HKEY_CURRENT_USER\Software\Classes\VirtualStore\MACHINE\SOFTWARE.

This file system and registry virtualization technology is aimed at legacy applications, so it is used only in the following circumstances:

► A process for an interactive user

► 32-bit executables

► No requestedExecutionLevel in the application manifest, which allows an application to request a specific execution level

► Run the command set LOCALAPPDATA in a command window to see what the variable equates to for your account. Note that this equates to the AppData\Local area of the profile, so it does not roam between machines, a concept discussed in Chapter 5.

Booting from a Virtual Hard Disk

The *virtual hard disk (VHD)* format enables a single file to simulate a physical hard drive, with its own volumes, file systems, and content. VHD was initially part of Virtual PC for use with its machine virtualization solutions, but has been enhanced and built upon for use by Hyper-V, the Microsoft server virtualization platform. Windows Server 2008 with the Hyper-V role installed enabled VHDs to be attached to and detached from an operating system instance and viewed like a real disk, although this had to be performed through scripts, which I have documented at http://www.windowsitpro.com/article/virtualization/q-how-can-i-mount-a-virtual-hard-disk-vhd-in-hyper-v-without-additional-programs-.

With Windows Server 2008 R2, the VHD format was upgraded to a core part of the operating system and was heavily re-architected, providing better performance—particularly for dynamically expanding VHDs. The capability to attach and detach VHDs was made part of the Disk Management graphical interface, in addition to PowerShell and the command-line Diskpart utility. Figure 2-16 shows the actions to create a VHD and attach a VHD to a Windows 2008 R2 operating system. VHDs can be attached with full read/write access or read-only, depending on need. Once attached, the VHD is assigned a drive letter like any other disk, and it can be accessed through all the normal Windows mechanisms, such as Windows Explorer. The only indication that the disk is a VHD is that the icon in the Disk Management tool is blue and an action to Detach the VHD is available on the context menu, as shown in Figure 2-17. Windows 8 makes it even easier to attach a VHD; just double-click on a VHD and it will automatically attach and be available with a drive letter.

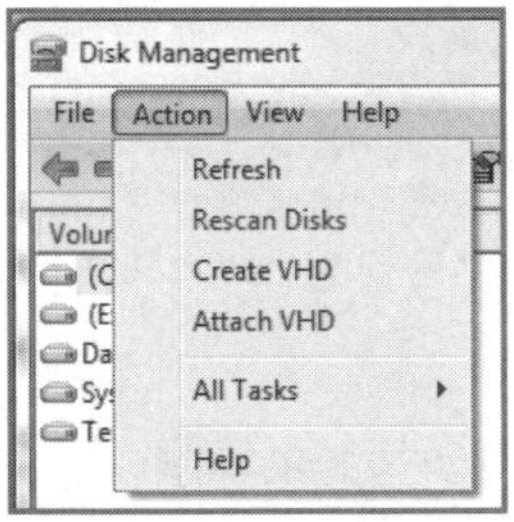

FIGURE 2-16: Creating and attaching VHD files is possible through the Disk Management ➜ Action menu.

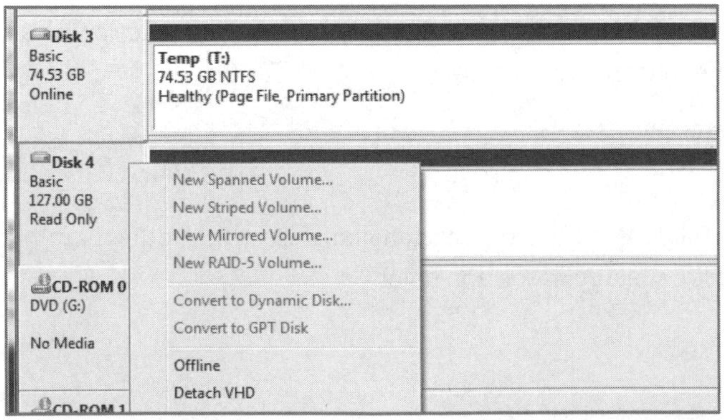

FIGURE 2-17: Actions available for an attached VHD on a Windows 7 machine that was attached as read-only

ATTACHING AND DETACHING VHDS FROM THE COMMAND LINE

Mounting a VHD with Windows 2008 R2 is easy using Disk Manager, but you can also perform this using PowerShell via the **Msvm_ImageManagementService** command as shown here:

```
$VHDService = get-wmiobject -class "Msvm_ImageManagementService"`
-namespace "root\virtualization" -computername "."
$VHDService.Mount("<path to vhd file>")
```

To unmount, use the **$VHDService.Unmount** command.

To achieve the same using a regular command prompt, **cmd.exe**, start **disk-part.exe** and run the following commands:

```
select vdisk file=c:\test.vhd
attach vdisk
```

To detach, use the **detach vdisk** command.

I mentioned earlier that the server and client Windows versions share a common codebase and that Windows 7 is the client equivalent of Windows Server 2008 R2. This means the VHD core integration with the operating system is also part of Windows 7, and Figure 2-17 was actually taken from my Windows 7 desktop. In addition to attaching and using VHD files, another great benefit is that you can boot a physical machine from a VHD file, a feature known as Boot from VHD. This works for Windows 7, Windows Server 2008 R2, and Windows 8, and it can be very useful for multi-boot scenarios in which multiple operating systems are installed on the same physical box or just to provide easy portability of the operating system.

To install Windows into a VHD on a physical box, perform the following procedure:

1. Boot from the Windows 7 or 2008 R2 media.

2. Select the language options as you would normally do and click Next.

3. At the Install Now screen, press Shift + F10 to open a command prompt window. Within this window, you will partition the disks and create the VHD file that the operating system will be installed to.

▶ For best performance when using Boot from VHD, use a fixed-size VHD file instead of a dynamic VHD. Boot from VHD is available only in Windows 7 Enterprise and Ultimate SKUs and all Windows Server 2008 R2 SKUs.

▶ It is possible to boot from a VHD that is used as a virtual machine and vice versa.

4. Select a disk and wipe the content as follows:

```
diskpart
list disk
select disk 0
clean
```

5. Create a 200MB system partition, which the Windows 7/2008 R2 installation procedure normally creates automatically:

```
create part primary size=200
format fs=ntfs label="System" quick
active
```

6. Using the rest of the space, create a partition that will hold the VHD files. I call it boot, but you could call it VHDStore or whatever is meaningful for you. I used the C drive but when you boot to the VHD, the drive letters will shift; therefore, you could assign the letter D, but just make sure you use D:\name.vhd in step 7.

```
create part primary
format fs=ntfs label="Boot" quick
assign letter=C
```

7. Create a VHD file on the drive. In this example I created it as a 25GB file that is an expanding disk. You can use type=fixed instead of type=expandable to create a fixed-size VHD, but this will use all the space during the VHD creation. However, this will give better performance and is the recommendation for use outside of testing.

```
create vdisk file=c:\win7ult.vhd maximum=25000 type=expandable
select vdisk file=c:\win7ult.vhd
attach vdisk
create partition primary
format fs=ntfs label="Win7Boot" quick
```

8. You can now list the volumes, as shown in Figure 2-18:

```
list vol
```

9. Exit Diskpart and then type **exit** again to close the command prompt window:

```
exit
exit
```

10. When you get to the step to select the installation target, select the VHD partition that was created. A warning will appear that you cannot install it on the partition, but you can ignore it.

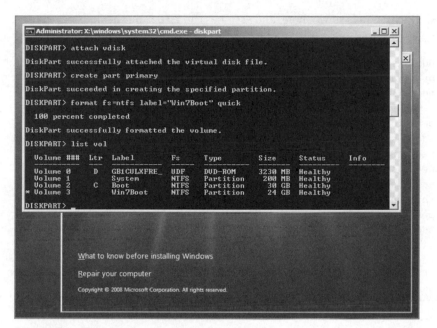

FIGURE 2-18: The completed process to attach a VHD and create a partition on which to install an operating system

Installation will now proceed as usual. Once the installation is complete, the VHD partition is now the C: drive while the partition containing the VHD files is demoted down to the D: drive. If you look at the D: drive, you see the VHD file, while the C: drive is the content of the VHD and looks like a normal windows installation. The 200MB partition you created does not have a drive letter and is essentially invisible to the OS.

Now imagine you have an existing VHD file that you wish to add to the boot menu and that you want to be able to boot from. This VHD could have come from another system or even a virtual machine. The command sequence is as follows:

```
bcdedit /copy {current} /d "Desired Name in Boot Screen for the VHD"
bcdedit /set {enter GUID output from previous line} device
vhd=[LOCATE]\<any directory structures used\><vhd filename>
bcdedit /set {previous entered GUID value} osdevice vhd=[LOCATE]\<any
directory structures used\><vhd filename>
bcdedit /set {previous entered GUID value} detecthal on
```

If the VHD is running Hyper-V, you also need to turn on the hypervisor:

```
bcdedit /set {previous entered GUID value} hypervisorlaunchtype auto
```

A full walk-through is shown here, and assumes the VHD is on the D: drive. Note that you have to type the square brackets.

```
C:\Windows\system32>bcdedit /copy {current} /d "Windows 2008 R2"
The entry was successfully copied to {63b38b1e-..-001c23449a2b}.
C:\Windows\system32>bcdedit /set {63b38b1e-..-001c23449a2b}
device vhd=[d:]\win2k8r2.vhd
The operation completed successfully.
C:\Windows\system32>bcdedit /set {63b38b1e-..-001c23449a2b}
osdevice vhd=[d:]\win2k8r2.vhd
The operation completed successfully.
C:\Windows\system32>bcdedit /set {63b38b1e-..-001c23449a2b}
detecthal on
The operation completed successfully.
C:\Windows\system32>bcdedit /set {63b38b1e-..-001c23449a2b}
hypervisorlaunchtype auto
The operation completed successfully.
```

When you boot from a VHD, the pagefile is actually created on the partition containing the VHD that is being booted, not in the actual VHD. This is why you always need more spare space on the partition than just the size of the VHD. If there is not enough space on the parent partition hosting the VHD, then the other partitions in the system are scanned and a pagefile is created where possible. If a pagefile cannot be created on any partition, then the OS in the VHD will boot and run without a pagefile. The pagefile is never created within the VHD.

It is possible to convert a physical installation of Windows to a VHD using the Disk2vhd tool from Sysinternals (see http://technet.microsoft.com/en-us/sysinternals/ee656415), shown in Figure 2-19. When executed, the tool displays all volumes on the system and allows you to select the drives that should be captured to a VHD and to name the VHD file to which the data should be captured. Once the volumes are selected, click Create. A differential snapshot is created, the data is copied from the snapshot into a VHD, and then the snapshot is deleted, all with no downtime.

> ▶ To see the differential snapshot, run the vssadmin list shadows command.

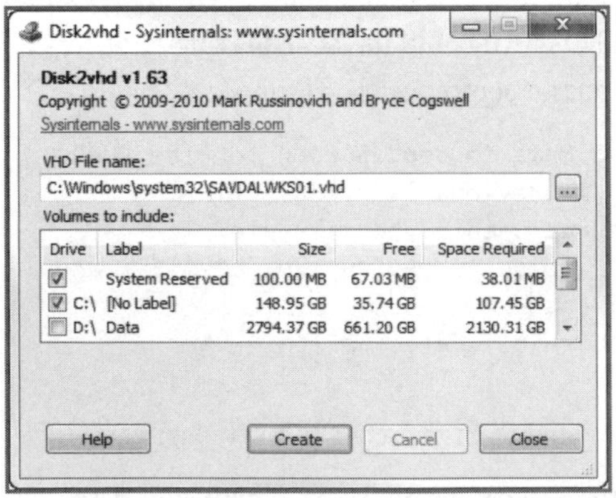

FIGURE 2-19: Run the Disk2vhd tool and select the volumes to be captured to a VHD file.

The VHDs created by Disk2vhd are fully bootable, unlike the VHDs created by Windows Backup, so you can use Disk2vhd to capture the system disk from an operating system installation and then copy that VHD to a virtual server like Hyper-V and use it as the boot volume for a virtual machine or use with Boot from a VHD to Boot a physical machine from the created VHD.

EXPLORING THE NEW FEATURES IN WINDOWS 8

Windows 8 represents a major shift in the Windows operating system, driven by changes in the consumer space that have in turn affected the enterprise. In other words, the organization has had to respond to changes in what users want and expect from devices and operating systems. The rapid adoption of very small slate devices that are controlled primarily with touch means using minimal hardware and as little power as possible to provide long battery life on devices, helping to minimize their physical size. To enable very small devices such as ARM-based devices and even system on a chip (SoC), a special version of Windows 8, Windows RT, will be available. This final section of the chapter explores some of the new Windows 8 features. However, although this information is accurate at the time of writing, keep in mind that it is based on the consumer preview of Windows 8 and is therefore subject to change.

Metro Interface, Touch, and Navigation

The Start menu, taskbar, system tray, and all the features introduced in the Explorer shell were first introduced in Windows 95, which was designed in 1993, 20 years ago. Times have changed, of course, and just as changes necessitated the introduction of the Explorer shell to replace Program Manager, current technology necessitates a change in the user interface because of changes to how Windows is used and the new types of hardware—in particular, touch-centric interfaces and easier access to applications.

Windows Phone 7 first introduced a new Metro interface, which was designed to provide a rich user experience that could be used in a "glance and go" manner, providing very fast access to information through live tiles that display information, rather than static icons. The Metro interface is very easy to use with touch, and it focuses on giving the application and its information the majority of the screen real estate, instead of a lot of operating system elements and controls. The Metro interface style was recently implemented on the Xbox 360 and is used in Windows 8, replacing the old Start button and its cascading menus with a new Start screen. The new Start screen is the launching point for new Metro-style and even non-Metro-style

▶ Minimizing the onscreen visual elements, known as chrome, provides a cleaner interface.

▶ These are also called immersive applications.

▶ To access the traditional desktop, click the Desktop tile on the Start screen or press the Windows key (⊞) + D. The desktop is not being retired or losing functionality. The primary focus has shifted to the new Start screen.

▶ Configuring a live tile to a double space typically enables live content to be displayed, which may not fit when a tile uses only a single space.

applications. The key principles behind the new Metro-style interface are that it's fast, fluid, intuitive, and consistent in its usage.

The Start screen with the new live tile layout is shown in Figure 2-20. Notice that the live tiles display information related to the specific application, rather than a generic icon that does not convey anything. Note also the five charms on the right side; these are displayed based on user input and provide system and application commands and configuration capabilities, which are covered in detail later. The Media application shows the video it is current playing, the Desktop tile shows my desktop wallpaper, the Mail tile shows new messages, Weather shows the current weather, and so on. You can get basic information without even launching the applications. The tiles can be configured to use either a single space or a double space.

FIGURE 2-20: A basic Windows 8 Start screen with a number of applications installed; the system commands, or charms, are pulled out from the right edge.

▶ The purpose of the snapped state is to be able to keep an eye on a running application that is not your primary focus. Perhaps you have a media file running in the snapped view or you are monitoring the weather or a flight's status.

Windows 8 also features a new application model using the new Windows Runtime (WinRT), whereby applications do not run on the old-style desktop but are chromeless, filling the entire screen and providing a very different appearance than traditional Windows applications. Figure 2-21 shows two Metro-style applications on the screen at the same time, but notice that no operating system controls are visible; controls and options are displayed as needed and in a consistent manner, as I will shortly explain. Two Metro applications can be displayed at the same time by pinning one of the applications to a small part of the screen (a set 320 pixels wide), giving the other application the rest of the screen. Metro-style applications are expected to implement modes whereby they are running on the entire display, known as the *fill view*, or snapped to one edge, the *snapped view*. An application can be snapped to the left or the right, but you cannot have more than two Metro applications on the screen at once.

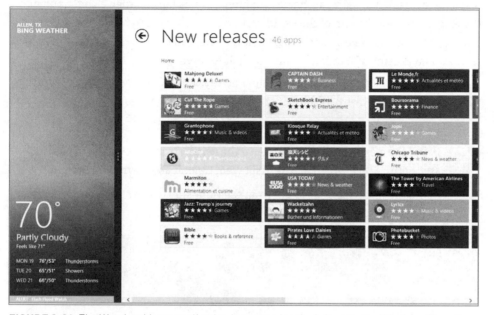

FIGURE 2-21: The Weather Metro application is snapped to the left while the Windows Store is shown in fill view using the rest of the screen.

You can easily customize the Start screen and organize tiles into groups. You can also unpin tiles you don't typically use from the Start screen, and it's very easy to quickly browse the icons it contains. Applications that are not on the Start screen, such as those not frequently used, can be found on the All apps screen, which you can access by pressing the Windows key + Q; or right-click on an empty place on the Start screen and select All apps; or with touch, swipe down from the very top of the screen and select All apps. When the All apps screen appears, all applications are displayed and an easy search capability is exposed to quickly find the applications required.

BASIC NAVIGATION

Before looking at some basic customization of the Start screen, it's important to understand how to interact with it, with Metro applications, and with the Windows 8 desktop. Windows users are used to interacting with mouse and keyboard, and that hasn't changed with Windows 8. However, the capability to also navigate and use Windows

▶ On the Start screen, you can just start typing letters to automatically search for applications containing the characters entered. No control sequence needs to be typed first.

▶ Although the new Start screen was initially a shock, after I organized everything it is actually faster to use than the old Start button cascading menus.

▶ The Windows 7 desktop is still available in Windows 8 for non-Metro applications, but there is no Start menu on it. Pressing Start launches the Start screen.

8 with touch has been added—as either a complement to mouse and keyboard where available or as the sole means of interaction when touch is the only interface option.

The first thing that will strike many users when using Windows 8 via touch is how responsive it is. When using a keyboard or mouse, some lag between a command and the response is not the end of the world, but when you are using touch to move things around, your gestures must have an immediate effect in order to have a useful interface, and my testing of Windows 8 has shown it to be very responsive.

The Start screen is accessed in a number of ways but all are consistent, including when using the Windows 8 desktop instead of Metro applications:

▶ From the keyboard, simply press the Windows key (⊞).

▶ Using the mouse, move the cursor to the very bottom-left corner of the display and a mini Start screen will be displayed. Click it as shown in Figure 2-22.

▶ Using touch, swipe your finger from the right side of the screen inward, and the charms will be displayed. Click the Start charm.

> ▶ In a multi-monitor configuration, all the corners and edges on all displays can be used with the Windows 8 gestures, including the bottom-left mouse hover to open the Start screen.

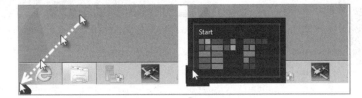

FIGURE 2-22: Mouse gesture to access the Start screen, which works on the Windows 8 desktop or within a Metro application

NOTE When using any of the touch swipe gestures in Windows 8, such as swiping from the right inward to bring up charms or swiping from the left, top, and bottom, it is very important to start the swipe from off the screen. The swipe gesture only registers when the outermost pixel starts the motion. Likewise, when moving the mouse to a corner, move the mouse as far into the corner as possible.

Recall the Start screen shown earlier in Figure 2-20. On the far right side of the screen are five icons, the Windows 8 charms that provide a way to navigate and interact with Windows 8 and Metro-style applications. The charms are considered the system commands for Windows 8. To access the charms use one of the following:

▶ From the keyboard, simply press the Windows key (⊞) + C.

▶ Using the mouse, move the pointer to the bottom-right corner of the screen to display the charms, and then move the mouse up to select.

▶ Using touch, swipe your finger from the right side of the display inward and the charms will be displayed.

With the exception of the Start charm, which always brings up the Start screen, the charms expose different information and actions depending on the context in which the charm is activated, be it from the Start screen, from a Metro application, or from the Windows 8 desktop. Keyboard shortcuts are also shown for each charm:

▶ Search charm (⊞ + Q): Used to search, including application-specific search when accessed from an application. Applications can register with Search to be displayed when the Search charm is selected. This registration is achieved through a contract between the application and the operating system.

▶ Share charm (⊞ + H): Used to share data to other locations and applications, including social applications like Facebook. For example, you might use a picture application and then select the Search charm to share that picture straight to Facebook.

▶ Devices charm (⊞ + K): Used to access and interact with devices, such as enabling display output to a second screen, printing information from the current Metro application, and so on. Figure 2-23 shows printing from within the Windows 8 Reader application; the print window is opened when the printer is selected from the Devices charm.

▶ Settings charm (⊞ + I): Used for Windows 8 Start screen configuration when selected from the Start screen, application-specific settings when selected from a Metro application, and control panel and other options when selected from the Windows 8 desktop. Windows 8 includes a new Settings interface that provides access to many configuration categories, but the old control panel is still included.

To access application commands for a Metro application, such as to open a new tab in Internet Explorer or to add a new connection in the Remote Desktop application, you can use a keyboard, mouse, or touch, as shown in Figure 2-24:

▶ From the keyboard, simply press the Windows key (⊞) + Z.

▶ Right-click anywhere on the application with the mouse.

▶ Using touch, swipe your finger from the top or bottom of the display inward.

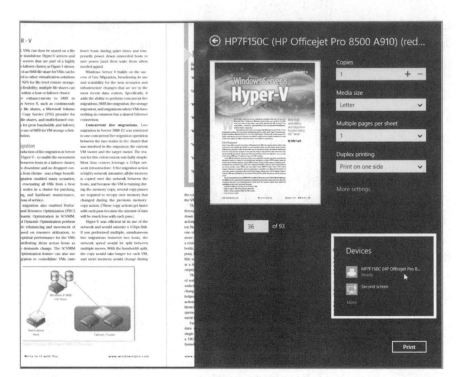

FIGURE 2-23: Select the printer to be used from the Devices menu, exposed via the Devices charm, and the print interface will be shown.

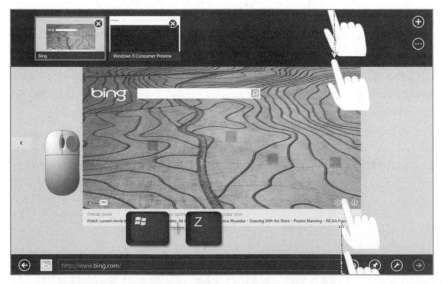

FIGURE 2-24: The application commands for the Metro version of Internet Explorer. By hiding them normally it gives the application the entire display surface.

Navigating the various open applications is the next skill to acquire, and after that using Windows 8 is just a matter of getting used to the new way of interfacing. The old Alt + Tab way of navigating through all applications (both Metro and traditional) still works, but the Win key + Tab combination has changed. Instead of displaying the Flip 3D interface of all applications, the Win key + Tab now shows all running Metro applications, the desktop (if open), and the Start screen, but it does not show each individual application running on the desktop. In addition, the Metro app history does not show the current application with the focus; the list is designed to facilitate switching to other applications. This means if you are currently on the Start screen, the Start screen is not shown in the list; if you are on the desktop, then the desktop is not shown; and so on. Figure 2-25 shows my Metro app history bar when running from a Metro application, so other Metro applications, the Start screen, and my desktop are shown. Note that the thumbnail is live for each application, showing the current content; and the thumbnails are organized in order of most recently accessed, with the previously used application shown at the top.

To access the Metro app history bar using the mouse, move the mouse to the top or bottom left corner and then move the mouse straight down or straight up, respectively. Using touch, swipe in from the left edge and then back left off screen in one motion (so you are swiping on and off screen from the left).

To access the last application used using the mouse, move the mouse to the top-left corner to display the last application thumbnail and click it. To move to the last application that was running using touch, swipe in from the far left inward, which will drag in the previously used application. If you decide you don't want it, just drag it back to the far left and the Metro app history will be displayed, enabling a specific application to be selected. Using this swipe from the left, you can snap Metro applications to the left or right side by swiping in from the left and then holding your finger toward the left or right side, which after a second brings up a separator bar to which you can drop your application to snap it. To snap an application to the right with the keyboard, use the Win key plus the period (.) key; to snap left, press Shift while pressing the Win key and period (.) key.

FIGURE 2-25: The Metro app history bar shows all open Metro applications, the Start screen, and the desktop.

▶ Pressing Ctrl while pressing the Win key + Tab opens the application list and keeps it open even after the keys are released, allowing navigation with the cursor keys or mouse. This also works with Alt + Tab.

▶ Feel free to play around in the Windows 8 interface. You won't break anything and it's the best way to get a good handle on Windows 8 and how to do things the way that works best for you.

If you are wondering how you close a Metro-style application, the short answer is you don't need to. When a Metro-style application is not displayed, Windows automatically suspends its processes, which means it is not consuming any processor or other system resources and is therefore not a drain on the battery. You can request that an application not be suspended, such as to play music or to retain the capability to perform some functions using the Windows broker service, but most Metro applications automatically suspend and then resume when brought back into focus. To close an application, press Alt + F4 on the keyboard; using touch or the mouse, hold near the top of the application and then drag down to the bottom of the screen.

USING AND ORGANIZING THE START SCREEN

▶ You can uninstall Metro applications directly from the Start screen, rather than use a specific uninstall control panel applet or program.

You can apply the basic navigation methods just described to the Start screen with a few extra little tips. The Start screen tiles can be added and removed in addition to being customized, such as showing live information or occupying either one or two tile spaces. To bring up the options for a tile it must be selected. To select with the mouse, right-click on the tile; with touch, just perform a small swipe down on the tile; with the keyboard, navigate to the tile with the cursor and then press space—any of these methods will place a small check on the tile and the options will be shown at the bottom of the screen. To unselect, repeat the gesture. The options enable you to unpin the application from the Start screen, make the tile large or small, uninstall the application, and specify whether live information should be shown or just a generic icon. Figure 2-26 shows the basic commands for a tile. Note that multiple tiles can be selected at once. Applications can be pinned to the Start screen from the All apps screen.

FIGURE 2-26: The commands for a tile are shown on the Start screen.

Tiles can be placed into tile groups by selecting one tile at a time and dragging it to another existing group on the Start screen. To create a new group, drag the tile outside the existing groups and a light-gray vertical bar will be drawn, indicating that a new group is being created. If you have a lot of icons on the screen, to avoid dragging past them all, select the tile and drag it to the bottom of the screen, which will zoom out the Start screen and make it easy to quickly move around. The Start screen can manually be zoomed using a number of methods:

► Hold down the Ctrl key and scroll the mouse wheel up or down to zoom in and out.

► Using touch, pinch the screen to zoom out or stretch (separate) fingers to zoom in.

Once the Start screen is zoomed out, you cannot select individual icons, only an entire group. You can reorder the groups horizontally by dragging with the mouse or touch. If you right-click or keyboard space, you access the group options, which enables you to name the group as shown in Figure 2-27.

► Take some time to personalize your Start screen, removing tiles you don't use and organizing tiles into groups and naming them. It makes a huge difference.

FIGURE 2-27: The zoomed out Start screen makes it easy to reorder the tile groups and name them.

Table 2-1 summarizes the major navigation items I've described in this chapter. You can also head over to http://www.savilltech.com/videos/win8nav/win8nav.wmv for a video demonstration of the history of Windows and how to use these navigation gestures.

TABLE 2-1: Windows 8 Navigation Items

TASK	KEYBOARD	MOUSE	TOUCH
Start screen	Press the Windows key (toggle)	Move from bottom-left corner of display and mini Start screen will be displayed. Click it.	Swipe from right edge of screen and press the Start charm.
Charms	Win + C	Move from bottom-right corner and move up to the charms.	Swipe from right edge of the screen.
Search charm	Win + Q		
Share charm	Win + H		
Devices charm	Win + K		
Settings charm	Win + I		
Application commands	Win + Z	Right-click on the application.	Swipe from top or bottom edge of the screen.
Metro app history	Win + Tab [+ Ctrl]	Move from top or bottom left corner, then move up/down depending on the corner.	Swipe from left edge inward, then back left off the edge.
Snap applications	Win + . [+ Shift]	Drag application from Metro app history near the left or right edge. Right-clicking on tile in Metro App history also gives snap options.	Swipe from left edge inward, then hold near the left or right edge.
Access last application	Win + Tab or Alt + Tab	Move to top-left corner of screen, then click displayed thumbnail.	Swipe from left edge inward.
Select/unselect a tile or group	Space	Right-click	Swipe down on the tile.
Close a Metro application	Alt + F4	Left-click near top of the application, then drag down to the bottom of the screen.	Press near the top of the application, then drag down to the bottom of the screen.

USING THE WINDOWS 8 DESKTOP

Although the Start screen and Metro-style applications are major features of Windows 8, the desktop is not going anywhere; and it is still used for any non-Metro applications, which will be the majority of applications until the Metro application model is widely adopted. Even then, some applications will not fit the Metro model and will use the desktop. You can access the familiar desktop using the Desktop tile on the Start screen or press Win + D. The taskbar and system tray are still present, gadgets can be placed on the screen, and it behaves and looks very similar to Windows 7 except that the Start button is missing and the curved look of Windows 7 has been replaced with a square look—but Aero Glass and all the Aero features are still present, such as Aero Peek. The only feature missing is Flip 3D, which is replaced by the Metro app history bar.

▶ Just move the mouse to the bottom-left corner and select the Start screen thumbnail to get to Start, or press the Windows key. Easy!

> **TIP** If you always use some applications from the desktop and you don't want to access them via the Start screen, you can pin them to the taskbar to make them instantly accessible. You can pin applications to the taskbar directly from the Start screen if the application is not Metro, and you have the option to Run as administrator, as shown in Figure 2-28.

FIGURE 2-28: Application commands for a non-Metro application have desktop-specific options.

Windows Explorer now uses the context-sensitive ribbon, providing access to commands based on the currently selected object. For example, if the computer is selected in Windows Explorer, then the ribbon displays a Computer tab that enables access to computer-specific items such as system properties and the control panel. Selecting a drive displays the Drive ribbon, enabling actions such as format and optimize (defragment the disk). Take some time to use the new Explorer, selecting different objects and noting how the ribbon changes; after some experimentation, it really does become a lot more intuitive to use.

FIGURE 2-29: The basic task icons for central control of the machine

From the desktop, the Settings charm provides quick access to some key configuration applets: Personalization, PC Info (System properties), Help, and the Control Panel. You can access a set of basic system tasks through the Settings charm, from both the desktop and the Start screen, as shown in Figure 2-29, including network configuration, volume control, notification configuration, and rebooting, shutting down, and sleeping the computer.

TASK MANAGER 2.0

Something that had not changed very much since its first incarnation in Windows NT 3.1 is the Task Manager, which provides information on processes running on the system and some performance metrics. Windows 8 brings an updated Task Manager. When first launched from the taskbar context menu or by pressing Ctrl + Shift + Esc, it looks very basic, as shown on the left in Figure 2-30; but clicking the More details button brings up the detailed Task Manager, shown on the right. Notice that the detailed Task Manager for processes now uses highlighting to indicate higher resource utilization, making it easy to see where resources are being used. Alternatively, you can still sort the entries on any column, placing the highest consumers at the top.

FIGURE 2-30: The basic interface to Task Manager (on the left) and the full-featured option (on the right)

The App history tab provides a new view of an application's resource utilization over time, making it easy to see where CPU and network bandwidth is being used, which is great for troubleshooting battery life and network bandwidth charges. The Startup tab lists the applications that start when the system boots, and their impact on the speed of booting. An application can be disabled and re-enabled if desired by right-clicking on the status entry. The Details and Services tabs provide detailed information about the process executables and the services running on the system.

LOGON EXPERIENCE

Passwords have served Windows users very well for a long time, but when using touch-only devices, typing a complex password on an onscreen keyboard is cumbersome and not very user friendly. Windows 8 introduces two new password options to complement the standard alphanumeric password: a pin and a picture password. To configure these sign-in options, select Settings ➜ More PC settings ➜ Users.

A pin is a simple four-digit code; a picture password enables you to select a picture and three gestures for that picture, using a specified combination of circles, lines, and taps. Both the pin and picture password are machine specific; and for a domain account they are not stored in Active Directory, so they need to be set on each machine a user logs onto. The pin and picture password are used to unlock the actual user password, which is securely stored on the Windows 8 client in an encrypted form. Figure 2-31 shows the option to create a picture password and the simple three-step process. Once created, you can use the picture password, the pin, or a regular alphanumeric password to log on to or unlock a machine.

▶ The onscreen keyboards in Windows 8 are far better than those in Windows 7 and have configurable size and layout options.

▶ Policies are available to block domain users from using pin or picture passwords.

FIGURE 2-31: For this picture password I swiped down each arm, then tapped the visor.

Windows 8 also introduces the capability to log on directly to a Windows 8 client using a Windows Live ID, and synchronizes various settings such as wallpaper, favorites, and more. This means the settings synchronized would be available on any Windows 8 device that logs on with the same Live ID. It is also possible to link a Live ID with a domain account for easier access to services that use Live ID or just to synchronize certain settings between machines.

There are no major profile changes in Windows 8, but there are some additional settings that allow a primary computer to be specified for users so that only when a user logs on to a primary computer are his profile and data roamed to the device. Additional settings related to the use of offline mode are available and documented at http://technet.microsoft.com/en-us/library/hh848267.aspx.

MULTI-MONITOR CONFIGURATION TIPS

I want to briefly cover multi-monitor configuration. The Start screen only occupies a single display; the other monitors show the desktop, and when the Start screen is open, the other monitors continue to show the applications running on the desktop. Selecting Desktop from the Start screen makes that display also show the desktop, meaning all displays are showing the desktop. The Start screen can be moved between displays using the Windows key and either the Page Up (PgUp) or the Page Down (PgDn) key, which cycles it left or right between the displays. While the Windows 8 Consumer Preview limited gestures and Metro applications to a single monitor, the Windows 8 Release Preview and final version allow the use of all monitors for the Start screen, gestures, and Metro applications.

One change from Windows 7 when using multiple monitors is that the taskbar appears on all displays, making it easy to move and launch applications; but the system tray shows only on the display used for the Start screen.

New Application Model and the Windows Store

▶ Metro applications are only available on Windows Server 2012 if the Desktop Experience feature is enabled.

Windows 8 introduces the new *Windows Runtime (WinRT)*, the foundation for Metro-style applications that enables them to not only be written in languages such as C++, C#, and VB.NET, but also using JavaScript, HTML5, and CSS. This enables developers to create an application that can run on different architectures such as x86, amd64, and even ARM. Metro applications have strict guidelines regarding the creation of clean applications that work well in the Metro environment and offer users great interaction in both snapped and full views.

To use a Metro application, the display must support a minimum resolution of 1024×768; and if the snapping of a Metro application to the left or right edge is required, the display must be at least 1366 × 768. If the display is not at least 1366 wide, then the capability to snap is not available.

Windows 8 introduces a new Windows Store that features Metro-style applications. In addition to providing a central location for purchasing and installing applications based on a user's Live ID, the Windows Store will track the applications installed; when updates for the application are available, the Windows Store will display them and perform the update when requested by the user, simplifying application management for the user and providing an experience similar to what users have grown to expect with mobile devices like the Windows Phone and the iPad. The Windows Store was enabled in the Consumer Preview and contains a wide range of applications that is growing rapidly.

The addition of support for the ARM architecture to Windows 8 with the Windows RT edition will enable Windows to run on a whole new range of devices that are far smaller and use less power than traditional Windows desktop devices, but these ARM devices will not be able to run traditional Windows applications that use the desktop. Windows RT devices will only run Metro-style applications that are built on WinRT.

Windows To Go

There is one final technology I want to mention regarding Windows 8, and that is the new Windows To Go capability that will be available for the Windows 8 Enterprise Edition SKU. *Windows To Go* enables a physical machine to boot from a USB drive that contains a complete Windows 8 installation, and Windows 8 runs fully from the USB drive without allowing any access to disk resources on the computer booting from the Windows To Go USB drive. Any internal disks on the machine booted from Windows To Go are actually placed in an offline state.

▶ Windows To Go is not supported on Windows Server 2012 and differs from the technology used by Hyper-V Server for a USB boot.

Computers must support booting from USB, and USB 3.0 computers and USB drives should be used for best performance. A special Windows To Go Creator wizard is used to create a USB drive with a special Windows 8 client configuration that can be used when booting from a USB device enabled with Windows To Go.

When using Windows To Go, the machine cannot be hibernated because hibernation stores computer-specific information on the disk, which would not apply to a machine booted from a USB drive. Nor is the Trusted Platform Module (TPM) in a computer used by Windows To Go because of the roaming nature of Windows To Go; and if BitLocker Drive Encryption is needed, a boot password is used instead of the TPM.

▶ If hibernation is required for Windows To Go, a Group Policy setting is available to enable it.

The reason I want to focus on Windows To Go is because this book is about Microsoft virtualization, technology that enables the operating system to be separated from the machine on which it is running and instead roam on a USB device. This is a great new capability that may be used by organizations in place of solutions such as VDI or session virtualization for some key scenarios. I see Windows To Go working well in scenarios such as the following:

▶ Contractors and temporary workers who have their own machines. A corporate Windows To Go USB drive can be given to the contractors to plug into their laptops and work in the corporate environment without any changes to their equipment and without access to the local content on the device. Similarly, they cannot copy corporate data onto their devices because storage devices are offline, so the corporate environment is secure in both directions.

▶ Users working from home as part of normal operations or in disaster scenarios using their own machines. Using a corporate Windows To Go USB drive, the home machine can be booted to the corporate image.

▶ Providing users with their own environment that travels with them on different corporate machines, such as in hot-desk organizations whereby users may use a different desk and computer each day. If all users have their own Windows To Go devices, they will have a consistent desktop experience.

Windows 8 Editions

There will be four versions of Windows 8, but only two of them will be available for purchase through retail channels. The four versions and their features are shown below, although other features may be added at the final release.

TABLE 2-2: Windows 8 Versions and Features

FEATURE NAME	WINDOWS 8	WINDOWS 8 PRO	WINDOWS 8 ENTERPRISE	WINDOWS RT
Upgrades from Windows 7 Starter, Home Basic, Home Premium	x	x		
Upgrades from Windows 7 Professional, Ultimate		x		
Start screen, Semantic Zoom, Live Tiles	x	x	x	x
Windows Store	x	x	x	x

FEATURE NAME	WINDOWS 8	WINDOWS 8 PRO	WINDOWS 8 ENTERPRISE	WINDOWS RT
Apps (Mail, Calendar, People, Messaging, Photos, SkyDrive, Reader, Music, Video)	x	x	x	x
Microsoft Office (Word, Excel, PowerPoint, OneNote)				x
Internet Explorer 10	x	x	x	x
Device encryption				x
Connected standby	x	x	x	x
Microsoft account	x	x	x	x
Desktop	x	x	x	x
Installation of x86/64 and desktop software	x	x	x	
Updated Windows Explorer	x	x	x	x
Windows Defender	x	x	x	x
SmartScreen	x	x	x	x
Windows Update	x	x	x	x
Enhanced Task Manager	x	x	x	x
Switch languages on the fly (Language Packs)	x	x	x	x
Better multiple monitor support	x	x	x	x
Storage Spaces	x	x	x	
Windows Media Player	x	x	x	

(continues)

TABLE 2-2: (*continued*)

FEATURE NAME	WINDOWS 8	WINDOWS 8 PRO	WINDOWS 8 ENTERPRISE	WINDOWS RT
Exchange ActiveSync	x	x	x	x
File history	x	x	x	x
ISO / VHD mount	x	x	x	x
Mobile broadband features	x	x	x	x
Picture password	x	x	x	x
Play To	x	x	x	x
Remote Desktop (client)	x	x	x	x
Reset and refresh your PC	x	x	x	x
Snap	x	x	x	x
Touch and Thumb keyboard	x	x	x	x
Trusted boot	x	x	x	x
VPN client	x	x	x	x
BitLocker and Bit-Locker To Go		x	x	
Boot from VHD		x	x	
Client Hyper-V		x	x	
Domain Join		x	x	
Encrypting File System		x	x	
Group Policy		x	x	
Remote Desktop (host)		x	x	
BranchCache			x	
DirectAccess			x	

FEATURE NAME	WINDOWS 8	WINDOWS 8 PRO	WINDOWS 8 ENTERPRISE	WINDOWS RT
AppLocker			x	
Windows To Go			x	
Windows 8 App Deployment side-load			x	
VDI enhancements			x	

Windows RT will only be available pre-installed on ARM tablets and devices, while Windows 8 Enterprise Edition will only be available to customers with enterprise agreements with Microsoft. Microsoft has a detailed blog entry on Windows 8 Enterprise at http://windowsteamblog.com/windows/b/business/archive/2012/04/18/introducing-windows-8-enterprise-and-enhanced-software-assurance-for-today-s-modern-workforce.aspx. The Microsoft Desktop Optimization Pack and Windows Intune remain additional components. Windows Media Center is no longer a core part of Windows 8 but will be available as an add-on media pack component.

SUMMARY

This brief introduction to Windows 8 covered the key items that enable you to navigate and work with it on the client and the server, but the best teacher is your own hands-on experience, so just install it and start playing. As mentioned earlier in the chapter, see http://www.savilltech.com/videos/win8nav/win8nav.wmv for a demonstration of the material covered in this chapter regarding interacting with Windows.

Windows 8 will bring Windows to a wide range of new devices and use scenarios, supporting both touch as a first-class interface method and much smaller form factor devices because of advancements in technology and the ARM version of Windows. The key point is that a device running Windows 8 will offer a no-compromise experience, with the ability to run all the Windows applications and enable all the manageability that has become standard with Windows. Devices running Windows RT will be able to run all the Metro-style applications and feature the same interface experience as the other Windows 8 editions. Like anything new, once people get past the initial shock of the changes and begin to use it, I think the experience will be positive.

CHAPTER 3

Virtualizing Client Operating Systems

This chapter looks at virtualizing operating systems on the client itself. There are two main purposes for virtualization on a client system: resolving application incompatibility with newer operating systems, and supporting power users who need different environments for testing and doing their jobs. Various solutions are available for client-side operating system virtualization, and in this chapter you learn about the Microsoft technologies and where they best fit.

VIRTUALIZING AN OPERATING SYSTEM: THE "HELLO WORLD" OF VIRTUALIZATION

As I described in Chapter 1, my first experience with virtualization was running VMware Workstation on my desktop computer, which enabled me to run many operating system instances on a single physical box. I used this for testing purposes, both for software I wrote and for exploring various configurations for Windows Server and Client that helped me learn and do my job. For many people who have been in the industry for a while, this type of desktop virtualization solution will be familiar. Although this form of machine virtualization was very basic, the principles underlying it still apply to the advanced server virtualization explored throughout this book.

To be clear, note that when I talk about client virtualization in this chapter, unless stated otherwise I am talking about machine virtualization, not other technologies for virtualizing applications and user data that are used on the client operating systems.

Two main components of a virtualization platform are aimed at a client platform. One is the virtualization technology itself that enables the creation of virtual machines and their assets, such as an amount of memory, processor resource allocation, network access, and some virtual storage in the form of a virtual hard drive. The second is the solution's management interface, which is typically in the form of an application that runs on the client operating system and allows actions such as creating, starting, and stopping a virtual machine.

The technology to enable virtualization on a client platform has traditionally been a type 2 hypervisor, whereby the hypervisor runs on top of the operating system that is actually installed on the hardware. In the Microsoft environment this means the hypervisor runs on top of Windows Vista or Windows 7. This is different from a type 1 hypervisor such as Hyper-V, whereby the hypervisor runs directly on the hardware and the operating systems run on top of the hypervisor, as shown in Figure 3-1.

A type 1 hypervisor offers better performance than a type 2 hypervisor. Because it runs directly on the hardware, it requires processors to have special virtualization technologies.

Most processor designs provide a hierarchy of instruction privilege levels, depicted as concentric *rings*, to support protection against faults and attacks. The Intel x86 architecture implemented four rings, with the innermost ring, 0, having the most privileges, while ring 3 has the most restrictions. Operating system functions are usually mapped to the rings: ring 0 runs the kernel, ring 1 runs device drivers, ring

> ▶ Many people believe Hyper-V is a type 2 hypervisor because it seems that Hyper-V is running on top of Windows Server. This is not true, however; Hyper-V runs directly on the hardware, and Windows Server actually sits on top of the hypervisor.

> ▶ The kernel is the core, and the most privileged part, of the operating system; it has full access to all the system and hardware resources and has its own protected memory area. Other parts of the operating system make requests to the kernel.

2 runs other types of driver, and ring 3 is where applications run. To be compatible with processors with fewer privilege levels, Windows uses only two rings, 0 and 3. The concept of *CPU mode* or *processor mode* parallels the privilege rings; Windows uses *kernel mode* and *user mode*, where kernel mode is anything running in ring 0, while user mode is anything running in ring 3.

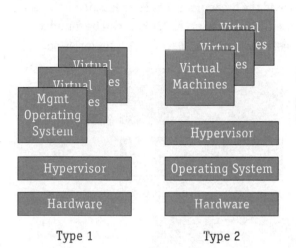

FIGURE 3-1: Basic composition of a type 1 hypervisor and a type 2 hypervisor

Many operating system instructions have to run in kernel mode, ring 0, but with the hypervisor running on the actual hardware, how can the guest operating system run in ring 0 and still be controlled by the hypervisor? Modern processor architectures provide hardware assistance for virtualization by inserting a new -1 privilege level below ring 0. The hypervisor instructions execute in *ring -1*, controlling access to the CPU and other resources while still allowing the operating system kernels in the virtual machines to run in ring 0. This allows the virtual machines running on a type 1 hypervisor to achieve performance almost equal to the operating system running on the bare metal without a hypervisor. This is covered in detail in Chapter 8.

The type 2 hypervisor architecture is very different. As described earlier, the hypervisor sits on top of an operating system that is installed on the physical hardware. The type 2 hypervisor places its core module as a driver at the kernel level, the *Virtual Machine Monitor (VMM)*, but the main hypervisor hardware virtualization and guest virtual machine kernel runs in either ring 1 or ring 3. This model is known as *ring compression* because instead of using rings 0 through 3, the hypervisor uses rings 1 through 3. When the virtual machine kernel mode needs to perform an action that requires true kernel mode on the processor, ring 0, the type 2 hypervisor has to trap that request and then pass it to the VMM in the kernel mode on the host OS. This

▶ Microsoft Virtual Server, which was Microsoft's initial server virtualization offering, was a type 2 hypervisor and therefore unable to compete with other major server hypervisors in terms of performance and features.

trapping and request process greatly degrades performance of CPU actions because of the added latency. In addition, all the virtual devices are running in ring 1, which means the input/output operations also have to be passed to the host operating system for actioning. This difference in their architecture explains why type 2 hypervisors have far lower performance than type 1 hypervisors. The type 2 architecture is shown in Figure 3-2. I highly recommend the great piece that Mark Russinovich wrote on the user and kernel mode changes in Windows Server 2008. It can be found at http://technet.microsoft.com/en-us/magazine/2008.03.kernel.aspx?pr=blog.

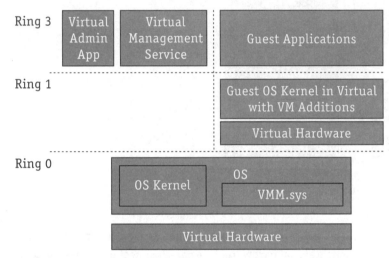

FIGURE 3-2: Basic architecture of Microsoft type 2 hypervisor solutions

In practical terms, however, this lack of bare-metal-level performance was not a big problem for client-side virtualization, as the requirements were not typically driven by high performance but rather a need to run some virtual machines with different operating systems. The hardware requirements for ring -1 and the additional complexity of a type 1 hypervisor didn't make sense for client machines.

Client virtualization has always been very basic, lacking many features of server-based virtualization solutions. Reasons for this include the following:

▶ There is also less money to be made in client-side virtualization solutions. Why spend money for what is now freely available? Less potential money means less development budget.

- ▶ A client machine typically has far fewer resources than a server, so it can run fewer virtual machines. Therefore, the client virtualization solution does not need the same scalability as a server virtualization solution.

- ▶ Client machines don't have the same access to advanced hardware, such as fibre channel and advanced networking equipment, so the virtualization solution doesn't need as many features.

► The demands and importance of virtual machines on a client machine are typically lower, meaning high-availability technologies are unnecessary.

► The type of work being performed in the virtual machines is likely to be more focused; and the virtual machines are directly accessed, rather than running background services.

Client virtualization requires some additional features because of the highly interactive nature of virtual machine usage, such as the capability to map USB devices from the local host to the virtual machine. In addition, consider that many client devices might only have wireless network connections, which are typically not supported by server virtualization solutions. Many users have laptop machines that run from a battery, so these machines are typically placed into sleep or hibernate mode to enable a quick resumption of work when the device is needed again. This capability is unnecessary on a server platform, so most virtualization solutions block these power-saving activities. In summary, client virtualization solutions lack many features of server virtualization solutions but have some additional needs.

Times have changed. Many users need to run 64-bit operating systems in virtual machines, which are typically not supported by type 2 hypervisors, and most client hypervisors are limited to 32-bit operating systems. Even with Windows Virtual PC in Windows 7, the 32-bit guest limitation was still present, even when running on 64-bit Windows 7.

EXAMINING THE BENEFITS OF VIRTUALIZING LOCALLY

While the limitations of current client virtualization seem apparent, before criticizing Microsoft for not offering a type 1 hypervisor for Windows 7 capable of supporting a 64-bit guest, consider why you really want client virtualization and the needs of client operating systems. The uses for client virtualization fall into two major classes:

► Application compatibility

► IT professionals and developers, usually considered "power users"

Currently, application compatibility is a huge challenge for organizations that want to move from Windows XP to Windows 7. Numerous applications will not run on Windows 7, for a variety of reasons. Some have dependencies in the operating system that are no longer present, and some have 16-bit components but the organization

► Fortunately, Microsoft plans to offer built-in client-based Hyper-V support for Windows 8.

► Most applications can be made to run on Windows 7 through application compatibility technologies, also known as shims. Fully explore any such options for an application before using client virtualization.

now wishes to use a 64-bit operating system. The most common issue, however, is that the original application was poorly written and used nondocumented methods to perform functions that worked at the time but no longer work with newer operating systems. For applications that cannot run on the client operating system, one solution is to run the application on a Windows 2003 Terminal Server, which is the same basic operating system as Windows XP, and then users access the application remotely using remote desktop technologies. The drawback with this approach is that the user must be connected to the network to access the application; and a potentially large amount of datacenter infrastructure is required, depending on the number of applications and the number of concurrent users. The other option is to use client-side virtualization, running the legacy operating system, such as Windows XP, in a local virtual machine along with those few specific applications that only run on Windows XP installed in the Windows XP virtual machine. If the majority of your applications are unable to function, then consider engaging a Microsoft partner to help troubleshoot your compatibility problems. Most applications can be made to work in Windows 7, or there is an update that will make it work from the vendor or through application shimming. Note that application virtualization such as App-V is not a solution to compatibility challenges related to applications and operating systems, a topic covered in detail in Chapter 4. The requirements for this application compatibility solution are fairly basic: a single virtual machine, typically running behind the scenes with minimal resource requirements, running one or two applications that are just surfaced to the user's desktop when needed.

The other use is for those power users, the IT professionals who want multiple operating system instances available to test scenarios or different operating systems on a single machine, or developers who require different environments and testing and debugging processes. These power users have different requirements than users who just need client virtualization for application compatibility. For example, a developer might need client virtualization for the following:

▶ Automating the deployment of multiple virtual machines to quickly set up new environments to meet current development or test requirements

▶ Testing using VMs, which may need to be fairly large in terms of resource usage and include multiple virtual machines communicating

▶ Debugging using snapshot technologies. This is a great benefit for developers. Consider a developer trying to fix a problem. Using snapshot technologies, which enable multiple point-in-time states of a VM to be saved and then reused repeatedly if required, a developer can get a virtual environment to a state that has a specific problem, snapshot that state, and then try different remedies without sacrificing the capability to revert back to that known state.

▶ Performing validation with testing on true server virtualization, which ideally means compatibility between the client and server virtualization technologies

That is a fairly hefty set of requirements; and as you'll see in the next section, they were really not met even with the latest Windows 7–based Windows Virtual PC solution, which was targeted for the application compatibility scenarios described earlier, which have far lower requirements. There are other use cases for client-side virtualization, but many of the scenarios are variations on the main two. Consider sales professionals who need to demonstrate their software to customers. Client virtualization would enable great demonstrations, running even server operating systems in the virtual machines.

Throughout this book I talk about virtual desktop infrastructure (VDI) and connecting remotely to a client operating system that is running in a virtual machine in the datacenter. VDI requires connectivity to the datacenter, but with client virtualization it is possible to check out a VDI image and run it locally on your laptop so it's available offline, and then check it back in when connected to the network again. This requires compatibility between the client and server virtualization platforms.

Two other scenarios I'm seeing more frequently are the Bring Your Own Device to work scenario and the contractor machine scenario. For these, a typical solution is VDI. However, another option, which is similar to checking out a VDI image, is to install a client hypervisor on the machine and run a corporate operating system side by side with the device's normal operating system, keeping them isolated from each other. The advantage of this over VDI is that you have no datacenter compute or storage requirements to host all the virtual machines used by devices, so it is cheaper.

Clearly, there is a need for client virtualization that meets the needs of a variety of scenarios and business requirements. As you will see in the next section, until very recently Microsoft's client solutions have been squarely aimed at the application compatibility scenario, rather than at providing a powerful client hypervisor for power users—but that is changing in Windows 8.

▶ This capability is available using the Citrix XenDesktop VDI solution, which leverages the Citrix XenClient as a local hypervisor running on the desktop machine.

▶ Other options are possible if the device doesn't require both the local OS and the corporate image to be running at the same time. Windows can boot from a VHD copied to the local disk; or for Windows 8, using the Windows To Go feature.

TRACING THE EVOLUTION OF CLIENT OS VIRTUALIZATION—FROM VIRTUAL PC TO CLIENT HYPER-V

▶ Connectix had virtualization solutions that enabled PlayStation games to be played on other platforms. After Sony failed to stop the product via a lawsuit, they bought the product from Connectix and then immediately dropped it.

I already talked about my first virtualization experience: sitting in a seminar where the presenter did magic using something called VMware that allowed him to run many operating systems on a single machine. Another major player in the desktop hypervisor space was Connectix, which I also tried. Connectix had a lot of technologies related to virtualization and optimization, including products to increase the amount of memory through compression, RAM disk solutions, plus Mac and Windows machine virtualization solutions for desktop and server—namely, Virtual PC and Virtual Server. The machine virtualization solutions are all type 2 hypervisors and run on top of Windows. They also had Mac machine virtualization solutions, which Microsoft continued to support and update.

In 2002, machine virtualization was becoming more prevalent, and a viable solution for the datacenter was needed because of increases in server hardware capability—and Microsoft did not have a solution. Rather than create something from scratch, which ultimately they do anyway, Microsoft purchased Connectix early in 2003 and rebranded the two Windows-based solutions to create Microsoft Virtual PC and Microsoft Virtual Server.

Microsoft released its first version as Microsoft Virtual PC 2004 SP1 in June 2006 as a free product, quickly following up in early 2007 with Microsoft Virtual PC 2007, which could take advantage of hardware virtualization capabilities to improve performance; it also supported viewing on multiple monitors and supported Windows Vista.

On the server side, Microsoft released Microsoft Virtual Server 2005 in Standard and Enterprise editions; however, in 2006 Microsoft got rid of the Standard edition and released Virtual Server 2005 R2 Enterprise as a free download. The Virtual Server was also a type 2 hypervisor, running on top of Windows, and it had a lot of limitations in terms of supported virtual machine configurations. These limitations limited its ability to compete, mainly with ESX from VMware but even with Xen from Citrix.

Behind the scenes, Microsoft was working on a new server virtualization technology, originally code-named Viridian, then named Windows Server Virtualization (WSV), and then finally called Hyper-V. Hyper-V was not an update to Microsoft Virtual Server but rather a completely new type 1 machine virtualization solution designed for server workloads. It was made available shortly after the release of Windows 2008. Hyper-V delivered a great server virtualization solution that continues to get better and better.

Why am I talking about how great Hyper-V is in the client virtualization chapter? The Hyper-V client and server products are basically the same operating system. They share the same base code and many of the same features. There are different components between the client and server, but fundamentally it's the same operating system with some tweaks related to performance and capabilities associated with the operating system. This is why the client and server operating systems release around the same time. Windows XP equals Windows 2003, Windows Vista equals Windows 2008, and Windows 7 equals Windows 2008 R2.

A major update to Hyper-V was made in Windows Server 2008 R2, and many people expected Microsoft to include Hyper-V in Windows 7 to address Microsoft Virtual PC's limitations and to support power users. After all, if it's the same fundamental operating system, why not just put Hyper-V in the client and make everyone happy? This did not happen, however; instead, in 2009 Microsoft released Windows Virtual PC, which exclusively ran on Windows 7 and was still a type 2 hypervisor. New features were added, particularly the capability to:

▶ Note the subtle name change from Microsoft Virtual PC to Windows Virtual PC.

- ▶ Attach USB devices to a virtual machine

- ▶ Redirect smart cards

- ▶ Publish applications in a VM directly to the host Windows 7 operating system Start menu and run seamlessly on the Windows 7 desktop with a small update

- ▶ Integrate with Windows Explorer, making management easier and actually less intrusive to the user

Although many people were surprised that Hyper-V was not in Windows 7, look again at the list of new features introduced with Windows Virtual PC. They are great for client virtualization, particularly for accessing and using applications running within the virtual machines. The reason goes back to different requirements between server and client, and the use case on which Microsoft focused for client virtualization. For Windows Virtual PC in general and Windows 7 specifically, the use case for client virtualization was application compatibility, not the power users.

Why not use the Hyper-V from Windows Server 2008 R2? Hyper-V cannot attach any USB device to a VM, and the only way to get any USB connectivity to a virtual machine on Hyper-V is to remote desktop to the operating system in the VM and then use the Remote Desktop Protocol device redirection features. Hyper-V does not easily integrate with the native operating system. In fact, it was designed with security in mind and actively obstructs links between virtual machines and the host operating system. This means that while using Hyper-V on the client would have been good for the power users, it would not have been good for application compatibility purposes or general use by basic users. Microsoft learned many lessons from Windows Vista

▶ This is exactly what Windows Virtual PC delivered and why just putting Hyper-V in the client would not have worked very well.

deployments at many organizations, and most problems involved applications not being compatible and stopping deployments of Windows Vista. For Windows 7, Microsoft wanted a workable solution for application compatibility to ensure that applications would not cause any delay of its deployment.

There would have been other problems putting Hyper-V on the client without some significant work. Consider initiatives around power saving and how people use a laptop. When people close the lid, the computer goes to sleep and hibernates to save the battery life. You cannot do this with Hyper-V, as Hyper-V would break any suspend or hibernate functions as part of its design. In addition, many laptops have only wireless network connections, and Hyper-V virtual networks cannot use wireless network adapters. This did not stop people from trying, however, and because Windows 7 and Windows 2008 R2 are effectively the same operating system, some power users deployed Windows Server 2008 R2 as their desktop operating system and enabled Hyper-V. I was one of them, and saw firsthand these functionality issues. On a desktop machine, however, these do not present a huge problem.

TIP   To make Windows Server 2008 R2 look and act like Windows 7, you need to install a few additional features and perform some customizations. This can also be carried out on Windows Server 2012 to make it act more like Windows 8 (client), but there will be less need to do this thanks to Client Hyper-V in Windows 8. Install the following features:

▶ **BitLocker:** If you want disk encryption

▶ **Desktop Experience:** This provides the Aero themes and multimedia capabilities. If installing on Windows Server 2012, the Desktop Experience feature is part of the User Interfaces and Infrastructure Feature group.

▶ **Wireless LAN Service:** Enables the use of wireless adapters, which is useful when installing Windows Server 2008 R2 on a laptop

▶ **XPS Viewer:** To view XPS documents

Make sure you install the latest audio and graphics card drivers for your equipment using the drivers designed for Windows 7 64-bit, which should work on Windows Server 2008 R2. The Windows 7 64-bit drivers should also work for any other hardware in the machine.

If you frequently use search, then install the Windows Server File Services role. Turn off the Shutdown Event Tracker, which is the dialog that pops up every time you shut down the server. I documented the process to disable the Shutdown Event Tracker at http://www.windowsitpro.com/article/configuration/how-do-i-enable-disable-the-shutdown-event-tracker-.

Launch **services.msc** and in the Themes and Windows Audio Services properties, set Startup type to Automatic and click Start. This enables the capability to
use Aero features and hear audio. The next step is to enable Aero Peek and hot
color tracking. Open the System control panel applet. From the Advanced tab,
select Settings under the Performance section. Under the Visual Effects tab,
you can then enable the features you want, such as Aero Peek. It is also possible to change the computer's processor priority from Background services,
which is the normal server configuration, to foreground applications by selecting Programs from the Advanced tab of the Performance Options dialog, as
shown in Figure 3-3.

Along with Windows Virtual PC, Microsoft released a feature called Windows XP
Mode, which works only with Windows 7
Professional, Enterprise, and Ultimate editions. This was designed to provide users
with a fully enabled and licensed Windows XP environment into which legacy
applications could easily be installed.
Those applications would be automatically displayed on the main Windows 7
desktop Start menu; and when launched

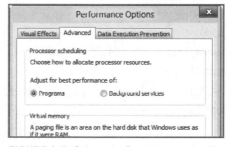

FIGURE 3-3: Select the Programs option if
you want Windows to prioritize applications
over background services.

they would appear on the Windows 7 desktop rather than a separate virtual machine
window. I cover this in more detail in the "Using Windows XP Mode" section in this
chapter. XP Mode was great for application compatibility for home users but it was not
manageable. For enterprises that needed similar capabilities to run legacy applications on Windows 7, Microsoft released Microsoft Enterprise Desktop Virtualization
(MED-V), included with the Microsoft Desktop Optimization Pack, which offered features similar to XP Mode but with additional capabilities. It was also manageable as
part of an organization's desktop management infrastructure. MED-V is also covered
in detail later in this chapter.

At the time of writing (2012), Microsoft is releasing Windows 8 and Windows
Server 2012, and the focus has shifted to client virtualization again. Remember the
two main use-case scenarios for client virtualization: application compatibility
and power users. Windows XP was released over 10 years ago, and most applications
now have versions that work with Windows 7, which means they will also work with
Windows 8. This shift enables Microsoft to focus on the power users and add the
engineering to take its Server Hyper-V solution to the client, which is exactly what

▶ While Windows
8 has a new
Metro-style
interface and a
new programming
model with WinRT,
applications that
were written
for Windows 7
should work on
Windows 8 without
modification.

has happened with Windows 8 and Client Hyper-V. Using Hyper-V on the client makes more sense than trying to update Windows Virtual PC to handle all the power user scenarios such as automation, power features, and server compatibility that are already present in Hyper-V on the server. As you will see in the section "Client Hyper-V in Windows 8" later in this chapter, the problems associated with using Hyper-V on a client have been addressed.

INTRODUCING WINDOWS VIRTUAL PC

Despite the release of Windows 8, many organizations will continue to use Windows 7 for some time. As previously discussed, *Windows Virtual PC* is the Microsoft client virtualization solution for Windows 7, so this section takes a brief look at using Windows Virtual PC under Windows 7, as it also forms the foundation for both XP Mode and MED-V.

Windows Virtual PC runs on 32-bit or 64-bit processors and runs on all versions of Windows 7 Home Basic and above. Initially, Windows Virtual PC required the processor to support hardware-assisted virtualization, even though it is only a type 2 hypervisor, but an update released shortly after Windows Virtual PC was released removed that requirement.

Windows Virtual PC is available at `http://www.microsoft.com/windows/virtual-pc/download.aspx` and includes the update. Once installed, Windows Virtual PC is available from the Start menu, and virtual machines can be started and stopped through a new integration with Explorer, as shown in Figure 3-4.

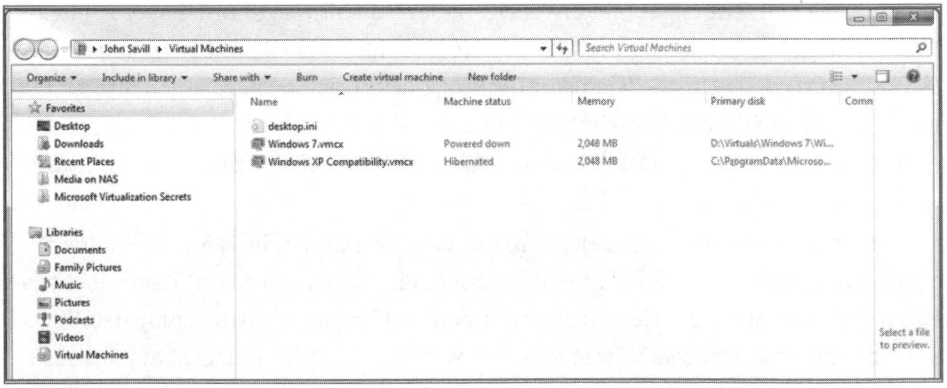

FIGURE 3-4: Viewing and controlling virtual machines with Windows Virtual PC

The virtual machines created with Windows Virtual PC can only have a single virtual processor assigned to them; and because only 32-bit guests can run in the VM, a maximum of 3.7GB of memory can be allocated. The guest operating systems supported by Windows Virtual PC are Windows XP SP3 and above, Windows Vista SP1 and above, and even 32-bit Windows 7.

Each virtual machine can have up to four virtual network adapters assigned, as shown in Figure 3-5. Each virtual adapter can be in one of four states:

▶ Not connected

▶ Connected to an internal network, which allows virtual machines to communicate with each other but not outside the physical machine

▶ Connected using Shared Networking, which uses network address translation (NAT), meaning the virtual machine does not have a unique address on the actual network

▶ Connected to an actual physical adapter using bridging technologies, meaning the virtual machine maps directly to the network adapter and therefore has an address, such as through DHCP or even static IP. Any adapters that are used by a virtual machine will have the Virtual PC Network Filter Driver enabled, as shown in Figure 3-6.

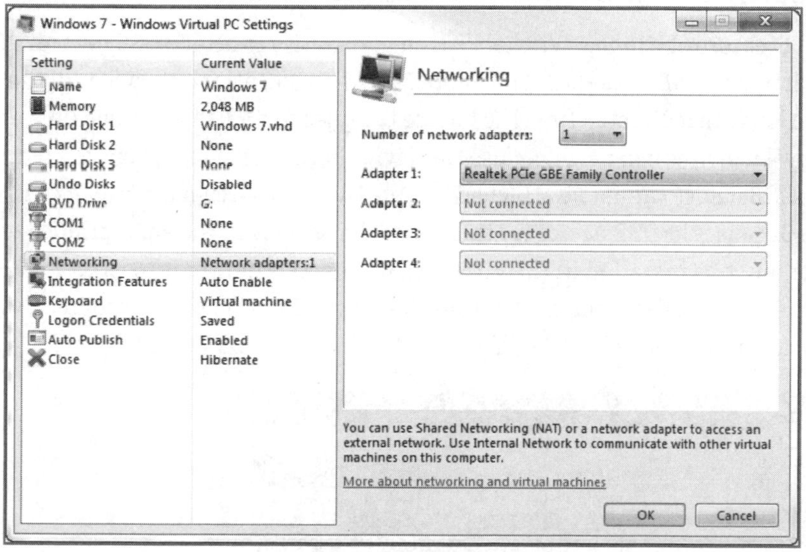

FIGURE 3-5: Viewing the networking configuration for a virtual machine

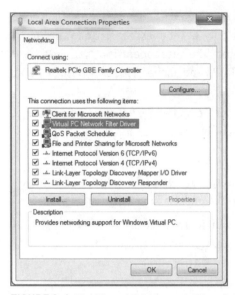

FIGURE 3-6: The Virtual PC Network Filter Driver is enabled for any network adapters used by a virtual machine.

Attaching USB Devices to a Virtual Machine

► You would not use this feature for devices that can be supported with normal Remote Desktop Protocol sharing, such as printers that are already well handled and can be shared between the host and guest OS.

A great feature of Windows Virtual PC is the capability to attach USB devices directly to a virtual machine, as shown in Figure 3-7. When you attach a device, all the I/O operations are redirected from the host to the guest operating system. This means the local machine can no longer use the device because its operations are redirected, and a USB device cannot be attached to more than one virtual machine at the same time. Because the USB device is attached at the port level, the appropriate device driver must be installed in the virtual machine in order for it to function. For an attached device, the associated option changes to Release; select it to free it up again for local use or to attach it to a different VM.

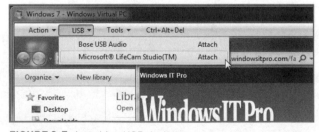

FIGURE 3-7: Attaching USB devices

Virtual machines are created from the Windows Explorer view of the Virtual Machines folder, using the Create virtual machine action, which runs the Create a Virtual Machine wizard. To start a virtual machine, just double-click on it in the Windows Virtual PC Explorer view, or select it and click Open. The virtual machine video output will open in a new window and operating systems can be installed.

After an operating system is installed in the virtual machine, you should install the Windows Virtual PC Integration Components in order to get maximum functionality and performance, including folder and clipboard integration between the virtual machine and the host operating system. In the Tools menu of the VM window, select Install Integration Components, follow the steps in the wizard, and then restart the VM.

When the window for a virtual machine is closed, the virtual machine is hibernated, meaning the memory and any device state are saved to disk. This enables the virtual machine to start faster the next time it is needed. If you want to shut down the virtual machine instead, run the following command from an elevated command prompt within the VM:

```
shutdown /s /t 0 /f
```

The key goal of Windows Virtual PC is overcoming application compatibility problems by running legacy applications in a virtual machine; and for the best user experience, the applications running in the virtual machine should be accessible from the host desktop. Windows Virtual PC enables this through the Auto Publish capability, shown in Figure 3-8, which automatically publishes any applications installed in the virtual machine Start menu to the host Start menu. When a user runs the application from the Start menu, the virtual machine that has the application will start automatically behind the scenes, and then the application itself will start. Instead of the entire virtual machine desktop displaying on the user's Windows 7 desktop, only the application's windows will show. To users it appears as though the application is running on their local machine. If your virtual machine is running Windows XP or Windows Vista, a seamless application update (RemoteApp) must be installed on it to enable this integration:

▶ If you install an application in the virtual machine that does not place a shortcut on the All Users Start menu, you will need to add one yourself for the application to show on the host operating system Start menu.

- ▶ Windows XP SP3 or Windows XP Professional SP3: http://www.microsoft.com/download/en/details.aspx?displaylang=en&id=4465

- ▶ Windows Vista SP1 and above, and Enterprise and Ultimate editions: http://www.microsoft.com/download/en/details.aspx?displaylang=en&id=10007

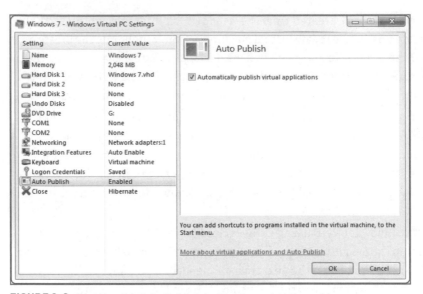

FIGURE 3-8: Enabling the Auto Publish feature for a virtual machine

Using Windows XP Mode Virtualization

Windows *XP Mode* is a download available for Windows 7 Professional, Enterprise, and Ultimate editions. It uses the Windows Virtual PC download but includes the RemoteApp update I just described. It delivers a Windows XP virtual machine that Microsoft provides preconfigured and licensed for installation on the Windows 7 machine. The Windows XP virtual machine download, which is 500MB in size, quickly provides average users with an easy way to get a Windows XP environment running, into which any legacy applications can be installed and then made available on the Windows 7 desktop.

The XP Mode feature is not any special technology beyond the basic Windows Virtual PC and application publishing that is available without XP Mode. XP Mode just provides a packaged solution and an XP license for users. Another purpose for which XP Mode may be useful is to maintain access to Internet Explorer 6. If Internet Explorer 6 is required, it's important to ensure that the Internet Explorer browser is not automatically updated by Windows Update or other mechanisms. To prevent Windows Update from updating the browser, use the Internet Explorer Blocker Toolkits, which provide registry key and group policy templates. The IE 9 Blocker Toolkit can be found at www.microsoft.com/download/en/details .aspx?displaylang=en&id=179.

▶ If the XP Mode VM does not meet your needs, instead use your own custom OS. To integrate with the Windows 7 desktop, ensure that the Integration Components and the published application update are installed.

XP Mode has other uses beyond just running an application in Windows XP or maintaining access to Internet Explorer 6. I have seen organizations using Windows Vista and even Windows 7 within a virtual machine. Suppose your desktop is running 64-bit Windows 7 and you have an application that does not run on a 64-bit operating system. Installing 32-bit Windows 7 in a virtual machine and integrating with the main 64-bit Windows 7 desktop provides access to the applications in the 32-bit Windows 7 virtual machine.

At www.savilltech.com/videos/winvpcandxpmode/winvpcandxpmode1024768.wmv I provide a walkthrough of Windows Virtual PC and XP Mode that also demonstrates the advanced USB attachment capabilities. The video also shows the seamless applications in action.

USING MICROSOFT ENTERPRISE DESKTOP VIRTUALIZATION (MED-V)

Windows Virtual PC and the packaged XP Mode provide a good solution when applications that only run on Windows XP must remain available in a Windows 7 environment. The challenge is that there is no easy way to manage the virtual machines in an enterprise environment, and no easy way to ensure that all the users of a machine get the shortcuts from the virtual machines. Additionally, for scenarios in which certain websites must open in Internet Explorer 6, users are responsible for launching IE6 from the XP VM.

Microsoft Enterprise Desktop Virtualization (MED-V) provides an enterprise solution for legacy application compatibility—in a nutshell, an XP Mode with manageability. MED-V is part of the Microsoft Desktop Optimization Pack (MDOP), so using MED-V requires the desktop to have the MDOP subscription.

▶ MDOP is only available for desktops that are covered by Microsoft Software Assurance or Windows Intune, as an additional option.

Implementing MED-V

MED-V, like Windows XP Mode, uses Windows Virtual PC to run virtual machines; however, MED-V also installs a MED-V agent on both the host and the guest desktops to provide additional capabilities. MED-V provides very granular control over the shortcuts added to the Start menu and allows configuration of specific URLs that should always be redirected to the Internet Explorer running inside the MED-V virtual machine.

MED-V is currently at version 2, which is very different from version 1 in terms of infrastructure requirements. MED-V 1 required specific MED-V servers that distributed the MED-V virtual machines and had the technology to update the virtual machines as needed. MED-V 2 no longer has any such infrastructure requirements. MED-V 2 has a wizard that is used to create an installer package, which includes a preconfigured virtual machine with applications installed and any enterprise configuration—including which URLs should be redirected to the browser inside the VM. The created MSI file can then be distributed to the desktops in the enterprise using any electronic software distribution (ESD) system, such as System Center Configuration Manager. To maintain the virtual machine, you leverage existing desktop management solutions; but because the virtual machine is running a legacy operating system, no significant updates should be required for the operating system, and the only applications within the virtual machine are legacy applications that are unlikely to ever be updated.

To create the MED-V package, the MED-V Workspace Packager is used, which is passed through the VHD that contains the legacy operating system and legacy applications, along with Start menu shortcuts and the URL redirection, as shown in Figure 3-9. *URL redirection*, also called Web redirection, is very useful when users access a number of URLs that require a legacy version of Internet Explorer. Rather than the user having to manually launch the legacy IE from the MED-V image, then type in the legacy URL, the user types the URL in the Windows 7 environment and URL redirection automatically redirects to the legacy IE instance in the MED-V environment. Once the Workspace Packager configuration is complete, an install package is created that contains the virtual machine and configuration of the MED-V environment, which can then be installed on desktops. The only requirement is that Windows Virtual PC and the MED-V agent must already be installed on clients.

After the MED-V package is installed on a machine, the Start menu will be populated with the applications inside the virtual machine that were configured to be published per the MED-V configuration. If you examine the properties of the Start menu shortcuts, you can see that the MED-V host agent is used to launch an application within a specific virtual machine. The following is an example shortcut (all on one line):

```
"C:\Program Files\
Microsoft Enterprise Desktop Virtualization\MedvHost.exe"
/LaunchApp %SystemRoot%\system32\vmsal.exe "Windows XP Compatibility"
"||39b215f5" "Microsoft Outlook"
```

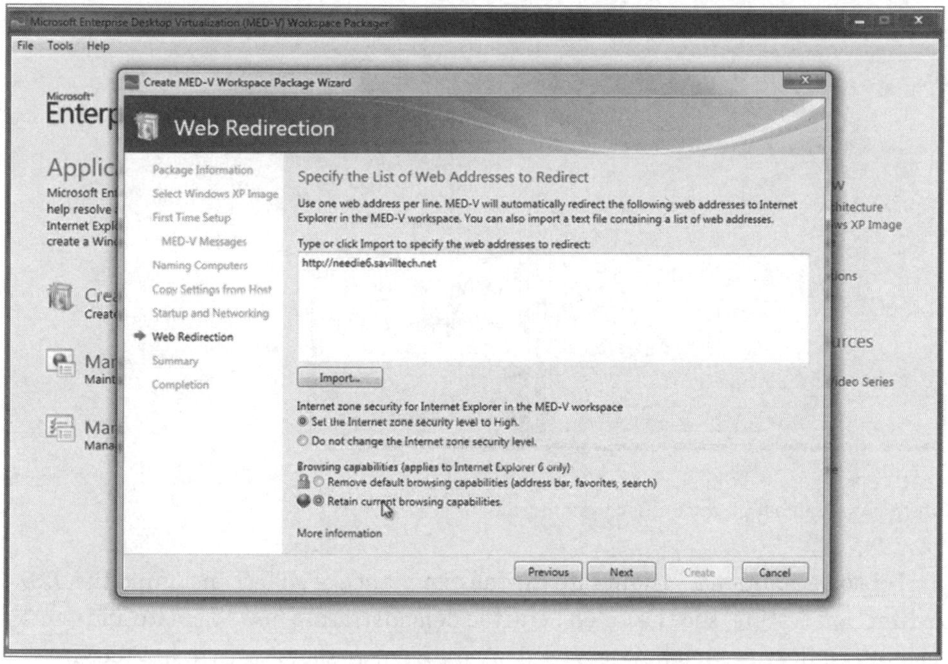

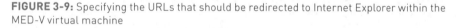

FIGURE 3-9: Specifying the URLs that should be redirected to Internet Explorer within the MED-V virtual machine

As shown in Figure 3-10, MED-V enables users to configure only one option: Fast start (the default) or Normal start. Remember that MED-V is dependent on the virtual machine that contains the applications and web browser. The user experience when first selecting a MED-V application depends on whether the virtual machine that contains those applications is already running. If the virtual machine is not running, then the user will experience a delay in the launch of the application because the virtual machine has to be restored from hibernation. By default, the MED-V virtual machine is configured to start when the user logs on, which makes the applications available immediately but means that the resources of the desktop machine are consumed, whether applications in the MED-V virtual machine are running or not. The other option is Normal start, which means the virtual machine is not started until a user first launches an application contained in the virtual machine, which saves resources until needed but delays the first launch of applications.

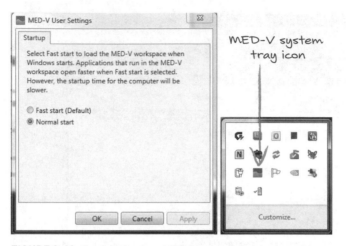

FIGURE 3-10: Configuring how MED-V starts its virtual machines, which is available from the MED-V system tray icon

For some additional insight into the full experience of MED-V, including the URL redirection feature, see the video I created demonstrating how to create and deploy a MED-V workspace, and how it is used, at `http://www.savilltech.com/videos/medv2quicklook/MedV2QuickLook.wmv`.

One problem sometimes happens when trying to directly access the virtual machine desktop for troubleshooting purposes. Normally the Windows XP desktop is never seen, as only the applications running inside the VM are available. The MED-V 2 host agent contains an administrative toolkit that is accessed by opening a command-prompt window and entering the following:

```
cd "%systemdrive%
cd Program Files\Microsoft Enterprise Desktop Virtualization"
medvhost /toolkit
```

This will open the Administration Toolkit interface, which provides access to the Event Logger and the MED-V workspace. It allows viewing of events related to MED-V, in addition to restarting or resetting the workspace, viewing the applications published inside the workspace, switching the MED-V workspace view to full screen, and viewing the web addresses configured to redirect to Internet Explorer within the XP workspace, as shown in Figure 3-11. Restarting a MED-V VM performs a reboot of the guest operating system, whereas performing a reset reverts the VM back to its initial configuration, deleting all data and configuration stored in the virtual machine.

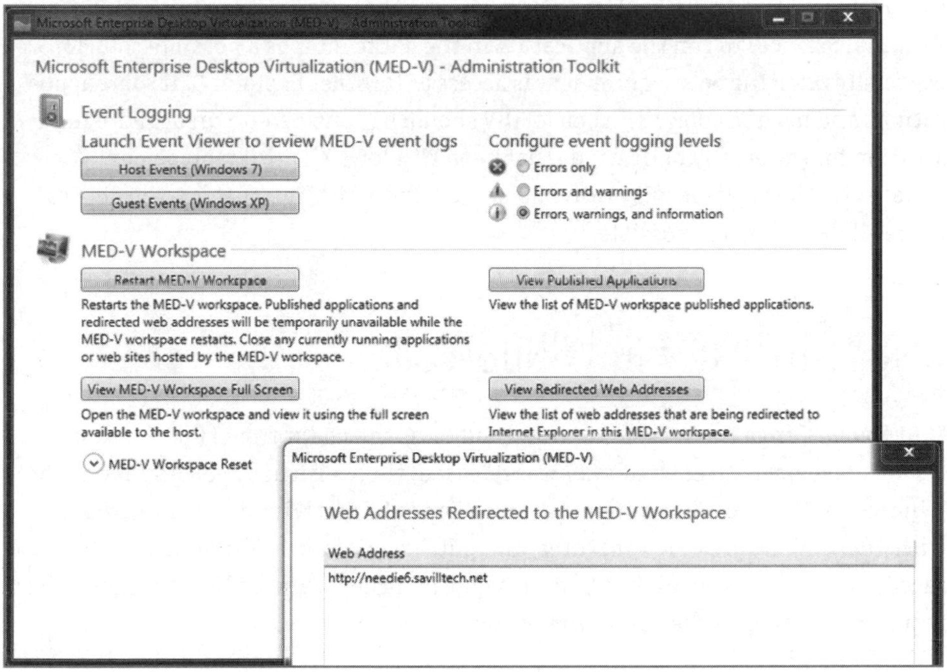

FIGURE 3-11: The MED-V Administration Toolkit interface is great for special troubleshooting and direct access to the MED-V virtual machine.

Knowing When to Use MED-V and When to Avoid It

MED-V is the enterprise application compatibility solution that should be used when your organization has critical applications that will only run on Windows XP or that require Internet Explorer 6. These applications should be of sufficient importance that the Windows 7 rollout would be delayed until these applications could be remediated. Additionally, all efforts should have been made to make the application work on Windows 7 using application compatibility settings, also known as shims, to find an updated version of the application that works with Windows 7 or even a replacement that works under Windows 7. Microsoft has numerous tools to help in application remediation, including the *Microsoft Application Compatibility Toolkit*, which is available to download from http://www.microsoft.com/download/en/details .aspx?displaylang=en&id=7352. Microsoft also offers its customers the *Application Compatibility Factory*, which provides consultants to come onsite to help remediate

▶ If you determine that a huge number of applications will run under Windows XP only, then either your company has not updated applications for 10 years or the application remediation exercise may need to be repeated.

the most troublesome applications. Also consider the use of Windows Server 2003 Terminal Services to run the application in the datacenter as a possible solution, especially when the only requirement is access to Internet Explorer 6. If some applications still need Windows XP, then MED-V should be considered a great short-term solution for those few applications that need Windows XP until replacements or updates for the applications are available for Windows 7. The goal is to be able to retire MED-V as soon as possible.

CLIENT HYPER-V IN WINDOWS 8

▶ Certain features in Windows Server 2012 Hyper-V such as a synthetic fibre channel and live VM migration are not included in Client Hyper-V, as they don't make sense on a client. More on this later in the chapter.

"Put Hyper-V from the server into the client" was the chant from IT professionals and developers after Windows 7 was released; their wish has been granted with Windows 8. Microsoft has taken the latest Hyper-V from Windows Server 2012, with nearly all its great new features, and put it straight into Windows 8 without sacrificing desktop capabilities like suspend and resume, and utilizing unique client requirements such as the use of wireless networks.

The Goals and Features of Client Hyper-V

As explained earlier, *Client Hyper-V* is targeted squarely at IT professionals and developers, enabling all the requirements those types of users require. Because Client Hyper-V is not designed for solving application compatibility issues, it does not currently work with MED-V. Client Hyper-V provides a virtualization platform that other vendors can build on to enable many scenarios, so although Microsoft targeted Client Hyper-V for IT professionals and developers, other usages may be offered in the future that extend the Client Hyper-V platform. In fact, some parts of Hyper-V have been built to be extended. The network switch, for example, is fully extensible, allowing third-party add-ins to be placed into the Hyper-V network stack. From a developer's perspective, this is very useful, enabling deep monitoring of network traffic going across the network and even the injection of network traffic.

Client Hyper-V has all the same scalability as Server Hyper-V, which means the capability to create virtual machines with 32 vCPUs, 1TB of memory, and use of the new VHDX format allowing 64TB virtual disks. I doubt any desktop system, or for that matter many server systems, will be creating virtual machines with 1TB of memory, but this degree of scalability means the hypervisor will never be a limiting factor for required configurations.

The dynamic memory feature is also available in Client Hyper-V, which allows memory to be added to and removed from virtual machines based on the needs of the operating system and the applications running on them. This feature is really aimed at maximizing the density of virtual machines on a physical machine, which is primarily a server requirement because density is not typically a huge requirement for clients; but it is still potentially useful, considering that desktops and laptops typically have fewer resources, so it could help run more virtual machines.

Some of the Server Hyper-V storage features are great for client virtualization. It is possible to add (hot-add) storage to running virtual machines on the virtual SCSI bus, and this storage can physically reside on IDE, iSCSI, USB flash drives, and even via SMB, which means the virtual machines could reside on a Windows Server 2012 file share. File shares enable users to easily share demo environments between different client machines and even the snapshots for the virtual machines.

Storage Live Migration is also included in Client Hyper-V, which means virtual machines can be easily moved between different storage mediums without having to turn off the virtual machines. A great example is running a virtual machine stored on a corporate file share on a user laptop, enabling use both at the office and at home or offline. With Storage Live Migration, the virtual machine can be moved to the laptop, without ever stopping the virtual machine. You can also move a virtual machine from the machine's local disk to an external USB drive; and it's still possible to use BitLocker, the volume encryption technology, with Hyper-V, so there is no loss of security.

While Windows Virtual PC had a basic disk undo capability, with Client Hyper-V users have the full snapshot capability that is part of Hyper-V, enabling many different point-in-time views of a virtual machine to be saved and reverted back to as needed—another requirement for developers.

In terms of what can be run within the guest operating systems, anything that works in Server Hyper-V will also work in Client Hyper-V, which includes Windows 8, Windows 7, Windows Server operating systems (both 32-bit and 64-bit), and even Linux. Remember that Client Hyper-V does not include any license rights to run the guest operating systems, so any operating systems being run need to be licensed. One way to license the guest operating systems is with the virtual rights included with various Microsoft SKUs and agreements, which could be Software Assurance or Windows Virtual Desktop Access (VDA), both of which provide up to four guest virtual rights. Another option is just buying additional Windows operating system licenses for the virtual machines.

▶ Server Message Block (SMB) version 2.2, which is part of Windows Server 2012, is required to host virtual machines on a file share. It will also be available on certain third-party storage appliances because the SMB 2.2 specification is public.

Client Hyper-V uses exactly the same virtual machine and hard disk format as Server Hyper-V, so virtual machines can easily be moved between client and server. For managing Client Hyper-V, the same Hyper-V manager tool, PowerShell, and WMI capabilities are shared between both client and server. Because the same tools are used on either platform, there is no need for additional training or ramp-up time when using Client Hyper-V if Server Hyper-V is already known.

Client Hyper-V Requirements and Installation

▶ I highly recommend using SLAT-capable processors with Server Hyper-V for best performance, although they are not required.

The requirements for Client Hyper-V are slightly different from those for Server Hyper-V. Server Hyper-V requires that the processor support hardware virtualization, such as the Intel VT and AMD-V technologies, and must be 64-bit. For Client Hyper-V, the processor must also support Secondary Level Address Translation (SLAT), which is not a requirement for a server unless it is using RemoteFX technologies. The SLAT technologies are Intel EPT or AMD RVI. SLAT is required on Client Hyper-V because it enables the processor to perform memory mapping between the physical memory and the memory within the virtual machine, which means the hypervisor no longer has to do it. This mapping is very important when a Windows Device Driver Model (WDDM) graphics driver is used, because the graphics driver uses noncached and write-combined memory to achieve the best performance, which causes the Translation Lookaside Buffer (TLB) in the CPU to be constantly flushed and rebuilt. This is very bad for performance, but SLAT accommodates and solves this problem. It is always required for Client Hyper-V because the primary environment on the client is the Windows 8 desktop, which typically has a good graphics card with WDDM drivers, and users expect good media playback and overall responsiveness. Therefore, if Client Hyper-V is needed, then the processor must support SLAT in order to ensure a good user experience. Fortunately, any Intel Core I processor, and all AMD processors since early 2011, should have SLAT support. To check, you can download a utility called coreinfo from http://technet.microsoft.com/en-us/sysinternals/cc835722 and run it with the /v switch to determine whether the processor in your machine supports virtualization extensions and SLAT. The command must be run in an elevated command prompt, which means it has administrative rights. From the Start menu, type command, then right-click on the displayed command prompt search result and select to Run as administrator. The following example shows a system that has hardware-assisted virtualization and extended page table support:

```
D:\temp\coreinfo>coreinfo /v

Coreinfo v3.04 - Dump information on system CPU and memory topology
Copyright (C) 2008-2012 Mark Russinovich
Sysinternals - www.sysinternals.com

Intel(R) Core(TM) i7-2640M CPU @ 2.80GHz
Intel64 Family 6 Model 42 Stepping 7, GenuineIntel
HYPERVISOR      -         Hypervisor is present
VMX             *         Supports Intel hardware-assisted virtualization
EPT             *         Supports Intel extended page tables (SLAT)
```

To install Client Hyper-V, open the Programs and Features control panel applet and select the "Turn Windows features on or off" action on the left side of the control panel. Select the Hyper-V feature as shown in Figure 3-12, and then click OK. A reboot is required to complete the installation, as the hypervisor has to be enabled.

▶ For several reasons, there is no policy to block enabling Client Hyper-V. One reason is because Windows features can be turned on and off even when the OS is offline, in which case such a policy would have no effect.

FIGURE 3-12: Enabling Hyper-V in the Windows 8 client

The enablement was very simple because Hyper-V is just a part of Windows, a fact that brings additional benefits. For example, no separate infrastructure is required to deploy, patch, and manage Client Hyper-V; it uses the same infrastructure that is used to deploy, patch, and manage Windows. Therefore, Windows Update, System Center Configuration Manager, and WSUS will all be able to update Client Hyper-V. The virtual machines running on Client Hyper-V are themselves just operating system instances that are managed and patched per normal processes. For example, it is possible to run the SCCM agent inside the virtual machines to manage them, or leverage WSUS or Windows Update.

Differences between Client and Server Hyper-V

I don't want to spend any time talking about how to manage Client Hyper-V, as the process is the same as Server Hyper-V, which is covered in detail in Chapter 8. Instead, it would be useful to look at the key differences. I have already mentioned the requirement for a processor that supports SLAT; and following are some of the key features with Client Hyper-V and its use of Remote Desktop Protocol 8 to communicate with the virtual machines from the Windows 8 desktop:

▶ Wireless networks can be connected to a virtual switch on Client Hyper-V, which is key for laptops.

▶ USB peripherals can be used within the virtual machine using the RDP 8 USB pass-through feature.

▶ Support is provided for up to 12 monitors on the virtual machine.

▶ You can save the virtual machine state when the client computer is put to sleep or hibernated, and resume the virtual machines when the computer is resumed. On a laptop this means that when you close your laptop lid, the virtual machine state is saved. When you open the lid again the virtual machines are started automatically.

▶ Support is provided for 3D graphics and rich multimedia in virtual machines.

▶ Bi-directional audio, including VOIP, is available.

▶ Touch support enables Metro applications in virtual machines.

Chapter 8 describes all the Server Hyper-V features; but as I mentioned earlier, some of those features are not present in Client Hyper-V. The following list includes the features not available in Client Hyper-V, and why (keep in mind that Client Hyper-V is aimed at running on a desktop machine):

▶ RemoteFX capability to virtualize the GPU and pass it to virtual machines, but Client Hyper-V does have the software GPU that is part of Windows 8 and RDP 8.

▶ Live migration and shared-nothing live migration of virtual machines, because moving virtual machines with no downtime is not a key requirement for IT professional use. Also, failover clustering is not available in client platforms, which normal live migration leverages (but not shared-nothing live migration, which enables virtual machines to be moved between hosts with no common infrastructure apart from a network connection).

- ▶ Hyper-V Replica, which enables an offsite replica of a virtual machine to be maintained. It's highly unlikely for a virtual machine running on a desktop machine to need offsite disaster recovery capability, and if it does it shouldn't be running on Client Hyper-V.

- ▶ SR-IOV network, which enables virtual machines to directly access SR-IOV-capable network adapters. No desktop machine would support SR-IOV, and the zero-latency network capability that SR-IOV provides isn't a requirement for desktop workloads.

- ▶ Synthetic fibre channel, because desktops will not have connectivity to fibre channel.

- ▶ Network virtualization, which enables the creation of networks that are abstracted from the underlying physical network fabric. This is useful for multi-tenancy environments or multi-location infrastructures, but not for desktops.

▶ Fabric refers to the components that make up the datacenter infrastructure.

If you need any of the aforementioned features, you probably shouldn't be using Client Hyper-V for hosting the virtual machines on a desktop. Use Server Hyper-V for virtual machines that require any of these features.

▶ If virtual machines are hosting non-Windows Server operating systems such as client operating systems or Linux, and the preceding features are needed, then the free Hyper-V Server product, which is covered in Chapter 8, can be used.

> **TIP** Processor and memory configurations in your desktop machine are normally not easily changed, and typically client virtual machines will not require large amounts of processor use. If you want to run many virtual machines, it may be possible to install extra memory, and dynamic memory may also facilitate some additional workload. If you were limited to making only one investment, purchase a solid-state disk (SSD) for the virtual machines, as this will greatly improve the performance of the virtual environment. After I implemented SSDs, the time required to start all my virtual machines went from 20 minutes to about 45 seconds.

I want to next share a few PowerShell commands that can be very useful on Client Hyper-V. These are my top three very simple cmdlets and a couple of combinations. Chapter 8 covers this in more detail when I dive into Hyper-V, but for now you should be aware that more cmdlets are available just for Hyper-V in Windows Server 2012 than there were for all roles and features in Windows Server 2008 R2. When working with PowerShell, commands tend to be simple and very likely state the action you want to perform. For example, to create a new virtual machine, the command is New-VM.

▶ A great way to learn the available cmdlets and switches is to work with the PowerShell ISE (Integrated Scripting Environment), which features IntelliSense to help automatically complete commands as you type.

For example, suppose you want to create a new virtual machine and then start it. The following command creates the VM and passes the path for the existing VHDX file:

```
New-VM VM1 -VHDPath d:\virtuals\vm1.vhdx
```

To start the VM in the same command, pipe the object created in the preceding command to the Start-VM cmdlet:

```
New-VM VMName -VHDPath d:\path\vm.vhdx | start-vm
```

You can combine creation of the virtual machine with other loop logic to bulk create, which is useful for testing. For example, the following command creates 10 virtual machines (see Figure 3-13):

```
foreach ($number in 1..10) {New-VM VM$number | Start-VM}
```

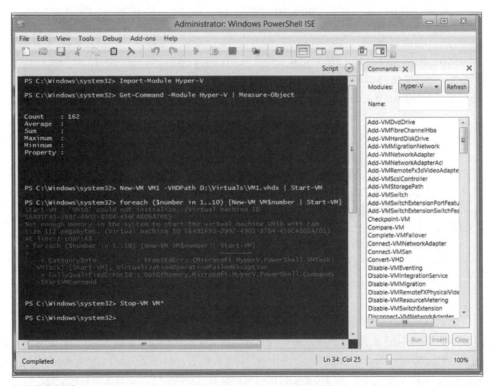

FIGURE 3-13: Creating virtual machines using the PowerShell ISE. Notice that number 10 failed due to lack of memory.

Another useful command enables you to move the storage for a VM using Power-Shell. The following example moves all the storage, including snapshots, to the new location (although it is possible to be more granular in the move operation):

```
Move-VmStorage VM -DestinationStoragePath D:\newpath
```

The last PowerShell cmdlet I want to cover is great for cleaning up. The following command stops and deletes all the virtual machines with a certain name:

```
Get-VM VM* | Stop-VM -Passthru | Remove-VM -Force
```

> **TIP** Windows 7 and Windows 2008 R2 included a new feature called Boot from VHD that enables a physical machine to boot from a virtual hard disk. It is possible to take a VHD that is used for a Client Hyper-V virtual machine and boot the desktop from it. There is no need to Sysprep or generalize the VHD; it can be taken from a VM and used directly to boot a machine. This enables an IT professional to test in a virtual machine and then take the environment to physical hardware to complete testing.
>
> First, mount the VHD from the virtual machine, which you can do by just double-clicking it with Windows 8. It will be mounted as a drive visible in Explorer. Next, add a boot option to that new mounted drive using an elevated command prompt (right-click on the bottom left of the Windows 8 desktop and select the Command Prompt [Admin] option):
>
> ```
> bcdboot <mounted drive>:\windows
> ```
>
> That's it. Upon reboot, there will be an option to boot from the VHD. It is also still possible to start the VM from the VHD, provided the physical machine is not booted from the VHD.
>
> Note that if you are using BitLocker on the host, you cannot boot using Boot to VHD from a VHD on a BitLockered drive. You would need an unencrypted volume to store the VHD.

SUMMARY

Client virtualization has two focus areas: application compatibility and IT professional usage. Application compatibility is a major focus for Windows 7 deployment; and for home users and small businesses, XP Mode with Windows Virtual PC can be a great short-term solution. For the enterprise, MED-V is a good option, providing additional manageability and automatic URL redirection for configured URLs to the Internet Explorer running inside the MED-V virtual machine. Windows 8 switches focus to virtualization for the IT professional and delivers the Hyper-V experience almost entirely feature-complete on the desktop.

CHAPTER 4

Virtualizing Desktop Applications

People often say that data is an organization's most important asset, but without applications to manipulate and display it, data is worthless. Therefore, enabling employees to work from anywhere and on any device must include not only access to the data, but also—and more important—access to the applications that allow them to work with the data. As computing capabilities have evolved exponentially, so have the applications that use these capabilities; they are well integrated and intuitive, but they are also big and, frankly, cumbersome to deploy and maintain. This chapter looks at the evolution of these applications and suggests a better way to manage and deliver applications within your organization using application virtualization.

LOOKING AT THE APPLICATION INSTALLATION PROCESS

Before I walk through the application virtualization technologies available with App-V, it's important to understand why virtualizing applications is beneficial. This understanding is best gained through an examination of the evolution of applications and how applications are installed on a modern desktop operating system.

The Early Years of Applications

Looking back to early desktop operating systems that ran on computers with a single processor, a single processing core, a few hundred KB of RAM, and a 10MB hard drive, it becomes clear that those early applications bore little resemblance to what you find today. Those early operating systems were not multitasking, so only one application could run at a time; therefore, applications didn't have to be designed for interoperation with other applications (except perhaps to be able to open data files from other applications).

Originally, applications were made available in the form of executable files, and the install process consisted of taking the application from media and copying it to a directory on the hard drive. If there was configuration specific for the application, it was stored in a file in the application's directory, maybe in an INI file.

▶ Each application was very much its own island, with no interaction with or concern for anything else on the system. Happy days!

As Windows and the hardware it ran on evolved, the process of *multithreading* was achieved, which enabled multiple applications to appear to run at the same time, an effect produced by the operating system quickly switching between tasks executing on the processor. Then systems with multiple processors and multiple processing cores came along, enabling true multiprocessing. Additionally, it became more common for applications to communicate and share resources with each other. All these enhanced capabilities and features increased the application's size, which made running an application as one big executable impractical.

Dynamic Link Libraries (DLLs) enabled functions to exist in a separate file from the main executable of an application and to be accessed as needed. These DLLs were shared by multiple applications. They were also widespread in development platforms, where they provided the common functions that interacted with the operating system and graphical interface. Many DLLs were actually supplied as part of the operating system, reducing the size of application installers.

Unfortunately, this new era of shared DLLs introduced a phenomenon known as *DLL Hell*, which manifested itself in the form of applications crashing, not starting, or generally misbehaving. The major causes of these problems were as follows:

▶ **Memory space limitations:** These problems were usually seen in older 16-bit operating systems that allowed only a single memory space and only one instance of a DLL to be loaded into memory at a time. Therefore, even if applications had different versions of the same DLL in their folders, only one instance could be loaded in memory.

▶ **Poorly written application installers:** Some installers installed a shared DLL even if a newer version already existed, which would break other applications on the system that needed the newer version.

▶ **Incorrect DLLs:** Frequently, the wrong DLL was used for COM (Component Object Model) registrations.

Fortunately, various solutions have been put in place to avoid DLL Hell, such as *Windows Resource Protection (WRP)*, formally known as Windows File Protection (WFP) in Windows XP, which monitors any replacements of key operating system files by application installations or other processes and restores the files to the correct version. Another key DLL Hell–fighting technology is *Windows Side-by-Side Assemblies (WinSxS)*, which allows multiple versions of the same DLL to exist and ensures that each application uses the appropriate DLL version. Look in your `%SystemRoot%\winsxs` folder to see all the different DLLs that are handled by WinSxS!

The registry was another advancement in the Windows operating system. Instead of applications maintaining their own configuration files, the registry enables every application to store its configuration in a standard way. By requiring applications to standardize their configuration data and the way they interact with the operating system, such as the capability to update the registry as part of a transaction, the registry ensured system integrity following any change. Over time, this shared configuration store started to experience issues of its own because of its lack of portability and its inability to adapt to having multiple versions of the same application on the system. Programs would fail because the different versions would try to install to the same location in the registry.

Because of all these shared components, a lot of testing is required when it is time to deploy a new version of an existing application or a brand-new application to ensure that the change does not conflict with or break other applications already being used. The potential for damage requires that you carry out numerous regression tests that go through all possible scenarios—such as "if application A and B are

▶ Although Windows Resource Protection (WRP) should catch replacements, it doesn't always. If you think something is wrong, manually run **SFC /SCANNOW** from the command prompt to scan critical files and fix any problems.

▶ A prime example of this is deploying mandatory security patches, which may not happen until several days after their release by Microsoft, leaving the business computers open to zero-day exploits.

installed but not C, then applications A, B, and C are installed before application D," and so on. This testing can cause significant delays before rolling out a new application across your enterprise, which in turn can affect the company's ability to remain competitive or gain market share and deliver services to its customers.

Understanding the Actual Installation Process

▶ Like a good boy scout, a good uninstalled application leaves no trace it was ever there. Windows Installer technology helps ensure that uninstall operations remove all components.

Now that you've seen how Windows has evolved, it's time to consider what typically happens when you install an application on a current version of Windows, such as Windows 7. Realistically, applications can install in different ways; however, for an application to achieve the Certified for Microsoft Windows logo, it needs to use the Windows Installer technology, among other requirements. The Windows Installer technology enables an application to be installed, maintained, and cleanly removed. If the installation fails, the Windows Installer can automatically roll back any changes to the system. These Windows Installer packages have an MSI file extension that defines all the elements of an application installation.

When you install an application, the installer program may elevate its privileges if it uses a Windows trusted installer. Normally processes run a basic set of privileges that are sufficient for normal, day-to-day activities such as running applications. Certain operations require greater privileges as they change the operating system, which is the case when an application is installed. The Windows trusted installer is part of Windows and handles the elevation of privileges during an application installation without requiring User Access Control (UAC) authorization. Trusted installers are able to perform the following actions:

- Pulling setup files from the media or from the network
- Running setup routines, which may include extracting and expanding files from Zip or other compressed setup files
- Registering components with the operating system
- Making changes to the registry
- Installing fonts
- Creating file type associations
- Performing optimization routines based on the operating system
- Requesting customization options from the installer

All these steps take time. Consider an application like Office 2010, for example. It may take 10 minutes to install, which is a lot longer than it takes simply to copy the install media files to your hard drive. This time discrepancy is caused by all the setup routines and optimizations that the installer program performs as part of the install process.

Now imagine deploying Office 2010 to hundreds of machines. That's hundreds of 10-minute time blocks being wasted as users wait for the application to be available, and hundreds of duplicate configurations. As you install more and more applications, your operating system has to deal with more applications registering components on the operating system, which ultimately leads to the kind of bloat that you see on older operating systems, and gradual slowdown and stability challenges.

Businesses today demand that users be able to use different machines in different places. Therefore, if users need to be able to walk up to any desktop and use their applications, then performing the application installation on demand and expecting users to wait is not practical. IT managers need a better way to make applications instantly available on any operating system instance while minimizing the bloat caused by traditional application installations and the conflicts that can arise through the sharing of computer resources, such as the file system and registry.

HOW VIRTUALIZING DESKTOP APPLICATIONS WORKS

As you saw in the preceding section, many application-to-application compatibility problems are caused by sharing, which is supposed to be a benefit; but, as any only child will tell you, sharing is no fun. It makes installing applications take too long, and the required testing before you can release new applications can delay vital new services. These problems didn't exist when nothing was shared between applications, but no one wants to go back to Windows 3.1. However, there is a solution: simply run each application in its own little bubble.

When I talk about a bubble for each application, I don't mean a separate operating system environment like you see in a virtual machine (VM) scenario. Although that would isolate each application, you would lose the benefit of having the applications running on a single operating system, and management and computer overhead would be enormous. Instead, think of the bubble as containing virtualized elements of the operating system that are specific to the installed application footprint; that is, each bubble would be a virtual layer, if you will, overlying the actual operating system resources, as shown in Figure 4-1. Note that each virtualized application has its own bubble with its own layers, which are hidden from the other virtualized applications.

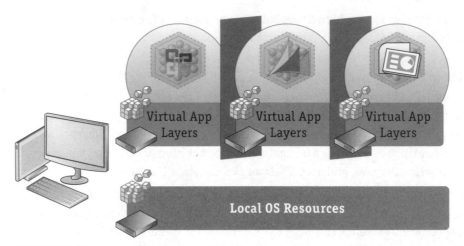

FIGURE 4-1: Each virtualized application has its own execution environment within a virtual computer layer—including, but not limited to, the virtual file system and registry.

The Microsoft solution for application virtualization is App-V. App-V is capable of supporting the virtualization of almost every desktop application available for Windows and has native 32-bit and 64-bit support. To understand how the App-V solution can accomplish this, it's useful to examine how the application is isolated from the underlying operating system.

Examining the Onion that Is Application Virtualization

▶ You can also think of each application's bubble environment as a sandbox within which application changes are limited to the borders of its own virtual environment, unable to affect the rest of the operating system.

The application installation process makes changes to the operating system. Typically, it copies files into its own folder under C:\Program Files, creates its own registry key and values under HKEY_LOCAL_MACHINE\SOFTWARE, registers any file-type associations for any types of data it handles, installs fonts, registers COM objects, and more. If you want to abstract the application from the operating system and allow it to run without making all these changes, you need a way to segregate the changes, containing them in a bubble within which the virtualized application can run. This is exactly what App-V does. It creates an application-specific bubble in which various layers overlie the true operating system resources, so when the virtualized application runs, it thinks its files are on the file system, its registry files are in the registry, its fonts are installed, and so on. A great way to come to grips with this concept is to look at a virtualized application's file-system activity.

Figure 4-2 shows an operating system's file system element and the virtual bubble of the virtualized application, which in this case is PowerPoint 2007. As you can see, the virtualized PowerPoint application has full read access to the true file system of the operating system, but all its file system activity must first go through its virtual file system layer. This virtual layer is created during the sequencing procedure. *Sequencing* is the process of creating a virtualized application. All the files copied during the application install process are stored in this virtual layer.

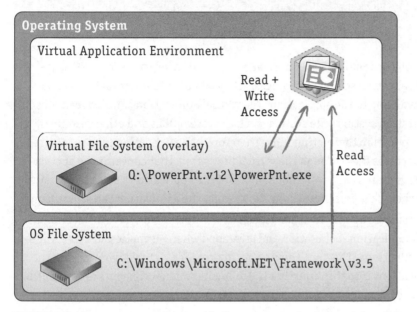

FIGURE 4-2: Here you can see the App-V's file system overlay that contains all the application files for the virtualized application.

You will notice that the application is not installed under the C:\Program Files folder as you would commonly see, but rather on a Q: drive, with an 8.3 format folder named for the specific application; for example, instead of Microsoft PowerPoint, the folder may be named PowerPnt.v12. The Q: drive is not a real drive on the client computer, but rather a virtual drive letter that is visible only within a virtualized application. You don't have to use the Q: drive for App-V, but you do need a specific drive letter that can be used consistently across the entire infrastructure, so you need to pick a drive letter that does not exist locally on any computer and is not used for home drive mapping, business unit storage, or anything else. Pick a drive letter that can be reserved for App-V and that won't need to change down the road.

Why do you even need this Q: drive (or whatever drive you select)? For now, think of the Q: drive as the interface to the cache of the virtual file system for the virtualized application. This cache contains all the application files and all the files that would normally be written to the C: drive (and anywhere else) during the sequencing process. In this case, there is a drive letter called Q: on this machine and the virtual

▶ Changing the drive letter used by App-V after deployment is labor intensive. Take time up front to pick the right drive letter. In most environments, Q: is not used in the existing network infrastructure, but be sure to triple check!

▶ The next version of App-V, version 5, no longer requires the use of the Q: drive, simplifying deployment and virtualization of applications.

application thinks it has been installed to `Q:\<your app>`, which is where it will look for all its files as it starts up and while it's executing.

> **CROSSREF** You'll learn a lot more about using the Q: drive, including best practices for working with it, when you read "Creating an App-V Virtualized Application."

If other application files would normally be placed in locations on the C: drive during the application sequencing process, they will be in the virtual file system as well and available to the application. The virtual application can also read files from the operating system's file system, such as system DLLs and other resources, to enable the application to function fully. Therefore, the application runs in its virtual bubble and accesses files through the virtual file system that contains the application's files. This means that even though none of the application's files are actually installed on the local operating system file system, the application can still run on it.

The same process applies to other aspects of the operating system affected during a typical application installation and leveraged when an application starts and performs its functions. The App-V environment provides virtual layers to trick the virtual applications into thinking that the following virtual elements represent the real operating system resources:

▶ **Registry:** App-V maintains a virtual registry layer visible only to the virtualized application (thereby avoiding any registry conflicts with locally installed applications). The virtual registry is not a complete copy of the local operating system registry because that would actually limit the application's ability to work with the operating system. Instead, the virtual registry is an overlay of the local operating system registry, where all application-specific registry settings are stored.

Remember also that the registry is the central configuration store for the entire operating system environment, which includes items like configured printers and Open Database Connectivity (ODBC) connections. Therefore, if your application maps to any printers or creates ODBC connections, either as part of the installation process or even while it's running, this configuration would also be contained within its virtualized registry layer.

▶ **Services:** Certain applications install services that run under the security context of the user and start when the application launches. Each virtual application will have its own virtual services, which means that different virtual applications can use the same service or multiple different versions of the service without issue. Note that virtualized services will be visible only to the application within the bubble and will run only while that application is being used. Therefore, if you need a service to run in the Local System security context or to be available all the time, you should not virtualize it because it will not be visible to the Services control panel applet or any service command.

▶ **COM environment:** Many applications use COM for communication and functionality. App-V virtualizes the COM communications, protecting them from one virtual application to another.

▶ **INI files:** Most of today's applications no longer use INI files; however, if an application does still use and modify INI files within the Windows INI environment, a virtual copy of the Windows INI file is used, protecting the real system INI files from being altered.

▶ **Process environment:** Each virtual application has its own virtual process environment, including environmental variables that can be modified or created without any impact on the underlying operating system.

▶ **Fonts:** Certain types of applications, particularly productivity applications, install fonts to the system. App-V captures these fonts and stores them in a virtual fonts layer. The virtual application will have access to the virtualized fonts, as well as any fonts installed on the local operating system.

Another operating system element handled by App-V is file type associations, including the icons used to represent them, along with shortcuts for the application. To understand how virtualized file type associations work with virtualized applications, let's look at a virtualized Word 2010 bubble. If the file type associations and icons are contained in the virtual environment, and a user tries to open a .doc file in Explorer, the file won't open, even if the virtual Word 2010 application is currently running. That is because virtualized file type associations are invisible to the local operating system. This would make a very unfriendly environment for users, who would always have to open documents directly within Word.

To avoid this scenario and enable virtualized applications to be as accessible as a locally installed application, file type associations, icons, and shortcuts, such as those on the desktop, need to be handled differently. The Microsoft Application Virtualization Sequencer (App-V Sequencer) tracks any file type associations, icons, and shortcuts created during installation. App-V stores this information outside the main virtualized application's bubble, which enables the shortcuts and associations to be applied to a user environment before the virtual application is executed. This makes the virtualization process invisible to the end user.

▶ One of the most useful reasons for modification is to change the Path environment variable, because it is commonly updated by application install processes and may be needed for an application to find its various executable files.

> **NOTE** When virtualizing an application, the question of virtualizing drivers needs to be addressed. That is, if an application installs a driver, do you virtualize it? Currently, App-V does not support the virtualization of drivers. If you virtualize an application that installs a driver, you still need to deploy the driver part of the application using traditional means, such as through Group Policy (GP) or another Enterprise Software Deployment (ESD) tool.

► In reality, only minor changes are made to the operating system, that being a single file cache of the virtualized applications and the application file type associations and icons. These changes are restricted to the App-V data areas.

The advantage of virtualizing an application is that you can run it on the local OS, and therefore use local computer resources, all without actually installing it in the traditional manner and hence without actually modifying the operating system. The ability to run an application on a local operating system without having to install it there is the key point of application virtualization.

Creating an App-V Virtualized Application

The best way to understand the App-V Virtual Desktop Infrastructure (VDI) solution is to create a virtualized application. In this section, I walk you through the App-V sequencing process. Once the virtual application has been sequenced, you'll learn how to deliver the virtual application to the end user.

UNDERSTANDING THE SEQUENCING ENVIRONMENT

The App-V solution comprises a number of components, one of which is the App-V Sequencer, which is used to create an App-V virtualized application. As you begin sequencing applications, it is very important to adhere to some best practices, so this section looks at what these are and why you should care about them.

If you've been in the IT industry a long time, you may remember the introduction of the Windows Installer more than 10 years ago, which moved away from the setup .exe, application installation file and introduced us to MSI installers. When the Windows Installer was released, a number of professional tools to create MSI installers became available as well. However, many organizations just wanted a quick way to create an MSI, so Microsoft provided WinInstall, which was licensed from a third-party vendor. WinInstall takes a snapshot of a clean operating system—one that includes only service packs and hotfixes—and then a second snapshot after the application is installed. All changes to the system, such as registry and file system modifications, between the before and after images are considered part of the application and placed into the MSI file. In order to be effective, it is critical that the clean operating system has no applications installed on it when you start.

Why does this matter? Consider what would happen if you started with an operating system that already had a shared library installed by another application. That existing shared library would be considered part of the "before" snapshot. If the application that you wanted to install typically installed the same shared library, the WinInstall program would not recognize that library as a change in the "after" snapshot. Therefore, the shared library would be omitted from the MSI file, causing the application to fail when installed on another computer, because it would be missing critical files.

Sequencing an application works in a similar, if not more sophisticated, way. When you sequence an application, the App-V Sequencer looks at changes that would typically be made to the system during the application installation process and makes those changes to the virtualized application package instead.

You need to start the sequencing process with a clean operating system image, with only service packs and patches applied—and, of course, the App-V Sequencer installed. You need to start with this clean operating system state every time you want to sequence a new application, so if you have already sequenced application A and now want to sequence application B, you need to wipe the operating system clean again.

Constantly re-creating the operating system environment for sequencing would be a major headache and a waste of time, but fortunately this book is about virtualization, which is absolutely the best solution here. What you want to do is create a VM on a Hyper-V Server and then use that VM as your sequencing environment.

To create a VM for sequencing, you'll take advantage of Hyper-V's machine virtualization feature known as a *Snapshot* to take a point-in-time copy of the environment before you install the application. Then after each application is sequenced, you can just roll the VM back to the initial snapshot to get a clean environment again. The process of creating the clean sequencing environment is as follows:

1. Create a new VM on Hyper-V.

2. Install Windows on the VM and apply the latest service pack and fixes, to match your corporate standard.

3. Install Internet Explorer 9, if that is your corporate standard.

4. If Microsoft Office is installed locally on all your desktop machines, you should also install Microsoft Office.

5. Install antivirus software and perform a full scan. Then disable the antivirus application.

6. Install the App-V 4.6 Service Pack 1 (SP1) Sequencer.

▶ The supported operating systems for the App-V Sequencer include Windows XP and later; for more information, see http://technet.microsoft.com/en-us/library/cc817142.aspx.

▶ It is easy to copy a VM and roll back any changes made, which makes it the perfect solution for an operating system you constantly need to revert to a clean state.

▶ Because you are looking for changes to the operating system, you don't want any services running in the background that might make changes to the operating system that would mistakenly become part of the virtualized application.

7. Ensure that Windows Update, Windows Search, Disk Defragmentation, and Windows Defender are all disabled. You can do this by opening the `services.msc` file or you can use the Run dialog, stop each service, and then set them to Disabled.

8. Close all Windows Explorer windows.

9. Shut down the operating system within the VM, which will also stop the VM once the operating system shuts down.

10. Create a snapshot of the VM.

> **CROSSREF** For an explanation of Hyper-V snapshots and how to use them, and other Hyper-V–related guidance, please see Chapter 8.

11. Start the VM and then sequence your application.

12. Once the sequencing is complete and you have copied the virtualized application to another location, shut down the VM's OS.

13. Using Hyper-V, apply the snapshot you created, as shown in Figure 4-3. Your VM is now back to its clean operating system state, and ready to sequence your next application.

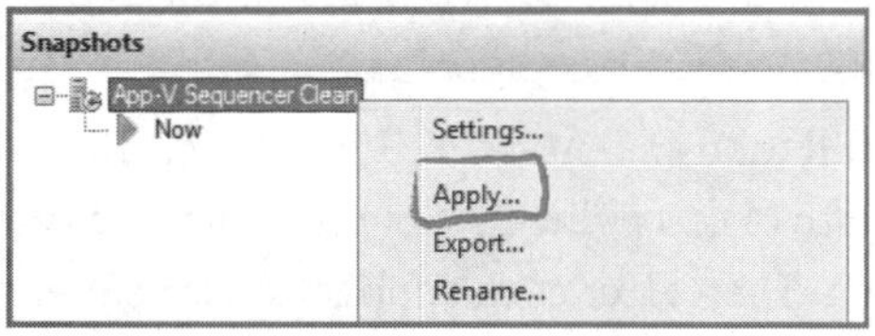

▶ You can store the virtual application anywhere other than your sequencing VM because you are about to roll back its state and would therefore lose your virtual application. Most IT departments have a special file share where they store virtual applications.

FIGURE 4-3: Select the snapshot you want to roll back to and then select Apply from the Actions menu.

> **NOTE** As an alternative to Hyper-V, you can create a clean operating system environment using Windows Virtual PC, which runs on desktop operating systems and does not require a server. The only change to the preceding procedure would be to enable Undo Disks on the VM instead of creating a snapshot. You would then discard the changes to the undo disk after sequencing to wipe the operating system clean.

When configuring your sequencing environment, there are too many variables to cover them all here. However, the preceding list should give you a good overview of the process of creating a clean operating system sequencing environment.

> **NOTE** If you'd like more guidance, download the App-V 4.6 SP1 Sequencing Guide from Microsoft from `http://download.microsoft.com/download/F/7/8/` `F784A197-73BE-48FF-83DA-4102C05A6D44/App-V/App-V%204.6%20Service%20` `Pack%201%20Sequencing%20Guide.docx`.

If I had been writing this book a year ago, before App-V 4.6 SP1 was released, a lot of additional steps would have been required to prepare your sequencing environment, and the sequencing process would have been a lot less user friendly. I would be talking about creating dummy ODBC connections and printers, and a new partition on the Sequencer. Fortunately, App-V 4.6 SP1 ensures that your sequences are successful by handling many of the best practices you would have had to perform manually. It also automatically creates a virtual Q: drive (or whatever your organization chose). App-V 4.6 SP1 is a usability release and it makes App-V a lot simpler to use and manage. If you used App-V in the past (or even its predecessor, SoftGrid), it's definitely time to get reacquainted.

You'll notice that I've mentioned the Q: drive that you'll be using during the sequencing a number of times. Before you look at what's involved in creating a virtual application, you should understand why you need this extra drive.

USING THE Q: DRIVE

Having a drive letter for the virtual file system makes a lot of sense from a functionality and performance perspective for a number of reasons, some of which go back to earlier versions of App-V and are still best practices today. To understand its importance, consider the virtual file system that exists inside the virtual application's bubble. Not only does it provide the virtual Q: drive, but it also overlies real partitions, such as the C: drive.

For example, if your virtualized application's files were stored as `C:\Program Files\Application1`, every time the `C:\Program Files\Application1` path was accessed, that access request would have to be intercepted by the virtual environment and redirected to your virtual file system store. This redirection used to have a performance penalty in SoftGrid, the early version of App-V. Although most of that penalty has been eradicated with the latest App-V release, why incur even a small performance penalty if it isn't necessary?

Remember also that the whole point of virtualization is to separate one layer from another. Using a separate drive letter as part of this separation is needed for the virtual application to abstract itself from the variety of different system infrastructures. Whereas one computer may use the C: drive for its system drive, another computer may use D: or even B:. If the virtual application was created based on installing to the C: drive but is then executed on a machine that uses D: as its system drive, what would happen? Most likely, the application would either fail to start or crash once it started. By using a consistent drive letter for virtual applications, you can remove a lot of the uncertainty.

In reality, App-V does a great job of removing these drive letter dependencies, but it's not perfect and problems can still occur. When you create a virtualized application, the App-V process parses for any hard-coded drive letter mappings and replaces them with a variable to the App-V virtual file system mount (SFT_MNT). But some applications may hard-code paths not available to the App-V process, such as configuration in a binary format. Using the Q: drive gives you the best chance of successfully virtualizing your application.

Additionally, when you virtualize an application, you are overlying the operating system's file system with your virtual file system. If the virtual application's files were just stored under C:\Program Files\Application1, for example, what would happen if Application1 were also locally installed on the desktop machine, maybe even a different version of the application? Your virtual application would be unable to access the folder on the true file system because it would always be redirected to the content in its virtual file system first. By installing your virtual applications to a unique drive, you ensure there is never a conflict with a locally installed application. This is critical behavior, because one of the main reasons for virtualizing applications is to avoid application-to-application conflicts and resolve compatibility challenges.

Ultimately, although you need a Q: drive as part of the App-V environment, you can choose to mostly ignore it. However, there is no real benefit to doing so because although most applications may still work without it, using the Q: drive guarantees you a higher success rate with virtualizing your applications, and you can be confident you won't introduce any virtual-to-local application clashes.

EXPLORING THE SEQUENCING PROCESS

At this point, it is assumed that you have created a sequencing environment and picked the drive letter you are going to use. In this section, you'll walk through the process of actually creating a virtualized application and customizing some of the application components, such as file type associations, shortcuts on the system, and file system and registry locations, that should be considered part of the virtual application based on the needs of your organization.

Before you log in to the clean sequencer environment, make sure you have gathered all the installation media you'll need for the application you want to sequence, including any updates or patches you want to include. In addition, make sure that your install media is pre-extracted; otherwise, the files generated during the extraction part of the application installation will become part of your virtualized application. You can clean up the files after the application is created, but if you keep the process as clean as possible, it makes everything simpler and helps ensure success.

Once you have all your installation media ready to go, launch the App-V Sequencer to start the sequencing process. You are presented with the main introduction screen, shown in Figure 4-4.

► If you launch Internet Explorer to apply updates or download installation media during the sequencing process, that activity could become part of your virtual application package.

► Minimizing activities is a key aspect of the sequencing process; you don't want to perform any actions you don't have to because any changes resulting from those actions become part of your virtualized application.

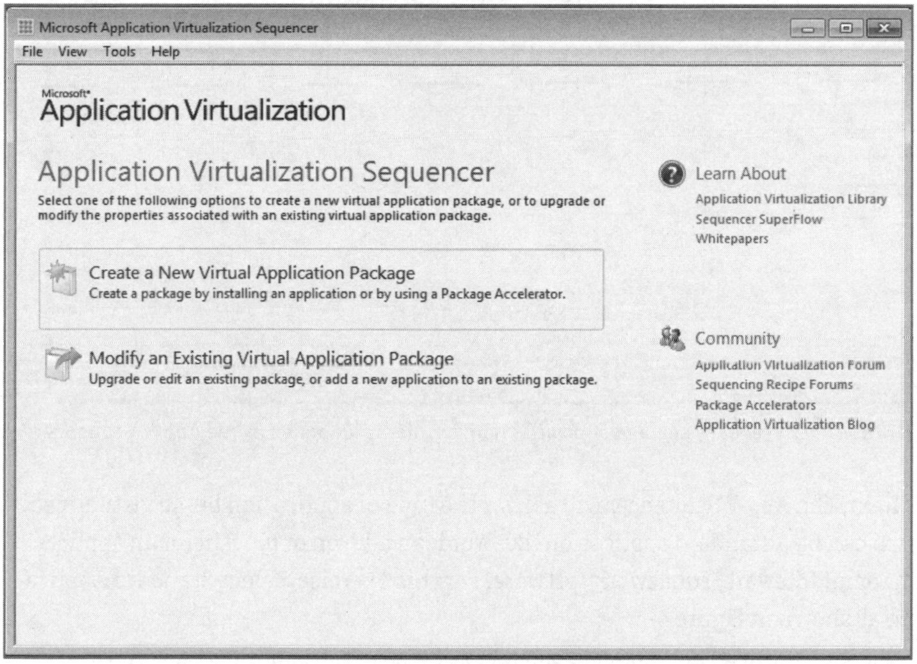

FIGURE 4-4: The App-V Sequencer's main screen

Select the option to Create a New Virtual Application Package. The App-V Sequencer then gives you another choice: Create Package (default) or Create Package Using a Package Accelerator. First, I'll walk through the default option, and then I'll show you how to use App-V 4.6 SP1's new Package Accelerator option.

The App-V Sequencer's new simpler-to-use methodology ensures that best practices are adhered to by first running a check of the sequencer environment to ensure that all services, such as Windows Update, Search, and malware protection are turned off. It also scans for anything that might be wrong with the environment, providing you with a list of items that need to be resolved before you can continue, as shown in Figure 4-5. Resolve any listed problems using the onscreen guidance and then click Refresh. When no issues remain, you can continue with the virtualization.

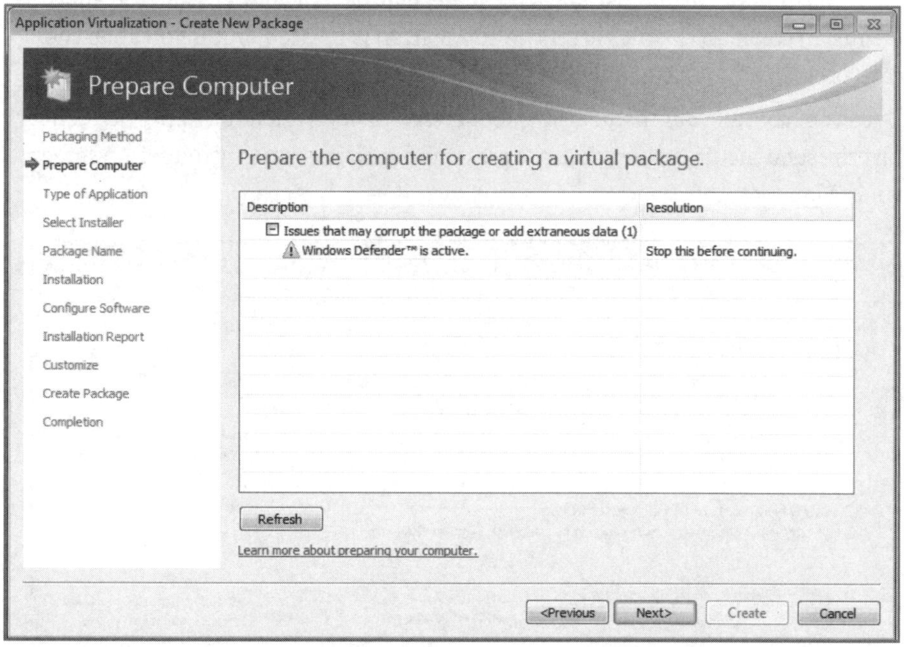

FIGURE 4-5: Correct any sequencer environment problems identified by the App-V Sequencer.

Next, the App-V Sequencer will ask for the type of application being virtualized, which can be a standard application like Word, an add-on or plug-in for an application, or middleware/framework software. For this exercise, select Standard Application, as shown in Figure 4-6.

The Sequencer will now prompt you for the name of the application's setup program so that it can launch the setup process when needed. Alternatively, you can choose not to let the App-V Sequencer launch the setup process. Instead, you can select a custom installation during which you, as the *sequencing engineer* (the person performing the sequencing of the application), will launch all the setup processes manually. The only real advantage of allowing the App-V Sequencer to run the application setup process for you is that it automatically elevates the privileges for installation, avoiding the UAC prompts. Whether you perform a standard or custom installation, it is still possible to perform custom commands and configuration steps. Once the type of installation is selected, click Next to proceed.

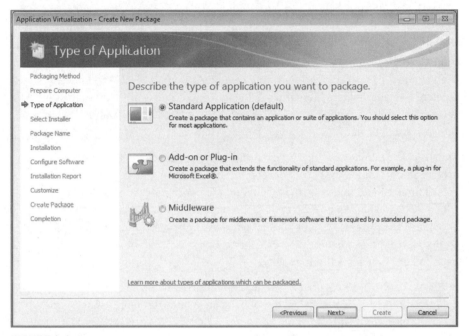

FIGURE 4-6: Select the type of application you want to sequence so that the Sequencer can provide the right guidance.

> **TIP** If you have any custom configurations or multiple installers to deal with, I would just run all the installers manually. You will have to deal with the UAC prompts, but it's worth it to have the extra level of control.

Next, the Sequencer asks you to name your virtual application—for example, Adobe Reader X. Notice that the Sequencer automatically supplies the installation path for the virtual application. By default, this path is Q:\<the name of virtual application>. If your organization has agreed on a letter other than Q, you can change this through the Edit option.

▶ This is when you create the famous Q: drive I have been talking about. Change this drive designation only if you have a valid reason; and don't change it to C:\Program Files unless you have fully researched the implications and understand them!

GOODBYE 8.3 FILENAME FORMAT

If you have had experience with previous App-V implementations, you'll be interested to know that you no longer have to use an 8.3 format folder on the root of the Q: drive to store your virtual applications. This was a welcome change with App-V 4.6 SP1. For readers new to the IT world, the idea of a filename limited to eight characters and a three-character file type might seem crazy; however, that is exactly the limitation you had with the initial FAT file system. App-V required the 8.3 character folder name because although NTFS and later versions of FAT allowed long filenames, an 8.3 format name is still automatically created behind the scenes for any 16-bit components of an application that only talk in the 8.3 format.

The problem with automatic 8.3 format filename generation is that the names are created using the first six characters of the program name. Therefore, if you virtualize multiple applications with long folder names, such as Microsoft Office 2010 and Microsoft Project 2010, both applications end up with the same short filename, `Micros~1`. This conflict prevents both virtual applications from being used at the same time. You can get around this problem by setting the 8.3 base folder name attribute manually.

In App-V 4.6 SP1, you no longer have to manually create a short folder name because the App-V Sequencer automatically generates a random short name for the folder, eliminating the collision issues. Another change that makes sequencing easier to use! If you do decide to manually assign the root folder an 8.3 format name, App-V will use the short name you chose.

Manually specifying the 8.3 format name does give you one major advantage in that the randomly generated names can actually make some troubleshooting operations harder. I still prefer to use 8.3 format names for the root folders so that I can maintain greater control.

TIP If you want to know what short name the Sequencer gave your virtualized application, you can open the project file (.sprj) generated at the end of the sequencing process. Look for the **Shortname** attribute, as shown in the following example:

```
<PACKAGEROOTFOLDER Longname="Q:\Adobe Reader"
Shortname="Q:\81KILROY.450"/>
```

Once you've confirmed the application install path, the next step is to monitor the system. At this point, the App-V Sequencer sees everything you run or change. Notice that the dialog also contains a Run button. If you specified an application install program earlier in the wizard, the Sequencer will launch it automatically when you click the Run button. If you didn't specify an application installer, you can now manually run the application installers, setups, and commands from anywhere else on the system. In Figure 4-7, you see not only the monitoring process, but also a notification balloon reminding the sequencing engineer to select the Q:\<path> folder for the install path, to prevent the application from installing to the default C:\Program Files.

▶ The monitoring phase of sequencing is definitely not the time to launch a web browser and start shopping on Amazon. Run only the application installer and items related to the application you are capturing, and nothing else!

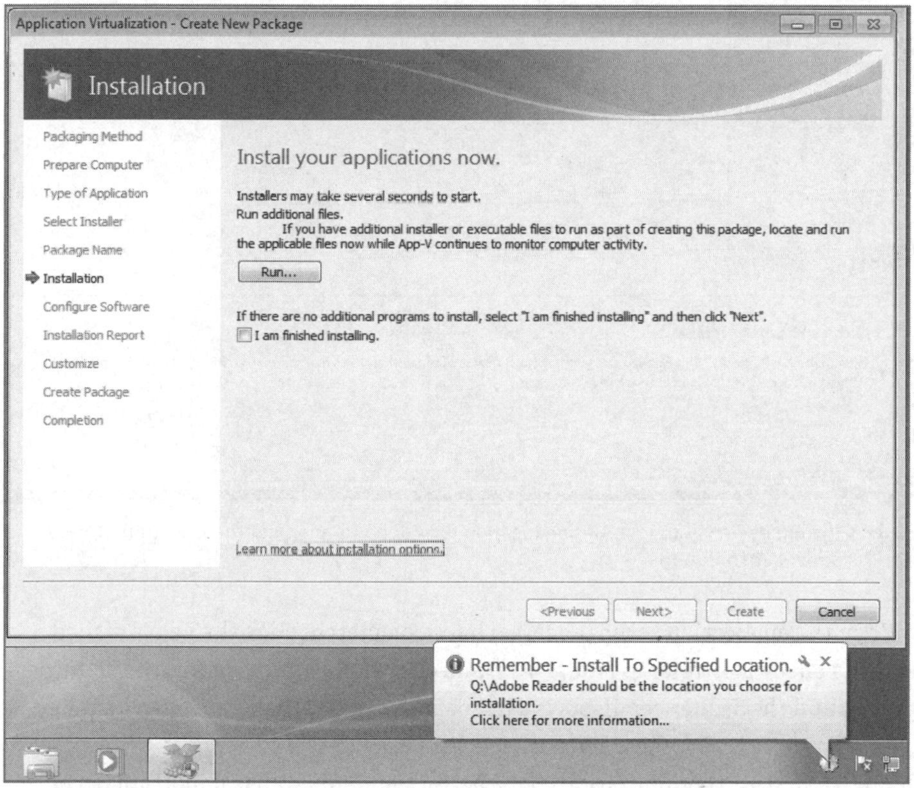

FIGURE 4-7: At this stage, every change to the OS will be made part of the virtualized application.

When you run the application installer, you need to change the install path to the Q: drive location. This is vitally important and the only way to ensure that most of the application files will be written to your virtual Q: drive. It's OK if some files are

▶ The exact method for creating a transform file varies for every application, so you will likely need to consult the documentation for your application for further instruction. Fundamentally, the transform file allows you to customize the installation and execution of the application it is transforming.

written to C:—they'll still be captured. However, for optimal sequencing you want most of the application files on the Q: drive. Although the exact location to install the application varies, the Q: drive should always be available; however, you will likely have to select the Custom install method for most application installers. For some applications, such as Adobe Reader X, you may need to create a transform file for the application installer to set the desired installation path, as shown in Figure 4-8.

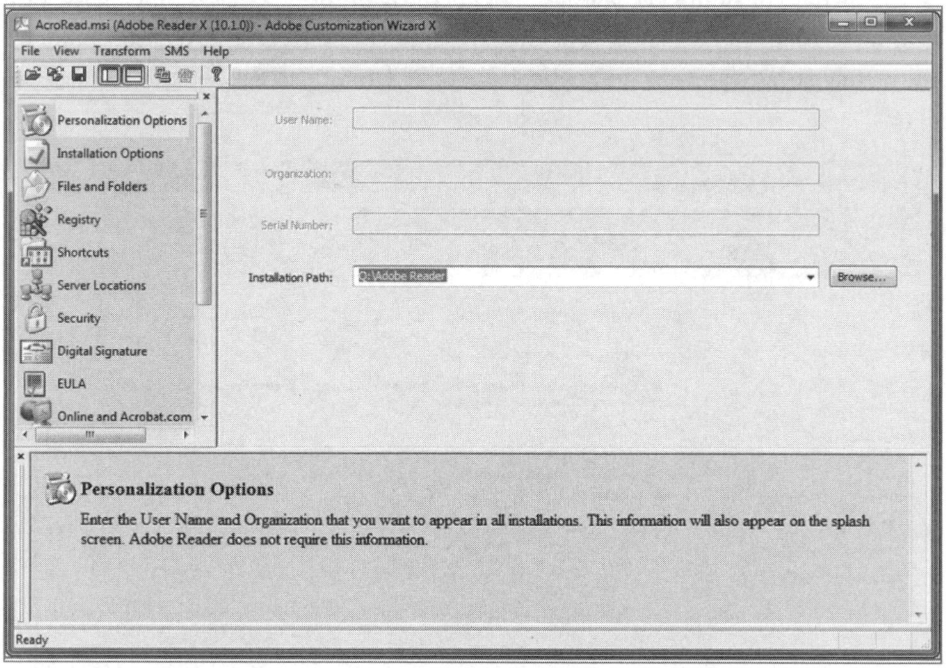

FIGURE 4-8: To set a custom installation location for Adobe Reader, set the Installation Path under Personalization Options.

When the application setup processes have completed, click the I am finished installing check box (refer to Figure 4-7), and click Next. At this point, the monitoring stops and the Sequencer displays a list of applications that have been installed as part of your virtual application package. Run each detected application to allow any kind of first-run configurations to be performed. This step is important because you don't want your virtualized application to have to run through initial configurations and potential changes every time it is deployed. During this initial execution process, disable any automatic updates, accept any agreements, and run anything else that would normally accompany using a program for the first time.

> **WARNING** Disabling automatic updates is important for any virtualized application, because any automated attempt to update a virtual application would lead to unexpected results.

After executing all the components of the virtualized application at least once and performing any necessary configuration, you can continue to the Installation Report by clicking Next. The Installation Report details the state of the application virtualization and lists any problems and any additional information. You can click any message to get more detailed information and assistance in resolving the problems. The next step is customization.

The customization stage is critical for optimizing the delivery of your virtual applications for real-time streaming when clients first use the application. When you prepare for streaming, an important process occurs. At this point, the Sequencer has created a large binary store, basically a single file, that contains all the virtual layers needed for the application, including the file system and registry. However, most applications don't use all their files when they launch; instead, they perform only the most common operations. Therefore, only a subset of the application installation file is actually needed to start the application.

This customization process will organize your virtualized application file such that the parts of the virtual layers needed to launch the application are at the start of the store, making them the first parts sent to the client, which enables the application to start quickly. The rest of the virtual layer is sent in the background after the application has launched. For the Sequencer to ascertain what parts of the virtual application need to be sent for the application to launch, known as *Feature Block 1 (FB1)*, you need to run each application within the virtualized application you just created. The Sequencer will watch what parts of the virtual layers are accessed to launch the application and then move the necessary parts into FB1 while leaving everything else in *Feature Block 2 (FB2)*. From your end, this process looks the same as when you performed the initial configuration of the applications (see Figure 4-9), but this time the Sequencer is looking for any components that are accessed so that it can place them in FB1.

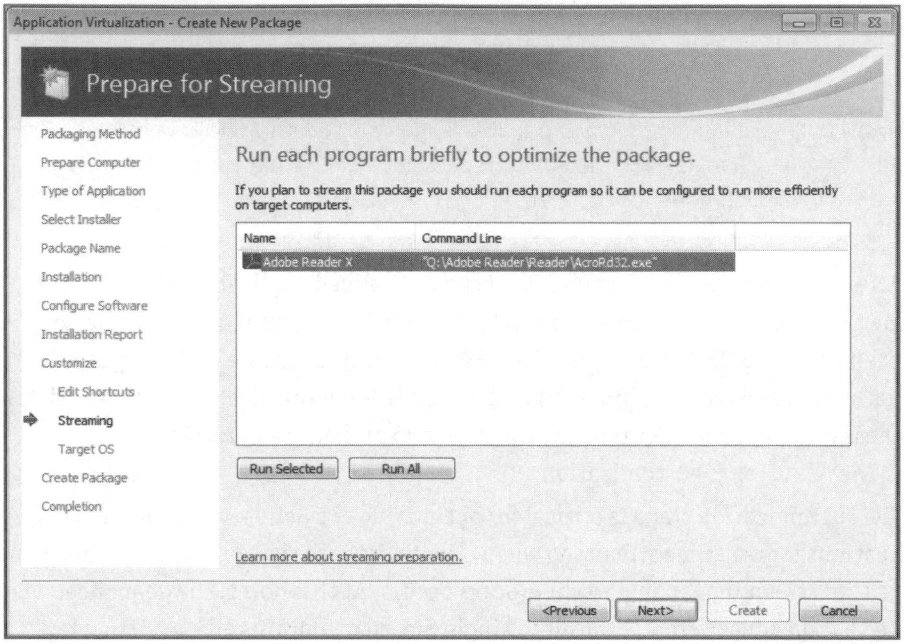

FIGURE 4-9: Launch each virtualized application so that the Sequencer can determine which virtual layers are needed to launch the application.

> **TIP** If you have virtualized a very large application that contains many different programs, such as Microsoft Office, you don't have to launch every application as part of this streaming optimization step. If the application contains programs that you don't want streamed as part of the initial FB1, don't run them. Likewise, if you will always perform certain actions when you first launch the application, such as File ➔ Open, go ahead and run that action at this time to ensure they are included in FB1.

After you have launched the applications you can move to the next stage of the wizard, where you select the operating system versions on which your virtual application can execute. This can be a tricky decision. By default, the Sequencer selects the operating system and architecture that you used to sequence the application—for example, Windows 7 32-bit. However, you can also choose to allow this virtual application to run on other operating systems and architectures, such as Windows 7 64-bit, Windows XP, and Windows Vista, as well as the Windows Server 2003 platform and later. For example, in Figure 4-10, the sequenced application will be supported on both 32-bit and 64-bit versions of Windows 7.

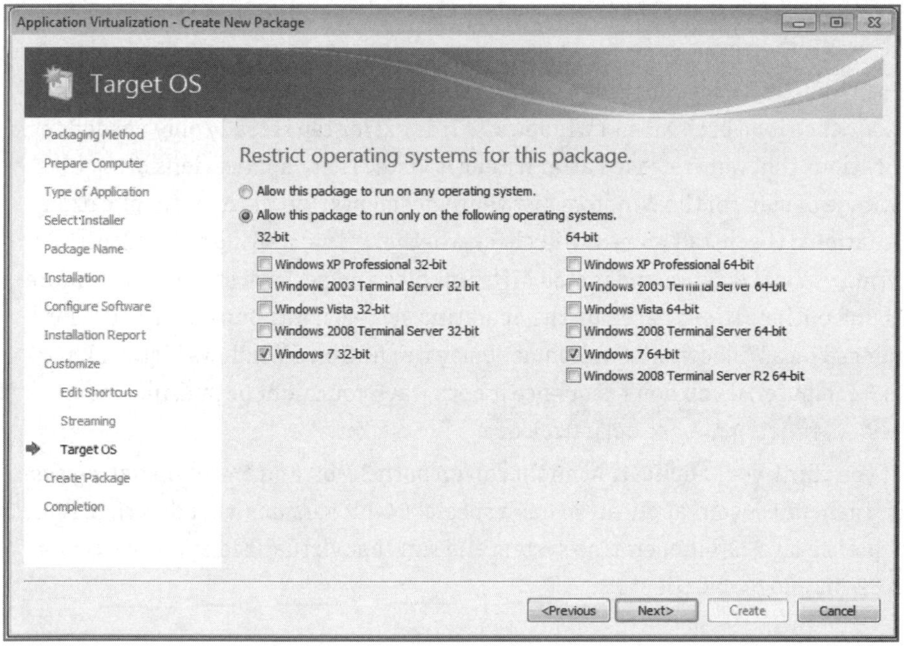

FIGURE 4-10: Check the appropriate boxes to indicate which operating systems will support your virtual application.

Which operating systems should you choose? Ideally, you would sequence the application separately on each operating system environment on which it will run. For example, if I had clients running Windows XP 32-bit, Windows 7 32-bit, and Windows 7 64-bit, I would sequence the application three separate times. In reality, unless the application has architecture-specific files, you could probably get away with sequencing once on Windows XP 32-bit and once on Windows 7 32-bit, and then use the Windows 7 32-bit sequence on Windows 7 64-bit as well. If it were an older application, you could probably sequence it on Windows XP 32-bit and it would work just fine on Windows Vista and Windows 7 as well.

The key point is if you intend to virtualize an application once and run it on multiple operating systems, *always* sequence it on the lowest operating system. In other words, if you intend to run the virtualized application on Windows XP, Windows Vista, and Windows 7, you should sequence it on a Windows XP machine. You should do this for the same reason that applications are sequenced on a clean operating system. If you sequence an application on the Windows 7 operating system and then try to run it in Windows XP, it may fail. This is because the Windows 7 operating system has certain DLLs and files built into it, so the application does not need to install them, but these files are not present on a Windows XP environment. As a result, when the

▶ This is a hugely important point to consider when you sequence post-Vista applications. You want to give users all the features and the best experience by taking advantage of the benefits of the latest operating systems. Don't take the shortcut and sequence only on Windows XP. Your users will thank you. Well, they won't, but they should!

application tries to start, key files are missing, causing errors. If you sequence on Windows XP, then even if the file is already on a Windows 7 system no harm is done.

If a Windows XP sequenced application will likely run on Windows 7, why should you sequence it on both XP and Windows 7? This extra step is really only needed for applications that were released after Windows Vista. These applications often take advantage of many of the Windows Vista enhancements. During many application installations, the install process will check whether it is installing to Windows XP or to Windows Vista or later, and install different files and perform different configurations and optimizations based on the operating systems. Although an application sequenced on a Windows XP environment may run fine on a Windows Vista or Windows 7 computer, if you don't sequence it both ways you might be missing out on additional functionality or optimizations.

If you think your application might run on both 32-bit and 64-bit operating systems, then unless your application has a special 64-bit version (most don't), it's safe to sequence on a 32-bit operating system and run that virtualized application on both 32-bit and 64-bit clients.

> **WARNING** Don't try to sequence an application on 64-bit Windows and run it on 32-bit Windows. Only bad things will happen!

The final step allows you to configure your packaged application by adding any desired comments; selecting a save location for your application; and, if you want, compressing it. Compression results in a smaller virtualized application that consumes less disk space and less bandwidth when transferring over the network to clients; however, it does consume extra CPU cycles to perform the decompression. Keep in mind that 4GB is the limit for a virtualized application. If your application is larger than that, you will need to use compression. Just click the Create button to complete the process and you have your first virtualized application. Next, copy the virtual application to a location outside of the sequencing environment, shut down the VM, and revert it back to the clean state, ready for the next application sequencing.

In summary, what you did wasn't too complicated, and it was wrapped up in a few steps driven by a wizard. The following steps highlight the main points in the entire process:

1. You created a clean operating system environment.

2. You launched the App-V Sequencer, which prepared your environment, and scanned the system to ensure that the Sequencer operating system was properly configured.

3. The App-V Sequencer asked for the type of application and you gave it the name of the setup file (or chose a custom configuration).

4. The App-V Sequencer started monitoring the environment, launched the application installer, and tracked all changes to the system.

5. You launched the application to allow the initial configurations and installed any necessary updates.

6. You ran the application again to allow the Sequencer to optimize the application by placing the data needed to launch it into FB1 and moving the rest into FB2.

7. You decided which operating systems you wanted to support your virtualized application.

8. You saved the virtual application.

UNDERSTANDING THE FILES OF A VIRTUALIZED APPLICATION

Once a virtual application is created, you can look at its folder and the files within it to get a deeper understanding of how your virtualized application works. Table 4-1 describes each of the files you see in the virtual application folder, as shown in Figure 4-11.

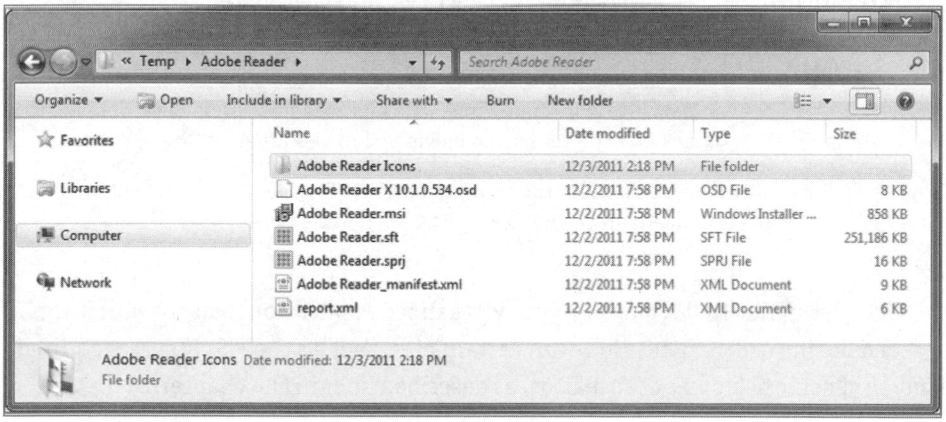

FIGURE 4-11: Open the virtual application's folder to see all the files.

TABLE 4-1: An App-V Virtualized Application's Component Files

FILE	DESCRIPTION
OSD	This file contains the description of the application, including details about the location of the binary file (SFT) that contains the assets of the virtual application, integration with the shell, scripts, details of the environment, and any dependencies. The OSD file is sent to client machines ahead of the virtual application to enable the App-V client component to know where to find the virtualized application and allow it to add the required shortcuts. You will have an OSD file for every program found during the sequencing process. For example, if you sequenced Microsoft Office there would be many OSD files, one for each of the different programs such as Word, Excel, PowerPoint, Outlook, and many others! Having a separate OSD for each program allows separate configuration options.
MSI	This may seem strange. You are creating a virtual application that runs in your virtual environment without needing to install to a machine, and yet an MSI file is created. This MSI file is not needed unless you want to deploy App-V in a standalone architecture. In that case, the MSI takes your virtualized application and precaches it onto a client, making it available to the user.
SFT	This is the big kahuna. The SFT file is the binary file that contains all the virtual layers you've created. It is organized into FB1 and FB2 if the virtualized application was optimized for streaming.
SPRJ	The SPRJ file is the virtual application's project file. It lists the settings for the virtual application and allows modification using the App-V Sequencer.
Manifest.xml	The Manifest.xml file contains details about all the file type allocations, shortcuts, and shell integrations.
Report.xml	The report.xml file contains details about the application's sequencing, including the same messages provided during the prerequisites check before sequencing began and the summary at the end.
Icons Folder	The Icons folder contains all the icon (ICO) files that were installed for application shortcuts and file type associations.

The files in this folder make up your virtualized application, most of which are needed during deployment. However, certain files, such as the MSI file, are required only in specific deployment scenarios, as described later in the chapter.

EDITING A VIRTUALIZED APPLICATION

For basic applications, the process of creating a working virtual application may entail only the sequencing exercise you just walked; however, other types of applications may require a bit of tweaking, which can mean many things. You may need to configure a script to run on first launch, or you may need to modify some of the settings in the virtual registry or virtual file system. Some of these changes you can do during the actual sequencing process, whereas you may need to do others after the sequencing is complete by editing your virtual application using the App-V Sequencer.

To edit a virtual application, launch your App-V Sequencer and select Open from the File menu. Select the option to Modify an Existing Virtual Application Package, which enables you to select the project file (SPRJ) for your virtual application. From there, you can view all the details about the virtual application and make any changes needed.

The editor window gives you access to eight configuration tabs: Properties, Deployment, Change History, Files, Virtual Registry, Virtual File System, Virtual Services, and OSD. The following paragraphs cover the most important edits you are likely to make to your virtual application, including several tips and gotchas.

The Properties tab is straightforward; it enables you to set the package name and a comment. The Deployment tab, shown in Figure 4-12, however, has some key items that might need tweaking. The first is the server URL, which includes the name of the server from which the App-V client will download the virtual application and the protocol to be used.

As Figure 4-12 shows, a number of different protocols are available for your App-V client to receive virtualized applications, including the Real Time Streaming Protocol (RTSP); Hypertext Transfer Protocol (HTTP), both secure and unsecure; and file share–based. The default protocol is Secure Real Time Streaming Protocol (RTSPS), but depending on your App-V infrastructure you may need to use another.

> ▶ You can install the App-V Sequencer on any supported operating system, which gives you easy access to open and edit a virtualized application outside the sequencing environment.

> **NOTE** I cover the hostname in the "Understanding the App-V Infrastructure" section; but even if you don't intend to have multiple download sources for virtualized applications, using **%SFT_SOFTGRIDSERVER%** gives you more flexibility in the future if you add other servers or assign the existing server a new name.
>
> The default hostname is the value of **%SFT_SOFTGRIDSERVER%**. This environmental variable needs to be defined on each App-V client. It should translate to the name of a local server that contains the virtual application for download by the client.

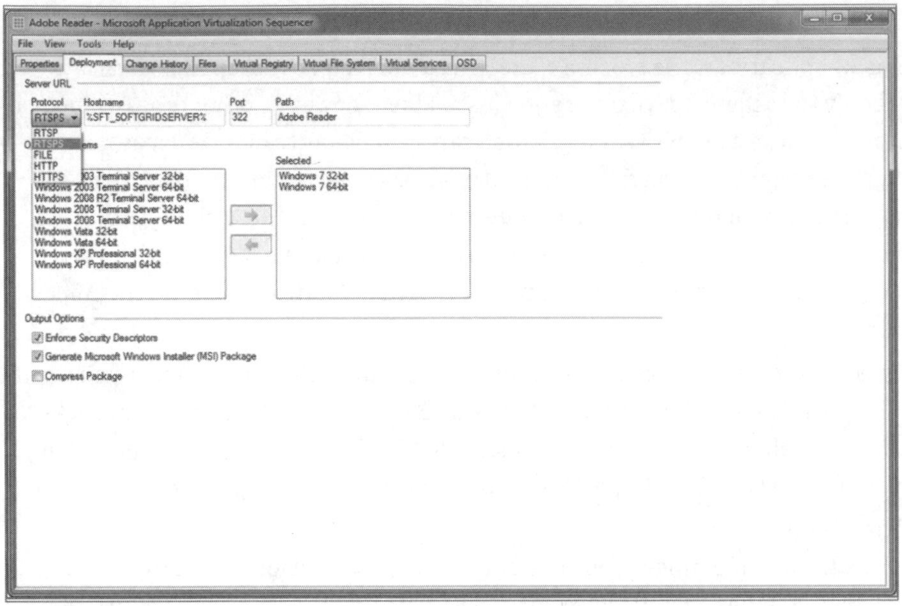

FIGURE 4-12: Select the Deployment tab to change the deployment settings for a virtual application.

The Properties tab also displays the path from which the App-V clients will pull the streaming file, which contains the same folder name you specified for the application's installation. The supported operating systems for the virtual application are also displayed and can be modified; and you can enable the options to compress the application, to generate an MSI package, and to set security descriptors that should be enforced, which is a topic worth taking a closer look at.

When applications install, they sometimes set permissions on files that prohibit normal users from making modifications or writing to the folder. By default, when you virtualize an application these security descriptors are maintained, brought into the virtual file system, and enforced. However, because the application is virtualized and not truly on the operating system, you can choose to uncheck the Enforce Security Descriptors check box, thereby allowing users to run the application as if they had full control rights. Note that the security settings defined in the registry by an application are *not* maintained when the application is virtualized.

> **TIP** Allowing users to run a virtual application as if they had full control rights without actually having to give them full control rights can be very useful, especially in session-based environments like Remote Desktop Services.

> **TIP** When files in the Files tab are selected, the option to configure the file as User Data or Application Data is available. If the file may need to be changed and retained for individual users, such as a configuration file, set the file type as User Data.

The Files tab, shown in Figure 4-13, exposes the virtual application's content through the Q: drive. If you examine this content, you will see all the files installed by the application and some App-V system files, such as `appv_manifest.xml` and `osguard.cp`, a key file that represents the actual virtual environment for the virtual application and ensures its isolation from the local operating system.

The VFS folder represents the virtual file system (VFS) overlay for everything other than the App-V logical Q: drive. This includes such content as files writing to the `Windows` folder, `Program Files` folder, and other system files. The strange folder names starting with CSIDL stand for Constant Special Item ID List, which are special folders on Windows systems. The CSIDL scheme is used because different systems may keep the Windows system files in different locations, such as `C:\Windows` or `D:\WINNT`, so using a special folder ID that always equates to the Windows system folder, `CSIDL_WINDOWS`, ensures that the VFS always overlies to the right place on the App-V client when running the application. For example, in Figure 4-13, the selected item is folder `Adobe\Acrobat` under `CSIDL_PROGRAM_FILES_COMMON`, which equates to `%ProgramFiles%\Common Files\Adobe\Acrobat`.

> ▶ In Windows Vista and later, CSIDL has been replaced with a new folder identification scheme called KNOWNFOLDERID.

> **NOTE** You can find a full list of the CSIDL special IDs and the typical paths they equate to at `http://msdn.microsoft.com/en-us/library/windows/desktop/bb762494(v=vs.85).aspx`.

To see how typical paths were replaced for your virtualized application, select Tools ➔ Options in the App-V Sequencer. Under the Parse Items tab is a list of every path found and its replacement CSIDL or environment variable—a result of the parsing App-V when it sequences an application. Anytime it sees a hard-coded path, such as to `C:\Windows`, it replaces it. This even applies to the Q: drive. Instead of having applications specifically mention the Q: drive, the App-V parser replaces it with a special environment variable, `%SFT_MNT%`, that represents the App-V virtual drive to try, ensuring the greatest flexibility for virtual application usage. A number of App-V–specific variables whose names begin with SFT are used throughout App-V.

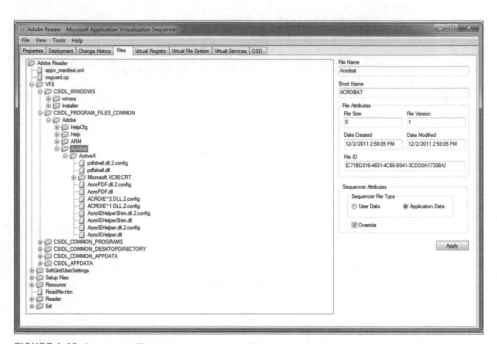

FIGURE 4-13: Select the Files tab to explore the files that overlie common system paths.

The Virtual Registry tab allows you to view the settings in the virtual registry overlay, and the Virtual File System tab gives a separate view into the VFS folder that shows only virtual file system entries. The Virtual Services tab displays any virtualized user-mode services for your application. On the Virtual Registry, Virtual File System, and Virtual Services tabs, you can add, modify, and delete entries. Any or all of these modifications may be needed to tweak your virtual application so that it performs as desired.

The final tab, OSD, allows editing of the OSD file in a structured fashion and includes some advanced configuration options, the shortcuts you want to present for the application, and the file type associations. Note one advanced setting in the OSD file that you may need to change: the LOCAL_INTERACTION_ALLOWED policy. This setting relates back to all the fantastic virtualized components of App-V applications I talked about earlier, including COM and also named objects including shared memory, that ensure that virtual applications do not conflict with any other virtual or local application, or modify their configuration. Imagine you have a locally installed application that your virtual application wants to leverage. A great example of this is a situation in which you have Outlook locally installed on your computer and your virtual application wants to send an e-mail. By default, the virtual application's attempt to interact with the local Outlook application would fail because interaction between the virtual application and local applications is disabled by default. To allow local interaction, you need to enable it by changing the LOCAL_INTERACTION_ALLOWED setting to TRUE, as shown in the following code:

```
<POLICIES>
        <LOCAL_INTERACTION_ALLOWED>TRUE</LOCAL_INTERACTION_ALLOWED>
</POLICIES>
```

TIP Personally, I find it easier to edit the OSD file directly in an XML editor or even good old Notepad, because the file is not huge and it's fairly intuitive.

WARNING Enabling local interaction means the virtual application's COM objects and named objects will register not inside the virtual bubble, but rather in the global namespace on the local operating system, which could potentially cause conflicts with local applications. Therefore, you should thoroughly test this modification before using it. In addition, although you are setting this option in the OSD file for a specific program, remember that the OSD setting applies to the entire virtual application. If you have different **LOCAL_INTERACTION_ALLOWED** values in each of the various OSD files of your virtual application's programs, the ability to interact locally would depend on which of the virtual application's programs was launched first. This could cause seemingly random behavior, so my advice is to ensure that all OSD files in a virtual application have the same setting for local interaction.

If you make any changes, you can save as a new package or just overwrite the package opened. Typically editing will occur after the initial sequencing to perform minor modifications to the virtualized application. Changes are saved using the File menu.

When tweaking your virtual application to ensure correct execution, how do you know what tweaks to make? For internal applications, this may involve some troubleshooting and trial and error based on testing. For common applications, it is likely that someone else has already ascertained the right tweaks to make. These predefined tweaks are known as *recipes*. Microsoft has a great repository that you can browse through to aid in the fast and proper virtualization of your applications.

NOTE You can find Microsoft's recipe collection at http://social.technet
.microsoft.com/Forums/en-US/prescriptiveguidance.

Now that you have your application in an installed state in your virtual environment, all you have to do is deliver it to an operating system; it's ready to run instantly—no installation or configuration is required on the OS. That is how App-V delivers the capability to run applications almost instantly for the first time; you just deliver the data of the binary stream you created over the network, which even for large applications is very fast on today's corporate networks.

UPDATING A VIRTUAL APPLICATION

At some point in your virtual application's life cycle, you many need to perform an update. This is an easy task, essentially the same as updating an application on a regular desktop. The difference is that instead of rolling out the update to every desktop, you only have to perform the update once.

> ▶ Be sure to copy the virtual application package to the App-V Sequencer environment so that the Sequencer can find it.

Use the App-V Sequencer environment (in a clean state) to update a virtual application. Once you launch the App-V Sequencer, select the option to Modify an Existing Virtual Application Package. Next, select Update Application in Existing Package, which allows you to specify the existing virtual application package. The Sequencer will open the application and load it into the virtual environment. The Sequencer then allows you to apply updates by running patch files, such as MSP files, or other setup files that may perform an update. You also have the opportunity to optimize the package for streaming again. Relaunch each application again to prepare the FB1 with the new updates.

When the updates are complete and the package is saved, you'll notice that the SFT file, which contains the actual virtual application, has a new filename reflecting the version change. For example, if you update AdobeReader.sft, the new version will be named AdobeReader_2.sft and the OSD file would now reference this _2 version of the SFT file. If you performed another update, the new SFT would be called AdobeReader_3.sft and the numbers would continue to increment with each new version.

You can then deploy the new version of the virtualized application to clients as an update. The great feature of an updated virtual application is that only the changed blocks of the virtualized application are sent over the network to the App-V clients, rather than the entire virtualized application.

USING PACKAGE ACCELERATORS

Every App-V engineer should manually sequence applications at least once to really understand the full process and gain insight into what is happening under the covers. For more complex applications, it can be quite an arduous process, and some recipes require a lot of steps to ensure an optimal virtual application.

Many organizations ask why vendors don't just ship them a virtualized version of the application, which the organization could just place in its infrastructure and instantly roll out without the need for sequencing. This seems like a reasonable request and something every organization would love, until you really look at what a generic, pre-virtualized version of an application would actually mean.

For any significant application, it's very common for organizations to perform some customizations, either through deployment settings or transform files, to ensure that the application behaves exactly as needed. If vendors provided a pre-virtualized application, no configuration would be possible unless the organization opened the App-V application in the Sequencer and began editing the virtual file system and registry values, which would be cumbersome and unpopular. However, it would be nice if vendors provided an accelerator to make it easier to sequence their applications. The accelerator could automatically apply any recipe steps that normally have to be manually actioned.

App-V 4.6 SP1 introduced the concept of *Package Accelerators*, which are actually cabinet files (CAB) that contain various configurations, scripts, and processes to enable the easy sequencing of a virtual application. Now vendors, or partners, can provide a Package Accelerator file that, when used with the App-V 4.6 SP1 Sequencer and the application's source media, will create a fully virtualized application—without requiring the standard sequencing process and the manual tweaks.

> ▶ Package Accelerators normally make the sequencing process faster, but they *always* ensure that the recipe for the application is correctly followed, which is much more important.

> **NOTE** You can find Package Accelerators at the TechNet Gallery, located at http://gallery.technet.microsoft.com/site/search?f%5B0%5D.Type=RootCategory&f%5B0%5D.Value=App-V&f%5B1%5D.Type=SubCategory&f%5B1%5D.Value=PackageAccelerators.

Sequencing an application with a Package Accelerator is different from standard sequencing. Although you use the same App-V Sequencer, when you create a new package you select the option to use a Package Accelerator. Then you are prompted to provide the Package Accelerator file. Remember, the Package Accelerator is not the virtualized application; it is simply a set of guided screens and processes that applies all the steps in a recipe to ensure the success of the virtualized application.

The exact steps to follow when using a Package Accelerator vary, but you are guided step by step, and customization is still possible if the application allows them. This guided process results in a virtualized application that meets the desired state for your organization, rather than a vanilla virtual application that may not be exactly what you want. The programs in the application may still launch to enable the streaming optimizations, and the process is similar to performing a basic sequencing, but you won't need to manually edit your virtual application once the Package Accelerator guided sequencing is complete.

BUILDING BRIDGES BETWEEN VIRTUALIZED APPLICATIONS

I have stressed how each virtual application has its own virtual environment that isolates it from any other virtual application, which solves application-to-application compatibility challenges because the virtual applications are not aware of each other; but what if you want specific virtual applications to be able to interact? For example, suppose you have virtualized a Java Runtime Environment (JRE) and then virtualize a Java application that you would like to be able to use the virtualized JRE. The same is true for virtualizing .NET and then having separate .NET applications.

Prior to App-V 4.5, the only way for separate virtual applications to see each other was to sequence them together as a single virtualized application, which meant all Office plug-ins would have to be sequenced with Office 2010 as a single virtual application. This was inefficient and resulted in a lot of duplicated effort to update a common program like the JRE.

▶ DSC basically allows configured virtual applications to run in the same sandbox or bubble.

App-V 4.5 included a new technology called Dynamic Suite Composition (DSC) that enables separate virtual applications to be launched in a shared virtual environment and then communicate with each other. This is not a systemwide configuration, nor would you want it to be. If every virtual application suddenly saw every other virtual application, one of the main benefits of virtual applications—solving application-to-application conflicts—would be lost. Instead, you manually configure specific applications to use DSC by setting a dependency from one virtual application to the virtual application upon which it is dependent. For example, you would configure your Java application to be dependent on the JRE virtual application, your .NET applications on your .NET virtual application, and your Office plug-ins on your Office 2010 virtual application. These dependencies can optionally be set as mandatory, meaning if the application that the dependent application depends upon is not available, then the dependent application cannot run. A good example is setting a mandatory dependency for a Java application to the JRE virtual application, because without JRE the Java application cannot run anyway. In Figure 4-14, the Word 2007 virtual application is dependent on the ODF plug-in, which enables the ODF plug-in to function with Office because it will share the virtual environment and therefore have a common named object and COM object space. I've done the dependency this way so the ODF plug-in is always loaded when Word starts.

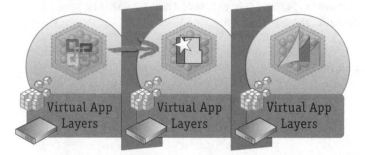

FIGURE 4-14: Here, Office is dependent on the plug-in, which means they share a virtual environment. The other virtual application is still isolated.

To configure this dependency, you add a reference in the Dependencies section of the dependent application's OSD file. In this example, you would update the Word 2007 OSD file as it is being configured to be dependent on the ODF plug-in virtual application, which means the ODF plug-in will load into the Word 2007 virtual environment every time Word 2007 is launched.

To create a dependency, you need to know the location of the SFT file, the GUID, the filename, the system guard instance, and the size of the application that it is dependent on to insert into your OSD file. This sounds extremely labor intensive until you realize you basically just copy the entire IMPLEMENTATION block from the OSD file of the virtual application that it is dependent upon, which makes it much easier!

In the following example, I added a dependency on the ODF virtual application. Notice how similar in structure the highlighted dependency section looks to the IMPLEMENTATION block of my Word 2007 virtual application OSD file. I just pasted it straight from the OSD file of my ODF plug-in virtual application. It looks complex but it is actually easy.

```
<?xml version="1.0" standalone="no"?>
<SOFTPKG GUID="CB6E0534-A1BA-494D-ABE8-11C95A65051E" NAME="XML Editor"
VERSION="12.0.4518.1014">
  <IMPLEMENTATION>
    <CODEBASE
HREF="RTSP://savdalappv01:554/MSWord.v12/Microsoft_Word_2007_3.sft"
GUID="A637675A-9EA1-4220-A769-C45BCA490588" PARAMETERS=""
FILENAME=
"%CSIDL_PROGRAM_FILES_COMMON%\Microsoft Shared\OFFICE12\MSOXMLED.EXE"
SYSGUARDFILE="MSWord.v12\osguard.cp" SIZE="489055926" />
    <WORKINGDIR />
```

```
<VIRTUALENV TERMINATECHILDREN="FALSE">
   <DEPENDENCIES>
      <CODEBASE
HREF="RTSP://savdalappv01:554/ODFplug.v31/ODF_Plug-in_v31.sft"
GUID="3E402536-FA2D-49F1-9EA8-745E7A659EA5" PARAMETERS=""
FILENAME=
"ODFplug.v31\Sun\Sun ODF Plugin for MSOffice 3.1\program\soffice.exe"
SYSGUARDFILE="ODFplug.v31\osguard.cp" SIZE="195455074"
MANDATORY="TRUE" />
   </DEPENDENCIES>
   <ENVLIST />
</VIRTUALENV>
```

> **NOTE** If playing around in XML files is not your idea of fun, Microsoft has a DSC Tool that enables you to graphically add dependencies between applications, configure whether they are mandatory, and then save the updated OSD file, all without ever editing XML. You can download this tool from http://www.microsoft.com/download/en/details.aspx?displaylang=en&id=6655 and it is recommended over manually editing OSD files.

SEEING APPLICATION VIRTUALIZATION IN ACTION

While it's helpful to read about all these processes to sequence applications, edit them, update them, and leverage Package Accelerators, seeing them in action can also clarify the steps. I highly recommend checking out the following videos I created that walk through the various application virtualization processes:

- ▶ **Overview of App-V:** http://www.savilltech.com/videos/App-VOverview/App-VOverview.wmv

- ▶ **Virtualizing an example application with App-V 4.6 SP1:** http://www.savilltech.com/videos/adobeseq46sp1/AdobeReaderXSeqwith46SP1PA.wmv

- ▶ **Virtualizing Office 2010 with App-V 4.6 SP1 manually and with a Package Accelerator:** http://www.savilltech.com/videos/office2010AppV46SP1Seq/office2010AppV46SP1Seq.wmv

- ▶ **Updating a virtualized application:** http://www.savilltech.com/videos/AppV46SP1AppUpdate/AppV46SP1AppUpdate.wmv

- ▶ **Dynamic Suite Composition with App-V:** http://www.savilltech.com/videos/appvdsc/appvdsc1024768.wmv

UNDERSTANDING THE APP-V INFRASTRUCTURE

The App-V technology represents a huge leap in software execution and delivery, and the ability to abstract the application from the operating system offers a lot of benefits for users and organizations. To fully realize App-V's benefits, you need to understand the infrastructure elements that are deployed so that clients can actually find, download, and run the App-V virtualized applications. There are three main infrastructure scenarios for App-V: standalone, full, and light; however, before digging into the server-side infrastructure, let's take a quick look at the client-side infrastructure.

Exploring the App-V Client

Various application virtualization solutions are available in the market today. Some solutions do not leverage any client-side service or client, embedding the virtual environment code in every virtualized application. Others install a small client on the operating system that provides the virtual environment for the virtual applications and can also help with management functions. App-V uses the second approach, so before an operating system can run an App-V virtualized application it must have the App-V client installed.

The App-V client for App-V 4.6 SP1 is supported on the following operating systems, and both 32-bit and 64-bit versions are available:

- ▶ Windows XP Professional SP2 and SP3

- ▶ Windows Vista Business, Enterprise, and Ultimate RTM, SP1, and SP2

- ▶ Windows 7 Professional, Enterprise, and Ultimate RTM and SP1

- ▶ Windows Server 2003 SP1 and SP2

- ▶ Windows Server 2003 R2 RTM and SP2

- ▶ Windows Server 2008 SP1 and SP2

- ▶ Windows Server 2008 R2 RTM and SP1

The server operating systems mentioned use the Remote Desktop Services (RDS) version of App-V, which allows your virtual applications to run in a session virtualization environment, whereby each user has his or her own session on a shared server operating system. Using session virtualization offers many of the advantages of the

▶ Session virtualization is the current term for what the IT world has traditionally considered Terminal Services type solutions.

standard App-V to your server environments, such as solving application-to-application compatibility challenges and avoiding cluttering the operating system with many locally installed applications. The App-V client for RDS has the same functionality and interaction as the desktop App-V client that I focus on here.

INSTALLING THE APP-V CLIENT

The desktop App-V client is provided as both a `setup.exe` file and a `setup.msi` file, which enables organizations to choose the file type that works best for their standard deployment method, such as an ESD solution like the System Center Configuration Manager (SCCM), a GP, or even manual installation. The App-V client also has a Support folder that includes an updated Microsoft Application Error Reporting (MER) component that is applied automatically if needed.

> **TIP** Even if you have the Visual C++ 2005 and 2008 redistributables already installed, the version you have is unlikely to be the exact version that App-V requires, which includes an Application Template Library (ATL) security update. Use the **setup.exe** if you can; it's the easiest and most dependable way to deploy the App-V client and it automatically installs any required dependencies.

▶ This type of manual configuration is not ideal for a mass rollout, for which you should instead use a silent installation and pass all the App-V client configuration settings as part of the command line.

Additionally, the `setup.exe` version of the App-V client install media contains any prerequisites, including specific versions of the Visual C++ 2005 and 2008 that are needed for App-V. The `setup.msi` installer will not automatically install the Virtual C++ redistributables. When the App-V client is manually installed using either method, the install wizard will prompt you for various settings, such as the name of the Application Virtualization (App-V) Management Server, the local cache size, and the drive letter to use for virtual applications. Alternatively, you can bypass the install wizard and do a *silent installation*, in which no dialogs are displayed during the installation process.

You want to configure a number of key settings, as shown in the following code. Type the entire command on one line (note that the ^ is the line continuation character).

```
Client\x64\setup.exe /s /v" /qn ^
SWIPUBSVRHOST=\"savdalappv01.savilltech.net\" ^
SWIPUBSVRTYPE=\"RTSP\" SWIPUBSVRPORT=\"554\" ^
SWIPUBSVRDISPLAY=\"SAVDALAPPV01\" ^
SWIFSDRIVE=\"Q\" SWICACHESIZE=\"4096\""
```

Key settings here include the parameter string for your Application Virtualization (App-V) Management Server (if you are using one), which specifies the hostname of the App-V server (SWIPUBSVRHOST); the protocol used (SWIPUBSVRTYPE); the port (SWIPUBSVRPORT, which should correspond to the protocol used); and the display name for the App-V Management Server within the App-V client (SWIPUBSVRDISPLAY). Note also how the preceding code specifies the drive letter that App-V should use as the virtual drive (which, remember, should be the same for the entire environment), the sequencer environment (SWIFSDRIVE), and the size of the App-V cache on the client (SWICACHESIZE), which is used to locally store the virtualized applications.

If you want to use the MSI installation for the App-V client, then you need to manually install each of the App-V dependencies as mentioned, and then pass the configuration through switches to the MSI. You can download the correct versions of the dependencies for App-V 4.6 SP1 from the following locations:

- **Visual C++ 2005 SP1 Redistributable Package ATL Security Update:** http://www.microsoft.com/download/en/details.aspx?displaylang=en&id=14431

- **Visual C++ 2008 SP1 Redistributable Package ATL Security Update:** http://www.microsoft.com/download/en/details.aspx?displaylang=en&id=11895

- **Microsoft Core XML Services 6.0 (needed only for Windows XP clients):** http://www.microsoft.com/download/en/details.aspx?DisplayLang=en&id=3988

After they are downloaded, create a folder hierarchy containing the App-V client, the MER component, and the prerequisites previously mentioned. To deploy and ensure that the prerequisites are installed, you can use the following script, which calls the prerequisites and then the setup.msi file with the same switches you used for the setup.exe file, but make sure you replace \\server\share with the real server and share containing your App-V client:

```
start /wait \\server\share\Client\prereq\vc2005\vcredist_x86.exe /Q
start /wait \\server\share\Client\prereq\vc2008\vcredist_x86.exe /Q
start /wait msiexec /i ^
\\server\share\Client\x64\Support\Watson\dw20shared.msi ^
APPGUID={342C9BB8-65A0-46DE-AB7A-8031E151AF69} REBOOT=Suppress ^
REINSTALL=ALL REINSTALLMODE=vomus
start /wait msiexec.exe /i \\server\share\Client\x64\setup.msi ^
SWIPUBSVRHOST="savdalappv01.savilltech.net" SWIPUBSVRTYPE="RTSP" ^
SWIPUBSVRPORT="554" SWIPUBSVRDISPLAY="SAVDALAPPV01" ^
SWIFSDRIVE="Q" SWICACHESIZE="4096" /q
```

The preceding script is for a 64-bit client installation; the 32-bit deployment would be the same except that the last two entries would specify the x86 folder instead of x64, as shown here:

```
start /wait \\server\share\Client\prereq\vc2005\vcredist_x86.exe /Q
start /wait \\server\share\Client\prereq\vc2008\vcredist_x86.exe /Q
start /wait msiexec /i ^
\\server\share\Client\x86\Support\Watson\dw20shared.msi ^
APPGUID={DB9F70CD-29BC-480B-8BA2-C9C2232C4553} ^
REBOOT=Suppress REINSTALL=ALL ^
REINSTALLMODE=vomus
start /wait msiexec.exe /i \\server\share\Client\x86\setup.msi ^
SWIPUBSVRHOST="savdalappv01.savilltech.net" SWIPUBSVRTYPE="RTSP" ^
SWIPUBSVRPORT="554" SWIPUBSVRDISPLAY="SAVDALAPPV01" SWIFSDRIVE="Q" ^
SWICACHESIZE="4096" /q
```

My full folder hierarchy containing all the App-V install files and the prerequisites is shown here for your reference:

▶ `App-V Client 4.6 SP1\x64install.bat`

▶ `App-V Client 4.6 SP1\x86install.bat`

▶ `App-V Client 4.6 SP1\Client\Prereq\vc2005\vcredist_x86.exe`

▶ `App-V Client 4.6 SP1\Client\Prereq\vc2008\vcredist_x86.exe`

▶ `App-V Client 4.6 SP1\Client\x64\setup.exe`

▶ `App-V Client 4.6 SP1\Client\x64\setup.msi`

▶ `App-V Client 4.6 SP1\Client\x64\Support\Watson\dw20shared.msi`

▶ `App-V Client 4.6 SP1\Client\x86\setup.exe`

▶ `App-V Client 4.6 SP1\Client\x86\setup.msi`

▶ `App-V Client 4.6 SP1\Client\x86\Support\Watson\dw20shared.msi`

TIP   If you want to deploy the App-V client using the System Center Configuration Manager (SCCM), you can use either the **setup.exe** file or the **setup.msi** file. If you choose to use **setup.msi** and the batch file, you cannot specify a server name and share because SCCM uses a distribution point model that allows clients to download software from the closest server. The solution is to replace the *server**share* in the batch file with **%~dp0**, which resolves to the distribution point and location of the App-V client package on the server. For example:

```
start /wait %~dp0Client\prereq\vc2005\vcredist_x86.exe /Q
```

Note there is no backslash (\) between **%~dp0** and **Client**. This is intentional because the **%~dp0** includes a trailing backslash when resolved.

USING THE APP-V CLIENT INTERFACE

The App-V client makes a number of changes to the operating system when installed. This may seem like I'm contradicting what I said earlier in the chapter about App-V virtual applications making no changes to the local operating system, but I'm talking about changes the App-V client makes, *not* the virtual applications themselves.

The most obvious change is a new shortcut under Administrative Tools for the Application Virtualization (App-V) client, which is a graphical interface into App-V. However, because it's part of the Administrative Tools Start menu group, it is not available to regular users. The shortcut is intended for help-desk staff in the event that troubleshooting procedures are needed.

The App-V client has three primary workspaces: Applications, File Type Associations, and Publishing Servers. The Applications workspace, shown in Figure 4-15, displays all the virtual applications that are available to the current user. If you look at the properties of a virtual application and select the Package tab, you can see details about the location of the virtual application on a server, as well as its total size and the size of its FB1 (the Launch Data Size), which is the data that needs to be available to initially launch the application. Notice the FB1 for Adobe is only 7MB compared to a total application size of 119MB. That means if this is the first time the application is being launched, only 7MB of data needs to be sent over the network until the application opens, after which the user can start using it while the rest is silently downloaded in the background.

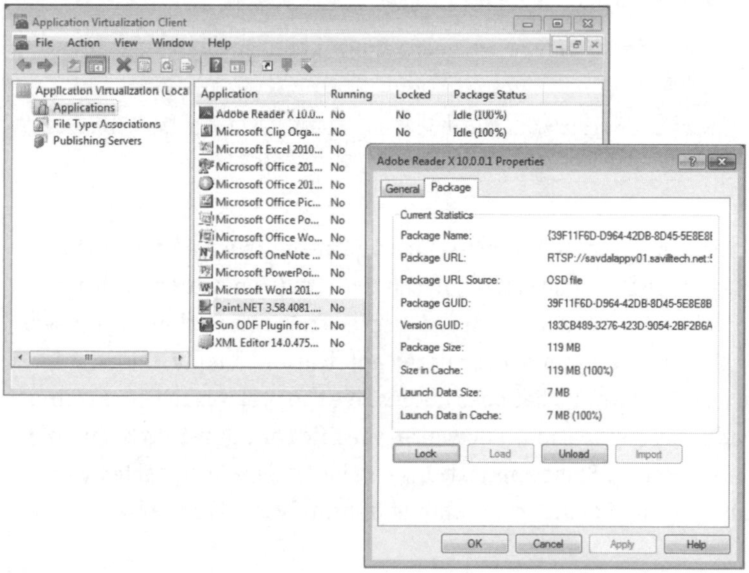

FIGURE 4-15: Use the Applications workspace of the App-V client to view the virtual applications; and select Properties to view details about the selected application.

The default size is 4GB and is configured using the SWICACHESIZE parameter. If the cache is full and another application needs to be cached, the least recently used virtual application is removed to free up space.

I've mentioned caching a number of times, so let me give you a bit more information about it. Although you don't have to install virtual applications on a local operating system, you don't want to constantly have to pull data over the network either. To avoid this, virtual applications are cached locally on the operating system in a cache file. You set the fixed size of this file when you install the App-V client.

With the virtual applications that have been cached to the local machine and therefore stored in the local cache file, you can perform various actions that are available through the App-V client's Action menu. The Action menu is displayed when you select a virtual application. Common actions you may perform are outlined in Table 4-2.

TABLE 4-2: App-V Application Actions

ACTION	DESCRIPTION
Load	Loads a virtualized application into the local client's App-V cache.
Unload	Removes a virtual application from the local client's App-V cache.
Delete	Removes a virtual application from the local client's App-V cache, including all shortcuts and file type associations for the application. The application shortcuts and file type associations are re-created if the application is offered to the client again.
Clear	Deletes any user-specific settings for the virtual application as well as application shortcuts and file type associations; however, the application itself is not removed.
Repair	Removes any user-specific configurations and reapplies the default settings.
Lock/Unlock	Locks or unlocks an application in the App-V client. Applications must be unlocked before they can be removed from the cache.

Virtual applications are protected from user modifications, such as deleting an application DLL or playing with some setting in the registry (all of which typically break an application). The App-V cache is also protected from corruption. If you ever do experience a problem with an App-V virtualized application, simply unload it from the cache and then load it again. If that does not resolve the problem, a user setting could be to blame, as many applications allow user-specific configuration to customize the application experience. Some applications can be rendered unusable by bad user settings. Performing the Repair action should definitely resolve the issue.

The File Type Associations workspace enables you to see which virtual application is associated with which file types and modify the associations if needed. You use the Publishing Servers workspace when you are using the App-V Server infrastructure model; it shows the App-V Management Server that your client communicates with to find available virtualized applications. You can also trigger a manual refresh of available virtual applications.

Aside from the App-V client, two additional services are installed on the machine, Application Virtual Client and Application Virtualization Service Agent, which handle the virtual applications and virtual services, respectively.

Another change to the local operating system is the appearance of the Q: drive (or whatever drive letter you chose). Any attempt to navigate to Q: will result in an Access Denied message because this Q: drive does not really exist. You can only see content there from within a launched virtual application, because the Q: drive is your interface to the App-V local cache. When you launch a virtual application and look at the Q: drive, you see all the virtual applications' root folders that are currently in the local machine's App-V cache, which is the key reason you needed to ensure that each virtual application had a unique root-level folder name. In Figure 4-16, I have navigated to the Q: drive from within my virtualized instance of PowerPoint 2007, so I can see all the virtual applications cached on my machine, which include Adobe Reader, Office 2010, and Word, in addition to an ODF plug-in for Word.

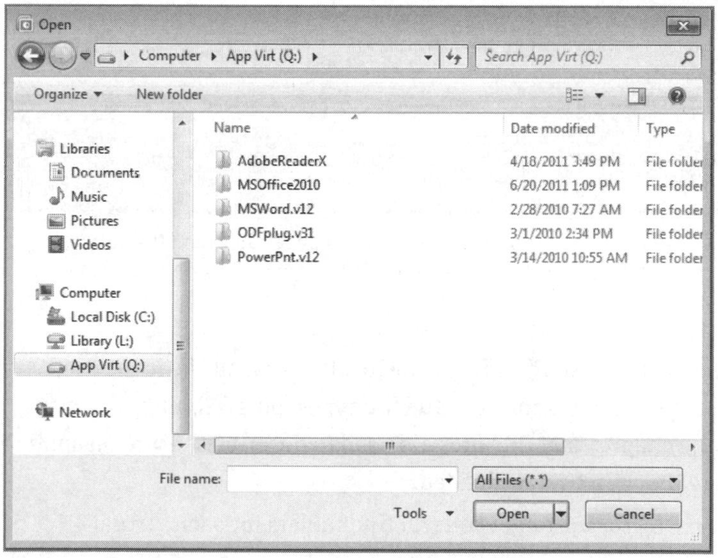

FIGURE 4-16: Looking at the Q: drive through a virtualized application

Aside from the Q: drive, there are other changes to the local computer's file system—in particular, that cache file to which I keep referring. The App-V cache is a shared file for all the computer's users, which makes sense. If you have 10 different people using the same machine, you don't want 10 copies of the same application cached, wasting disk space. Security is enforced for the virtual applications, so users who don't have permission to run an application won't be able to run it even though it's visible in the shared cache.

The App-V shared files for all users are stored under the C:\ProgramData\Microsoft\ Application Virtualization Client\SoftGrid Client folder; the key file is sftfs .fsd, which is the single cache file that contains all the cached virtual applications. As shown in Figure 4-17, the cache file on my system is more than 2GB in size because I have quite a few virtualized applications, and it could continue to grow up to the maximum cache size specified during installation, which was 4GB.

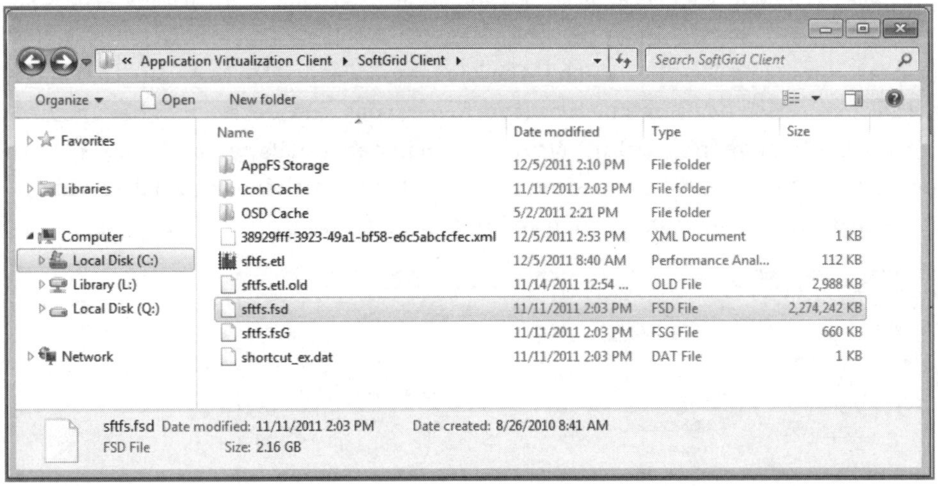

FIGURE 4-17: The **sftfs.fsd** file is the physical store for your App-V cache and the data exposed through the Q: drive, and it can be seen using any file system explorer tool such as Windows Explorer.

The SoftGrid Client folder also includes cache locations for all the icons used for the known virtual applications' shortcuts and file types, plus OSD files. You may recall from earlier in the chapter that OSD files are used to describe the virtual applications and from where they can be downloaded.

If you look in the AppFS Storage folder you will find folders for each virtual application, named *<short folder name of virtual application>-<GUID of virtual application>*. Each folder contains a number of files, one of which is

`GlblVol_sftfs_v1_<SID of the service App-V runs as, normally S-1-5-20>`, which contains writes to operating system objects that the virtual application makes, such as the file system or registry, that are not per-user settings. The virtual applications cannot write to the shared cache file, so this `GlblVol` file is where the writes are stored. This file acts as a write filter for the virtual file system.

If you navigate up to `C:\ProgramData\Microsoft\Application Virtualization Client`, you will find an `sftlog.txt` file, which is a great log file for obtaining information about the virtual applications' activities and any potential issues.

I mentioned deleting user settings through the Application Virtualization Client, but you might be wondering where these are stored. As mentioned, the virtual application cache cannot be written to by applications; the cache just stores the cache for a virtual application, and the cache is shared between all users. Therefore, user settings aren't stored there. What happens if an application tries to perform a write to one of its assets, such as its location on the virtual file system or registry? In addition to the shared cache file, all users have their own App-V storage area for each virtual application. The user-specific application settings **are** stored in the roaming part of their profile, typically the `C:\Users\<user name>\AppData\Roaming\SoftGrid Client` folder. Within that folder, each application has a subfolder, which is named *<short folder name of virtual application>*-*<GUID of virtual application>*, the same naming convention used for the global per-application folders. Within this folder is a `UsrVol_sftfs_v1.pkg` file, which is essentially another overlay for the file system and registry where per-user writes made to the assets of the virtual application are stored.

> ▶ These are the entries that were configured as User Data when you edited the virtual application in the Sequencer application.

Remember that all the writes written to these `GlblVol` and `UsrVol` files are only for writes to assets of the virtual application, and by assets I mean file system and registry locations that were identified as part of the virtual application's installation. If a virtual application tries to write to locations that are not its assets—that is, locations other than those created during its installation—the writes will be written to the local file system and registry *if* the user has sufficient permissions to write to those locations based on the operating system security configuration.

A great troubleshooting tip if you are having problems with a virtual application is to launch another application under the context of a virtualized application so it can interact with the virtual environment through the eyes of the virtual application. To launch another application such as `regedit.exe` or Explorer in the virtual environment of a virtual application, you need to use two App-V command-line applications.

The first command-line tool is `sftmime`, which enables you to interface with the App-V environment. The following example requests a list of all the virtual applications, using their official, friendly names:

```
C:\>sftmime /query obj:app /short
Adobe Reader X 10.0.0.1
 Microsoft Clip Organizer 14.0.4750.1000
 Microsoft Excel 2010 14.0.5130.5003
 Microsoft Office 2010 Language Preferences 14.0.4750.1000
 Microsoft Office 2010 Upload Center 14.0.4757.1000
 Microsoft Office Picture Manager 14.0.4750.1000
 Microsoft Office PowerPoint 2007 12.0.4518.1014
 Microsoft Office Word 2007 12.0.6425.1000
 Microsoft OneNote 2010 14.0.4763.1000
 Microsoft PowerPoint 2010 14.0.4754.1000
 Microsoft Word 2010 14.0.5123.5000
 Paint.NET 3.58.4081.24586
 Sun ODF Plugin for Microsoft Office 3.1 9.0.0.9398
 XML Editor 14.0.4750.1000
```

Once you know the correct name for each virtual application, you can launch an application of your choice within the virtual environment of a virtual application, such as a command prompt (`cmd.exe`) or the registry editor (`regedit.exe`). The following example launches a command prompt within the virtual environment for PowerPoint 2007. `Sfttray.exe` is used for virtual application execution behind the scenes, and you can use it if you need to run an alternate program within the virtual environment. You see this in action in Figure 4-18. In the opened command prompt you can navigate the Q: drive and open the VFS folder within the virtual application's root folder, in which you see all those special folder names that are overlaid on the local OS paths such as `C:\Windows`, and so on. If you were to navigate to a folder such as `C:\Windows\winsxs`, you would see files contained both in the virtual file system (`CSIDL_Windows\winsxs`) and the local file system, which is exactly what the virtual applications see.

> ▶ In a managed App-V environment, when the virtual application launches, it actually does a quick check with the servers hosting the virtualized application for any updates to the virtual application.

```
C:\ >sfttray /exe cmd.exe ^

"Microsoft Office PowerPoint 2007 12.0.4518.1014"
```

Note that all these items—the App-V Client, the Q: drive, the files on the file system—are items searched for specifically. If you were just a user running a virtualized application, what is different? Looking at the Task Manager, you would see the regular process name, nothing special. The only notification users get when they run an App-V virtual application is in the bottom right-hand side of the screen, just above the system tray, when the application is loaded into the virtual environment at startup (as shown in Figure 4-19) and then again when the application closes.

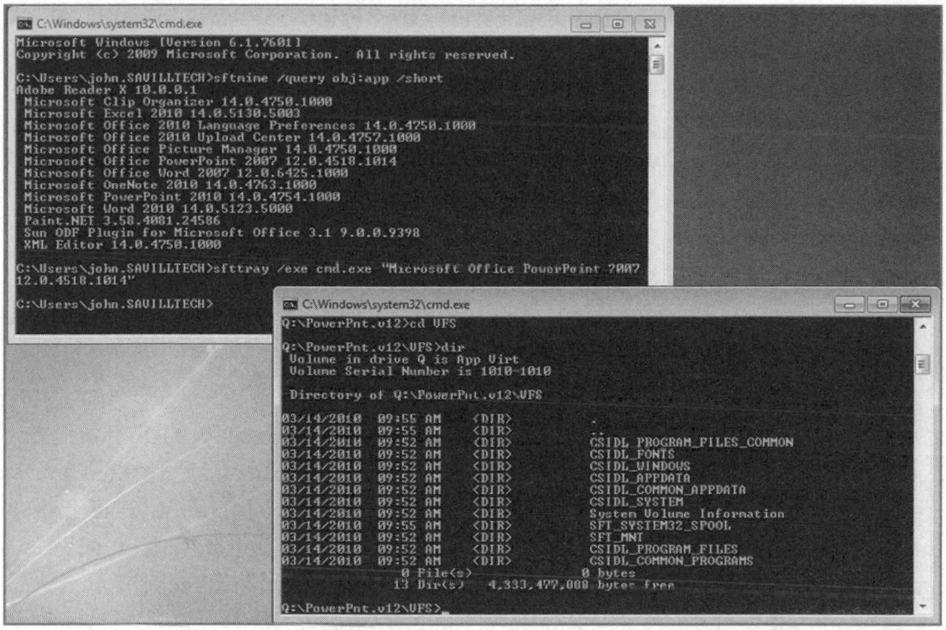

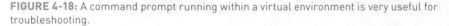

FIGURE 4-18: A command prompt running within a virtual environment is very useful for troubleshooting.

The final piece of your App-V infrastructure is the server-side infrastructure itself, which with App-V is entirely optional. Before you read on, I definitely recommend downloading the Microsoft Application Virtualization 4.6 Infrastructure Planning and Design guide from http://technet.microsoft.com/en-us/library/ee354207.aspx, which provides much more detail than space allows here and will help you implement the right infrastructure for your organization.

FIGURE 4-19: Blink and you'll miss it: the only indication users get that an application is virtualized with App-V. Well, that and the fact that they can't break it!

Using Standalone Mode

The simplest App-V server infrastructure to document is using App-V in standalone mode, which requires no server infrastructure at all. You still need the App-V Sequencer VM to create the virtual applications, but you use your own method to get the virtual applications to your clients, to which you have deployed the App-V client. This could include users connecting to a file share that contains virtualized applications that they can then load using the App-V client.

One method to import a virtual application directly into the App-V client is to launch the Application Virtualization Client application, select the New Application action in the Applications workspace, and then select the OSD file for the virtual application. This action imports the virtual application into the client, including the shortcuts and file type associations, and the binary stream into the local cache.

> NOTE Although the standalone mode works fine and can be a good solution for test purposes, it's not really suitable for widespread enterprise use. Standalone mode does not enable a number of the App-V benefits, such as streaming and user-based access control.

If you have an existing ESD solution that can deliver setup files or MSI files, another option is to leverage the MSI file that was created automatically when you created your virtual application. Create a package in your ESD system and specify the MSI file for the virtual application, which, when executed on the client, will import the virtual application to the App-V client, which in turn makes the application available to the user. The MSI file actually leverages the `sftmime` command shown earlier to publish the virtual application to the App-V client and then load it into the cache.

Using Full Infrastructure Mode

A full infrastructure App-V deployment offers the top-end App-V experience and provides a number of unique features. It requires you to designate servers to fulfill several App-V server roles, and leverages SQL Server and Active Directory (AD) for storing App-V application and infrastructure configuration and application assignment, respectively.

APPLICATION VIRTUALIZATION MANAGEMENT SERVER ROLE

The first server role is the App-V Management Server, which allows the importing of virtual applications through the Application Virtualization (App-V) Management Console into the App-V Management Server content area, customization of file type associations, license metering of virtual applications, and assignment of virtual applications to AD users or groups of users. The capability to closely track and control application usage is a huge benefit of the App-V Management Server. One great feature is the capability to set a license based on the number of concurrent users, which prevents more than that number of users from running a virtual application

▶ Remember that you had the option to configure this server when you installed the App-V client. Doing so provides the best App-V experience in terms of speed of application availability to clients.

at the same time; an expiration date can also be configured to prevent a user from accessing the application after the date specified. The App-V client communicates with the App-V Management Server based on the logged-on user; the App-V Management Server communicates with all the virtual applications that should be available to that user and sends the OSD files for the virtual application along with the various icon files. This enables the shortcuts for the virtual applications to be placed on the desktop and Start menu, and the various file type associations to be configured; and because the App-V infrastructure also sends the icon files, the correct icons are also displayed. However, App-V has not actually sent the virtual application to the machine yet.

The App-V Management Server also enables streaming of the virtual application to the App-V client using the Real Time Streaming Protocol (RTSP), or Secure RTSPS, which is the next step to actually launch an application when a user clicks one of the application shortcuts that were sent or opens a data file that is of a file type associated with the virtual application. When the virtual application needs to start up, it is the App-V Management Server that streams that initial FB1 of the virtual application to the App-V client, enabling the virtual application to launch very quickly for immediate use while the rest of the application, FB2, is sent to the background.

What if the FB2 is very large and the user attempts to access a feature of the application that was not in FB1 and has not yet been pulled down from FB2? Imagine being in Word and selecting Word Art: Unless you launched Word Art when you were performing the streaming optimization phase of your sequencing, the Word Art components will be in FB2 (and Word Art definitely belongs in FB2 unless you really need fancy words when you first launch Word). App-V streaming handles this rapid need for FB2 content by being able to pull chunks of FB2 on demand in 64KB blocks from the virtual application store, the App-V Management Server, if the content is not yet in the local cache. Prior to App-V 4.6, the on-demand block size was 32KB, which could be changed in the Sequencer, but given the stability of networks today and the ability to handle larger blocks of data, the 64KB standard was adopted and the option to change removed from the GUI.

▶ If you really want a smaller block size, you can use the /BLOCKSIZE command-line parameter with the Sequencer, which allows 4KB, 16KB, 32KB, or 64KB block sizes, but only use this if absolutely necessary and you know what you are doing!

The virtual application is then kept in the App-V client cache so that subsequent launches of the virtual application do not require downloading of the binary stream over the network; only a quick check is performed upon application launch to determine whether the application has been updated. The virtual application is removed only if it is unloaded or deleted manually, or the App-V cache fills up and the application has not been recently used. Figure 4-20 shows the interaction of the App-V Management Server and the App-V client for a new virtual application, starting after the user logs on.

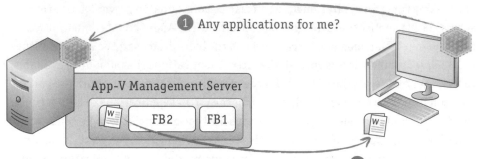

1 Any applications for me?

App-V Management Server

FB2   FB1

Here is Word OSD and its icons. Add a shortcut on the Start **2** menu and associate .doc with this virtual application.

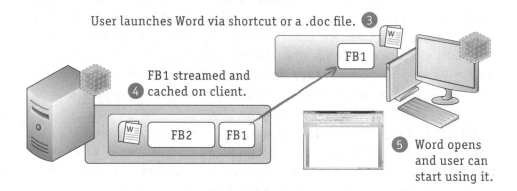

User launches Word via shortcut or a .doc file. **3**

FB1

4 FB1 streamed and cached on client.

FB2   FB1

5 Word opens and user can start using it.

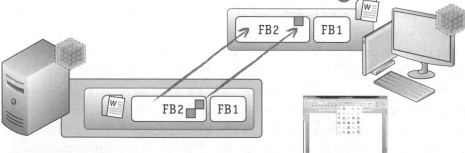

FB2 is cached in the background and 64KB blocks are pulled on demand when required if the FB2 content is not yet cached on the client. **6**

FB2   FB1

FB2   FB1

FIGURE 4-20: The three main steps of App-V Management Server and client interaction for a new virtual application

Make sure you consider network bandwidth when using on-demand streaming of applications. Performing a standard deployment of an application over the network sends the same amount of data as streaming a virtualized application (maybe more, maybe less, depending on compression usage). When you stream on demand, however, the user has clicked the application icon and is waiting for that FB1 to download before the application launches, whereas with a standard application deployment the user does not see the application until all of it has been sent over the network and installed. For traditional application installations, the application may be deployed outside of standard business hours to minimize congestion on the network, especially when rolling out a large application. Streaming virtual applications is unlikely to be a problem for most organizations, but it is certainly something to consider—especially for users on wireless networks, which are typically much slower than wired connections. One solution for large virtual application deployments, such as a new or updated application, is to stagger the availability of the virtual application, or you can precache the application on App-V clients outside of business hours through scripts.

Another important aspect to consider for streamed virtual applications is your laptop and mobile users. If you send only the OSD file, shortcuts, and icons when the user is connected to the network, and then the user disconnects and later tries to launch the application for the first time when still disconnected, the launch will fail because the application cannot be streamed. To resolve this problem, you should configure precaching of virtual applications for your mobile users so that the binary stream is sent to the client as soon as possible, rather than waiting for the user to launch the application. You can use numerous methods to enable this precaching, including user-initiated caching by loading the application from the Application Virtualization Client or through performing a script-based load by leveraging the SFTMIME command-line LOAD function, specifying the name of the virtual application using the PACKAGE:<package name> option, as shown in the following example. If you use a traditional ESD solution, the capability to precache the virtual application should be standard functionality, as you will see in the next section.

```
SFTMIME LOAD PACKAGE:<Package name>
```

FILE TYPE ASSOCIATIONS WITH APP-V AND LOCAL APPLICATIONS

One topic that has been mentioned several times in this section is file type associations, which do require some consideration—both for different virtual applications that define the same file type associations and for virtual applications and local applications that have the same file types. This is not an issue specific to virtual applications, but rather something to consider anytime you have multiple programs trying to configure associations for the same file type. Whichever application performs the file type association last owns the file type association, and the same applies to local applications and virtual applications.

For example, if you have Office 2010 installed locally, then the local Word 2010 will be associated with .doc. If you then publish a virtualized Word 2003 to the same machine that has file type associations for DOC files enabled, the App-V Word will be the default application for DOC files. You can manually change the file type association or you can remove the file type association from the virtualized application so the locally installed Word would still own the file type association.

WARNING You need to be very careful when deploying multiple applications with the same file type associations to avoid random behavior based on installation order. Therefore, always make a spreadsheet of applications and their file type associations, and decide which application should own the file type association. Never have more than one application defining an association for a single file type.

The App-V Management Console, shown in Figure 4-21, communicates with the App-V Data Store (hosted on SQL Server) via the App-V Management Web Service, which is installed automatically when the App-V Management Server is installed. As you can see in the figure, the App-V Management Console allows modification of items such as shortcuts and file type associations for virtual applications. From the Access Permissions tab, you can define which users can use the virtual application.

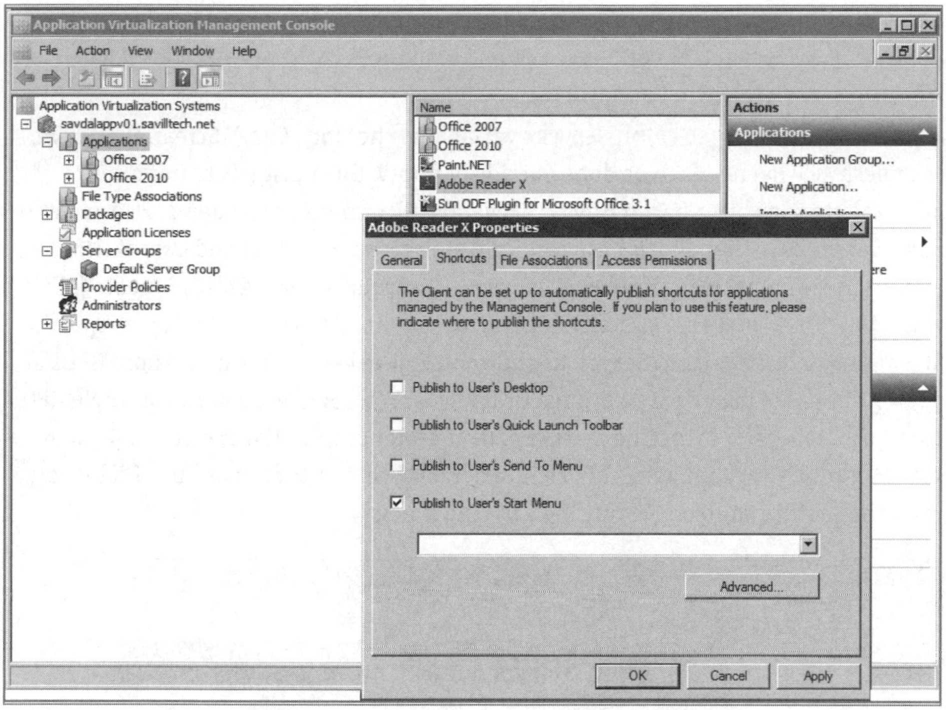

FIGURE 4-21: In the App-V Management Console, select the properties of a virtual application to customize it.

APPLICATION VIRTUALIZATION STREAMING SERVER ROLE

Another App-V server role is the Application Virtualization Streaming Server. I mentioned previously that the App-V Management Server can stream the binary content of the virtual application (using RTSP or RTSPS), but you can also configure servers that just provide the streaming capabilities without the actual management functions. You may want streaming-only servers to provide greater scalability for your App-V environment, and to have a local App-V Streaming Server in different geographical locations. Multiple App-V Streaming Servers can be created and configured with a common set of content (the virtual applications).

This use of multiple App-V Streaming Servers is exactly why by default the virtual applications did not specify a server name from which App-V clients should download the binary stream, but rather used the %SFT_SOFTGRIDSERVER% variable. For

App-V clients in different locations, this variable can resolve to different local App-V Streaming or Management Servers in order to balance the streaming traffic and avoid WAN links when they are not needed.

Setting the %SFT_SOFTGRIDSERVER% variable to the right App-V Streaming Server is something that needs to be done outside of App-V. One option is to use a script at machine startup; but a better way is to leverage GP preferences, a new feature in Windows Server 2012 that allows easy configuration of many system and user attributes, including environment variables. You can create various Group Policy Objects (GPOs) with the %SFT_SOFTGRIDSERVER% system variable defined to resolve to a local App-V Streaming or Management Server, as shown in Figure 4-22, then apply those GPOs at appropriate AD site or Organizational Unit levels. You could even define a single GPO, using the Item-level targeting feature of GP preferences, so that each definition of %SFT_SOFTGRIDSERVER% applies only to a specific AD site or IP subnet—but I'll let you work that out for yourself (Figure 4-23 is a big hint)!

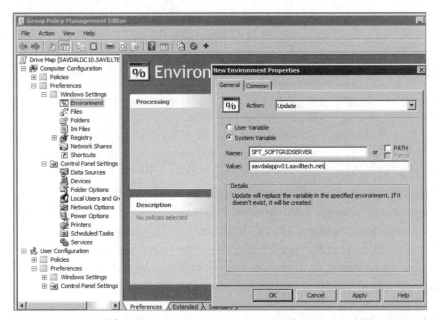

FIGURE 4-22: Use GP preferences to create a system environment variable without the need for scripts.

Whether you should use RTSP or RTSPS depends on a few factors. The most obvious is whether you need the virtual application encrypted as it's streamed in. If so, you must use RTSPS, but you might also want to use RTSPS to restrict the streaming traffic to a single port. By default, RTSP listens on port 554 to configure the connection, but the actual transfer of traffic is a random port between 1024 and 49151. This means any firewall has to have all those ports open. Conversely, RTSPS uses only port 322 for all communications between the streaming server and the client, which means only a single port needs to be open on any firewalls between them.

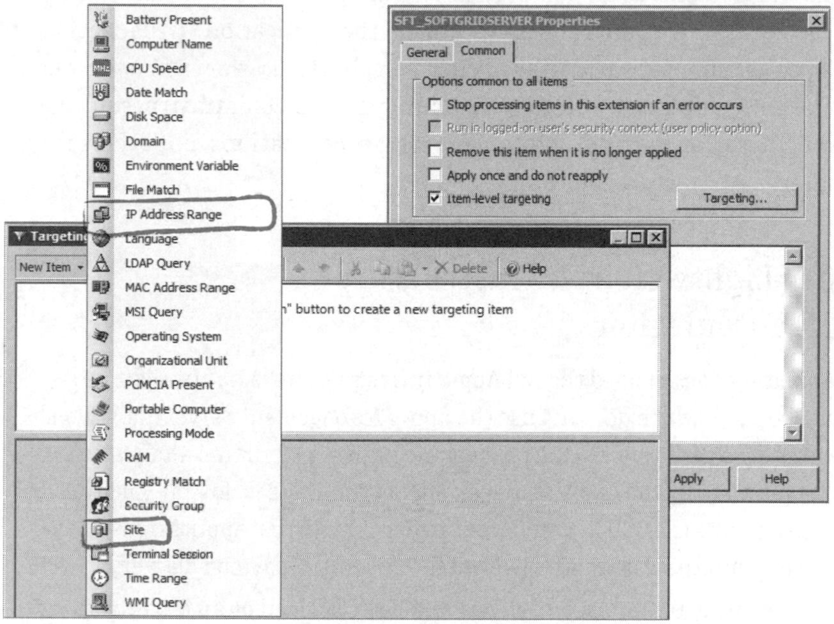

FIGURE 4-23: GP preferences enable a huge range of item-level targeting options.

Another reason to use a single port is if you want to use a hardware load balancer to distribute App-V client traffic to multiple streaming servers in large environments, because load balancers typically require a single port to be used in the configuration. To use RTSPS on the streaming servers, the only requirement is installation of a valid certificate that is trusted by both the App-V server and client, matches the Fully Qualified Domain Name (FQDN) of the App-V Streaming Server, and is configured for Server Authentication. It is best to decide to use RTSPS when you first deploy your App-V infrastructure, because switching after deployment requires updating all your OSD files for virtual applications to specify the RTSPS and port 322. If you have hundreds of virtual applications, the protocol and port update is cumbersome and would certainly warrant automation through a script (or getting an intern for a few weeks).

It is also possible to use IIS (HTTP/HTTPS) or file server (SMB) as an alternative to RTSP and RTSPS. You do lose some functionality, such as the capability for updated applications to be detected automatically and sent via Active Update, which sends the updated application the next time the user launches the application; but the capability to leverage existing IIS and file server resources may be preferable to setting up App-V RTSP servers.

What is great about the full infrastructure is that it offers full, on-demand streaming of the virtual applications, which can be made available based on the currently logged-on user. Checks for new applications are performed automatically at logon and can easily be triggered manually through the Application Virtualization Client, plus you get automatic updating of virtual applications when a new version is available. The downside is that you are maintaining a complete infrastructure just for App-V, which may be the right solution for some organizations, but others may prefer a lighter infrastructure solution.

The App-V Lightweight Infrastructure and SCCM Integration

If your organization doesn't need the full App-V infrastructure, a lightweight infrastructure can be used, which does not use the App-V Management Server but still uses App-V Streaming Server to enable the on-demand delivery of virtual applications. Because you are not using the App-V Management Server, there is no App-V method to deliver to App-V clients the OSD files and icons needed for virtual applications to be visible to users, so an alternate method is needed for this initial payload delivery.

Typically, the initial OSD and icon delivery will be performed by an organization's existing ESD system, and then the streaming capabilities of the App-V Streaming Server can be leveraged when the user launches the application. Organizations get the benefit of leveraging their existing software deployment investment for the application targeting and management, plus the streaming capabilities of the App-V Streaming Server.

The Microsoft ESD solution is the System Center Configuration Manager (SCCM), which with version 2007 R2 introduced full integration with App-V. Using only your existing SCCM infrastructure, this integration enables a rich App-V experience, including the streaming of applications.

▶ Although the comparison is not perfect, you can consider an App-V Management Server = a SCCM Management Point, and an App-V Streaming Server = a SCCM Distribution Point in terms of functionality.

You'll learn more about SCCM later in this book, but for the present discussion suffice it to say that it provides a number of server roles, two of which are of interest in terms of App-V integration:

▶ **Management Point server role:** The SCCM client communicates with this role to report information and find out about software available to the client.

▶ **Distribution Point server role:** This is a server from which SCCM clients can download available software; such servers are typically geographically distributed.

SCCM enables both the delivery and streaming of App-V applications using the SCCM infrastructure and the on-demand streaming and delta-based updating of virtual applications in a very similar fashion to using the native App-V infrastructure. Delta-based updating allows only the changes to an application update to be sent to clients instead of the entire application after each update. SCCM also offers a second option known as *Download and Execute*. With Download and Execute, the SCCM client will not see any application shortcuts or file type associations until the App-V binary stream has been completely delivered and cached on the client, which is great for those laptop and mobile work scenarios I discussed previously.

SCCM also allows virtual application targeting on a per-machine basis, in addition to user-based targeting; and it has very powerful reporting capabilities. It can leverage the BITS protocol to deliver applications, which is great for achieving more controlled delivery of applications using bandwidth controls, and the download will resume if interrupted. Again, this is great for laptops and mobile workers!

If your organization is already using SCCM and wants to implement App-V, the smart money would use your existing SCCM infrastructure, rather than set up any App-V servers.

USING APP-V IN YOUR ORGANIZATION

At this point, you have taken a deep look at App-V, including how it works at a technical level and what the infrastructure requires. This section looks at why an organization might benefit from using App-V, how to determine whether your business needs are a good match for it, and how others use App-V. It also describes some complementary technologies.

Benefits of App-V

I've touched on some of App-V's benefits in previous parts of this chapter, but this section focuses on them because they are a critical aspect of the total cost of ownership (TCO) of virtualizing your applications, and justifying the adoption of App-V to senior management and C-level executives. App-V is a great technology and I personally believe it has a place in every IT infrastructure, but as an IT specialist you need to be able to explain to the people writing the checks why it's needed.

Eliminating the application installation on the client is a key feature of App-V and solves a number of common challenges in organizations:

▶ First, application-to-application compatibility problems caused by conflicts are solved by App-V because applications are not installed on the operating system. This removes the possibility of conflicts because virtual applications cannot see each other.

▶ Second, the common performance degradation of a desktop system over time—as more applications are installed, partially uninstalled, repaired, and updated, and more components are registered, bloating the registry—is a thing of the past. Because applications are not installed to the operating system, the only application footprint is in the shared cache file and some icons, shortcuts, and file type associations—nothing that affects the operating system's performance or degrades it over time.

▶ Third, because the applications are not installed, there is far less chance of them becoming corrupted through system failure or user "configuration," as no application assets are available to users to change. In a worst-case scenario, virtual applications can be removed from the local cache and streamed to the client again. Virtual applications are able to self-heal in many respects: If a user deletes a shortcut or removes a file type association, it is automatically resolved the next time the App-V client communicates with the server infrastructure.

▶ Finally, because no application installation is required, applications are available to clients nearly instantly, even on first usage. The binary stream is sent to the client with the blocks required to open the application sent first (FB1), which even for a large application like Office 2010 may take 10 seconds on most networks. Making applications available to users on demand is absolutely critical to enable flexible and productive working scenarios in which users can quickly access their applications on different machines and environments.

The isolation of virtual applications and the sequencing process provide an organization with many opportunities to streamline application testing and rollout processes throughout the organization:

▶ Because virtualized applications are isolated from one another, the regression testing and app-to-app compatibility testing usually required when introducing a new or updated application is unnecessary. This reduces the delay in introducing a new application into the organization—sometimes from many weeks to days—which is critical for getting the tools and applications into the hands of the business sooner and enabling it to stay ahead of the competition. Virtualizing applications can actually simplify your Windows rollout!

▶ Creating a virtualized application through sequencing and with Package Accelerators is normally faster than creating an MSI for custom applications.

▶ User customizations for virtual applications are stored as part of their roaming profile area, so they travel with the users no matter which operating system instance they use.

Securing access to applications and ensuring that application licensing is adhered to can be a huge challenge for organizations. App-V has numerous capabilities to ensure user access control through AD integration, license reporting, and metering capabilities, including concurrent usage restrictions and automatic application license expiration.

App-V can leverage your existing PC life-cycle management solutions, avoiding the need to deploy additional infrastructure for App-V. Organizations have many options in terms of how they deploy App-V, with different levels of infrastructure investment possible. Twenty-three localized versions of App-V 4.6 SP1 are available, making it suitable for most global businesses.

If the task of convincing management to pursue a virtualization solution falls to you, focus on the value it brings to the business, with any initial costs quickly offset by long-term savings. That is the bottom line for any business: using new tools faster, cutting down time lost waiting for software deployments, and accessing the tools from any operating system to enable more flexibility. It also reduces the costs of testing applications, solves application compatibility challenges, and minimizes desktop problems caused by corrupt application installations. Look at how other organizations are currently using App-V and read their stories, which help drive home the App-V message and sell the idea of adopting App-V within your organization.

> **NOTE** A great place to read these stories is on Microsoft's case study site at `http://www.microsoft.com/casestudies/default.aspx`. Some of my personal favorites are as follows:
>
> ▶ BMW case study at `http://www.microsoft.com/casestudies/Microsoft-Desktop-Optimization-Pack/BMW-Group/Virtualization-Helps-BMW-Simplify-and-Speed-Application-Packaging-Deployment/4000009332`
>
> ▶ Login Consultants at `http://www.microsoft.com/casestudies/Microsoft-Application-Virtualization/Login-Consultants/IT-Services-Firm-Helps-Clients-Ease-Speed-Application-Packaging-with-Virtualization/4000009346`.

▶ Having a member of the budget board or senior leadership representing your project and selling it to other senior leaders is of huge value and greatly increases the chance of success.

▶ You are probably thinking that makes sense if you were wondering why you kept seeing SoftGrid Server and SFT (SoFTgrid) everywhere. Microsoft hasn't finished renaming everything yet and probably won't for some time.

Always try to secure the support of a senior executive to act as your sponsor for any new technology or IT outlay. Make them understand the value of the technology and get them to act as its champion.

Acquiring App-V

As you have seen in this chapter, the benefits of App-V are numerous, and I'm sure organizations have found some that I have not covered, so the next question from most organizations is "how much is this going to cost me?" This section explores two costs: the cost of the package that includes App-V, and the cost of the Software Assurance (SA) on each desktop that you'll need to purchase to be able to buy that package. Everyone loves licensing.

App-V is actually an evolution of an acquisition Microsoft made in July 2006 of a company known as Softricity (http://www.microsoft.com/presspass/press/2006/jul06/07-17SoftricityPR.mspx). Softricity provided an application virtualization solution called SoftGrid.

Around the same time, Microsoft purchased a number of other companies, including AssetMetrix, Winternals, and DesktopStandard, which all had great solutions to enable better management of enterprise desktop environments. These acquisitions were rebranded and combined to form the first version of the Microsoft Desktop Optimization Pack (MDOP) described in Chapter 3.

Organizations with SA on Windows Client can add MDOP to their agreements on a subscription basis, which is typically around $10 per desktop per year (the price varies according to customer agreement). Considering how much useful software you get with today's MDOP, which has grown a lot from the initial version and now includes the Microsoft Enterprise Desktop Virtualization (MED-V) technologies and enterprise BitLocker management, that price amounts to a rounding error for most organizations.

The challenge for some organizations is actually SA for Windows Client, which is a bigger financial commitment. However, it also offers many advantages, not the least of which is the Enterprise version of Windows Client, which provides true enterprise-class features such as DirectAccess, BranchCache, BitLocker, AppLocker, and more. MDOP is tied to SA to provide another benefit for organizations that have chosen SA, and the MDOP feature set does complement the Enterprise edition of Windows to provide a true enterprise desktop experience.

Another option for acquiring MDOP is through a Windows Intune subscription, which is the Microsoft public cloud Software as a Service (SaaS) solution for desktop management. Think of Windows Intune as a cloud-based version of the on-premise SCCM solution, except Windows Intune lacks some SCCM capabilities, such as operating system deployment, mobile device management, and server management. Nonetheless, it can complement SCCM nicely for certain user scenarios, such as contractors, highly mobile users, and noncorporate assets. For machines covered with Windows Intune, the Enterprise edition of Windows Client can be used, and MDOP can be added on a per-device, per-year subscription basis.

Finally, I mentioned App-V running on session-based virtual environments such as Remote Desktop Session Hosts (RDSHs) and Terminal Services (the pre-Windows Server 2008 R2 name for RDSHs), and there is great news in this respect also. Your Windows Server 2008 R2 Remote Desktop Server Client Access Licenses (RDS CALs) include App-V for RDS rights, which means you can run your App-V virtualized application on your RDS servers at no additional cost! Running App-V on your RDS servers makes a lot of sense because typically you need many applications on session-based servers where many users share a server operating system, and by leveraging App-V you avoid app-to-app conflicts and keep the operating system clean of application installation "baggage."

Knowing What to Virtualize and When

For most organizations, the decision to use application virtualization is a no-brainer, but when is the right time to virtualize applications, and what should be virtualized? Although you can start the application virtualization process at any time, a significant amount of effort is required to create your virtualized applications, roll them out, and perform the application and user acceptance testing. Unless you have just performed a desktop update, a great way to implement App-V is as part of a desktop refresh or upgrade to a new version of the desktop operating system.

When organizations perform a desktop upgrade, a lot of testing is done to ensure application compatibility, so the additional effort to virtualize the applications is minor relative to the entire operation and may actually save time in terms of the total application testing process. Using application virtualization, you can remove most of the app-to-app testing scenarios for the reasons already described.

If you are not expecting a desktop update anytime soon, rolling out App-V can still save your organization money by reducing the number of problems associated with application management and resolution. Many organizations that choose to deploy the App-V client prioritize particular problem applications to be virtualized first; then, over time, more applications are moved over to App-V as time and resources allow.

The next decision is what applications you should virtualize. In my opinion, once you have decided to use application virtualization with App-V, you should virtualize all your applications except the ones you can't.

First, you need a list of all applications used within the organization and the number of users who access them; typically, you would virtualize applications that are used by more than *x* number (varies by company) of users in order to warrant the effort. There will likely be exceptions for applications that don't meet the user criterion but have specific issues that would be resolved by using App-V.

Next, examine the applications to identify any that you cannot virtualize or shouldn't virtualize. Remember, with App-V you cannot virtualize device drivers, system services, or operating system components. If your application uses a device driver, which includes file system filters such as those used in anti-virus solutions, you cannot virtualize it. You cannot virtualize old versions of Internet Explorer because that is a system component, and MED-V is the right solution for that. Commonly, items you won't virtualize include the following:

▶ Malware protection such as anti-virus

▶ System management agents

Everything else is an option. Even if your application does have a device driver (for example, something like Adobe Reader, which has a Print to PDF driver), you could virtualize all of it except for the driver component and deploy the driver part using a traditional software deployment method.

The next consideration is related to applications that need to interact with each other. Remember that App-V has the DSC capability that enables you to define dependencies between applications, but you will need to manage those relationships manually. If you have an application or component that is used by many other applications, it may be deemed easier to install that application locally to the operating system. This could be something such as the .NET Framework.

When you look at how other organizations adopt virtualization, three distinct approaches emerge. Many organizations start with the first approach and move to the last over time:

1. Only virtualize problem applications or applications that currently require frequent updates (because delivering application updates is easier with App-V than traditional application updates). Adobe Reader is often virtualized as one of the first applications in many organizations because it's used often and is fairly easy to virtualize.

2. Virtualize applications as described in the approach above and business unit/ specialist applications that are used only by specific users. Applications that are used on all machines are just installed locally on the operating system at operating system install time or even made part of the base image.

3. Virtualize everything except for applications that cannot be virtualized.

Then there is Office, which I have left until last because there is no easy, one-size-fits-all solution for it. Many applications leverage Office capabilities to function, and likewise many users have add-ins for Office that would need to be virtualized as well to be able to run in the virtualized Office 2010. Dependencies have to be defined between all the various applications/add-ins that integrate with Office. If you have a very controlled desktop environment and understand all these interactions, then Office can be virtualized, and virtualized successfully. Conversely, if you don't have a deep understanding of Office usage, then installing Office 2010 locally on desktops may be a safer option until you have a better grasp. You may want to virtualize earlier versions of Office, which might still be needed to run legacy add-ins and macros. It is very common to see organizations run Office 2010 locally on desktops but virtualize the legacy version just for compatibility with older documents or spreadsheets, and it works great.

If you do virtualize Office 2010, there is one additional challenge: Office 2010 integrates very deeply with the operating system for features such as search integration for Outlook and Office document types, printing to OneNote, and Outlook integration with URLs and the mail control panel applet. With a virtualized Office 2010 implementation, none of the previous features would function. However, Microsoft provides the Microsoft Office 2010 Deployment Kit for App-V at http://www.microsoft .com/download/en/details.aspx?displaylang=en&id=10386, which is a piece of software you deploy locally to the operating systems, enabling all the functionality listed with a virtualized Office 2010 deployment.

The Microsoft Office 2010 Deployment Kit for App-V also performs another function that makes it mandatory for Office 2010 virtual deployments: handling the licensing of Office 2010. Office 2010 needs to be activated, and you could quickly run into problems with activation in a virtualized Office 2010 installation because it may constantly reactivate with each user of the machine, and if the virtual application was deleted and re-streamed. To solve this, the Deployment Kit handles Office 2010 activation and communicates this to the virtual Office 2010 application. Note that using the Office 2010 Deployment Kit requires a version of Office 2010 that uses a volume license Key Management Server (KMS) or Multiple Activation Key (MAK);

▶ Don't forget to delete the file type associations for file types that should still be associated with the locally installed Office 2010. You don't want to deploy Office 2003 via App-V and have it become the default application for all your Office documents!

you cannot use any kind of retail, Microsoft Developer Network (MSDN), or Office 365 version of Office 2010.

I currently see many organizations deploy Office 2010 locally to the operating systems partly because of the application management required to virtualize and set dependencies between all the applications and add-ins that use Office. Another reason is that Office is an application that typically resides on every desktop; it does not need to be delivered on demand, which is one of the benefits application virtualization brings. As I previously mentioned, though, many organizations do virtualize the legacy versions of Office if they are still needed for certain data documents or add-ins. This mixed solution of using Office 2010 locally and virtualizing older versions works well and offers users access to everything they need without the complexities of trying to install multiple versions of Office on a single operating system instance.

I want to finish this section with a brief word about licensing, a topic you never really want to finish on, start on, or even mention in most polite conversations. However, in talking with customers about App-V, on-demand streaming, and concurrent metering, the question always comes up: "Does this mean I no longer need to buy as many copies of my application?" The answer is an emphatic *no*. App-V is an application execution and delivery solution; it does not change anything about how you license your applications. Sorry!

Playing Nicely with App-V

For organizations that have looked into application virtualization solutions, comparisons to XenApp from Citrix will naturally be made. The question of whether to use XenApp or App-V is very common, so let me give you my opinion on this. Microsoft and Citrix have a very close relationship, with each company focusing on specific technology aspects; and as part of the joint Microsoft-Citrix solution, the strongest technologies from each company have been chosen. Both Citrix and Microsoft have application virtualization solutions, but App-V is recommended for a number of reasons:

▶ It has a more flexible and powerful sequencing process to actually capture the application compared to the XenApp profiling process.

▶ It virtualizes user mode services and DCOM (Distributed Component Object Model), which XenApp does not.

▶ It offers better isolation of virtualized applications, resolving more app-to-app compatibility challenges.

- ▶ Major Independent Software Vendors (ISVs) are starting to ship App-V Package Accelerators in addition to the MSI version, which will make deployment even easier and accelerate the adoption of App-V as the application virtualization standard.

- ▶ It offers improved support for Microsoft-created software.

- ▶ It integrates with SCCM.

- ▶ It supports a shared cache, which is key for VDI environments.

- ▶ It can also create an MSI version, which when installed populates the machine's cache with the App-V sequenced application.

It is important to understand that although XenApp does have an application virtualization component, it is actually a small part of XenApp. XenApp provides great flexibility in presenting the application to the desktop, so many organizations use App-V to virtualize the application and then XenApp to actually deliver and present the application to desktops.

Another close partner for Microsoft is Flexera (which I still think of as InstallShield). Flexera offers a solution called AdminStudio, which, in addition to helping create traditional MSI files for software deployment, now supports the automatic generation of virtualized applications. Organizations can bulk-convert standard application installers into virtualized applications, which can greatly speed up the sequencing phase of a virtual application adoption. Don't assume that an automated solution like AdminStudio will be able to virtualize every application automatically. However, it can definitely automate a large portion of your application sequencing, enabling you to focus on the more complex applications to virtualize.

SUMMARY

For many organizations, application virtualization with App-V will be the second virtualization technology to see widespread adoption after server virtualization, and it offers huge opportunities for cost savings and improvements in efficiency. In any organization that wants to implement VDI, session-based virtualization, or flexible workspaces, or in any environment where people can use different operating system instances, the capability to quickly access applications is critical. App-V is the solution of choice for many organizations.

In addition to providing a faster way to deliver applications within your organization—fewer regression testing requirements, which provides value to the business faster—App-V really transforms how the entire user workspace is deployed and managed, but requires careful planning. The existing application landscape must be well understood, interactions between applications ascertained, and the cost benefits that application virtualization will provide calculated. App-V is one part of a complete desktop virtualization solution and has some new features coming to make it even simpler to deploy, use, and manage.

Virtualizing User Data

When asked to name their greatest asset, many organizations will claim that it is their employees, but what they really care about is their data. Without data, no organization in the world would be able to do business. Whether the data is valuable intellectual property, invoices, personnel records, application data, configuration data, contracts, or any of the other possibilities, data is crucial to a business; and so, therefore, is the manner in which users interact with and leverage the data. Outside of the corporate world, data is also important to individuals—wedding-day photos, that video of baby's first steps, or Chapter 5 of a book you are collaborating on and can't afford to lose because you are already behind schedule. As our world becomes ever more mobile, users want quick and reliable access to their corporate and personal data no matter where they are, and in this chapter you learn about technologies that make data easily available to users in a transparent fashion and increase the data's security.

UNDERSTANDING DATA VIRTUALIZATION TECHNOLOGIES AT HOME

When I talk about *data virtualization*, the key principle is separation of the data's physical storage from how and where it can be accessed. Data virtualization enables ongoing access to the data.

The line between work life and private life has blurred considerably because the way people work has changed. It is now common to have corporate data at home on noncorporate devices. Likewise, users want to be able to access important personal data across the multiple devices they own, as well as on devices they access but do not own. To demonstrate the best way to make data "always available," I want to first explore how Windows actually stores user data.

Examining How Windows Organizes User Data

▶ This separation of the data's physical path from how it is perceived and manipulated is precisely what is meant by virtualization of data.

Windows 7 tries to guide users toward an efficient organization of data through its Libraries feature, which, in a default installation, provides folders for Documents, Music, Pictures, and Videos. If you install the Zune application, a Podcasts library is also created; install Windows Virtual PC and a Virtual Machines library is created. Think of a *library* as a way to organize your data into easy to use collections and eliminate the need to know where the data is physically stored. A library consists of a number of folders whose contents it displays for browsing; and more important, it indexes that content for searching, making it very easy to find the desired data.

Every library has a default folder that is used when data is saved to the library. But the component folder locations can be anywhere, local or remote; the only requirement for a remote location is that it support the indexing of data. While a number of built-in libraries are automatically available in Windows, it is also possible to add custom libraries containing any type of data to meet the needs of the user. Figure 5-1 shows a custom library for Family Pictures. As you can see from its properties, this library contains the contents of multiple physical folders, including remote folders. During creation of the library, the user also selects the type of library, which affects how the content is organized and displayed.

Folders in the default libraries include the familiar My Documents, My Music, My Pictures, and My Videos that were included in earlier versions of Windows, in addition to the shared data folders in the Public profile. All the "My" folders are still around and located in the user's profile area, which is covered in detail in the next chapter. Because the My folders are still used by many applications that have not been updated to leverage libraries, they are the default locations for data saved to libraries; so most users' data will exist within their profile My folders.

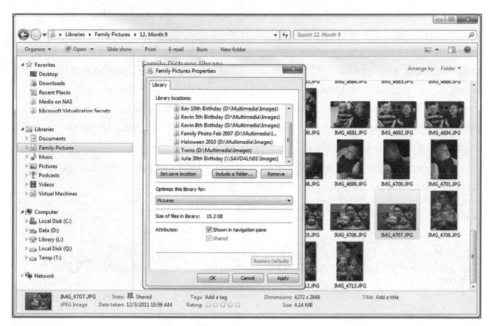

FIGURE 5-1: Selecting the properties of a library via the Properties context menu (right click) enables you to add folders to it, which can be searched as a single entity.

Enabling Data Replication at Home

As a mobile user, you want your data available to you wherever you go. One option is to store your data on a USB drive, and then you can just plug it into whatever machine you are currently using. Of course, the problem with this approach is that if you lose your USB drive, you've lost all your data; and unless you use a technology such as 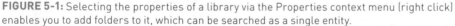 BitLocker-To-Go to encrypt the content, someone else can easily access all your data. Another drawback is that performance will likely suffer, as the transfer speeds of removable USB drives are not comparable to those of a local hard drive.

Another option is to use a USB drive as a synchronization device. For example, I typically work with three computers: the desktop in my home office, my laptop, and my slate device. Using synchronization software, I can keep two storage devices synchronized, which enables me to store my data locally on all three machines. When I'm done working on one machine, I run the synchronization tool to quickly sync the changed files between my current machine and the USB drive. When I use a different machine,

▶ Anytime you store private data or your company's intellectual property on some kind of portable media, you need to protect it. Don't be the next story on the news about a huge corporate leak caused when you left your unencrypted USB stick in a taxi.

I pop in the USB drive and sync again, which copies the new data from the USB to the computer I'm about to use. Once I'm finished, I synchronize to the USB again.

In this scenario, the USB drive serves as the definitive source of truth, and if I were to lose it, I would still have the complete data set on at least one of my machines. I've used a number of different synchronization tools, but I've had great success with the free Microsoft SyncToy, which enables you to configure folder pairs to synchronize and track file changes, including renames and deletions, to ensure there is no corruption during synchronizations. You can download the SyncToy application from: `http://www.microsoft.com/download/en/details` `.aspx?displaylang=en&id=15155`.

As shown in Figure 5-2, SyncToy has a clean interface—one that is simple to get started with—but also offers power synchronization if needed.

FIGURE 5-2: Using SyncToy, you can select a particular folder pair for targeted synchronization or configure all pairs using the All Folder Pairs view.

A synchronizing drive is a good option, but this is 2012! Cloud services offer huge amounts of disk space online, and since nearly everyone has lightning-fast Internet connectivity, why replicate to a USB drive using a manual process? As part of its Windows Live service, Microsoft provides a cloud-based storage solution called SkyDrive, available free to anyone with a Windows Live ID. At the time of writing, SkyDrive, available at `https://skydrive.live.com/`, offers 25GB of storage, which enables you to save a lot of data and access it anywhere using a web browser or a custom application for Windows Phone, iPhone, and iPad.

INTEGRATING SKYDRIVE WITH EXPLORER

Several third-party add-ons can expose your SkyDrive content to Windows Explorer, but you can also achieve this by copying some information from Office 2010. Through its SkyDrive integration feature, Office 2010 has an option to Save to Web, which accesses SkyDrive directly via your Windows Live ID.

To copy this shortcut to Explorer, open Office 2010, select the Save & Send menu option, and select Save to Web. After entering your Windows Live credentials, your SkyDrive content will be displayed. Select your folder and select Save As. The address bar displays your unique WebDAV address, so copy the address bar as text.

Now, use this path as the target to which to map a drive using Explorer, making sure you select "Reconnect at logon." To avoid any annoying authentication requests, link your Live ID with your Windows user account, which is accomplished through the Link Online IDs action in the User Accounts control panel applet.

I prefer not to work directly off SkyDrive because of the latency introduced when working with data stored on the Internet. And, while I could manually copy data back and forth, there is a better solution: Windows Live Mesh. Using Windows Live Mesh, you can select folders for synchronization between multiple devices and optionally SkyDrive. Windows Live Mesh can also synchronize Internet Explorer and Microsoft Office settings. You can download Windows Live Mesh at: `http://www.microsoft.com/downloads/details.aspx?FamilyID=7044F719-612E-4336-8ABF-F06632317891&amp;displaylang=ml&displaylang=en`.

As shown in Figure 5-3, configuration of Windows Live Mesh is simple. The user selects a folder to synchronize within the Windows Live Mesh application and then the target of the synchronization, which can be SkyDrive, to copy to Microsoft's cloud servers. Data does not have to synchronize to SkyDrive; you could choose to

▶ Windows Live Mesh also enables an easy way to remotely connect to your computer either using the Windows Live Mesh client application or through the Windows Live Devices website. Click the Remote tab to see the options.

synchronize between your devices, but that requires both computers to be turned on at the same time, whereas using SkyDrive means your various devices don't need to talk directly.

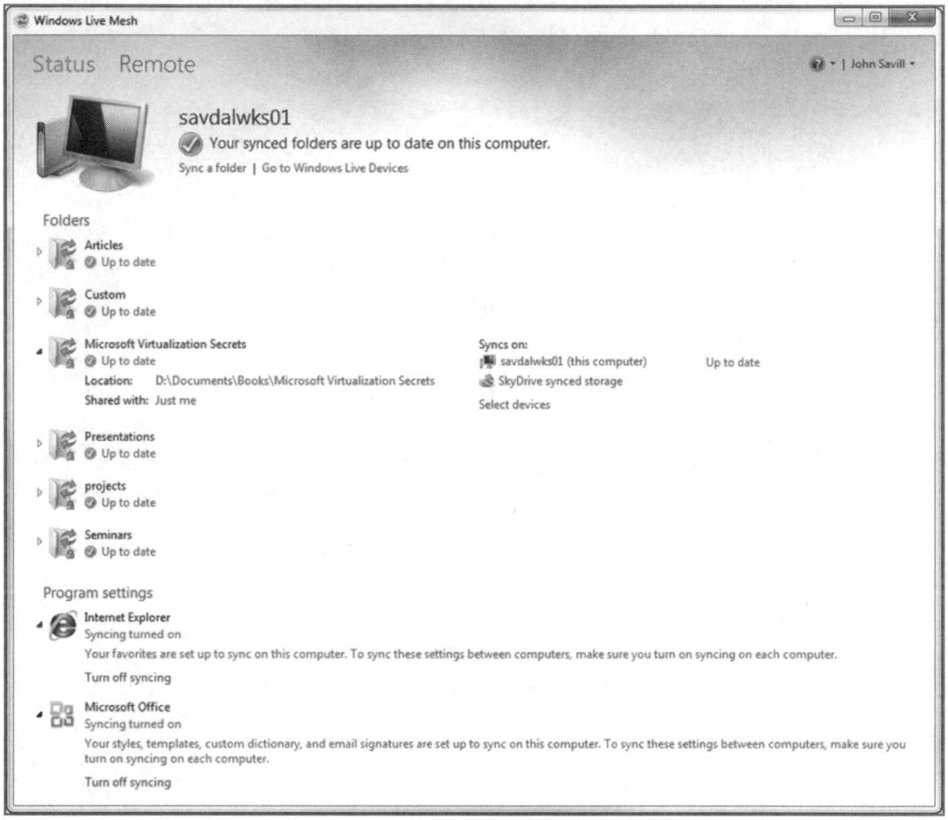

FIGURE 5-3: Windows Live Mesh enables you to configure the synchronization of specific folders between devices and with SkyDrive.

Once Windows Live Mesh is configured and working, your data is available to you on whatever device you are currently using, assuming you have an Internet connection to enable the synchronization and you configured the data to synchronize to SkyDrive. Currently, Windows Live Mesh replicates the entire folder if any part of it is changed, but the capability to replicate only changes to files is on the list of future updates.

So, is Windows Live Mesh a solution for corporate users? Could every Windows user just sign up for a Windows Live ID and configure their My Documents and other data locations to replicate to SkyDrive, making that data available on any device and providing data protection? The answer is no, and the next section explains why.

UNDERSTANDING DATA VIRTUALIZATION TECHNOLOGIES AT WORK

While protecting data at home is important, protecting corporate data can sometimes be the difference between success and failure, or even between relaxing at home and sitting in jail. Numerous regulatory requirements affecting companies today require data to be kept for a certain period of time, and failure to produce this data is a criminal offense. When a company has to perform data discovery for auditing or legal proceedings, it needs to be done as efficiently and swiftly as possible to avoid prolonged legal issues (after all, lawyers are not cheap). Following are three common regulatory requirements that affect data retention:

- **The Basel II Accord:** Many financial institutions must retain data for seven years.

- **Sarbanes-Oxley Act (SOX):** U.S. organizations retain audits for seven years.

- **Health Insurance Portability and Accountability Act (HIPAA):** Typically, healthcare providers must ensure the privacy and retention of patient records for six years.

On the flip side, to simplify the discovery process, should it ever be required, many organizations don't want to keep data longer than necessary. Indeed, sifting through Zip drives with information from 10 years ago isn't the most efficient use of time.

Separating the user data and profile from the operating system is important in an environment where users typically work from multiple machines, meaning their configuration and data need to always be available. For example, consider a scenario in which the IT department wants to roll out a new desktop operating system. If the user configuration and data are not local to the desktop, then the upgrade process is far simpler and involves less risk. Another benefit of having data available separately from the desktop machine is protection from hardware loss or failure.

Unfortunately, using a service such as Windows Live Mesh for organizational data fails on many levels in terms of both protecting the data and making it available, because:

- The organization has no access to the data on the user's personal SkyDrive, making discovery and any kind of auditing impossible.

- Data is stored in the cloud, so when a user logs onto a new machine, he must set up the Windows Live Mesh service and then synchronize, pulling all the data from the Microsoft servers. This takes time and valuable bandwidth; and, most important, it is not transparent to the end user.

- Organizations may not want certain types of data to be stored on the Internet or even outside of corporate datacenters.

- SkyDrive maintains a current view of the data but has no capability to view previous versions.

- SkyDrive does not have capabilities to support rich collaboration and check-in/check-out of data.

Using Folder Redirection

Fortunately, Windows Server and Windows Client offer a great solution for handling user data: *Folder Redirection*. It ensures the data is available to clients no matter which corporate machine they use, and the data is stored centrally on corporate servers, allowing full backup and searching where needed. Essentially, this feature redirects the familiar folders in which users store data, such as My Documents, My Pictures, Desktop, and Favorites, to a network location. This means whenever the user saves to My Documents, for example, the data is actually stored on a corporate file server.

This solution caches the content locally on the client machine as well, providing synchronization in a highly efficient way. It enables access to the data even when the machine is offline but brings the corporate copy up to date as soon as connectivity is reestablished. By bringing these two technologies together, Folder Redirection solves all the problems associated with a consumer solution, such as Windows Live Mesh—except for rich collaboration, which is covered later in the chapter.

▶ Consider a scenario in which a laptop is sometimes connected and sometimes disconnected. User data needs to be available even when the device is not connected to the network.

Evaluating Folder Redirection

> CROSSREF   I discuss user profiles in greater detail in Chapter 6.

Most users save their data to their Desktop or to My Documents. Both of these folders are actually part of the user profile; however, the mechanisms used for profile synchronization are not designed to deal with large amounts of data. In order for user data to be available to any machine in the corporate environment, it must be saved to a corporate file server. As described in the previous section, this is actually achieved by redirecting the data folders of the user's profile to the corporate file servers. By redirecting these common folders to the file server, users do not have to change their habits—the user merely saves to any redirected folder and it's automatically saved on the file server. Having all the data residing on the corporate file servers provides many benefits, including:

- Only one location needs to be backed up and archived.
- Only one location must be searched during data discovery operations.
- Data deduplication is facilitated.
- Point-in-time views of data can be created, enabling users to self-restore deleted or overwritten data.
- Unwanted data can be easily purged.
- Corporate policies can enforce the type of data that can be saved—for example, blocking MP3 files.

▶ Alternatively, you can specify where certain file types are stored on the file server. This enables administrators to easily harvest the files for their own collection. For more information, research the File Server Resource Manager (FSRM).

Getting started with Folder Redirection is simple. An organization just needs a file server, a file share that will store the content, and a Group Policy (GP) specifying the users who can perform redirection of the selected folders. However, it is important to understand the implications of this process. With redirection, all user data moves from individual machines, where a hardware failure means one user loses his or her data, to centralized storage, where a failure could mean the loss of *all* users' data. This risk means that the file server infrastructure needs to be properly architected to provide resiliency to failure, which likely involves using a cluster of file servers and a storage area network (SAN) to meet the performance and capacity requirements of hundreds or thousands of users. It's also important to ensure that backup procedures are in place to provide protection from data corruption or even site loss.

In other words, before adopting Folder Redirection, carefully consider the needs of the users, including how they work, such as whether they are located in a main corporate office or a branch or mobile; their connection speed; and the types of important data they use and where it's stored. You also need to consider whether quotas will be used to limit the amount of data that can be stored and what services are expected or would be useful, such as self-recovery capabilities; and then you need to architect your solution accordingly. Rushing into Folder Redirection without careful planning could end in disaster.

TIP If you decide to set a quota on user data, there is a GP setting to limit the total profile size; however, a better option is to use an FSRM quota on the file server. That way, users can be alerted via e-mail when their quota is reached or a certain percentage threshold is crossed.

Keep in mind that some user education may also be needed to ensure that users understand the new capabilities that will be enabled and that only data stored in the "My" folders will be redirected. If your organization decides not to protect folders like My Pictures, or certain file types like MP3 files, it's important to communicate this clearly to users. That way, if they have important data that won't be protected they can arrange to store it elsewhere, perhaps manually on a separate corporate file server. Again, these considerations reinforce the need for a proper understanding of user requirements to ensure that the right solution is architected.

Implementing Folder Redirection

Once your organization has decided to move ahead with Folder Redirection and you've identified the folders that will be redirected, the next step is the actual implementation. Guidelines for implementing the file system requirements for Folder Redirection can be found at http://technet.microsoft.com/en-us/library/cc781907(WS.10).aspx, which explains the security permissions on the file system and the share. Essentially, the *share* is a single root under which each user has a folder automatically created by the system, making it easy to get up and running.

To configure the folders to redirect, you must first create a Group Policy Object (GPO) and apply it to the users whose folders will be redirected. Don't edit the Default Domain Policy, but rather create a new one for your custom settings, which is accomplished with the Group Policy Management Editor found in the Administrative Tools Start Menu group and shown in Figure 5-4.

After the GPO is created, you must link it to either the domain or the organizational units that contain users. Next, you configure the Folder Redirection settings. The branch of the GPO that needs to be set is User Configuration ➜ Policies ➜ Windows Settings ➜ Folder Redirection.

The first thing you need to do when configuring Folder Redirection settings is select the folders to redirect. In Windows Vista and 7, 13 distinct folders can be redirected, which covers just about every area of the user profile that may contain data, enabling the actual remaining user profile components to be very small. Nevertheless, many organizations choose not to redirect all the areas. For example, a business environment might redirect Documents but not Music or Videos.

▶ Windows XP could only redirect five folders: Application Data, Desktop, My Documents, My Pictures, and Start Menu. Notice the subsequent introduction of items like Favorites and Saved Games.

> CROSSREF The importance of having a small user profile is discussed in more detail in Chapter 6.

Most of the items shown in Figure 5-4 are self-explanatory, such as Documents, Pictures, and Start Menu, but there is one folder whose purpose may not be clear: AppData\Roaming. Many applications have associated data that may be machine- or user-specific. Applications will write user-specific data, such as a custom dictionary in Office, to the AppData\Roaming subfolder of the user's profile. This user data can be redirected to a specified central location on the server. It is important to understand that when you redirect AppData\Roaming, you are redirecting file system based application settings and configurations that are tied to the user portion of the registry. So, you'll need to also use Roaming Profiles. Otherwise, applications may encounter inconsistencies between file system content and registry content. If the application data is machine-specific, or simply too big to follow the user, then that data might be written to the AppData\Local subfolder of the user's profile.

> If you look in your profile under AppData, you will also see a LocalLow folder. This is the low-integrity folder used for Internet Explorer add-ons running in protected mode to store files and settings.

CROSSREF Roaming Profiles are discussed in detail in Chapter 6.

Within the Group Policy settings for each folder that can be redirected there are three options possible for configuration (and sometimes one more):

- **Not configured:** The item is not redirected.
- **Basic:** Redirect everyone's folders to the same location.
- **Advanced:** Specify locations for the redirected content based on users' security group membership.
- **Follow the Documents folder:** For folders that are normally children of the Documents folder, such as Pictures, Music, and Videos, the redirection can be configured to follow whatever redirection is specified for Documents.

When selecting the target folder location for the redirection, the most common configuration is to select Create a folder for each user under the root path, which is the share you manually created. With this option, folders are automatically created for each user and Windows takes care of setting all the right permissions. Another option is Redirect to the following location, which means manually creating a folder for every user. The final option, Redirect to the local user profile location, redirects the folder to the local profile path instead of the file server.

For the Documents folder, you can choose a fourth option, Redirect to the user's home directory, if a user already has a home drive configured and you just want to redirect Documents to that. It's not generally recommended because security and ownership are not checked; it is assumed that proper security is already in place. However, if your organization has already configured a home drive, it's certainly an option.

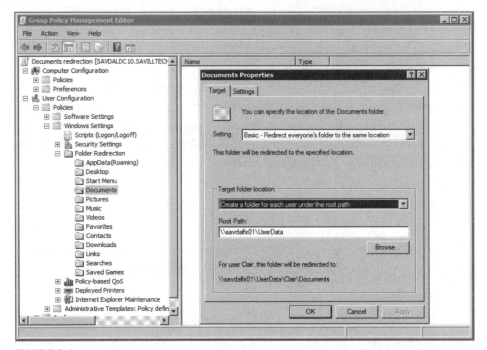

FIGURE 5-4: Select the properties of the folder you want to redirect, and under the Target tab, specify how to perform the redirection.

The next setting to configure is the exclusive rights option under the Settings tab. By default, the option to Grant the user exclusive rights to <folder> (for example, Documents) is enabled, which means when Windows creates the target folder only the user will have permission to read it—not even administrators will be able to see the content. Note that the Local System, which is the computer account, can still see the data; a local administrator is NOT the same as Local System and would not have access. So, if you want administrators to be able to see the content, uncheck the exclusive rights option. However, if you want the user to have exclusive rights to a folder, it is good to know that even though administrators cannot see the data, cor-rectly configured backup accounts will still be able to see the data for backup pur-poses using the Back up files and directories user right.

To enable users to see previous point-in-time views of the data stored on the file server, you need to enable the Shadow Copies feature on the volumes that contain the user data. Users will be able to access the previous views of their data through

▶ Access the properties of the volume in Explorer, and on the Shadow Copies tab, select the volume and click Enable. Click the Settings button as well to specify the schedule for creating the shadow copies and the maximum disk space.

the Previous Versions tab when they select the properties of a share; alternatively, users can directly select the Restore Previous Versions action for a share. Understand that enabling previous versions consumes additional disk space, the amount of which varies according to the number of changes on the volume. The more changes there are, the greater the amount of change data that has to be stored. The good news is that the Shadow Copy feature only stores changes to files, not the entire file. For example, if you have a 32MB PowerPoint file and you just change the title, this change should only use a couple of kilobytes of actual Shadow Copy storage.

With Folder Redirection configured and applied, the next time a user logs on, any local content that has been configured for redirection will be replicated to the specified file server. In pre-Windows 7 versions, this initial duplication process delays the first logon because the data must be replicated to the server first. However, beginning with Windows 7, a local cache is used to populate the server in the background, avoiding this delay.

Enabling Offline Files and Synchronization

Separating user data from the machine has huge advantages, but it's critical not to limit the way users work. Forcing users to always be connected to the corporate network to access their data would hurt productivity, especially for users with laptops. Users need to have access to their data when not connected, which is where another technology comes into play: *Offline Files*, which is sometimes also referred to as *Client Side Caching* (CSC).

Once the user's data has been redirected to a file server using Folder Redirection, the next step is to enable that same data to be cached locally on the clients to enable fast access and availability offline. For the folders redirected with Folder Redirection, you don't have to do anything; local caching of the content happens automatically. I should point out that almost any data on a file server can be locally cached on a client machine if desired.

When changes are made to a file in a redirected folder while a user is offline or on a slow link, the data is actually modified on the local machine's cache. Offline Files has the capability to assess the connection speed of the user to the network folder; and if the link is considered slow, then it will present the user with the data on the local cache. This whole process happens automatically and is transparent to the end user.

By default, Windows 7 and later clients automatically go into slow-link mode if the round-trip latency is greater than 80 milliseconds. However, you can configure this value on a per-share level for greater control using the GP setting Computer

▶ For situations when corporate data should not leave the premises, policies to block removable media usage, restrict e-mailing of certain document types, and even virtual desktops can be leveraged.

Configuration ➜ Policies ➜ Administrative Templates ➜ Network ➜ Offline Files ➜ Configure Slow-Link Mode.

The Offline Files synchronization feature replicates these changes to the file server in the background at regular intervals. This replication of only the changes made to the file, called *Bitmap Differential Transfer*, is a huge improvement over the technology used in Windows XP, which copied the entire file anytime a change was made. Bitmap Differential Transfer tracks the specific blocks of a file that have changed in the local cache, and then sends only those changed blocks to the server. Note that Bitmap Differential Transfer only applies to the replication of changes from the client local cache to the server. Anytime data is pulled from the server to the local cache, then the entire file is copied.

When a user is not working with a strong connection to the server storing the content, nearly all operations occur first on the server. Once the server confirms that the file I/O operation succeeded, such as a write to a file, it is performed against the local cache copy. Only when both the server and the local cache are updated does the process performing the operation get confirmation that the operation completed.

Windows Vista made improvements in the transitions between offline and online activity, making them seamless to the user; Windows 7 improves on this by adding seamless transitions between states: online, offline, and offline (slow-link) scenarios. Windows 7 also has a nice transparent caching feature that automatically caches data from file servers when it is detected that the connection to the file server is below a defined latency and the file is not already cached through Offline Files.

While Offline Files is valuable for redirected data, it can also be used for other shared folders on the network. Unless an administrator specifically removes the capability to make content available offline, a user can select the option on the properties of the shared data to make content always available offline at a share, subfolder, or even file level, which causes the data to be cached on the client. It's also possible for administrators to specify that certain content on a file share always be available to end users through properties on the share. The exact same technology, including Bitmap Differential Transfer, is used anytime Offline Files is configured, resulting in more efficient use of the network.

> **WARNING** If you dig around on the Internet or your machine, you will find the actual location of the Offline Files cache—C:\Windows\CSC. Never try to edit or delete anything in this folder directly. It can cause serious harm to your data. The correct way to manage Offline Files is via the Sync Center control panel item, which has an option to manage offline files and provides full access to cached data, including deletion..

MANAGING CENTRALIZED DATA STORAGE

While the price of storage has come down, a huge amount of work is still required to handle backups and maintain data, so ensuring that file server resources are used efficiently is very important. This section briefly covers two key technologies that will become an administrator's best friend as more and more data is centralized and stored on file servers in the datacenter.

Using File Server Resource Management

Windows Server 2003 R2 introduced a brand-new suite of tools called File Server Resource Manager (FSRM). The goal of FSRM was to give administrators a better handle on the data stored on file servers. Prior to FSRM, the only tool administrators really had was the Quota capability on NTFS volumes; however, the quota could only be set for an entire volume and it was based on the logical size of the data, not the physical size. With the initial release under Windows Server 2003 R2, and in Windows Server 2008, the FSRM functionality was divided into three areas:

▶ Logical size would differ from physical size if, for example, the data were compressed. If the logical size of a compressed file is 10MB, the physical space used on disk may only be 2MB.

- ▶ Storage Reports Management

- ▶ Quota Management

- ▶ File Screening Management

An additional component, File Classification Infrastructure (FCI), was added in Windows Server 2008 R2, which I will cover in the Using File Classification Infrastructure section.

STORAGE REPORTS MANAGEMENT

The Storage Reports Management node enables you to run several predefined reports, which can be output to many formats, including Dynamic HTML (DHTML), HTML, XML, CSV, and of course a good old TXT file. You can schedule the reports to run on a defined schedule or on demand, and they can also be automatically e-mailed to specific users or groups of users. The available reports are shown in Table 5-1.

Although reports can be run manually through the Storage Reports Management interface, you can combine storage reports with the Quota and File Screening capabilities to generate exception reports that can be e-mailed to offending users when they exceed a given quota. For example, if a group with a shared quota nears its threshold, a Files by Owner report can be sent automatically to its members, showing them which users are consuming the most space.

TABLE 5-1: The Storage Reports Available in the FSRM

REPORT NAME	OUTPUT	PARAMETERS
Duplicate Files	Lists files with the same size and last modified date	None
File Screening Audit	Lists violations of file screening policies	Number of days since occurrence and users
Files by File Group	Lists files grouped by their file group type	File groups to include in report
Files by Owner	Lists files grouped by their owner	File owners to include in report
Files by Property	Lists files based on classification property	The classification property to match
Large Files	Lists files larger than the specified size	Minimum file size and file specification
Least Recently Accessed Files	Lists files that have not been accessed for a specified period	Minimum number of days and file specification
Most Recently Accessed Files	Lists files that have been accessed in a specified period	Maximum number of days and file specification
Quota Usage	Lists all quota entries and the mount used	Minimum % of quota used to list in report

The Files by Property report, shown above, was added in Windows Server 2008 R2 as part of the FCI capability.

Figure 5-5 shows another example. It is a Large Files Report that I recently ran on the C: drive. It indicates the files that are larger than 50MB per my configuration, including who owns the files and details about all matching files.

QUOTA MANAGEMENT

Quotas have always been a pain point for most organizations. On the one hand, and for all the reasons mentioned earlier, organizations want users to store data on the file servers; on the other hand, they need to control how space is allocated. Often a network location may be shared by an entire team or business unit, but traditional NTFS quotas could only be assigned per user per volume, not per group or per share. FSRM overcame this limitation with a quota mechanism that is far more granular and configurable.

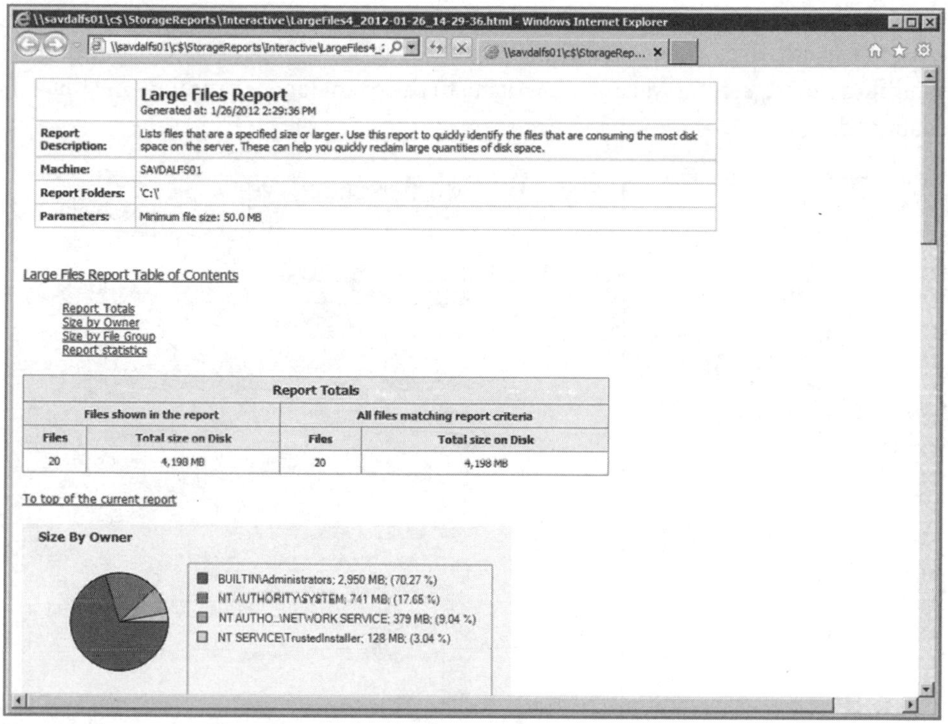

FIGURE 5-5: A Large Files Report, showing the number of files larger than my configured size and a breakdown of ownership.

First, FSRM Quota Management is based on the physical size of the data on disk, not the logical size. This aspect encourages users to be more conscientious about compressing their files, because compressed files are physically smaller and therefore use less of the user's disk quota.

Second, the FSRM Quota Management feature is configured at a folder level, rather than the entire volume, and the quota is shared by all users who can, based on NTFS permissions, write to that folder. Quotas can be manually configured, but they are typically based on a *quota template* that defines the quota size and what action should be taken when the quota reaches specified percentages of the available size. Figure 5-6 shows an example of a quota template. The "200 MB Limit with 50 MB Extension" template clearly highlights most of the FSRM quota functionality.

Notice the quota has a name, a description, and a space limit, which can be defined in KB, MB, GB, or even TB. The quota can also be set to be hard or soft. A *hard quota* prevents the folder from exceeding the specified size by rejecting I/O operations in real time if users break the quota. A *soft quota* can be exceeded; it is typically used to notify users when they are using more than a specified amount of space

> ▶ If you don't want users consuming quota from a particular folder, then don't let them write there. You can prohibit this with NTFS permissions.

and to trigger reports. Thresholds can also be defined at various percentages of the limit usage, which can trigger any combination of actions, such as generating and sending a report, sending an e-mail, writing to the event log, or running a custom command.

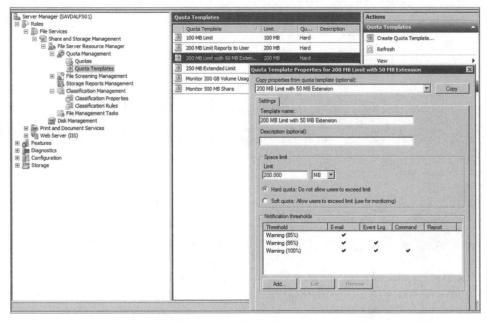

FIGURE 5-6: Access a quota template's Properties to view and modify information about the quota.

Each of these actions can be designed to match your custom specifications. To configure the actions you want to trigger, select the Quota item to be changed and select the Edit Quota Properties action. Once the properties for the quota are opened for each notification threshold, the different actions can be set. For example, to set a Report trigger, click the Report tab and select any combination of Storage Reports that you want run and e-mailed to appropriate users/administrators to provide practical information about data use.

On the E-mail tab you can configure the e-mail option by specifying the recipients (administrators and/or user), the subject line, and the message body. The subject and body are custom text that can include various variable values appropriate to the template settings and the action the user was performing. For example, the E-mail action for the quota template has the following message body, where anything in square brackets is a variable that will be replaced with the current value when actually sent. Note that the same variables can be used to define what and when event logs should be written, as configured under the Event Log tab.

"User [Source Io Owner] has reached the quota limit for quota on [Quota Path] on server [Server]. The quota limit is [Quota Limit MB] MB and the current usage is [Quota Used MB] MB ([Quota Used Percent] % of limit). An automatic one-time extension has been granted, and the quota limit has been increased to 250MB."

The Command option enables any command or script to be run. In the preceding example, this quota template has a limit of 200MB, but when the quota is hit an additional one-time 50MB extension is added. This is configured using a command argument that calls the command-line interface for FSRM quotas to change the quota template on the folder to the "250 MB Extended Limit" template, as shown in Figure 5-7. This demonstrates the power of the quota templates.

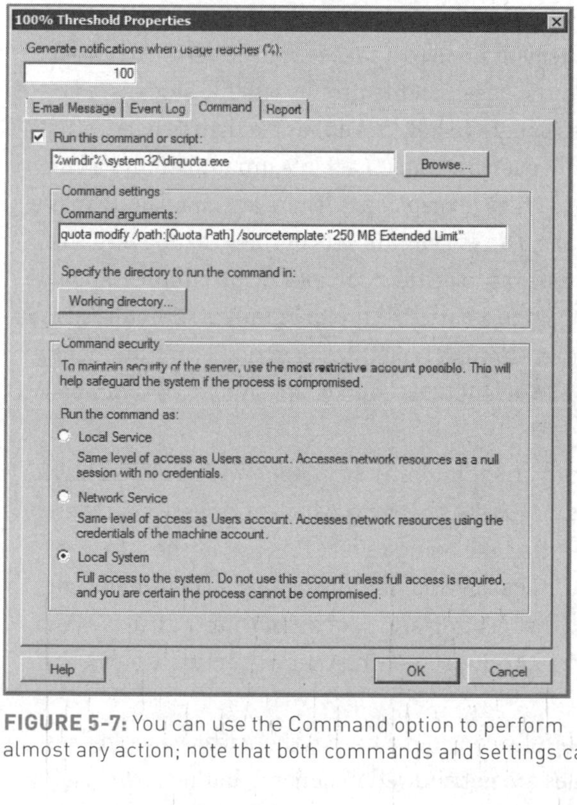

FIGURE 5-7: You can use the Command option to perform almost any action; note that both commands and settings can be passed.

Another nice feature of FSRM Quota Management is the capability to apply a template at a root folder, which automatically applies it to any existing or new subfolders. For example, imagine you had a root `Projects` folder. If you applied the 100MB Limit quota template to `Projects` with the setting to Auto apply template and create quotas on existing and new subfolders, then any folders under `Projects` would automatically get their own 100MB quota. The setting to auto apply a template is configured when a new quota is created.

FILE SCREENING MANAGEMENT

While FSRM Quota Management helps limit how much data is stored on the server, it doesn't really help to control what data is stored. Your idea about how to best use a 5-million-dollar SAN might be very different from that of your CEO's executive assistant, a Britney Spears fan who wants to ensure that her (or his) valuable MP3 collection is never lost. Assigning the assistant a 1GB quota may be plenty for that MP3 storage, but it really wasn't what you had in mind.

The FSRM File Screening Management node provides real-time verification about what kind of data is written to folders, based on file groups and file screens. *File groups* are used to specify the types of data to be blocked, using filename patterns typically based on the file extension, such as *.mp3. Each file group specifies a list of included files and a list of excluded files (exceptions). There are many built-in file groups, such as Audio and Video Files. *File screens* are sets of rules that govern the file groups allowed or blocked and actions to be taken in exception circumstances. You can configure a file screen to apply to a particular folder (and its subfolders) and specify the file groups to block, either through templates or manual configuration. Like quotas, a combination of e-mails, event logs, commands, and reports can be triggered by a file screen.

Also like quotas, file screens can be set to *Active screening*, which blocks any attempts to write blocked file types, or *Passive screening*, which notifies users of policy infractions without preventing the file from being saved. It is usually best to start using File Screening Management in Passive mode, telling users they shouldn't write the specified types of data to the location and suggesting alternate locations. Then, after a period of time, switch to Active screening that will actually block the file types.

Before blocking a file type, carefully consider whether there may be valid uses for it. For example, perhaps MP3 files are not allowed in general, but recordings of meetings could be created as MP3s, which you would want to allow. To resolve this conflict, you could create a specific exception folder where this file type could be stored. That way, you control where the various types of data are stored, rather than having them scattered randomly around your entire file server infrastructure.

Using File Classification Infrastructure

As mentioned previously, Windows Server 2008 R2 introduced a new module to the FSRM family, FCI. Up to this point, the active components of FSRM, Quota Management and File Screening Management, operated on data as it is written. File Classification Infrastructure (FCI) operates on the existing stored data; it enables files to be classified and then allows actions to be performed automatically based on the classification. You start by defining a set of file classification properties, and then create file classification rules that assign a classification to specific files. For example, imagine searching data for digit strings in the format of ###-##-#### and if found, classifying the file as sensitive because it contains a social security number. File classification rules can also be configured to classify based on the path in which a file is located and can be applied to any folder.

An example of configuring a file classification rule is shown in Figure 5-8, which uses a file classification property I created called Sensitive. This file classification rule sets the property value to Yes if a match for the social security number format is found in the file.

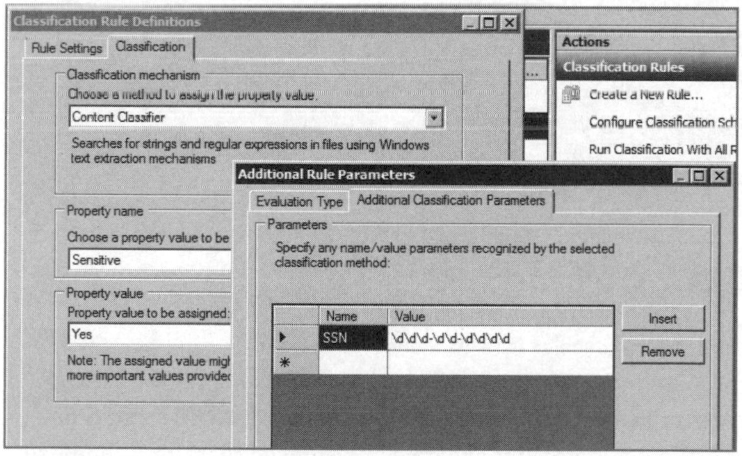

FIGURE 5-8: A file classification rule that uses the Content Classifier rule to examine the contents of files; in this case, searching for the social security number format.

▶ Lower tier of storage means cheaper. Why use your expensive SSD RAID 10 storage for data that no one has even looked at for three months? Move it to that legacy spindle based on RAID 5 (or RAID 0 if you don't want the data)!

Once data is classified, you can define several file management tasks for it. *File management tasks* are actions that you want performed based on the classification of the data. For example, for data classified as sensitive, you could configure a file management task to apply a Rights Management policy that encrypts all such data. This helps protect the data and prevents data leakage. File management tasks can also be triggered on built-in file properties, such as how much time has elapsed since the file was created, was last modified, or last accessed; as well as matching the name of the file against a (wildcard) pattern. For example, using these built-in properties, it is easy to set up a file management task that automatically moves data that has not been accessed for over 60 days to a lower tier of storage. The example shown in Figure 5-9 would trigger such a task for any Word document created more than 120 days ago that has not been accessed for 60 days.

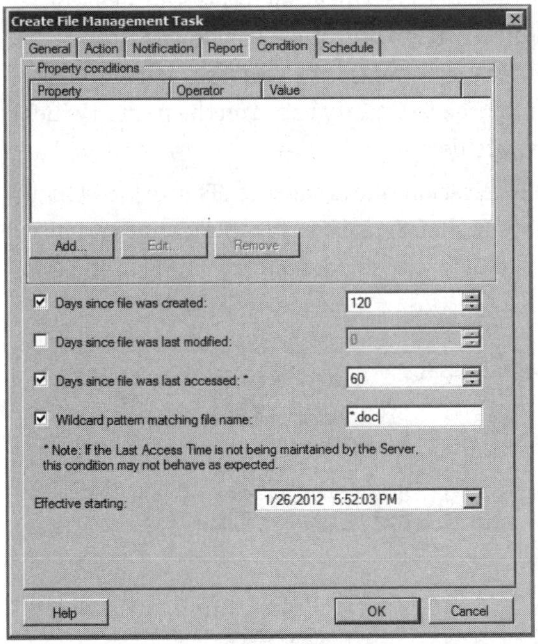

FIGURE 5-9: Select any combination of properties, file dates, and name wildcards as the condition for a file management task.

Tests have been performed using FCI with Windows Server 2008 R2 on environments with millions of files and terabytes of data, which proved that the technology is viable in larger environments. Even if you don't want to use the classification capabilities of FCI, the capability to use file management tasks based on the creation, modification, and access dates of files is significant.

LEVERAGING SHAREPOINT AND OFFICE TECHNOLOGIES

I would be remiss to not at least mention SharePoint when talking about user data. While it is still more common for data to be stored on file servers, a better option for many types of data storage is SharePoint. Not only does SharePoint provide a platform for storing and managing documents, it also offers a rich collaboration environment that enables many users to check out and check in documents and even work on the same document simultaneously (with the new versions of Office).

SharePoint is a very extendable platform that covers several areas of functionality, of which the most relevant here are content management, search, and data "insight." The SharePoint portal can be accessed through comprehensive interfaces that leverage specialized Web Parts, such as a calendar Web Part or a picture Web Part; many third parties create Web Parts to integrate their functionality with SharePoint. Any data storage solution must take into account the type of data stored and how it is handled by the users. SharePoint can provide a much more robust experience with better organization than just placing files in an ever-growing file structure. SharePoint also provides the capability to maintain versions of documents and metadata and offers highly configurable workflow and search capabilities.

Another nice feature of SharePoint is that Office documents can be accessed directly from a browser using Office Web Apps. Office 2010 and SharePoint are very tightly integrated, enabling documents to be directly opened from and saved into SharePoint. In addition, a very efficient transport protocol enables the easy transfer of data between the Office application and SharePoint.

One point that is hotly debated by many IT administrators is the question of when data should be stored in SharePoint and when it should stay on a file server. Typically, legacy data can be left on the file server, acting as an archive of sorts, leveraging SharePoint for new documents to enable collaboration. For file server data that is still heavily used and would benefit from SharePoint capabilities, a migration to SharePoint is certainly a possibility, but it's important to plan the SharePoint architecture and migration process appropriately. For example, some types of data just don't belong in SharePoint—your large streaming media files and your ISO library will probably not be well served by SharePoint. For some things the file server is still the best option. You can find a really nice blog post at `http://sharepoint .microsoft.com/blog/Pages/BlogPost.aspx?PageType=4&ListId={72C1C85B-1D2D-4A4A-90DE-CA74A7808184}&pID=844` that outlines many considerations about when to

use SharePoint and when to use file servers. Also check out http://technet.microsoft
.com/en-us/library/dd163523.aspx for a useful discussion on replacing file servers
with SharePoint.

Ultimately, SharePoint provides a lot of value and should at least be considered
as an option to improve efficiency with data management and collaboration. Many
of today's mobile devices have built-in support for SharePoint sites, such as Windows
Phone, which provides a very nice end-user experience.

SUMMARY

Folder Redirection and Offline Folders do a great job of making user data and even
certain configuration files available wherever the user may work, and with Windows 7,
the technologies are highly efficient and mostly transparent to the user. It is critical,
however, to understand that much more than just the user's data must be considered.
Equally important are the user settings; in the next chapter you learn about virtualizing the user profile, which should always go hand in hand with virtualizing user
data. Don't neglect other technologies such as SharePoint to provide a capability
for great collaboration between users, which is typically far more functional than a
simple file share. Using the File Services Resource Management capabilities provides
an excellent set of tools for really managing, controlling, and reporting on all the
centrally stored data and should definitely be evaluated.

CHAPTER 6

Virtualizing User Profiles and Settings

A user's data and applications are only useful when they can be easily accessed. If shortcuts or application customizations are missing, productivity is greatly reduced as users struggle to find information and work with their applications. User-specific shortcuts and application settings are stored within the user's profile, which is typically specific to the operating system instance. So if users log on to multiple computers, they would have different profiles and therefore different settings on each machine. This issue is compounded with server virtualization, whereby users may be working with different operating system instances daily. This chapter explores different methods to make the user's profile available no matter what operating system instance or version is being used.

UNDERSTANDING THE FUNDAMENTALS OF USER PROFILES

The world of the computer user fundamentally comes down to three things: the user's applications, data, and customizations. While a new operating system is nice and holds the promise of better productivity through new and improved features, each new version of the operating system must enable fast and efficient access to these three things that the user needs. If users are going to use multiple operating system instances, such as when Virtual Desktop Infrastructure (VDI) or session virtualization are used, or even just where multiple physical desktops are used, those three fundamental requirements need to follow them. Chapters 4 and 5 described how to use virtualization to make users' applications and data easily available no matter what operating system they are using. That only leaves the user's customizations—or, more specifically, using virtualization to make their user profile available from any operating system or device.

> **NOTE** A profile folder could already exist for a username if, for example, there were a local user account with the same name as a domain account, or if a domain user account were deleted and then re-created, in which case, even though the account would have the same name, it would have different identifiers and be considered a different account. Therefore, it would not reuse the existing profile. This is why, if an AD account is deleted accidentally, just re-creating the user account won't provide the desired results—all group memberships would also be lost. The AD account would need to be recovered using AD recovery features.

Before you can understand how to make a roaming profile, you need to understand what is included in a profile. The user's profile is stored in a user-specific folder under the %SystemDrive%\Documents and Settings folder in Windows XP and the %SystemDrive%\Users folder in Windows Vista and later. SystemDrive is an environment variable that points to the partition on which the Windows operating system is installed, typically C:. For example, John's profile on a Windows 7 machine would typically be stored in the C:\Users\John folder, but if a folder with the same name already exists, John's profile might be stored in a different folder.

Within the user's profile folder are a large number of subfolders that match up fairly closely to the folders that can be redirected with Folder Redirection, which was covered in Chapter 5 and allows that which appears to be local content to actually be stored on a remote file server and then cached locally. These folders contain the file system–based content of the user's profile, which includes the data stored in My Documents but also Internet Explorer Favorites, shortcuts on the Start menu and the Desktop, and application-specific content. For example, if you look in the AppData\ Roaming folder of a profile, you'll see that it contains many application-specific files, such as Office custom dictionaries, and items that should follow the user, hence the "roaming" in the folder's name. There is an AppData\Local folder that is also used for user-specific file-system data, but the data in this folder could be machine-specific or, in some cases, too large to move, and therefore it should not travel to other machines. The AppData\LocalLow folder is where low integrity applications such as Internet Explorer running in protected mode are permitted to write. These folders need to be made available to users no matter which machine they use, and all of these folders (except AppData\Local and AppData\LocalLow) can be redirected with Folder Redirection; and if you want them to follow the user, they must be redirected—and essentially removed from the profile.

If all the folder data is taken out of the profile, what is left? The user's profile also consists of file-system data and registry information. The user-specific registry information is in the HKEY_CURRENT_USER hive and contains a lot of the operating system and application configurations that are user-specific and not file-system-based. Figure 6-1 shows the basic registry structure of the HKEY_CURRENT_USER hive.

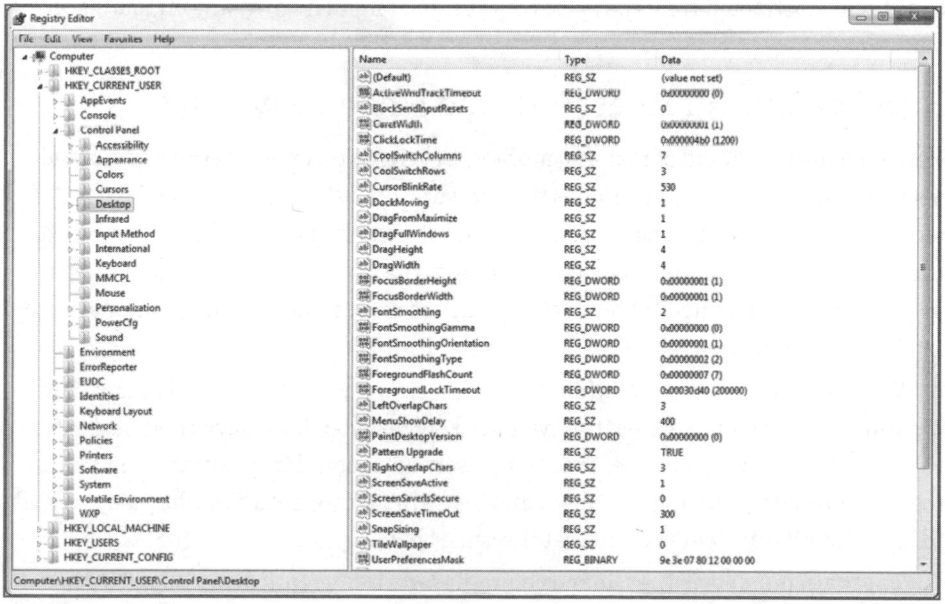

FIGURE 6-1: The Desktop area of the user's registry hive contains the desktop area configuration settings, such as the background picture and screensaver.

▶ The actual content is in the NTUSER.DAT file. There are other files as well, such as ntuser.dat.LOG* and transaction files. In case you were curious, the ntuser.pol file contains an archive of registry policy settings.

The user area of the registry, HKEY_CURRENT_USER, whose content varies according to which user is currently logged on, is actually stored in the NTUSER.DAT file at the root of the user's profile folder. When a user logs on, his NTUSER.DAT content is mapped to the HKEY_CURRENT_USER registry hive. This is the main file that needs to roam with the user after the rest of the profile has been virtualized through Folder Redirection. Even for a user with a lot of registry configurations, the NTUSER.DAT file is still relatively small; mine is around 12MB and I have a lot of applications with configuration data stored in the registry.

Without loading the same NTUSER.DAT file into HKEY_CURRENT_USER when a user logs on, most of the application and operating system settings would be lost. It's therefore necessary to abstract the NTUSER.DAT file, along with any necessary data from the operating system, to create a roaming profile that is available no matter which machine the user logs on to.

USING ROAMING PROFILES FOR VIRTUALIZATION

Roaming profiles provides one option for making the primarily registry-based configurations available on the many operating system instances a user may use. By making the user's profile available across operating system instances, it can be thought of as being abstracted from the operating system, and in its own way virtualized.

How Roaming Profiles Work and When They Don't

Many people have heard of roaming profiles, but they don't necessarily understand what they are. The Roaming Profiles feature works in a similar fashion to Folder Redirection, basically taking the user's profile and storing it on a network server. When the user logs on, the profile is pulled down from the server and cached; and when the user logs off, the (changed) files in the profile are copied back to the server, overwriting the older profile.

This sounds like a neat solution, but in practice, if you suggested that an IT organization use Roaming Profiles, they would likely feel you don't have their best interests at heart, and with good reason. Many users have noted frequent problems with roaming profiles becoming corrupted and behaving very erratically when a user tried to log on or off different machines at the same time.

The main problem is that Roaming Profiles works by replicating an entire file whenever there is a change, rather than just recording the change itself. Roaming

Profiles was not really designed to handle huge amounts of data, but many organizations enabled Roaming Profiles without employing Folder Redirection, so the profile still contained all the user's data. This meant that the Roaming Profile process potentially was trying to replicate gigabytes of data during each logon and logoff sequence, which made the process take a long time, congesting the network, especially at peak hours, such as the start and end of the day, and therefore made for a very poor user experience. Because the logoff time could take so long, users would just turn off their machines rather than wait for the copy process to complete, corrupting the network profile. And if a user was logged on to multiple machines, the profile from the last machine to log off would become the network profile, overwriting the others. It is therefore not generally advised to use Roaming Profiles in configurations where a user may be able to log on multiple times using the same profile. In today's environments, the concurrent use of multiple operating system instances is becoming more common, making roaming profiles even more problematic.

Windows 7 introduced some enhancements to the replication process—in particular, the capability to synchronize the profile periodically in the background. To enable background synchronization, you need to create a Group Policy Object (GPO) and enable the background upload of a roaming user profile's registry file while user is logged on setting, which is found under Computer Configuration ➜ Policies ➜ Administrative Templates ➜ System ➜ User Profiles. Once enabled, various settings allow the NTUSER.DAT file to be synchronized—either at a certain interval or at a specific time of day. Note that only the NTUSER.DAT file is replicated with the background synchronization; nothing else in the profile is included. Everything else is still replicated at logoff.

> ► This is useful for users who don't typically log off, such as laptop users who only ever put their machines to sleep. This way, their NTUSER.DAT is still synchronized to the server periodically.

Enabling Roaming Profiles is actually very easy. First you create a network file share to store the roaming user profiles and permissions, as documented at http://technet.microsoft.com/en-us/library/cc757013(v=WS.10).aspx. To create a roaming profile for a user, open Active Directory Users and Computers and find the user account, right-click, and select Properties. Click the Profile tab and specify the profile path on the share, as shown in Figure 6-2. Conventionally, the path is a folder on the base share named for the user. You do not need to create the folder beforehand, as Windows will automatically create it and set the file system permissions required to protect the content.

To enable users in bulk, it is possible to select multiple users with the Active Directory Users and Computers tool and then select Properties. This will bring up a modified Properties dialog box that will enable specific settings, such as the profile path, to be configured for all selected users. Since you are updating multiple users

▶ This works even when updating a single user's properties, saving time if the person has a very long name!

you cannot specify the actual usernames for each but rather use the **%username%** variable, for example \\fileservername\share\%username%. This variable will automatically be substituted with the specific usernames when the profile path is used and created.

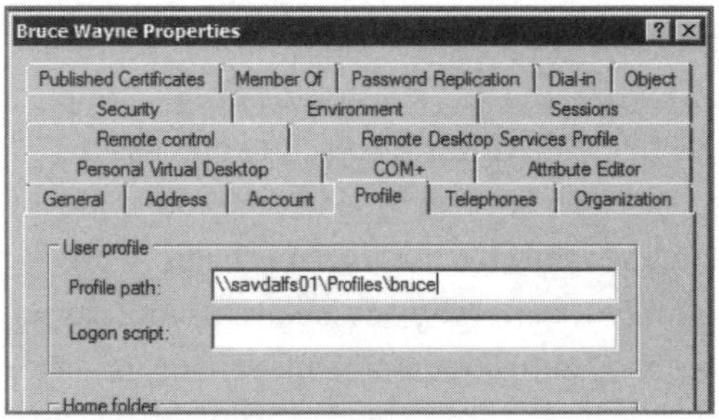

FIGURE 6-2: Specify the base file share for storing a user profile and username.

Minimizing Profile Size and Working with Folder Redirection

Some of the problems mentioned in the preceding section could be solved by minimizing the size of your roaming profiles and therefore the time required to download and upload the profile at logon and logoff. One of the quickest ways to shrink a roaming profile is to use Folder Redirection to redirect much of the data out of the profile. Folder Redirection can have such a huge impact on the integrity of your roaming profiles that I would go so far as to say that trying to use the Roaming Profiles feature without it is doomed to failure, as it is not architected to handle the replication of large amounts of data and will incur corruption and performance problems. And with the improvements introduced to the granularity of Folder Redirection in Windows Vista, organizations can now fine-tune their folder redirection, making profiles even smaller.

CROSSREF Folder Redirection is discussed in more detail in Chapter 5.

So, if Folder Redirection is so vital, what do you do about all the folders within the user's profile that the company doesn't want on the network and therefore shouldn't be redirected with Folder Redirection—such as a user's My Music folder? You might not want these folders on your network, but you don't want them bloating your roaming profiles either.

While it is possible to limit the size of a profile through the Limit Profile Size Group Policy setting, if you have already taken care of data and application file storage through Folder Redirection, then limiting the profile space will result in users getting errors until they shrink their profile size. Many users won't have a clue about how to reduce the size of their profile, just adding to their frustration.

Alternatively, you can reduce the amount of data replicated with Roaming Profiles by excluding certain directories from being replicated. The registry value ExcludeProfileDirs controls which directories should not be synchronized between the local profile and the roaming profile. After your organization has decided what data areas they want redirected using Folder Redirection, look at the folders that remain and decide which folders you want to exclude with ExcludeProfileDirs; the rest of the data will be part of the roaming profile.

The best way to configure folder exclusions is by using a Group Policy. Open or create a new GPO and select User Configuration ➜ Policies ➜ Administrative Templates ➜ System ➜ User Profiles and enable the Exclude directories in roaming profile setting. By default, when you enable this option, the Appdata\Local and Appdata\LocalLow folders (which include Temporary Internet Files, Temp, and History) are excluded from the roaming profile. You will also have the option to create a list of additional folders to be excluded from replication.

One item that may require some extra consideration is the AppData\Roaming folder that I mentioned earlier. The AppData\Roaming folder contains application file system configurations and information that may also relate to application settings stored in the user's registry area. If you use roaming profiles, it's critical that you also roam AppData\Roaming using Folder Redirection or the Roaming Profiles functionality. Otherwise, there will be inconsistencies between the file system and registry configurations for applications.

Additionally, Folder Redirection and Roaming Profiles may synchronize at different times due to different technologies being used to synchronize the content, and that could potentially add some inconsistencies between the stored state of the registry and file system. Roaming profiles are normally replicated at logon and logoff, whereas Folder Redirection with Offline Files occurs on an ongoing basis. One option is to configure certain folders under AppData\Roaming to only synchronize at logon and logoff, using the Network directories to sync at Logon/Logoff time only Group Policy setting (also found under User Configuration ➜ Policies ➜ Administrative Templates ➜ System ➜ User Profiles) for any application that is known to store configuration in both the registry and file system. By making this change, the replication will happen at the same time for file system and registry information.

Normally, even when you use roaming profiles, a local cache of the profile is left on the machine. However, if you want the local profile cache deleted at logoff for either security or space reasons, then you can find several helpful Group Policy settings under Computer Configuration ➜ Policies ➜ Administrative Templates ➜ System ➜ User Profiles, including:

▶ **Delete cached copies or roaming profiles:** Deletes any cached profile when the user logs off

▶ **Delete user profiles older than a specified number of days on system restart:** Keeps profiles cached until they are older than a configured number of days, after which they are deleted

Challenges of Roaming Profiles in Mixed Environments

Using Roaming Profiles definitely has some limitations, but when it is configured the right way and combined with Folder Redirection it can meet most needs. However, roaming profiles will often behave unexpectedly in environments with a mix of operating systems.

As described earlier, a number of profile structures changed between Windows XP and Windows Vista, which enabled better granularity of data types and separation of application data from other areas of the profile. This restructuring resulted in a new profile version (v2) being introduced with Windows Vista, with Windows XP being a v1 profile. Windows XP cannot use a v2 profile; and Windows Vista and Windows 7 cannot use a v1 profile. If you have a mix of clients in your environment running both Windows XP and Windows 7, then each user will need to have two profiles (a v1 profile and a v2 profile) if you want to use roaming profiles. Both profiles will be visible on the file share used to store profiles, with the v2 profile having the .V2 extension after the username—for example, my v2 profile is stored in the folder John.V2 on the file share. Unfortunately, this means users will have to maintain two separate profiles and repeat customizations. After doing so, anything roamed using Folder Redirection will be available on Windows XP, Windows Vista, and Windows 7 clients without issue.

There are additional considerations. If session virtualization is used, such as Remote Desktop Services (RDS), described in Chapter 7, it is not advisable to share a profile between a client operating system such as Windows 7 and a server operating system, such as the Windows 2008 R2 Remote Desktop Session Host, because of differences in configuration, application setup, and so on, which means configuring a separate profile for session virtualization. The separate RDS profile is set through the user's AD properties, and a separate file share would be used for the session virtualization profile.

Furthermore, suppose you have a mix of 32-bit and 64-bit Windows 7 client machines. Although Folder Redirection works fine between 32-bit and 64-bit clients, sharing a profile can cause problems because of the configuration differences in the way each version stores data. These factors need to be examined and should be considered when deciding whether to have different architectures used within the organization.

UNDERSTANDING WINDOWS LIVE INTEGRATION IN WINDOWS 8

Windows 8 introduces a new, deep integration with its Windows Live service. Windows Live provides a collection of services and software products, but one of its primary features is Windows Live ID, which provides a single sign-on identity service that enables a user with a Windows Live ID to sign on to many Microsoft websites. Traditionally, in order to log on to a Windows computer you needed to log on with a local user account that is stored in the computer's local security account database or with a domain account. Provided that a Windows 8 computer is connected to the Internet, it is possible to log on directly using a Windows Live ID, which simplifies the process of logging on and account management for many home users.

What makes Live ID a truly great feature is that in addition to logging on with a Live ID, you can configure synchronization of user settings to the Windows Live service. Once synchronization is configured, users can log on to any Windows 8 computer with their Live ID and have the same settings available. Figure 6-3 shows the Sync your settings page of the new Metro-style Windows 8 PC settings interface. To access the PC settings interface, select the Settings charm from the Start screen and click the More PC settings option at the bottom of the Settings bar.

As shown in the figure, you can configure which types of settings should be synchronized, such as basic personalization, which includes lock screen options, account picture, background, and colors, to more advanced types such as Ease of Access, Language preferences, Browser settings, and even some application configuration.

This capability to synchronize settings using the Windows Live service is also possible when you do not log on using a Live ID. You can link a local account or even a domain account to a Live ID, as shown in Figure 6-4. This simplifies a number of actions within Windows. For example, when you visit a website, your Live ID will automatically be used, and when you access the new Windows Store, any purchases

▶ The data associated with the Windows Live service is stored using the SkyDrive cloud-based storage service, but it is not possible to browse the data stored in SkyDrive for the synchronization of settings using the standard UI.

are linked to your Live ID, which means you can download on any machine on which you use the same Live ID. Only one Live ID can be associated with an account, but one Live ID can be linked to many different local and AD accounts. Once a Live ID is linked to a local or domain account, the synchronization of user settings to the Windows Live service can be configured, and are then synchronized at logon and logoff.

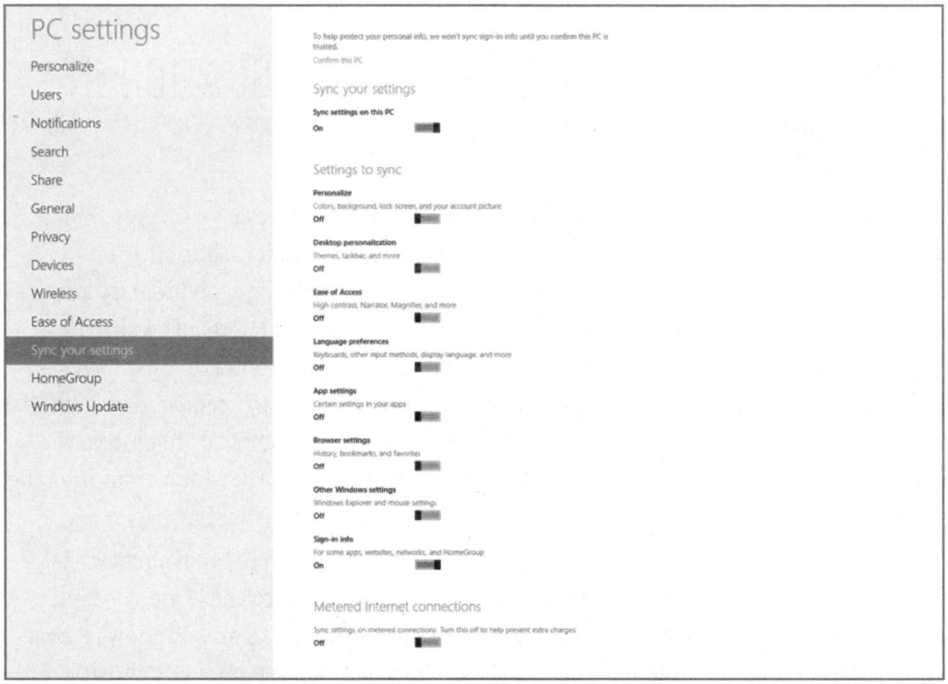

FIGURE 6-3: Specifying which settings to synchronize with the Windows Live service

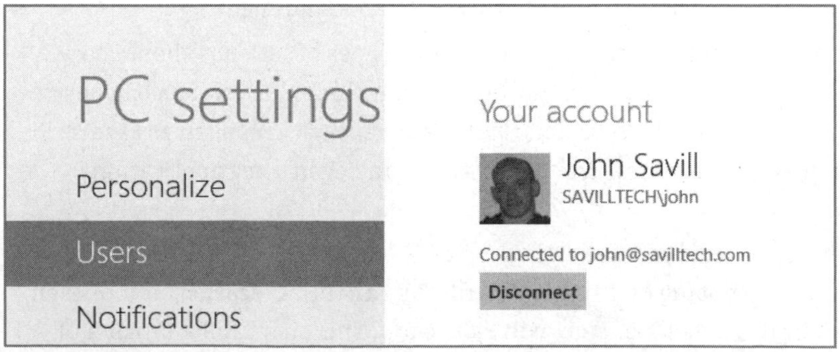

FIGURE 6-4: Linking my domain account to my Live ID through the Users page of PC Settings

In a corporate environment the use of the Windows Live synchronization raises an interesting question. Should Roaming Profiles be used or should Windows Live ID synchronization be used? While the Windows Live synchronization feature is a great capability for home users, it is not something corporations should rely on or recommend the use of on corporate assets. A corporate profile solution like Roaming Profiles or one of the other technologies I'm about to cover should be used. If your organization does not use Roaming Profiles and you want some synchronization of settings between your machines, then go ahead. If an organization has Roaming Profiles enabled and users turn on the Windows Live synchronization, then the Windows Live synchronization will not function because it detects that Roaming Profiles is used.

▶ Even if the synchronization of settings is not required, linking your Live ID to your domain account is still useful for site access and the Windows Store. Just skip turning on settings synchronization.

> **NOTE** As mentioned earlier, there is no graphical interface to view the data stored in Windows Live that is the result of synchronizing PC settings, which means it's not possible to just delete files that contain the synchronized data. When Windows 8 is released, there should be an option at `http://account` `.live.com` that will clear your settings saved in the cloud.

THIRD-PARTY USER PROFILE VIRTUALIZATION SOLUTIONS

It should be fairly clear that Roaming Profiles is a viable option in a single operating system, single concurrent logon environment. If your environment potentially requires multiple concurrent user logons and/or using different operating system versions and architectures, then the Roaming Profiles feature is extremely problematic. That's primarily because Roaming Profiles, like Windows, treats the entire user registry area as a single replicated file, NTUSER.DAT, with no application-level granularity.

The top initiatives of many organizations today involve VDI, session virtualization, Bring Your Own Device (BYOD), and many more, all of which require users to log on to different devices and likely involve multiple logons at the same time. Roaming Profiles just doesn't fit the bill. Fortunately, several third-party solutions have been designed to remedy the problems associated with Roaming Profiles.

Citrix has a basic solution as part of its session virtualization and VDI solutions that can help with some issues. However, the most powerful solutions are desktop virtualization products that focus purely on profile virtualization and the application-level granularity of settings, such as those from AppSense and RES Software. These solutions, which differ slightly in implementation, actually inject agents into the operating system that "hijack" an application or operating system component that tries to talk to the user's profile. The agent detects the application or operating system component performing the action and separates the profile into application-specific and operating system component–specific areas. Each of these areas is stored separately on either a file system or a database and is synchronized with the local machine when applications start and stop, rather than at the traditional logon and logoff.

Synchronizing only the profile changes related to a specific application when the application starts and stops introduces some powerful new capabilities. First, because the application-specific settings are separate from the rest of the profile, they can therefore more easily move between different operating systems and architectures, provided the software has an agent for the operating systems and architectures being used. This means the same settings can be used across all available operating systems and architectures, meaning only one profile for the user.

Second, because the settings are synchronized as the application starts and stops, multiple logons are more easily handled. In a common scenario, a user who is logged on to a Windows XP machine launches PowerPoint and makes a change to the layout, opens a file, then closes PowerPoint but doesn't log off. As PowerPoint closes, its application-specific profile settings (both registry and file system) are sent to the profile solutions storage, such as a SQL database. Now imagine the user also has an open session on a Windows 7 machine and starts PowerPoint. As PowerPoint starts, any changes to the configuration for PowerPoint are automatically downloaded and the application launches with the new layout; and the document previously opened on the other machine should appear on the recent document list. The same process would apply to using a session virtualization solution such as RDS, which can even replicate application settings between locally installed applications and virtualized applications—such as those with App-V, which typically do not work well with normal roaming profiles.

▶ *This download and upload on a per-application basis is very fast because only changes to the application's configuration are synchronized.*

Beyond Profile Portability with Profile Component Rollback

Separation of the user's profile into application-specific chunks introduces another powerful capability. Sometimes part of a user's profile becomes corrupted and the entire profile has to be restored from a backup. However, if you're using a third-party user virtualization solution that separates the profile into application-specific blocks, it is possible to view the profile at the application level. In the event of profile corruption for a specific application, you can just roll back and restore that application's area to a previous point in time without having to modify the rest of the user's profile. For example, Figure 6-5 shows the different elements of the profile visible through the AppSense interface, and the shortcut menu that allows you to roll back a specific part of the profile for only one application.

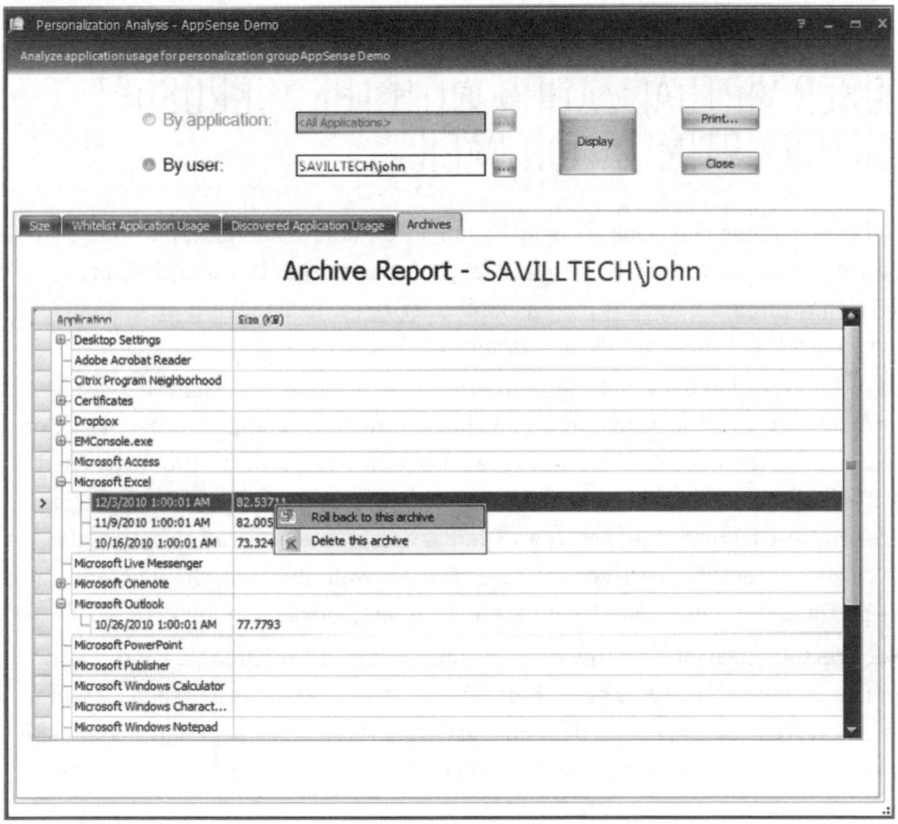

FIGURE 6-5: Using AppSense to roll back Excel to a previous point in time

Using Settings Management

This section touches on one other aspect of many third-party user virtualization solutions: user settings management. Many solutions allow settings to be configured and enforced on users. I'm generally not a fan of using this aspect of products because the Group Policy tool already provides a great solution, which is fully supported by Microsoft and does an excellent job. You can customize a Group Policy for most areas of the registry and pretty much every aspect of the operating system. I urge any clients of mine who are thinking about using the settings management component of a product to carefully consider why they might do so. If it's for a specific group of settings that are not possible with Group Policy, then that makes complete sense. Otherwise, it is best to stick to using the Group Policy tool, considering other solutions only when Group Policy cannot meet the requirements.

USER EXPERIENCE VIRTUALIZATION: THE EVOLUTION OF USER VIRTUALIZATION WITH THE MICROSOFT DESKTOP OPTIMIZATION PACK

If I had been writing this book six months ago, I would have spent far more time on AppSense, recommending it as the best user profile virtualization solution. Prior to that, Microsoft did not really have a viable user virtualization option. That all changed with *User Experience Virtualization (UE-V)*.

UE-V delivers a flexible and full-featured virtualization solution for the user's settings where previously organizations would have to deploy Roaming Profiles or a third-party solution. Where roaming profiles are worked as a single object—the entire user registry synchronized at logon and logoff—UE-V separates each application's settings into its own settings package that is synchronized when the application both starts and is closed. For desktop settings and ease of access configuration, the synchronization is performed at logon, logoff, connect, disconnect, lock, and unlock.

Not every application's settings are virtualized with UE-V. Organizations can determine which applications need their settings made available between different operating system instances and UE-V enable those, while other applications will keep their settings local to each operating system instance.

Understanding UE-V Templates

When a user customizes an application or even his or her desktop, those user-specific customizations are written to the registry or the file system, and sometimes both. UE-V works by capturing those registry and file system locations where nominated applications store user settings and saving them to a settings package file. A settings package file contains all the user-specific settings for one application, so one user may have many different settings package files; for example, one for each application plus one for desktop settings and one for accessibility settings. The settings package is saved as a .pkgx file. When a UE-V virtualized application starts, the package for that application is processed and settings applied to the computer currently in use, making all customizations available. Once the user closes the application, those settings are recaptured and saved in an updated settings package.

The settings packages are stored on a file share, and that is the only server-side infrastructure required for UE-V. There is no UE-V server or special management tool. The file share that is created has a subfolder for each user, in which each user's settings packages are stored. The settings packages are also cached locally on each machine using the Windows Offline Files functionality. It is very important to enable Offline Files when using UE-V; otherwise, UE-V cannot function. Caching the settings locally enables the application settings to be available even when a client is not connected to the network. Another option, if home folders are defined in Active Directory for each user, is to store the settings packages in the user's home folder.

▶ This is very similar to the folder structure created for Roaming Profiles!

To define what applications should have their settings virtualized with UE-V, templates are used. These tell UE-V which process filenames identify a specific application—for example, CALC.EXE represents Microsoft Calculator—and then which areas of the file system and registry contain user-specific settings for that application. UE-V includes a number of templates to virtualize some of the most common applications and Windows accessories, including Microsoft Office 2010, Microsoft Lync 2010, Calculator, Notepad, WordPad, Internet Explorer 9, Internet Explorer 10, along with desktop themes and ease of access settings. Listing 6-1 shows the template that is supplied for the calculator. It includes the name of the application, its UE-V ID (MicrosoftCalculator6), and the version of the template. The next section identifies the processes that comprise the calculator application, which is just a filename, CALC.EXE, and you can specify a product version. In this example only a major version of 6 needs to be matched, but it is also possible to specify a minor version in order to precisely specify the versions of an application to which a particular UE-V template should apply. Finally, the settings that should be virtualized are specified, which for Calculator are all in the registry under the Software\Microsoft\Calc key. You can browse all the templates at C:\Program Files\Microsoft User Experience Virtualization\Templates, which is a great way to learn the template format.

▶ All settings in the registry must be within HKEY_CURRENT_USER, which is why the registry hive is not specified. If an application is writing a setting to HKEY_LOCAL_MACHINE, then it is not a per-user setting.

LISTING 6-1: UE-V Calculator Template

```
<?xml version="1.0" encoding="utf-8"?>
<!--
Do not modify this settings location template. Changes to this
template can result in User Experience Virtualization not working
for the designated application now or in the future.
```

```
-->
<SettingsLocationTemplate xmlns='http://schemas.microsoft.com/
UserExperienceVirtualization/2012/SettingsLocationTemplate'>
  <Name>Microsoft Calculator</Name>
  <ID>MicrosoftCalculator6</ID>
  <Version>0</Version>
  <Processes>
    <Process>
      <Filename>CALC.EXE</Filename>
      <ProductName>Microsoft&#174; Windows&#174; Operating System
       </ProductName>
      <ProductVersion>
        <Major Minimum="6" Maximum="6" />
      </ProductVersion>
    </Process>
  </Processes>
  <Settings>
    <Registry>
      <Path>Software\Microsoft\Calc</Path>
    </Registry>
  </Settings>
</SettingsLocationTemplate>
```

▶ If a template should apply to different versions of an application, it is possible to just delete the minor version in the wizard page—for example, version 5.5 could be changed to 5. To support more than one major version, edit the XML Major, Minimum, and Maximum values.

> **TIP** As the use of UE-V becomes more widespread, there is going to be a growing number of templates made available to download, so it is worth searching for an existing template (www.technet.com) before doing it yourself.

You can create new templates manually with an XML editor, but Microsoft also provides a UE-V Generator, which enables easy creation and modification of UE-V templates, as shown in Figure 6-6. Clicking on the Create a settings location template option starts the Create wizard, in which you first specify the file path of the executable file for the application, along with any command-line arguments and working folder. The UE-V Generator will launch the application and monitor the registry and file system areas that are user specific, displaying them for review, as shown in Figure 6-7, using MagicISO Maker as an example. Notice the separate tab for reviewing file locations. Finally, details about the application are shown, such as the product name and version. At this point you can modify any of the generated values under the corresponding tab (Properties, Registry, or Files) before creating the XML template.

FIGURE 6-6: The User Experience Virtualization Generator provides an easy way to quickly create new templates.

FIGURE 6-7: The UE-V Generator auto-launches the selected application and performs a scan of the user locations that are accessed for its settings, which are then displayed before finalizing the template.

The UE-V Agent Service

The engine behind UE-V that enables it to perform actions is the User Experience Virtualization Agent Service, UevAgentService. The agent is the only piece of UE-V code that needs to be deployed, and it must be installed on all operating systems that will use the UE-V technology. A single installer is used to deploy both the 32-bit and 64-bit versions of UE-V, and the standard installation also includes all the built-in templates. To install custom templates, the templates can either be registered using the Register-UevTemplate PowerShell cmdlet, which could be done when the UE-V agent is installed or at any later time, or a network folder can be created in which all templates are placed. The UE-V agent will parse this folder every 24 hours and load in any new templates. A folder is specified using the Set-UevComputerSetting Power-Shell cmdlet and setting the SettingsTemplateCatalogPath registry value to the file share you use.

UE-V is supported on Windows 7, Windows 8, Windows Server 2008 R2, and Windows Server 2012; and because each application has its settings virtualized in its own settings package application, the configuration for each application (or version) can be shared between any of the supported operating systems. This means a user could have a local Windows 7 desktop, a remote Windows 8 VDI, and numerous sessions on Remote Desktop Session Hosts running a mix of Windows Server 2008 R2 and Windows Server 2012, and have all the same application customizations available. Contrast this with the monolithic roaming profiles where you need a separate profile for different combinations of OS and applications. At the time of writing, Metro applications cannot have their settings virtualized with UE-V, as Metro applications use a different process model than regular applications. UE-V also works across applications that are installed locally on an operating system and that are virtualized with technologies like App-V.

How UE-V Works

This section puts everything together by looking at how an application that has settings virtualized with UE-V runs:

1. The user launches an application.

2. The UE-V Agent Service sees the new process and compares it to the list of processes that UE-V is monitoring based on registered templates. When it finds the match, it hooks into the process and prevents the process from starting immediately.

3. The UE-V Agent Service checks the file share (or AD home folder) for an updated settings package for the application. If the remote settings package is different from the local cache of the settings package, then the Offline Files functionality synchronizes the local cache from the file server. If the remote settings package is the same as the local cache, then no synchronization is required.

4. The service takes settings from the local cache of the applications settings package and applies them all to the local operating system's file system and registry.

5. The service then allows the application to start.

6. Because the UE-V Agent Service is still hooked in to the application process, it is notified when the application is closed and the application process ends. The service gathers all the registry and file settings specified in the template for the application, writes them to the local settings package, and then notifies Offline Files to replicate the local cache of the settings package to the file share.

Notice UE-V does not require any changes to the application; it simply delays an application from starting, gets the settings and applies them to the registry and the file system, and then allows the application to start, which reads the user settings from the normal local computer file system and registry user locations as defined by the application. Internet Explorer is just another application to UE-V—synchronizing settings as Internet Explorer starts and is stopped. Because of differences between Internet Explorer 9 and 10, settings are stored separately for them, which is reflected in two separate UE-V templates. Similarly, for desktop and ease of access settings, there are implementation differences between Windows 7/2008 R2 and Windows 8, which means there are separate templates and settings packages for each. If you disable the option to Hide protected operating system files and enable the option to Show hidden files, folders, and drivers in Folder Options, it's possible to see the folders UE-V created for each application's settings package, as shown in Figure 6-8.

I have often seen problems in which users have changed settings for an application to a point where the application no longer functions; that part of their profile has become corrupted. With typical profile solutions the only solution is to delete the entire profile, as a profile is a single object. With UE-V, each application has its own settings package, enabling application-level settings rollback. The first time a user starts a UE-V–enabled application, all the current settings defined to be captured in the template for that application are stored in the application's settings package in a

▶ Rollback is not something performed by a typical user, who would instead raise a ticket with the help desk.

special "rollback" mode and saved, no matter what future settings are made. To roll an application back to its initial configuration, you can use the `Restore-UevUserSettings` PowerShell cmdlet, passing the name of the application template ID.

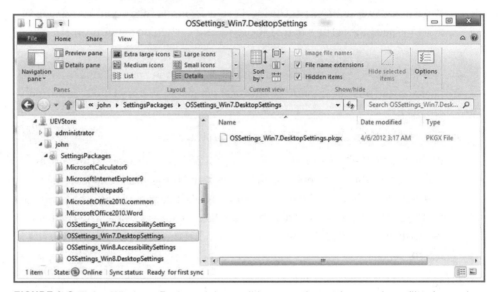

FIGURE 6-8: Using Windows Explorer it is possible to see the settings package files for each UE-V-enabled application.

UE-V is designed to replace Roaming Profiles, so organizations should not try to run both on the same machines; the results would be unpredictable, although it would probably be safe to assume that UE-V would overwrite any settings in Roaming Profiles. For organizations looking for a complete desktop virtualization solution, UE-V enhances the user experience when combined with folder redirection and application virtualization technologies. Check out `http://www.savilltech.com/videos/UEVOverview/UEVOverview.wmv` for a video walk-through of UE-V that shows the technology in action.

SUMMARY

I am a huge Microsoft fan. I love Microsoft technologies and I believe their solutions are often the best. The Windows Roaming Profiles solution, however, is really not something I could recommend for any kind of heterogeneous environment because of the many limitations described in this chapter. Now, with UE-V, Microsoft has a truly powerful solution that will meet many customer requirements—and one that offers a high degree of granularity. In environments where UE-V does not meet the requirements, perhaps due to operating system support, you can still deploy great third-party solutions.

Not covered in this chapter are features such as User Profile Disks (covered in Chapter 7), which is available in Windows Server 2012 RDS. These features are limited to pools of servers and, therefore, are not general user virtualization solutions but should still be considered in specific circumstances.

When you combine all the technologies covered up to this point with application virtualization, Folder Redirection/Offline Files, and user profile virtualization, it is now possible for users' entire view of the world to travel with them no matter what machine or operating system they use.

CHAPTER 7

Using Session Virtualization

Session virtualization, which is also called presentation virtualization, is one of the most well established and highly used forms of virtualization. Separating the presentation of a session from an operating system or a specific application by using remote desktop protocols enables users to use a range of devices in various locations, while all the actual resources reside and computation takes place in corporate datacenters on a shared server infrastructure. For many IT professionals, Microsoft session virtualization means Terminal Services, technology that was most current 10 years ago. In reality, the technology has evolved a great deal in recent versions of Windows, offering a complete solution for organizations in many scenarios without the need for complementary solutions from companies such as Citrix and Quest, which were considered a necessity prior to Windows Server 2008.

EMBRACING RETRO VIRTUALIZATION: WHY AN OLD FORM OF VIRTUALIZATION IS STILL ONE OF THE BEST

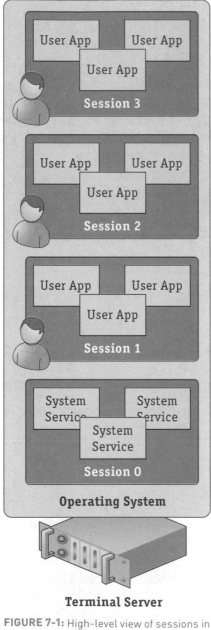

Terminal Server

FIGURE 7-1: High-level view of sessions in the Windows operating system

▶ Prior to Windows Server 2008, users logging on to the console of a system used session 0, which was the same session used for system services. Windows 2008 reserves session 0 for key services, and user sessions use 1 and above.

Many people mistakenly assume that *virtual desktop infrastructure (VDI)*, which virtualizes a client operating system and makes it available remotely, is a *replacement* for session virtualization. In fact, both VDI and session virtualization are viable technologies; in some scenarios one makes more sense than the other, and for most organizations both VDI and session virtualization will be used. Session virtualization is by far the more economical of the two technologies. Compared to VDI, it serves more users for each dollar spent while offering the same user experience for most use cases.

As described in Chapter 1, various forms of session virtualization have been around for a very long time. I recall my early days of remotely connecting to a large server that hosted my session along with many other users, and my interaction was achieved through a dumb terminal that simply displayed text sent from the server and then sent back to the server keystrokes I typed in. My interaction with the session was abstracted from where the session was actually running. In the Microsoft world, this type of session virtualization was originally called Terminal Services.

First I want to clarify what a session really is in the Windows world. Think of a *session* as a collection of processes that are providing services for a single logical entity, such as for a logged-on user, a logon session, or even services running on the operating system.

Sessions are isolated from each other, which provides protection for information within the session and gives users a protected workspace even though the actual operating system is shared with other users. Each time users log on, a session is created for them in which they function. Figure 7-1 shows the basic idea of sessions on a Windows server, with session 0 reserved for system services, and sessions 1 and beyond for remote connections. It is obviously still possible to log on to the console of a server, but there is no special reserved session number for a console logon anymore—it just uses the next available session number.

Each interactive logon session on Windows has a number of key processes used to manage the session and maintain the graphical interface. You can view these processes using an application like Task Manager or even using the Windows session virtualization management tools. Figure 7-2 shows a list of processes on a Windows Server 2008 R2 server that is enabled for session virtualization and remotely connects three users: administrator, john, and Cortana. The list of processes is ordered by session ID. The top of the screen shows the last few processes running in session 0 (reserved for the system), which includes wininit.exe, which is used to initially manage the starting of key Windows processes, and smss.exe, which is the session manager, used for starting user sessions. Then, four different session IDs are shown: three for users and one, session 4, used for the console. The console is currently not being used, which is why the only processes associated with it are to enable logon. Take some time to look at all the processes for each of the three user sessions (2, 3, and 5). Notice that for each session, most processes are owned by the user logged on to that session, and those processes include the following:

- explorer.exe (the shell)
- dwm.exe (desktop window manager, responsible for compositing the display)
- rdpclip.exe (remote desktop clipboard management)
- msseces.exe (malware protection provided by Microsoft Security Essentials)
- taskhost.exe (a container process for running a variety of DLLs)

Some sessions have additional processes—for example, session 2 for user john also has WINWORD.EXE because the user is running Word in his session. Notice also that for each session, two processes are running as user SYSTEM, which is the core operating system security context. These processes are winlogon.exe and csrss.exe, which have an instance created for each user session but are maintained by the SYSTEM because they are responsible for the security of the session and the Client/Server Runtime Subsystem, respectively, which are too critical to run as part of the users' security context.

▶ When a server is virtualized it still has a console, which is accessed through the virtualization management software option to connect to the VM, which opens a window to the server; this is its "console."

▶ This was previously called a Terminal Server, but in Windows Server 2008 R2 and beyond it is called a Remote Desktop Session Host.

▶ Because WINWORD.EXE is a 32-bit application, the splwow64.exe process also runs. It handles translation of 32-bit application requests to the 64-bit driver model.

Server	User	Session	ID	PID	Image
savdalts0...	SYSTEM	Services	0	464	wininit.exe
savdalts0...	SYSTEM	Services	0	412	csrss.exe
savdalts0...	SYSTEM	Services	0	324	smss.exe
savdalts0...	john	RDP-Tcp#0	2	3984	msseces.exe
savdalts0...	john	RDP-Tcp#0	2	2960	explorer.exe
savdalts0...	john	RDP-Tcp#0	2	3324	dwm.exe
savdalts0...	john	RDP-Tcp#0	2	1264	rdpclip.exe
savdalts0...	john	RDP-Tcp#0	2	2664	taskhost.exe
savdalts0...	john	RDP-Tcp#0	2	4232	WINWORD.EXE
savdalts0...	john	RDP-Tcp#0	2	3732	splwow64.exe
savdalts0...	SYSTEM	RDP-Tcp#0	2	1256	winlogon.exe
savdalts0...	SYSTEM	RDP-Tcp#0	2	3256	csrss.exe
savdalts0...	administrator	RDP-Tcp#1	3	2548	mmc.exe
savdalts0...	administrator	RDP-Tcp#1	3	3508	msseces.exe
savdalts0...	administrator	RDP-Tcp#1	3	3360	explorer.exe
savdalts0...	administrator	RDP-Tcp#1	3	3244	dwm.exe
savdalts0...	administrator	RDP-Tcp#1	3	3028	rdpclip.exe
savdalts0...	administrator	RDP-Tcp#1	3	2404	taskhost.exe
savdalts0...	SYSTEM	RDP-Tcp#1	3	788	winlogon.exe
savdalts0...	SYSTEM	RDP-Tcp#1	3	2844	csrss.exe
savdalts0...	SYSTEM	Console	4	2056	LogonUI.exe
savdalts0...	SYSTEM	Console	4	3532	winlogon.exe
savdalts0...	SYSTEM	Console	4	612	csrss.exe
savdalts0...	Cortana	RDP-Tcp#2	5	4700	mmc.exe
savdalts0...	Cortana	RDP-Tcp#2	5	4436	msseces.exe
savdalts0...	Cortana	RDP-Tcp#2	5	4208	explorer.exe
savdalts0...	Cortana	RDP-Tcp#2	5	4128	dwm.exe
savdalts0...	Cortana	RDP-Tcp#2	5	1632	rdpclip.exe
savdalts0...	Cortana	RDP-Tcp#2	5	3476	taskhost.exe

FIGURE 7-2: A list of processes for some remote sessions on a Windows Server 2008 Remote Desktop Session Host

The concept of enabling multiple interactive user sessions on Windows Server that could be remotely accessed was first introduced as part of Windows NT 4 Terminal Services Edition using the *Remote Desktop Protocol (RDP)*. RDP provides the services to send graphical interface content for the user's session from the server, where the session actually resides, to the user's workstation that is accessing the session. RDP also sends the keyboard and mouse input from the user's workstation to the remote session; and, as I will show, it adds support over time for other types of device, bi-directional audio, and more advanced graphics techniques. This basic RDP access is shown in Figure 7-3.

Microsoft provided client software for a number of platforms that enabled the RDP connection to the Terminal Server and remote connectivity to a client operating system. RDP clients were initially available for Windows NT, Windows 95, Windows 98, and even Windows for Workgroups. In addition to software RDP clients, a number of vendors produced small "thin clients" that could be attached to a monitor, mouse, and keyboard and whose sole purpose was to serve as an RDP client for connectivity to a desktop hosted on a Terminal Server. These thin clients were much cheaper than a normal PC and were useful for certain locations, such as a basic kiosk and particular users—for example, those highly restricted. The key point was that no matter what device a user was using, once they used RDP to connect to a Terminal Server they enjoyed exactly the same processing performance and application availability.

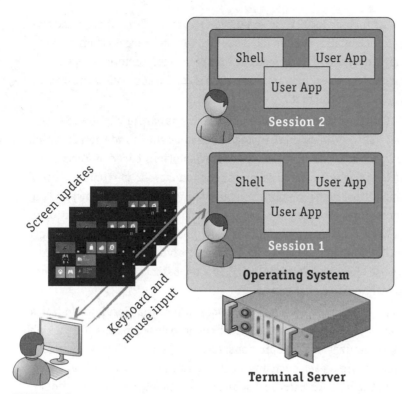

FIGURE 7-3: High-level view of RDP session interactions

The RDP functionality became a core part of the server operating system with Windows Server 2000 and Windows XP, and in all subsequent versions of Windows. The built-in nature of remote desktop made available both the server-side component, enabling a machine to accept remote desktop connections, and the RDP client, enabling the remote desktop connection to be initiated. Notice that server-side and client-side components are present in both the server and client operating systems.

For servers, the built-in RDP was used in two ways. By default, servers used RDP in a Remote Administration mode, which enabled a server to accept two simultaneous RDP connections that were to be used by administrators to manage a server. This enabled administrators to avoid manually servicing a server console. A server could also be placed in Application Server mode, traditional Terminal Services, which no longer restricted RDP to two simultaneous connections and was designed for user sessions, although licensing had to be in place for users accessing the server on a per-device or per-user basis. In this chapter, I focus on the Application Server mode and the use of RDP for user sessions.

▶ The Application Server nomenclature is not used anymore. Instead, a server is placed into the mode of accepting user sessions when the Terminal Services or Remote Desktop Session Host role is installed.

▶ Prior to the inclusion of RDP as part of the operating system, many administrators found themselves either sitting in very cold and noisy server rooms to manage servers or using expensive KVM solutions.

Clients used the included RDP functionality in two ways. First, it provided the Remote Desktop functionality that enabled users to remotely access their desktop from another machine. Second, it formed the foundation for Remote Assistance, which enabled users to request help from someone else who could view the user's desktop and even take control of it.

Although RDP with Terminal Services was available as part of Windows Server 2000 and 2003, it was not widely used; instead, it became the foundation on which other solutions were built. The most widely adopted solutions based on Terminal Services came from Citrix, which offered several such products—in particular, XenApp, which added capabilities such as application publishing (described below) and an enhanced protocol with better capabilities and less bandwidth requirement. The Citrix solutions were very widely used, but it's all good for Microsoft, as in order to use Citrix XenApp solutions, licenses for Terminal Services must be purchased because XenApp uses Terminal Services. Citrix is a key partner with Microsoft for remote desktop technologies of all kinds.

Windows Server 2008 made some major changes to Terminal Services, adding a number of key capabilities that made the built-in remote desktop capability a viable solution for many organizations that previously required Citrix. That is not to say Citrix is no longer required; each company must determine its own needs and then ascertain whether the built-in Microsoft solutions will meet those or whether a partner solution from someone like Citrix or Quest should be considered. The major changes to Windows Server 2008 include the following:

▶ **Application Publishing:** Also known as Remote Programs and RemoteApp, this capability enables publishing an application to a remote user instead of an entire desktop. Normally with remote desktop, when a connection is made a window is opened that displays a complete desktop from the remote server—with Start, taskbar, system tray, and so on. With application publishing, the only window that opens is for that specific application, such as Word. The application is still running on the remote server, but it integrates seamlessly with the user's local desktop, including system tray integration. This is a much better and less confusing experience for the user. Figure 7-4 shows this exact scenario, with Word running on a remote server on my main Windows 8 desktop on the right. Notice that the remote instance of Word has a different window style (theme) compared to the native Windows 8 Word instance, and Task Manager shows that instead of running winword.exe, the remote Word's local process is the RDP client. For a detailed demonstration, see http://www .savilltech.com/videos/TSRemoteApps/tsremoteapps1rg.wmv.

▶ XenApp has had many name changes. When I first used it, the name was WinFrame Server, then MetaFrame Server, then Presentation Server before becoming XenApp. Microsoft Terminal Services technology was originally licensed from Citrix!

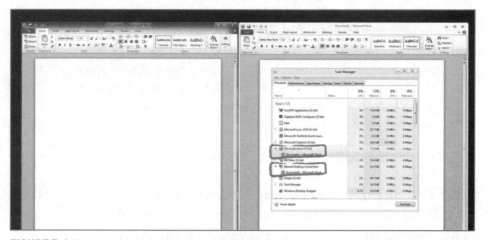

FIGURE 7-4: Word running locally on the machine on the left and from a session host on the right

▶ **Web Portal:** Terminal Services (TS) Web Access provides a website that can be accessed to view a list of all sessions and remote applications that are available, providing fast access for users. The same web portal can also be used with RemoteApp and Desktop Connection, which was a new Windows 7 feature that enabled remote applications and desktops to be published to users' Start menus through a subscription model, providing users with very easy access to remote services.

▶ **Terminal Services (TS) Gateway:** This provides the capability to encapsulate RDP traffic in HTTPS packets, allowing RDP to pass through firewalls that had exceptions for port 443 (HTTPS) and avoiding the need for firewall exceptions for RDP traffic (port 3389) or the use of virtual private network (VPN) technologies to establish secure connections. This is explained in a video at http://www.savilltech.com/videos/tsgateway/tsgateway800600.wmv.

▶ **Driverless printing:** Prior to Windows Server 2008, printing was a major problem with RDP. To print to a printer that was local to the client device, the correct printer driver had to be installed on the Terminal Server because when a print was performed, the rendering of the document for the printer was performed on the Terminal Server and then sent over the RDP connection to the client for actual printing. If the print driver was wrong, a corrupted print output would occur or even crash the operating system. Windows Server 2008 introduced TS Easy Print, which enables printing without a driver being installed on the Terminal Server. The new process works by rendering the print job to an XML Paper Specification (XPS) file and then sending the XPS

▶ XPS contains both the data and the formatting for a document. Think of XPS as Microsoft's version of PDF.

file over RDP to the client, which then renders the XPS for the printer using the local printer driver. This avoids any issues with printer drivers on the Terminal Server. TS Easy Print enables the advanced printer features of the local printer by asking the local client to display any printer property dialogs over RDP when printer properties are opened in a remote session. For a demo of this technology, see `http://www.savilltech.com/videos/tseasyprint/tseasyprint800600.wmv`.

There were other changes as well, which I cover later in this chapter along with more detail on the Web Portal and TS Gateway technologies. The Remote Desktop Protocol itself has also gone through a large number of changes, including support for RemoteFX with Windows Server 2012 for session virtualization.

A key point to remember about session virtualization and Terminal Services is that although the user is connecting to a server operating system, from an aesthetic and functional perspective the user's session looks identical to one running on a client operating system. Microsoft client and server operating systems are built on a shared codebase that is then customized for the different priorities of the client vs. server operating system. If an application runs on a client operating system, then it should run on the equivalent version of the server operating system. In terms of equivalence, the following can be used:

- ▶ Windows XP = Windows Server 2003
- ▶ Windows Vista = Windows Server 2008
- ▶ Windows 7 = Windows Server 2008 R2
- ▶ Windows 8 = Windows Server 2012

▶ *Windows Server 2008 R2 solves this with IP virtualization, enabling each session or specific application in a session to have its own unique IP address.*

There will be some exceptions. Some applications won't handle multiple instances of the application running at the same time on a single operating system instance even when running in different sessions, possibly because of some interaction with an installed service. Some client/server applications will struggle when running on a Terminal Server because all the user sessions on a Terminal Server will have the same IP address, the IP address of the Terminal Server, which might confuse the server end when trying to differentiate clients communicating with the same address/port. Consider also that the users are sharing a common operating system, so one user cannot reboot without shutting down everyone else's session; nor should a user be able to customize the operating system, as this would change the operating system for everyone on the Terminal Server.

Session virtualization on a Terminal Server is best used for task workers who do not need to customize or reboot the operating system and who run a fixed set of applications such as line-of-business applications, Office, and Internet Explorer, which will all work without issue in a session virtualization environment.

> **CROSSREF** For a detailed discussion about the relative advantages of session virtualization vs. VDI, see Chapter 13.

Another big shift with Windows Server 2008 is how session virtualization is used. In the past, users wanted the remote server to provide an entire desktop in which they ran a number of applications; and while a session desktop is still required in some scenarios, in most cases users just want to access a specific application remotely. This change is the result of the shift in devices used by clients and how they are used. If a user is on an iPad, a full desktop is hard to interact with; but presenting only the window of an application to the user provides a much easier interface. Even for users on full desktops, having remote applications seamlessly integrated with their local desktop provides a better experience. This focus on application publishing rather than entire desktops is seen in Windows 8, where publishing applications is the default.

UTILIZING THE CAPABILITIES OF REMOTE DESKTOP PROTOCOL (RDP)

Initially, RDP only needed to handle the sending of changes to the display as bitmap updates and passing the keyboard and mouse input. Considering the variety of current use cases and the reality that a remote desktop could be a user's primary workspace, RDP has had to evolve to offer a lot more. As RDP has evolved, so too has the built-in Remote Desktop Client (RDC) that provides the remote connections over RDP; and as enhancements to RDP are made, the RDC is updated to take advantage of the new capabilities. Often the RDC is updated for the version of Windows that offers the new RDP features, but sometimes a new version of the RDC is created for older versions of the operating system, enabling these systems to connect to newer operating systems and take advantage of new features.

Because RDP supports a number of virtual channels, different types of traffic and use scenarios can be enabled, including third parties that want to create additional capabilities on top of RDP. Windows 8 currently supports version 8 of RDP as both client and server. To verify the RDP version supported by your Remote Desktop Client, start the client and click the About link, which opens a window containing the RDP

▶ When RDP 7 was introduced in Windows 7 and Windows 2008 R2, a Remote Desktop Client that supported RDP 7 was also made available for Windows XP and Windows Vista.

▶ Up to 64,000 separate virtual channels are available for an RDP connection! The new RemoteFX technology takes advantage of RDP virtual channels to offer its functionality.

version supported, as shown in Figure 7-5. The Remote Desktop Client is available from the Start menu or just launch `mstsc.exe` directly.

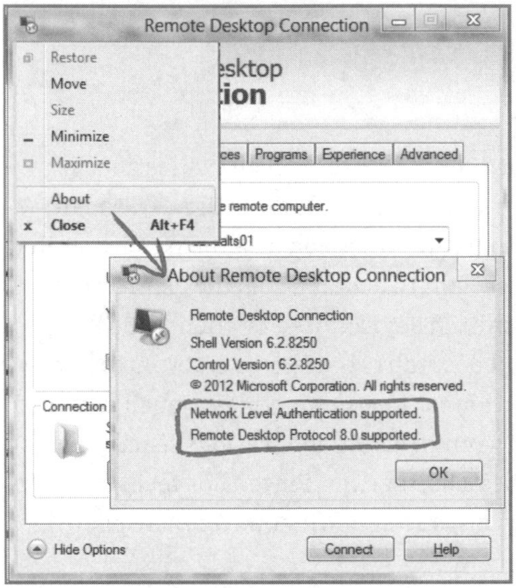

FIGURE 7-5: Checking the RDP version supported on the Remote Desktop Client

Looking at the RDP capabilities today, it quickly becomes apparent that a full desktop experience is possible using an entirely remote session while still accessing local devices, including printers. Key capabilities include the following:

▶ Full keyboard, mouse, and touch redirection, including keyboard hooks, which allow special key combinations to be redirected to a remote session

▶ Support for 32-bit color and desktop composition, enabling a full Aero Glass experience

▶ True multi-monitor support, enabling individual displays to be selected for use in a remote session. Prior to RDP 7.0, although multiple monitors could be used, they were treated as a single display with a combined dimension, meaning dialogs would be displayed in the center of a dual-display environment. Treating each display separately resolves this.

▶ Multimedia redirection, enabling certain types of media—such as those that are typically played in Windows Media Player—to be redirected to be played natively on the client device if the client device has the capability, providing cleaner media playback and saving bandwidth. For example, if you play a WMV file in a remote session, the actual WMV primitive is sent over RDP to the local client and rendered locally.

▶ While this chapter focuses on session virtualization, the same RDP is used for VDI and for remotely accessing a physical workstation, which means the same capabilities are generally available, except for RemoteFX.

▶ Progressive rendering of images, enabling a lower-quality version of the image to display initially and then increasing in quality as bandwidth allows. Other items on screen, such as text, would still be rendered with full fidelity, including font smoothing.

▶ Bi-directional audio, enabling sound to be sent to and from the local client. This enables audio applications such as Voice over IP softphones to be run remotely.

▶ Print redirection. Using the TS Easy Print functionality, driverless printing is available in remote sessions (this also works for Windows 7 target machines running RDP server service and above).

▶ Full encryption where required using 56-bit or 128-bit keys, enabling FIPS compliance if needed and Network Level Authentication (NLA) to ensure authenticity of both the server and the client

▶ Clipboard, drive, port, device, and smart card redirection. Certain types of device can be redirected to a remote session in an abstracted fashion, which obviates the need to install a driver for the specific hardware on the remote server. Devices with in-boxes, such as cameras, are one example.

▶ Port-level USB redirection with RemoteFX, enabling any USB device to be redirected to a remote session. However, because the redirection is at a port level, the driver for the USB device must be present on the remote server; and the device is available to only one remote session at a time and is no longer available to the local client.

When using a Windows operating system as the client for RDP, install the latest Remote Desktop Client version possible to gain the highest level of RDP support and therefore the best experience. Windows 8 includes a new Metro RDP client that follows the Metro principles of very clean design and standard ways to interact. Figure 7-6 shows the Metro RDP client with the Settings open, which you can access by selecting the Windows 8 Settings charm. If you are not using a Windows operating system as the client, but a thin client or a third-party application for another device such as an iPad, check what RDP version is supported and whether technologies like RemoteFX are enabled.

This brings up an interesting dilemma. Many organizations have an aging desktop infrastructure, so a choice must be made between replacing the desktops with newer equipment to run the latest operating system or switching to session virtualization and VDI. One great use for older desktops is to use them as RDP clients; but rather than use a full legacy operating system such as Windows XP and then use the RDC, Microsoft has created Windows ThinPC, a version of Windows specifically

▶ Start RDC and look at every tab and every option on a Windows 7 or Windows 8 desktop. This is a great way to become familiar with the options and capabilities. Notice you can save different configurations for fast future use.

targeted for use as an RDP client that is built on the Windows 7 codebase, providing full RDP functionality. Windows ThinPC is a replacement for Windows For Legacy PCs (WinFLP), which was built on the Windows XP codebase.

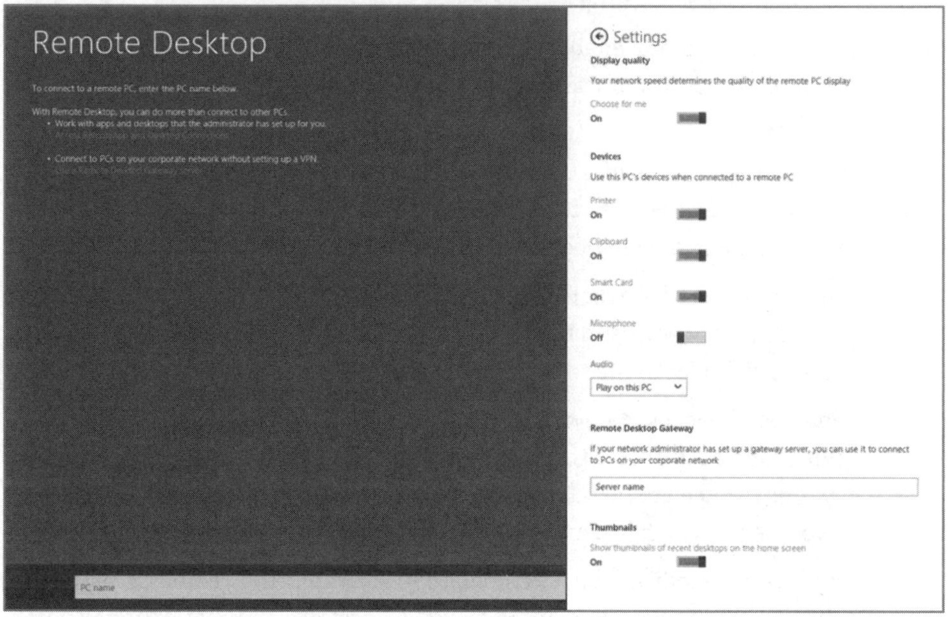

FIGURE 7-6: Windows 8 offers a newly styled RDP client that follows Metro design principles.

USING REMOTE DESKTOP SERVICES (RDS) IN WINDOWS SERVER 2008 R2 AND WINDOWS 8

Windows Server 2008 was a major turning point in session virtualization for Windows, offering the key capabilities described earlier in the chapter, such as TS Gateway, driverless printing, TS Web Access, and RemoteApp, in addition to a vastly improved Remote Desktop Protocol. Windows Server 2008 R2 provided incremental improvements to these features but its major difference was the addition of a built-in VDI solution, which is why Terminal Services was renamed Remote Desktop Services. None of the previous session virtualization technology was removed; it was improved, and the new name was chosen to highlight that it wasn't just about session virtualization now but rather providing remote access to desktops, which could include VDI. For those familiar with the Terminal Services nomenclature, Table 7-1 provides a quick reference for the naming changes between Windows 2008 and Windows 2008 R2. Windows Server 2012 uses the same Windows Server 2008 R2 naming.

TABLE 7-1: Changes in Terminal Services Naming

WINDOWS SERVER 2008	WINDOWS SERVER 2008 R2
Terminal Services	Remote Desktop Services
Terminal Server	Remote Desktop Session Host (RD Session Host)
TS Farm	RD Session Host Farm
Terminal Services Licensing (TS Licensing)	Remote Desktop Licensing (RD Licensing)
Terminal Services Gateway (TS Gateway)	Remote Desktop Gateway (RD Gateway)
Terminal Services Session Broker (TS Session Broker)	Remote Desktop Connection Broker (RD Connection Broker)
Terminal Services Web Access (TS Web Access)	Remote Desktop Web Access (RD Web Access)

▶ A farm is a collection of session hosts offering a shared service to provide high availability and load balancing.

There are two huge changes between Windows Server 2008 R2 and Windows Server 2012 that I think have the most impact: how RDS is managed and how it's deployed. Windows Server 2008 R2 includes a number of tools that must be used to administer RDS, and each tool is required to complete an RDS deployment, so knowing which tool to use can sometimes be confusing. Windows Server 2012 has one tool: Server Manager. Everything is in one place and organized in a highly logical way. Likewise, deploying RDS in Windows Server 2008 R2, whether using session virtualization or VDI, requires configuring many different servers, which can be fairly complex. Windows Server 2012 Remote Desktop Services is the only Windows Server 2012 role that enables scenario-based installation and configuration for servers that are part of an Active Directory domain. With scenarios, a simple, step-by-step wizard is used from a single instance of Service Manager. It asks a few questions, has you specify the servers that it should use for each RDS role, and then performs the installation of RDS and the configuration on all the servers for you—whether you chose VDI or session-based. There is even a Quick Start option that deploys all the components to a single server.

▶ Microsoft offers step-by-step guides on deploying RDS in Windows Server 2008 R2. Go to bing.com and search for "step-by-step remote desktop services 2008 R2" and you will find various guides for VDI and session host deployments.

▶ Quick Start is for evaluation and test purposes. Never use it in a production environment!

Exploring the Components of RDS

While Windows Server 2012 makes the deployment and management of RDS simpler, the component roles required are the same as those for Windows Server 2008 and 2008 R2, with a small change related to the Session Host in redirection mode, which is no longer required, as you will see later in this section. First, I want to cover at a high level what is required for a session virtualization deployment, and then we'll dive into the components. If you look at Chapter 11 and the components for VDI, you'll note it looks very similar. That's because it is the same technology; only the back-end infrastructure differs. For all components, load balancing and redundancy options are available, which should be used for production rollouts for which the RDS deployment is important to business operations. Following are the steps that a user must take to establish a connection to a Remote Desktop Session Host using all the Remote Desktop Services components.

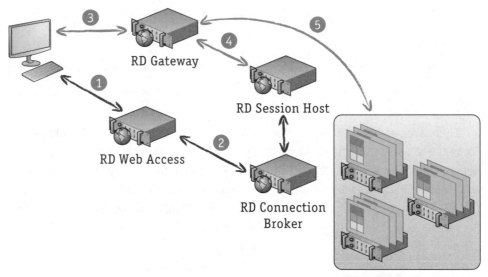

FIGURE 7-7: Setting up a virtualized session process with Remote Desktop Services

1. Users first need to find the Session Hosts or remote applications that are available. Although an RDP file can be created and deployed to users using various methods, a more dynamic approach is to use the Remote Desktop Web Access service, which presents a browser-based list of available connections from which the user can choose. Using the RemoteApp and Desktop Connection feature, you can publish this same list to a user's Start menu on a computer running Windows 7 (or later).

2. To create the list of published applications and connections that is presented to the user, the Remote Desktop Web Access server communicates with the Remote Desktop Connection Broker, which has knowledge of the Session Hosts and applications through its own communications with configured RemoteApp sources. The same RD Web Access and RD Connection Broker infrastructure can also be used with VDI targets if both are used.

3. No matter what method is used, be it Remote Desktop Web Access, RemoteApp and Desktop Connection, or a deployed RDP file, the users will end up with an RDP file that can be used to initiate a connection. If the user is outside of the corporate network, a direct RDP connection would be blocked by a firewall in most organizations, meaning the user would need to initiate a VPN-secure connection. However, you can use an alternative solution that does not require any end-user action or additional client-side software—namely, RD Gateway, which I describe shortly.

4. The user needs an initial RDP connection point. With Session Hosts it is possible for a user to initially connect directly to a Session Host in a farm using a shared name, which could be any Session Host. Then the Session Host that the user contacts queries the Connection Broker to determine whether the user has an existing session somewhere else. If so, then it redirects the user. If no existing session exists, the RD Connection Broker determines to which Session Host the user should be redirected, based on each host server's load. An alternative method is to use a dedicated Remote Desktop Session Host in redirection mode, which means the server acts as the connection point for the user's initial RDP connection, queries the Connection Broker, and then redirects the client to a specific Session Host. For Windows Server 2012 implementations, the initial contact point is the Connection Broker itself, and a Session Host in redirected mode is no longer required, which simplifies the infrastructure.

▶ A shared name can be achieved using DNS round robin, Network Load Balancing, or a hardware load balancer. All provide a single initial target for requests, which are distributed among all servers that are part of the shared name.

5. The client now makes an RDP connection to the destination Session Host (via the RD Gateway if connecting from outside of the corporate network) and your connection is complete. The logon process for the user would now commence.

The preceding process is certainly simpler than implementing a VDI solution but it still has many components; and while it might not look too daunting, a lot of configuration is required for each part, which gets more complicated when high availability with multiple instances of each role are set up. As already mentioned, some of these roles are also discussed in Chapter 11 because part of the infrastructure is the same, but it bears repeating.

RD WEB ACCESS

The *RD Web Access* server provides an initial entry point for users to select, via a web portal, the desired application, session, or VDI desktop target that is available to them. While not a required component, it does simplify the user experience. The same RD Web Access component is also used to populate the user's Start menu in Windows 7 and above using the RemoteApp and Desktop Connection feature.

The RD Web Access portal supports form-based authentication and single sign-on, in addition to differentiating between public and private computers for credential caching. The Web Access portal utilizes HTTPS to ensure the protection of credentials that are passed and could otherwise be exposed to the Internet, through publishing enabled by gateway services such as Microsoft User Access Gateway.

RD GATEWAY

▶ The SSL certificate of the gateway server is used for initial secure communications, so the client must trust this certificate, which may mean obtaining an SSL certificate from a public certificate authority.

The *RD Gateway* allows RDP traffic to be encapsulated in HTTPS packets, which enables a secure RDP connection through corporate firewalls without having to open firewall ports or use additional VPN solutions. With RD Gateway, you can configure who can connect through the service, what they are allowed to connect to, and the RDP settings they can use, such as device redirection.

The RD Gateway is placed in a basic DMZ or behind some kind of firewall/proxy for more security. External clients connect to the RDP destination via the RD Gateway, which is enabled by adding the RD Gateway server to the RDP file configuration that is provided to the client. The client then encapsulates the RDP traffic in HTTPS and sends it to the RD Gateway, which extracts the RDP and forwards it to the RDP destination. When traffic comes back from the RDP destination bound for the client, the RD Gateway encapsulates it in HTTPS and sends it to the client. This technology allows users outside the corporate network to access all the RDP resources without additional steps or software. Users who are on the corporate network can bypass the RD Gateway and communicate directly with the RDP destination.

▶ The RD Gateway is typically used by clients on the Internet, so the name used should be resolvable on the Internet DNS and resolvable to a publicly reachable IP address to your DMZ.

The key point of the RD Gateway is that it does not care about the final target of the RDP communication; it just handles the traffic, removes the HTTPS wrapper and encryption, and forwards it to the final recipient, which could be a Windows Server 2012 Session Host or a Windows XP physical desktop. It's a great feature to have available. Figure 7-8 shows the basic communications flow and client configuration entries. To configure the use of RD Gateway, you select the Advanced tab in the Remote Desktop Client and enter the name of the gateway, as shown at the bottom left. You specify the final RDP target, a Session Host in this example, under the

General tab, as shown at top left. Notice that the target server to be connected to does not require an Internet addressable name because this name is not used until the gateway server where the actual RDP packets are inspected. The key component that must be contactable from anywhere is the gateway. You can create different connections with different target hosts that can all use the same gateway.

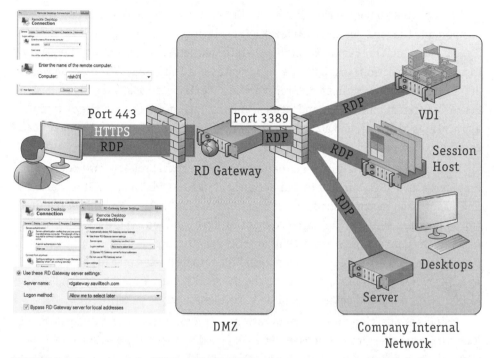

FIGURE 7-8: The wrapping of RDP traffic in HTTPS and the interaction with RD Gateway

The RD Gateway has controls that enable you to configure which users can connect via the gateway, which targets are allowed, and what client capabilities should be permitted—for example, is cut and paste allowed or can local drives be redirected and made available between the RDP client and target? It is vital to lock down the RD Gateway configuration, as this component represents the boundary between the Internet and internal systems. It is possible to deploy security solutions such as Forefront Unified Access Gateway (UAG) and Network Access Protection (NAP) in front of the RD Gateway to ensure the health of the client computers connecting.

> **CROSSREF** For more information on Forefront Unified Access Gateway (UAG) and Network Access Protection (NAP), see Chapter 12.

RD CONNECTION BROKER

The *Connection Broker* is the intelligence of Remote Desktop Services. It knows about all the servers, it knows how busy the servers are, it knows where users have disconnected sessions so they can be redirected. All Remote Desktop processes involve the Connection Broker in some way.

The updated RD Connection Broker in Windows Server 2008 R2 is one of the major components that enables an all-Microsoft VDI solution, because it gives RDS the ability to balance and track connections to non-terminal servers—specifically, the ability to manage connections to client operating systems. Additionally, Windows Server 2008 R2 enables the Connection Broker to balance RemoteApps and support servers with different published applications, enabling the user to see all the different applications gathered from all the servers in the farm. This eliminates the need for all servers to have exactly the same applications.

Windows Server 2012 further enhances the Connection Broker in two key ways. Previously, an RD Session Host in redirection mode was mandatory for VDI scenarios and was strongly recommended for large Session Host farms. This is no longer required; the Connection Broker is the initial connection point and redirects as needed. Additionally, the Connection Broker in Windows Server 2012 uses a SQL database to hold its configuration, enabling the Connection Broker to be hosted on a failover cluster in an active-active configuration using the shared SQL configuration, which provides higher availability and better scalability to this key service.

A single Connection Broker configuration can provide services for many farms of Remote Desktop services, which could be VDI on RD Virtualization Hosts or session virtualization desktops/published applications on RD Session Hosts. Because of the heavy communication between the RD Connection Broker and RD Web Access roles, it is common to install them on the same server.

RD SESSION HOST

The most important part of the session virtualization experience is the RD Session Host itself, and in many ways it is the simplest part. The *RD Session Host* is a Windows Server operating system with the RD Session Host role service installed, which switches the server from remote administration mode to a full Session Host. Providing the RD Session Host can communicate with an RD licensing server, users can connect if they are members of the local Remote Desktop Users group on the Session Host.

Applications are installed on the Session Host that should be available to the users, and it's important to lock down Session Host servers so users can only run applications and access components such as Internet Explorer but not make changes

▶ Active-active means multiple hosts in a cluster can host a service at the same time. Active-passive means only one host is offering the service, with other hosts waiting to take over should the active host fail.

▶ A 120-day grace period is provided and should be sufficient to purchase RDS CALS and configure the licensing server.

▶ Use Group Policy to prevent users from tampering with configurations that affect all users.

to the operating system or perform reboots. Additionally, after the Session Host is configured and applications are installed, the applications can be published, making them available to users directly outside of a full desktop while still enabling the option to have a full desktop. Multiple Session Hosts with the same configuration can be grouped into a farm, which is managed on the Connection Broker and provides a distributed service.

Note one major change in Windows Server 2012 session virtualization: A Session Host is configured to provide full desktops or remote applications; it cannot do both. The default configuration for a Session Host is to provide remote applications, but a server can be reconfigured to provide full desktops by unpublishing all the applications from the server. This change enables the Session Host to optimize the experience based on full desktops or individual applications.

IP virtualization, a new feature introduced in Windows Server 2008 R2, enables even more applications to use session virtualization, including many client-server applications. IP virtualization allows either each session or specific applications running in the session to have their own virtual IP address, which is leased from a DHCP server on the network. This avoids application conflicts whereby multiple instances of an application have the same IP address, which would normally be the case running on a Session Host because all sessions share the IP address of the Session Host.

RD SESSION HOST IN REDIRECTION MODE

While a requirement for VDI in Windows Server 2008 R2, the use of an RD Session Host in redirection mode is optional for session virtualization because of the RD Session Host's inherent ability to redirect RDP connections directly after communicating with the Connection Broker, but is advisable in large RDS implementations for performance and scale reasons. In Windows Server 2012, redirection mode is no longer required because the Connection Broker handles the redirection as previously discussed.

RD LICENSING

While Remote Desktop Services is a core role of Windows Server, clients that use anything that is part of RDS, such as a Session Host, VDI, RemoteFX, Connection Broker, or RD Gateway, must have an RDS Client Access License (CAL). There are two types of RDS CAL available: you should choose the most appropriate based on how your organization will use RDS.

▶ **Per-device:** Each device that accesses RDS services has an RDS CAL that is tracked by the RD Licensing server, and precise measurement of the CALs purchased vs. used can be viewed and enforced.

▶ Use IP virtualization with specific applications instead of the entire session where possible. Issues can arise with Active Directory communications and other services when IP virtualization is used at a session level instead of just an app.

▶ **Per-user:** Each person who uses RDS services must have an RDS CAL. Because this is per-user and not per-AD account, there is no way to truly track, because a single user could have multiple accounts or multiple people could share a single AD account. Per-user RDS CAL usage is essentially administered by the honor system and license counts are not enforceable; but reports are available to view user accounts that have requested RDS CALs.

An organization may use a mix of per-device and per-user CALs, but in some scenarios one type of CAL clearly makes more sense than another. For example, if you have a single user who might use many machines and the sum of users using RDS is less than the total number of machines that are ever used, then use per-user CAL licensing. Conversely, if you have a small number of machines that many different users use, such as shift workers, or you have a single shared machine used by many people in order to occasionally access an application, then per-device RDS CALs will be most economical.

The licensing server does not use many resources and it can be installed on a domain controller to provide instant integration with Active Directory, making it easy for RDS components to automatically find the RDS licensing server; but even if it is not installed on a domain controller, it is possible to configure automatic discovery at a domain or forest level. Remember that even if you use another technology on top of RDS, such as Citrix XenApp or Quest, you still need to purchase RDS CALs. Vendors do not always mention this fact.

RDS Management and Deployment

The step-by-step guides I mentioned earlier provide details about how to deploy and configure Remote Desktop Services with Windows Server 2008 R2, and there are a number of separate management tools:

▶ **RD Connection Manager:** Used to perform configuration of the Connection Broker and create VDI pools

▶ **RD Gateway Manager:** Used to configure the RD Gateway, including creating policies for connection based on user, client computer, and authentication method; and resource access policies, specifying what targets can be communicated with based on user group membership. RD Gateway Manager can also be used to monitor all connections using the RD Gateway service.

▶ **RD Licensing Manager:** Used to manage RDS CALs and run reports

▶ **RD Session Host Configuration:** Used for configuration of a Session Host, including licensing configuration and diagnostics. Farm membership and IP virtualization configuration are also performed using this tool.

▶ **RD Services Manager:** Used to monitor users, sessions, and processes on a Session Host or a group of Session Hosts

▶ **RD Web Access Configuration:** This is a web page within the RD Web Access that enables configuration of where the RD Web Access gathers its list of applications, which can be from the local Session Host (if Web Access is running on a Session Host) or from one or more RemoteApp sources, which is common where Web Access is run on a separate server and publishes applications from separate Session Hosts.

▶ **RemoteApp Manager:** Used to configure which applications are published on a Session Host. It can also create RDP files for users that include all settings, such as RD Gateway and custom RDP settings for specific RemoteApps, such as an RDP file for Word running on a Session Host. It's also possible to export the configuration of RemoteApp settings from one server into others, which is useful for farms of identically configured servers that all have the same applications installed. Figure 7-9 shows the RemoteApp Manager and some of the settings available. Notice near the bottom that it is possible to configure whether each published application should appear in RD Web Access.

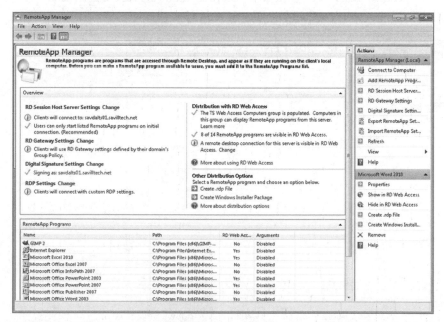

FIGURE 7-9: Performing configuration of the applications to publish with RemoteApp Manager

▶ Scenario-based deployment does not have to be used with RDS, but manually installing and configuring each RDS role instance is not recommended due to its complexity compared with the relative ease of a scenario-based install.

As mentioned previously, Windows Server 2012 eliminates the need for all these by providing one tool that is fully integrated with Server Manager, not only making management much simpler but also totally changing the deployment experience. It is still possible to deploy individual RDS roles in Windows Server 2012 and then perform configuration manually to get the different RDS role instances to communicate and provide a complete RDS solution, but there is another option. RDS is the only Windows Server 2012 role to use the new scenario-based deployment method, which is available for domain-joined machines. When the Add Roles and Features action is selected, the option to perform an RDS scenario-based installation is displayed, as shown in Figure 7-10. Selecting this enables the installer to choose whether the deployment is a VDI deployment or a Session Host deployment, and the option to perform a Quick Start is available. The Quick Start installs everything on a single server for testing purposes, whereas the standard deployment allows multiple servers to be selected for the various roles required (for either a VDI or Session Host deployment) and then automatically performs all configuration tasks and installations on all servers selected. Once the wizard completes and the servers reboot, a complete RDS environment configured to best practices will be available—all with a few mouse clicks. This is a great improvement over following a 40-page configuration step-by-step guide. In the video at http://www.savilltech.com/videos/win8rdsdeploy/win8rdsdeploy.wmv, I demonstrate a basic deployment using the new Quick Start option in addition to the manual options. Expect more scenario-based deployments in future Windows Server editions to provide a much simpler deployment method for other Windows Server roles.

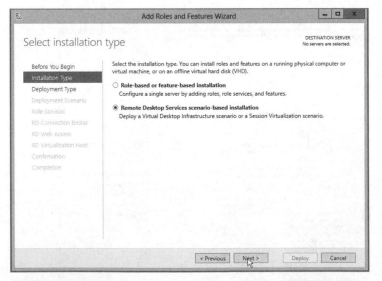

FIGURE 7-10: The new Add Roles and Features Wizard in Windows Server 2012, showing the scenario-based installation option

Figure 7-11 shows the initial entry point for managing Remote Desktop Services in Windows Server 2012. Notice it graphically shows the roles currently configured and those currently not used. This makes it easy to quickly identify where to go to configure specifics for each role and activities you may still need to perform, but remember that if you use the scenario-based deployment all required roles will be configured and available already.

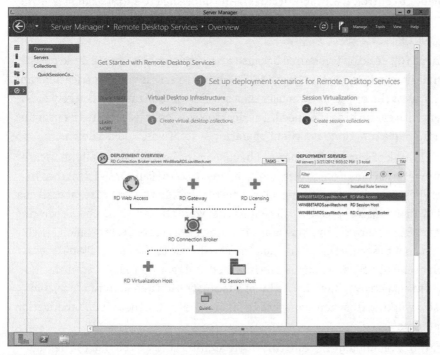

FIGURE 7-11: The main Windows Server 2012 Server Manager RDS overview screen with configuration info displayed

Utilizing the Key Capabilities and Scenarios for RDS Session Virtualization

There are many scenarios for which RDS session virtualization is the perfect fit, and Chapter 13 describes in detail how to compare VDI with session virtualization to determine the right choice when it is not clear. This section covers some of the use cases I see in the industry and explains how the different aspects of RDS work together.

When an application only needs to be published to a device instead of an entire desktop, 99 percent of the time I would argue that session virtualization is the right

▶ If an application does not run on a server OS or does not support multiple instances running on one OS, VDI publishing the application may still be the only option, but these applications should be few and far between.

choice over VDI. That's because publishing applications is very efficient with session virtualization. Consider that a single operating system could be used by hundreds of different users all running an application. VDI is not designed for publishing an application. It is possible with some third-party solutions, but running a whole VM for one application is a huge waste of resources unless absolutely necessary. In addition, VDI is useful for power users, people who need to modify the OS, reboot it, and have complete control. If an application is being published to a user, that means the rest of the operating system is basically being hidden and therefore locked down, so the reasons to use VDI do not apply.

Even if a full desktop is required because a user is using the remote desktop as their primary interface, such as from a thin client or to access many applications and services, unless the user is a power user then session virtualization will likely provide them with everything they need. The desktop will look the same to the user and perform the same functions as a client operating system when locked down.

When I think of some RDS scenarios I have seen in the field that really showcase some unique situations beyond offering an application to iPads or full desktops to various types of device, two in particular come to mind. In the first case, a retail customer had an extensive spread of call centers that were staffed using people working from home. Each user working from home required a corporate desktop, along with VPN equipment to secure the connection from the house to the corporate datacenter; and each user had a separate phone line installed and required a lot of training. Not only was this expensive, it required a lot of administration and maintenance, and these users working from home only used a single line-of-business (LOB) application to enter orders.

As part of a technology refresh, this whole architecture was changed. The call center staff were required to have their own machines running at least Windows XP and a broadband connection (which was already required as part of the VPN solution), and they were compensated for the cost of broadband. The staff were sent a USB headset and Voice over IP (VoIP) software and e-mailed an RDP configuration file. This RDP configuration file had an RD Gateway defined in it to allow access over the Internet, and the LOB application was published from an RD Session Host farm. On the datacenter side, Network Access Protection was used to ensure that the client machines met a certain health standard in order to not expose the company to security vulnerabilities or malware; and users now just clicked an RDP file to perform their job—no VPN or special hardware was required. This new architecture provided a huge cost saving, drastically reduced the amount of time needed to get a new call center person provisioned, and improved the work environment.

You may be wondering why the VoIP client was not served by session virtualization, with the audio stream sent to the agents over RDP, as I previously mentioned as the way RDP now supports bi-directional audio. It really came down to how the VoIP software optimized its performance based on its view of network connectivity, which didn't account for carrying audio over RDP. The VoIP server handling customer calls will be in a datacenter; if the agent VoIP client software runs on a Session Host server also in the datacenter, the software configures itself for zero latency and high bandwidth. However, the agent is actually connecting to that Session Host server over a WAN link with high latency and jitter, which means the VoIP optimization does not match the reality, so quality problems can ensue.

In the second case, an organization could not afford to perform a desktop refresh but needed Windows 7 features and an updated desktop experience. The client set up session virtualization in the datacenter at a fraction of the cost of replacing all the desktops and deployed an RDP client minimal OS to the desktops so they acted as a thin client. Each machine got a new monitor, keyboard, and mouse; and the users initially thought they had been upgraded to new machines. The experience was great and they had no idea their desktops were actually running in the datacenter. As an unexpected benefit, the organization had some client-server applications that transferred a huge amount of data between the client and the server. These applications ran much faster after this switch because the desktop was now actually running in the datacenter on the same local network as the server, enabling faster communication.

Evaluating the End-User Experience with RDS — Do They Know It Is a Server?

I've mentioned a number of times that session virtualization looks the same to a user as a client OS running in VDI. Is this really true? Look at Figure 7-12. This is a standard user connected to a Windows Server 2008 R2 Session Host, which is confirmed by the OS Name in the MSINFO32.EXE output in the bottom-right corner. The user has Internet Explorer running, a media file playing, Office applications available, and any line-of-business applications needed. The desktop is fully customizable, including a personalized background, an image, and other environment settings. Aero Glass is being used for best graphical fidelity. On the Start menu, the option to shut down and restart are not available because this would affect all the other users; but apart from that the user can do anything in this environment that a client operating system would allow, as long as the user is not a power user who needs to be able to change the actual operating system, such as installing applications and other customizations. Users can look around and determine that they are running on a server OS, but the point is to provide a productive environment for users that still enables them some level of customization, which session virtualization supplies.

FIGURE 7-12: A logon from a normal user to my Windows 2008 R2 Session Host

This solution works very well for task-based workers who run a defined set of corporate applications that can be made available on the Session Host. Application virtualization technologies like App-V complement session virtualization, keeping the server operating system free of numerous application installations and providing flexibility in terms of the applications available—including different versions of the same application, which is typically not possible because of application conflicts. See http://www.savilltech.com/videos/RDSUserView/RDSUserView.wmv for a video of this user session in action and a quick view of the tools you can use to manage RDS in Windows Server 2008 R2.

Best Practices for Architecting RDS for Your Organization

As I have already discussed, it is critical to identify the activities users will need to perform in the session virtualization environment and determine whether they require a full desktop or specific applications. It may be that some users have several different devices and while on a slate device they need a published application, on a normal desktop they want a full session-based desktop environment. Understand the applications they need to do their work, what add-ons may be required, whether Internet access is required, and whether Internet Explorer or an alternate web browser should be made available. Ensure that the applications needed by users are available, as users will not be able to install additional applications.

Not being able to install applications is related to locking down the environment. Never make a user a local administrator on a Session Host. Ideally, users should not be administrators on desktop machines, but on a Session Host it would be a nightmare; you could expect the entire environment to be unusable in a matter of hours, with servers constantly being rebooted. Users should only be members of the Remote Desktop Users group on each box, which should protect the Session Host from damage by users. Additionally, Group Policy can be used to block features that should not be available to users. Some organizations decide to block most of the control panel or block several applications aside from just the few the users need. Blocking items may be done not to protect the Session Host but rather to simplify the user environment, reducing clutter and therefore minimizing IT support, which is a major consideration for organizations. AppLocker is a recent feature in Windows Server 2008 R2 that enables the use or blocking of specific applications.

Because users often disconnect instead of logging out, administrators must make a related configuration decision. Users may disconnect for valid reasons and intend to reconnect. For example, the user may be going to lunch or going home to resume work from there. Conversely, users may just close their Remote Desktop Client instead of logging off, and not connect again for days, which just consumes Session Host resources unnecessarily. In the RD Session Host Configuration tool, administrators can configure not only whether users are allowed more than one concurrent session (which is the normal configuration), but also after how long disconnected sessions should automatically be ended and logged out, as shown in Figure 7-13. Understand the work habits of users and ensure that the configured automatic logout settings are communicated to users, so they understand when their sessions will time out and be automatically disconnected and that saving their work before logging off (or just walking away) will prevent loss.

▶ If all users should have access to all Session Hosts, add the Domain Users group to the Remote Desktop Users group. If only a subset of users require access, create a domain global group with those users and add to the RDU group on each host.

▶ Do not set the value too low; the default one hour may be too short. If users disconnect to go to lunch, take a few minutes extra, and return to find their sessions logged out (and potentially work lost), they will not be happy.

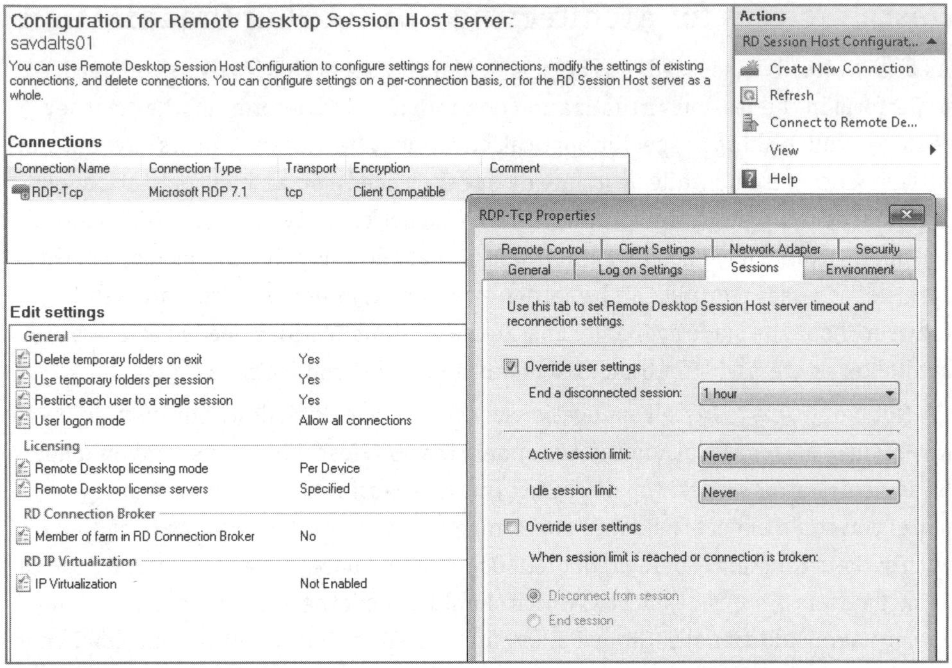

Configuration for Remote Desktop Session Host server:
savdalts01

You can use Remote Desktop Session Host Configuration to configure settings for new connections, modify the settings of existing connections, and delete connections. You can configure settings on a per-connection basis, or for the RD Session Host server as a whole.

Connections

Connection Name	Connection Type	Transport	Encryption	Comment
RDP-Tcp	Microsoft RDP 7.1	tcp	Client Compatible	

Actions

RD Session Host Configurat... ▲

🖥 Create New Connection
🔲 Refresh
🖥 Connect to Remote De...
   View ▶
🛈 Help

Edit settings

General
- Delete temporary folders on exit — Yes
- Use temporary folders per session — Yes
- Restrict each user to a single session — Yes
- User logon mode — Allow all connections

Licensing
- Remote Desktop licensing mode — Per Device
- Remote Desktop license servers — Specified

RD Connection Broker
- Member of farm in RD Connection Broker — No

RD IP Virtualization
- IP Virtualization — Not Enabled

RDP-Tcp Properties

| Remote Control | Client Settings | Network Adapter | Security |
| General | Log on Settings | Sessions | Environment |

Use this tab to set Remote Desktop Session Host server timeout and reconnection settings.

☑ Override user settings
   End a disconnected session: [1 hour ▼]

   Active session limit: [Never ▼]
   Idle session limit: [Never ▼]

☐ Override user settings
   When session limit is reached or connection is broken:
   ◉ Disconnect from session
   ○ End session

FIGURE 7-13: Changing the disconnected session timeout value using the RD Session Host Configuration tool

If session virtualization is being used as an important part of the business, make sure your deployment is fault tolerant. Have multiple Session Hosts in a farm, have multiple RD Web Access servers, and load balance RD Gateways. Place the Connection Broker in a cluster to provide protection from a node failure. In Windows Server 2012, the Connection Broker can run on multiple servers simultaneously in an active-active configuration, as previously mentioned.

To help you with RD Session Host capacity planning, I recommend reading an excellent paper from Microsoft, available at `http://www.microsoft.com/download/en/details.aspx?displaylang=en&id=17190`, which will be updated for Windows Server 2012. Additionally, when creating a new session virtualization environment, it's a good idea to perform load simulation, and Microsoft provides a nice tool set at `http://www.microsoft.com/download/en/details.aspx?displaylang=en&id=2218` to help with automated load simulation.

USING RDS WITH OTHER VIRTUALIZATION TECHNOLOGIES

In the preceding chapters I have talked about application virtualization with App-V, data virtualization with folder redirection, and user settings virtualization with roaming profiles and other technologies. All these technologies should be used with RDS. The goal is to provide users with access to a common environment and have their data and applications available.

App-V is recommended in a Session Host environment because it typically contains a large number of applications that need to be installed for the different users of the Session Host. Every application installed on an operating system makes changes, increases the size of the registry, registers components, uses resources, and potentially slows down startup times. By virtualizing applications there is no footprint on the operating system, keeping it clean and making it easy to quickly provision new Session Hosts without having to go through long application deployment processes. App-V for Remote Desktop Services is part of the standard RDS CAL, so it's a technology to which you have access.

Do not share a profile between desktop operating systems and Session Hosts using standard roaming profiles. Have a separate profile for each, which is possible using an Active Directory user configuration. Settings from a server operating system that is 64-bit are unlikely to play well with a 32-bit desktop operating system and vice versa. Using a roaming profile for virtualized sessions is still important in scenarios where a farm of Session Hosts are used to ensure that users get the same configuration no matter which Session Host they connect to.

Windows Server 2012 does introduce a new option for user customizations and even data virtualization through the new User Profile Disk capability, shown in Figure 7-14. The User Profile Disk is a virtual disk that is configured to store the user settings and data that are automatically connected to whatever Session Host (or VDI client when used with virtualization host) to which a user is connected. This gives users a consistent experience without having to use roaming profiles. Remember that the User Profile Disk is specific to each farm of RDS servers; it is not shared between different farms. For example, if you have three different environments—a virtualization host farm for VDI, a Session Host farm for desktops, and a Session Host farm for published applications—and you use User Profile Disks in all farms, there would be

▶ I prefer to not synchronize data through User Profile Disk, as it makes the data available only when using a specific farm. Folder Redirection will work no matter where the user logs on, so it is the preferred approach.

three User Profile Disks for each user. Also consider the User Experience Virtualization technology discussed in Chapter 6, which provides the best solution—providing portability between VDI, Session Hosts, and physical desktops.

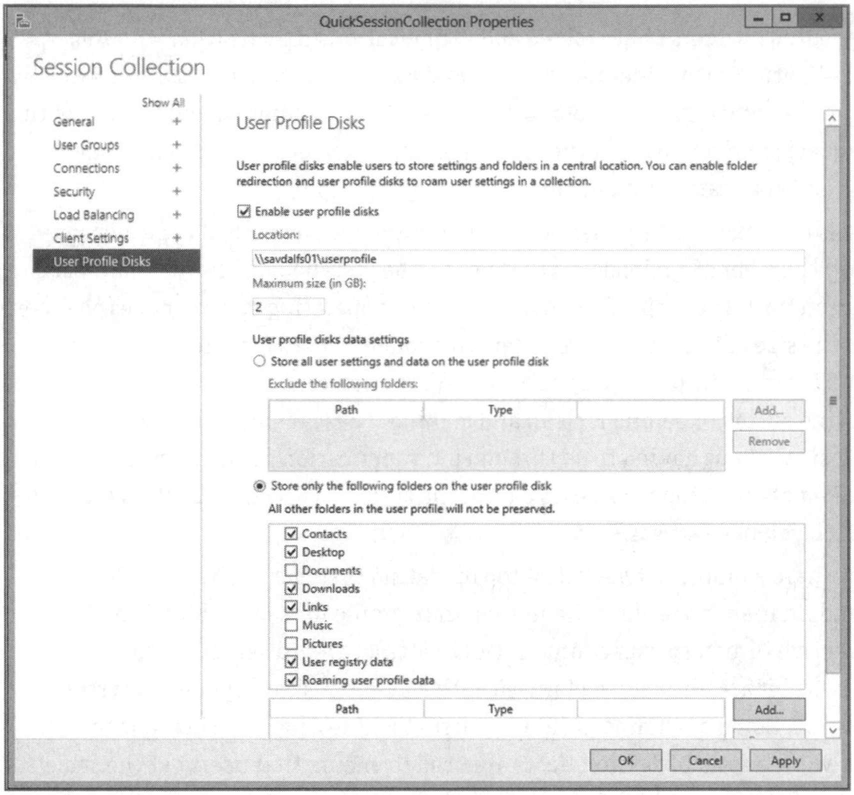

FIGURE 7-14: Enabling User Profile Disks for specific aspects of the user profile

THIRD-PARTY PRESENTATION SOLUTIONS FOR REMOTE DESKTOP VIRTUALIZATION

It would be remiss to not talk about key partners that build on Remote Desktop Services for session virtualization. For many organizations, session virtualization means Citrix XenApp, and both Citrix and Quest have great solutions. The strong built-in session virtualization solution that began with Windows Server 2008 improved with 2008 R2 and is even better in Windows Server 2012, but there are still compelling features in the partner offerings. I always ask clients about what features they need, their environment, types of client device, and typical connectivity, and then explain what would or wouldn't be possible with the purely Microsoft RDS solution and what the solution would look like by adding Citrix or Quest. The customer can then decide if the additional cost of third-party solutions is worth the added functionality. The following sections briefly cover the major features each of these products adds to session virtualization.

Using Citrix XenApp for Session Virtualization

Citrix has been supporting session virtualization longer than Microsoft, and it originally created much of the technology on which the first version of Terminal Services was based. Citrix continued to work closely with Microsoft during the development of RDS and still builds additional value on top of what Microsoft provides.

Citrix XenApp provides a few key features beyond the Microsoft RDS session virtualization solution:

- ▶ A different protocol for communication (HDX) that offers better redirection of content and works better over high latency and slower networks than RDP

- ▶ Rich graphical capabilities and progressive rendering, although many of these capabilities are present in RDP 8

- ▶ Clients for the Citrix protocol for nearly every platform that exists, including Windows, iOS, Android, Unix, Symbian, Java, Macintosh, and web browsers. Being able to access Citrix from any device is a big selling point.

- ▶ A more powerful Connection Broker that distributes connections based on resource utilization of each server instead of the number of connections

- ▶ A single interface that enables users to subscribe to applications, which are then made available no matter what device is being used

- ▶ Simplified management and installation of large deployments

- ▶ The capability to publish applications from a VDI client OS

- ▶ Support for Voice over IP and video conferencing within a session

For a complete list of differences, download http://www.citrix.com/site/resources/dynamic/salesdocs/xenapp6onRDS.pdf, which offers details about every feature that might be needed and compares XenApp against Windows Server 2003, 2008, and 2008 R2 (but does not include Windows Server 2012 at the time of writing). Although I have only scratched the surface here, XenApp offers a robust and complete solution.

Using Quest vWorkspace for Session Virtualization

The Quest vWorkspace solution is aimed at both session virtualization and VDI, providing a single solution to manage and provision both. Unlike Citrix, Quest leverages the RDP that is part of Windows, although support for other protocols is available. The focus of this product is providing a strong management solution with a single tool to manage VDI, session virtualization, and even blade PC users, simplifying the whole process. Quest also focuses on providing a single broker for all the different services, offering a solution that can dynamically use the right technology. The Quest broker also handles a heterogeneous environment that might contain a mix of technologies, such as from Microsoft, Citrix, and VMware. For the organization, this all equates to cost savings, which is a big selling point for Quest.

SUMMARY

Session virtualization is not going away and is in no way a "yesterday" technology. While it is one of the oldest technologies, it has evolved with changing needs and has not been eclipsed by VDI; it complements VDI, with each handling different use case scenarios. Taking into account the shift in technology and new form factors and operating systems that need access to Windows applications, the very efficient publishing of applications made possible by RDS session virtualization makes it more critical than ever.

Windows Server 2008 R2 established a very rich set of features for virtualized desktops, and Windows Server 2012 makes them easily available to all organizations with the new scenario deployment feature, which deploys and configures a multiple-server RDS environment. For evaluation purposes, the Quick Start scenario deployment is a great way to quickly see what is possible and learn about the product.

As Microsoft improves its RDS solution, the complementary partner solutions also improve, offering customers a wide range of solutions that cover any possible business requirements. Take time to carefully ascertain what is needed by the organization and its users, and then evaluate the various options to ensure that the right solution is selected—one that meets the return on investment goals. Finally, don't automatically bypass the Windows RDS solution. It's great in Windows Server 2008 R2. In Windows Server 2012, it rocks.

CHAPTER 8

Working with Hyper-V

Machine virtualization is the default type of technology that most IT administrators associate with the term "virtualization." This is because machine virtualization is usually an organization's first experience with virtualization, and it is still the predominant and most critical type of virtualization within a company. Although virtualization now includes session virtualization and data virtualization, it was machine virtualization that first attracted mainstream attention and adoption as companies realized what they could accomplish with virtualization technologies. Microsoft's first true enterprise-ready machine virtualization technology was Hyper-V, which in a relatively short amount of time has become one of the top three hypervisors in the market today. This chapter dives into the capabilities of Hyper-V and how you can use it in your organization. It also tackles the inevitable comparisons made against other available hypervisors.

VIRTUALIZING THE DATACENTER OS

In my role as a consultant and technical specialist, I talk to IT managers, directors of IT, and C-level executives, and each group can have a different perception of machine virtualization. What they all agree on, however, is that the benefits of moving from one physical box per operating system instance to a virtualized environment, which enables many OS instances to share a single physical server by creating virtual machines, are clear. Key benefits that organizations obtain through virtualization include the following:

▶ **Higher utilization of resources:** Prior to virtualization it was very common to see physical servers running at 10 percent CPU utilization, leaving a large amount of memory unused. This was because servers were purchased with worst-case scenarios and years' worth of potential growth in mind. Virtualized servers have much greater utilization. Storage is also more efficient with the move from direct attached storage for each server to shared storage on storage area networks (SANs) or network attached storage (NAS) devices.

▶ **Cost savings:** Less hardware means less money spent purchasing hardware. It also means less rack space and less power used, and less power equals less money. Similarly, less hardware also means less cooling requirements, which also translates into less power and therefore more cost savings. Software licensing can also be reduced, as a number of products, including the Windows operating system and the System Center product, can be licensed in a datacenter model whereby each processor in a physical server is licensed and then an unlimited number of virtual machines can be run on that server.

▶ **Faster provisioning of environments:** In a physical setup, each new operating system instance requires purchasing a server, which requires time for ordering, delivery, racking, and installation. Virtualization allows you to maintain sufficient spare capacity to create new environments in a matter of minutes, assuming the right processes are in place.

▶ **Increased mobility and resiliency:** Virtualization abstracts the guest operating system running in the virtual machine from the underlying hardware. This means a virtual machine can be moved from one brand of server to a completely different brand of server with different processors, network adapters, and storage, and started without problems, providing the same hypervisor is used. This mobility is very useful for disaster-recovery scenarios.

Additionally, hypervisors such as Hyper-V have high-availability capabilities that can provide increased protection from hardware failures by automatically restarting virtual machines on other virtualization servers in the event of a problem.

The use of virtualization is very well established in some organizations, which have aggressively moved from physical to virtual using migration technologies, while other organizations are moving to virtualization over time as new servers are required and old systems are retired. Either way, virtualization is an accepted standard today. Most server applications are supported in virtual environments, including applications like SQL Server and Exchange.

▶ Many CIOs consider virtualization in the datacenter to be a "done" initiative and their thoughts have moved on to the next phase, such as migrating to the private cloud.

UNDERSTANDING THE TYPES OF HYPERVISOR

Before looking at Hyper-V in detail, this section briefly expands on some of the content I introduced in Chapter 3. When I talk about hypervisors, I am referring to the technology that enables the deployment of virtual machines and their assets, such as an amount of memory, processor resource allocation, network access, and some virtual storage in the form of a virtual hard drive. Hypervisors do much more than this, but at a fundamental level this is their primary function. In addition to the hypervisor, there needs to be some kind of virtual machine manager that facilitates the creation and management of virtual machines that run on the hypervisor and provides insight into the state of the virtual machines.

There are two main types of hypervisor: type 1 and type 2. A type 2 hypervisor runs on top of an operating system that is installed on the physical hardware. This is commonly seen on desktop virtualization solutions such as Windows Virtual PC. Typically, these solutions are not very efficient because all operations have to run through the host operating system installed on the hardware, and virtual machines cannot directly access the processor's ring 0, which is where kernel mode instructions are executed. The advantage is that no special hardware is required.

A type 1 hypervisor runs directly on the hardware, and the virtual machines and the management operating system (if there is one) sit on top of the hypervisor and access hardware through the hypervisor. A type 1 hypervisor enables the performance of guest operating systems in virtual machines to match that of running the same guest operating system directly on bare metal hardware. This matching of performance is achieved by allowing the virtual machines direct access to the processor's kernel mode, ring 0, in addition to other performance optimizations such as high performance virtual hard disks, low latency and high throughput networking stacks, and efficient memory handling.

Allowing virtual machines to directly access the processor's kernel mode while the hypervisor manages processor access is achieved through the use of virtualization technologies implemented in the processor that expose a ring -1. This ring sits below ring 0, giving the hypervisor complete control over the processor while the virtual machines natively access ring 0, as shown in Figure 8-1. All three main datacenter hypervisors are type 1: VMware ESX, Citrix XenServer, and Microsoft Hyper-V.

▶ Any server, or even desktop processor, made within the last five years should have the virtualization extensions. Look for Intel VT or AMD-V as a feature on your processor.

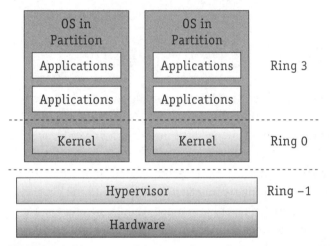

FIGURE 8-1: Placement of the hypervisor and operating system components

Type 1 hypervisors can implement the management of non-CPU and memory resources in two different ways: *monolithic* and *microkernelized*, as shown in Figure 8-2. In the monolithic hypervisor, all drivers for all hardware are part of the hypervisor itself. This means drivers for network adapters and storage are part of the actual hypervisor. This results in a larger hypervisor and a very specific set of supported hardware, as the driver has to be contained in the hypervisor. A microkernelized hypervisor is smaller, as it does not contain drivers for non-CPU and memory devices. Instead, a microkernelized hypervisor uses a parent partition to host the drivers for the hardware on the server, and then the other virtual machines use the parent partition for access to the disk and network resources. When implemented correctly, the microkernelized model does not introduce latency in resource access; and it enables much greater variation in supported hardware because drivers are not part of the hypervisor. The driver stack of the parent partition is used for the actual network and storage access.

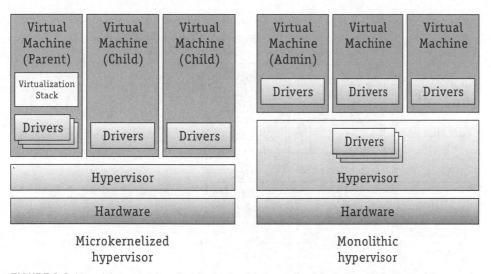

FIGURE 8-2: How drivers are handled for both microkernelized and monolithic hypervisors

Architecture of Hyper-V

Not surprisingly, when the vast array of hardware that Windows supports is considered, Hyper-V is a microkernelized type 1 hypervisor. The parent partition that acts as the virtual machine manager also hosts the drivers for the non-CPU and memory hardware, which the parent partition then provides as services for the virtual machines to access. To ensure there is no latency in resource access, Hyper-V uses a *Virtual Machine Bus (VMBus)*, which is a kernel-level memory bus between the parent partition and each virtual machine used for the transport of disk and network-related data. Figure 8-3 shows the Hyper-V architecture, including both the parent partition and two virtual machines. Although the figure shows the VMBus as a single shared bus between the parent partition and each child virtual machine, in reality there is a separate VMBus between each child virtual machine and the parent, ensuring data security and isolation between the virtual machines.

Hyper-V is a complete machine virtualization solution that is comprised of not only the hypervisor component but also the virtual machine management system and other processes related to enabling virtual machines. These processes run in the virtualization management partition, which for Hyper-V is the Windows Server operating system. It is by using Windows Server as the management partition for Hyper-V that all the features of Windows can be surfaced to Hyper-V: all the drivers for various types of hardware, failover clustering for high availability, backup, encryption, and more. Within the parent partition, each virtual machine also has a virtual machine

▶ People sometimes ask if Hyper-V can be used without the Windows Server management partition. The answer is no. Hyper-V is the hypervisor plus the management functions, which are part of the Windows Server OS.

worker process (VMWP), which runs as a user-mode process to manage the virtual machine, which is created by the overall virtual machine management service (VMMS).

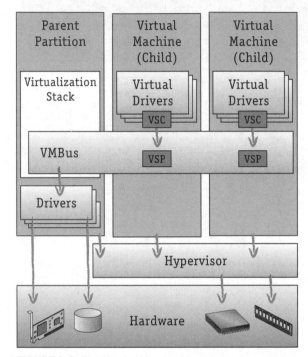

FIGURE 8-3: The Hyper-V bus architecture

Deployment of Hyper-V consists of installing Windows Server onto a physical box—this OS installation will become the parent partition—and then enabling the Hyper-V role, which enables the hypervisor to load at system startup. The Hyper-V role is enabled using Server Manager, PowerShell, or DISM; it's just another role within the operating system. What is special about Hyper-V is that when it's enabled, it makes a change to the boot configuration; it instructs the boot loader to load the Hyper-V hypervisor and therefore enable virtualization. This can be seen by running the following bcdedit command. Note the hypervisorlaunchtype entry at the bottom for a server that has the Hyper-V role enabled:

```
C:\ >bcdedit


Windows Boot Manager
--------------------
identifier              {bootmgr}
device                  partition=\Device\HDVol2
description             Windows Boot Manager
```

▶ Deployment Image Servicing and Management (DISM) is a command-line utility in Windows 7 that replaced Package Manager.

▶ The server must have a processor that supports virtualization technologies in order to enable the Hyper-V hypervisor to load, and the virtualization technologies must be enabled in the server's BIOS.

```
locale                      en-US
inherit                     {globalsettings}
default                     {current}
resumeobject                {7f62ada7-..-c5af989ba6db}
displayorder                {current}
toolsdisplayorder           {memdiag}
timeout                     30


Windows Boot Loader
-------------------
identifier                  {current}
device                      partition=C:
path                        \Windows\system32\winload.exe
description                 Windows Server 8 Beta
locale                      en-US
inherit                     {bootloadersettings}
recoverysequence            {7f62ada9-..-c5af989ba6db}
recoveryenabled             Yes
testsigning                 Yes
allowedinmemorysettings 0x15000075
osdevice                    partition=C:
systemroot                  \Windows
resumeobject                {7f62ada7-..-c5af989ba6db}
nx                          OptOut
hypervisorlaunchtype        Auto
```

Much of the Hyper-V code runs inside the Windows Server parent partition, which provides not only the services to manage the virtual machines but also access to non-CPU and memory resources via the VMBus, as previously mentioned. Because the VMBus is at the kernel level and purely in-memory, it does not introduce any significant latency between a virtual machine accessing a resource, such as a disk or network adapter, and the parent partition performing the actual communications with the physical hardware.

There is a catch, though. Remember that a main reason for virtualization is to abstract the virtual machine operating systems from the physical hardware, enabling better mobility of guest operating systems. This means the guest operating systems do not see the true hardware present in the server, but rather *emulated hardware* or *synthetic hardware*. The two types are very different and provide different performance. Emulated hardware is achieved by Hyper-V telling the virtual machine it has a specific "real" network or storage controller. This is normally an older piece of hardware for which most operating systems have a built-in driver. Hyper-V then emulates that legacy piece of hardware and converts the legacy hardware I/O operations to operations on the actual physical hardware, using the driver in the parent partition. For example, Hyper-V has a legacy network adapter available that emulates the Intel 21140-based PCI Fast Ethernet Adapter. One problem with emulated hardware is that the emulation degrades the communication performance because the operations have to be converted between the virtual and physical devices. The bigger problem is that the virtual machine worker process in the parent partition, which runs in user mode, provides the emulated hardware. This means every time a virtual machine talks to an emulated device, the I/O passes first to the kernel of the guest operating system; Hyper-V then redirects it up to the user-mode worker process for that virtual machine in the parent partition, which then passes the converted traffic to the kernel-mode driver for the (physical) networking adapter in the parent. This context switching is very slow and a lot of performance is lost.

The advantage of using legacy network adapters is that they are supported across almost any operating system and can be used to boot a guest virtual machine over the network, such as with PXE boot. The IDE controller also uses emulated hardware, which is why SCSI is preferred for all disks except boot volumes. However, the Hyper-V team has greatly improved the IDE controller, so there is no longer a significant performance difference between IDE and SCSI with Hyper-V.

The preferred hardware approach is to use synthetic drivers, which is achieved through *Enlightened I/O*, so named because the guest operating system is aware that the resources available, such as network, storage, input subsystems, and graphics, are actually virtual devices. The guest OS is aware of these virtual devices through the installation of *Integration Services*, which provides the necessary drivers and components to interact directly with the VMBus, eliminating the need to emulate physical hardware. Instead, it enables the guest to directly communicate using higher-level protocols such as SCSI directly over the VMBus, obviating the need for I/O to switch between kernel and user mode, as VMBus is provided purely in kernel mode. Enlightened I/O leverages a virtual service provider (VSP) and a virtual service client (VSC) for each type of communication between the parent partition and the guest. The VSPs run in kernel mode on the parent partition, and the VSCs run in each guest and communicate via the VMBus. You should always use synthetic devices if possible, as they offer better performance than emulated hardware; however, if you are running an operating system on which Hyper-V does not have Integration Services, you need to use emulated hardware.

Figure 8-4 highlights the difference between an unenlightened machine and an enlightened machine. On the left is a machine running Windows 2000 that does not have Hyper-V Integration Services, and on the right is a Windows 2003 installation

▶ The Intel 21140 adapter is a quad-port card, which is how Hyper-V can easily support four legacy network adapters in one virtual machine; each legacy network adapter is actually a port on the emulated 21140 device.

▶ Without Integration Services installed, keyboard and mouse interaction is very problematic and the mouse will get "stuck" in virtual machines, requiring a key sequence to release the mouse.

that does have Hyper-V Integration Services. Notice that because IDE is being used, both virtual machines see an emulated Intel 82371 IDE Controller; however, the enlightened virtual machine has native hardware performance. Also shown are the other emulated devices vs. Hyper-V synthetic devices that use the VMBus, in addition to the Hyper-V synthetic video and SCSI controller.

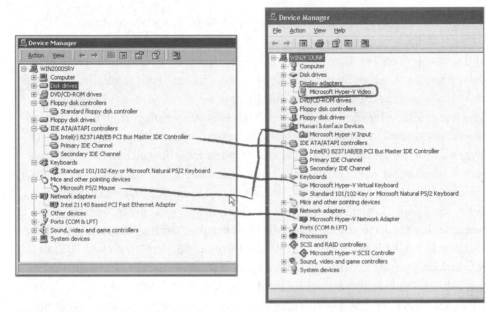

FIGURE 8-4: An unenlightened virtual machine vs. an enlightened virtual machine

The Hyper-V Integration Services provide additional services beyond just synthetic devices, which offer nearly bare-metal performance. The Integration Services also enable the following capabilities, which help provide a rich set of services for virtual machines running on Hyper-V. Note that not all services are available on all operating systems.

- ▶ **Operating system shutdown:** Enables the guest operating system to be cleanly shut down from the Hyper-V manager or the management interfaces Hyper-V provides, such as PowerShell and Windows Management Instrumentation (WMI)

- ▶ **Time synchronization:** Keeps the time of the guest OS synchronized with the host operating system. This should be disabled for guests such as domain controllers that have their own time synchronization processes.

- ▶ **Data exchange:** Allows the exchange of specific registry location values between a guest and the parent partition

▶ For each Integration Services component, an agent service is installed in the guest operating system. These can be seen by running the command wmic service where (name like "vmic%") get name, displayname which will list the names and display names of all such services, as all their names start with vmic.

▶ **Heartbeat:** Allows Hyper-V to check the responsiveness of the guest operating system by using a heartbeat check

▶ **Backup (volume snapshot):** A very powerful feature I will touch on later that allows backup requests at the host level to be passed to the guest operating system

▶ When running Linux on Hyper-V, if it is a supported Linux distribution then Microsoft will help support any Linux issues related to virtualization on Hyper-V.

Windows 7 and 2008 R2 have the Integration Services for Windows Server 2008 R2 Hyper-V built in. If updates are made to Hyper-V that introduce a newer version of Integration Services, then an update is required for the guests. Likewise, Windows 8 has the Windows Server 2012 Hyper-V Integration Services built in. For older Windows operating systems, Hyper-V in Windows Server 2008 R2 has Integration Services available for Windows Server 2000 and above, but support for operating systems is not limited to Windows. Microsoft has a whole team of engineers who create Hyper-V Integration Services for Linux, offering symmetric multiprocessing virtual environments that leverage the VMBus synthetic drivers for a number of the major Linux distributions, including Red Hat Enterprise Linux, SUSE Linux Enterprise Server, and CentOS. Microsoft supports Integration Services only for operating systems that are supported by the OS vendor; for example, because Windows Server 2000 reaches the end of support with the release of Windows Server 2012, there will not be Integration Services for Windows 2000 as part of Windows Server 2012 Hyper-V. You can use the Windows Server 2008 R2 Integration Services for Windows 2000 guests if you need some synthetic device support even though you are using the Windows Server 2012 Hyper-V hypervisor. Hyper-V supports both 32-bit and 64-bit guest operating systems.

Before diving deeper into the features of Hyper-V, I want to address a very common concern related to Hyper-V, and that is the use of Windows Server as the management partition. Every hypervisor has some kind of management system—it could be Linux-based, or it could be very thin and baked into the hypervisor code base itself; however, some management system is needed for the virtual machines and services to enable interaction with the virtual environment. Microsoft uses Windows Server as the management partition because of the benefits Windows Server brings, as mentioned earlier, but there are often concerns related to the size of Windows Server and its maintenance.

▶ While Hyper-V has a basic management tool, for a full-featured management capability Hyper-V should always be managed with System Center 2012—specifically, Virtual Machine Manager, although the other components also offer great value.

In reality, although Windows Server takes up noticeable disk space, on most systems even 10GB of disk space is really not a big deal. There is also a memory overhead for the Windows Server management partition, but here again, consuming even 2GB of RAM is not a problem on most systems, especially considering the functionality and flexibility that using Windows Server as the management partition provides. A real concern is the amount of patching that is required for Windows Server, as some patches require reboots and every time the management partition has to be rebooted it means taking down all the virtual machines during the reboot. Great advances have been made with each release of Windows to reduce the number of times servers need to be rebooted due to patching, but there will still be times when a reboot is required. For this reason, *Windows Server Core* is the recommended installation mode for the Windows Server OS. This is a server installation without the graphical shell, management tools, Internet Explorer, and many other non-essential Windows components; it provides only a command-line interface. As a result, it requires far less patching and therefore fewer reboots than a normal Windows Server installation, and it should always be used with Hyper-V. Critical patches required for Windows Server 2008 R2 were reduced by 50 percent for Server Core compared to a Full Server installation. Because it lacks many components, a Server Core installation also uses less disk space and less CPU and memory resources, although the main benefit is the reduced maintenance. Windows Server 2012 provides a more flexible configuration process, allowing you to switch easily between Server Core and Full Server installation without rebuilding from scratch. For more details, see Chapter 15.

▶ Using failover clustering and migration technologies, it is possible to reboot servers within a cluster with no downtime to virtual machines by moving the VMs between servers. No downtime to the virtual machines is what really matters.

USING HYPER-V WITH WINDOWS SERVER 2008 R2

This section introduces the key Hyper-V features available with Windows Server 2008 R2. Please keep in mind that this is a high-level overview of the features that are of most interest to the majority of people; it is not exhaustive. Therefore, even though a feature is not covered here, that does not mean it isn't available with Hyper-V or System Center.

Although Hyper-V was first available shortly after Windows Server 2008 was released, it is with Windows Server 2008 R2 that Hyper-V has really found its footing and it is now considered a serious hypervisor for enterprises. For organizations looking at Hyper-V, there is no reason to deploy the Windows Server 2008 version of Hyper-V. Instead, you can start with Windows Server 2008 R2 SP1 Hyper-V for the best set of features available, and Windows Server 2012 may have shipped by the time you are reading this—it is covered in the next section. The features that are part of Windows Server 2008 R2 Hyper-V have been carried over into Windows Server 2012, many with some improvements.

Capabilities and Features

I've already explained that Hyper-V enables the creation of virtual machines that can run 32-bit and 64-bit guest operating systems. The following sections go into more detail about the capabilities of Hyper-V virtual machines, including the amount of hardware Hyper-V can utilize and its features.

PROCESSOR RESOURCES

Windows Server 2008 R2 and Hyper-V differ in terms of the number of processors, cores, logical processors, and memory they support. Because newer processors have multiple processing cores and technologies such as hyper-threading, which add more complexity, a review of logical and virtual processors would be useful here. Motherboards contain one or more sockets in which processors can be installed, which is why the terms "socket" and "processor" are sometimes used interchangeably. Each processor has one or more processing cores. Whereas early processors had only one core, multi-core processors are now predominant—following dual-core processors were quad-core processors, and today 10-core processors are available. Each core acts like a separate processor, capable of performing its own execution of program instructions. However, the cores share a common bus interface and certain types of on-processor cache.

In many types of program instruction execution, not all of the core's execution resources are utilized. That's why Intel introduced a hyper-threading technology that makes a single processor core look like two processor cores, known as *logical processors*, enabling two instruction threads to run on each processor core. This increases overall throughput by enabling the processor to switch between the two instruction threads, keeping the cores busy, as it's common for instruction threads to stall while waiting on a resource. With hyper-threading, if one thread stalls the other thread can be executed. There is still only a single execution resource on the core, so hyper-threading does not double performance; the actual improvement varies, but an increase of 10 to 15 percent is typical. Microsoft has a great article on hyper-threading at http://msdn.microsoft.com/en-us/magazine/cc300701.aspx.

Figure 8-5 shows the Performance tab of Task Manager on one of my Windows Server 2012 boxes—a single Intel Core i7 processor, which is a quad-core processor and has hyper-threading enabled. Notice that the physical processor count is 4, while the logical processor count is 8 because the hyper-threading splits each core into two logical processors.

▶ The future is multi-core processors, and Intel already offers a 32-core processor.

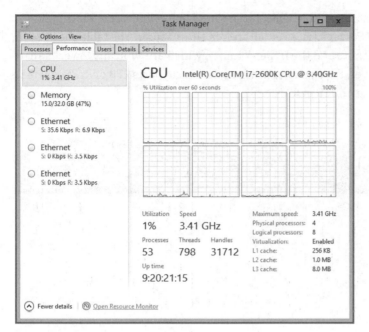

FIGURE 8-5: Task Manager in Logical Processor view showing the physical processors and logical processor details

Having multiple logical processors is very useful for virtualization. In order for a non-virtual system to take best advantage of many logical processors, the applications being used have to be written to take advantage of multiple threads of execution. Additionally, running many applications concurrently on an operating system instance would take advantage of multiple logical processors, as the operating system would distribute each application's execution thread over the available logical processors. With virtualization, each virtual machine is assigned a certain number of virtual processors, which are mapped to logical processors, which means high utilization of processor resources.

Windows Server 2008 R2 is available in several editions; for Hyper-V, the versions considered are Standard, Enterprise, and Datacenter. I will talk more about the different versions later with regard to licensing and features, but Table 8-1 summarizes some key details related to Hyper-V. I have also included the Microsoft Hyper-V Server 2008 R2 standalone product, which is a special version of Windows Server that is available as a free download. It is a Server Core version of Windows Server with the Hyper-V role that is aimed at hosting Windows client operating systems, such as virtual desktop infrastructure implementations, and non-Microsoft operating systems. I cover Hyper-V Server in more detail later in this chapter. The table shows both the Windows Server limits and the Hyper-V limits, which are typically lower than those of Windows Server. For example, Windows Server supports 2TB of RAM, whereas Hyper-V can only use up to 1TB of RAM.

TABLE 8-1: Windows Server 2008 R2 Editions

SPECIFICATION	STANDARD	ENTERPRISE	DATACENTER	MICROSOFT HYPER-V SERVER
Maximum Physical Memory Supported	32GB	2TB	2TB	1TB
Maximum Physical Memory Supported with Hyper-V Enabled	32GB	1TB	1TB	1TB
Physical Socket Support	4	8	64	8
Maximum Logical Processors Supported (Native, No Hyper-V)	256	256	256	N/A
Logical Processors supported with Hyper-V Role Enabled	64	64	64	64
Maximum Memory per VM	~31GB*	64GB	64GB	64GB
VMs per Host	384	384	384	384
Clustering Support	No	Yes, 16 nodes	Yes, 16 nodes	Yes, 16 nodes
VMs per Cluster	N/A	1000	1000	1000
Virtual Instances per License	Host + 1	Host + 4	Unlimited	None

*Technically, Hyper-V in Windows Server Standard could support up to 64GB of memory per VM; but the Standard SKU is limited to 32GB, thus Hyper-V is constrained by this limitation.

As shown in the table, Windows Server 2008 R2 Hyper-V supports 64 logical processors; any logical processors present above number 64 are not initialized by the operating system kernel on startup and are effectively parked and not used. This limit can easily be reached, with today's processors commonly having between six and 10 cores and then taking account of hyper-threading. For example, a machine with only four 10-core processors and hyper-threading enabled would have 80 logical processors. This would mean the OS would not initialize the last 16 logical processors (those over the 64 supported count). That means eight physical cores of processing power unused—almost an entire processor's worth. It is not possible in Windows to turn on hyper-threading for some processors and not for others; currently hyper-threading is enabled or disabled at the BIOS level. Therefore, for best performance on this machine, do not enable hyper-threading and let Hyper-V use all the cores on the system, which would be seen as 40 logical processors.

Now that you have looked at logical processors, the rest of this section examines the concept of *virtual processors*, which are processors configured on a virtual machine. For Windows Server 2008 R2, each virtual machine can have between one and four virtual processors, or vCPUs. Hyper-V does not create a hard association between a virtual processor and a logical processor, which is known as processor affinity. Each time a virtual processor needs to execute an instruction, the hypervisor schedules that instruction on an available logical processor. It is this capability to use different processors based on need, and thus increase overall utilization, that enables virtualization to consolidate operating systems onto a smaller number of physical servers.

The number of virtual processors that can be assigned in total across all virtual machines on a server depends on the number of logical processors in the server. While there is no hard limit, Microsoft supports a ratio of 8:1 for virtual processors to logical processors, as this has been tested in real-world scenarios. This means if your server has four logical processors, then 32 virtual processors can be assigned in total to all the virtual machines. This could be 32 single vCPU virtual machines, or eight quad-vCPU virtual machines, or any combination. There is an exception: for Windows 7 virtual machines, Microsoft has tested and supports a ratio of 12:1, which helps increase the density of virtual machines for Windows 7 virtual desktop infrastructure (VDI) implementations.

Discovery and planning in terms of the placement of virtual machines and the actual virtual processor to logical processor ratios used are vital. While a ratio of 8:1 is supported, virtualization cannot magically enable more processing resource than is physically available. For virtual machines with very low CPU utilization, such

▶ Anytime hyper-threading pushes a server over the supported number of logical processors, which is 64 for Windows Server 2008 R2, turn off hyper-threading. Or leave it on; it won't hurt performance.

▶ Processor affinity is not possible with Hyper-V. Processor affinity subverts the idea of abstracting a virtual machine from the hardware.

as around 10 percent, planning on eight virtual processors to one logical processor would be fine, yielding an average utilization of around 80 percent on the physical core. If virtual machines have high processor utilization, then a ratio of 8:1 would yield very poor performance because the virtual machines must constantly wait for cycles on the physical cores.

Some applications, such as SQL Server and Exchange, have their own individual supported ratios of virtual processor to logical processor, which can be as low as 1:1. I cover this in more detail in the section "The Importance of Discovery and Planning," but understand that because of the fairly low additional performance gain that hyper-threading provides, I prefer to count only processor cores when thinking about my virtual to physical ratios. For example, if I have a Hyper-V host with four processor cores, I would consider 32 my maximum number of virtual processors even if hyper-threading were enabled. Figure 8-6 shows a high-level view of the breakdown of physical processors to cores to logical processors and the mapping to virtual processors. As shown in Table 8-1, each virtual machine can have up to four virtual processors assigned.

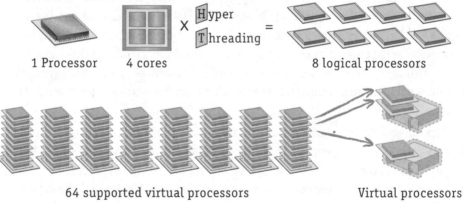

FIGURE 8-6: A view of physical processor to virtual processor breakdown

When assigning processors to a virtual machine, between one and four can be assigned, depending on what the guest OS supports. It is also possible to set three other values that help control processor resource usage—virtual machine reserve (percentage), virtual machine limit (percentage), and relative weight:

► **Virtual machine reserve (percentage):** This is the amount of the virtual machine's total processor resource reserved for it and therefore always available. Consider a host with four logical processors. If the virtual machine is allocated two virtual processors, and the reserve is set to 50 percent, then half of two of the logical processors is reserved for this virtual machine. The VM will not start unless 50 percent of two processors is available. This does not mean the resource has to come from the same number of cores as vCPUs or all from the same core, just that amount of overall CPU resource from the system. Thereafter, the hypervisor ensures that the virtual machine always has half of two logical processors of processing available. If the virtual machine is not using its full reserve, then other virtual machines may access the processor resource; however, as soon as the virtual machine with the reserve needs the CPU, it has priority and is guaranteed its full allocation.

▶ **Virtual machine limit (percentage):** This is the maximum amount of processor that the virtual machine can use. The default is 100 percent, which means this virtual machine can use the entire resource of the allocated processors. Note that during periods of resource contention, the virtual machine may not get a full 100 percent but will always get its reserve amount.

▶ **Relative weight:** During periods of resource contention, the weight value is used to determine the importance of a virtual machine getting shares of CPU time. For example, a virtual machine with a weight of 200 would get twice the number of CPU cycles as a virtual machine with a weight of 100.

Windows Server 2008 R2 Hyper-V has two other processor-related check-box settings that are set on a per-virtual-machine basis. The first is "Migrate to a physical computer with a different processor version." Using migration technologies, it is not possible to migrate a virtual machine between Intel and AMD processors due to their completely different architecture and instruction sets. However, by default, nor can you migrate between servers with different versions of the same processor family. This is because although both servers may have Intel processors, the different processors may have different capabilities and instructions. This is a problem because some applications perform tests when they start up to check the capabilities of the processor. If an application starts in the context of the availability of a certain set of instructions for the processor and is then moved, using migration technologies, to a server with a different processor that does not support a particular instruction, when the application makes the call it might crash. To resolve this problem, Hyper-V adds the capability to hide many higher-level functions of processors from the guest operating systems. This means you can move guest operating systems between nodes in a cluster even if the processor versions are different, because the virtual operating systems are exposed only to the generic instructions that are present in all versions of the processor family. Note that this functionality does not scan the processors and

▶ Do not enable this unless necessary, as it hides more advanced capabilities of the processor that may be useful to the applications running in virtual machines and provide better performance or features.

expose the lowest common set of functionality of all the processors in the cluster, it just limits access to a generic, basic set lower than all the processors in the cluster.

The second processor-related setting is "Limit processor functionality"; enabling it essentially dumbs the virtual processor down to improve the chances of very old operating systems such as Windows NT running on Hyper-V. Note that although this setting exists, the use of Windows NT 4 is not supported on Hyper-V, as the operating system itself is no longer supported.

▶ This setting has been removed in Windows Server 2012. If you still have NT 4 servers in your environment, it really is time to upgrade to an operating system of this century!

MEMORY RESOURCES

When looking at resources other than the processor used in virtual environments, memory is the other major one that typically dictates the total number of virtual machines that a host can support. Whereas logical processors are divided up and shared by virtual processors assigned to different virtual machines, memory works differently because the content of memory can't constantly be swapped with different content for different operating system instances. For Windows 2008 and Windows Server 2008 R2 prior to Service Pack 1, each virtual machine was assigned an amount of memory that was allocated when the virtual machine started, and it could not be modified while the virtual machine was running. This means for a Hyper-V server with 16GB of memory, assuming 1GB was reserved for the Windows Server parent partition, that 15GB could be used by virtual machines running on the server—in any supported combination of memory amounts per virtual machine. It could be one virtual machine with 15GB of memory assigned or 30 virtual machines each using 512MB of memory. The problem with this very static type of memory assignment is that the amount of memory given to each virtual machine has to be based on the most memory it will ever need, rather than the amount it currently needs. This can result in a lot of wasted memory during normal usage, which reduces the number of virtual machines that can be hosted on each server.

Windows Server 2008 R2 Service Pack 1 introduced a new memory optimization feature, *Dynamic Memory*. This new technology allows the amount of memory allocated to a virtual machine to increase and decrease based on the amount of memory the processes running in the guest operating system actually need at any given moment in time.

▶ Dynamic Memory is different from the memory overcommit used by other hypervisors. Memory overcommit tells the VM it has a very large amount of memory and allocates it as the VM writes to memory—and hopefully not all VMs try to write to all the visible memory.

Dynamic Memory uses two memory values for each virtual machine, an initial amount of memory and a maximum amount of memory. Hyper-V's virtualization management can intelligently allocate a virtual machine additional memory beyond its initial size, up to the maximum value based on its needs and the amount of physical RAM available in the server. The additional memory might be reallocated from other virtual machines with less need.

Figure 8-7 shows the dialog used to configure memory in Windows Server 2008 R2 SP1. The legacy Static memory option is still available, which allocates a set amount when the virtual machine is started, but the Dynamic Memory management options enable you to set the Startup RAM, the memory allocated to the virtual machine when it is initially turned on, and the Maximum RAM, the size to which the memory for the virtual machine can grow. The default Maximum RAM is 64GB, but you should configure this to a more reasonable limit based on expected and tolerated memory use, because the virtual machine could grow to whatever value is set here, possibly depriving other virtual machines of needed memory.

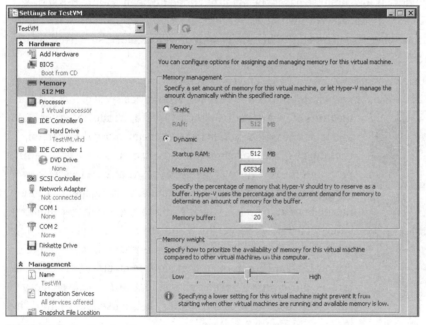

FIGURE 8-7: Configuring Dynamic Memory settings for a virtual machine

The last two options enable you to specify a free memory buffer, set as a percentage, and a memory priority, relative to other virtual machines. When you consider an operating system's use of memory and the mechanics to add additional RAM, it's not desirable to let the OS exhaust all memory entirely and then wait for Hyper-V to start adding RAM, which may take a few seconds. In those few seconds the virtual machine's performance could be severely adversely affected, and it would have started to swap out memory to its pagefile—something that you want to avoid.

To prevent this memory starvation, a default amount of 20 percent is reserved for use in the virtual machine. When the virtual machine has less than this memory percentage available, Hyper-V will add more if it is physically available in the host to

▶ The pagefile is a file on disk that can be used by an OS's virtual memory manager to temporarily store pages from RAM when physical memory is low. This can diminish performance, as disk is much slower than RAM to use.

bring the virtual machine back to the desired percentage. You can set the memory buffer based on the needs of the virtual machine, and you can even make an adjustment while the virtual machine is running. The slider enables you to prioritize memory allocation when not enough physical RAM is available to meet all the desired amounts for the VMs; this works just like CPU allocation, with a VM with a higher memory priority receiving additional memory before VMs with a lower priority.

What makes Dynamic Memory special in terms of its optimization technique is how the decision to add or remove memory is made. I used the word "intelligently" earlier because Dynamic Memory not only adds more memory to a virtual machine if its free memory is low, but also bases the amount added on need. Figure 8-8 shows part of a Task Manager view of a Windows Server 2008 R2 server that has 8GB of RAM. At first glance this server appears to have only 4MB of free memory, so it needs more, right? Wrong.

Windows XP, Windows Server 2003, and earlier operating systems were designed to use as little memory as possible, so it was very common to see systems with large

▶ It is because nearly all memory is always used that memory overcommit technologies like "allocate on first write" don't work well with modern operating systems and why Hyper-V does not use that memory optimization technique.

FIGURE 8-8: An operating system with only 4MB of free memory—or has it?

amounts of free memory. Windows Vista, Windows Server 2008, and later operating systems use all the memory they can for caching purposes to help improve performance, by pre-loading programs into memory. If memory is available, it makes sense to use it to try to improve performance. Leaving memory idle has no benefit, which is why it's rare to see a high free memory value on Windows Server 2008 and above. The memory used for caching can be used by applications as needed, so it is largely still available. Therefore, looking at free memory isn't particularly meaningful; you need to consider the *available* memory (which includes most of the memory being used for cache). This is shown in Figure 8-8 as well.

It is this available memory value that Dynamic Memory uses, and it is key to the intelligence of its memory allocation. The newest update to Hyper-V Integration Services provides a new Dynamic Memory VSC (virtual service client) in the guest OS that communicates with its corresponding VSP (virtual service provider) in the parent partition to report its use of memory. Specifically, it reports its amount of available memory; and based on the amount of available memory in the guest, the memory buffer percentage configured for the virtual machine, and the amount of physical RAM available in the host, additional memory may be allocated to the guest. This type of intelligent memory allocation is only possible because of the insight provided by the Dynamic Memory VSC; it would not be possible for the hypervisor to do this by looking at which memory is being used by a virtual machine externally, because it would be impossible to determine whether the memory is being used by an application or just for disposable purposes like pre-caching.

Certain versions of Windows have long had the ability to hot-add memory to the operating system, but this is not what Dynamic Memory utilizes. The scenario for hot-add memory is the rare addition of an entire slot of memory, which is very different from frequently adding memory in very small amounts; and hot-add memory was not the right solution. Instead, the Integration Services for Hyper-V that run inside the guest operating systems were enhanced with a new kernel-level *memory enlightenment* that communicates with the parent for instructions that additional memory has been allocated. It then presents this new memory to the guest operating system, which can begin using it.

While adding memory to a virtual machine is fairly simple, the process to remove memory that is no longer needed by a virtual machine is more complex. It is not possible to just remove memory from an operating system and expect it to continue to function. The process to reclaim memory is known as *ballooning*, which is a clever technique that enables the guest operating system to decide which memory it no longer needs. The balloon is implemented as a kernel-mode device driver, which means when it asks for memory the operating system has to fulfill the request. The virtualization manager instructs the guest component to grow the balloon driver to a certain size. The balloon driver requests an amount of memory from the operating system, and the operating system looks at its memory for the best way to meet the request. In a best-case scenario, it can just allocate free memory, potentially using memory currently allocated for cache and perhaps paging out memory to the guest OS page file. Once the memory is allocated to the balloon driver, these addresses are communicated to the virtualization manager, which tells the hypervisor it can now effectively unmap those address ranges from physical RAM (because the balloon driver will never actually touch them and no other part of the guest OS is allowed to). This way, the memory has been reclaimed by Hyper-V and can be used with other virtual machines. This process is shown in Figure 8-9. If the virtual machine needs additional memory in the future, then the VM management can instruct the balloon to deflate—either fully or by a certain amount—and reallocate physical RAM previously allocated to the balloon back to the memory given to the guest OS.

While Dynamic Memory is great for client operating systems in virtual desktop infrastructure implementations, it also works very well for many server workloads. I've seen several organizations use Dynamic Memory on all types of server workloads, including file servers, domain controllers, System Center servers, and more, and obtain huge memory savings. Using Dynamic Memory can enable running many more virtual machines on a server, thanks to the optimized use of memory.

▶ The key point is that it is the guest OS that intelligently decides how memory should be allocated in the most unobtrusive way with the least hit to performance, rather than an external process that does not understand how memory is being used.

▶ It is still critical to understand and carefully plan the placement of virtual machines based on expected memory usage and to set realistic maximum values. Poor planning will result in the host running out of memory and virtual machines not getting enough RAM.

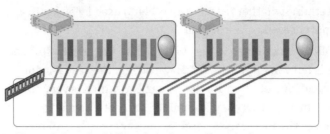

Balloon driver is deflated and not allocated any memory in the guest.

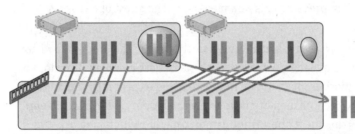

These addresses do not map to physical memory now.

Hyper-V under memory pressure sets a desired size for the balloon driver in a virtual machine. The balloon driver requests the memory from the guest, and as allocated, reports the pages to Hyper-V, allowing the memory to be unmapped from physical memory.

FIGURE 8-9: Inflating the balloon driver allows Hyper-V to reclaim memory from a virtual machine.

Conversely, some types of services need special consideration when using Dynamic Memory, and some should not use it at all. The following list contains some caveats, but check with each application vendor for its support of Dynamic Memory:

▶ Linux VMs cannot currently use Dynamic Memory because they do not support hot-add memory, so there is no way to give the Linux OS more memory while running. However, this may change in the future.

▶ The Exchange 2010 Mailbox server role checks the amount of memory when the mailbox server starts and then does not recheck again, so it will not take advantage of additional memory if added to the virtual machine after the mailbox service has started.

▶ The Enterprise SKU of SQL Server 2005 introduced support for the hot-add of (physical) memory into the operating system, and SQL Server treats virtual memory added to the VM by Hyper-V's Dynamic Memory feature in the same way. That means in order for SQL Server to take advantage of additional virtual memory, you must be running the Enterprise or Datacenter SKU edition. SQL Server checks the OS memory every second, and if the memory has increased, it recalculates its target memory size, which is how additions from both hot-add memory and Hyper-V Dynamic Memory are recognized. Because SQL Server has its own mechanisms for managing its buffer pool within the allocated memory, the buffer should be set to 5 percent for a SQL Server virtual machine, rather than the default 20 percent. This will enable Hyper-V to reclaim virtual memory that is not needed.

▶ Like SQL Server, Java also has its own memory management mechanisms, which means the buffer should be set to 5 percent for virtual machines running Java workloads, rather than the default 20 percent.

As emphasized earlier, Dynamic Memory is not a memory overcommit technology. Instead, it gives a virtual machine an initial amount of memory and then adds more as needed if available in the host. This ensures the best use of memory without running the risk of overcommitting the amount of memory available to virtual machines.

The maximum amount of memory that can be assigned to a virtual machine with Windows Server 2008 R2 Hyper-V is 64GB. While it is possible to assign a virtual machine a static amount of memory greater than what is available on the host, the virtual machine will not be able to be started.

> **NOTE** When virtualization technologies are used, it's common to run many similar versions of operating system instances on one physical piece of hardware. For example, on my main server I have 18 virtual machines all running Windows Server 2008 R2 SP1. These are the same operating system version, which means a large part of their memory content has the same data as other virtual machines running the same guest operating system.
>
> *Page sharing* enables the storage of duplicate pages of memory from all the virtual machines only once in physical RAM—basically, Single Instance Storage for virtual machine memory. In one form of page sharing, the hypervisor creates a hash value for every page of memory for every virtual machine and then compares the hash values. If a duplicate hash is found, a bit-by-bit comparison of the memory pages is performed to ensure that the memory pages are truly identical. If they are, then the content is stored only once in memory and the duplicate virtual machine page addresses point to the singly stored page, now shared. This seems like a great idea; unfortunately, with newer operating systems, Windows Server 2008 and later, it does not work well for many reasons.
>
> *(continues)*

(continued)

First, page sharing works best on empty pages; however, as you learned in the previous section, with Windows Vista and later, memory is rarely left empty—it is used to cache as much as possible.

Second, memory pages are getting bigger, much bigger. In the past, memory pages have been 4KB in size, so the chances of finding two or more 4KB pages with the same content across operating system instances were quite high; therefore, significant physical memory space would be saved by page sharing. However more recent Intel and AMD processors support large memory pages with a 2MB memory page size. At the OS level, Windows Vista and Windows Server 2008 and above (along with newer Linux operating systems) enable the use of large pages by default. The chances of finding duplicate 2MB memory pages is very slight, and the cost of comparing two large pages is very high, which is why as operating systems adopt large memory pages, page sharing loses its benefit.

Another factor is that Windows Vista and above use Address Space Load Randomization, which is a security technology that on Windows loads key components of the kernel into 1 of 256 possible locations, making it harder for malware to attack the kernel based on component location in memory, as the locations will vary on different instances of the OS and at each reboot. This means duplicate instances of the same operating system will not have the same content in the same locations for this memory content, which minimizes the effectiveness of page sharing—but only for a small part of the operating system content.

▶ *The Hyper-V host cannot access a disk that is passed through to a VM. It must be offline on the Hyper-V host. Pass-through disks may be used for very high I/O applications like SQL Server, but this is typically not required.*

VIRTUAL HARD DISKS

Processor and memory are very important resources to virtual machines, but storage is also critical. There are ways to enable a Windows Server 2008 R2 Hyper-V virtual machine to boot from a SAN by attaching to the LUN (Logical Unit Number, which is essentially a portion of space carved from a SAN) from the Hyper-V host and then mapping the disk directly to the VM using the pass-through disk capability of Hyper-V; however, in most cases virtual machines will have some dedicated storage.

As I just mentioned, one option is to use a *pass-through disk* whereby a virtual machine has connectivity mapped directly to physical disks; however, this requires the physical disk to be used exclusively by a single virtual machine, losing the benefits of abstraction because the virtual machine is now directly linked to a physical piece of hardware. Other features such as using *snapshots*, which provide a point-in-time saved state of a virtual machine, are not possible.

The most common, and the recommended, storage for a virtual machine is a virtual hard disk (VHD). In Windows Server 2008 R2, the VHD format is a core part of the operating system; and the performance of a VHD differs only negligibly from that of a pass-through disk. A VHD can be up to 2TB in size, and several different types of VHD are available:

▶ **Dynamically expanding:** This is the most popular format. Essentially, the virtual hard disk is created using a minimal amount of disk space, and as the disk is used the file expands on the file system to accommodate the data written to the disk up to the maximum size specified. This option makes the most efficient use of the disk space because space is not used on the physical hard drives unless necessary. In Windows Server 2008 a performance penalty was associated with dynamic disks because when a write was performed the file had to grow. Fortunately, the VHD implementation was rewritten in Windows Server 2008 R2 and this performance penalty is negligible. A dynamically expanding disk does not shrink as data is deleted unless a compact operation is performed.

▶ **Fixed size:** In this case the size specified for the virtual hard disk is allocated and used when the disk is created. For example, creating a 127GB fixed size virtual hard disk creates a 127GB VHD file on the Hyper-V server. This option is likely to result in a less fragmented virtual hard disk.

▶ **Differencing:** A differencing disk is a particular type of dynamically expanding disk that is linked to a parent virtual hard disk and only stores the changes from the parent hard disk. The parent may be either a fixed or dynamically expanding VHD; it may even be a differencing disk itself, relative to a further parent VHD.

Although there is little performance difference between a dynamic VHD and a fixed VHD in Windows Server 2008 R2, the recommendation for production environments is to use a fixed VHD. The primary reason is because when using dynamic VHDs, there is always the possibility that the underlying storage will run out of space, so as the dynamic VHD tries to grow it will fail, causing unpredictable results. That said, if a system has very well-defined processes to monitor disk space usage and issue alerts as needed, then the use of dynamic VHDs in production may be acceptable.

> ▶ VHDs can be mounted using Windows Server 2008 R2 disk management tools, and physical computers can boot from VHDs using the Boot from VHD feature available in Windows Server 2008 R2 and Enterprise and above versions of Windows 7.

> ▶ VHD is a standard published by Microsoft and used by other vendors, such as Citrix. You can find the specification at http://www.microsoft.com/download.

Virtual machines can have a number of VHDs attached to them, but a single VHD cannot be used by multiple virtual machines at the same time. Hyper-V supports both an IDE bus and a SCSI bus to connect VHDs to virtual machines. While the IDE bus must be used for DVD drives and the disk from which the virtual machine will boot, for all other VHDs the SCSI bus is recommended for best performance and maximum flexibility.

▶ A mix of pass-through and VHD disks is supported on any of the controllers.

Up to four devices can be connected over the two IDE controllers (two per controller), while up to 64 disks can be connected to each of the four supported SCSI controllers, enabling a possible total of up to 256 SCSI-connected disks. The SCSI controller also supports the hot-add of storage, enabling the addition of disks while a virtual machine is running, which can be very useful.

It is possible to perform conversions between dynamic and fixed VHDs using Hyper-V Manager and command-line tools. The conversion process creates a new VHD and copies the content from the source VHD to the target.

VIRTUAL NETWORKS

The last big resource for an operating system is network connectivity, and Hyper-V provides a number of network options for virtual machines. Each virtual network effectively creates a virtual switch on the VMBus within the host OS. Three different types of virtual networks, shown in Figure 8-10, can be created on the Hyper-V host, each with its own accessibility and use:

▶ **External virtual networks:** These are bound to a physical network card in the server, and both the Hyper-V host and virtual machines have access to the external network via the physical NIC and can also communicate with each other. The virtual machines each see one virtual network device, while the Hyper-V host sees two network devices. The first network device on the Hyper-V host is the physical NIC, which is bound only to the Microsoft Virtual Network Switch Protocol—meaning it is being used by a Hyper-V virtual network. The second network device seen on the Hyper-V host is a virtual network switch adapter that uses the created external network for communication, essentially bound to the physical NIC. This second network device that allows the Hyper-V host to use the virtual network is only available if the option to allow the management operating system to share this network adapter is configured on the virtual network, which is enabled by default. A great site to look at is http://technet.microsoft.com/en-us/library/ff428137(WS.10) .aspx, which describes the supported network configurations for Hyper-V servers depending on the use of services such as Failover Clustering, Live Migration, and iSCSI.

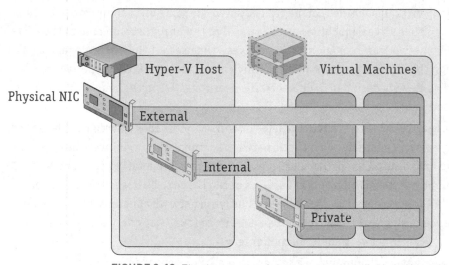

FIGURE 8-10: The three types of virtual network available in Hyper-V

▶ **Internal virtual networks:** These are not bound to a physical NIC and therefore cannot access any machine outside the physical server. An internal network can be used only for communication between virtual machines and between virtual machines and the Hyper-V host. This can be useful if you are hosting services on the parent partition, such as an iSCSI target, that you want the virtual machines to be able to use. On both the Hyper-V host and the virtual machines, a network device is visible that represents the interface to the internal virtual network.

▶ **Private virtual networks:** These enable the virtual machines to communicate with each other but not the host, and without any external connection. You may use this for a test network for VMs on a single box, or perhaps for VM-to-VM communication such as a guest cluster communication.

Once virtual networks are created, they can be connected to virtual network adapters that are added to virtual machines. The virtual machines then have access to whatever network to which the virtual network has connectivity. For access outside of the Hyper-V host, external networks must be used. In production environments, the network adapters used as part of an external network are often *teamed adapters*, a technology that enables multiple network adapters to be used as if they were a single network adapter. This can aggregate available bandwidth and provide resiliency against a network or switch failure by teaming multiple network adapters connected to different switches. NIC teaming is a feature of the network driver in Windows Server 2008 R2, not an actual Hyper-V or Windows Server feature.

▶ When connecting a virtual machine to an external network, ensure that the virtual machine is configured with an IP address and VLAN that match that of the network connected to via the external network; otherwise no communication is possible.

Many virtual machines can be connected to the same virtual networks; and when multiple virtual machines on the same Hyper-V host are connected to the same external network and communicating between themselves, the traffic never travels through the physical network adapter, which is a nice feature. The Hyper-V virtual switch is cleverly designed to detect traffic to another VM on the same host and pass it directly.

Virtual machines can have multiple network adapters added, which can be either legacy network adapters or synthetic network adapters. Legacy network adapters should only be used for virtual machines that will run an operating system that does not support Hyper-V Integration Services or that have to be booted over the network. All other scenarios should use the synthetic network adapter for optimal performance. A single virtual machine can have up to four legacy network adapters and eight synthetic network adapters configured.

If you have multiple Hyper-V servers that are configured in a cluster, it is important to have the same virtual networks defined on each server with the same name to ensure no loss of network connectivity when virtual machines are moved between servers. Use a consistent virtual network naming convention to avoid any confusion.

BASIC HYPER-V MANAGEMENT

The Hyper-V Manager is installed as part of the Hyper-V role, which enables configuration of the Hyper-V server settings, virtual networks, and virtual machines. The management tool also handles all the basic functions related to Hyper-V and VMs, such as starting, stopping, snapshots, exporting, and importing, although it is not intended for use with large-scale Hyper-V deployments. For a robust, full-featured Hyper-V management experience, the System Center 2012 product should be used, specifically System Center Virtual Machine Manager, which I cover in the next chapter.

Figure 8-11 shows the Hyper-V Manager (it actually shows the Windows Server 2012 Hyper-V Manager, but the Windows Server 2008 R2 Hyper-V Manager is nearly identical except for a few missing actions, like Virtual SAN Manager and Replication). As you can see, multiple Hyper-V servers can be managed using this tool, which displays all the virtual machines on the selected server along with key details such as its state, CPU usage, and assigned memory. Selecting a virtual machine will display actions related to it in the bottom-right corner, including connecting to the console of the virtual machine.

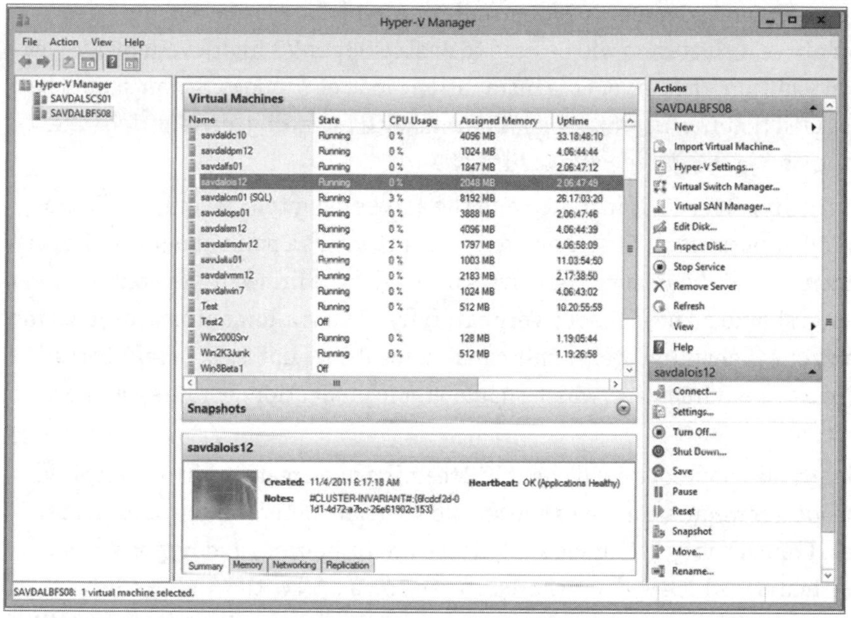

FIGURE 8-11: The basic Hyper-V Manager tool connected to two Hyper-V servers

Enabling remote management of a Hyper-V server requires performing a fairly complicated set of steps related to WMI Access, DCOM permissions, firewall exceptions, and Authorization Manager access. Fortunately, you can download a utility at http://code.msdn.microsoft.com/HVRemote/Release/ProjectReleases .aspx?ReleaseId=2338 that enables you to set up a user with the appropriate permissions for remote management on the Hyper-V server and make other necessary configuration changes on the server and client. Note that this utility makes the specified user an administrator of Hyper-V.

If you want to manage Hyper-V using PowerShell, there is no native Hyper-V PowerShell support in Windows Server 2008 R2. The solution is to use the PowerShell cmdlets that are part of System Center Virtual Machine Manager; alternately, there is also an excellent free PowerShell cmdlet library available at http://pshyperv .codeplex.com/releases/view/38769 that works with PowerShell v2.

HYPER-V SERVER SETTINGS

Once you understand the basic types of resource that can be assigned to a virtual machine, it's important to understand the configuration options possible on the Hyper-V server itself. As I have already discussed, Hyper-V is just a role that is enabled on a Windows Server 2008 R2 installation, which needs to be Enterprise Edition or above if clustering will be used to enable Hyper-V's high-availability capabilities. In addition, the Server Core installation mode of Windows Server should be used, provided that the organization is familiar with installing, configuring, and managing a Server Core Windows installation.

After the Hyper-V role is installed and the server rebooted, several configurations should be performed. First, however, I want to stress a point about your Hyper-V environment: its configuration, the drivers used, and the firmware versions of server components should all be managed very carefully. Do not allow automatic updating of servers via Windows Update, as this can include driver updates. Carefully test all updates in a test environment, which should mimic production, before applying them to production.

Earlier in the chapter I talked about NIC teaming and creating virtual networks, which are vital configuration items you should complete before adding any virtual machines. Connectivity to storage should also be configured, and Hyper-V hosts joined to clusters, which will use shared storage on a SAN with Windows Server 2008 R2, should all have the same storage connectivity. Ideally, MultiPath I/O (MPIO) is used for the connectivity to external storage, which, like NIC teaming, provides multiple paths to storage to minimize the chances of losing connectivity in the event of a hardware failure. You can also configure the default path for virtual machines and virtual machine hard disks, which should be set to one of the storage areas created for virtual machine storage.

VIRTUAL MACHINE SETTINGS

I have already emphasized the importance of carefully considering the configuration of processor, memory, disk, and network resources, including which networks the VM needs to connect to, based on demonstrated needs. The following list describes a few other key virtual machine attributes that may need to be configured:

► **BIOS startup order:** Remember that if a virtual machine needs to boot from the network, the virtual machine must have a legacy network adapter attached.

► **Virtual DVD drive:** Can be mapped to an ISO file or to a physical CD/DVD drive in the Hyper-V server

► **Two available COM ports:** Can be connected to a named pipe on a remote computer

- ▶ **Diskette drive:** Can be mapped to a virtual floppy disk (VFD) file
- ▶ **The name of and various notes about a virtual machine:** Can be stored in the configuration
- ▶ **Integration Services:** Select which should be offered on the virtual machine. A good example would be to disable the Time synchronization service for domain controllers, which have their own time synchronization technologies.
- ▶ **Snapshot storage location:** This is normally the same location as the virtual machine.
- ▶ **Default Start and Stop actions for virtual machines:** This can be useful because these actions dictate what happens to the virtual machine when the Hyper-V host is shut down and started. For the Stop action you can choose to save the virtual machine state to memory, shut down the virtual machine, or just turn it off. For Start actions, virtual machines can be configured to never start, to start if previously running at shutdown, or to always start. You can also specify a delay to starting the virtual machine, which is useful if, for example, you have a SQL Server virtual machine and a server application in another virtual machine that uses that SQL Server instance. On the server application virtual machine, a delay of 5 minutes could be set to ensure the SQL Server has started before starting the dependent virtual machine. I wrote my own MngVMs solution for shutting down and starting virtual machines; it is freely available at www.sav111tech.com/mngvms/.

▶ Do not use this for production virtual machines unless you are sure it won't harm the OS or the applications running in it. It's the same as pulling the plug on the server with no graceful shutdown.

REMOTE DESKTOP PROTOCOL AND HYPER-V

The link between Hyper-V and the Remote Desktop Protocol may not be apparent initially, but when you are looking at the list of configurable features for a virtual machine, you may notice one missing item: mapping of a USB device. Hyper-V does not support mapping a USB device on the Hyper-V host to a virtual machine. If a USB device needs to be connected to a virtual machine, then the only solution is to connect the USB device to a user's workstation and then use RDP to connect the workstation to the virtual machine, which can access the USB device via RDP. This may not meet every USB requirement but it's the best option available. RDP is also used to connect to virtual machines for interactive sessions.

CROSSREF Interacting with virtual machines over RDP, including connecting USB devices, is covered in Chapter 11.

LICENSING

I want to touch on only one aspect of licensing regarding Windows Server 2012 and Hyper-V, and that is virtual instance rights. The final row of Table 8-1 provides the following information about virtual instances per license:

- ▶ Windows Server 2008 R2 Standard: Host + 1
- ▶ Windows Server 2008 R2 Enterprise: Host + 4
- ▶ Windows Server 2008 R2 Datacenter Edition: Unlimited
- ▶ Microsoft Hyper-V Server 2008 R2: None

▶ Only the Hyper-V role can be enabled. If the physical server is running other roles as well, such as a print server or domain controller, then that server counts as a virtual instance, so only three virtual machines would be covered.

Before virtualization, different editions of Windows Server were purchased because of enhanced features, such as Failover Clustering in Enterprise editions and above, and additional hardware capabilities. Those reasons still apply, but with virtualization there is another consideration: virtual instance rights. When you purchase Windows Server you have purchased the right to install the operating system on a specific piece of hardware. Virtual instance rights also provide permissions to run that operating system on a virtual machine on that same piece of hardware. This means if the Enterprise Edition is purchased, then Windows Server 2008 R2 Enterprise is installed on a physical server and the Hyper-V role is enabled. The Enterprise license also allows you to install Windows Server 2008 R2 on four virtual machines running on that server. The virtual machines are still tied to that physical server; the virtual instance rights cannot be moved around between servers. Additional virtual machines can be created on the server and have Windows Server installed on them, but only four can be running on that server at any one time. Licenses can be moved between servers every 90 days. This is important in some scenarios. For example, suppose you create a two-node cluster of Hyper-V servers running Enterprise Edition that allows the two nodes to share storage and move resources, such as virtual machines, between them. Each Hyper-V host could run four virtual machines per the Enterprise Edition virtual instance rights. Now suppose you want to move the virtual machines from host 1 to host 2 so maintenance can be performed on host 1. You can do this, but you could not move them back for 90 days, as that would be moving the license between servers. This is not a Hyper-V restriction; these are the terms of the Microsoft Windows Server license and would also apply if Windows Server virtual machines were running on any other available hypervisor.

The solution is to use Windows Server Datacenter Edition, which is licensed on a per physical processor basis and allows an unlimited number of virtual machines to be running on the server. This means there is no problem moving virtual machines between servers in a cluster or even outside of clusters.

In my experience, organizations always use the Datacenter Edition unless Hyper-V is running in a branch location with a single server that only runs a couple of virtual machines. For any other scenario Datacenter is a better option. There is a caveat. The virtual instance rights are for Windows Server operating systems and not Windows client operating systems. You cannot install Windows Server Datacenter Edition and then run 200 virtual machines running Windows 7; you would need to license each version of Windows 7, and license it in the correct way, to be able to use it in a virtual environment. If a server is running only client virtual machines, such as in a virtual desktop infrastructure environment, or even running non-Windows operating systems such as Linux, then the virtual instance rights that are part of Windows Server are not usable to legitimize the virtual machines.

This is why Microsoft released Microsoft Hyper-V Server 2008 R2, which is a free download that is essentially Windows Server 2008 R2 Enterprise Edition with only the Server Core install option and only the Hyper-V role available. It supports clustering and other features of Windows Server and is designed to be used in environments where the Hyper-V solution is required but the virtual instance rights are not. Why pay for Windows Server if you just need the free Microsoft Hyper-V download? It behaves exactly the same as a Server Core installation of Windows Server.

Using Backups, Exports, Imports, and Snapshots

With virtualization the number of operating system instances running on a single piece of hardware is increased greatly, which also means the effect of any hardware failure or disk corruption is that much greater. When virtualizing in production environments, it's very rare to use disks that are local to a server. Instead, external disk subsystems like SANs are used, as they offer better performance, higher utilization of storage, better redundancy protection against hardware failure, and the capability for volumes to be accessed simultaneously by multiple Hyper-V servers in the same cluster. However, all these capabilities of a SAN cannot protect against logical corruption due to file system failures, so the use of backups is still critical.

▶ A logical corruption is a corruption that is within the stored data.

BACKING UP WITH HYPER-V

For many generations, Windows Server has used the Volume Shadow Copy Service (VSS), which provides facilities that enable application vendors to register special VSS Writers with the operating system when the application is installed. All VSS Writers registered on an operating system are called during a shadow copy backup initiated by a VSS-aware backup program. The VSS Writers ensure that all data on disk for

▶ This is a fancy term for pausing writes to disk during the shadow copy process.

the application is in an application-consistent state and that further writes are quiesced while the backup is taken, maintaining the integrity of the on-disk data being backed up. An *application-consistent backup* means that the data is in a suitable state to be restored and used without corruption problems.

When a backup is taken at the Hyper-V host level of all the virtual machine assets—primarily the VHD files—ordinarily the virtual machines are unaware of it, so the data backed up is probably not in an application-consistent state. The Hyper-V Integration Services includes a backup (volume snapshot) service that enables the Hyper-V host to notify each virtual machine when a VSS backup is taken. The following steps outline the process to ensure that backups of the virtual machines are in an application-consistent state:

1. The backup software (the VSS Requestor) on the Hyper-V server makes a request for a VSS snapshot and enumerates the VSS Writers on the system to ascertain the data that can be backed up with VSS—for example, the Hyper-V VSS Writer.

2. The Hyper-V VSS Writer (in conjunction with the VSS Coordination Service) forwards the VSS snapshot request to each guest operating system via the Backup Integration Service.

3. Each guest operating system acts as though it is receiving a native VSS Request and proceeds to notify all VSS Writers on the guest to prepare for a snapshot.

4. Each VSS Writer in the guest operating systems writes any outstanding information to disk that relates to its service (e.g., Exchange, SQL Server) and notifies the VSS Coordination Service that it is ready for a snapshot and which data to back up (although this part is ignored because we'll be backing up the entire VHD from the Hyper-V host).

5. The Backup Integration Service for each VM tells the Hyper-V VSS Writer it is ready for a snapshot to be taken, and the Hyper-V VSS Writer notifies the backup application via the VSS Coordinator that it is ready for a snapshot.

6. The backup software takes a VSS snapshot of the file system containing the virtual configuration files and the virtual hard disks. All data on the virtual hard disks is consistent, thanks to the VSS Request being passed into the virtual machines. Once the snapshot is taken, the VSS Writer notifies the Hyper-V guests that the snapshot is complete, and they continue their normal processing.

Note that only VHD content is backed up using this method. If a virtual machine has pass-through storage or iSCSI storage connected through the guest OS iSCSI Initiator, then that content is not part of a backup at the Hyper-V server level through the Hyper-V VSS Writer. The scenario just outlined describes an *online backup*, also known as Child VM Snapshot, where the guest operating system meets the following requirements:

▶ Integration Services are installed, with the Backup Integration Service enabled.

▶ It supports VSS.

▶ It uses NTFS file systems with basic disks (not dynamic).

If you have guest operating systems that use dynamic disks, use non-NTFS partitions, don't have Integration Services installed, or don't have the Backup Integration Service enabled, or if the OS is just not supported (Windows 2000), then an offline backup of the virtual machine will be taken, also known as a *saved state backup*. This is because virtual machines that can't support an online backup are placed into a saved state during the VSS snapshot, which means there is a period of downtime for the virtual machine during the backup. Operating systems that have to use saved state include Windows 2000, Windows XP, NT 4, and Linux. Windows 2003, 2008, and Vista and above all support the online backup method with no virtual machine downtime.

If you have guest operating systems that can't use the Hyper-V pass-through VSS capability, then perform backups within the virtual machine guest operating system. However, even when it's not required there are times when backing up within the virtual machine guest operating system provides a better level of functionality than a Hyper-V backup, depending on the backup application. As an example of a backup solution I use System Center Data Protection Manager (DPM), which is Microsoft's premium backup and recovery solution for Microsoft workloads. When you have installed the DPM agent on the Hyper-V server, the main DPM administrator console provides a level of granularity at the virtual machine level, which means you can select which virtual machines to protect but not what to protect within them. Conversely, if you deploy the DPM agent into each guest operating system, from the console you have complete access to the detailed information available through DPM. For example, if the virtual machine were running SQL Server, you would be able to select which databases to protect, including the capability to capture the transaction logs, and so on. The restore granularity would be the same, so sometimes the best functionality can be realized by performing backups from within the guest OS.

▶ Be sure to regularly test restoring the backups you take. I have often seen companies try to restore a backup when it was really needed and it failed, or the right information was not actually being backed up.

▶ Snapshots cannot be taken if a virtual machine uses pass-through storage.

Regardless of what other technologies are used, such as replication, multiple instances of applications, or even snapshots, none of these can replace backups. Backups should always be taken regularly for complete protection against all types of failure.

CREATING AND USING HYPER-V SNAPSHOTS

One frequently overlooked feature of Hyper-V is the snapshot feature. Snapshots enable point-in-time views of a virtual machine to be saved. A snapshot can be created when the virtual machine is turned off or when running. If a snapshot is taken when a virtual machine is running, the current memory and device state is saved in addition to the virtual hard disk state that is taken when a snapshot is taken of a stopped virtual machine. Taking a snapshot creates a number of files:

- ▶ **XML file:** Contains a copy of the VM configuration file prior to the snapshot
- ▶ **VSV file:** Contains the state of devices associated with the virtual machine. This is created only when a snapshot is taken of a running virtual machine.
- ▶ **BIN file:** Contains the memory content of the virtual machine. This is created only when a snapshot is taken of a running virtual machine.
- ▶ **AVHD file:** To capture the state of the virtual hard disks, the differencing VHD capability is used. The current virtual hard disk state is frozen and marked read-only, and this is what the snapshot points to. A new differencing disk is created that uses the existing VHD as the parent. The VM configuration XML file is updated to point to this new differencing AVHD file so all future disk writes are written to the new file.

Entire hierarchies of snapshots can be created and each snapshot can be custom-named, making it easy to understand what each snapshot represents. Snapshots can then be applied to a virtual machine, reverting it back to the state it was in when the snapshot was created.

How snapshots should be used is frequently debated. They are not replacements for backups, but they are very useful in development and testing environments. Snapshots enable you to save the state of an operating system, make some changes, and then revert back to the state before the changes were ever made. For a developer, the capability to freeze a system at the point of a problem and be able to revert back to that problem state repeatedly is invaluable.

Using snapshots in production environments is generally discouraged, and in some cases it is hazardous. For example, it is known to cause problems for some types of services, such as Active Directory Domain Services. Taking a snapshot of a domain controller and then reverting the domain controller to that snapshot can result in replication problems, duplicate security identifiers, and therefore security vulnerabilities; I cover this in some detail in Chapter 15.

EXPORTING AND IMPORTING VIRTUAL MACHINES

Sometimes you need to move a virtual machine between Hyper-V hosts that are not clustered, or you simply no longer need a virtual machine but want to keep it in storage in case it is ever needed. Just copying the virtual machine's folder that contains its configuration and virtual hard disk files will not allow the virtual machine to be read back into Hyper-V. Instead, you need to use the Export action, which saves a copy of the virtual machine's storage and configuration to a specified folder in a format that can then be imported back into a Hyper-V server later. To export a virtual machine, the virtual machine must not be running and should be in an off state.

▶ Windows Server 2012 Hyper-V can do exactly this!

When importing a virtual machine it is possible to perform the import using new identifiers for the virtual machine, which enables exported virtual machine files to be used to create another virtual machine. Alternatively, the import can be performed reusing the old identifiers in the export, in which case the export will re-create the original virtual machine.

Implementing High Availability, Live Migration, and Cluster Shared Volumes

Before covering high availability and other mobility technologies, I want to quickly review the failover clustering capabilities of Windows Server at a very high level, as they are the foundation for all the Hyper-V high-availability capabilities. *Failover Clustering* is a Windows Server 2008 R2 Enterprise and Datacenter feature that needs to be enabled on each server. Once the Failover Clustering feature is enabled, adding servers to a cluster enables the servers to share access to external storage, and services defined in the cluster can be moved between the servers. Figure 8-12 shows a basic two-node cluster that is offering a single service. In this example one of the nodes is offering a service, which has a name, an IP address, and uses some shared storage. The other node is passive, but if something happens to the active node the service can move over to the passive node, which would then become active.

▶ *Node* is the term used for a server that is part of a cluster.

When designing your cluster environments, be careful to avoid any single points of failure. The whole point of a cluster is to provide a high-availability environment. Use redundant power supplies in servers, uninterruptable power supplies, multiple network connections using different switches, and multiple paths to storage. Examine every connection and component and try to ensure there are no single points of failure.

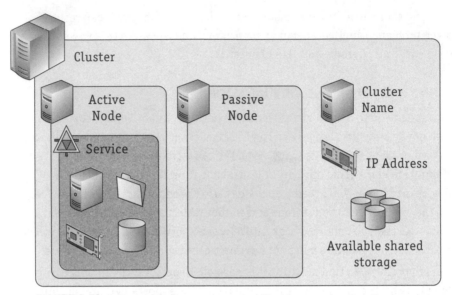

FIGURE 8-12: A cluster has its own name and IP address and optionally shared storage, which is available to all nodes in the cluster.

In Windows Server 2008 R2, a cluster can have up to 16 nodes. There is no need to have passive nodes: all nodes in the cluster can be offering services (*active/active* mode), although it is recommended to have at least one node not normally running services (*active/passive* mode). Either way, you must ensure that there is sufficient spare capacity on the remaining nodes to run services in the event of one or more nodes failing or being taken offline for maintenance. Failover Clustering provides many capabilities, including handling splits in communication between parts of the cluster, using quorum calculations to ensure that only one partition of the cluster runs services, avoiding, for example, the risk of database corruption. For overviews of failover quorum, creating and validating a failover cluster, and high-availability networking, see www.savilltech.com/videos/ClusterQuorum/ClusterQuorum .wmv, www.savilltech.com/videos/clustercreate/ClusterCreate.wmv, and www .savilltech.com/videos/2008R2Networks/2008R2Networks8006001mbps.wmv.

Hyper-V uses Failover Clustering to provide its high-availability capabilities, to allow the migration of virtual machines between nodes, and to automatically restart virtual machines on another node in the cluster if the node a virtual machine is running on crashes. There is a big difference between unplanned and planned outages. In an unplanned outage, a server just turns off without warning, and without a clean shutdown process. This might result from a worker pulling out the power supply by mistake or a server suffering a critical hardware failure. Whatever the reason, there is no opportunity to move virtual machines to another host cleanly, maintaining state from before the failure. Therefore, in the event of an unplanned failure, when the failover cluster logic determines that the server is not available, its only option is to distribute the virtual machines across the remaining hosts in the cluster and restart them. The virtual machines will be in a crash-consistent state because the operating system was not cleanly shut down within the VM when the host crashed.

Planned scenarios, obviously, enable a much richer set of features that allow virtual machines to be moved without any disruption of availability and therefore no impact on end users. Planned scenarios include taking a Hyper-V host down for hardware maintenance or rebooting to apply patches. The functionality to move virtual machines between hosts in a cluster has been greatly improved between Windows Server 2008 and Windows Server 2008 R2 Hyper-V.

Windows Server 2008 had a feature called *Quick Migrate* that enabled a quick migration by suspending the virtual machine on the source node, writing the content of the memory, processor, and device registers related to the VM to a file on the shared storage, moving the LUN containing the configuration and virtual hard disks to the target node, and then reading the memory and so on from the file into a new VM created on the target node. After all this is done the VM is available again. If this sounds like a time-consuming operation, it is; and it results in a period of unavailability, meaning clients with connections to the VM experience service interruption (in real terms, the process requires around 8 seconds per 1GB of memory configured to the VM).

Quick Migrate was not seen as a production-quality solution, as other vendors offered the capability to move virtual machines between servers with no downtime. This capability is needed for features such as *dynamic placement optimization*, which moves virtual machines between hosts automatically to balance out load among multiple servers. Quick Migrate requires a service interruption for two reasons:

▶ The virtual machine has to be paused to freeze its memory so it can be copied to the target node.

▶ The LUN ownership has to be moved from one node to another, requiring a dismount and mount operation of the physical disk resource, which takes time. NTFS is a "shared nothing" file system, which means two different computers cannot mount the same NTFS volume at the same time. That's why the NTFS LUN containing the virtual machine must be dismounted and then mounted on the new target server.

To enable a zero downtime migration solution, both these challenges had to be overcome, and this is exactly what happened in Windows Server 2008 R2, which introduced the zero downtime Live Migration capability, which works in conjunction

▶ Crash-consistent state refers to the state of an operating system and its applications when the OS is turned off without a clean shutdown. The OS and application data may be in a dirty state, and recovery processes may be required.

▶ Of course, users don't care if Hyper-V hosts have to be taken down for maintenance. Users only care if the virtual machines are taken offline, interrupting access to services.

with the Cluster Shared Volumes (CSV) feature, also new to this version. By pairing these two features, the virtual machine no longer had to be paused to copy its memory, and LUNs no longer had to be moved between hosts because all hosts in a cluster could access CSVs at the same time.

It is not possible to copy a running virtual machine's memory to another node in a single-copy pass because as the memory is being copied, the VM is still changing parts of it. Although the copy is occurring from memory to memory over very fast networks, it still takes a finite amount of time. The virtual machine cannot be paused to perform the copy, as that would interrupt connections and cause an outage. The solution is to take an iterative approach, as shown in Figure 8-13 and explained in the following steps:

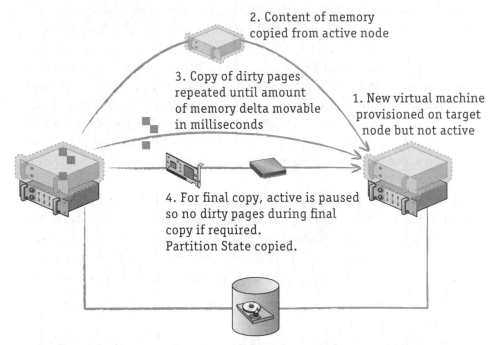

2. Content of memory copied from active node

3. Copy of dirty pages repeated until amount of memory delta movable in milliseconds

1. New virtual machine provisioned on target node but not active

4. For final copy, active is paused so no dirty pages during final copy if required.
Partition State copied.

FIGURE 8-13: Four main stages of the live migration process

1. The first step of live migration copies the virtual machine's configuration and device information from the source node to the target node, which creates a shell virtual machine to act as a container and receive the virtual machine's memory and state.

2. This stage transfers the virtual machine memory, which is the bulk of the information copied and takes up the bulk of the time required for a live migration. Remember that the virtual machine is still running, so a

mechanism is needed that tracks pages of memory that change during the copy. To achieve that, the virtual machine worker process on the source node creates a "dirty bitmap" of memory pages used by the virtual machine and registers for modify-notifications on those pages. When a memory page is modified, the bitmap is updated to indicate that. Once the first pass of the memory copy is complete, all the pages of memory that have been marked dirty in the memory map are recopied to the target. This time, only the changed pages are copied, which means there are far fewer pages to copy and the operation should be much faster; however, keep in mind that while these pages are being copied, other memory pages may change, so this memory copy process repeats itself.

3. With each iteration of memory copy, the amount of data to copy should shrink and the time to copy should decrease; eventually a point should be reached where all the memory has been copied and the VM can be switched. However, this may not always be the case, which is why there is a limit to the number of memory copy passes that are performed; otherwise, the memory copy might repeat forever.

4. When the memory pages have all been copied, or the maximum number of copy operations is reached, it is time to switch the virtual machine to execute on the target node. To make this switch, the VM is suspended on the source node, and any residual dirty memory pages are copied to the target along with the device and register state of the VM.

5. Control of any storage associated with the VM is transferred from the source node to the target node.

6. The virtual machine is resumed on the target node.

7. The final step is the target node sends out an unsolicited ARP reply indicating that the IP address used by the virtual machine has moved to a new location (MAC address), which causes routing devices to update their tables. It is from this moment that clients resume communication with the VM, but on the target node. While there is a momentary suspension of the virtual machine, which is required to copy the state information, it lasts only milliseconds, below the TCP connection timeout threshold. This is the goal, as it means client connections are not broken during the live migration process and users are unlikely to notice anything.

8. Once the migration to the target is complete, a notification is sent to the previous host indicating that it can discard the migrated VM and clean up the virtual machine environment.

While Live Migration takes care of moving the memory of a virtual machine with no downtime, recall that the second reason for downtime with Quick Migrate was caused by moving the LUN containing the virtual machine's assets, as an NTFS LUN cannot be accessed by multiple nodes simultaneously. Cluster Shared Volumes (CSV) solves this by making LUNs with NTFS volumes available to all nodes in a cluster simultaneously. Cluster disks are configured to be CSV, which makes them available to every node in the cluster as part of a shared ClusterStorage namespace. The ClusterStorage namespace is visible as C:\ClusterStorage on every node, with LUNs that are CSV-enabled viewable on every node as subfolders of ClusterStorage, such as C:\ClusterStorage\Volume1, C:\ClusterStorage\Volume2, and so on. With every node in the cluster being able to see the CSV content at the same time, it is no longer necessary to move LUNs between hosts, removing the other obstacle to a zero downtime migration solution. For details on Hyper-V use of networks in a CSV scenario and how CSV works behind the scenes, see my video at www.savilltech.com/videos/CSVDeepDive/CSVDeepDive.wmv. In Windows Server 2008 R2, CSV can only be used to store virtual machines; it is not supported for any other type of workload.

WARNING I recently purchased a box cutter from the hardware store. I rushed home to use the new box cutter but found it packaged in hard plastic that could only be opened *with a box cutter*. The irony of this was not lost on me: I needed the instrument within the packaging to get the instrument out of the packaging. This is the same situation you may face when hosting domain controllers on Hyper-V hosts that are part of a failover cluster.

For a failover cluster to function, it must contact Active Directory, which provides its security and cluster objects. This means a domain controller for the domain must be available. Until the cluster is started, the virtual machines within it cannot be started. If the domain controllers are virtual machines on the cluster, then the cluster cannot start because the domain controller virtual machines are not running—and the domain controller virtual machines cannot start because the cluster is not started.

The solution is to have at least one physical domain controller available, or at least have a domain controller on a Hyper-V server that is not clustered. Putting domain controllers on different Hyper-V clusters does not provide protection because in the event of a complete site power down, all clusters would be shut down.

This problem is resolved in Windows Server 2012, which can start the cluster without having to contact a domain controller. (By the way, I was eventually able to get the box cutter out with only a few plastic cuts to my hands.)

USING HYPER-V WITH WINDOWS SERVER 2012

Windows Server 2008 R2 SP1 provided solid virtualization capabilities with features such as Dynamic Memory, Cluster Shared Volumes, and Live Migration; and all those capabilities are present in Windows Server 2012 Hyper-V, too. However, the additional changes related to Hyper-V and the complementary Windows Server 2012 features are nothing short of phenomenal. Microsoft Hyper-V Server 2012 and Windows Server 2012 provide the best platform for virtualization.

I have done a lot of Windows Server 2012 briefings, and Figure 8-14 shows the first slide I use for Windows Server 2012 Hyper-V features. It shows the main new capabilities—not all of them, just the major ones. This gives you some idea of the sheer scale of improvements in this version. In this section, I cover the major Hyper-V features introduced in Windows Server 2012 that can greatly affect how machine virtualization is implemented in your organization and how it stacks up against the competition.

▶ Live Migration is critical to organizations. No new feature breaks the ability to move a virtual machine between servers without downtime.

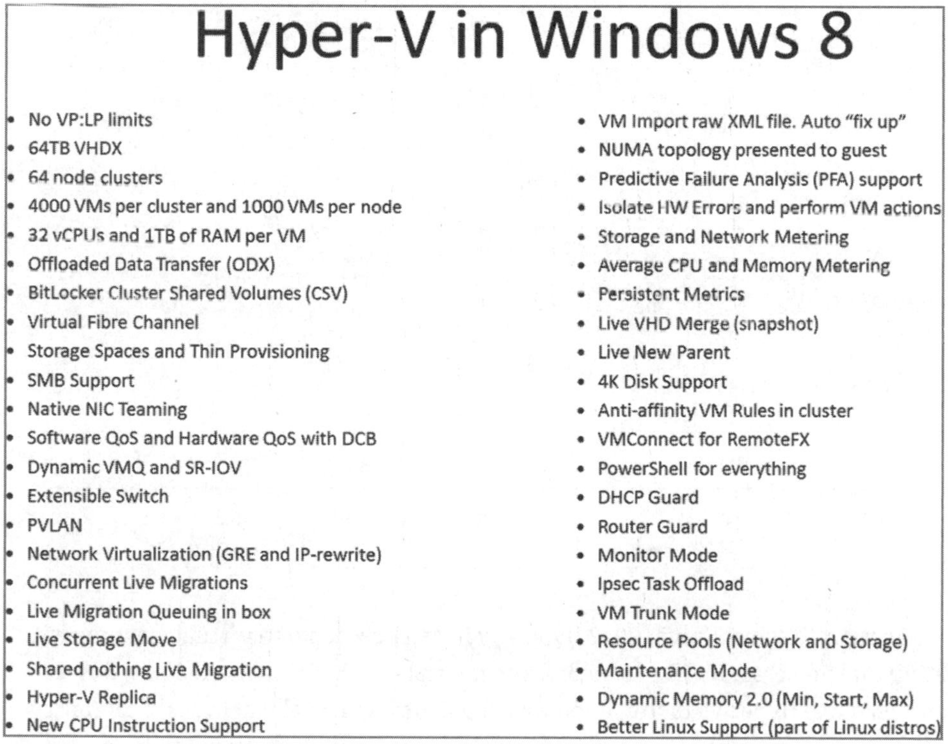

Hyper-V in Windows 8

- No VP:LP limits
- 64TB VHDX
- 64 node clusters
- 4000 VMs per cluster and 1000 VMs per node
- 32 vCPUs and 1TB of RAM per VM
- Offloaded Data Transfer (ODX)
- BitLocker Cluster Shared Volumes (CSV)
- Virtual Fibre Channel
- Storage Spaces and Thin Provisioning
- SMB Support
- Native NIC Teaming
- Software QoS and Hardware QoS with DCB
- Dynamic VMQ and SR-IOV
- Extensible Switch
- PVLAN
- Network Virtualization (GRE and IP-rewrite)
- Concurrent Live Migrations
- Live Migration Queuing in box
- Live Storage Move
- Shared nothing Live Migration
- Hyper-V Replica
- New CPU Instruction Support

- VM Import raw XML file. Auto "fix up"
- NUMA topology presented to guest
- Predictive Failure Analysis (PFA) support
- Isolate HW Errors and perform VM actions
- Storage and Network Metering
- Average CPU and Memory Metering
- Persistent Metrics
- Live VHD Merge (snapshot)
- Live New Parent
- 4K Disk Support
- Anti-affinity VM Rules in cluster
- VMConnect for RemoteFX
- PowerShell for everything
- DHCP Guard
- Router Guard
- Monitor Mode
- Ipsec Task Offload
- VM Trunk Mode
- Resource Pools (Network and Storage)
- Maintenance Mode
- Dynamic Memory 2.0 (Min, Start, Max)
- Better Linux Support (part of Linux distros)

FIGURE 8-14: New features of Windows Server 2012 Hyper-V

Scalability Changes

Four virtual CPUs and 64GB of memory per virtual machine seemed like plenty when Hyper-V was first introduced, as did 2TB VHD files; but as larger workloads are being virtualized, including very large-scale servers, more scalability needs to be available to virtual machines and to the Hyper-V host itself. Windows Server 2012 provides a big increase to all the scalability numbers related to Hyper-V, as summarized in Table 8-2, which compares the Windows 2008 R2 number and the Windows Server 2012 number. Note that this table is accurate at the time of writing; these numbers could be higher for the final release.

TABLE 8-2: Scalability Improvements from Windows Server 2008 R2 to Windows Server 2012 Related to Hyper-V

SYSTEM	RESOURCE	WINDOWS 2008 R2 MAXIMUM	WINDOWS SERVER 2012 BETA MAXIMUM	IMPROVEMENT FACTOR
Host	Logical processors	64	160	2.5x
Host	Physical memory	1TB	2TB	2x
Host	Virtual processors per host	512	1024	2x
Virtual Machine	vCPUs per VM	4	32	8x
Virtual Machine	Memory per VM	64GB	1TB	16x
Virtual Machine	Max virtual disk size	2TB	64TB	32x
Cluster	Nodes	16	64	4x
Cluster	Virtual Machines	1000	4000	4x

So with Windows Server 2012 Hyper-V you can now deploy a virtual machine with 32 virtual processors, 1TB of memory, and multiple 64TB virtual hard disks, hosted on a 64-node Hyper-V cluster along with 3,999 other virtual machines. Scalability is just one aspect of the improvements, but it helps Hyper-V be a good fit for even the largest workloads. Additionally, the previous ratio of logical processor to virtual processor supported has been removed, with Windows Server 2012 enabling any ratio that works in your environment.

Before moving on to other functionality areas I want to briefly touch on *Non-Uniform Memory Access (NUMA)*. As central processors got faster, access to the memory became a performance bottleneck because the CPU stalled waiting for data. Subsequent developments included the introduction of high-speed, on-chip cache memory, in an attempt to limit the memory accesses required, and direct memory access channels that linked memory banks directly to processors. Newer systems have multiple processors, which tend to exacerbate the problem. One common multiple-processor architecture is *Symmetric Multi-Processing (SMP)*, in which all the processors have the same access to all memory, but this clearly does nothing to resolve the performance problem. A multi-processor chip design conforming to NUMA solves this by pairing certain memory banks with specific processors, together known as a *NUMA node*. With NUMA, while executing an instruction thread of a process, the operating system scheduler attempts to use memory and processor from the same NUMA node, ensuring the fastest memory access. Figure 8-15 shows my Intel dual-processor server, which has two NUMA nodes, one for each processor, and attached memory; Windows Server 2012 enables Task Manager to show a NUMA node view.

▶ Ensure that your server BIOS has the memory mode option set to NUMA, not SMP, for best performance with Hyper-V.

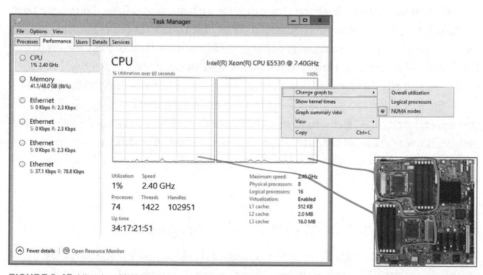

FIGURE 8-15: Viewing NUMA nodes in Windows Server 2012

▶ The best NUMA configuration leaves the settings alone, as Hyper-V will determine the best configuration. The settings are available for advanced scenarios, but you should never need to change them for normal operation.

NUMA was not a big concern previously with virtual machines that had a maximum of four virtual CPUs; but when you have virtual machines with 32 virtual CPUs, NUMA becomes a much bigger issue because virtual machines could start to cross NUMA nodes and memory usage becomes very important. The mapping of virtual processors onto logical processors becomes a performance issue for the hypervisor, which needs to be NUMA-aware. With Dynamic Memory enabled, the memory used by a VM can grow, which increases the chances that it will use physical memory outside the NUMA node. The capability to span NUMA nodes, which means virtual machines can access memory on other NUMA nodes, is a configurable option for the Hyper-V host, enabled by default; and for each virtual machine, several NUMA configurations are possible related to NUMA topology and usage. Fortunately, the default settings are optimal for nearly all environments and should not require modification.

Dynamic Memory has also been improved. In addition to the startup and maximum amount of RAM, you can set a new minimum amount of RAM. The idea behind the minimum amount of RAM is that some virtual machines might initially require 1024MB of RAM for startup, so those VMs have to be configured with that amount of memory; after the virtual machine is started, however, it no longer needs that amount, but Hyper-V couldn't take back memory below the startup RAM value. With the new minimum RAM option, the example virtual machine can have a minimum value of 512MB set, allowing Hyper-V to reclaim memory when the virtual machine no longer needs it.

▶ You can specify a particular disk as the Smart Paging file location, so using a solid-state disk would be a good fit for best performance.

Another memory-related setting is *Smart Paging*, which Microsoft has introduced to resolve an anomalous situation that can arise with minimum RAM. Consider a host running many VMs around their minimum RAM allocation but below their startup requirement, for example a densely populated VDI server with many idle desktops. The host can be running steadily, having allocated all the physical memory, but a VM cannot be restarted as there is insufficient free memory to cover the startup requirement. Smart Paging is an enhancement to Dynamic Memory that is applicable in these specific circumstances to ensure that virtual machines have enough memory to restart. It uses disk as additional temporary memory just to bridge the gap; once the VM has restarted, Hyper-V can shrink the memory used back down to the minimum, which will be within the physical memory.

Storage Enhancements and Live Storage Move

▶ The share must be running on Windows Server 2012 and the virtual machine must be hosted on Windows Server 2012 Hyper-V.

Windows Server 2012 introduces a new version of the Storage Message Block (SMB) protocol, version 2.2. This new version offers several improvements, described in Chapter 15, but the one that concerns us here makes it possible to host Hyper-V virtual machines on an SMB file share. Different Hyper-V servers that are part of clusters or even standalone can access virtual machines on the same SMB share. The SMB file share itself can be standalone or part of a cluster, and a great new feature in Windows Server 2012 enables multiple file servers in a cluster to serve the same file share namespace. The use of file shares is shown in Figure 8-16. Note that both the virtual machine configuration and virtual hard disks are stored on the file share.

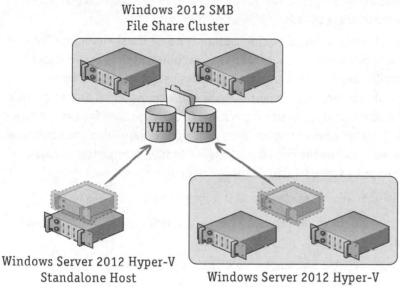

FIGURE 8-16: Windows Server 2012 Hyper-V environments with virtual machines stored on a Windows Server 2012 file share

Specific permissions are required on the NTFS file system and the SMB share itself in order to use the file share to store virtual machines. The computer accounts of each Hyper-V server need full control of both the folder and the share, and the administrator creating the virtual machines also needs full control on the file system and share. The easiest way to do this is from the command prompt. Run the following commands to create the folder and set the NTFS permissions for Hyper-V servers (serva and servb) plus the domain administrators:

```
md C:\HVShare
ICACLS C:\HVShare /Inheritance:R
ICACLS C:\HVShare /Grant "domainname\domain admins:(CI)(OI)F"
ICACLS C:\HVShare /Grant domainname\serva$:(CI)(OI)F
ICACLS C:\HVShare /Grant domainname\servb$:(CI)(OI)F
```

Next run the following PowerShell cmdlet to create the share with the same full control permissions (run within a PowerShell window as a single line):

```
New-SmbShare -Name HVShare -Path C:\HVShare -FullAccess
        "domainname\domain admins:(CI)(OI)F",
        domainname\serva$, domainname\servb$
```

▶ You cannot host the SMB file share on a Hyper-V server that will then have virtual machines stored on the file share. It does not work and is not supported. Host the SMB share on another server or even a virtual machine.

Many other scenarios, such as clustering, are possible, and Microsoft has a very good blog at http://blogs.technet.com/b/josebda/archive/2012/03/06/windows-server-quot-8-quot-beta-test-cases-for-hyper-v-over-smb.aspx that covers several and the permissions required.

The support of running virtual machines stored on SMB file shares means Hyper-V now supports both block-level storage for virtual machines, such as direct attached storage and storage area networks, and file-level storage using SMB. This new storage flexibility makes it even more important to be able to move the virtual machine's storage without downtime to the virtual machine. *Live Storage Move* is a new feature that enables a virtual machine's storage, such as its virtual hard disks and configuration files, to be moved while the virtual machine is running. Moving the storage of a virtual machine can be very useful in a variety of scenarios:

- ▶ Moving a virtual machine from local storage to a SAN

- ▶ Moving virtual machines between SANs for rebalancing of I/O or to perform maintenance on a SAN

- ▶ Moving some virtual machines to an SMB share

- ▶ Emptying an NTFS volume of VMs so you can run a chkdsk operation

▶ Another storage improvement is that merging storage when a snapshot is deleted no longer requires the virtual machine to be stopped. Merging now happens while the virtual machine is running—a big improvement over 2008 R2 Hyper-V!

Whatever the reason, Live Storage Move enables you to move VM files between all supported storage media—direct attached, SAN, and file-based (SMB)—with no downtime to the virtual machine. Live Storage Move works using the following three phases (as shown in Figure 8-17):

1. An initial copy of the data is made to the destination storage, which includes the VHD files, configuration files, snapshots, and everything related to the virtual machine. During this time the virtual machine continues to read and write to the source storage.

2. Once the initial copy is complete, the VHD stack mirrors all writes to both the source and the destination storage location, while a single pass of copying any blocks changed during the initial copy occurs.

3. Now that the source and the destination are synchronized, the VHD stack switches the VM to read and write only to the target storage. It then deletes the data on the source storage. This completes a full move of the storage associated with a VM with no downtime.

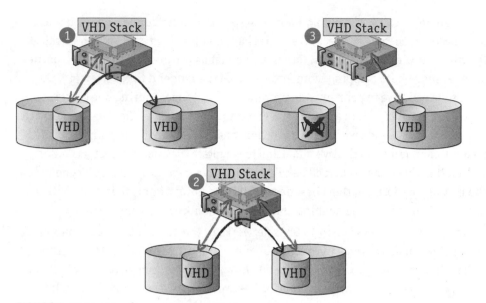

FIGURE 8-17: The Live Storage Move process

Virtual Machine Mobility

The addition of Live Migration in Windows Server 2008 R2 was a huge improvement for virtual machine placement flexibility, enabling moving virtual machines within a cluster with no downtime; however, in some scenarios even more flexibility is needed. One aspect of Live Migration that was poorly understood by many organizations was that only one live migration operation was supported concurrently between a pair of hosts in a cluster. A live migration action is highly network intensive because all the memory is copied over the network between the hosts. As I explained earlier in this chapter, because the VM is still running during the memory copy, several copy passes are required to recopy memory that changed while performing the previous memory copy action (getting faster with each pass because the amount of data is much less). Most datacenters deploy a 1 Gbps network infrastructure; Hyper-V was very efficient in its use of the network and would saturate a 1 Gbps link, so if you performed multiple live migrations between two hosts simultaneously, the result would be to divide the network capacity between multiple moves. With the bandwidth split, the copy would take longer for each VM and the amount of memory changing during the copy would be greater, actually increasing the total time to move the VM.

By analogy, think of pouring a bottle of soda through a funnel. Pouring four bottles down the same funnel at the same time will take four times as long, because the funnel is the limiting factor. Now imagine that as you are pouring out the bottles of soda, someone is dripping more into them, so the longer it takes to empty, the more soda you have to pour away, increasing the total time. Pouring one bottle at a time will actually result in a faster total emptying of the bottles. Replace funnel with network, bottle of soda with a live migration, and the extra soda dripping in with memory change during the live migration to complete the analogy. System Center Virtual Machine Manager helped handle multiple live migration actions by queuing them up and performing them in series, enabling administrators to initiate bulk live migrations in the management interface and then walk away.

Fast-forward to now, when 10 Gbps networks in the datacenter are becoming more prevalent and a single live migration is not likely to saturate a 10 Gbps network link (think a really big funnel). To take advantage of this, Windows Server 2012 now allows multiple concurrent live migrations between hosts. There is no fixed maximum number of concurrent live migrations, although you can specify a maximum number as part of the Hyper-V host configuration.

▶ Hyper-V will examine the network capability and the amount of available bandwidth and tune the number of concurrent live migrations based on current conditions to ensure the best performance.

Beyond improvements to Live Migration, additional migration scenarios are now supported by Hyper-V, starting with SMB Live Migration. In Windows Server 2008 R2, live migration could be only be performed for hosts within a cluster, using CSV. Now, when a virtual machine is stored on an SMB file share, the same process can be used to move a virtual machine between two Hyper-V hosts that are not part of a cluster.

In the SMB Live Migration scenario, both Hyper-V hosts must have connectivity to the same SMB file share, which contains the virtual hard disks and configuration files of the virtual machine that is being migrated. The only requirement for the SMB file share is that both Hyper-V host computer accounts have full control rights on the folder and share. The basic mechanics for the SMB Live Migration is the same as a live migration within a failover cluster, but some extra steps are needed because the VM is not a shared resource between the Hyper-V hosts:

1. A TCP connection is created between the host currently running the virtual machine (the source host) and the destination host. The virtual machine configuration data is sent to the destination, which enables the creation of a skeleton VM on the destination host and a reservation for the required memory.

2. The memory of the virtual machine is copied from the source to the destination, which, like a typical live migration, consists of an initial complete memory transfer and then a number of iterations to copy changed memory pages.

3. When the amount of memory left to transfer is very small, the virtual machine is temporarily stunned and the remaining memory, plus the CPU and device state, are copied to the destination host.

4. The handles to the files on the SMB file share are transferred from the source host to the destination host along with any physical storage that may be attached through the new virtual Fibre Channel adapter (another great feature in Windows 2012 Hyper-V!).

5. The virtual machine on the destination is now unstunned and running. The virtual machine on the source is deleted.

6. Finally, a reverse Address Resolution Protocol (ARP) packet is sent out, which forces network switches to update their mapping of the virtual machine IP address to the MAC of the new host.

The time between the stunning and unstunning of the virtual machine is typically milliseconds, and way below any TCP connection timeouts, so there is no impact to users of the virtual machine. If you watched a ping to the VM being live-migrated, you might see a longer than normal response time for one ping packet or even a dropped packet, but nothing that a user would ever notice or that would cause a disconnection.

Windows Server 2012 Hyper-V goes a step further with a *Shared Nothing Live Migration* capability, the other new migration scenario. This is the ability to migrate a virtual machine between two standalone Hyper-V servers that are not part of the same cluster and share no storage, needing only a Gigabit Ethernet connection between them—all with zero downtime.

The shared nothing live migration looks very similar to the SMB live migration, except this time Hyper-V also has to move the storage using the process I described in the earlier section on live storage move. Hyper-V is essentially performing everything in the SMB live migration scenario, plus a live storage move of the virtual machine's storage from the source to the destination, and then maintaining the mirroring of writes to both the source and destination storage, while a live migration of the memory and state is performed before a final switch of the host running the virtual machine.

With shared nothing live migration, you can move virtual machines between any Hyper-V Windows Server 2012 hosts with nothing in common but a shared Ethernet cable. I've demonstrated shared nothing live migration between two laptops that have only local storage. The running virtual machine using local storage on the first laptop moves to the second laptop without any downtime to the virtual machine.

▶ The flexibility that Shared Nothing Live Migration brings to environments is unmatched by anything else in the industry.

Note that the same capability can be used to move VMs between different clusters, different hosts, and potentially even between private and public cloud Infrastructure as a Service (IaaS) providers.

Hyper-V Replica

Migrating virtual machines is a great capability that's clearly applicable in the planned deployment of virtual machines, but this technology won't help in unplanned situations when a disaster strikes. Many Microsoft customers requested a disaster recovery feature for virtual machines that does not require expensive networking or storage subsystems and does not limit the virtual machine capabilities.

Hyper-V Replica is a new feature in Windows Server 2012 that enables asynchronous replication of a virtual machine's storage from one Hyper-V host to a second Hyper-V host, where they can be using completely different types of storage. An initial replication of the source virtual machine's storage is performed, either over the network using a direct connection between the primary and replica server or using a save of the VM's storage to a location on the network, which the replica server reads from—a process known as *off-the-network seeding*. If sufficient bandwidth isn't available for the initial storage seeding on the replica over the network, such as when creating a replica at a remote location of a VM with very large amounts of storage, then a backup can be taken of the VM on the primary server, shipped to the replica server, and restored. Once the initial replication of the VM is completed, a delta replication of the virtual machine storage is performed periodically, every 5 minutes. Because this replication is asynchronous and periodic, this is not a real-time replication solution; and in the event of an unplanned outage, a few minutes' worth of storage data could be lost when failing over to the replica. Therefore, this should be considered when architecting a solution utilizing Hyper-V Replica, but the benefit of this asynchronous replication is that there are no limitations to the scale of VM that can be replicated and there are no high network requirements between the primary Hyper-V server and the replica. The exact bandwidth needed between the servers depends on the amount of storage change, but one of the supported scenarios of Hyper-V Replica includes a replica in a secondary site connected via a WAN link.

▶ Hyper-V Replica is not an automated failover solution, but processes such as those provided through PowerShell and System Center could automate failover if required.

In the event of a disaster an administrator could manually activate the replicated virtual machine. Within Hyper-V Replica, options exist to test the failover process and run the replicated VM connected to a separate test network so it does not interfere with the production primary virtual machine. In planned failover scenarios, the primary VM would be shut down manually and a final delta sent to the replica site, where Hyper-V Replica would apply the delta, start the VM, and begin a reverse replication to what was previously the primary VM, providing the original Hyper-V server was configured to accept Hyper-V replicas.

Configuring Hyper-V Replica is a fairly simple process. All Hyper-V servers now have a Replication Configuration setting where you can enable replication and select the transport protocol to use. The two options are Integrated Windows authentication, with replication of the changes over port 80 (HTTP), or certificate-based authentication, with replication over port 443 (HTTPS); this also encrypts the virtual machine update data when sent over the network. Whichever option you choose, you can change the port it uses from the default. Finally, you can configure the server to accept replication requests from all Hyper-V servers or just from specific Hyper-V servers. The only additional step on the replication target is to enable firewall rules to allow communication over the selected ports.

Once a Hyper-V server with replication enabled is available, you configure individual virtual machines to have a replica through the Enable Replication action, which starts up the Enable Replication wizard. Within the wizard you are prompted to select the target replica server and how the initial replication should be performed; you can specify the number of optional recovery points to be created, which are hourly VSS snapshots that ensure the integrity of the specific replica recovery point. Once the virtual machine is replicating, you can view its replication health at any time by requesting a health report, which shows the number of replication cycles, the average size of the replications, and the length of time a replication has been running. It is also possible to specify an alternate TCP/IP configuration for the replica VM when it is activated, which is injected into the VM. This is required if the replica is hosted in a different network and network virtualization is not being used (which is another great feature of Windows Server 2012). Figure 8-18 shows a report of the overall health of a replica VM, which is available using the Replication Health action.

It is important to understand what Hyper-V Replica is and what it isn't. Hyper-V Replica is not a real-time, zero-loss, large-enterprise, disaster recovery solution. Hyper-V Replica is aimed at small and medium-size businesses that want a secondary site disaster recovery capability, and it works by sending the storage updates of the virtual machine periodically to the second location. In the event of a disaster, the replica is activated and the OS starts in a crash-consistent state at the point when the last storage delta was sent from the primary site. If this crash-consistent state is not adequate, then provided the recovery point feature was enabled, the administrator can select a recovery point. This starts the replica at a VSS snapshot point in time, ensuring that the VM is in an application-consistent state. It's an out-of-the-box feature that provides a good level of disaster recovery protection without requiring high network speeds, and it works with any type of Hyper-V-supported storage.

▶ Although Hyper-V Replica is a great out-of-the-box feature, if you need a higher level of functionality, you can find third-party solutions that build on Hyper-V.

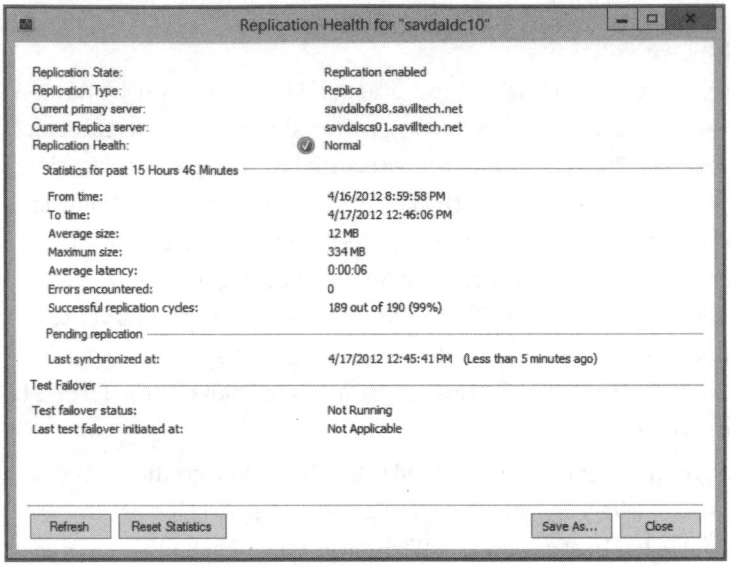

FIGURE 8-18: Looking at a replicated virtual machine's health using Hyper-V Manager

Network Virtualization, Extensible Switch, and Quality of Service

Virtualization has done a great job of virtualizing hardware for virtual machines, but for network connectivity the virtual machines have to adhere to the addressing and VLAN configuration of the physical network fabric. Windows Server 2012 introduces a new network virtualization capability that separates the network view of virtual machines from the underlying physical network fabric.

NETWORK VIRTUALIZATION

The virtual network capability is enabled through the use of two IP addresses associated with each virtual machine, along with a virtual subnet identifier to indicate the virtual network to which a particular virtual machine belongs. The first IP address is the standard IP address that is configured within the virtual machine, which is referred to as the *customer address (CA)* using IEEE nomenclature. The second IP address is the IP address with which the virtual machine communicates over the physical network; this address is known as the *provider address (PA)*.

Consider a single physical network fabric on which two separate organizations are running, the red and the blue. Each organization has its own IP scheme that can overlap the other, and the virtual networks can span multiple physical locations. This is shown in Figure 8-19. Each virtual machine that is part of the virtual red or blue

▶ Virtual networks can span multiple Hyper-V hosts and even multiple datacenters, which could extend to hosts on-premise and those in the public cloud.

network has its own red or blue customer address, and a separate provider address is used to send the actual IP traffic over the physical fabric.

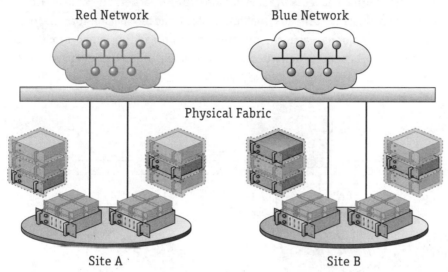

FIGURE 8-19: Two different virtual networks on the same physical network fabric

Two solutions enable network virtualization in Windows Server 2012. Both solutions enable completely separate virtual networks with their own IP schemes, which can overlap, to run over a shared fabric. The first option is *IP Rewrite*, which does exactly as the name suggests, it rewrites the packet addresses from CA to PA. The Hyper-V switch looks at traffic being sent out from the VM, checks the virtual subnet ID to identify the correct virtual network, and rewrites the IP source and target from the CA IP addresses to the corresponding PA IP addresses. This has a disadvantage in that it requires a lot of IP addresses from the PA address pool, as every VM needs its own PA IP address. The good news is that because the IP packet is not being modified, apart from the IP addresses, hardware offloads continue to function, such as Virtual Machine Queue (VMQ), Checksum, and Receive-Side Scaling (RSS). IP Rewrite adds very little overhead to the network process and provides very high performance. The IP Rewrite process can be seen in the upper part of Figure 8-20, along with the mapping table maintained by the source Hyper-V host.

The second option is *Generic Routing Encapsulation (GRE)*, an IETF standard, which wraps the originating packet from the VM containing CA addresses inside a packet using the PA addresses that can be routed on the physical network. Because the wrapper also includes the virtual subnet ID, each individual VM does not require its own PA address, as the receiving host can identify the targeted VM based on its CA address within the original packet combined with the virtual subnet ID in the wrapper. The

▶ The use of a shared PA means far fewer IP addresses from the provider IP pools are needed, which is good news for IP management and the network infrastructure.

only information the Hyper-V host on the originating VM needs to know is which Hyper-V host is running the target VM, and it can then send the packet over the network.

Because the original packet is wrapped inside the GRE packet, any kind of NIC offloading will break, as the offloads won't understand the new packet format. Fortunately, many of the major hardware manufacturers are now adding support for GRE to all their network equipment, which will once again enable offloading even when GRE is used. Both options are shown in Figure 8-20.

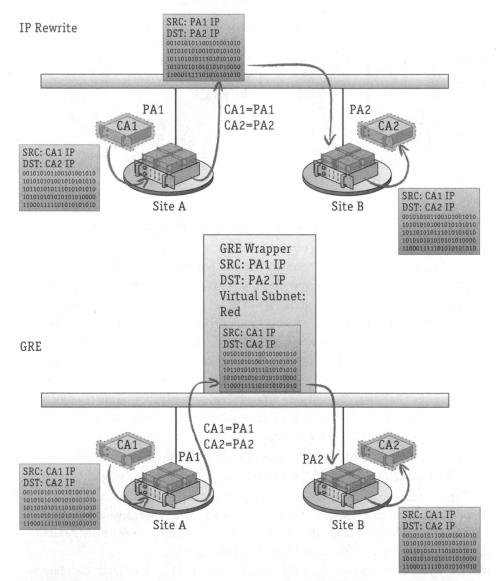

FIGURE 8-20: IP Rewrite and GRE in action with network virtualization

In both solutions, virtualization policies are used between all the Hyper-V hosts that participate in a specific virtual network to enable the routing of the CA across the physical fabric and to track the CA-to-PA mapping. The virtualization policies can also define which virtual networks are allowed to communicate with other virtual networks. You can configure the virtualization policies using PowerShell, which is the direction for all things Windows Server 2012 because when you are working with massive scale and automation, a GUI does not cut it. The challenge when using the native PowerShell commands is the synchronous orchestration of the virtual network configuration across all Hyper-V hosts that participate in a specific virtual network. The long-term solution is for the virtualization management solution to manage the virtual networks, not to do it manually using PowerShell. This is where System Center Virtual Machine Manager 2012 managing Windows Server 2012 is useful; it will automate the management of network virtualization.

Both options sound great, but which one should you use? GRE is the network virtualization technology of choice. It simplifies address management because of the reduced provider address requirements. In addition, GRE offload will be offered in new NIC cards very soon. For those who want to deploy today on existing hardware, use IP Rewrite. All existing performance offloads currently work with IP Rewrite.

EXTENSIBLE SWITCH

The Hyper-V switch enables the routing of network traffic between virtual machines and other network devices, which could be other virtual machines, physical systems, or pieces of network hardware. Windows Server 2012 introduces the capability to extend the features of the Hyper-V switch. Windows already offered very rich capabilities related to APIs and interfaces for third parties to integrate with the operating system—specifically, Network Device Interface Specification (NDIS) filter drivers and Windows Filtering Platform (WFP) callout drivers. The new Hyper-V Extensible Switch uses these same interfaces that partners are already used to working with, making it very easy for vendors to adapt solutions that integrate directly into the Windows Server 2012 Extensible Switch. Table 8-3 describes the four specific extensions available for the Hyper-V switch.

TABLE 8-3: Supported Hyper-V Switch Extensions

EXTENSION	PURPOSE	EXAMPLE	EXTENSIBILITY COMPONENT
Network Packet Inspection	Inspecting network packets but not making changes	Network monitoring	NDIS filter driver

(continues)

TABLE 8-3: Supported Hyper-V Switch Extensions *(continued)*

EXTENSION	PURPOSE	EXAMPLE	EXTENSIBILITY COMPONENT
Network Packet Filter	Injecting, modifying, and dropping network packets	Security	NDIS filter driver
Network Forwarding	Third-party forwarding that bypasses default forwarding	Virtual Ethernet Port Aggregator (VEPA) and proprietary network fabrics	NDIS filter driver
Firewall/Intrusion Detection	Filtering and modifying TCP/IP packets, monitoring or authorizing connections, filtering IPsec-protected traffic, and filtering RPCs	Virtual firewall and connection monitoring	WFP callout driver

Note that these extensions do not completely replace the Hyper-V switch but rather enhance it, enabling an organization to be very specific about the exact layers of additional functionality required within the environment and without requiring a complete switch replacement. Because the extensions are embedded within the Hyper-V switch, the capabilities apply to all traffic—including virtual machine–to–virtual machine traffic on the same Hyper-V host and traffic that traverses the physical network fabric. The extensions fully support live migration and can be managed using the graphical interface tools, WMI scripting, and PowerShell cmdlets, providing a consistent management experience across the extensions and the core Hyper-V capabilities. Third-party extensions for the Hyper-V switch will be certifiable under the Windows Server 2012 Certification Program, which ensures that the extensions meet an expected level of quality.

Extensions require only a simple installation routine, and once installed they are enabled on a per virtual switch basis. Figure 8-21 shows the sFlow packet sampling filter extension enabled for my external virtual network switch. I can connect to this from the sFlowTrend software application to report on trends in my network usage. This is just one of the many extensions available for the Hyper-V network switch.

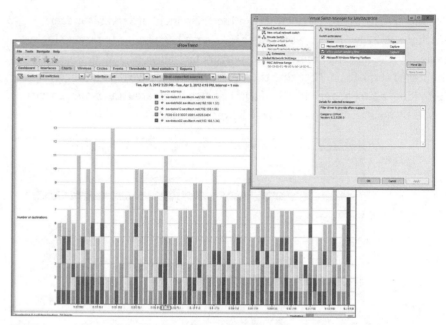

FIGURE 8-21: Enabling an extension for the virtual network switch and viewing report information

NIC TEAMING

While it is not specifically a Hyper-V feature, the addition of native NIC teaming in Windows Server 2012 is great news for customers, who typically want NIC teaming to provide network bandwidth aggregation and protection against NIC or switch failure but don't want to rely on vendor-specific driver implementations. NIC teaming is now a standard part of Windows Server 2012, enabling up to 32 different network adapters, which can be from different vendors, to be teamed together in one of three different modes, the first two of which are switch-dependent:

▶ **Static Teaming:** Configuration is required on both the switches and the computer to identify links that make up the team. Since this is statically configured, it cannot detect incorrectly plugged cables.

▶ **LACP (dynamic teaming):** The Link Aggregation Control Protocol (LACP) is used to dynamically identify links between the computer and specific switches, and thus enable automatic configuration of the team.

▶ **Switch-Independent:** The switch does not participate in the teaming, so each NIC in the team can connect to a different switch; this is not required but it's possible. This mode is the default.

> ▶ I don't think there are 32 NIC vendors, but if there were, their cards could be made part of one team!

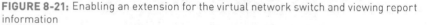

▶ NIC teaming is often referred to as LBFO, which stands for Load Balancing and Failover, the two features that NIC teaming provides.

NIC teams are created using the NIC Teaming component of Server Manager, as shown in Figure 8-22, which shows that two NICs have been added to form a single team named "VM Team." Also shown is the Network Connections dialog, which displays the status of the team. Note that the bandwidth of the two NICs has been aggregated, providing a 2.0 Gbps speed. NIC teams can also be created and managed with the New-NetLbfoTeam and Get-NetLbfoTeam PowerShell cmdlets.

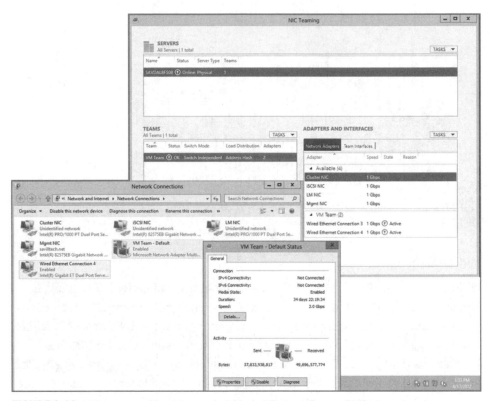

FIGURE 8-22: NIC team configuration and status in Windows Server 2012

The addition of NIC teaming in Windows Server 2012 does not mean that NIC teaming capabilities will no longer be provided by network card vendors. Some vendors differentiate their cards based on teaming capabilities, but customers will have the option to use teaming capabilities from the network adapter driver or the Microsoft NIC teaming functionality, which is fully supported by Microsoft, of course. The decision should be made based on required functionality and supportability needs.

QUALITY OF SERVICE

As more systems are virtualized and the trend continues toward a shared virtual infrastructure used by different business units and even different companies, it's critical that one virtual machine does not consume all the network bandwidth, starving other virtual machines. Similarly, in current converged fabrics where network and storage use a shared physical cable, it's vital to ensure that one type of traffic does not use more than its fair share.

Windows Server 2012 includes a Hyper-V Quality of Service capability, which through PowerShell makes it easy to set network utilization weights for virtual machines in addition to setting minimum bandwidth allocations, thereby ensuring that virtual machines get the bandwidth they require in times of contention but use up as much as is available otherwise, making them as efficient and responsive as possible. The software QoS is focused at a virtual switch port level.

Hardware QoS is also available by utilizing a new capability in many currently available network infrastructures, *Data Center Bridging (DCB)*. DCB enables classification of all the network traffic that is being sent over one physical NIC, whether the traffic is from the Hyper-V host or from a virtual machine. In Windows Server 2012, the traffic can be divided into eight classification buckets—for example, one bucket could be iSCSI traffic, another SMB, and then general IP traffic. For each of the buckets, DCB can configure the amount of bandwidth allocated, ensuring that no single type of traffic consumes all available bandwidth.

When you consider software QoS and hardware QoS with DCB, the main difference is that software QoS is at a VM level and works through the Hyper-V switch, whereas hardware QoS is VM-independent and works across all the types of traffic going over the network.

Other Key Features in Windows Server 2012 Hyper-V

The enhanced mobility, storage, replication, scalability, and networking features of Hyper-V in Windows Server 2012 get the most attention; but if you refer back to Figure 8-14, I've covered less than one quarter of all those items in the list, and remember that the list is not exhaustive. This section takes a brief look at some of the other interesting technologies; they may not make the headlines but they certainly provide other useful capabilities to your infrastructure.

▶ This is very useful for situations in which an export was not performed on a virtual machine and it needs to be used on another Hyper-V server. In planned scenarios, use Export where possible.

One of the first features I found the most useful when I started testing Windows Server 2012 was Simplified Import, which I used to move my virtual machines from Windows Server 2008 R2. Previously I needed to export each virtual machine and then import them to the new Hyper-V server. That is no longer required. With Windows Server 2012, you just run the Import wizard, point it to the folder containing a virtual machine, and Windows Server 2012 Hyper-V imports the raw virtual machine XML configuration file, fixing any problems it finds along the way.

Offloaded Data Transfer (ODX) is a technology that works in conjunction with the SAN solutions to enable large move/copy operations to occur internally and nearly instantaneously. Without ODX, if Hyper-V needs, for example, to move a virtual machine from one location on a SAN to another location, or copy a template to create a new virtual machine, the process consists of repeatedly reading in blocks of data from the SAN to memory and then writing it back out to the new location. This can take a long time, and consumes processor and memory resource. ODX enables Hyper-V to just tell the SAN to move or copy data from one location to another without the data having to pass through the Windows operating system. This can reduce an operation that previously took 30 minutes to one that takes less than 30 seconds. The major SAN vendors are looking for ways to implement this technology.

Staying with external storage for virtual machines, up till now to use a SAN you had to connect to it over iSCSI, which operates over TCP/IP and uses the Windows built-in iSCSI Initiator. However, many organizations use fibre connections to SANs, and Windows Server 2012 Hyper-V introduces a Virtual Fibre Channel capability that is managed through a new Virtual SAN Manager tool, which works in a similar way to the Virtual Network Manager. Through the manager you can create Virtual Fibre Channel SANs on the host, which are then attached to virtual machines so they can directly access the SAN over the host's fibre channel connection. This extends the capabilities for storage access and the clustering scenarios for virtual machines.

▶ In addition to operating system support, which for Windows Server means Windows Server 2012, SR-IOV requires that both the server motherboard and the network adapter support it.

There are two nice improvements in the area of networking adapter hardware: *Single Root I/O Virtualization (SR-IOV)* and *Dynamic Virtual Machine Queue (DVMQ)*. SR-IOV enables a single PCI Express network device to represent itself as multiple separate devices that can be attached directly to virtual machines. In the case of SR-IOV and virtual machines, this means a physical NIC can present multiple virtual NICs, which in SR-IOV terms are called virtual functions (VFs). Each VF is of the same type as the physical card and is presented directly to specific virtual machines. The communication between the virtual machine and the VF completely bypasses the

Hyper-V switch, as the VM uses direct memory access (DMA) to communicate with the VF. This results in very fast communication between the VM and the VF and very low latency, because neither the VMBus nor the Hyper-V switch are involved in the network flow from the physical NIC to the VM. Because the Hyper-V switch is bypassed, any features exposed through the virtual switch, such as switching, ACL checking, QoS, DHCP Guard, and third-party extensions will no longer apply to the traffic that uses SR-IOV.

SR-IOV does not break live migration, even when moving a virtual machine to a host that does not support SR-IOV. Behind the scenes, when SR-IOV is used the Network Virtualization Service Client (NetVSC) inside the virtual machine creates two paths for the virtual machine network adapter inside the VM. One path is via SR-IOV and one is using the traditional VMBus path through the Hyper-V switch. When the VM is running on a host with SR-IOV, the SR-IOV path is used and the VMBus is closed; but if the VM is moved to a host without SR-IOV, then the SR-IOV path is closed by NetVSC and the VMBus path is opened, all of which is transparent to the virtual machine. This means you don't lose any mobility even when using SR-IOV.

Dynamic Virtual Machine Queue (VMQ) is a similar technology. VMQ itself enables separate queues to be configured on a VMQ-capable network adapter, based on hardware packet filtering. Windows Server 2008 R2 introduced Hyper-V support for VMQ, with each queue mapped to a specific virtual machine. This eliminates some of the switching work on the Hyper-V switch because if the data is in a particular queue, the switch knows it is meant for a specific virtual machine. The difference between VMQ and SR-IOV is that with VMQ the traffic still passes through the Hyper-V switch, because VMQ is presenting different queues of traffic, as opposed to presenting entire virtual devices with SR-IOV. In Windows Server 2008 R2, the assignment of a VMQ to a virtual machine was static—typically, first come first served, as each NIC supports a certain number of VMQs. VMQ produces the highest performance gain when each queue is handling heavy receive traffic, so if the VM workloads vary, a static assignment will not be optimal. In Windows Server 2012, this queue assignment is made dynamically, so the Hyper-V switch now constantly monitors the network streams for each VM, and if a VM that was very quiet suddenly becomes busy it is allocated a VMQ. If no VMQs are available, then the VMQ is taken from a VM that may have previously been busy but is now quiet. Figure 8-23 shows a normal virtual machine connection through the Hyper-V switch; a connection using VMQ; and one using SR-IOV.

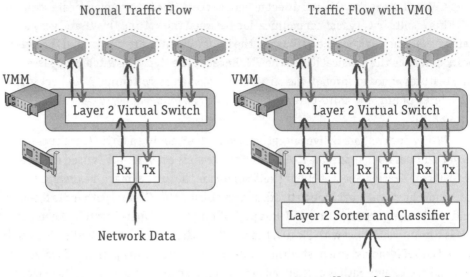

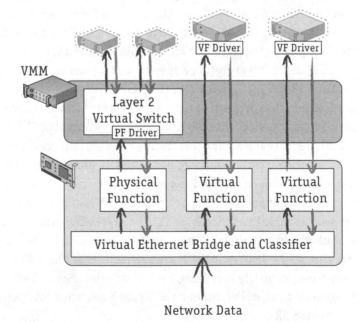

FIGURE 8-23: Comparison of the VMQ and SR-IOV network technologies

Windows Server 2012 also adds metering capabilities for virtual machines, and those measurement metrics follow the virtual machine even if it is moved to another Hyper-V host. This metering data can be very useful to show business units how busy their virtual machines are, to assign monetary costs based on usage, or just to obtain trending information for virtual machines.

Enhancements to Failover Clustering in Windows Server 2012 have enabled a management action for easy patching of an entire cluster of Hyper-V hosts with a single click—this initiates a process that evacuates a host of all virtual machines, patches the host, reboots it, and then brings the virtual machines back, repeating the process on the next host. Failover Clustering also adds the capability to set anti-affinity rules, which try to ensure that certain virtual machines are never running on the same Hyper-V server. In addition to anti-affinity, Failover Clustering enables the setting of priorities for virtual machines; highest priority virtual machines can be configured to start first, and low-priority machines can even be stopped if resources are needed to start high-priority virtual machines. Maintenance mode is also available, enabling you to easily drain a node of virtual machines to perform maintenance on it and then return them when maintenance mode is turned off.

▶ For example, consider multiple domain controllers. Anti-affinity can try to make sure they don't all run on the same Hyper-V server, which would negate your redundancy from hardware failure strategy.

The last item I want to touch on, but by no means the least, is PowerShell. Windows Server 2012 has a tight integration with PowerShell, and Hyper-V is probably the biggest user of PowerShell compared to other features. Windows Server 2012 Hyper-V has more PowerShell cmdlets than all of the PowerShell cmdlets in Windows Server 2008 R2 put together. On a Windows Server 2012 server with the Hyper-V role, run the following command to see a list of all the PowerShell cmdlets available:

```
get-command -module hyper-v
```

If you are interested in large-scale Hyper-V automation, then you will definitely want to look at PowerShell capabilities and the System Center 2012 product.

DECIDING WHAT AND HOW TO VIRTUALIZE

Windows Server 2012 offers a very rich hypervisor and a complete platform for virtualization, and when partnered with System Center 2012, a complete solution for the entire datacenter and even the private cloud. Once you have decided to find a virtualization solution, you must next figure out what to virtualize and how to go about the process.

The Importance of Discovery and Planning

▶ Make sure
monitoring includes
any peak times,
such as end-of-
month processing.

Whether you are moving from physical to virtual or migrating from another virtu-alization technology, the first step in a virtualization project is to understand the requirements of the virtualization solution and the current usage patterns of the operating systems and applications that are being virtualized. Just knowing the average use of operating systems is not enough; it's important to know their peak usage scenarios in addition to the average counts. This means that the monitoring of resource usage will likely need to be performed over a period of weeks.

To help gather the performance metrics reflecting operating system usage, Micro-soft provides the Microsoft Assessment and Planning (MAP) Toolkit. It runs in an agentless mode and gathers key performance counters, and then provides a report that not only shows performance usage but also provides guidance on the placement of operating systems once virtualized. The MAP Toolkit supports the gathering of information from both physical servers and virtual machines running on Hyper-V and VMware. You can download the MAP Toolkit from `http://technet.microsoft` `.com/en-us/library/bb977556.aspx`, and it contains detailed implementation docu-mentation; but the key point is to ensure that this gathering of performance data is carried out. You should also understand whether workloads work with Dynamic Mem-ory, as some applications do not; and be aware whether tweaks to Dynamic Memory buffer configurations will be required.

Once your workload requirements and compatibility with Dynamic Memory are well understood, you are in a position to create a very well-designed virtual environ-ment and migrate your operating systems. Remember that the placement of virtual machines is not static. As resource needs change, virtual machines can easily be moved without downtime, as can the virtual machine storage; and the movement of virtual machines based on resource utilization and balancing between Hyper-V hosts can be automated using System Center 2012.

▶ I recommend
engaging
consultants
for any kind of
virtualization
implementation
or migration—at
least for the
planning phase,
to avoid mistakes
and problems that
consultants have
seen before and can
help you avoid.

Take time to consider the right tools to assist the migration of operating systems to Hyper-V. System Center 2012 Virtual Machine Manager has physical-to-virtual and virtual-to-virtual tools, and you can also use migration tools from other companies, such as Double-Take Move, which can help in planning larger-scale migrations by providing richer migration functionality than SCVMM.

The actual migration needs planning and extensive testing. Hyper-V is a proven platform with rock-solid reliability, but the end-state is just one aspect of the risk of virtualization. For many organizations the transitory risk, the process of moving to virtualization, is a bigger issue; and it can be a blocker to adopting virtualization or migrating to a different virtualization technology even though the end-state may provide better functionality and cost savings. By using good migration technologies, performing thorough testing, understanding the relationships between operating system instances, and performing detailed planning, you can migrate to Hyper-V without destabilizing your environment and risking the availability of systems.

Virtualizing with SQL Server, Microsoft Exchange, and Other Enterprise Services

The question of virtualizing SQL Server, Exchange, System Center, and other major Microsoft services is a hot topic, but the answer today is much simpler than it was even a couple of years ago. All Microsoft products support running on Hyper-V—even components such as Exchange 2010 Unified Messaging that previously did not support virtualization are now supported with Exchange 2010 Service Pack 1. Microsoft products are tested using Hyper-V and are fully supported with a "single throat to choke" approach if you ever experience support issues with a Microsoft product running on Hyper-V. Microsoft's Server Virtualization Validation Program (SVVP), at `http://www.windowsservercatalog.com/svvp.aspx`, can be used to search for virtualization support and it applies not only to Hyper-V, but any hypervisor that is part of the SVVP program, which includes ESX and XenServer.

There are often very specific guidelines for virtualizing products on Hyper-V, such as the use of Dynamic Memory discussed earlier in this chapter, logical-to-virtual processor ratios, networking requirements, and storage recommendations. The following links provide some of the major guidelines for Microsoft products:

- ▶ Exchange 2010: `www.microsoft.com/download/en/details.aspx?id=2428`

- ▶ SQL Server 2008 R2: `http://technet.microsoft.com/en-us/library/ff898403(v=sql.105).aspx`

- ▶ SharePoint Server 2010: `http://technet.microsoft.com/en-us/library/hh295699.aspx`

- ▶ BizTalk Server 2010: `http://social.technet.microsoft.com/wiki/contents/articles/6986.biztalk-server-2010-virtualization.aspx`

COMPARING HYPER-V WITH VMWARE'S VSPHERE AND CITRIX XENSERVER

The final topic is that of comparing Hyper-V against other major server virtualization solutions on the market, the two key ones being Citrix XenServer and VMware vSphere. Ultimately, all three are great server virtualization solutions; it would be wrong to claim anything else. Each offers some features the others do not, which helps to meet the different needs of different customers. For some workloads, one product may support a few more virtual machines, while for other workloads another product may have higher density.

In reality, if you compare Windows Server 2012 Hyper-V and the latest versions from Citrix and VMware purely in terms of their hypervisor core capability set, there are not huge differences between them in their coverage of base requirements; it is when you look at more advanced features that gaps appear. For example, from talking to customers running VMware who were considering Hyper-V, the following capabilities were missing from Windows Server 2008 R2 Hyper-V:

- ▶ Storage migration
- ▶ Extensible network switch
- ▶ Large-scale virtual machines
- ▶ Fibre Channel connectivity for virtual machines

Not only are all of these missing items available in Windows Server 2012 Hyper-V, but Hyper-V leapfrogs the features. Some technologies are offered only by Hyper-V; some of the major ones that come to mind are as follows:

- ▶ Shared Nothing Live Migration
- ▶ Network virtualization
- ▶ A fully extensible network switch using existing Windows standards
- ▶ Built-in asynchronous replication technology
- ▶ Encrypted cluster volumes using BitLocker
- ▶ SR-IOV support

As time passes and new versions of each virtualization product are released, new features will be introduced; but the bottom line for any organization is determining what features you need. The beauty of Windows Server 2012 is that it's not just a temporary solution to your current problems that meets basic requirements. It offers the strongest set of features of any virtualization solution on the market. It provides not only the best server virtualization, and not only the best server operating system; when everything is considered together, it is the best platform for virtualization and the cloud.

It's very important to look beyond just server virtualization, though. What matters to most organizations is the manageability of the virtual infrastructure. I cover the full story of the Hyper-V partnership with System Center in Chapters 9 and 10, but essentially, with System Center 2012, there is a full management solution for your virtual and physical environments, for your hardware through to the actual applications and for your servers and desktops—a single solution for everything that can also provide management for VMware and Citrix virtualization infrastructure and gives visibility to your public cloud services. If you consider manageability, nothing comes close to Hyper-V and System Center; and when those two are put together you have the best private cloud available.

SUMMARY

Server virtualization is very much a standard in today's organizations, and Hyper-V offers a rock-solid and feature-rich platform for use in organizations of any size. Technologies like Dynamic Memory enable the creation of high-density virtual machine server environments, and dynamic placement technologies can help rebalance virtual machines that may not have been optimally placed. As highlighted in this chapter, however, any successful virtualization migration first requires the discovery of resource usage and proper planning to ensure the long-term stability of the Hyper-V environment.

The new features in Windows Server 2012 provide enhanced mobility features for virtual machines, enabling the movement of virtual machines between Hyper-V servers that are not clustered together. Using the Shared Nothing Live Migration capability, a virtual machine stored on local storage can be moved—without downtime—to a completely different server using any supported Hyper-V storage, which can be direct attached, on a storage area network or even on an SMB share with nothing but a single-gigabit network connection. Migration will even be possible to public cloud Infrastructure as a Service solutions as the cloud vendors adopt Windows Server 2012 Hyper-V. Combine this complete flexibility in mobility of virtual machines with network virtualization that enables the complete abstraction of the virtual machine networks from the physical network fabric, and you have the capability to host virtual machines anywhere—with no impact to network connectivity or reconfiguration.

As powerful as the features of Hyper-V are, however, keep in mind that server virtualization is not the same as the cloud. The cloud is focused on providing management infrastructure, but Hyper-V with System Center 2012 provides a complete private cloud solution for your environment.

▶ For a fun look at virtualization competition, have a look at www .vm-limited.com.

Using System Center Virtual Machine Manager

The tools that are used to manage and interact with Hyper-V are critical to a successful virtualization endeavor. I would not fault any administrator who blames his tools for an inefficiently run Hyper-V implementation if all he or she had access to was the management tool supplied with the product. System Center Virtual Machine Manager (SCVMM) 2012 is a necessity for truly effective and comprehensive management of a Hyper-V-based environment and, as I will demonstrate, a heterogeneous virtualization environment, including ESX and XenServer. Behind every great Hyper-V implementation is a great SCVMM.

This chapter explores the full capabilities of SCVMM for a great management experience. It covers all the features you'll need, although a comprehensive discussion about how to implement every feature is beyond the scope of one book. However, the chapter does include additional resources that provide step-by-step instructions. My goal is to explain why you should use SCVMM's tools and to provide you with tips and best practices you won't find in other places.

While SCVMM 2012 is the current version, I realize that some organizations may still be running SCVMM 2008 R2, so where the functionality discussed is also available in 2008 R2, I try to point that out. However, I urge any organization using SCVMM 2008 R2 to upgrade, because SCVMM 2012 has a lot more to offer. SCVMM 2008 R2 also offers an in-place upgrade procedure to simplify migration to 2012. Because this chapter is focused on SCVMM 2012, anytime I write SCVMM, I mean SCVMM 2012; and when talking about earlier versions, I specify the exact version.

A BRIEF HISTORY OF SYSTEM CENTER VIRTUAL MACHINE MANAGER

System Center Virtual Machine Manager is one of the components of Microsoft System Center. As the name suggests, SCVMM is focused on helping you manage your virtual environment. It has always been a useful tool, but with the latest 2012 release it moves from handy to essential. But before getting into SCVMM 2012's newest enhancements, I want to take a step back and go over the highlights of previous versions. SCVMM has always done a great job of enabling organizations to embrace Microsoft server virtualization through capabilities such as the following:

- ▶ Creating templates for virtual machines to enable fast deployment of new environments
- ▶ Managing large clusters of Hyper-V hosts
- ▶ Converting physical operating system instances to virtual machines
- ▶ Optimizing resources through automatic movement of virtual machines between hosts for best performance based on resource usage data enabled by connectivity to System Center Operations Manager (SCOM)
- ▶ Enabling end users to self-provision virtual machines based on quotas using a web-based portal

SCVMM 2008 R2 introduced the capability to manage VMware ESX–based virtual machines, which is a competitive hypervisor to Hyper-V. However, the ESX management feature was not widely used because of its limited management capabilities. This management, although limited, was a first step towards System Center managing non-Microsoft infrastructure elements, and is a theme continued and improved in System Center 2012, providing a management capability for a heterogeneous datacenter.

Over the years, when I talked to IT administrators about their experience with previous versions of SCVMM, several common issues emerged. Some were directly related to the management tool, but others were simply requests to make the lives of the IT department personnel easier, to help the organization be more efficient, and to ensure adherence to regulatory requirements, some of which are highly sensitive. The following reflect some of these typical concerns:

- ▶ "I would like to have visibility through SCVMM into the storage area networks that store my virtual machines."

- ▶ "Deploying server applications requires following a 100+ page procedure, which has a lot of potential for human error and differences in implementation between development, test, and production. I want to be able to install the server application once and then just move it between environments, making changes only to configuration."

- ▶ "My organization has many datacenters with different network details, but I don't want to have to change the way I deploy virtual machines based on where they are being deployed. The management tool should understand my different networks—such as production, backup, and DMZ—and set the correct IP details and use the right NICs in the hosts as needed."

- ▶ "I need to save power, so during quiet times I want to consolidate my virtual machines on fewer hosts and power down unnecessary servers."

- ▶ "Performing patching on the Hyper-V clusters is a painful and highly manual process; there must be a way to automate this so I can just push a button and patch the entire cluster."

- ▶ "I want to implement a private cloud and need the tools to enable this."

I have many more, but their common denominator is the fact that these organizations are, or plan to be, predominantly virtualized in the datacenter. Consequently, they need tools that enable easier management, particularly over large-scale implementations that span multiple datacenters.

The virtualization landscape and the demands organizations make on their environments and management tools have changed radically over the past few years; and as demands change, so must the toolset. I feel confident in saying SCVMM has seen the greatest increase in functionality of all in the System Center 2012 suite, due to the increased focus on virtualization and the desire for a single tool that could perform the majority of management activities.

SCVMM 2012 improves nearly everything offered in the previous versions, and adds a huge amount of new functionality that can be broken down into two main themes: fabric and service management.

▶ I have run into very few organizations that are all Hyper-V. Many have a mixture of Hyper-V, ESX, and XenServer; and, looking at industry reports, the trend is toward multiple hypervisors.

Figure 9-1 shows these two management areas and breaks them down further into the key areas of investment that were made in SCVMM 2012. This makes it the tool of choice not only for Hyper-V management, but also for the heterogeneous virtual environment nearly every organization has.

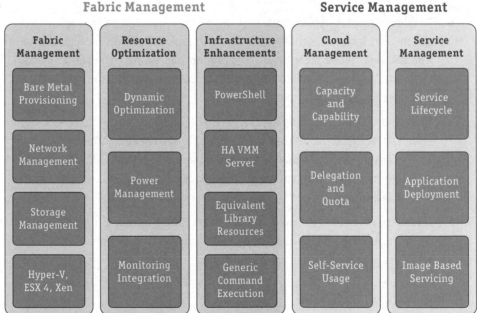

FIGURE 9-1: The five functionality pillars of SCVMM 2012

One initiative that almost every organization is considering right now is implementing a *private cloud*. If you ask five people for the definition of private cloud, you will likely get seven different answers. That's probably because the definition evolves along with the concept, but at a fundamental level I like to think of a private cloud as an internal deployment of virtualization technologies that enables a highly scalable, flexible, and elastic collection of resources that is easily accessible to designated users and groups for the deployment of operating systems and applications. As I walk through the SCVMM 2012 capability stack, it will become apparent that one of its primary directives is to enable the implementation of private clouds.

CROSSREF I dive much deeper into implementing a private cloud in Chapter 10.

Implementing SCVMM 2012

SCVMM 2012, like the rest of the System Center 2012 components, only supports installation on Windows Server 2008 R2, which requires a 64-bit server. If you want to create a highly available installation of SCVMM 2012, you need to use the Enterprise or Datacenter edition of Windows Server 2008 R2, because only those versions include the Failover Clustering feature required for high availability. A number of other software requirements exist, however these are fairly minimal. The only one you will have to install manually is the Windows *Automated Installation Kit (AIK)*, which includes components for creating and managing operating system images that are required for SCVMM's bare-metal deployment features. The other requirements are already part of the Windows Server 2008 R2 operating system, such as Windows Remote Management (WinRM) and Microsoft .NET Framework 3.5 SP1, and are added automatically by the SCVMM installation process. SCVMM must be installed on a server that is part of an Active Directory domain, but it does not have any specific requirements, such as a Windows Server 2008 domain or a forest-level domain.

NOTE You can download the correct Windows AIK version from http://www .microsoft.com/download/en/details.aspx?displaylang=en&id=5753..

SQL Server 2008 or SQL Server 2008 R2 is required for SCVMM to store its configuration and data, but this does not need to be installed on the SCVMM server itself. I recommend using a separate SQL Server for SCVMM and, ideally, leveraging an existing SQL server farm in your organization that is highly available and maintained by SQL administrators. If you are testing SCVMM in a lab with a small number of hosts, installing SQL on the SCVMM server is fine; but where possible, leverage an external, dedicated SQL environment.

The required hardware specifications vary according to the number of virtualization hosts being managed by SCVMM. A single SCVMM server can manage up to 400 hosts containing up to 8,000 virtual machines, and an SCVMM instance managing that many hosts should have 8GB of RAM and four cores running at around 3.6 GHz with 50GB of disk space. For smaller installations (fewer than 150 hosts, which

▶ These limits are the same for SCVMM 2008 R2 SP1 and are numbers tested; therefore, they are supported by Microsoft but are not actual hard limits.

is still a lot) the amount of memory recommended drops to 4GB; however, four cores are still preferred, running at around 2.8 GHz and 40GB of disk space. The Microsoft recommendations actually state that when you have fewer than 150 hosts per SCVMM, you can run the SQL Server on the SCVMM instance. However, I still prefer to limit the number of SQL instances in my environment, and it's better to invest in a well-designed and -maintained, highlyavailable SQL farm rather than a local SQL install. Also, if you are planning to implement a highly available SCVMM installation, you need SQL Server separate from your SCVMM server.

Can you virtualize the SCVMM installation? Yes! It would be pretty sad if Microsoft's flagship virtualization management tool had to run on physical hardware. Virtualizing SCVMM is fully supported and indeed recommended, and all the clients I work with virtualize SCVMM.

▶ Remember, this is not just CPU. Think CPU, memory, disk IOPS (input/output per second), and network bandwidth. Disk requirements in particular are often neglected, resulting in very poor performance because underlying storage fails to keep up with demand. Think IOPS, IOPS, IOPS.

As with any virtualized service, you should ensure that the necessary resources are available to meet your virtualized loads and you don't overcommit resources beyond acceptable performance. Because SCVMM is so important to the management of a virtual environment, I like to set the reserve on the vCPUs for my SCVMM to 50 percent to ensure that CPU resources are always available during times of contention. Of course, as you will see, SCVMM should be doing a great job of constantly tweaking your virtual environment to ensure optimal performance and that the virtual machines get the resources they need. You can move the virtual machines between hosts if necessary, but if you have severely overcommitted your environment by putting too many virtual machines on the available resources, performance will suffer. This is why proper discovery and planning is vital to a successful virtual environment.

One of the new features in Hyper-V 2008 R2 SP1 was dynamic memory, which is fully supported by SCVMM. When specifying the dynamic memory setting for a production environment, my recommendation is to set the startup memory to 2048 and the maximum to 4096 (the Microsoft minimum and recommended values) for environments managing fewer than 150 hosts; set the startup memory to 4096 and the maximum to 8192 for SCVMM instances managing more than 150 hosts. This way, your environment can efficiently manage the amount of memory it's using while staying within Microsoft-supported limits. You can certainly exceed these maximums if you find memory is low (although that should be unlikely), but I don't recommend going below the minimum supported for the startup unless it's in a small lab environment with only a couple of hosts and you are very short on memory.

You must specify an account during the installation of SCVMM that is used to run the actual SCVMM service. During installation, you are given the option to either specify a domain account or use Local System. Don't use Local System. Although it may seem easiest, it limits a number of SCVMM's capabilities, such as using shared ISO images with Hyper-V virtual machines, and it can make troubleshooting difficult because all the logs will just show Local System instead of an account dedicated to SCVMM. On the flip side, don't use your domain Administrator account. It has too much power and would cause the same troubleshooting problem, because you would just see Administrator everywhere. Create a dedicated domain user account just for SCVMM that conforms to your organization's naming convention, such as svcSCVMM. Make that account a local administrator on the SCVMM server by adding the account to the local Administrators group, which you can do easily with the following command or by using the Server Manager tool, navigating to Configuration ➜ Local Users and Groups ➜ Groups, and just adding the account to the Administrators group.

▶ If your organization does not have a naming convention for accounts, create one, now! You should also create an Organization Unit hierarchy in Active Directory for the types of accounts to help in the delegation of management and Group Policy application.

```
C:\ >net localgroup Administrators /add savilltech\svcSCVMM
The command completed successfully.
```

> **TIP** During the installation of SCVMM, the install process performs a check for the minimum amount of memory. If the OS has less than 2,000MB of RAM, the install process will error and refuse to continue. If you are using dynamic memory and set the startup to less than 2048, you will likely encounter this problem. If so, turn off the VM, set the startup memory to 2048, start the VM, and restart the installation. You will get a warning that the memory does not meet the recommended amount of 4,000MB, but it's just a warning and won't stop the installation process. When the SCVMM install is complete, you can power down the VM, modify the startup value to less than 2048, and continue using SCVMM. It does not check for minimum memory anytime other than during install, but remember that using less than 2048 really is not recommended and definitely should not be used in any production environment.

If you have multiple SCVMM servers in a high-availability configuration, the same domain account would be used on all servers; it's actually a requirement to use a domain account in an SCVMM high-availability scenario or if you have a disjointed namespace in your domain. For information on disjointed namespaces, see http://support.microsoft.com/kb/909264. Hopefully this is not something you have in your environment, because it can be a huge pain for many applications.

During the installation of SCVMM there is an option to specify the storage location of the distributed keys that are used for the encryption of data in the SCVMM database. Normally these keys are stored on the local SCVMM computer; however, if you are implementing a highly available SCVMM installation, the keys need to be stored centrally. For SCVMM this means Active Directory. For details on creating the necessary container in Active Directory for the distributed key management, refer to http://technet.microsoft.com/en-us/library/gg697604.aspx.

> **WARNING** Do not use a generic domain service account for different applications, which can cause unexpected results and makes troubleshooting difficult. Use a separate account for each of your services—one for SCVMM, one for System Center Operations Manager (in fact, you need more than one for Operations Manager), another for System Center Configuration Manager, and so on. What do I mean by unexpected results? When SCVMM manages a host, it adds its management account to the local Administrators group of that host—in this case, svcSCVMM. If that host is removed from SCVMM management, that account is removed from the local Administrators group of that host. Now imagine you used a shared service account between SCVMM and another application that also needed its service account to be part of the local Administrators group. When you remove the host from SCVMM management, that shared service account is removed from the local Administrators group on that host, and you just broke that other application. Ouch!

The actual installation process for SCVMM is a simple, wizard-driven affair that guides you through all the required configuration steps, so I won't go into detail here. Just remember to specify your domain account for the service.

A number of other SCVMM server roles related to its library feature, self-service portal, reporting, bare-metal deployment, and update management need to be configured at installation. I cover these in more detail in the relevant sections of this chapter.

MAKING SCVMM HIGHLY AVAILABLE

Many of the major enhancements related to virtualization are centered upon making the virtual environment more available, surviving host failures, and moving virtual machines and storage without any downtime. SCVMM is a management tool for the entire virtual environment. If SCVMM is unavailable, you have lost your link to your virtual environment.

However, even if SCVMM is unavailable, this does not mean that the virtual environments managed by SCVMM will shut down. The virtual machines will continue running and failover of resources in host failure scenarios will still occur, but you won't be able to create new virtual machines, and key technologies like balancing of virtual machines based on utilization will no longer occur.

So, it's important to ensure that the SCVMM service is available. Prior to SCVMM 2012, the way to make SCVMM highly available was to install it into a virtual machine and make that virtual machine highly available, essentially relying on the capabilities of the hypervisor to keep the VM running. In the event of an unplanned failure on the host running the SCVMM VM, the VM would be moved automatically to another host in the cluster and then restarted, which would introduce a period of unavailability for the VM.

SCVMM 2012 now supports being installed on a failover cluster, which means the SCVMM service becomes highly available and can be moved in both planned and unplanned scenarios using failover clustering technologies. Installing SCVMM to a highly available configuration is very simple. Start the installation on an operating system instance that is part of a failover cluster. The SCVMM install process detects the presence of the Failover Clustering feature and prompts whether the SCVMM installation should be made highly available. If you answer yes, you are prompted for an additional IP address and a name that will be used for the cluster SCVMM service, and that is really the only change in the installation process. You must specify a domain account for the VMM service to run as, and use Active Directory for the storage of the encryption keys. You also need to install SCVMM on all the other nodes in the failover cluster so the SCVMM service can run on all of them. And, as mentioned earlier, an external SQL Server should be used to host the SCVMM database.

Remember that failover clusters do not mean physical hosts. Failover Clustering works great in virtual machines. The core SCVMM service does not require any shared storage to operate, although the VMM library does need to be on storage that is accessible on all nodes or hosted on a separate file server (which should also be highly available). In addition, if you are making SCVMM highly available, ensure that the SQL database is also highly available using SQL clustering; SCVMM is not much use without its SQL database.

▶ Using a domain account is what you were going to do anyway based on my earlier recommendations. Right?

Administering SCVMM 2012

Once SCVMM is installed, you will want to configure all the features and begin managing your environment. The rest of this chapter dives into the details of performing the various management functions, but I want to first briefly introduce SCVMM's two key administrative technologies: Administrator Console and Windows PowerShell.

USING THE SCVMM ADMINISTRATOR CONSOLE

The SCVMM Administrator Console, shown in Figure 9-2, looks different from consoles you may be used to. System Center has moved away from the Microsoft Management Console (MMC) standard in favor of a new workspace-based layout. The new console for SCVMM is divided into five main elements (also known as *panes*):

▶ **Ribbon:** However you feel about ribbons, you will quickly begin to appreciate the dynamically changing ribbon. It shows the actions available for the selected object and highlights those that are most popular based on *a lot* of research by the SCVMM team.

► If you are European you can use a German accent and say, "Voondairbars," which is a lot more fun.

► **Workspaces:** The entire console is workspace-based. In the Workspaces pane in the lower-left corner, you select the workspace you want to work in, which is reflected in all other areas of the console. The Workspaces pane shows the five available standard workspaces: VMs and Services, Fabric, Library, Jobs, and Settings. You will also hear workspaces unofficially referred to as Wunderbars. After the initial configuration of SCVMM, you will not use Settings very often, but you will use the other workspaces as you enhance your environment.

► **Navigation:** This shows the areas of management available in the current workspace.

► **Results:** This pane shows results based on the current navigation node selected. Note that the Results pane is also affected by selected ribbon elements, which determine what appears in the Results pane based on the current Workspace and Navigation areas.

► **Details:** The Details pane is not always shown, but when available it displays detailed information about the currently selected object in the Results pane.

The best way to learn your way around the SCVMM console is to fire it up and just look around. Explore all the workspaces, select the different nodes in the Navigation pane, and pay attention to the ribbon, which changes dynamically to display some interesting options with which you will want to play.

The Microsoft Management Console (MMC) was great for its original purpose of providing a standardized interface that could enable different snap-ins to be placed and organized in a single console. However, its capabilities were limited, particularly in terms of Role Based Access Control (RBAC), which is a key tenet of System Center 2012. Note that I'm talking about System Center 2012 here, not SCVMM 2012, because the focus on RBAC is common to all of System Center 2012, not just SCVMM 2012.

As System Center 2012 is used more broadly across an organization, it's very likely different groups of users will be given access to only certain functionality areas of System Center 2012 components, and within those functionality areas be able to perform actions only on a subset of all the objects. In the past, although delegating different permissions was possible, users with delegated rights would still see all the elements of the management console, and would get Access Denied messages. With the new System Center 2012 model and RBAC, delegated users see only the areas of the console to which they have rights, and only the objects with which they are allowed to work.

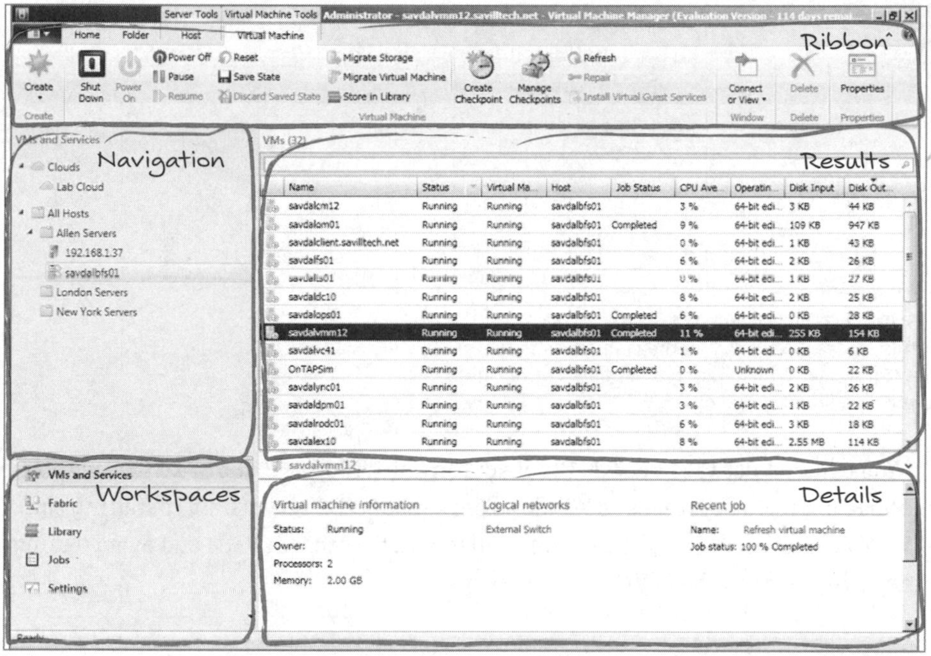

FIGURE 9-2: Elements of the SCVMM console vary according to the current workspace and selected elements of the workspace.

For example, in SCVMM 2012 you might grant delegated administrative rights to a group of users for only a specific collection of virtualization hosts. As Figure 9-3 shows, a full administrator sees the entire host hierarchy and all the available clouds, whereas a delegated administrator for the Allen servers cannot see any of the clouds and has no knowledge of other host groups except for Allen. Showing delegated users only the console elements and objects to which they have rights makes the console easier to use and more intuitive, and avoids the "Why don't I have access to x, y, and z?" questions. It also makes the administrative tool available to normal users, such as self-service users.

In SCVMM 2012, user roles are created and assigned in the Settings workspace in the Security – User Roles navigation area. By default, user roles exist for Administrator and Self-Service, but additional roles can be defined. Other profiles beyond Delegated Administrators include Read-Only Administrators, which is great for users such as the help-desk staff who need to see everything but should not be able to change anything and can be scoped to specific host groups and clouds; plus additional Self-Service User roles, which can be scoped to different clouds and can have different actions and quotas available to them. I cover the cloud and Self-Service roles in detail in the next chapter. Adoption of the new interface also enables the ribbon, which greatly facilitates user interaction with System Center 2012.

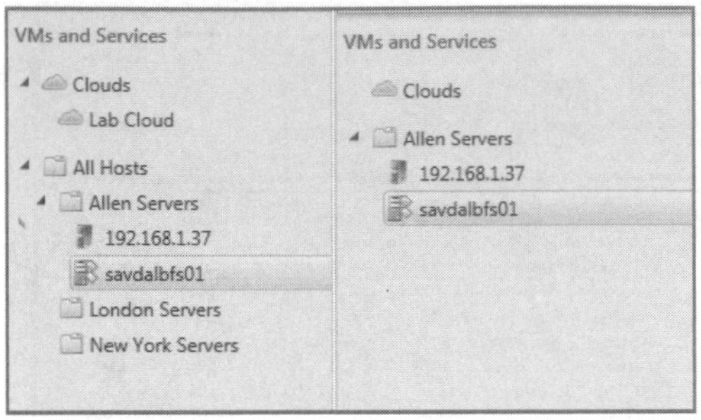

FIGURE 9-3: On the left is a normal SCVMM administrator view; and on the right you see the view for a user with delegated administrative rights to the Allen host group only.

You can install the SCVMM 2012 console on any Windows 7 x86 or x64 Professional or above operating system and Windows Server 2008 R2 servers. By installing the SCVMM 2012 console on machines, you can remotely access SCVMM and avoid having to actually log on to the SCVMM 2012 server.

> **TIP** I like to install all the various consoles from System Center 2012 components, Exchange, and anything I have to manage on a Remote Desktop Session Host (RDSH) (aka Terminal Server). Then I publish the applications to the desktops in my environment for easy access anywhere I log on. This way, my configurations for each administrative tool are consistent no matter which machine I use. If I'm not using one of my regular machines, I can use Remote Desktop Protocol (RDP) to access the RDSH directly and still access all the administrative tools. Publishing applications is covered in Chapter 7.

Once you start using SCVMM for management of your Hyper-V environments, you should not use Hyper-V Manager or the Failover Cluster Management tool for normal virtualization resource management. If you do make changes using Hyper-V Manager directly, SCVMM may not be aware of the change and it can take some time for SCVMM to detect it, which gives inconsistent views between Hyper-V Manager and SCVMM. For best results, once SCVMM is implemented and managing virtualization resources, don't use other management tools to manage the same resources.

UNLOCKING ALL POSSIBILITIES WITH WINDOWS POWERSHELL

When you look at any resource on System Center 2012 or Windows Server 2012, one common theme is the prevalence of Windows PowerShell. Everything that is done in the System Center consoles is actually performed by an underlying PowerShell cmdlet.

As you make a selection in a console and click an action, behind the scenes the console composes the correct PowerShell command and executes it. There are many actions you can only take with PowerShell, and as you become more acquainted with System Center you will start to use PowerShell more and more. I'm not talking about manually running actions, but when you consider that you can perform every management action for the entire System Center 2012 product using PowerShell, you will truly appreciate the automation possibilities and likely start automating more and more processes.

A good way to get started with PowerShell is to use the graphical interface to perform an action, such as creating a new virtual machine. In the Summary stage of the wizard you see a View Script button at the bottom right-hand corner. Click the button and you are shown all the PowerShell commands the console is going to run to perform the actions selected, as shown in Figure 9-4. You can add all these commands to your own scripts or automation processes.

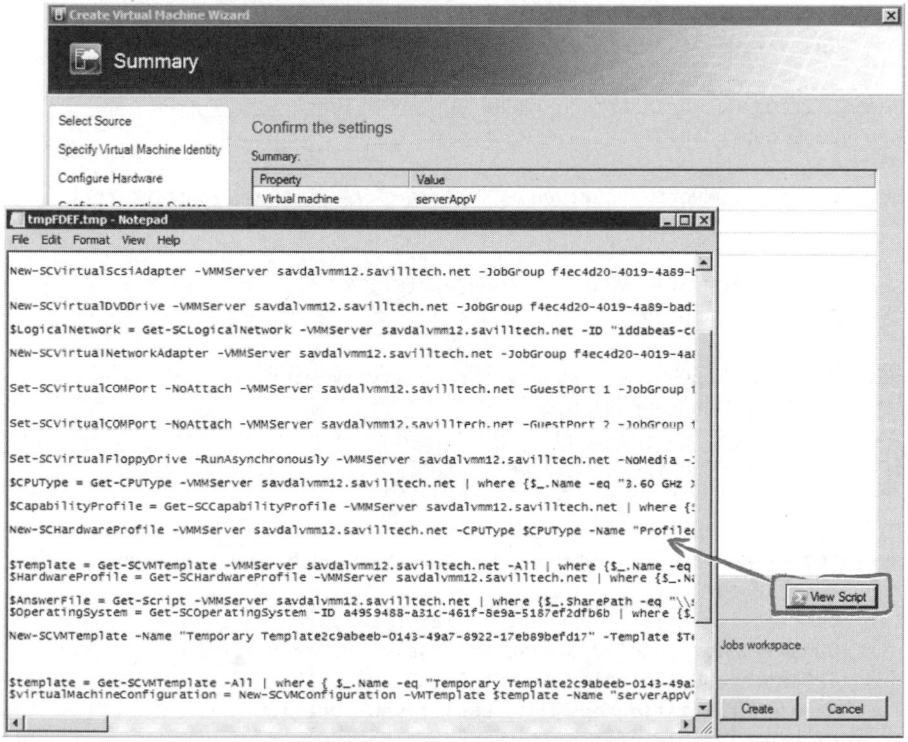

FIGURE 9-4: Click the View Script button to open a temporary file in Notepad that contains all the PowerShell commands needed to perform the current action.

Creating a virtual machine from a template is a great example, and Listing 9-1 shows the PowerShell script used to create a new VM—an empty VM to minimize the number of commands and start small. I also removed some of the large GUIDs for readability and added the PowerShell line continuation character (`` ` ``), but you could write each command as a single line. As you create VMs from templates, and use logical networks and tiered storage, the number of PowerShell commands grows.

Reading through the commands in the listing, most of them are self-explanatory. The majority of the commands are creating new objects such as DVD drives and network adapters, which are all bundled into the current job and finally used in the last command, New-SCVirtualMachine, which actually creates the virtual machine.

LISTING 9-1

```
New-SCVirtualScsiAdapter -VMMServer <VMM Server> -JobGroup <JobID> `
    -AdapterID 7 -ShareVirtualScsiAdapter $false `
    -ScsiControllerType DefaultTypeNoType

New-SCVirtualDVDDrive -VMMServer <VMM Server> -JobGroup <JobID> `
    -Bus 1 -LUN 0

New-SCVirtualNetworkAdapter -VMMServer <VMM Server> `
    -JobGroup <JobID>

Set-SCVirtualCOMPort -NoAttach -VMMServer <VMM Server> -GuestPort 1 `
    -JobGroup <JobID>

Set-SCVirtualCOMPort -NoAttach -VMMServer <VMM Server> -GuestPort 2 `
    -JobGroup <JobID>

Set-SCVirtualFloppyDrive -RunAsynchronously -VMMServer <VMM Server> `
    -NoMedia -JobGroup <JobID>

$CPUType = Get-CPUType -VMMServer <VMM Server> | where {$_.Name `
    -eq "3.60 GHz Xeon (2 MB L2 cache)"}

New-SCHardwareProfile -VMMServer <VMM Server> -CPUType $CPUType `
    -Name "ProfileXYZ" `
    -Description "XYZ" -CPUCount 1 -MemoryMB 512 `
    -DynamicMemoryEnabled $false -VirtualVideoAdapterEnabled $false `
    -CPUExpectedUtilizationPercent 20 -DiskIops 0 `
    -NetworkUtilizationMbps 0 -CPURelativeWeight 100 `
    -HighlyAvailable $false -NumLock $false -BootOrder "CD", `
    "IdeHardDrive", "PxeBoot", "Floppy" `
    -CPULimitFunctionality $false `
    -CPULimitForMigration $false -JobGroup <JobID>

New-SCVirtualDiskDrive -VMMServer <VMM Server> -IDE -Bus 0 -LUN 0 `
    -JobGroup <JobID> -VirtualHardDiskSizeMB 40960 -Dynamic `
```

```
        -Filename "Dummy_disk_1" -VolumeType BootAndSystem

$HardwareProfile = Get-SCHardwareProfile -VMMServer <VMM Server> | `
    where {$_.Name -eq "ProfileXYZ"}

New-SCVMTemplate -Name "Temporary Template" -HardwareProfile `
    $HardwareProfile -JobGroup <JobID> -NoCustomization

$template = Get-SCVMTemplate -All | where { $_.Name -eq `
    "Temporary Template" }

$virtualMachineConfig = New-SCVMConfiguration `
    -VMTemplate $template -Name "Dummy"

Write-Output $virtualMachineConfig

$vmHost = Get-SCVMHost -ComputerName "<Hyper-V Host>"

Set-SCVMConfiguration -VMConfiguration $virtualMachineConfig `
    -VMHost $vmHost

Update-SCVMConfiguration -VMConfiguration $virtualMachineConfig

$operatingSystem = Get-SCOperatingSystem | where { $_.Name -eq `
    "64-bit edition of Windows Server 2008 R2 Enterprise" }

New-SCVirtualMachine -Name "Dummy" '
    -VMConfiguration $virtualMachineConfig `
    -Description "" -BlockDynamicOptimization $false `
    -JobGroup "<JobID>" `
    -RunAsynchronously -StartAction "NeverAutoTurnOnVM" `
    -StopAction "SaveVM" -OperatingSystem $operatingSystem
```

The opportunity to use the View Script button is everywhere. For example, look at the properties of a virtual machine and modify something small, such as changing from static memory to dynamic memory. Once the change is made, the View Script button will become active, and clicking it will display the PowerShell script used to implement the changes made in the console. Other objects, such as some of those in fabric, don't even require a change: The View Script button is available when an object's properties are viewed and will show the PowerShell script used to create it.

To see all the PowerShell cmdlets that are available in SCVMM 2012, open the Virtual Machine Manager Command Shell and run the following command:

```
Get-Command -Module VirtualMachineManager
```

▶ This is just a Windows PowerShell console that automatically imports the Virtual Machine Manager module. The module can be loaded in any PowerShell console with the Import-ModuleVirtualMachine Manager command.

This will return a list of all 442 possible commands you can run. If you are looking for a PowerShell command related to creating something, you can pipe, or send, the output of Get-Command to a search for anything with "New" in the name, as shown in the following example:

```
Get-Command -Module VirtualMachineManager |
        where {$_.name -match "New"}
```

There are only 50 of those. Change the matching word from New to whatever you are looking for help on, such as LoadBalancer, LogicalNetwork, or UpdateServer.

> **TIP** To get a count of the results in PowerShell, just enclose a command in brackets and add `.Count` to the end. For example, `(Get-Command -Module VirtualMachineManager).Count` returns a total of 442.

If you have not had the opportunity to learn PowerShell, I strongly recommend taking some time to get at least a basic level of understanding. You can get a good idea of how to do things using the View Script capability within System Center, but knowing PowerShell will definitely help when you want to perform more sophisticated actions.

MANAGING THE FABRIC

Now that you understand the ways to interact with SCVMM, this section dives into what you can actually do; managing the fabric is really where you will spend a lot of time. When you think of fabric, images of material used to make your clothing and linens likely spring to mind, and this is exactly what it means in terms of your virtual environment—the underlying source material that enables you to virtualize your environment. In terms of virtualization, three types of fabric are most important for visibility and management:

- **Compute:** The virtualization hosts and clusters of hosts
- **Network:** The underlying network and network devices such as load balancers
- **Storage:** External storage arrays, such as SANs, that are used to store the virtual machines and other assets

Although previous versions of SCVMM did a good job of exposing the compute fabric and enabling management, they really didn't provide much information about the network and storage fabrics. Network and storage fabric intelligence and management are necessary when environments are housed in many different locations, and each location may have different types of storage, different IP subnets, and different load-balancing equipment. Administrators need to be able to deploy a virtual machine or multi-tiered service and only specify the networks to connect to, such as Production, and the tiers of storage to use, such as Gold for the highest IOPS storage and Green for lower capability loads. A good management tool needs to automatically create and configure the environments correctly, using the right physical storage and networks at each location where a virtual machine is created, based on logical selections made by the administrator. This abstraction and management of the network and storage fabric is exactly what SCVMM provides. SCVMM has not been idle in the compute fabric department either, so the following sections look at the compute fabric capabilities first and then explore storage and network.

▶ IOPS provides a measurement of the transfer speed of a disk or set of disks. The higher the number, the faster the storage. The highest performing workloads need storage with very high IOPS.

Managing Compute Resources

Hyper-V Manager and the Failover Cluster Management tool provide functionality out of the box to manage basic settings for a Hyper-V host or Hyper-V hosts within a cluster in addition to the virtual machines themselves. A major goal in IT is to use as few tools as possible to get the job done and ultimately attain the utopia of a single pane of glass for everything you do, which means a single interface. SCVMM's first requirement is to provide all the features in the native Hyper-V and Failover Cluster Management tools related to virtualization, so administrators don't have to use SCVMM *and* Hyper-V Manager *and* Failover Cluster Management. Looking at these capabilities is a great way to become familiar with System Center Virtual Machine Manager.

MANAGING HYPER-V SERVERS

Of course, a brand-new SCVMM 2012 installation isn't actually managing anything yet. It will have a default library with some blank disks in it and not much else. The first item of business is to add a Hyper-V server to SCVMM, or ideally a cluster of Hyper-V servers, which is where SCVMM can really demonstrate its worth. You add Hyper-V hosts through the Fabric workspace by clicking the Add Resources ribbon button, as shown in Figure 9-5.

When you add any kind of external system to SCVMM, you are prompted for credentials. You can enter these manually, but a better option is to use *Run As accounts*, a common capability available through SCVMM 2012. Run As accounts are sets of credentials stored securely in SCVMM that can be used when performing actions that require authorization, typically on remote systems. Good examples of Run As accounts are ones with permissions on the following:

▶ Remote ESX hosts

▶ Load balancers

▶ Storage arrays

▶ Administrator actions on Hyper-V hosts

FIGURE 9-5: Click the Add Resources ribbon button and then select Hyper-V Hosts and Clusters to launch the wizard to add Hyper-V servers to SCVMM.

By using a Run As account when an action is performed, only the Run As account needs to be selected, rather than requiring a user to enter full credentials, including username, password, and potentially a domain depending on the authentication scheme of the target device. You can manage Run As accounts in the Settings workspace, found under the Security node in the Navigation pane.

When a Hyper-V server is added to SCVMM, the SCVMM server must communicate with the Hyper-V host, add the SCVMM service account to the local Administrators group on the host to give SCVMM full management permissions, and install the SCVMM agent, which allows SCVMM to manage and collect information from the host. You can add Hyper-V servers selected individually, from a search of Active Directory, or as part of a Hyper-V cluster. If you add a Hyper-V host to SCVMM that is part of a cluster, it will automatically add all the hosts in the cluster and add the cluster objects into SCVMM.

You can add Hyper-V hosts that are in trusted domains, perimeter networks, and even untrusted domains. See http://technet.microsoft.com/en-us/library/gg610646.aspx for full information about the process for various scenarios.

SCVMM enables you to create a hierarchy of virtualization hosts using host groups, which can in turn contain other host groups The host groups also contain your virtualization hosts, which can be any mix of Hyper-V, ESX, and XenServer, enabling the hierarchy to reflect how you want to manage and allocate resources rather than which hypervisor is being used.

When architecting your host group hierarchy, consider carefully your reasons for creating it. Organizations typically design a host group hierarchy based on a number of factors, including the following:

- Geographic location

- Business unit ownership if not a shared infrastructure

- Capabilities of the hardware, including redundancy capabilities

- Type of hypervisor

- Network location, such as differentiating between hosts on the internal and DMZ networks

- Delegation of management

- Hosts or clusters that require a common configuration, such as reserve settings, optimization settings, placement logic, network and/or storage configuration

Once your host group structure is created, hosts and clusters are allocated to their appropriate group by the administrator using the SCVMM console. In a hierarchical design, host group members can be configured to inherit properties from the parent group, which means you can specify a certain level of the hierarchy to mirror delegation of management and common configuration, and then apply those settings across all successor groups. The child host groups can be created for other reasons, such as based on capabilities or placement.

Figure 9-6 shows a typical example of a geographical hierarchy: a top-level host group consisting of locations of corporate datacenters in London, New York, and, of course, Allen (in Texas, north of Dallas and where I live, which is why it ranks with those other major cities). To these top-level geographic host groups I applied management delegation and set common configurations around reserve and optimization settings. Note that settings common to every host group can be applied to the All Hosts container, under which all other host groups reside. At the second level down, I separated hosts based on network location, where I apply configurations for network and storage connectivity in addition to placement rules.

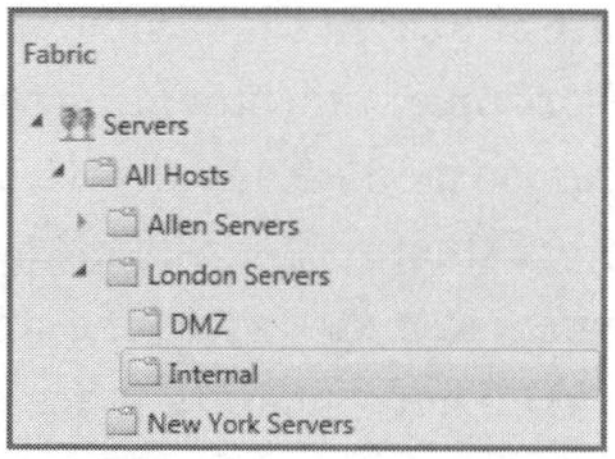

Selecting the properties of a host group exposes the configuration categories possible: Placement Rules, Host Reserves, Dynamic Optimization, Networks, Storage, and Custom Properties (see Figure 9-7). You can create custom placement rules to automate virtual machine

FIGURE 9-6: A two-tier hierarchy based on geographic location and then network location

placement based on custom attributes of the virtual machines. For example, a property of the VM might be "GeoLocation: London," and the placement rule could specify that custom properties of the VM must match the custom property of the host group that also says "GeoLocation: London." This ensures that VMs that should be created in London are actually created on London-based resources. Host Reserves enables you to allocate a certain amount of the virtualization host's resources to the virtualization management partition to ensure it can do its job. For Hyper-V this management partition is the Windows Server operating system you installed on the physical hardware. It's vital to ensure that the management partition always has enough resources to manage all those virtual machines, so reserving a certain percentage of resources prevents resource starvation on the management OS. These settings prevent virtual machines from starting if doing so would break these reserves for the host. Network and Storage provide insight into the access the host group has to those fabric resources (which are explored in the following sections).

With the virtualization hosts now in a well-architected host group hierarchy, some key features of SCVMM are available. Select a host group, then select the Overview action in the Show group in the Home tab on the ribbon. This provides a dashboard view summary of the health of the virtualization hosts in the host group; utilization information on CPU, memory, disk, and network for the current month and day; and the number of computer hours saved through the use of power optimization. Select the Fabric Resources action in the Show group to see some basic details about the hosts in the host group. The data to be shown is fully configurable; by default it's basic host status, CPU, and memory details, but it can be extended to show any combination of metrics such as VM count, cluster information, placement availability, custom fields, and a lot more. Right-click the Results pane column heading to see a list of all the possible properties that can be displayed.

Properties and actions for specific hosts are available once a host is selected within either the Navigation pane or the Results pane. Basic management options are shown in the ribbon, which include options to restart the host and power the host on or off (providing the BMC is configured). Options to start or stop maintenance mode are available. When a host is placed in maintenance mode, if it is in a host cluster then SCVMM evacuates all the VMs on the host to another host; otherwise, it simply saves the state of all virtual machines on that host. When a host is taken out of maintenance mode, VMs are moved back to the host or their state is restored from disk.

DYNAMIC OPTIMIZATION AND POWER OPTIMIZATION

These are new features in SCVMM 2012 that build on the Host Reserve feature, also setting minimum thresholds on free resources. *Dynamic optimization (DO)* is designed to ensure that the hosts within a cluster (Hyper-V, ESX, or XenServer) are spreading the virtual machine load as evenly as possible. This avoids some hosts being heavily loaded (potentially degrading the performance of virtual machines) while other hosts remain fairly lightly loaded. Dynamic optimization is one of the most frequently used features in almost all virtualized environments, because it dynamically balances the virtual machines across the hosts, automating a lot of the manual activities required of administrators related to the placement of virtual machines. Note that no amount of dynamic balancing can compensate for a poorly architected or overloaded environment, so it's still critical to perform accurate discovery and design of virtual environments.

DO is not considered a replacement for Performance Resource Optimization (PRO), which was present in SCVMM 2008 and leveraged System Center Operations Manager for details about utilization of the environment. Instead, DO is a complementary technology that does not rely on Operations Manager and is considered very much a reactive technology. DO works by periodically checking the resource utilization of each host in a cluster; and if the available resource drops below its defined threshold, DO will consider moving VMs onto other hosts with more free resources, thus rebalancing the virtual machines to better equalize host utilization throughout the cluster. As Figure 9-7 shows, you can define minimum thresholds for CPU, memory, disk, and network, in addition to how aggressive the rebalancing should be. The more aggressive the setting, the quicker DO will be to move virtual machines for even a small gain in performance. This means more live migrations, the technology used to move the virtual machines while ensuring no downtime.

Although any host group can have the DO configurations set at the group level, the optimizations are applied only to hosts in a cluster; and that cluster must support zero-downtime VM migrations, such as live migration on Hyper-V and XenMotion and vMotion on ESX. You can initiate a DO manually at any time by selecting a host cluster (in the SCVMM Navigation or Results pane, right-click on the name) and running the Optimize Hosts action, which will display a list of recommended migrations. The advantage of this manual DO is that it can be used even if DO is not configured on the actual host group, allowing one-off optimizations to be performed. The thresholds may be configured each time or defaulted.

▶ Dynamic optimization works only with clusters of hosts and not all the hosts in a host group. Virtual machines are moved around without user intervention using Live Migration or its equivalent, which operates only within a cluster.

▶ PRO is still present in SCVMM 2012 and is used as a more long-term placement technology. It is also the only extensible placement technology, allowing third-party PRO packs to be installed to extend the placement logic.

(continues)

(continued)

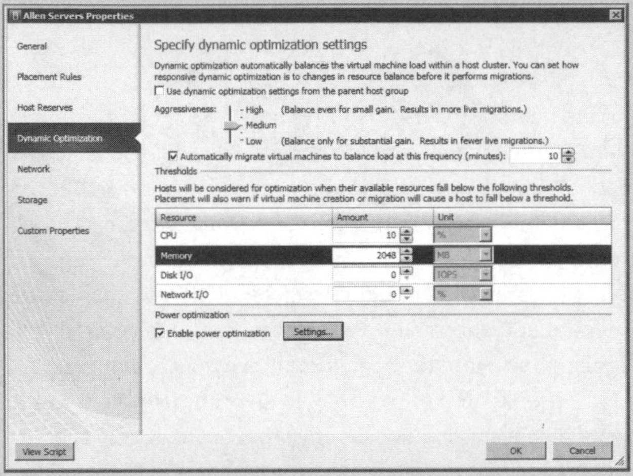

FIGURE 9-7: Uncheck the Use dynamic optimization settings from the parent host group box to allow specific DO settings for this host group based on resource thresholds.

Also shown in Figure 9-7 is an option to enable power optimization. Whereas dynamic optimization tries to spread load across all the hosts in a cluster evenly, *power optimization* aims to condense the number of hosts that need to be active in a cluster to run the virtual machine workload without negatively affecting their performance, powering down those not required. Consider a typical IT infrastructure that during the working day is busy servicing employees and customers, but is otherwise relatively idle. Using power optimization, you can set thresholds that ensure that VMs are consolidated and that evacuated hosts are powered down, provided the remaining hosts don't drop below their configured thresholds for CPU, memory, disk, or network resource. These are very similar to the configuration options set for DO, but instead of moving VMs off hosts below the threshold, you are controlling how much load you can move onto a host and remain above the threshold. Your power optimization thresholds should be set higher than those for dynamic optimization, because the goal of power optimization is consolidation in quiet periods. If the power optimization thresholds were lower than the dynamic optimization thresholds, hosts would be powered off, and then a lot of live migrations would occur, moving VMs around; and the hosts that were just powered off would be powered on again.

The power optimization thresholds also need to leave a significant margin of spare resource. First, resource utilization fluctuates even in quiet periods, and you don't want to be starting and stopping servers. Second, when resource utilization picks up again during busy periods, it takes time to power on and boot the servers that were powered down. Therefore, plenty of buffer capability is required to ensure that there is no resource shortage during the ramp-up.

Additionally, as Figure 9-8 shows, you can set at what times power optimization can occur. In this example I don't want power optimization to occur during business hours, except for a few exceptions. However, there is no reason to stop power optimization during the working day if you set sufficiently high thresholds to ensure that hosts have sufficient spare resources and won't suddenly be overtaxed during the time it takes to power up servers that were powered down.

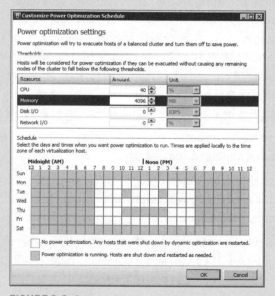

FIGURE 9-8: Set comfortable resource thresholds to ensure sufficient resource availability.

The capability to wake servers remotely is actually very important, because you don't want to power down servers that are not needed at a certain time and then be unable to start them up when needed again. Powered-down hosts are started using the host's Baseboard Management Controller (BMC), which needs to be configured on a per-host basis. If the BMC is not present in a host or is not configured, it will not be able to be powered off as part of power optimization.

One feature I'm a huge fan of that was added in SCVMM 2012 is the option to run scripts on hosts via the Run Script Command action. This enables an SCVMM administrator to run essentially any command on the selected host and see the response. Follow these steps to take a quick test drive:

1. Select a host and click the Run Script Command from the Host group within the Host tab on the ribbon.

2. Enter the name of the executable program and the parameters. In this walk-through you're going to use cmd.exe as the executable, which means for the parameters you must add /q to turn off echo and /c to run the command and then terminate it, which ensures that the result of the command you want to run will be returned to SCVMM. After /q and /c enter your actual command. For this example you just want to start the Print Spooler. My full parameter is /q /c net start spooler as shown in Figure 9-9. The Script resource package option allows an additional custom resource to be used as part of the remote script execution; these are just folders that contain resources, such as scripts or executables that are stored in the SCVMM library and whose names end with .cr. In my environment I created a folder named PSTools.cr in the SCVMM library containing my SysInternals PS suite of tools, which are very useful. A Run As account can also be used if needed for the script execution.

3. Click the Advanced button to configure options for standard and error output, how to detect execution failure, and handling restarts.

4. Once all options are set, click the OK button (although the View Script button will be available if you want to grab the PowerShell that is actually triggering this remote script execution for future use).

5. Select the Jobs workspace and order by Start Time. A new job will have been created by SCVMM invoking the specified Run Script Command, which will show the status and any information related to its output.

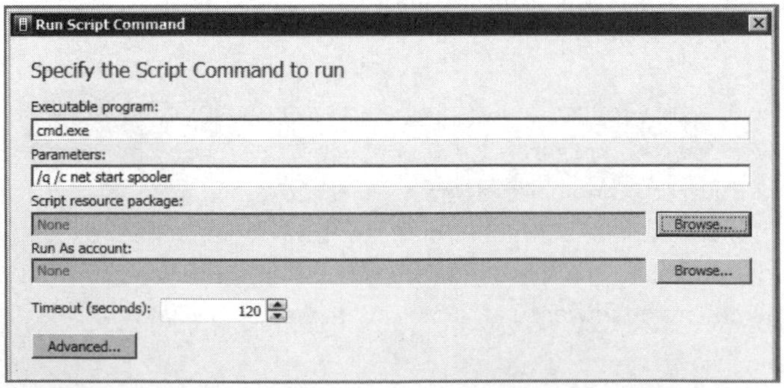

FIGURE 9-9: A very basic remote command execution that starts a service using the net start command

> **TIP** If you have problems with script commands, connect to the host that is being sent the command and in the `C:\Windows\Temp` folder will be a file named `gce_stderrorxxxxxxxxx.log` containing the error that matches the content in the job object within SCVMM.

Opening the properties of a host enables configuration of all the standard elements you would expect, such as hardware, network, paths for virtual machines, servicing windows, and machine-specific reserves, if required. There is also a Status section, which provides a health summary of the host, the Hyper-V role, and the SCVMM agent components, as shown in Figure 9-10. In the event of a problem, you can attempt remediation by clicking the Repair All button. Though this is not a deep monitoring solution comparable to Operations Manager, it does provide a low level of basic health and remediation that is useful when hosts are not behaving or responding as expected.

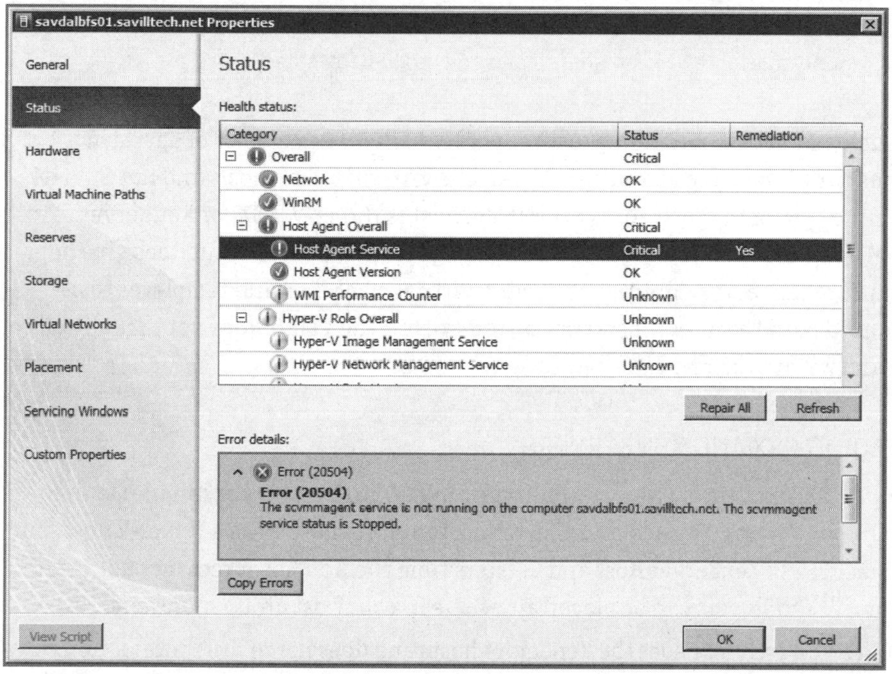

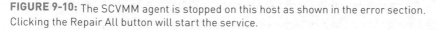

FIGURE 9-10: The SCVMM agent is stopped on this host as shown in the error section. Clicking the Repair All button will start the service.

Properties of host clusters are also accessible, including Available Storage and Cluster Shared Volume information. One feature you will likely want to use, under the General section, is the Cluster reserve (nodes) setting, which allows you to specify the number of host failures the cluster can withstand without affecting its ability to host the virtual machine load.

For example, if you have a four-node cluster, you might set a Cluster reserve of one node, which constrains SCVMM from placing more virtual machines than are able to run on only three of the nodes; that is, the cluster could handle a loss of one node and still run all the virtual machines. If you have a 16-node cluster, you might set a cluster reserve of two nodes. In this case, the Cluster reserve value is used in two ways. If the cluster has more virtual machines configured than what can be supported based on the total number of nodes in the cluster *minus* the number of nodes configured for Cluster reserve, it will have a state of over-committed. When a host cluster is in an over-committed state, it receives a rating of zero during any virtual machine placement operations. Note, however, that virtual machines can still be placed on the cluster through administrator manual override, but this is not advised.

> NOTE SCVMM 2012 allows you to create virtual machines that are not highly available on a host that is part of a highly available cluster using shared or local storage. Prior to SCVMM 2012, if a host were part of a highly available cluster, only highly available VMs on shared storage could be created.

Finally, I'd like to mention guest support, which is the support of operating systems running inside virtual machines. The virtualization host, and not SCVMM, determines guest support, so it varies if the host is Hyper-V, ESX, or XenServer. SCVMM does not change the guest operating systems supported, but does give better management and visibility by allowing virtual machines and templates to be configured with the guest operating system within the VM. It does not actually alter anything within the VM.

MANAGING ESX AND XENSERVERS

Managing XenServers is a new capability in SCVMM 2012 and is very similar to managing Hyper-V hosts. You add a XenServer host in the same way as a Hyper-V host, but you select Citrix XenServer Host and Clusters from the Add Resources menu instead of Hyper-V. XenServers can be placed anywhere in your host group hierarchy.

SCVMM directly manages the XenServer hosts and does not require interaction with a Citrix XenCenter server, which is the Xen version of SCVMM. A SCVMM package must be installed manually on the XenServers before being added to SCVMM, which enables communication between the XenServer and SCVMM. Go to http://www.citrix.com/lang/English/lp/lp_2305185.asp to download the Microsoft System Center Integration Pack for XenServer, which can be installed on existing XenServers or during the XenServer installation as documented at http://blogs.citrix.com/2011/06/16/managing-xenserver-with-system-center-virtual-machine-manager-scvmm-2012/.

A Run As account will be needed that has root access on the XenServer host to enable the connection and management of the XenServer. Once SCVMM is connected to Xen-Server, all the major virtual machine management capabilities will be available.

ESX management differs quite a bit from XenServer management. VMware does not make public APIs available for direct management of ESX hosts; instead, the management APIs are accessed through vCenter, which is the VMware version of SCVMM but for ESX. This means the process to add ESX hosts to SCVMM requires the addition of the vCenter server to SCVMM. Once vCenter is known to SCVMM, the ESX servers that are managed by those vCenter servers can be added to SCVMM and placed into the host group hierarchy, as shown in Figure 9-11, which has both an ESX host and a Hyper-V host in the same host group. The capability to place the ESX hosts anywhere in the SCVMM host group hierarchy is a change from previous versions of SCVMM, which required the ESX hosts to exist in a separate, one-time static import of the vCenter datacenter tree.

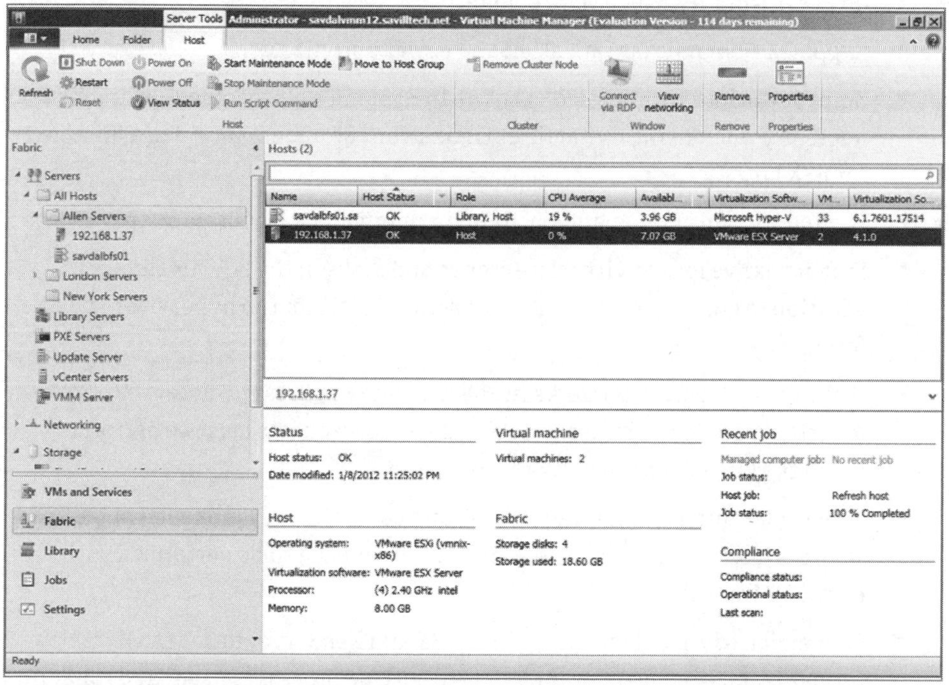

FIGURE 9-11: As with a Hyper-V or XenServer host, basic management of the ESX host is possible through SCVMM, as shown in the ribbon.

All management actions to ESX hosts from SCVMM are actually actioned by vCenter, which is sent commands by SCVMM. SCVMM no longer uses Secure File Transfer Protocol (SFTP) to transfer files to ESX hosts, instead leveraging HTTPS. This also means SCVMM no longer requires root Secure Shell (SSH) access to ESX hosts, which was a security concern for many ESX environments.

The capabilities available for ESX and XenServer management are basically the same, and are shown in the following list. What is key to understand is that SCVMM is focused on virtual machine management (hence SCVMM's name) of these external hypervisors, not on the management of the hypervisor itself. This is different from SCVMM's approach to Hyper-V hosts, for which it offers full host management as well:

- ▶ Adding hosts and clusters/pools

- ▶ Configuring placement logic based on current virtual machine deployment and VM migrations

- ▶ Support of SCVMM Service Deployment (SCVMM will not deploy VMware vApps for ESX users.)

- ▶ Availability of private cloud functionality (For ESX the SCVMM private clouds do not integrate with VMware vCloud.)

- ▶ Support of dynamic optimization and power optimization

- ▶ Zero-downtime VM migrations between hosts in a cluster/pool, which is a necessity when using dynamic optimization; Storage vMotion is available for ESX hosts.

- ▶ Placing hosts in maintenance mode and bringing them out of maintenance mode

- ▶ Storing native format virtual machines and disks in the SCVMM library in addition to creating new templates within SCVMM for the hypervisor-specific formats

- ▶ Utilization of logical networks in SCVMM and IP address pools; actual creation of virtual network switches on ESX and XenServer hosts must be performed using the virtualization native tools.

- ▶ Support for thin provisioning storage and basic storage management on ESX, whereas most storage operations on XenServer need to be performed with Citrix native tools

- ▶ Conversion of virtual machines from ESX and XenServer format to Hyper-V format (For ESX conversion a virtual-to-virtual process is used, and for Xen-Server conversion a physical-to-virtual process is used.)

- ▶ Full utilization of the virtualization host's capabilities related to virtual machine creation, such as 8 vCPUs and 255GB of RAM when deploying to ESX hosts

For anything other than basic host management of ESX and XenServer, administrators will use the natively provided tools from VMware and Citrix. The great news for ESX organizations is that SCVMM now works with vCenter side-by-side, rather than trying to take over, meaning both tools can be used in tandem (which is very different from the SCVMM 2008 R2 experience). Note that the preceding list does not refer to the overall capability of the hypervisor—only the capabilities exposed through SCVMM.

The next section covers the library, but one huge change in SCVMM 2012 is the handling of templates imported from vCenter. In previous versions of SCVMM, when templates were imported from vCenter the template and associated VMDK files would be imported into the SCVMM library and removed from the vCenter library, which meant the templates had to be deployed from SCVMM, and the file copy from SCVMM to the ESX host was slow compared to deployment from vCenter. In SCVMM 2012, only the template metadata is imported from vCenter; the actual template and VMDK are left in place. When an ESX template is deployed from SCVMM 2012 to an ESX host, SCVMM instructs vCenter to deploy the template, taking advantage of the native file transfer capabilities of vCenter to ESX, and therefore providing the best performance. This is a common theme with SCVMM 2012 and vSphere management: SCVMM 2012 works *with* vCenter rather than trying to take over and block its use.

USING LIBRARIES

You will want to have many resources available in your virtual environment, both for virtual machine creation and for host management. Although it is possible to store all these resources in various locations, the best way is to utilize the SCVMM library feature, which allows one or more file shares to be used by SCVMM as a central repository for assets that can be used in virtualization management. Typical assets placed in the library include the following:

- Virtual machine templates, which include the virtual machine hardware configuration, OS configuration information such as domain membership, product key, and other configuration options, enabling very fast creation of new virtual machines

- Virtual hard disks, which are primarily VHD for Hyper-V virtual machines (and XenServer), but they can also store VMDK for ESX. VHD files can also be used to deploy physical Hyper-V servers.

- Virtual machines that are not in use

- ISO files, which are images of CDs and DVDs that can be attached to virtual machines to install operating systems or applications

▶ You can save disk space on the virtualization hosts or shared storage for unused machines by storing them in the SCVMM library, which is very useful. You can deploy them again if needed. For end users, this prolongs their VM quota!

- ▶ Drivers
- ▶ Service templates, which describe multi-tiered services
- ▶ Various types of profiles, such as hardware profiles and guest OS profiles, which are used as building blocks for creating templates. Also host profiles (for physical deployments of Hyper-V servers), capability profiles (which describe the capabilities of different hypervisors or environments), SQL Server profiles for installing SQL Server, and Application profiles for application deployment. Think of profiles as building blocks for use in other activities within SCVMM.
- ▶ Baseline and catalog updating
- ▶ Scripts and commands used for management, which can be grouped together into packages called *custom resources* (which, as previously mentioned, are just folders with a `.cr` extension).

I want to be clear that although the library does have a physical manifestation by storing content on the file shares you specify when you add new library servers, not everything in the library is saved as a file. You will not find virtual machine templates or profiles as files on the file system; instead, templates and profiles are stored as metadata in the SCVMM SQL database.

You can access the filesystem that corresponds to a location in the library by right-clicking a library branch and selecting Explore, as shown in Figure 9-12, or by selecting Explore from the ribbon. To add non–virtual machine type content such as drivers and ISO files, you would just use the Explore feature and then copy content onto the file system using Windows Explorer. When the library content is refreshed, the new content is displayed; you can force this to occur by selecting the library server and selecting the Refresh action in the Library Server ribbon tab. By default, library content is automatically refreshed once per hour, but you can change this in the Settings workspace. In the General navigation area, select the Library Settings and change the refresh interval per your organization's requirements.

I cover the creation and usage of templates in the next section when I walk through administering virtual machines, so I'm going to move on to using other types of resources, but templates are a major reason to use SCVMM and we won't be glossing over them.

Although a single SCVMM library server is added during the installation of SCVMM, you can add other library servers. It's very common to add multiple library servers, particularly to have a library server in each datacenter where you have virtualization hosts, to ensure that content that may need to be accessed by the hosts is locally available, obviating the need to traverse a WAN connection. After you have added a library server and selected the share, check the Add Default Resources box to copy the entire SCVMM default library content to the share, which is useful content. It is fully supported to host the file share that stores the library content on a highly available file server, which means it's part of a failover cluster and therefore helps ensure the content is available even if a node fails.

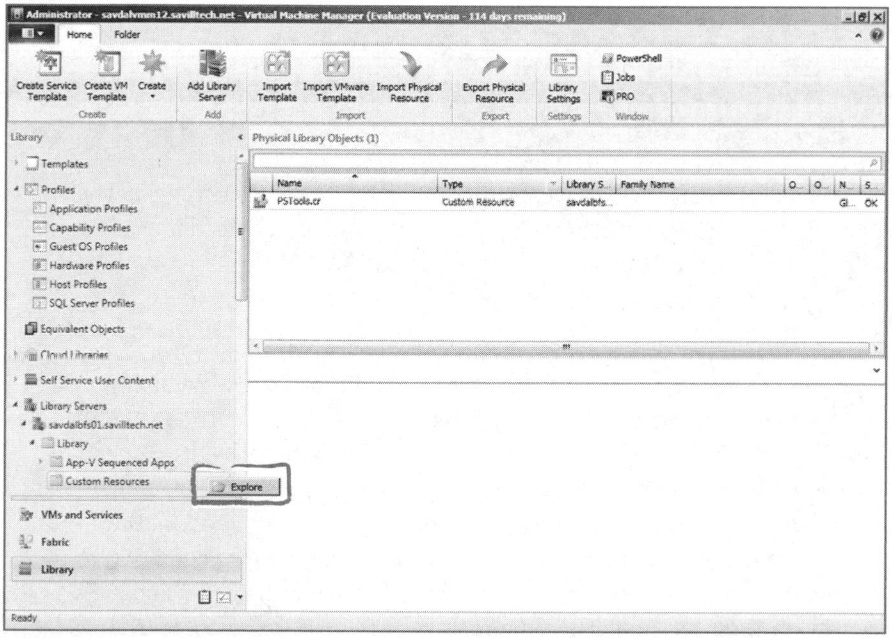

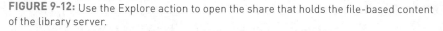

FIGURE 9-12: Use the Explore action to open the share that holds the file-based content of the library server.

To ensure hosts use a library server that is closest to them, you can assign library servers to host groups by selecting the properties of the library server and setting the host group, as shown in Figure 9-13. It is recommended that virtualization hosts should be connected by at least a 100 Mbps link to the library server they use, and ideally 1 Gbps.

If you have multiple libraries you will end up with the same content on many different library servers, and your templates will refer to the content on a specific library server such as \\londonlib\SCVMM\VHDs\2008R2.vhd. However, if you are deploying to a server in, for example, New York and there is a library server in New York (\\newyorklib\ SCVMM) that has exactly the same file, you would use that rather than copy the content across the North Atlantic. SCVMM allows equivalencies to be created in the library, which as the name suggests enables you to specify that various content from all the different libraries is actually the same object. This means that even though a template may, for example, deploy to \\londonlib\SCVMM\VHDs\2008R2.vhd, because you created an equivalency between the \\londonlib\SCVMM\VHDs\2008R2.vhd and \\newyorklib\SCVMM\VHDs\2008R2.vhd files, if you deployed the template in New York it would use the VHD from the New York share. This also provides redundancy because if the New York library were not available, the London library could be used.

REPLICATING LIBRARY CONTENT BETWEEN MULTIPLE SCVMM LIBRARY SERVERS

SCVMM has no capability to replicate the content of the library servers. If your organization has 20 SCVMM library servers, for example, you need to maintain 20 file shares, each with its own content. If you add a VHD to one library, you need to add it to the other 19 manually.

A number of solutions exist to keep the content replicated, but all involve initially having a single "master" library, which is the library whose content you update, add to, and remove. A technology is then used to synchronize this master copy to all the other library servers. One way to replicate the content is to use the Microsoft Robust File Copy tool (Robocopy), which copies the content from the master to all the other libraries in the organization. Once the copy is complete, a manual refresh of the library is performed in SCVMM to load in the new content, which can be performed in PowerShell using the **Read-SCLibraryShare** cmdlet. Another option is to use Distribute File System Replication (DFSR), which allows master-slave relationships to be created and automatically replicates changes from the master to the slave library shares, but the new content is not displayed until a library refresh is performed. You *cannot* use Distributed File System Namespaces (DFSN) as a location for libraries, only the DFSR replication component.

If your organization is using another replication technology, that is fine; the two listed here are free, Microsoft-provided technologies.

To create an equivalency, select the root Library Servers node in the Navigation pane in the Library workspace. You can then add a filter in the Results pane to show only the objects of interest. For example, in Figure 9-14 my filter is set to show virtual hard disks only. Select the objects that are the same and then select the Mark

Equivalent action. A dialog will open that asks for a Family for the objects and then a Release. Both of these values are just text values, but they are used to help find other objects that match the Family and Release, so be consistent in your naming. As you type in the values, autocomplete will show existing values or you can select from the drop-down.

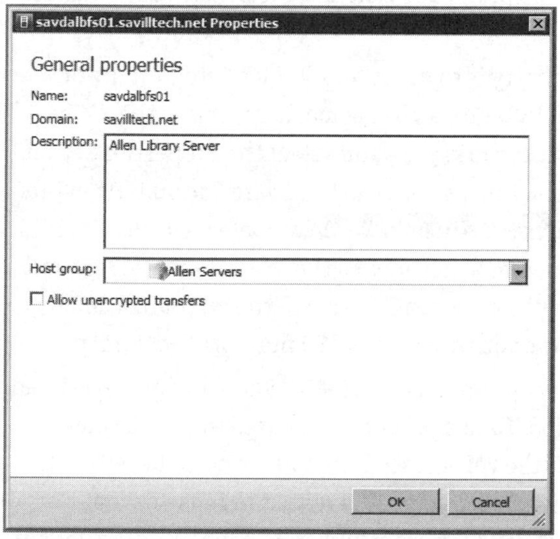

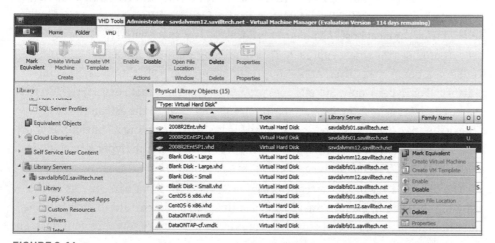

FIGURE 9-13: To assign a library server to a host group, select the library's properties and then select the host group to which it should belong.

FIGURE 9-14: To create an equivalency, select multiple objects that are the same across multiple library servers, and then select the Mark Equivalent action to make usage of the object interchangeable based on closest location to the host.

The content in the library is used in many different ways throughout SCVMM. Earlier when I talked about the Run Script Command, I explained that custom resources from the library could be used for additional script or executable access when running the command. Later, when I talk about deploying templates, you will see that virtual hard disks from the library are specified for the deployment in addition to using the hardware and guest OS profiles as building blocks for your template information.

One interesting purpose for the library is to use it for ISO files, which contain the content of a CD or DVD. To inject a CD/DVD into a virtual machine, select the VM in the Results pane of the VMs and Services workspace and select the Properties action. Within the properties of the virtual machine, select the Hardware Configuration tab, and under Bus Configuration ~~you will find a Virtual DVD drive.~~ Select the Virtual DVD drive. Note there are options for No media, which means the drive is empty; Physical CD or DVD drive, which links it to the physical optical drive in the virtualization host; or Existing ISO image file, which allows you to select an ISO file from the library.

Note also an interesting secondary option in Figure 9-15, "Share image file instead of copying it." Why is that there? A CD/DVD image is normally used to install some software onto an operating system. If the VM accessed the ISO file over the network and that connectivity was lost, it may cause unexpected results because it would appear the media was suddenly ripped out. To prevent this from happening, by default when an ISO is attached to a VM drive, the ISO is first copied using BITS over the HTTPS protocol to the Hyper-V host in the virtual machine's folder, and then the VM attaches to the local copied ISO file. This means any network interruption would not stop the access to the ISO. When the ISO is ejected from the VM, the copied ISO file is deleted from the local host. Although this does use disk space while the ISO is being used, it provides the safest approach. This same copy approach is used for ESX and XenServer, but using a different file copy technology specific to the virtualization platform. For Hyper-V only, SCVMM does provide the option of not copying the ISO to the virtualization host, instead attaching the virtual drive to the ISO on the SCVMM library file share (which is the "Share image file instead of copying it" option). If you want to use this, a few special configurations are required on the Hyper-V host, documented at http://technet.microsoft.com/en-us/library/ee340124.aspx.

The library is one of the key capabilities of SCVMM. All types of resources can be stored in the library, even entire virtual machines, so it's important to architect the right number of library servers to ensure proximity of a library server to your hosts in all your datacenters.

▶ You should find a DVD drive—it's the default for virtual machines. If there is not a DVD drive, stop the VM and add a DVD drive through the New: DVD action in the Hardware Configuration dialog and then restart the VM.

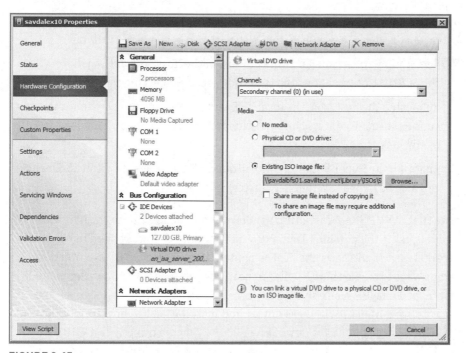

FIGURE 9-15: Once an ISO file is selected, you can choose to share the image file. Note the New: DVD option at the top of the dialog if you don't have a DVD drive.

PERFORMING BARE-METAL HYPER-V DEPLOYMENTS

One area of focus for SCVMM improvement was better capabilities to manage the actual Hyper-V hosts—for example, actually deploying Hyper-V to a bare-metal server and creating clusters. SCVMM 2012 supports the capability for virtualization servers to boot over the network using PXE; SCVMM acts as a PXE Boot Server and provides a Windows PE image for the server to use temporarily. Once the server has booted into the Windows PE environment, SCVMM can continue with the configuration of the new host, which includes the following:

1. Running any generic commands that have been defined, such as performing hardware-specific actions like RAID configuration

2. Partitioning and formatting disks for the Windows operating system, including creating the system partition containing the boot configuration database

3. Downloading from the SCVMM library a defined VHD file that contains Windows Server 2008 R2

4. Placing the VHD file on the local host storage and setting up the boot configuration database to use Boot from VHD with the downloaded VHD file

5. Performing a check on hardware present in the host, and pulling drivers from the SCVMM library that match the hardware and injecting them into the VHD

6. Rebooting the host from the local VHD and performing final customizations such as static IP address configuration from SCVMM IP pools and domain join operations

7. Enabling the Hyper-V role and installing the SCVMM agent installed. The host can also be joined to a Hyper-V cluster.

Note that SCVMM is not installing Windows Server 2008 R2 onto the hardware; instead it is using the new Boot from VHD functionality that was added in Windows Server 2008 R2, which allows physical computers to boot from a VHD file. You have numerous ways to create this VHD file. You can use a standard Windows Server 2008 R2 Sysprepped image in your library, you can capture a different image using the `imagex` command from the Windows Automated Installation Kit, or you can even convert the WIM file on the Windows Server 2008 R2 media directly to a VHD using the WIM2VHD tool (at `http://archive.msdn.microsoft.com/wim2vhd`). I like to use SCVMM capabilities to create a template and use the generated VHD from a 2008 R2 VM, keeping it in the family.

> **TIP** For best performance, use a fixed-size VHD file, especially for production environments. If the VHD in the library is dynamic, it will be converted to fixed during the deployment by default unless you deselect the option to convert in the host profile properties. For all Boot from VHD file configurations, the `pagefile.sys` file is not created in the VHD but on the physical hard disk. Though you can change the physical hard disk used, you cannot configure `pagefile.sys` to run within the VHD file. Because `pagefile.sys` is stored on the physical disk, make sure the physical partition containing your VHD is large enough to store both the fixed-size VHD and the size of the `pagefile.sys` file that matches the size of your memory.

There are a few prerequisites and configuration steps needed to use the bare-metal deployment capability in SCVMM 2012, but it's a straightforward process and relatively easy to get up and running quickly:

1. Deploy Windows Deployment Services (WDS), a role of Windows Server 2008 R2, to a server and add the PXE Server to the Fabric workspace of SCVMM. Once this is added, SCVMM performs configuration on the WDS to deliver the

SCVMM Windows PE environment and to check with SCVMM for authorization for machine boot. Network drivers for the physical servers are added to a folder called Drivers in the SCVMM library.

2. Create a Run As account in SCVMM with credentials for the Baseboard Management Controller (BMC) as the root account.

3. Create a host profile in the SCVMM library that specifies which VHD in the library is to be used for the physical host, in addition to IP address configuration, how driver installation will be handled, the OS configuration, and default paths for virtual machines.

4. Add the new servers to SCVMM. Using the Fabric workspace, Add Resource - Hyper-V Host and Cluster option, specify to Add physical computers to be provisioned as virtual machine hosts. At this point the BMC in the host will be contacted to confirm manageability by SCVMM. You specify the host profile and the IP address settings, such as DHCP or IP pool usage.

5. Enable the physical server to PXE boot (to enable boot over the network) and ensure virtualization features are enabled (which are Hyper-V requirements).

Whether your organization chooses the bare-metal deployment capability will depend on your existing OS deployment capabilities. Deploying the Hyper-V hosts from SCVMM is a nice feature, but if System Center Configuration Manager is already deploying your servers, and you have all the drivers installed and other hardware add-ins for BIOS and RAID configuration, it would be easier just to add a step in the SCCM task sequence to enable the Hyper-V role and install the SCVMM agent, rather than maintain an entirely separate OS deployment solution just for Hyper-V hosts. It's certainly worth a look if you don't have any kind of existing server deployment capability. SCVMM's ability to create clusters of Hyper-V hosts automatically is useful no matter what system you use to deploy the actual operating system, and most organizations are very interested in it.

▶ The physical server must have a BMC that allows management by SCVMM during deployment—that is, it must support the Intelligent Platform Management Interface (IPMI) protocol or Systems Management Architecture for Server Hardware (SMASH) out of the box.

UPDATING HYPER-V SERVERS

Windows requires patching occasionally (OK, sometimes monthly), and in a virtualized world every time you patch the hypervisor or management partition there is a chance the update requires a reboot. In a clustered implementation, patching means moving all the VMs on the host to other hosts in the cluster using Live Migration (to ensure no downtime in VM availability), patching the host, rebooting, and then moving the VMs back. If a reboot is required in a nonclustered scenario, the VMs on the host are unavailable for however long it takes to apply updates, and during shutdown/startup and the reboot itself.

SCVMM 2012 supports patching of Hyper-V hosts, including the capability to patch an entire cluster of Hyper-V hosts in a one-click operation through its orchestration capabilities. SCVMM will take care of evacuating a node, placing it in maintenance mode if connected to System Center Operations Manager, patching it, rebooting it, bringing it out of maintenance mode, moving VMs back, and then repeating the process for the next node until every node in the cluster is patched.

Windows Software Update Services (WSUS) is used to discover all the available patches through a connection to the Microsoft Update servers, and then a baseline is created in SCVMM that contains all the patches you want applied to the Hyper-V hosts. The baseline is then assigned to host groups and/or individual Hyper-V hosts and a scan can be performed (see the ribbon in Figure 9-16), which indicates whether the hosts and clusters are compliant. If a host or cluster is not compliant, the action to Remediate will be available, which applies the patches. To remediate an entire cluster, you trigger the previously described orchestration for all hosts in the cluster. As shown in Figure 9-16, you can click Compliance Properties for a host to see compliance for individual updates in a baseline.

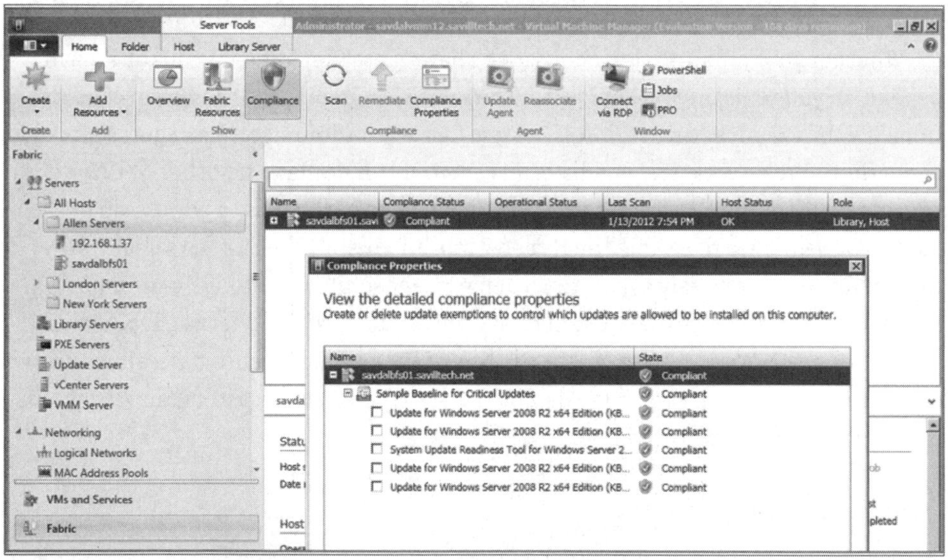

FIGURE 9-16: Selecting Compliance from the Show section of the ribbon displays detailed compliance status for a host.

If your organization is using SCCM for the patching of servers, it is currently not possible to leverage the SCCM update deployment packages you already have for servers managed via SCVMM. However, SCVMM *can* use the same WSUS server that is used by SCCM, with a few tweaks to both SCVMM and SCCM. As with the bare-metal deployment scenario, if you are already using SCCM to patch servers, it is probably easier to leverage SCCM to patch your Hyper-V servers rather than configure SCVMM to manage patches for the Hyper-V servers separately. The advantage that SCVMM has over SCCM is the orchestration of patching an entire cluster. Note, however, that the same process could be achieved fairly easily using System Center Orchestrator (discussed in the next chapter), which could use the SCVMM maintenance mode capability to evacuate the VMs and then the SCCM update services for the actual patching.

Managing Network Resources

You could create the best virtual machine environment in the world—with a library full of awesome content and templates for every situation—but if the VMs cannot talk to each other or the rest of the organization, then they are of limited use. Most organizations have many networks—production, testing, development, backup, DMZ, Internet, and more; and virtual machines will almost certainly need to connect to these.

USING LOGICAL NETWORKS

Virtualization tries to abstract each layer of functionality from the others, but traditionally the network has been closely tied to your virtual machines and virtual machine templates. This hard link means you may need different templates depending on the datacenter to which you deploy a virtual machine. Moreover, you need to understand which (virtual) external switch on a Hyper-V host has connectivity to the right networks, or which connected physical switch port is trunked the right way to allow connectivity to the required VLAN.

Ideally, a consistent naming scheme should be used among the virtualization hosts to make this simpler; but when deploying a virtual machine you still need to pick which virtual switch to use, and you'll likely customize the IP address for the VM based on where you're deploying it to. For example, if I deploy my virtual machine to London, my production network may be on the 192.168.25.0/24 subnet with a VLAN of 24, whereas deploying to New York may use an IP subnet of 192.168.40.0/24 with a VLAN of 18. That's a lot to handle for IT administrators; now imagine you are exposing your virtual machine templates and your fabric resources to business units and end users, through self-service portals and various service catalogs, for them to deploy their own virtual machines and services to all of the datacenters. Good luck with getting them to get those details right.

> *All problems in computer science can be solved by another level of indirection.*
>
> *—David Wheeler*

▶ The proper term for a site is logical network definition, but the GUI refers to it as a network site. If you look at the PowerShell script to create a site, it uses the cmdlet New-SCLogicalNetwork Definition, which is always the source of ultimate truth.

This first part of a longer quote captures exactly the solution for handling all the networks in an organization and the different network configurations at the various datacenters an organization may have. SCVMM 2012 supports the concept of *logical networks*, which model within SCVMM the various networks that exist in your organization. These logical networks contain sites that are created and allow the definition of the IP subnet and/or the VLAN for the network at each specific location. Additionally, the host groups that exist in a site can be selected through the interface. Figure 9-17 shows the three datacenters in my organization and the single logical network I defined for my external switch, which has three sites, one for each location. Each site is linked to the correct host group that represents the datacenter and has the appropriate IP subnet and VLAN definition for the external switch network in that location.

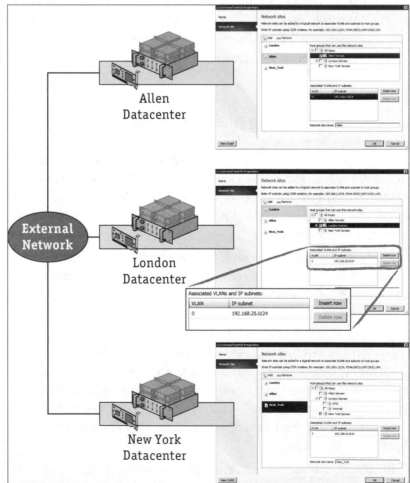

FIGURE 9-17: With three datacenters for each logical network, I defined three sites, each with the correct IP and VLAN detail for the network at the specific site.

Once the logical network is defined and the sites for the logical network are created, you can go one step further. For servers in a virtual environment, it is unlikely you would want to use regular DHCP to allocate IP addresses to the guest operating systems running in the virtual machines, as most IT administrators prefer static IP addressing for servers. SCVMM 2012 allows IP pools to be defined and linked to a site from which SCVMM will allocate an address when it creates a virtual machine that is connected to the parent logical network. When creating an IP pool, various parameters must be defined:

▶ The start and end IP addresses that define the IP pool (within the subnet for the site)

▶ Default gateway, DNS, and WINS server addresses

▶ IP addresses from the pool that are to be used as virtual IP addresses in load-balancing scenarios, and those reserved for other purposes

SCVMM is not acting as a DHCP server to allocate the IP addresses from the pool. When a VM is created and connected to a logical network that has an IP pool defined, and the VM is configured to use a static IP address, SCVMM will select a free IP address from its pool, mark it as used, and inject the IP information into the Sysprep answer file. As the VM goes through the customization phase, it reads in settings from the Sysprep answer file and the static IP address is configured within the guest operating system.

If a VM is no longer needed, it is important to delete it from within SCVMM so that the IP address is allocated back into the pool of available addresses, where it is placed at the bottom to prevent it from being reused again too quickly. If a VM is deleted outside of SCVMM, the IP address will appear in an Inactive addresses area within the IP address pool, from which it can then be manually placed back in the available pool.

There is one other prerequisite for using static IP addresses within virtual machines: assigning a static MAC address to each virtual NIC within the VM to ensure correct assignment of IP addresses to interfaces. Whereas SCVMM 2008 R2 allowed a single MAC address for the entire SCVMM installation, in SCVMM 2012 different MAC address pools can now be created. This is especially useful when managing Hyper-V and ESX because previously, with only one pool, the ESX MAC pool would have to be used even for Hyper-V servers. Default MAC address pools are defined for VMware and non-VMware, but you can create additional pools that can be assigned to hosts and host groups.

Once the logical networks and all dependent resources are defined, just a few other steps are required to get the logical networks in use throughout the environment. First, update the properties of the physical NICs on each virtualization host through the Hardware tab of the host's properties and select the logical networks that are connected through the particular NIC. This allows SCVMM to understand which NICs and switches to use when virtual machines need connectivity to specific logical networks.

Finally, the VM templates are updated to set the logical network that should be connected to the virtual network adapters within the template definition. For a detailed step-by-step guide on creating and using logical networks, go to http://www.ntfaq.com and search for "How do I use a logical network in System Center Virtual Machine Manager 2012?"

When you now deploy a template to one or multiple locations, SCVMM will take care of the correct NIC mapping and IP address/VLAN configuration. From an end-user self-service perspective, the users can now request virtual machines in particular datacenters connected to logical networks, such as development or production, and everything else will be taken care of behind the scenes.

INTEGRATING WITH HARDWARE LOAD BALANCERS

With today's virtual machines hosting critical services, the need for integration with high-availability and load-balancing components is vital. To safeguard network traffic and services it is very common to use a hardware load balancer, which employs a virtual IP address for the clients to use to connect to a service. The load balancer accepts requests on that virtual address and intelligently distributes them to operating system instance IP addresses that are part of the pool that the virtual IP address services. A good example is web servers.

For example, suppose you have five web servers with IP addresses 1.1.1.1 through 1.1.1.5; these IP addresses would be in a pool on the load balancer. A virtual IP address is created on the load balancer (which confusingly is known as a virtual service)—for example, 1.1.1.50—and as web requests are sent to 1.1.1.50, the load balancer distributes them through various rules to the web servers in the pool. If the load balancer detects from assorted health indicators that a web server is not available, requests are not sent to that particular server.

Windows itself has a software load-balancing component, but many organizations utilize hardware load balancers for the highest performance and functionality, such as the F5 Big-IP. In the past, the virtual machines could be deployed through SCVMM, but the administrator would still need to manually configure the hardware load balancer.

SCVMM 2012 can be configured to create the pools and virtual services automatically on supported hardware load balancers as part of a service template deployment

(I cover service templates shortly) or using the SCVMM PowerShell cmdlets. This means the entire web farm of VMs can be deployed automatically and the virtual IP created and configured on the hardware load balancer with no manual intervention.

As a prerequisite, the load balancer provider from the hardware manufacturer must be installed on the SCVMM server, and the management service restarted. The load balancer can then be added in the Fabric workspace in the Networking - Load Balancers area. When adding specific hardware load balancers to SCVMM, you must specify a Run As account with administrator credentials on the load balancer, the make and model, and the provider to use. You also specify the host groups that can use the hardware load balancer, which is commonly based on location or network segmentation, and finally the logical networks that the load balancer is connected to, both front end and back end (which can be the same). For example, you might have two logical networks, DMZ and Internal. Your front-end logical network for the load balancer may be the DMZ, which is where requests for the web services are coming from, while the back-end logical network will be Internal, which is where the actual web servers reside. Telling the hardware load balancer to which logical networks it's connected enables the correct assignment of virtual IP addresses from the IP pools defined for each site on the logical network.

In order for services to use the load balancer, you need to create a VIP template that defines which load balancer to use, which protocol and port to use, whether persistence should be enabled, the type of load balancing to perform (as shown in Figure 9-18) and finally which, if any, health monitors should be used to check the availability and health of the IP addresses within the pool being fronted by the load balancer. Note that you can create many VIP templates that all use the same physical load balancer to provide load-balancing configurations for different use case scenarios within the organization.

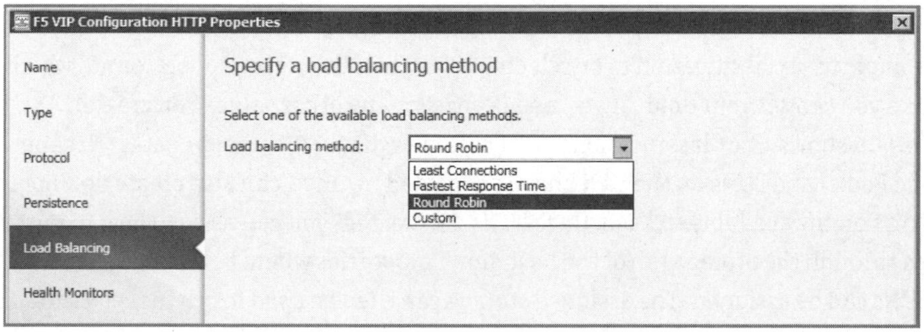

FIGURE 9-18: Select the Load balancing method from the drop-down to customize how incoming requests are distributed to servers in the pool.

Managing Storage Resources

The same challenge with network resources applies to storage. Traditionally, the actual volume that is used to store virtual machines needs to be selected during virtual machine deployment; if SAN storage is used, this is probably based on which tier of SAN storage is required, how connectivity is made to the SAN, and which SAN is used, because many datacenters have multiple SANs. Additionally, different datacenters may use different SANs.

The challenge with storage is greater than with networks because often virtualization administrators have no visibility into the back-end storage configuration, which makes troubleshooting and management difficult. Lack of access to the back-end storage can also make automation difficult, and even with access there may be no consistent method to connect to a SAN, to create a LUN, and then assign to a host. Every SAN entails a different management method, and many organizations have different SAN vendors and different models of SAN. Trying to automate storage management with many different management tools is cumbersome.

Fortunately, a new industry standard, Storage Management Initiative-Specification (SMI-S), provides a common approach for interacting with storage systems such as SANs. The major storage vendors are creating SMI-S providers to enable a consistent way to interact with storage. These SMI-S providers offer full access to the SAN configuration, exposing the back-end structure and enabling the administrator to manage the SAN, such as creating LUNs and unmasking to hosts.

SCVMM 2012 has a new Storage Fabric capability that enables connection to SMI-S providers from SCVMM. Once SCVMM is connected to the SMI-S provider of the storage (which just requires the IP address of the SMI-S provider and a Run As account with permissions on the provider), it performs a discovery of the data known to the provider (which by default refreshes its information from the SAN every 10 minutes) and populates the SCVMM Storage Fabric view of the known arrays. During the addition, the wizard prompts for a classification to be selected for each of the storage pools found, which is where you can set your Gold, Silver, and Bronze (or any other values you create). As Figure 9-19 shows, the Classifications and Pools view displays the aggregates (NetApp Storage Pools) and LUNs on the SAN I have connected to, and I can also create new Logical Units on the available storage. Once LUNs are created, you can assign them to host groups through the Storage tab of the host group properties where both storage pools and LUNs can be assigned. The assigned storage can then be used for virtual machine storage for any host in the host group.

▶ Storage is often defined in tiers such as tier 1, tier 2, or Gold and Silver tiers. The higher the tier, the higher the performance and redundancy capabilities. Gold tier could be Raid 10 on SSD storage, whereas Tin tier might be a disk found in the trash.

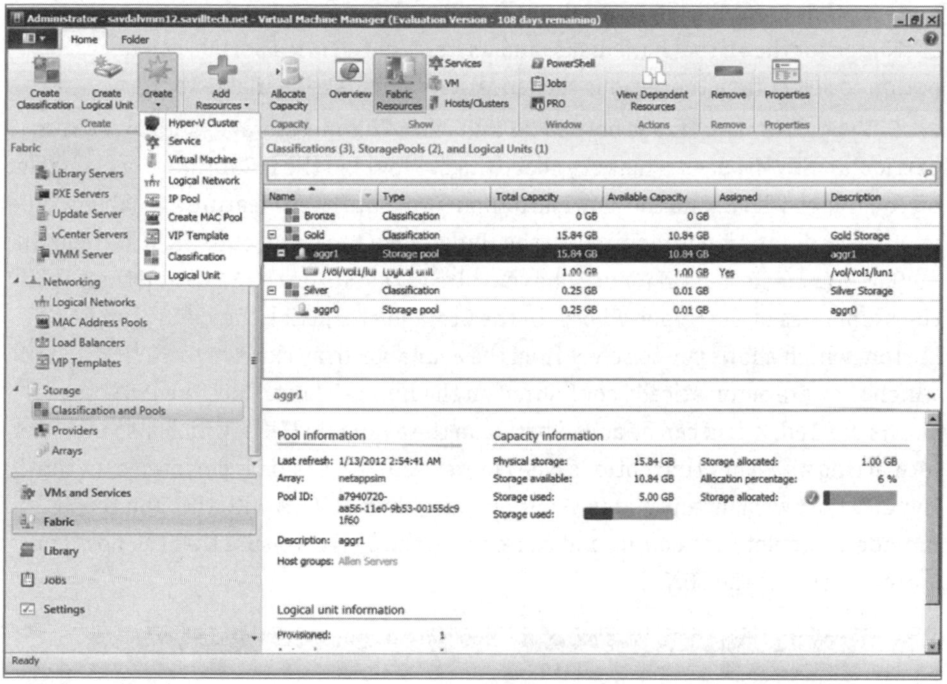

FIGURE 9-19: Select Logical Unit from the Create menu to create a new LUN for additional capacity.

> **WARNING** Many SAN implementations do not have the SMI-S provider on the actual SAN, instead, the SMI-S provider must be installed on a Windows server operating system. Do *not* install the SMI-S provider on the SCVMM server. Though it may work in some scenarios, very strange behavior can occur and it is not supported by Microsoft.

Getting back to the scenario of multiple datacenters with multiple SANs, all the SANs are added to SCVMM and all the storage is allocated to the classifications, such that all the Gold tier storage is grouped together for all the datacenters, all the Silver tier storage is grouped together, and so on. The storage has been assigned to the host groups by geographic location, so storage in the Gold and Silver tiers located in London is allocated to the London host group, storage in New York is allocated to the New York host group, and so on. Now, when a new virtual machine is created, you only need to specify which tier of storage should be used, and SCVMM will automatically use available storage on LUNs with enough free space from the specified tier in the location that hosts the VM. Virtual machine templates can be updated to specify tiers of storage for the virtual hard disks, and users in self-service portals can have the option to select from the various classifications you make available to them.

SCVMM 2012 can manage both iSCSI and Fibre Channel storage; and for iSCSI in particular, SCVMM does some very cool things. Provided the iSCSI Initiator is enabled on the Hyper-V host, and the Multipath Input/Output (MPIO) feature is enabled, no manual configuration is required on the Hyper-V host to connect to iSCSI storage. In SCVMM you create an LUN (or use one that already exists on the SAN) and then open the properties of the Hyper-V host. In the Storage area, click the iSCSI Array Add button, which allows you to select from the available arrays known to SCVMM, after which they are automatically configured on the Hyper-V host. Once the iSCSI session is created, a disk can be added based on the available LUNs, which also includes formatting and mounting options (see Figure 9-20). All of this is performed on the Hyper-V host without any manual configuration; and SCVMM will, through the SMI-S provider, complete any zoning and masking on the SAN to ensure that the host has correct access to the LUN.

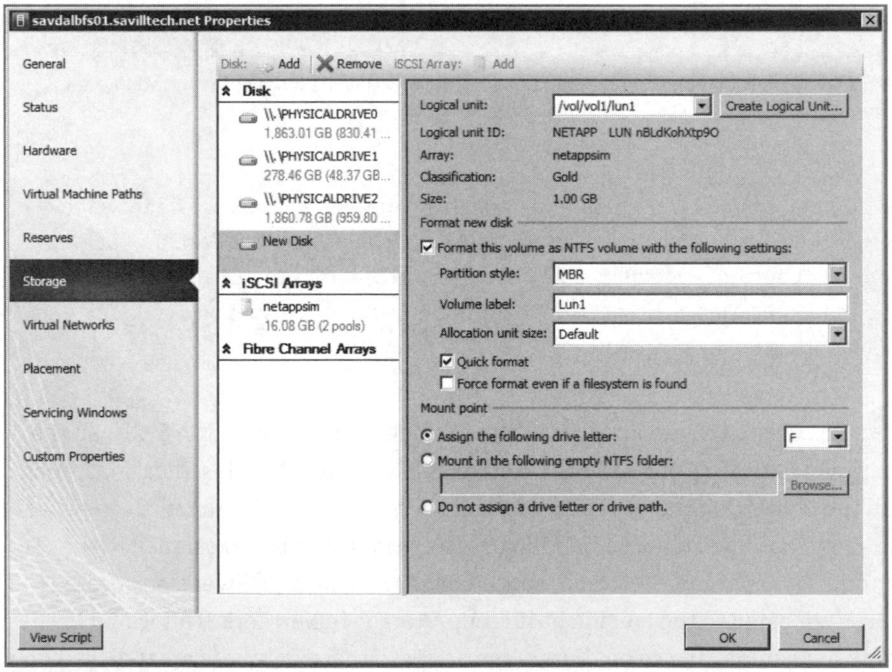

FIGURE 9-20: Creating a new NTFS volume on an LUN that is assigned to the host group on my NetApp filer

For Fibre Channel storage, SCVMM can perform the configuration of LUNs on the Hyper-V hosts; however, the host must already be correctly zoned with the Fibre Channel SAN. The same level of automatic zoning and SAN configuration possible with iSCSI is planned for Fibre Channel in a future SCVMM release.

The integration of SMI-S into SCVMM provides another capability where supported by the SAN: rapid provisioning. Most SANs can clone or snapshot an existing LUN to a new LUN in seconds. Now imagine that LUN had a Sysprepped VHD file containing Windows Server 2008 R2. Instead of having to perform a file copy operation, the SAN would just duplicate the LUN containing the template to a new LUN in seconds. Once the LUN was duplicated, SCVMM would still need to boot the guest OS to customize it, but all the time needed to copy the VHD file has been eliminated.

Enabling a VHD to be available for rapid provisioning requires the following steps:

1. Create a new LUN from the available storage pool capacity.

2. Unmask the LUN to the SCVMM library host and assign the LUN to the correct host.

3. Initialize the newly visible disk, create a partition, and format the volume.

4. Mount the new volume using a folder mount path (not a drive letter). Note that this folder should be an existing library share. For example, if the SCVMM library is path D:\Library, then the new partition could be mounted under path D:\Library\2008R2EntVHD.

5. Place the Sysprepped VHD in the D:\Library\2008R2EntVHD path.

6. Refresh the library.

Once the library refresh is complete, SCVMM will see the new VHD and mark it as SAN copy-capable, enabling rapid provisioning to be used when the VHD is duplicated. Each duplication results in the creation of a new LUN, because this technology currently requires 1 VHD per LUN. The rapid provisioning does not support adding the new LUN as part of a CSV volume in the current version.

The other great capability gained through the SMI-S integration with SCVMM is that now the SCVMM PowerShell cmdlets provide a consistent method for interacting with storage, enabling greater orchestration throughout the datacenter. Even if you don't automate storage allocation with SCVMM, the standardization of management is a huge benefit.

CREATING VIRTUAL MACHINE TEMPLATES AND SERVICE TEMPLATES

Because a lot of virtual machine administration is very intuitive in SCVMM, I won't spend time covering that. Basically, all the actions you can perform in Hyper-V Manager can be done in SCVMM, and they are available through the dynamic ribbon. The following sections focus on the creation and migration of virtual machines.

Creating and Migrating Virtual Machines

Ultimately your virtual environment is there to support virtual machines, which contain the guest operating systems and applications. Creating and migrating virtual machines is a large element of your virtual management but can be simplified and automated using some of the solutions presented in this section.

NEW VIRTUAL MACHINE CREATION OPTIONS

▶ The default synthetic network adapter does not support PXE boot because of the reliance on the VMBus and the synthetic nature of the NIC. To boot over the network the VM must have the legacy NIC, which emulates an Intel NIC.

When creating a new virtual machine, it is possible to create an empty virtual machine that could be configured entirely from scratch, or you could use a Hardware Profile from the library to set the virtual hardware, insert an operating system install ISO into the virtual DVD drive, and then perform a full operating install inside the VM. Another option is to have a legacy network adapter in the virtual machine, boot the VM from the network, and deploy an operating system to it via PXE boot. Both of these options require a lot of effort and are generally very slow. All operating system installers for Windows Vista/Windows 2008 or later are actually based on an image file in Windows Imaging Format (WIM), which is a Sysprepped Windows installation that has been captured. During installation, this image file is deployed to the local storage and then a mini setup routine is performed. Sysprep is a component part of the operating system; when run on an OS installation, it strips out all unique information, such as security identifiers (SIDs) and globally unique identifiers (GUIDs), and performs other actions to prepare the operating system for duplication. Without first running Sysprep, duplication of the operating system may cause problems for certain software applications and would be unsupported by Microsoft.

In a virtual world you don't need to invoke the actual install process. It's far easier and much faster to create a virtual hard disk that has the operating system deployed to it already and is Sysprepped so it's ready to be duplicated, and then save that VHD to the library. The prepared VHD is then combined with virtual hardware and guest OS configuration to create a virtual machine template (although it is fine to just use Sysprepped VHDs with manually created VMs, which entails copying the Sysprepped VHD to the new VM location and then creating the actual VM). You have a number of options to create a template.

TO SYSPREP OR NOT TO SYSPREP, IS THERE A QUESTION?

Some readers might remember a great blog post a few years ago by Mark Russinovich (`http://blogs.technet.com/b/markrussinovich/archive/2009/11/03/3291024.aspx`), who determined that machines with duplicate SIDs would not actually cause a security problem. However, although the OS may work fine, certain applications depend on the SID, and there have been security issues related to removable media when SIDs are not unique, Windows Update may not function correctly, Key Management Server activations have problems, and more. In addition, there is more to Sysprep than just resetting the SID and GUID; in fact, in Windows 7 Sysprep uses 26 separate Windows component providers that perform functions necessary for preparing a machine for duplication, known as the `GENERALIZE` operation. The bottom line is that you need to run Sysprep if you plan to duplicate a client or server operating system.

The first option is to create the Sysprepped VHD manually by deploying the operating system to a VM, customizing, running Sysprep, and turning off the the VM. You then copy the VHD from the VMs folder to the SCVMM library, renaming it to something more descriptive, such as `Srv2008R2EntSP1.vhd`. Then you create a template manually, either from scratch or by using Guest OS Profiles and Hardware Profiles that exist in the library, which uses the new VHD. Remember that you can create many different templates that point to the same VHD file; this enables you to create templates that meet the various requirements of your organization without having to manage and maintain a large number of VHD files. Within the Guest OS Profile settings (see Figure 9-21), you can specify not only which roles and features to install, which is great for the various server role scenarios, but also custom Answer Files, to further tailor the OS installation, as well as add custom scripts that could install additional applications.

▶ A better option for more complex software installations is to use service templates, but it's good to know it is possible within the Guest OS Profile.

The second option is very similar and can still be customized, including changing the hardware and guest OS configuration; however, it avoids manually copying the VHD and then creating a template. The initial process is the same: Create a virtual machine that matches the hardware you want for the template, install the operating system, and then customize, ensuring that the local Administrator password is blank. However,

stop there; don't Sysprep and shut down the VM. Within the VMs and Services workspace, select the VM and then select the Create VM Template action. This will perform
the Sysprep operation automatically, allow the virtual hardware and guest OS to be customized, and then create the template and accompanying VHD in the SCVMM library. In
the process, this action will destroy the original VM, so if you don't want to lose it, use
the Create ➔ Clone action first to create a duplicate of the VM, and then create the VM
template from the clone.

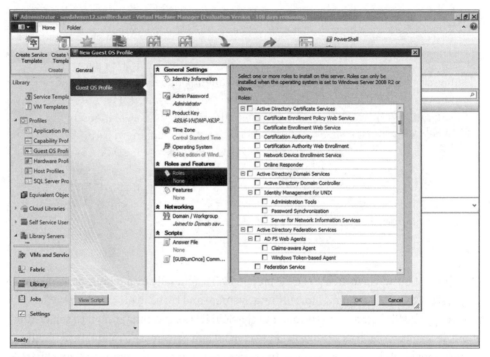

FIGURE 9-21: Most of the common operating system configurations can be defined within a
Guest OS Profile; and all OS server roles can easily be added.

Once you have created some templates you can easily create new ones based on
them. Select an existing template and then select the Create VM Template action
again. After giving it a new name, all the current values from the source template will
be populated in the new template, and you can modify any configuration related to
the virtual hardware and guest OS.

With the templates defined, you can create new virtual machines by selecting a
template in the Library workspace and selecting the Create Virtual Machine action.
Alternatively, in the VMs and Services workspace, choose Create Virtual Machine,
selecting one of the three options—to use an existing virtual machine, a VM template,

or a virtual hard disk—on the first screen of the Create Virtual Machine Wizard. You can also use PowerShell to create virtual machines based on templates, as described in the section Unlocking All Possibilities with Windows PowerShell.

At this point, I hope the advantage of using templates over traditional installation methods is apparent. Remember, too, that templates are not limited to Hyper-V; you can also create and manage templates for ESX and XenServer in SCVMM.

MIGRATING EXISTING OPERATING SYSTEM INSTANCES

For brand-new operating system deployments using SCVMM, using a template is the logical choice, but what about existing operating systems? These operating systems could be on physical systems, or they may be on another hypervisor, such as ESX, and you want to move them to Hyper-V.

SCVMM provides two technologies, *physical-to-virtual (P2V)* and *virtual-to-virtual (V2V)*, to help migrate operating systems. Despite its name, P2V can actually be used to migrate virtual machines, and it is the technology you must use to convert a virtual machine from XenServer. However, the V2V technology is specifically designed for the conversion of virtual machine configuration and storage assets to the Hyper-V format, so it should be used whenever possible.

V2V is supported for virtual machines on ESX and works by creating a new virtual machine on Hyper-V without deleting the original virtual machine. Focusing on the migration from ESX, the V2V process can convert virtual machines that are powered off directly from the ESX host. It can also convert VMs from the SCVMM library, provided the full virtual machine and VMDK are in the library; however, in SCVMM 2012 this is unlikely because only the metadata is imported from vCenter. Virtual machines on a file share can also be converted by using the New-SCV2V PowerShell cmdlet (which is also used to perform the other conversions).

> **WARNING** When performing a V2V conversion from an ESX virtual machine, a critical step is ensuring that the VMware tools are uninstalled from the VM prior to trying to convert it; otherwise, it will likely crash when the VM tries to start on Hyper-V.

Converting a physical machine to a virtual machine using P2V is more interesting. Two different types of conversion are possible: online and offline. Online P2V is used for operating systems that support the Microsoft Volume Shadow Copy Service (VSS). It deploys an agent to the physical computer operating system (although this could also be a VM as previously stated), which captures the hardware configuration and maps it to a virtual machine configuration. The content of the hard drives is then captured using a VSS backup, which ensures the integrity of the backup, and written to a VHD on the Hyper-V host. The application must be stopped during this process; otherwise, once the backup is taken to Hyper-V, any subsequent changes on the physical host would be lost. This is not a problem if the application running in the VM doesn't store application data or state locally. Because of the VSS requirement, the online P2V is available for Windows XP SP2 and Windows 2003 SP1 and later.

FIGURE 9-22: Initiate a P2V or V2V through the VMs and Services workspace Convert Physical/Virtual Machine action.

For those Windows 2000 SP4 machines that don't support VSS, or for the other operating systems where perhaps you don't want to use online P2V because a VSS writer for the application is not available, an offline P2V is performed. With the offline P2V, a Windows PE OS is temporarily installed on the source server and the computer is rebooted into the Windows PE environment through a modification to the boot record. The VMM agent in the Windows PE environment captures the disk content and streams it to the Hyper-V server; once complete, the machine boots back into the regular operating system, the final P2V processes are completed, and the actual VM is created on the Hyper-V host.

You can also use the New-SCP2V PowerShell cmdlet to perform P2V conversions, and I definitely recommend running a P2V through the wizard and looking at the generated script for all the required actions. In my experience, where V2V operations fail, the P2V will often succeed. Therefore, even if V2V is available, if at first you don't succeed, try P2V; and if the online P2V fails, the offline P2V is very likely to work. Other tools are available that can perform migrations with additional capabilities, such as performing an initial capture and then sending delta updates of the source machine to the target virtual machine until you are ready to flip the switch. This enables the VM to be tested before going live. If the built-in SCVMM tools don't meet your needs, check out third-party solutions, such as those from Double-Take, Quest, PlateSpin, and many others.

There is a steep learning curve when carrying out migrations of existing operating system images, so start with noncritical operating system instances so you don't get fired if things go badly, and be sure you thoroughly test the new converted VM before destroying the source OS! When you are confident with migration technologies and troubleshooting, move on to more critical workloads.

Utilizing Server Application Virtualization

Insanity: doing the same thing over and over again and expecting different results.

—Albert Einstein

One of the customer requests at the beginning of this chapter was a way to simplify the deployment and servicing of applications and avoid the use of large application implementation documents, which are prone to inconsistencies through human error. Reversing the preceding quote, sanity is doing the same thing over and over again and expecting the same result. In other words, sanity equals consistency. Consistency results in greater reliability and easier manageability, and SCVMM helps to achieve this through *Server Application Virtualization* or Server App-V, which enables server applications to be virtualized and run on server platforms without actually having to be installed.

HOW SERVER APP-V DIFFERS FROM CLIENT APP-V

Chapter 4 details Client App-V, and to be very clear, Server App-V is based on Client App-V 4.6 SP1. The process to create a server-virtualized application using Server App-V is almost exactly the same, except the Sequencer is called Microsoft Server Application Virtualization Sequencer, as shown in Figure 9-23. Some steps in the Client App-V sequencing process are missing in Server App-V, particularly the Type of Application and Customize (optimize package) steps. This is understandable because the goals for Client App-V are different from those for Server App-V. Once an application is sequenced it is copied to the SCVMM library, and the library is refreshed to find the new content and make it available.

The goals for Client App-V are to provide application isolation to solve application-to-application compatibility problems and reduce the number of testing scenarios; to enable optimized streaming of applications to desktops for improved user productivity and mobility; and to avoid cluttering the desktop operating system. Those are not the goals for server applications. It's uncommon to encounter server application-to-application problems; typically you could just stand up another server and separate the applications onto separate operating systems, especially in a virtualized environment. In fact, just the opposite is true: Server applications typically need to see each other. Optimizing server applications so they can quickly start running on a server by streaming down only the part of the server application that is immediately required is not a usual requirement. Server deployments are typically better planned out and executed.

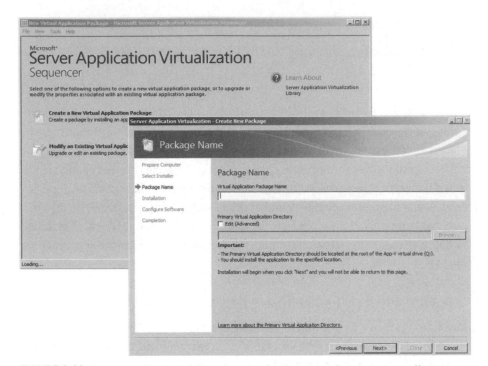

FIGURE 9-23: Server applications follow the same basic sequencing process as client applications.

All the same guidance for the Sequencer from Client App-V applies, so review that material in Chapter 4. That includes custom installing the application to the created folder on the Q: drive.

The goals for Server App-V are primarily related to the deployment and management of applications, essentially making life easier for the IT administrator and reducing the number of those hugely complex application installations that have to be performed in development, in test, in production, and various other environments. Server App-V enables the server application to be installed once onto a clean Windows Server operating system that has the Server App-V Sequencer installed. After those complex installation procedures are followed, that virtualized server application can be deployed to multiple environments without requiring re-installation.

However, there is one hiccup. This is not Office or Adobe Reader, for which no instance-specific configuration is needed. If a server application is installed, configured, and then virtualized, how do you modify the configuration for the various deployments in the diverse environments, which absolutely require different configurations? One of the key features of Server App-V is that once applications are virtualized, it scans the configuration files for configuration items and extracts them into *deployment configuration items*. The deployment configuration item values are configured on a per-instance basis when the virtualized server application is actually deployed. This allows different configurations for different environments, including credentials, server name, ports, and any other configuration in the registry, service, text file, and so on. As Figure 9-24 shows, in addition to auto-discovered configuration items, which is not much for a basic Apache installation, you can add deployment configuration items and set the locations where the items can be discovered. Use the wildcard (*) character in the search for configuration items, such as DB* for any string starting with DB. In the current release of Server App-V, only XML files can be searched for configuration items, so the Apache example would not find any matches. At some point in the future, text file searching should be implemented.

Deployment configuration items can be made optional or mandatory and default values can be specified. Details about the deployment configuration items are in an additional file in the Server App-V package (not found in Client App-V packages), deploymentconfig.xml.

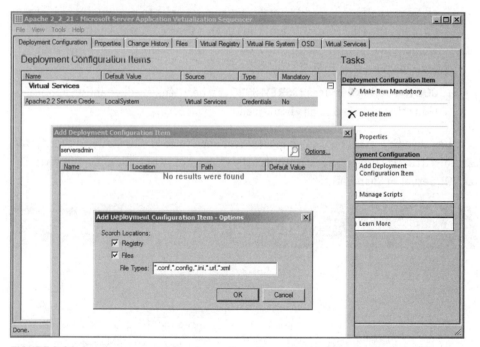

FIGURE 9-24: Apache uses .conf files for configuration, so I added *.conf to the list of files to be searched.

Client App-V and Server App-V also differ in terms of what can be virtualized. Naturally, Server App-V can virtualize more aspects of the operating system than Client App-V because it must handle server applications, which typically communicate with Windows components such as IIS, services, WMI, and COM+. In addition, once a Server App-V package is deployed to a server, it is available and interacts with the system—it just needs to be started. Additional areas of virtualization possible with Server App-V are as follows:

▶ **Windows services:** Client App-V can only virtualize user services running in the user security context. Server App-V will support system services that are displayed in Windows Service Control.

▶ **COM/COM+/DCOM:** These components are all captured and visible with tools such as dcomcnfg.

▶ **WMI:** WMI providers and classes installed by an application are virtualized.

▶ **Local users and groups:** Any local users or groups created during application installation are captured and re-created on the deployed server.

▶ **IIS:** IIS 6, 7, and 7.5 websites, virtual directories, and application pools can all be virtualized. An additional requirement prior to sequencing is installation of the IIS server role and the IIS Management tools, along with the Web Deploy application (`http://www.iis.net/download/webdeploy`) that enables the packaging of IIS sites.

▶ **SQL Reporting Services (SSRS):** SSRS can be virtualized, enabling applications that use SSRS to be virtualized.

▶ Web Deploy is included in the default SCVMM library in the Application Frameworks folder, where you can also find the Server App-V Client and Sequencer.

The preceding list should cover most server applications. Currently, Server App-V cannot virtualize drivers, a restriction of the Client App-V as well, nor can it virtualize SQL Server or SharePoint.

MAKING SQL AVAILABLE IN A VIRTUAL MACHINE TEMPLATE

Although you cannot virtualize SQL Server, that does not mean you can't make SQL Server available as part of your virtual machine templates, making it available for service usage. SQL Server supports a Sysprep operation, so SQL Server can be installed onto a VM, and then you can Sysprep that OS so it can be duplicated. Once an OS image has SQL Server Sysprepped, the SCVMM templates have a SQL Server Configuration option that enables you to specify the media source for the SQL Server installation files needed to complete the SQL Server specialization phase, the accounts for the various services, who should be SQL Server administrators, the security mode, and custom SQL Server configuration files. This SQL Server configuration can be combined with application configuration to run SQL Server configuration scripts to create new databases on the SQL Server deployment. See `http://technet.microsoft.com/en-us/library/ee210664.aspx` for some good information on Sysprep and SQL Server.

PROVIDING SERVER APPLICATION CONFIGURATION PORTABILITY WITH SERVER APP-V

The next piece of the puzzle for Server App-V is helping server applications to be more portable. The goal is to take a running Server App-V application and move it to another operating system, maintaining all the configuration and data that belongs to the virtualized application. This is exactly what Server App-V delivers.

Server App-V virtualized applications are deployed primarily using service templates, which are covered next. Part of that service template functionality is the ability to service the template, such as replacing the OS VHD used; if so, and a deployment based on the service template has a Server App-V application, then the configuration and data associated with that virtualized application are automatically backed up and then restored once the VM has been updated.

TIP For testing purposes you will likely want to use the virtualized application outside of a service template. Once the Server App-V agent and PowerShell cmdlets are installed, you can use the following to manually deploy a Server App-V application outside of a service template:

```
Add-ServerAppVPackage -Name <Name of app>
   -Manifest <Manifest location and name>
   -SFT <SFT location and name>
   -configuration <configuration>
```

Any services that are normally autostarted during the package add operation can be started with the following cmdlet:

```
Start-ServerAppVPackage <package name> cmdlet.
```

Behind the scenes, a few PowerShell cmdlets are actually being used, which are available once the Server App-V agent and PowerShell cmdlets are installed. When the state needs to be backed up, the Backup-ServerAppVPackageState cmdlet is used to back up the changed data to a specified folder, and then during a restore that same folder is referenced by the Restore-ServerAppVPackageState cmdlet.

Taken all together, the features of Server App-V enable administrators to easily deploy server applications in a consistent fashion, because the installation is performed only once while allowing different settings at each deployment. Server App-V also provides complete portability of the virtualized application while maintaining all data and state, enabling a deployed Server App-V application to be moved to a completely different operating system instance.

Creating and Using Services

Now it is time to bring all these aspects of virtual machines and virtual applications together to provide a packaged service. Very few server applications work in isolation; server applications talk to other server applications, and often multiple instances of server applications are required for availability and load-balancing needs.

SCVMM provides the ability to create virtual machine templates, which can be easily deployed. Server applications can be easily virtualized and quickly deployed while providing portability with Server App-V. By using these technologies together, multi-tiered services can be deployed manually, for example by creating eight virtual machines: four for the web front-end tier, two for the middle tier, and two for the back-end storage/database tier. When it is time to update the service, each virtual machine would need to be updated manually, because once a normal virtual machine is deployed there is no ongoing relationship between the virtual machine and the template from which it was created, so it isn't possible to refresh a virtual machine if the virtual machine template is updated.

Service templates, new in SCVMM 2012, enable you to define complete services in SCVMM, which by default can be one-, two-, or three-tiered applications, as shown in Figure 9-25; and additional tiers can be added if required. You can specify the virtual machine template for each tier, in addition to which applications should be deployed. For example, on an IIS site, you could use Web Deploy for the front end, a regular virtualized application for the middle tier, and a Database Application using SQL DAC for the back-end tier.

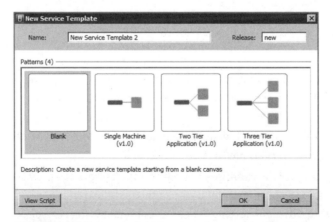

FIGURE 9-25: Select the initial pattern for a new service template.

These three types of applications—web applications (WebDeploy), virtual applications (Server App-V), and database applications (SQL DAC)—are considered *first class* in service templates, which understand the metadata of these types of applications and can enable parameters to perform the configuration when the application is deployed, such as by the end user. Other types of application install are fully supported through the Service Template Generic Command Execution (GCE) feature, as many organizations are not using SQL DAC, Server App-V, or even Web Deploy yet. By using GCE, scripts can be run both before and after any type of application installation. Customizing applications not considered first class would need to be handled through the application's native unattended configuration capabilities or scripting, and would not integrate with the service deployment interface in the same way as first-class applications. Standard Windows Server Roles and features can also be added through regular virtual machine guest OS definitions.

For each tier, a minimum, maximum, and initial number of instances are specified, which enables easy scaling based on utilization. Service instances created from a service template maintain a link back to the template, which becomes read-only. Therefore, it becomes the definitive source of truth about the service. If an update is required, a new version of the service template is created and applied to deployed instances. Deploying the new service template updates the services while maintaining application state through the Server App-V state backup and restore feature.

Defining a service from a service template removes the need for the IT department to manage so many individual OS images, because it abstracts the actual services, roles, features, and applications needed that traditionally may have been part of the OS image. Another very nice bonus feature is realized if SCVMM is integrated with Operations Manager, in which case Operations Manager understands the service definition and displays the VMs as part of a service.

As suggested earlier, the service template life cycle is comprised of four stages:

► Create the service template.

► Customize the deployment upon deployment of the service template.

► Deploy the service to environments.

► Update the service template to a new version and apply to running instances of the service.

When updating an existing instance of a service, three update types are possible. First is a Settings-only update mode, which changes only application settings but does not replace the OS images. Second is a new (in SCVMM 2012) update type, an

▶ Although a new OS image is deployed, details about the OS it is replacing are maintained, so AD information, SID, machine name, and everything else is the same.

In-Place update, whereby updates to the template settings are applied but the actual OS images are not replaced. This would be used to update applications and modify configuration of the virtual machines in the service. Last is the Image-based update, which replaces the deployed instances of operating system images with the new OS image and performs a reinstallation of applications, but maintains the application state through the backup and restore capabilities of Server App-V.

For example, if you have modified a virtual machine configuration that is part of a service—such as changing the memory from 1GB to 4GB and then applying an update to the service from a new version of the service template—then any customizations you made to the configuration would be lost. Remember, when you are talking about services, the service template is always the source of truth. In some circumstances this can be useful; perhaps your service instance has lost some VMs and you want to restore it to the parameters of the service template. You can refresh instances from the service template, which will look for any missing instances of virtual machines in the template's tiers that have less than the minimum number of instances and fix them by deploying additional required VMs.

Within a service template, in addition to specifying which virtual machine templates to use, which applications to install, and various other settings, you can also utilize load balancers and logical networks, as described earlier. By using the other fabric elements, service templates can enable very rich capabilities in a completely automated fashion.

Service templates are created and maintained in the Service Template Designer, shown in Figure 9-26. The interface consists of the familiar ribbon, a designer canvas, which is the majority of the interface, and a small properties area at the bottom that shows the properties of the currently selected object. In Figure 9-26 the options to add applications to the various tiers are shown; note I have a connection to the F5 load balancer for my web tier, which would be automatically configured when the service deployed. Once configurations are complete, run the Save and Validate action, which checks for any problems in the service template definition.

Once a service is deployed within the VMs and Services workspace in SCVMM, it is viewed as a single unit in addition to the individual virtual machines that make up the service. You can view the application settings configured for the service within the VMs and Services workspace view, which helps to identify individual instances of deployed services.

A great benefit of using the service template is how easy it makes it to scale out and in as required. Selecting the service within the VMs and Services workspace exposes a Scale Out action under Update, which launches the Scale Out Tier wizard. This enables you to select the tier and then the amount of scaling to be specified.

Additional VMs will be created based on the scale properties. To scale in, instances of the VM in the tier are just deleted. Scaling can also be performed through System Center AppControl and through System Center Orchestrator.

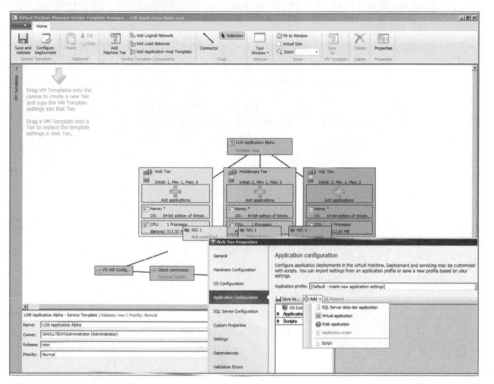

FIGURE 9-26: Using the Service Template Designer, you can select an application type to add or specify a script to deploy custom application types.

The best way to really understand the service templates is to just fire up the Service Template Designer and start playing with the settings and looking at the options available. Even for basic services, using a service template should make management far easier, especially when you want to make the service available for end-user deployment with some deployment-time configuration options.

SUMMARY

This is a very large chapter, and yet it only touches the surface of many of the most important capabilities. Management of your virtualization solution is critical to its success, and SCVMM 2012 delivers a fantastic management capability—not only in terms of the hypervisors but also through integration with storage and network fabrics. One feature that organizations should definitely look at is the capability to automate with Windows PowerShell, which is even more relevant in the next chapter, which describes integration with System Center Orchestrator and System Center Operations Manager.

One topic not covered in this chapter, and an area that particularly benefits from new capabilities in SCVMM 2012, is implementation of a private cloud and end-user self-service portals. This chapter contained numerous references to clouds, but I've saved the specifics for the next chapter, where you will see exactly what a Microsoft private cloud implementation looks like and learn all about SCVMM cloud capabilities and the end-user self-service options and capabilities.

CHAPTER 10

Implementing a Private Cloud

Every client and vendor I talk to refers to the "private cloud." Some of them know they want it, and some of them are adamantly against it—typically because of misunderstandings about what it means—but in fact every organization can benefit from the private cloud in some way. As organizations look for ways to stream-line not only IT but the entire organization, adopting the private cloud and shifting the focus to the application, rather than the operating system, creates entirely new, and more productive, ways to work and support business goals. This chapter brings together many of the concepts you've examined up to this point in order to demon-strate what the private cloud really is, how your organization can benefit from it, and what it takes to get a private cloud running in your company.

WHAT IS A PRIVATE CLOUD?

In order to talk about the private cloud, it's helpful to have a working definition and a common set of assumptions about the type of solution it provides. Therefore, for the purposes of this book, you can think of the private cloud as a form of IT infrastructure having the following attributes:

▶ It is both scalable and elastic, meaning it can grow and shrink as the load on the application changes.

▶ It enables better utilization of resources.

▶ Its functionality is independent of the underlying fabric.

▶ Because it is accountable, it can also be chargeable!

▶ It offers self-service capabilities.

▶ It is focused on the application.

> ▶ Although you might not log on to the actual console of a server, you are still remoting directly into the operating system to perform management tasks, which is basically still managing at the console level.

Beginning in reverse order, consider what it means to say that the private cloud is focused on the application. When you think about the shift from physical to virtual, what really happened? In the physical world, each physical server has a single operating system instance, which translates into a lot of wasted resources and money. The shift to virtualization consolidates these operating system instances into a smaller number of physical servers by running each operating system instance in a virtual machine. Although virtualization saves hardware and money, it doesn't actually change the way IT is managed. Administrators still log on to the operating system instances at the console and still manage the same number of operating system instances. In fact, now administrators also have to manage the virtualization solution.

Moving the focus to the application as part of the private cloud solution means focusing on the service being delivered and the applications used in that service offering. The private cloud infrastructure is responsible for creating the virtual machines and operating system instances that are required to deploy a service, removing that burden from the administrator.

Recall the service templates covered in the last chapter. Service templates in System Center Virtual Machine Manager enable the design of multi-tiered services, with each tier capable of using different virtual machine templates and different applications and configurations, as shown in Figure 10-1. Service templates enable administrators (and users, as you will see later) to easily deploy complete instances of services without any concern for the actual virtual machine configuration or placement. Those service templates also integrate with network hardware, such as load balancers that enable automatic configuration of network hardware when deploying services that require hardware load balancing.

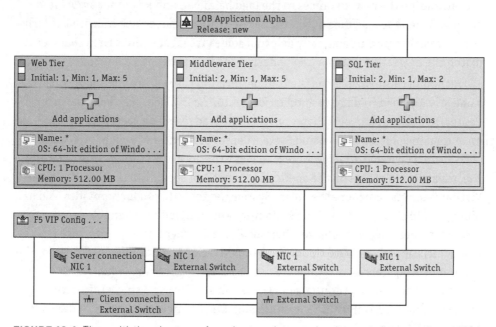

FIGURE 10-1: The multi-tiered nature of service templates makes it easy to focus on the application and the service it delivers.

Of course, initial deployment is only part of the solution. What about maintenance, patching, and scaling? Although later in this chapter I'm going to cover other components of System Center 2012, such as Configuration Manager, which can greatly simplify automated patching of both server and desktop operating systems, you can still use service templates. Unlike a normal virtual machine template, which loses any relationship with a virtual machine deployed from the template, any instances of a service deployed from a service template maintain their relationship to the template. This means you can update the service template, perhaps with a new operating system virtual machine template or configuration change, and then refresh the deployed instances of the service 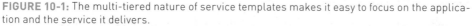 without losing the application data and configuration. That is truly focused on the application, and eliminates any additional management of operating system instances.

In terms of scalability and elasticity, those same service templates enable a minimum, maximum, and initial instance count of each tier of service. Using the web tier as an example, suppose you configure the tier to have a minimum of 2, a maximum of 20, and initially 4. This means when load increases, the tier can be

▶ It's even possible to update a deployed service instance in such a way that it is not taken down during the update. Through upgrade domains, a seamless update can be provided with no interruption to users.

scaled out to a higher number, such as 10, and the back-end infrastructure automatically takes care of creating the new virtual machines, setting up any configuration, adding the new instances to the load balancer, and any other associated actions. When the load dies down, the service can be scaled back in, with the back-end infrastructure automatically deleting some virtual machines from that tier to match the new target number and updating the hardware load balancer.

Although this example has the user performing the scaling out and in, that same private cloud could have automatic monitoring in place, such as with System Center Operations Manager. That way, when the load reaches a specified threshold, an automated process is run using System Center Orchestrator, which interconnects with System Center Virtual Machine Manager to perform the scaling. In other words, the private cloud's focus on the application is not just specific to the System Center Virtual Machine Manager—the entire System Center 2012 product provides a complete private cloud solution. This scalability and elasticity that enables access to resources when needed but leaves them available to other services otherwise is a key characteristic of the private cloud. Many organizations charge business units for the amount of computer resource that are used by their applications, which is why this scaling is important. By running many different services on a single infrastructure, you can achieve very high utilization of available resources, getting more bang for the infrastructure buck.

Independence from the underlying fabric can be confusing. What I mean by this is offering services to users regardless of who they are: IT department, business units in the organization, or individual users. This menu of offerings is known as a *service catalog* in ITIL terms. When users deploy a virtual machine or service, they should not need to know what IP address should be given to the virtual machine or machines. Nor should a user need to be aware of which storage area network is used, or which part of it.

For example, suppose you have multiple datacenters and multiple types of network and hypervisor. If you want to allow non-IT users to deploy virtual machines and services, you need to abstract all that underlying fabric infrastructure. That is, the user needs to be able to say (or request through a self-service interface), "I want an instance of this service in datacenter A and B and it should connect to the development and backup networks on a Silver tier of storage." Behind the scenes, the private cloud infrastructure can determine that for the development network in datacenter A, the network adapter needs an IP address in a certain subnet connected to a specific VLAN, and some other subnet and VLAN in datacenter B. It also determines that Silver tier storage in datacenter A means using the NetApp SAN and only these specific logical unit numbers (LUNs), while in datacenter B the EMC SAN

▶ The capabilities to scale out and in as needed and to run many different services on a single infrastructure are great, but the department running the infrastructure must still carefully plan and monitor usage to ensure that sufficient resources are available.

▶ Information Technology Infrastructure Library is a globally accepted collection of best practices for IT Service Management.

is used with other LUNs. This entire process is transparent to users, who get the service and connectivity they need with zero knowledge of the underlying infrastructure, which is exactly as it should be.

The idea of "self-service," or the user provisioning services, is a useful way to distinguish between virtualization and the private cloud. Consider the most basic case: creating a new virtual machine for a user. When I talk to clients about their current process for provisioning VMs in their virtual environment, the process is typically as follows (see Figure 10-2):

1. The user decides to make a request to the IT department.

2. The request is made via phone call, e-mail, or through the help desk.

3. The IT department gets the request and may do some validation, such as obtaining management approval.

4. IT then launches its virtualization management tool, creating a virtual machine from a template.

5. IT contacts the user to provide the IP address of the new VM.

6. The new VM is accessible to the user.

This sounds fast, but in reality this process ranges from a few days to six weeks in some companies I've worked with. It's a manual process, IT teams are busy, they may not like the particular business user, or there could be "solar activity disrupting electronics," which is really shorthand for not liking the user. Whatever the reason, it's a slow, manual process that is often fairly low on the priority list.

Note that it can be difficult to track the actual allocation of virtual machines—that is, their usage—which means it isn't possible to charge business units for the virtual machines they requested. This leads to virtual machine sprawl because, to the business units, the virtual machines are free!

In the private cloud, this process changes to what is shown in Figure 10-3. The resources used are the same, but the order of the steps and the methodology has changed:

1. The IT team uses its management tool to carve out resource clouds that include compute, storage, and network resources, assigning these clouds to users or groups of users, with certain quotas. This is all done before any users request resources, and it is the only time the IT team has to do this work.

2. The user accesses a self-service portal and fills out a basic request for the type of VM or application, and the cloud in which they want to create it, based on allocations and quotas in place.

▶ Use your favorite browser to search "solar activity disrupting electronics operator from hell" if this does not mean anything to you.

▶ Keep in mind that IT teams do a lot of other work. Moving to the private cloud frees IT teams from manually performing basic tasks needed to meet provisioning requests, enabling them to focus on initiatives that help the business to function.

3. The private cloud infrastructure receives the request and automatically provisions the VM, which might entail a workflow that includes receiving authorization from management. The user can view details about the new VM in the self-service portal, and perhaps receive an automated e-mail containing those details.

4. The user is very happy.

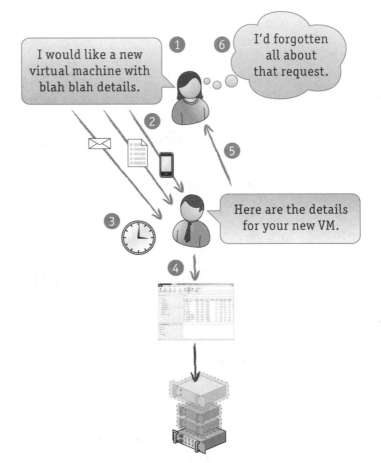

FIGURE 10-2: The traditional process for virtual machine provisioning is very hands-on and slow.

Note the inclusion of "allocations and quotas" in step 2 of the preceding process, which points to the number one fear of many IT departments I talk with about the private cloud: If users and business units can self-serve virtual machines, won't that result in millions of virtual machines being created for no good reason, plunging the IT infrastructure into a dark age of misery and VM sprawl beyond any previously envisioned nightmare scenario? No, because the allocations and quotas will prevent that from happening.

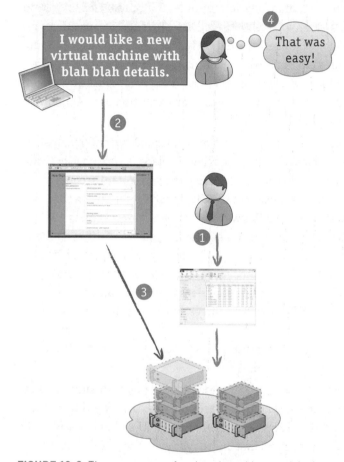

FIGURE 10-3: The new process for virtual machine provisioning when using the private cloud

Note what you are doing. First, you are creating clouds of resources and defining what these clouds can access: which virtualization hosts, how much memory on those hosts, and virtual CPU and disk IOPS consumption. Then you are setting which tiers of storage that cloud can access and how much space. You are setting which networks that cloud can connect to, and which VM templates can be used by the users to create the virtual machines. For each user or group of users, you are setting quotas for how many virtual machines can be created or how much memory and how many virtual CPUs they can use in each cloud. You can even specify what kind of virtual machines they can create in terms of CPU and memory allocations (you'll see how later).

▶ I'm not a fan of this type of automated deletion unless it's for some type of lab environment and the time limit is well advertised to the user beforehand.

With a private cloud solution you can set charge-back and show-back capabilities, so if a business unit consumes a large amount of virtual resource they are charged accordingly—creating a solution that is fully accountable. You can set the expiration of virtual machines so they are automatically deleted after a period of time. Users can create only on the resources you have defined and within the limits you configured. For example, if users are limited to five virtual machines and want to create a sixth, they would have to either delete a virtual machine, save a virtual machine by exporting to a library that you have granted them, or request an extension of their quota, which typically includes an approval process.

In case you missed it, the preceding process is more controlled and enforceable than any manual process most companies currently have in place. Although users who request a VM may eventually get it, the long delays usually involved can discourage business units from asking for virtual resources until it is past the time when they should have received them, which is a terrible way to control resources. Frustrated business users will sometimes go elsewhere for their services, such as setting up their own infrastructures or using public cloud services, which I've seen happen at a lot of organizations. It's far better to establish a good process and enable the business to function in the most optimal way, using internal services where possible. With a private cloud, you can configure costs for virtual resources and charge the business units. Therefore, if more virtual resources are required because the business units can now provision resources more easily, the IT department has the ability to gain the funding to procure more IT infrastructure as needed.

You can start slowly, maybe using the private cloud for development and test environments first, getting used to the idea and familiarizing users with working within quotas. The private cloud infrastructure can be used in production, but more often it's the IT department using the private cloud first and maybe even the self-service portal initially; then, over time, it can be turned over to end users.

UNDERSTANDING THE CAPABILITIES NEEDED TO OFFER A TRUE PRIVATE CLOUD

At this point, you're probably thinking that everything about the private cloud sounds great but wondering how you actually realize and implement it. I want to be clear that there is no single product called "Private Cloud"; you create a private cloud offering within your organization using Microsoft products and guidance based on your requirements.

A Brief Introduction to System Center 2012

The Microsoft private cloud solution encompasses Windows Server, Hyper-V, and System Center 2012. System Center 2012 consists of seven separate major components, as shown in Figure 10-4, and it also includes Endpoint Protection (anti-virus), which was previously part of the Forefront suite, and a new Unified Installer that enables fast deployments of the entire System Center 2012 product for testing proof-of-concept environments (but not production).

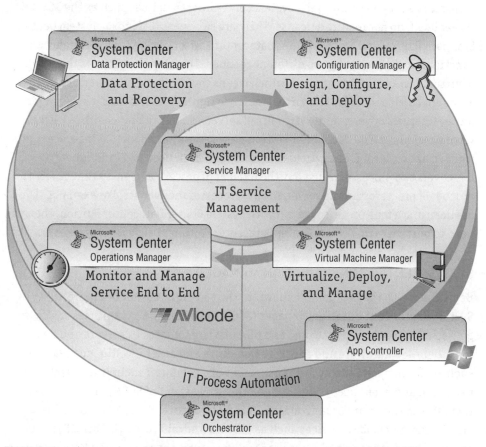

FIGURE 10-4: An overview of System Center 2012's integrated management capabilities

For readers unfamiliar with System Center, let me take you on a 10-cent tour; I go into more detail about the App Controller and Service Manager components toward the end of this chapter. Previously, System Center was a family of products that could be purchased individually or as a suite—you could buy System Center Configuration Manager, you could buy System Center Virtual Machine Manager, and so on. For the servers being managed by the products, users purchased Server Management Licenses (Server ML). Similarly, Client Management Licenses (Client ML) were needed for desktops, and Management Server Licenses were needed to run the server components of the products.

▶ There were previously more than 30 different SKUs (stock-keeping units) of System Center products, which made licensing very complex. The change to two makes it much easier to buy System Center.

System Center 2012 is now a single product that includes the components previously purchased separately, plus some extras (everything you see in Figure 10-4). You only have to buy Management Licenses for the servers being managed; you can deploy all the System Center management servers you need for your desired architecture. The servers running the System Center infrastructure, such as the SCVMM server itself, do not require a license. There are two types of license: System Center Standard Edition and System Center Datacenter Edition. There is no difference in functionality between the two different versions. The only difference is the number of virtual instance rights granted, which means the number of virtual machines. Standard Edition includes two virtual instance rights, which means it's meant for physical servers or very lightly virtualized servers, such as a branch office with two virtual machines. The Datacenter Edition provides unlimited virtual instance rights, which makes it ideal for the virtual environment. Each license, Standard or Datacenter, covers two processors. Just buy the number of processor licenses that covers the number of processors in the server, in two-processor increments. For example, if you are licensing a four-processor server with System Center Datacenter Edition, then you need to purchase two System Center Datacenter Edition licenses for that server.

SYSTEM CENTER CONFIGURATION MANAGER

▶ While SCCM can deploy operating systems, it is geared toward physical environments. You could deploy an OS to a VM using SCCM, but the VM would require legacy network adapters and this would not be as efficient as using a VM template.

Beginning with the component shown in the top-right corner of Figure 10-4, System Center Configuration Manager (SCCM) provides the capabilities to deploy operating systems, applications, and OS/software updates to servers and desktops. Detailed hardware and software inventory and asset intelligence features, such as the complete life cycle management of a computer including installation, patching, and event decommissioning, are a key aspect of SCCM, enabling great insight into the entire organization's IT infrastructure. SCCM 2012 introduces management of mobile devices such as iOS and Android through ActiveSync integration with Exchange and a user-focused management model. One key feature of SCCM for servers is settings management, which enables you to define a configuration baseline of desired configuration items, such as OS and application settings that can be applied to a collection of servers (or desktops). This can be very useful for compliance requirements.

SYSTEM CENTER VIRTUAL MACHINE MANAGER AND APP CONTROLLER

The SCVMM is covered in detail in Chapter 9, so it isn't necessary to repeat that material here. In short, it's the virtualization-specific management functionality across multiple hypervisors, and it provides insight into, and management features for, storage and network fabric resources. The App Controller provides a very rich Silverlight web-based, self-service interface for management of private and public cloud resources. You'll learn more about this later in the chapter.

SYSTEM CENTER OPERATIONS MANAGER

System Center Operations Manager (SCOM) provides a robust monitoring solution for both Microsoft and non-Microsoft operating systems, applications, and hardware. Any monitoring solution can tell you when something is broken, but SCOM's real power lies in its ability to proactively identify and fix problems and its adherence to best-practice functionality. SCOM management packs are sets of object definitions and rules about a specific application or component—for example, there is an Exchange management pack and a Domain Name System (DNS) for Windows Server management pack, and Microsoft has mandated that any Microsoft product should have a management pack that is written by the product team responsible for the application or operating system component. This means the same people who created the best-practice documents in the first place also created these management packs, which you can then just deploy to your environment. Operations Manager will raise alerts regarding potential problems or when best practices are not being followed. Note that new customers often complain that Operations Manager floods them with alerts when it is first implemented. This could occur for a number of reasons, perhaps because there are a lot of problems in the environment that should be fixed; in any case, Operations Manager can be tuned to ignore configurations that may not reflect best practices but are acceptable to the organization.

▶ The Operations Manager product team hates the short name of SCOM, possibly because it's so close to SCUM, so it is often referred to as OpsMgr.

Many third-party vendors provide management packs for their applications and hardware devices. Keep in mind one of the key tenets of the private cloud: It is "all about the application." In this regard, Operations Manager's capabilities to monitor the system—from the hardware, storage, and network all the way through the OS to the application—has been impressive, and it actually goes even further in Operations Manager 2012.

System Center Operations Manager 2012 introduces a number of changes, but two critical ones are related to network monitoring and custom application monitoring. Microsoft licensed from EMC a technology called Smarts (now Ionix), which enables a deep level of discovery and monitoring of network devices. With the network discovery and monitoring functionality, Operations Manager can identify the relationship between network devices and services—for example, understanding that port 3 on a given switch connects to server A, so if there is a switch problem Operations Manager can identify the affected servers. Information such as CPU and memory usage, among other information, is available for supported network devices.

The other big change was Microsoft's acquisition of AVIcode, which is now Application Platform Monitoring (APM) in Operations Manager 2012. APM provides monitoring of custom applications without any changes needed to the application. APM currently supports .NET applications and Java Enterprise Edition (J2EE); and to understand why this is important, consider what happens in your current environment, without APM, when performance problems related to a custom web application occur:

> *User phones IT: "Application X is running slow and sucks."*

> *IT phones the app developer: "Users say Application X is running really slow and really sucks."*

> *App developer to self: "I really, really suck and have no clue how to troubleshoot this. I should leave the industry in disgrace unless there are currently solar flares."*

With System Center Operations Manager, configuring Application Platform Monitoring to manage this custom application changes the preceding scenario dramatically:

> *User phones IT: "Application X is running slow and sucks."*

> *IT phones the app developer: "Users say Application X is running really slow. I see in Operations Manager the APM shows that in function X of module Y, the SQL Server query 'select blah from blah blah' to SQL Server database Z is taking 3.5 seconds."*

> *App developer to self: "It must be an indexing problem on the SQL Server and the index needs to be rebuilt on database Z. I'll give the SQL Server DBA the details to fix it."*

> *App developer to SQL DBA: "Your SQL Server database sucks."*

Operations Manager can be used in many aspects of the private cloud. In addition to monitoring the entire infrastructure to keep it healthy, which is obviously critical, because Operations Manager can monitor resource usage and trends, you can also use it to plan growth and trigger automatic scaling of services when resource usage reaches defined thresholds. Figure 10-5 shows an example Operations Manager view of the lab system design I created using SCVMM.

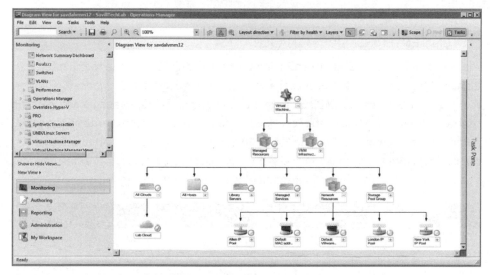

FIGURE 10-5: A nice view of the SCVMM and its various services visible through Operations Manager

SYSTEM CENTER DATA PROTECTION MANAGER

System Center Data Protection Manager (DPM) is Microsoft's best-of-breed backup, continuous data protection, and recovery solution for key Microsoft servers, including SharePoint, SQL Server, Dynamics, Exchange, and Hyper-V, file services, and support for Windows desktops. DPM enables very granular recovery of information within the supported options for the product, including end-user self-recovery in certain scenarios. In the private cloud, DPM can be very useful for protecting the environment. DPM can back up and protect the Hyper-V servers, the SQL databases that are used by most of the System Center 2012 components, the management servers running the System Center components, and all the virtual machines that are created and running on Hyper-V.

DPM supports backing up at the Hyper-V server level, and that backup request is passed by Hyper-V to the virtual machines running on it, enabling the virtual machines to ensure that information on disk is in a backup-ready state, thereby ensuring the integrity and usability of the backup.

To be very clear, being able to create a backup at the hypervisor level does not mean you should only back up at the Hyper-V level. If you want granular restoration capabilities of applications like SharePoint, SQL Server, and Exchange, the DPM agent must be installed within each virtual machine, and the backup must be from the VM directly in order for DPM to identify the application configuration and data.

SYSTEM CENTER SERVICE MANAGER

You'll learn more about System Center Service Manager (SCSM) later in the chapter, but for now think of Service Manager as the *Configuration Management Database (CMDB)* for the entire infrastructure; CMDB is another ITIL key term. Service Manager occupies the central location of System Center for a good reason—it has connectors into all the surrounding components, as shown in Figure 10-6, receiving feeds of information that it consolidates into a single view of everything related to an asset (such as a computer or a person), in turn providing a single point of truth for the entire organization.

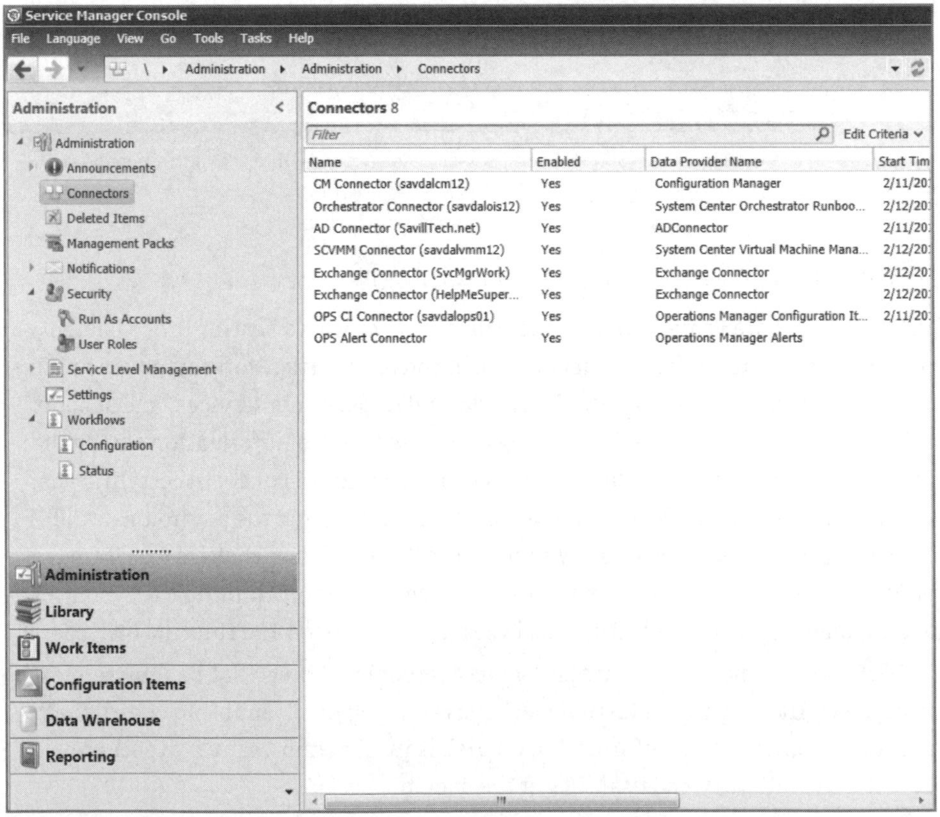

FIGURE 10-6: My Service Manager has connectors to all the other System Center components, plus Active Directory and Exchange in my configuration.

Service Manager has capabilities commonly associated with a help-desk solution—for example, logging requests such as incidents, problems, and change requests, but it also handles change management and release management, and provides a powerful workflow engine to enable your organization's processes (e.g., approvals) to be replicated in Service Manager.

One key feature of Service Manager that is covered later is Service Catalog, which enables an organization to request services, including software and virtual infrastructures. Many companies have a help-desk solution already in place, but Service Manager is far more than a ticketing system, and it can be implemented and integrated with another ticketing solution but leveraged for its other powerful capabilities and CMDB functionality.

SYSTEM CENTER ORCHESTRATOR

System Center Orchestrator actually began its life as a product called Opalis, acquired by Microsoft and renamed System Center Orchestrator as part of System Center 2012. Like Service Manager, Orchestrator is covered in more detail later in the chapter, but at this point it is useful to understand that it provides two key capabilities.

First, Opalis was acquired because it offered connectivity to many of the major existing datacenter applications and systems, which with the acquisition now includes the Microsoft solutions. Integration Packs for many systems exist and provide activities that are specific to the Integration Pack target, but Orchestrator can connect to targets that don't have Integration Packs using many types of communication, including WMI, SSH, PowerShell, SNMP, and many more.

Second, Opalis had very powerful runbook automation capabilities that leveraged all this connectivity. Runbooks that were typically manually actioned by IT administrators and business users can be migrated to Orchestrator using a full-featured flowchart-type interface and completely automated. Orchestrator has a Silverlight console that provides access to not only launch the defined runbooks but also to see their progress.

▶ Many organizations have procedures that must be followed. Perform this action on server A, depending on the result perform these actions on server B and C, and so on. These written collections of instructions are known as runbooks.

It is because of these capabilities that it appears as the foundation of System Center 2012 (refer to Figure 10-4), as all the other System Center 2012 components can leverage Orchestrator to perform actions on other systems and execute complex processes; and Orchestrator can connect to the rest of System Center 2012, enabling the automation of processes that use System Center components and other systems through a single runbook. As you will see later in this chapter, Orchestrator has a central role in the private cloud because of its ability to communicate with systems like Service Manager, Operations Manager, and Virtual Machine Manager to "orchestrate" the creation of virtual machines and scaling actions.

Using Hyper-V as the Private Cloud Foundation

Although I have written about Hyper-V a number of times up to this point, the Microsoft private cloud does not have to leverage Hyper-V. System Center is largely independent of the hypervisor; and if an organization is using ESX, for example, pretty much everything I have described is still possible. However, premium features are available when Hyper-V is used. Examples include full support of all System Center components, the capability to deploy and intelligently patch Hyper-V hosts, and automatic connectivity to external storage. Moreover, it's important to understand that Hyper-V is one of the top hypervisors available. It's one of the three machine virtualization hypervisors in the Gartner magic quadrant (along with VMware and Citrix); and with Windows Server 2008 R2 SP1 and Windows Server 2012 in particular, its feature set and scalability make it a solid choice.

> ▶ Gartner is a leading technology research firm that is consulted by many top companies. Solutions for a given technology are arranged into four quadrants with the most complete and forward-thinking technologies placed in the top (magic) quadrant.

DESIGNING A PRIVATE CLOUD WITH HYPER-V AND SYSTEM CENTER 2012

I've introduced the main applications and platforms that make up the Microsoft private cloud solution. I now want to spend a little time explaining how the components work together, and how to build a private cloud with SCVMM. Then you will see how System Center App Controller, Orchestrator, and Service Manager really round out the solution.

This section describes an ideal Microsoft private cloud solution; and unsurprisingly, this solution reflects what is described in the preceding section: System Center 2012 and Microsoft Hyper-V running Windows operating systems. Although aspects of the private cloud were supported in the previous version of System Center and it offered some self-service capabilities, I believe an ideal private cloud requires abstraction from the underlying fabric and a focus on the application. That is why I believe System Center 2012 is Microsoft's first true private cloud enabler.

You can also build a great private cloud with Windows Server 2008 R2 SP1; but once Windows Server 2012 is released with the new version of Hyper-V, features available with a private cloud will skyrocket. Just looking at the Windows Server 2012 Hyper-V Network Virtualization feature alone, the capability for a virtual network infrastructure completely independent of the physical network—enabling virtual machines to move anywhere within your infrastructure and even out to the public cloud without having to change IP address or any configuration—is amazing. Even better, what you build now will be able to take advantage of Windows Server 2012 when it's available.

> ▶ Service Pack 1 is important, as it introduces Dynamic Memory, which provides a level of VM density previously not possible.

Creating a Cloud with System Center Virtual Machine Manager

In the previous chapter I spent a lot of time writing about System Center Virtual Machine Manager. I introduced its powerful capabilities around fabric management, such as management and visibility into computer, network, and storage resources. I also described creating virtual machine templates and complete service templates of multi-tiered applications, but I stayed away from clouds, which were present in a number of the workspaces I walked through. Now I want to harness all the capabilities of Virtual Machine Manager and actually create private clouds for use in your organization.

I'm going to assume System Center Virtual Machine Manager is fully configured with all your hypervisor compute resources, such as placing all the Hyper-V servers into failover clusters that have been Dynamic and Power Optimized in order to achieve the most performant and highly available solution—one that minimizes power wastage by turning off hosts when not needed.

In addition, SCVMM should be connected to your hardware load balancers, all the SANs should have their SMI-S providers connected into SCVMM, and the storage should be classified for all locations, such as Gold, Silver, and Bronze. Logical networks and sites have been defined. Virtual machine templates for all common configurations have been created, and common services modeled as a service template. System Center Operations Manager is performing monitoring of the environment, System Center Data Protection Manager is backing up and protecting the environment, and System Center Configuration Manager is providing patching and desired configuration and inventory information. In other words, you are ready to create a cloud—which, assuming everything is well configured, is an easy exercise.

▶ *This material makes a critical assumption: that your environment is well designed and healthy. If it isn't, nothing will make it fall apart faster than enabling private clouds. Make sure your environment is the best it can be.*

The best way to truly understand what is involved in creating a cloud in System Center Virtual Machine Manager, and all the options, is to walk through the process of creating one and granting users access to it. This will demonstrate all the capabilities and the delegation options for different groups of users.

The Virtual Machine Manager console is used to create a new cloud. From the VMs and Services workspace, select the Create Cloud action from the ribbon. Specify a name and description for the cloud. For example, you might use "Development" for the name and then "Cloud for development purposes with access to development network only and Silver tier storage" for the description. Make sure the description is something meaningful.

Next, select the resources that will be included in the cloud, as shown in Figure 10-7. The host groups identified will govern the computer resources (virtualization hosts) that will be included in the created cloud, in addition to the various storage and networks that are available in those host groups. Remember that just because a host group is specified it does not mean the entire capability or connectivity of that host group is exposed to the cloud; you can specify exactly what you want to allow access to later in the wizard. The same host groups can be included in multiple clouds. Note in the dialog that you can select a VMware resource pool directly.

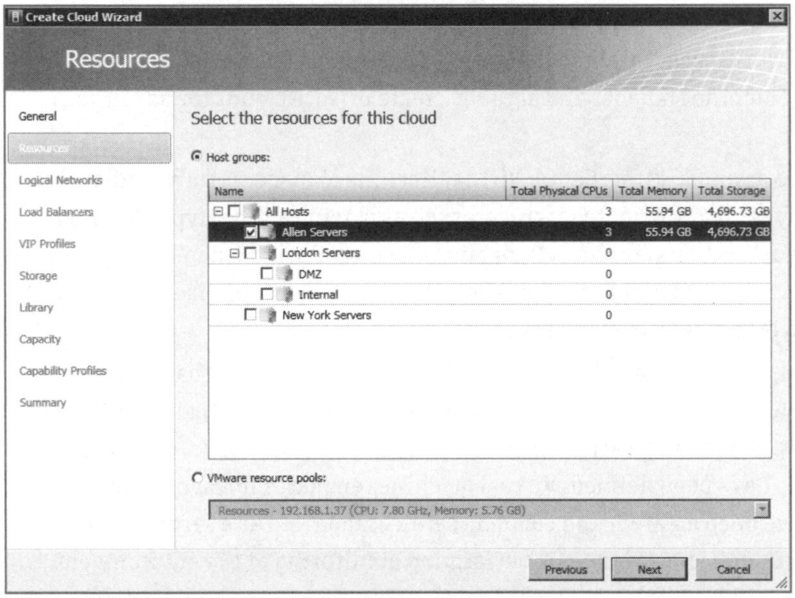

FIGURE 10-7: Select the host groups that will be available to the created cloud.

Next, select which logical networks are available to the cloud. The logical networks displayed will vary depending on the connectivity available to the hosts in the host groups specified in the previous dialog. Select the logical networks this cloud should have access to as shown in Figure 10-8 and click Next to continue with the wizard.

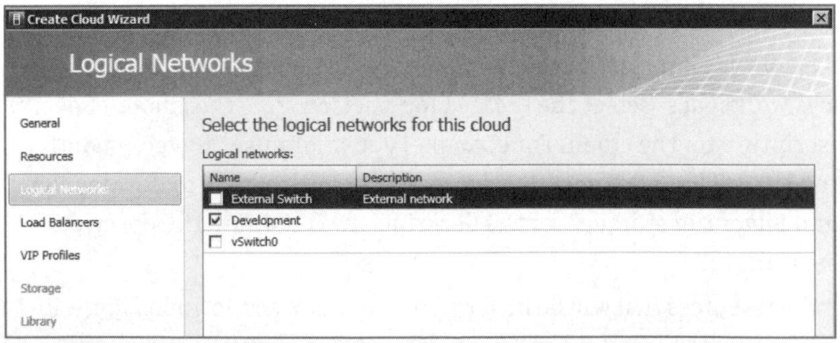

FIGURE 10-8: Select the logical networks available for connectivity within this cloud.

In the next dialog that appears, select the hardware load balancers that can be used. These also vary according to the host groups and logical networks selected, as a hardware load balancer is tied to these items. Click Next to continue. In the dialog that appears, select which virtual IP profiles should be available to the cloud. What you select here varies according to which load balancers were selected in the previous dialog (you likely see the pattern now). Make your selections and click Next.

The Storage dialog, shown in Figure 10-9, displays all tiers of storage that are available within the selected host groups. Select the tiers of storage that should be available to the cloud. For example, for a development cloud you would select lower tiers of storage such as Silver, Tin, or Crappy. Click Next when you are done.

▶ One of my clients named their lower-tier storage this, but quickly changed it when they realized end-users could see it through the self-service portal. Pick names that won't be offensive to any users.

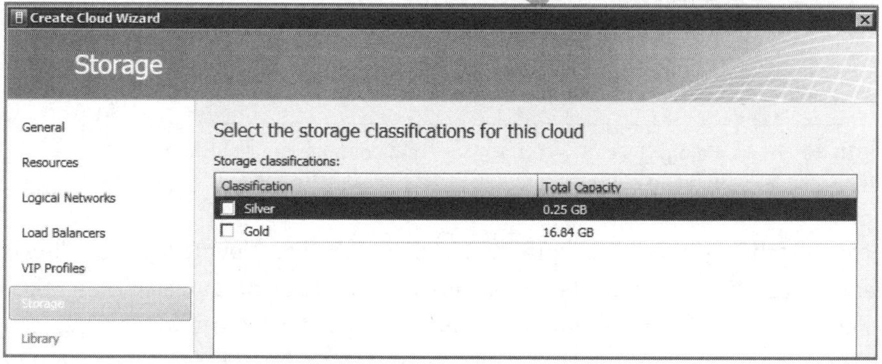

FIGURE 10-9: Select the tiers of storage available to the cloud.

The next step is selecting a library configuration. As shown in Figure 10-10, there are two parts to this, which I will cover in reverse order because the second part is not as commonly used. This option is related to selection of the read-only library shares, which are standard SCVMM libraries in the environment to which you want to grant this cloud access, and the contained resources that can be used to create virtual machines and services. You can choose to create libraries with a subset of ISO images to limit what can be created in the clouds. The read-only library needs to be unique for the private cloud and it is not used as part of a normal library.

▶ This step can get a little messy, requiring multiple read-only libraries for various clouds, so unless you need this just skip it.

Next, specifying a stored VM path identifies where users of the cloud can store content. To understand why you would want to give cloud users a writable library area, consider that cloud users will have a quota limiting the number of virtual machines they can create. However, it is very possible they may reach their quota but need to create another VM, or they may not currently need a VM but don't want to lose its configuration. Giving users a place to store their VMs removes the VMs from the virtualization host, thus freeing up their quota but enabling the VM to be later deployed from the library back to a virtualization host (and again counted against their quota). Note that the path specified for the storage of VMs cannot be part of a library location specified as a read-only library. An easy solution is to create a new share on a file server, add it to SCVMM as a library, and then use it as the writable area for a cloud. When everything is configured as you want it, click Next.

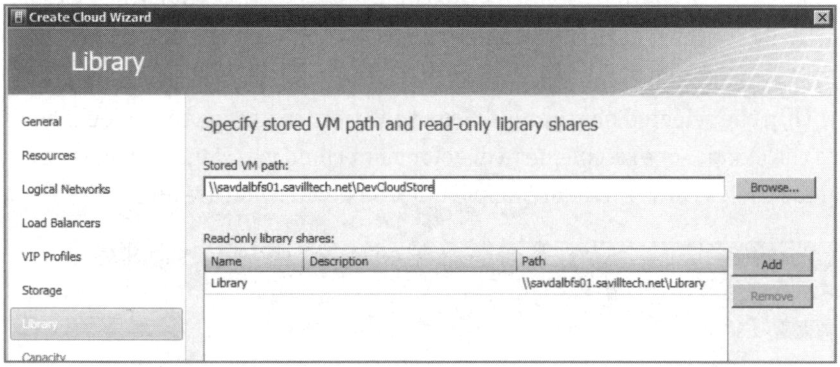

FIGURE 10-10: In this dialog, you can select a library that contains read-only items such as ISO files, and a single folder from an available library for VM storage purposes.

In the next dialog, shown in Figure 10-11, you set the new cloud's capacity. This is an interesting setting that reflects the various approaches an organization can take to managing capacity for the cloud. By default, the capacity is unlimited; but you can change any of the capacity dimensions; Virtual CPUs, Memory, Storage, Custom quota (which is carried over for compatibility with SCVMM 2008 R2), and Virtual machines. You can set the values to use the maximum, or a smaller or higher amount as shown in Figure 10-11. Keep in mind that this is the capacity available to this particular cloud, so you don't have to expose the full capabilities of the underlying host groups; you might have 10 different clouds on a single set of host groups and want to divide up the resources between clouds.

If you looked at the figure closely, you likely noticed that I set the memory higher than the total available in the underlying hosts in the selected host groups. How does this work? It's quite acceptable to set the capacity of a cloud to exceed that of its current underlying resources. However, if you do so it is very important that the proper resource utilization mechanisms and processes are in place so that when a cloud starts to approach the capacity of the underlying resources, additional resources are added to the host groups. This is where System Center Operations Manager really shines; it can monitor the usage of resources and then work with System Center Virtual Machine Manager and System Center Orchestrator to add new Hyper-V hosts to host groups. The same could be done for storage by adding new LUNs to the required storage tiers. Remember? That's a key attribute of the private cloud: scalability. Set the capacity for the cloud and click Next.

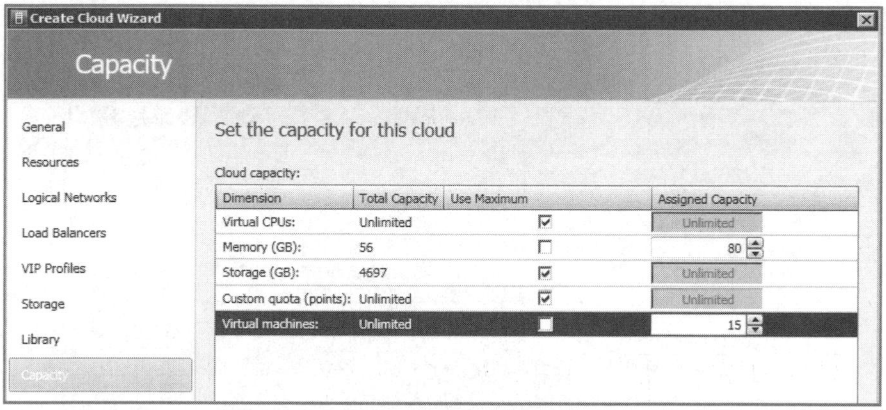

FIGURE 10-11: Set the capacities for this cloud per requirements.

The next dialog, Capability Profile, shown in Figure 10-12, is very different from capacity. Under Capacity you specify limits on the total of each resource type available to the whole cloud, whereas Capability defines what each virtual machine created in the cloud is capable of providing. For example, what is the maximum number of virtual CPUs that can be assigned to a virtual machine, and what is the maximum amount of memory for a VM? By default, three Capability Profiles exist, one for Hyper-V, one for ESX, and one for XenServer, which profile the maximum capabilities for each hypervisor platform. For example, the Hyper-V Capability Profile sets the processor range from 1–4 and the memory from 8MB to 64GB, which are the limits for Hyper-V 2008 R2 SP1. The ESX Capability Profile sets the processor range from 1–8 and the memory from 4MB to 255GB, which are the ESX 4.1 limits. Obviously, these limits differ for Windows Server 2012 and vSphere 5, which will result in an updated Capability Profile once an update to SCVMM ships to support Windows Server 2012 and vSphere 5. By default, you can select any combination of the three built-in, locked Capability Profiles for your cloud based on the hypervisors used in the cloud—but you don't have to.

Imagine you are creating a development cloud in 2013. Windows Server 2012 has been released, with its support for virtual machines with 32 virtual CPUs and 1TB of RAM. Suppose you give a user a quota of 20 virtual CPUs and 24GB of memory; do you want that user consuming their whole quota with a single VM? Not likely. Instead, you could create a custom Capability Profile in the SCVMM Library workspace, and under Profiles → Capability Profiles create a new profile specifying the capabilities you want to make available in a specific cloud. The custom Capability Profile shown in Figure 10-12 has a limit of two virtual CPUs and a memory range from 512MB to 4GB. You could also mandate the use of Dynamic Memory. Note that you can also set the number of DVD drives allowed, whether shared images are used, the number of hard disks allowed and their type and size, the number of network adapters, and even whether high availability is available or required.

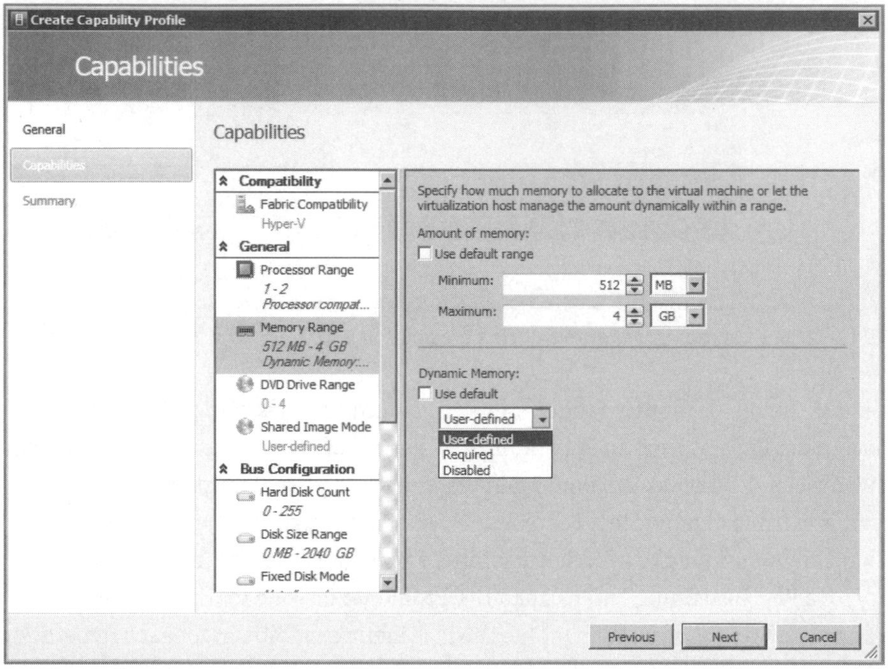

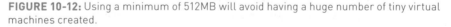

FIGURE 10-12: Using a minimum of 512MB will avoid having a huge number of tiny virtual machines created.

> **WARNING**   There is a potential pitfall in creating custom Capability Profiles if you don't plan well. Many resources, such as virtual machine templates, have a configuration that sets the required Capability Profile. If the VMM administrator doesn't update the resources with the created custom Capability Profile, you won't be able to assign any resources to your new cloud. This is configured through the Hardware Configuration area of the VM template. Select the Compatibility option and ensure that the new Capability Profile is selected.

Once you have created your custom Capability Profiles you can elect to use them for your cloud. As shown in Figure 10-13, custom Capability Profiles can be used in addition to, or instead of, the built-in Capability Profiles. Multiple Capability Profiles can be selected, and remember these are just limits which are then linked to various templates, so the Capability Profile used will depend on the template selected during VM creation. Click Next when you are done.

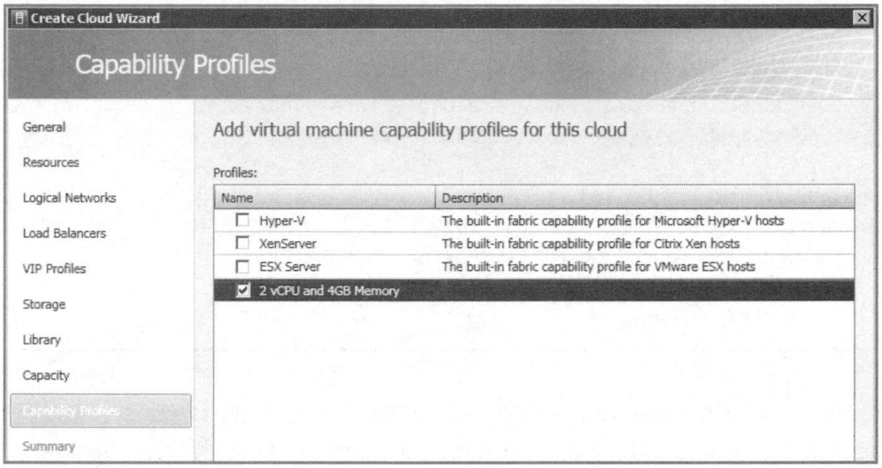

FIGURE 10-13: Selecting a custom Capability Profile for use within this private cloud

The last dialog shows a summary of all your choices, along with the magical View Script button that displays the PowerShell script used to create the corresponding new cloud. The following very basic example creates a cloud without hardware load balancers or Virtual IP templates, but it demonstrates what is going on. This enables you to use the PowerShell commands in other components such as System Center Orchestrator to automate the creation of clouds based on requests from Service Manager.

LISTING 10-1: Creating a Private Cloud Using PowerShell

```
Set SCCloudCapacity -JobGroup "GUID"
      -UseCustomQuotaCountMaximum $true
      -UseMemoryMBMaximum $false -UseCPUCountMaximum $true
      -UseStorageGBMaximum $true -UseVMCountMaximum $false
      -MemoryMB 81920 -VMCount 15

$resources = @()
$resources += Get-SCLogicalNetwork -ID " GUID "

$resources += Get-SCStorageClassification -ID " GUID "

$readonlyLibraryShares = @()
$readonlyLibraryShares += Get-SCLibraryShare -ID " GUID "

$addCapabilityProfiles = @()
$addCapabilityProfiles += Get-SCCapabilityProfile
      -Name "2 vCPU and 4GB Memory"
```

```
Set-SCCloud -JobGroup " GUID " -RunAsynchronously
        -ReadWriteLibraryPath "\\savdalbfs01\DevCloudStore"
        -AddCloudResource $resources
        -AddReadOnlyLibraryShare $readonlyLibraryShares
        -AddCapabilityProfile $addCapabilityProfiles

$hostGroups = @()
$hostGroups += Get-SCVMHostGroup -ID " GUID "
New-SCCloud -JobGroup " GUID " -VMHostGroup $hostGroups
        -Name "Development" -Description ""
        -RunAsynchronously
```

You now have a cloud but no one can use it yet, so the next step is to assign the cloud to users and groups. For now, however, grab a drink and congratulate yourself—you have entered the world of the private cloud. To assign access to clouds, user roles are used, which can be any of the following:

▶ **Delegated Administrator:** Can do anything to the objects within their scope

▶ **Read-Only Administrator:** Can view information about everything but cannot change anything, which is useful for auditors and interns

▶ **Self-Service User:** Can create and manage virtual machines

Each user role has a scope that defines the clouds it applies to, and the capabilities and users/groups within that user role. It is very common, therefore, to create a new Self-Service user role and possibly a Delegated Administrator user role for every cloud you create to enable granularity in the assignment of cloud access.

In SCVMM, open the Settings workspace and navigate to Security → User Roles and select the Create User Role action on the Ribbon. When the Create User Role Wizard opens, add a name and description for the object being created as requested. If the user role is cloud-specific, then include the name of the cloud in the name. Click Next. The next dialog that appears requests the type of user role. Select Self-Service User and click Next.

The next dialog prompts for Members: the users and groups that are part of this role. In general, my recommendation is to always use Active Directory groups, adding users into the AD group that needs access to the user role so it's not necessary to keep modifying the user role. When users are added to the AD group, they automatically receive the cloud rights of the AD group. This works great if you are creating a cloud for a certain business unit and that business unit already has an AD group. Just grant that business unit AD group access to the cloud-specific Self-Service user role; then, as users join the business unit, they gain access to the cloud. Even if the cloud is not specific to a business unit, if you have good processes in place to add users to groups, an AD group could be used—such as developers who have access to a development cloud. This recommendation differs when good processes are not in place to add users to groups and it's beyond the control of the team implementing the private cloud to fix it or affect change. In those cases, you might add users directly to user roles within SCVMM, which can be automated through PowerShell, and thereby eliminate potentially long delays associated with adding users to an AD group. Add the users and/or groups and click Next.

In the next dialog of the wizard, shown in Figure 10-14, define the scope of the user role—that is, the clouds to which it applies. Note that no host groups are shown, only clouds. System Center Virtual Machine Manager is the cloud or nothing. Select the clouds and click Next.

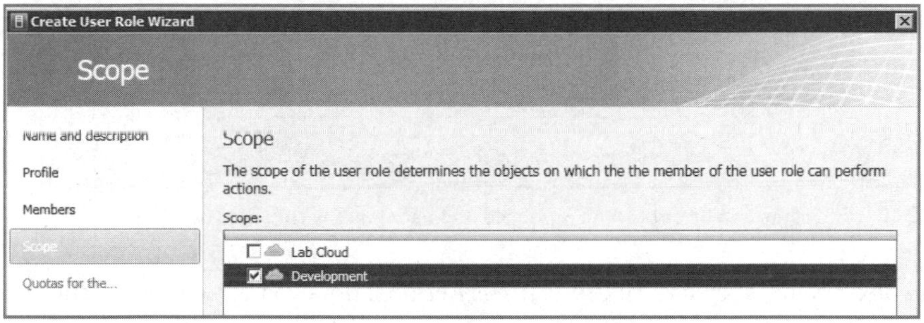

FIGURE 10-14: Select the clouds to which the user role will apply.

In the next dialog, shown in Figure 10-15, set the quotas for the user role. Recall that when you created the cloud you set its total capacity; now you are setting both the total quotas for the specific user role within the cloud and the quotas of individual users within the user role. Note that you may have multiple Self-Service user roles for a single cloud with different quotas and constraints. In Figure 10-15, I set an unlimited quota for the role, allowing it to access the full capacity of the cloud; but each user is much more limited. Make your selections and click Next.

The next dialog is Resources (not shown), where you can specify which resources should be available to the role, such as virtual machine templates, hardware profiles, service templates, and so on. Keep in mind that these resources will be available when the users of this role create virtual machines, so ensure that the right templates are available for them. Additionally, a library share can be specified for users' own uploaded data and prepared resources that are shared between all members of the role. Click Next when you are done to continue.

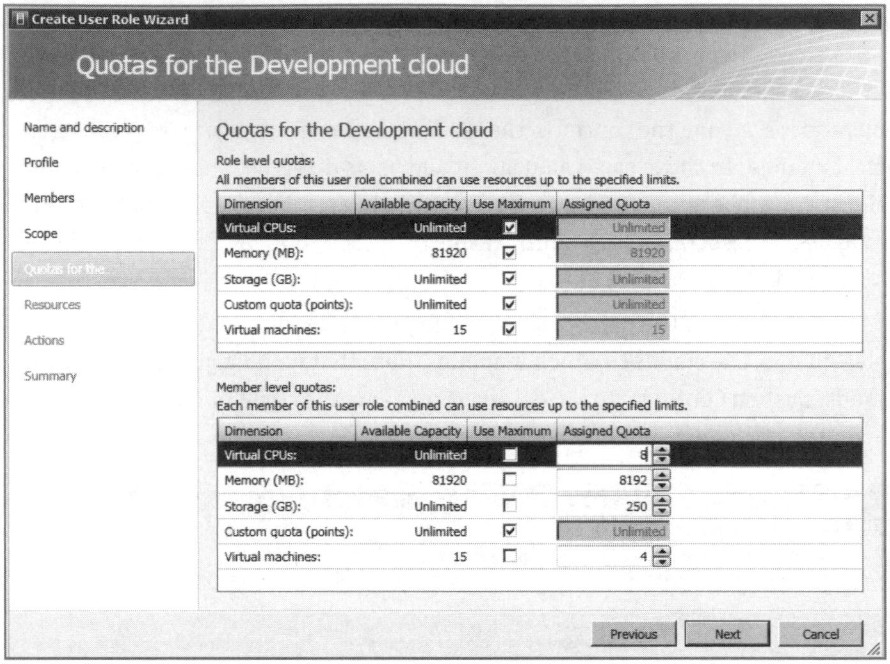

FIGURE 10-15: Quotas can be set for the user role and each user within the role.

The next dialog, shown in Figure 10-16, is Actions. Here you can configure the permitted actions for the user role. Note that these can be configured at a fairly granular level (they are fully documented at http://technet.microsoft.com/en-us/library/gg610613.aspx). For very basic users who just need to create and manage their own virtual machines based on defined templates, consider giving the following actions:

- ▶ Checkpoint
- ▶ Deploy and Deploy (from template only)
- ▶ Local Administrator (only needed if users can deploy from templates to enable the local administrator password to be set)
- ▶ Pause and resume
- ▶ Remote connection
- ▶ Remove
- ▶ Shut down
- ▶ Start
- ▶ Stop

After you have configured the actions, the next dialog enables you to specify any specific Run As accounts to be made available to the user role. Be careful when assigning which Run As accounts are made available, as you don't want to give basic users access to highly privileged Run As accounts. Click Next when you are done. A Summary dialog will appear. Click Finish to create the role. Again, you could export the PowerShell for reuse.

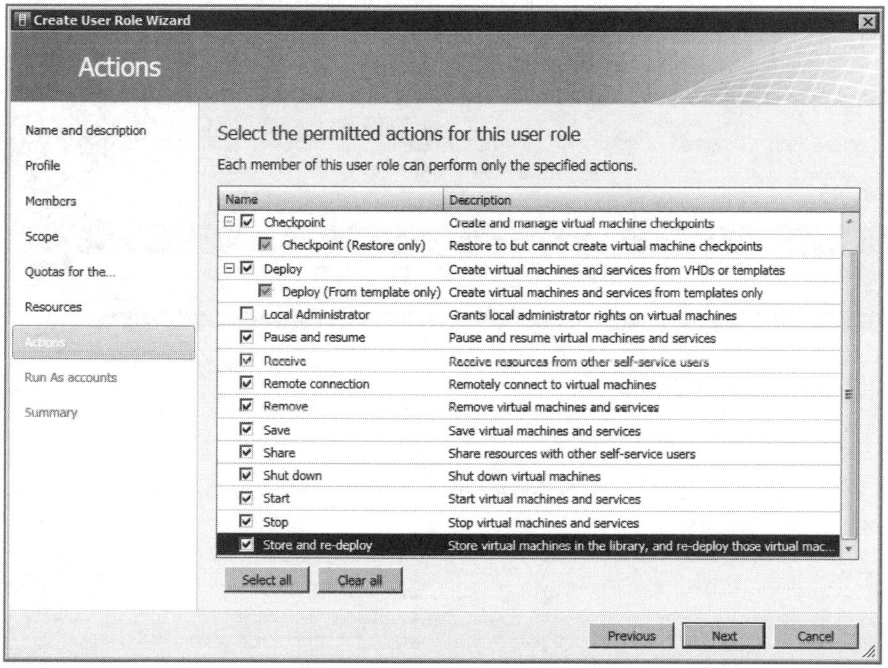

FIGURE 10-16: Configure the actions for a specific user role. If different sets of permissions are needed for different users, then create multiple user roles.

You have now created a cloud and configured the people who are allowed to use it. Now let's get the end users using it.

How End Users Experience System Center Virtual Machine Manager

One way to deploy virtual machines and services is to give users access to the System Center Virtual Machine Manager Console, which is fully role-based access controlled—meaning users see only the clouds they have access to and the functions they are allowed to perform.

Because people want to use the web, SCVMM 2012 comes with a web portal to enable end-user virtual machine provisioning, but not service provisioning, based on service templates (nor does it understand tiers of storage or many of the new SCVMM 2012 features). The built-in SCVMM 2012 web portal is very much the same as the web portal included with SCVMM 2008 R2, but it uses clouds instead of host groups. Figure 10-17 shows the SCVMM 2012 web portal. Notice the very basic nature of the interface and the fact that it only understands quota points, not the more granular options that are available in SCVMM 2012 itself.

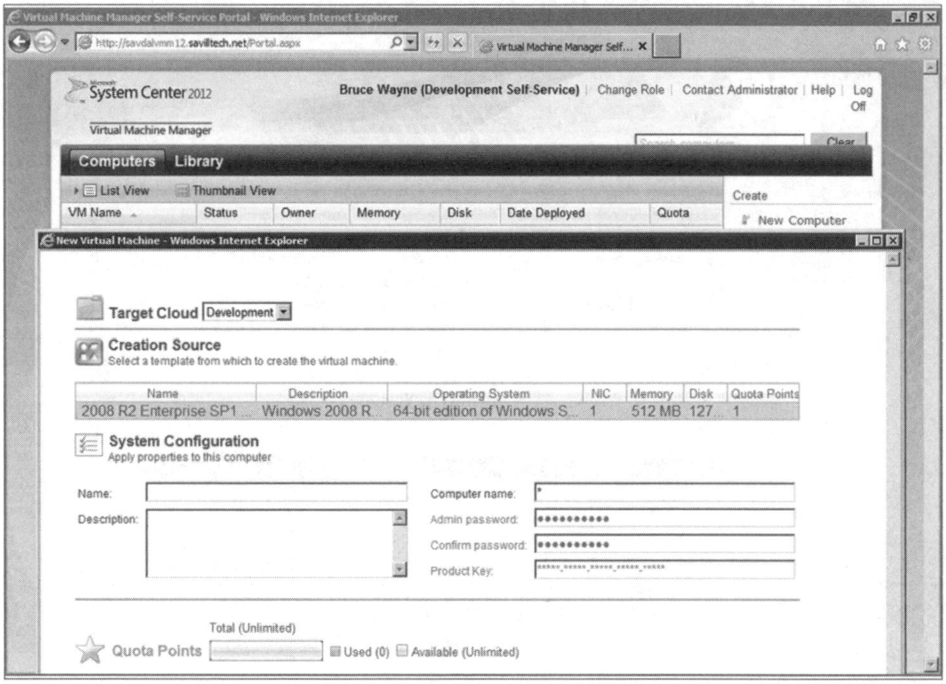

FIGURE 10-17: The built-in SCVMM 2012 web portal is very basic but it allows the user to create basic virtual machines.

However, I don't want to spend any more time on the SCVMM 2012 web portal—you won't use it. It's there for backward compatibility with SCVMM 2008 R2 and is very much a throwback to when System Center was comprised of separate products. With System Center 2012, you now get the entire set, including access to System Center App Controller, which is so much nicer for VM and service deployment, and you have System Center Service Manager for a service catalog approach.

WORKING WITH SYSTEM CENTER APP CONTROLLER 2012

System Center App Controller is a very thin installation. It can be installed on the System Center Virtual Machine Management server, but for busy environments better performance will be gained by running App Controller on its own server. App Controller does use an SQL Server database for its configuration storage, but the rest of its requirements are very light and the install media is around 11MB at the time of writing. System Center App Controller delivers a web-based Silverlight experience that provides access to both private clouds provided by System Center Virtual Machine Manager and public cloud services such as Windows Azure, as shown in Figure 10-18.

▶ This is not a typo; the App Controller installer is indeed 11MB. When is the last time you saw a Microsoft server product that could be installed from a few floppy disks?

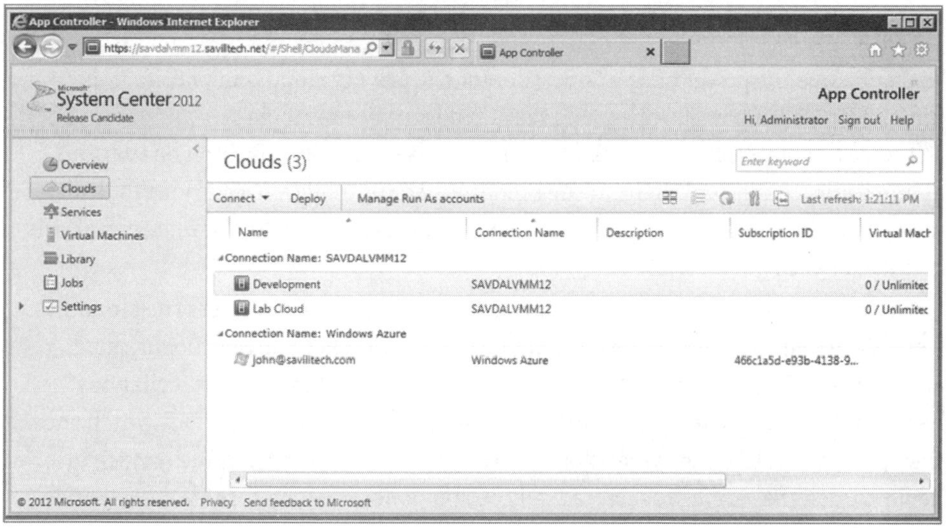

FIGURE 10-18: The Clouds screen of SC App Controller, showing my private clouds and public clouds

The Application Is What Matters

Note that the name of this component is System Center App Controller, not System Center Virtual Machine Controller. Remember, the focus of the private cloud is the application, not an operating system instance, which is typically what we mean when we talk about virtual machines. That does not mean SC App Controller cannot deploy individual virtual machines. It can do so easily and shows the user the amount of quota the VM would use, the amount of quota that would be left, and whether the user has access to multiple clouds. Users can select the correct cloud and configure any customizations, such as which network to connect to. Clearly, managing virtual machines within SC App Controller provides a very rich experience. It can also do so much more, such as deploy entire services that are based on those service templates you created in SCVMM that might have many tiers with different applications at each tier level.

If you have a Windows Azure application, it can be deployed to your Windows Azure subscription from within App Controller and fully managed and scaled, instead of having to use the Windows Azure website. Services can actually be moved between your on- and off-premise clouds, providing both powerful flexibility and portability.

Using App Controller to Manage Cloud Services

To emphasize the power of App Controller for the private cloud and facilitate an understanding of how it works, this section describes how to deploy an instance of a service template. My service template has three tiers, each of which has various applications configured. Behind the scenes it's configured to use various logical networks and tiers of storage, and as an end user you need to deploy an instance of this service for your business unit.

After logging on to System Center App Controller, the user selects the Clouds workspace and then the Deploy action tab, which launches the New Deployment activity. App Controller uses a canvas-type interface that dynamically changes based on the user's selection. Figure 10-19 starts with the basic canvas, which shows the options to select the target cloud for the deployment and then the service to deploy. Once the service is selected, all the components of the service are expanded, enabling user configuration such as setting OS names (if desired); network connectivity, if options are available based on the template and cloud; and any other options. The user then clicks Deploy and behind the scenes SCVMM takes care of all the VM provisioning and configuration required. You can view the Jobs workspace in SCVMM to see the VM creation process.

SC App Controller allows full management of any resources in the private and public clouds, including performing scaling options such as adding instances to a service and more basic management such as creating snapshots and managing VM state. If you compare the SC App Controller interface to the SCVMM self-service portal there really is no contest. This is very exciting when you consider that SC App Controller is only in its infancy. Imagine when Windows Azure has Infrastructure as a Service (IaaS), which allows virtual machines to run on the Azure public cloud, and when Windows Server 2012 has virtual networks that could span on and off premise. SC App Controller will enable not only application deployment to private and public clouds but also virtual machine and service deployments, including the capability to move resources between clouds. This is obviously in the future, but I don't think it's that far off.

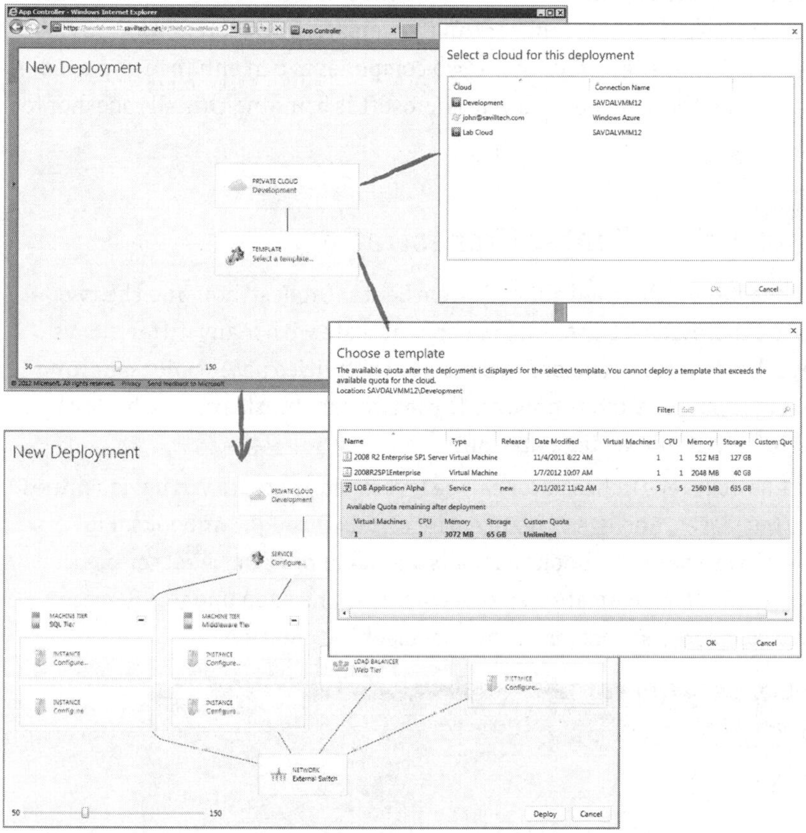

FIGURE 10-19: After selecting the target cloud and service to deploy, the user just completes basic details to complete the deployment.

SYSTEM CENTER 2012—MOVING BEYOND THE VIRTUAL MACHINE MANAGER AND THE APP CONTROLLER

When most people think private cloud, the primary enabler is System Center Virtual Machine Manager, with System Center App Controller providing a great user interface for managing private and public clouds, which is basically correct. SCVMM provides much of the functionality around abstraction of computer, storage, and network resources, creation of clouds and user roles, plus great template and virtual application capabilities. In some scenarios, however, clouds will need to be created outside of the Virtual Machine Manager Console, deploying virtual machines and services instances separately from VMM or App Controller interfaces as part of automated processes—and as I've previously mentioned, this is really where System Center Orchestrator and System Center Service Manager can participate. Therefore, I want to close this chapter by looking at a few ways these two components can enhance and enable the private cloud, and then introduce a way Microsoft is bringing this all together for the customer.

Leveraging System Center Orchestrator

Earlier in this chapter you learned about System Center Orchestrator and the two great capabilities it provides: the ability to communicate with many different systems and the ability to automate a defined series of activities potentially spanning these different systems through runbooks. These two capabilities can be highly beneficial to your private cloud implementation.

At the most basic level, Orchestrator can be leveraged to create virtual machines, deploy service templates, and even create entire clouds through runbooks. Figure 10-20 shows a very basic runbook that calls a number of PowerShell scripts that communicate with SCVMM to create a virtual machine, and then updates Service Manager with a completed status for the virtual machine creation.

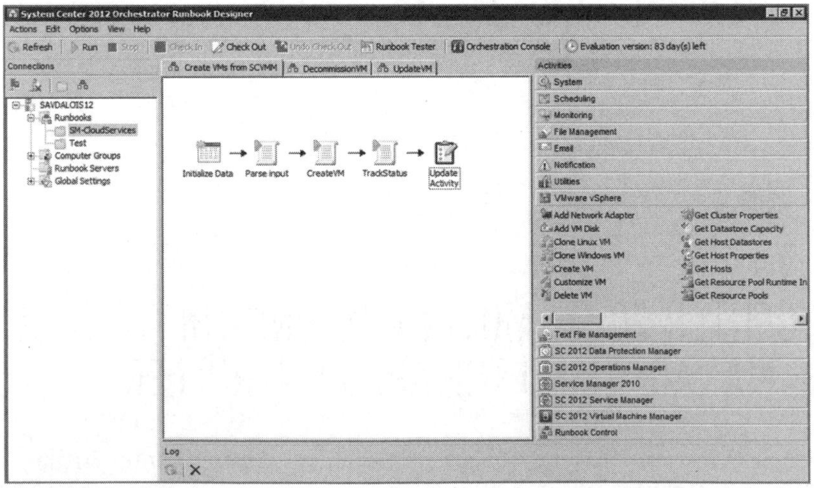

▶ Remember the numerous examples in the discussion of SCVMM in which a PowerShell script could be generated that shows the actions performed through the console? Those scripts fit perfectly into Orchestrator for automated running as part of a runbook.

FIGURE 10-20: A basic runbook receives an input request for a VM, creates the VM, and then updates the status of the request.

This is really just the tip of the iceberg. Running PowerShell scripts to perform actions through Orchestrator is great, and error checking and updating of other applications like Service Manager is a benefit, but you can run PowerShell without Orchestrator. If you look again at Figure 10-20, on the right is a list of activity groups, known as Integration Packs, including System Center Virtual Machine Manager, System Center Data Protection Manager, and VMware vSphere. Each Integration Pack contains activities specific to the target product for which the Integration Pack was created. vSphere includes activities for virtual machine creation and management; the same types of activities are available for SCVMM; and for Data Protection Manager, the activities include backup actions. Using Integration Packs for systems and the built-in Orchestrator activities, it is possible to automate any action related to the private cloud, and it can be customized to reflect exactly how your organization functions. Once you create the runbooks they can then be triggered automatically by the rest of the System Center components. Some great example scenarios in which you could use Orchestrator include the following:

► Create a new cloud based on an IT request through a service catalog that calls a created Orchestrator runbook.

► Deploy a new virtual machine or service instance.

► Offer a runbook that automatically patches and reboots all virtual machines for a particular user or business group.

► Automatically scale up and down deployed services by triggering runbooks that perform the scaling based on performance alerts from Operations Manager.

► Deprovision virtual machines or services that have passed a specified length of time or date in development environments.

Remember that the point of the private cloud is that it's automated; and you can't automate by using graphic consoles, so as you learn System Center and Virtual Machine Manager in particular, look at the series of actions you perform, look at the PowerShell scripts, look at the activities in Integration Packs, and then start creating runbooks in Orchestrator that can be used instead. Once the runbooks are created, they can be manually triggered using the Silverlight web-based Orchestrator interface or triggered from other systems, such as an item in Service Manager's Service Catalog. Given Orchestrator's capability to connect to almost any system, with a little bit of work any manual procedure you perform today should be able to be automated—and more important, automated through System Center Orchestrator.

Offering Virtual Services as Part of a Service Catalog with System Center Service Manager

I mentioned System Center Service Manager a number of times in this chapter and quite a few times in the last section. As previously explained, Service Manager is the Configuration Management Database (CMDB) of your organization. It has feeds and connections to all the other System Center 2012 components and can offer various services, such as managing basic ticketing-type activities like incidents (things not doing what they should), problems (something is broken), and change requests (someone wants something).

When there are problems in the environment, Service Manager is especially helpful because it connects to all the different systems, providing both an overview and a single point of truth about each asset, which aids in finding a solution. In Service Manager you can see all the hardware, software, and patch status information gathered from Configuration Manager. You can see AD information that was pulled from AD. You can see any alerts that were generated by Operations Manager, plus any more complex service dependencies, such as all the systems responsible for providing messaging services to the organization.

These multiple connections to systems enable Service Manager to provide a premium level of service for your private cloud. Keep in mind, however, that the discussion so far has been focused on creating clouds, virtual machines, and services with SCVMM console, App Controller, PowerShell, and Orchestrator. These are not tasks typically associated with end users, who have a different set of goals. Users worry about many different things: their primary job (which is not IT), applications, data, hardware, and so on—and virtual environments are just one small part of making all of that work. Users don't really want a separate interface just for requesting a virtual machine. They are not going to run PowerShell scripts you make available, and giving them a list of runbooks they can run through a web interface is likely to baffle them.

Service Manager 2012 introduces a new feature called the Service Catalog. The Service Catalog provides a single source for all the different types of services offered. This could include creating a new user, requesting the installation of a software package through SCCM, asking for a new keyboard, pretty much anything that Service Manager can enable through its connections to other systems. The Service Catalog is available to end users primarily through a SharePoint site that

▶ I'm talking about the typical user here. Power users and users whose job focuses more on virtualization and applications would absolutely benefit from SC App Controller, particularly for the control and insight it provides into private and public clouds.

uses Service Manager Silverlight Web Parts. Users can browse the Service Catalog as a single repository for all their needs, which makes it a perfect place to offer virtual services on the private cloud.

To offer the private cloud services in the Service Catalog, you just import the runbooks into Service Manager using the Orchestrator connector. When a user makes a request from the Service Catalog, the normal Service Manager workflows can be used, such as request authorization, and then the Service Catalog calls the runbook in Orchestrator to actually perform the actions. Service Manager and Orchestrator have great bi-directional communications in System Center 2012, enabling the status of the runbook's execution to be visible within Service Manager; and once the process is done, the service request is marked as completed and the user could even be notified by e-mail.

Using the System Center Cloud Services Process Pack

I'm sure everything described in this section sounds great: creating runbooks to create resources in the private cloud, connecting Orchestrator to Service Manager, and then adding the runbooks to the Service Catalog for end-user purposes. However, a fair amount of work is involved. You have to create the runbooks, configure all the System Center 2012 components to correctly communicate, set up the Service Catalog in Service Manager, and more.

To help speed you on your way, Microsoft provides a Process Pack to enable the private cloud using System Center 2012 and Hyper-V. The System Center Cloud Services Process Pack contains detailed guidance on actually configuring Virtual Machine Manager, Operations Manager, Orchestrator, and Service Manager—and it includes runbooks, which you install to your Orchestrator environment, and an additional Management Pack, which is installed into Service Manager, to enable the private cloud offerings. Figure 10-21 shows a new view in Service Manager Console once the Cloud Services Process Pack is installed. Notice it shows step-by-step actions that must be performed to complete the private cloud configuration.

The Cloud Services Process Pack is available from http://www.microsoft.com/en-us/download/details.aspx?id=28726, or just perform a search for System Center Cloud Services Process Pack. It includes the detailed installation and setup procedure. After following the instructions, you will have a complete private cloud that can be extended and modified as your requirements evolve.

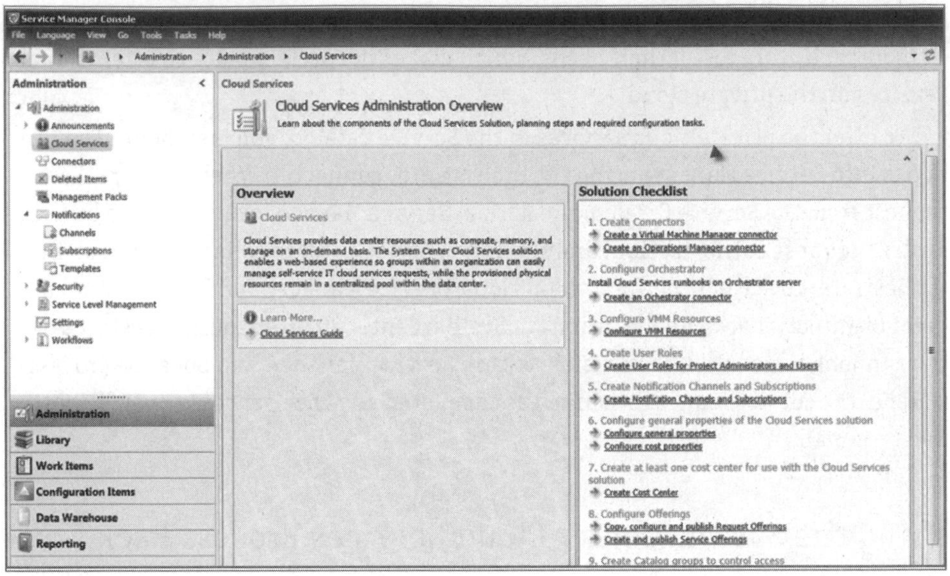

FIGURE 10-21: Completing a private cloud offering in the Service Catalog of Service Manager with step-by-step guidance

SUMMARY

Whether you find the term "private cloud" exciting or terrifying, I hope this chapter has demonstrated the capabilities it offers—to the IT department in particular and to the organization in general. Easier provisioning, higher utilization of resources, better accountability, less management overhead, and a focus on the application translate into greater efficiency and productivity for the business.

It's not easy. I wish it were a matter of installing some software and clicking Next a few times. In reality, a properly enabled private cloud requires a lot of up-front effort: deploying all the System Center 2012 components, connecting them, and offering services. Fortunately, the Cloud Services Process Pack greatly helps these efforts with detailed guidance and tools; and once this initial effort is done, the user's day-to-day work will be drastically reduced, enabling IT to focus on new services and initiatives rather than keeping the lights on and manually creating virtual machines.

CHAPTER 11

Architecting a Virtual Desktop Infrastructure

In recent years, at the top of nearly every Chief Information Officer's list of priorities is Virtual Desktop Infrastructure (VDI). VDI has been pushed as the solution to a multitude of problems and as the enabler for a whole new way of working. However, the reality is somewhere in the middle, and often other, more cost efficient solutions are available that don't require full VDI deployment.

This chapter walks through what exactly VDI is, the components required to implement VDI, and the complementary virtualization solutions that are needed to ensure a successful VDI solution. Windows Server 2008 R2 introduced a basic in-box VDI solution, which was improved with Windows Server 2012. In addition, Microsoft has several key partners with add-on VDI solutions, which are discussed at the end of the chapter.

UNDERSTANDING VIRTUAL DESKTOP INFRASTRUCTURE (VDI)

Virtual Desktop Infrastructure (VDI) is currently hugely popular and top of mind in most companies; nevertheless, not many companies are actually implementing it. Why? Typically, once VDI is understood and the other options explored, it shifts from being the strategic way forward to a solution for specific subsets of an organization's population. Personally, I have gone into countless meetings with clients who want to implement VDI, and by the time I walk out of the meeting having explained what it is, what is required, and some other options that offer exactly the same user-experience capabilities, they decide it's not for them or scale down its planned usage. This is not to say VDI is not a great solution for certain scenarios, but it's not the global solution it's made out to be by certain virtualization vendors who don't have session-based virtualization solutions and so have to push VDI.

Understanding What VDI Means to Users

VDI enables users to have their own desktop operating system instances, which are hosted on a back-end virtualization infrastructure. Users remotely connect to this desktop from some type of client device: it could be a specialist thin client, a full Windows client, or an iPad. Users can connect from anything that has a client that supports the protocol used to communicate with the virtualized client operating system, which for native Windows is the Remote Desktop Protocol (RDP). This means none of the users' desktops, applications, or data actually reside on their local devices. To the end users it looks like they have a full Windows 7 desktop on their local device, and the fact that it's running remotely is transparent. One of the great assets of this model is that users can connect to their VDI desktops from anywhere and from any device and get exactly the same desktop, the same data, the same applications, and the same experience. This is great for the users and for security, because the data never actually leaves the datacenter. All that is sent over the network are the screen updates from the remote client OS in the virtual machine (VM) to the end device and keystrokes and mouse actions back to the remote OS.

Figure 11-1 shows a very simplistic picture of the VDI environment, with users connecting through the RDP to a virtual machine running Windows 7 on a Hyper-V server. Though technically this basic setup could be considered VDI, it requires all users to have their own static virtual machines on Hyper-V configured as static connections from the users' end devices. Because users need to connect to their own VMs, scalability is difficult and is a huge maintenance pain when all those virtual machines have to be patched. In reality, VDI implementations need to be more sophisticated to handle these concerns.

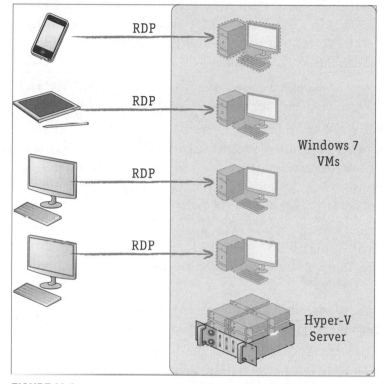

FIGURE 11-1: In the most basic sense, VDI consists of client devices connecting to a Windows client operating system that is hosted in a virtual machine.

Knowing When and How to Use VDI

So far I might sound like I'm fairly negative about VDI, but that isn't really the case. At times VDI is definitely a great solution. I'm just negative when it's used in scenarios where it's not the right solution and other solutions would make more sense.

CROSSREF I talk about how to decide what the right architecture is for both your desktop and datacenter environments in Chapter 13.

The following is a list of key scenarios in which VDI is often considered. I'll come back to many of them later to discuss if alternatives exist that should at least be investigated. This list is not definitive, but it does cover many of the scenarios I've heard in my consulting time.

▶ Disaster recovery situations in which users cannot access their normal work or work offices. Consider a huge blizzard that prevents workers from leaving their homes. With a VDI environment, users can just connect to their virtual desktop and access their complete desktop.

▶ Contract users with their own computers who need a corporate desktop environment. Rather than rebuild their computers, you can just give them access to a desktop in the corporate VDI environment.

▶ Bring Your Own Device (BYOD) situations in which organizations allow users to bring their own computers into the office (and may even pay them an annual allowance to do it). In this case, installing the corporate image on these devices does not make sense, so VDI can give the users a corporate desktop experience.

▶ Users who need to use many different devices and require a consistent desktop experience. This could include users who use shared devices, such as in hospitals.

▶ High-security situations where data cannot leave the datacenter. It's not practical to seat users in the actual datacenter, so remotely accessing a desktop located in the datacenter is the best of both worlds.

▶ Use of certain applications that access huge amounts of data in the datacenter. Sending a large quantity of data over the network may be impractical or result in poor performance, so hosting the desktop in the datacenter with the application effectively running on the same local network as the data improves performance.

▶ Critical desktops that need high resilience. Consider that with VDI, the desktop operating system is actually running on server hardware, which means server-class performance, high availability, and redundancy, including Redundant Array of Independent Disk (RAID)–based storage.

▶ Remote developers who need to be able to customize their operating system environments, install applications, reboot, and so on.

▶ Users of the iPad who need to access Windows applications that "for some reason" don't run on iOS.

▶ Datacenters are also generally cold and very noisy, so consider placing only users who are badly behaved in the actual datacenter.

▶ Out of all the reasons, this is the one I hear the most, and it really is the worst reason. There are many Windows slate alternatives that avoid the need to create a complete infrastructure and could run the application natively.

Notice that none of these reasons are along the lines of "reducing desktop management costs" or "simplifying management," although those reasons are sometimes given. In general, VDI will not save money. In fact, it is likely to actually increase costs. Likewise, although a well designed VDI environment may ease management, it is probably only because the existing desktop environment is not well architected. For far less money and upheaval, the existing desktop architecture could be improved and made easier to manage. Remember also that to use the VDI environment, users must be able to connect to the corporate network, and therefore, the VDI is unavailable in offline scenarios, such as when sitting on a plane.

Do remember that you will still have client operating systems that require management and maintenance, so you are not removing the management of the desktop; you are just moving it to the datacenter. In a well architected VDI, the management can be streamlined.

▶ This is very important. If you take a mess of a desktop infrastructure and just put it into the datacenter with VDI, all you have done is moved the mess from the desktops to the datacenter, which is often worse.

ARCHITECTING A MICROSOFT VDI SOLUTION

This chapter focuses on the Windows Server 2008 R2 VDI implementation, which was a new feature in Windows Server 2008 R2 and is part of the Remote Desktop Services role. Remote Desktop Services (RDS) was previously known as Terminal Services prior to Windows Server 2008 R2, which focused on session-based virtualization. Terminal Services was renamed to show the shift in focus from pure session-based virtualization to session-based and VDI scenarios.

Reviewing the Components of a Successful VDI Implementation

Figure 11-1 shows users whose devices are directly connected to a virtual machine. Although this is a basic form of VDI, it is completely impractical and likely wouldn't work in the real world. For a successful VDI implementation, a number of components are needed:

▶ Machine virtualization to host the virtual machines

▶ Virtualization management to enable the creation of virtual machines, to stop/start them as needed, and to pass information back to the VDI components

▶ Client platform to run inside the virtual machines, such as Windows 7 or Windows 8

▶ Access protocol to communicate with the virtual desktop OS, which is Remote Desktop Protocol

▶ Session Broker to decide which virtual desktop a user should be connected to and to remember which desktop a disconnected user was last using

▶ Gateway capability for users connecting from outside of the corporate network, avoiding the need for virtual private network (VPN) connections

▶ Licensing (Yes, you have to license. Sorry.)

The following steps walk you through the typical process of connecting to a hosted desktop in a Microsoft VDI implementation, from the initial user contact all the way through to a usable VDI session with an empty Windows 7/8 operating system, including the actual Microsoft role services used and how they interact. Figure 11-2 gives a visual representation of each of the major steps required for VDI functionality.

▶ Key point! All these components just get the user to an operating system instance, and that doesn't include the user's applications or data yet.

1. **Provide the user with an initial portal.** Users need to find the remote desktops they can connect to, which can include presentation virtualization sessions (Remote Desktop Session Host), published applications, and VDI sessions. Although an RDP file can be created and deployed to users using various methods, a more dynamic approach is to use the Remote Desktop Web Access role service, which presents a browser-based list of available applications and connections from which the user can choose.

2. **Populate the list of available connections.** To create the list of published applications and connections that is presented to the user, the Remote Desktop Web Access server communicates with the Remote Desktop Connection Broker, which has knowledge of the VDI pools, personal desktops, and other published connections and applications through its own communications with configured RemoteApp sources.

3. **Identify any personal desktop configurations.** To ascertain which applications and connections a user can access, the Connection Broker communicates with Active Directory, which also supplies any personal desktop configurations.

4. **Provide the user with an RDP file.** No matter what method is used, be it Remote Desktop Web Access, RemoteApp and Desktop Connection, or a deployed RDP file, the user will end up with an RDP file that can initiate a connection. If the user is located outside of the corporate network, a direct

RDP connection will be blocked by a firewall in most organizations, meaning that the user will need to initiate a VPN secure connection. However, you can use an alternative solution that does not require any end-user action or additional client-side software. Windows Server 2008 introduced TS Gateway, which allows the RDP traffic to be encapsulated in HTTPS (port 443) packets; in Windows Server 2008 R2 it was renamed RD Gateway.

5. **Enable the initial RDP connection.** The user needs an initial RDP connection point, because unless the user has a personal desktop configured, his or her VDI-client VM destination will not yet be known. A Remote Desktop (RD) Session Host is configured in redirection mode, which means it acts as the connection point for the user's RDP connection and then redirects the client to the true endpoint, the VDI session. The RD Session Host communicates with the RD Connection Broker to ascertain what the RDP target should be for the requesting client.

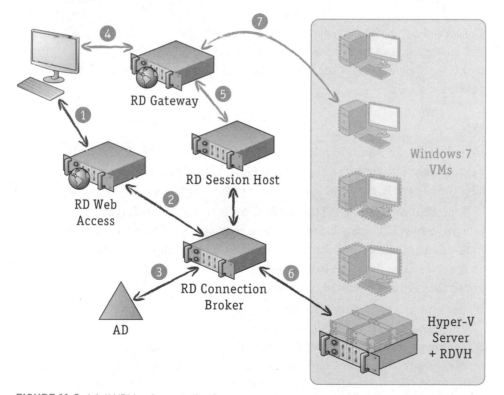

FIGURE 11-2: A full VDI implementation has many components, providing the end user with a rich capability set while staying invisible.

6. **Start the target VM.** The RD Connection Broker communicates with the Remote Desktop Virtualization Host role service that is enabled on the Hyper-V boxes to check the state of the VMs, start a VM if required, and gather any needed information such as the IP address of the client VM OS. This information is then passed back via the RD Connection Broker, the RD Session Host in redirection mode, and then back to the client.

7. **Client connects via RDP.** The client now makes an RDP connection to the destination VM via the RD Gateway (if connecting from outside of the corporate network). The logon process for the user would then commence.

> **CROSSREF** One component I've not shown in Figure 11-2 is the role of System Center Virtual Machine Manager (SCVMM). Although not a requirement, this definitely helps in the management, bulk creation, and updating of virtual machines. I cover SCVMM in detail in Chapter 9.

Certainly a lot of moving parts are required. Let's spend a little time looking at each component in a bit more detail as it applies to VDI. It should go without saying, but I'll say it anyway: All of the roles can be virtualized on Hyper-V, and it is common practice to do so.

HYPER-V

You probably know more about Hyper-V than I do by now and I've already talked about it extensively, but when it comes to VDI environments, there is another factor to consider. You'll need to decide which version of Hyper-V to use.

Typically, when you install the Hyper-V role onto a Windows Server 2008 R2 or Windows Server 2012 installation, the Datacenter version is recommended, because it allows an unlimited number of virtual machines running Windows Server. In addition to scalability, using the Datacenter version means the virtual machines can be moved between hosts without concern about license relocation rights and times.

However, in a VDI scenario, the virtual machines are not running Windows Server; they are running a Windows client operating system. The Windows Server Datacenter license does not cover client operating systems. The client licenses still need to be handled separately from the server operating system. So, why pay for the unlimited virtual rights of Windows Server Datacenter if they're not going to be used?

Enter *Hyper-V Server*, a free Microsoft environment based on Windows Server Core edition with the Hyper-V role enabled. It includes high-availability features, such as failover clustering and RemoteFX. Although Hyper-V Server has no guest operating system instance rights, you don't really need them, because you are licensing the client operating systems separately, which also means you don't pay extra for the hypervisor. Furthermore, you can use the same Microsoft management tools to manage Hyper-V Server because it is still essentially Windows Server at heart.

> **CROSSREF** I'll talk more about failover clustering and RemoteFX later in this chapter. For details on the RDS roles which are common between session virtualization and VDI, see Chapter 7, but I include a basic summary here.

RD WEB ACCESS

The RD Web Access role provides a web-based interface for the initial entry point for users to select the desired VDI or published desktop/application target. RD Web Access provides a simple-to-use portal but is not a mandatory component of a VDI infrastructure.

Another advantage of using RD Web Access is that you can use it to populate the same content shown in the website directly into the Start menu using the RemoteApp and Desktop Connection feature that was introduced in Windows 7. This feature eliminates the need for a web interface. Figure 11-3 shows how the user's desktop applications appear on the Web Access server using Internet Explorer. It also shows how the same content appears in the Start menu when using the RemoteApp and Desktop Connection feature.

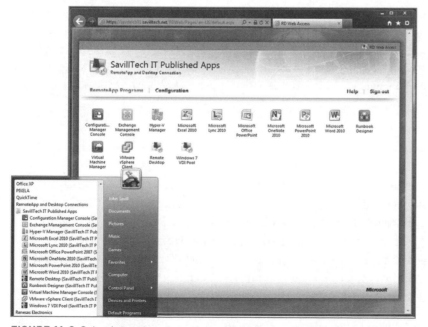

FIGURE 11-3: Selecting an icon from the web interface or the Start menu initiates the RDP connection, with an option to connect to the VDI environment.

RD CONNECTION BROKER

The updated RD Connection Broker in Windows Server 2008 R2 is one of the major components that allows an all-Microsoft VDI solution, because it gives RDS the ability to balance and track connections to non-terminal servers, specifically the ability to manage connections to client operating systems.

The Connection Broker really is the brain of the VDI environment, as it communicates with and controls the other components. It works closely with the RD Session Host in redirection mode, which is why they are frequently placed on the same OS instance. However, when you start having more than 250 simultaneous connections, you may need to consider breaking the roles onto separate servers.

It is through the RD Connection Broker role that VDI pools are created, specifically using the Remote Desktop Connection Manager, which manages the published applications, published sessions, and virtual desktop resources. When you create a VDI pool, you specify the Hyper-V servers that are hosting the VMs and then select the client VMs that will be part of the pool. The VDI pool creation wizard takes care of most of the other configuration required. The Connection Broker handles all incoming VDI requests. It first checks to see if the user has a disconnected session within the VDI pool, and, if so, the user is reconnected; otherwise, a currently unused virtual desktop is assigned to the user.

> NOTE   The management of VDI and session-based environments is improved in Windows Server 2012 with Server Manager. This single tool can not only create the VDI pools, but as part of that creation process, it can also configure the RD Virtualization Host, RD Web Access, the RD Session Host (including placing it in redirection mode), and RemoteApp servers, saving you the overhead of manually configuring each service for its VDI role.

▶ If the term Remote Desktop Session Host is new to you, it's simply what you used to think of as a terminal server—a server that provides the hosting of sessions. The name changed with Windows Server 2008 R2.

RD SESSION HOST IN REDIRECTION MODE

When you have a large farm of Remote Desktop Session Hosts (RDSH) that can all host user sessions, the users need an initial connection point that can then redirect them to the correct Remote Desktop Session Host. The RDSH in Redirection Mode provides that initial connection point. You do exactly the same thing in a VDI environment; you still need an initial RDP connection point for the RDP clients, which is exactly what the RDSH in redirection mode provides, redirecting the RDP clients to the right client OS VM that will be providing their desktop OS.

You can manually configure an RDSH to be in redirection mode, but if you use the Remote Desktop Connection Manager's VDI pool creation wizard, the RDSH will be configured for you. It should be noted that once an RDSH server is placed in redirection mode, it cannot also be used to host normal sessions; it will only perform redirections.

> **TIP** It is common practice to install the RD Connection Broker and RD Session Host on the same operating system instance because they work so closely together. It's not a requirement, but more of a best practice.

RD VIRTUALIZATION HOST

The RD Virtualization Host role service is installed on any Hyper-V host that will be participating in a VDI pool. The RD Virtualization Host enables the Connection Broker to communicate with the Hyper-V host, start/stop VMs, and gather information about the host required to enable client connections.

RD GATEWAY

The RD Gateway allows RDP traffic to be encapsulated in HTTPS packets, allowing secure RDP connection through corporate firewalls without having to open up firewall ports or use additional VPN solutions. Users that are on the corporate network can bypass the RD Gateway and communicate directly with the RDP destination.

Maximizing Client OS and VM Configuration

In the Windows Server 2008 R2 VDI solution, all the client virtual machines that will be used must be created in advance, configured, and then allocated to the VDI environment. This is known as a *static VDI implementation*. Although third-party solutions add *dynamic VDI*, which is the ability to create a single gold image that is then streamed to the virtual machine on demand (so there is only one VM to actually maintain), that is not the case with the in-box Microsoft solution. The creation and maintenance of virtual machines is where System Center Virtual Machine Manager is so important.

Because the client operating system is being used remotely and managed by the Remote Desktop Virtualization Host (RDVH), specific settings must be applied within the guest OS. These include enabling Remote Desktop and adding the VDI users to the Remote Desktop Users security group, which specifies the VDI users authorized to connect remotely to the OS using RDP. Remote Procedure Call (RPC) must be enabled for RDS, and firewall exceptions and RDP permissions must also be set for the management of the guest by the RDVH.

> **NOTE** All of these steps can be manually performed and are detailed at `http://technet.microsoft.com/en-us/library/ff603843(WS.10).aspx`. Or you can use a Microsoft-provided script, which is available from `http://gallery.technet.microsoft.com/ScriptCenter/en-us/bd2e02d0-efe7-4f89-84e5-7ad70f9a7bf0`, to automate the whole process.

▶ Sysprep is used to prepare an operating system for duplication by removing unique installation information such as Security Identifiers.

To create all the virtual machines needed, create and configure the client VM once and then use Sysprep. This Virtual Hard Disk (VHD) can then be stored in the SCVMM library and deployed hundreds of times to create the complete VDI environment; however, there is a challenge. Many different users will be using the same client OS, which means the OS may start to get "dirty" over time as different users perform different actions, so you will want to clean the guest OS after each logoff.

For each VM, you create a snapshot that must have RDV_Rollback somewhere in the name. This snapshot should be taken when the VM is in the clean state you want to reset to each time a user logs off. It can be taken either when the VM is running or not, but you must make sure no one is logged on when you take the snapshot. When a user logs off from a VDI VM that was connected via the Connection Broker, the VM resets back to the RDV_Rollback snapshot, thus restoring the VM to a clean state. Note that this RDV_Rollback capability applies only to VMs in a pool and not personal desktops.

▶ Capturing a snapshot while someone is logged on creates an unfriendly environment for users to log on to, but more importantly, it is a security risk to snapshot a session and distribute it many times.

If you choose to use an RDV_Rollback snapshot to ensure each user gets a clean OS environment, you'll need to consider how you want to handle Active Directory (AD) domain membership. Normally, the computer account password of the OS instance changes automatically every 30 days. If you restore to a checkpoint periodically, for example, after each logoff, the old machine account password that is present in the RDV_Rollback will no longer be valid once the computer has changed its password.

A number of options are available to resolve this. One solution is to disable the machine account password change, which you can accomplish through Computer Configuration → Policies → Windows Settings → Security Settings → Local Policies → Security Options → Domain member: Disable machine account password changes. Another option is to delete all the client VMs, re-create them, and create a new RDV_Rollback snapshot periodically, at an interval less than the AD machine account password change interval. This sounds ridiculous until you realize you can use SCVMM and scripts to automate the bulk creation of VMs for your VDI environment, which makes the option to periodically re-create a realistic option.

TIP You can simplify the bulk creation of VMs using the scripts provided at: http://gallery.technet.microsoft.com/scriptcenter/en-us/904bd2c8-099d-4f27-83da-95f5536233bc.

Using the frequent re-creation approach solves another issue. If you keep the VMs around for a prolonged period of time, you need to patch them and perform normal desktop maintenance. If you re-create the VMs every four weeks, all you need to patch is a single master image. Changes and new application deployments are made to the virtual desktop template, which is then replicated to create all the VMs in the VDI pool. This is another area that is improved in Windows Server 2012, which has an automated pool creation capability that leverages a virtual desktop template.

The client virtual machines will use a lot of storage space; however, there is one Hyper-V feature that can help. *Differencing disks* allow a parent-child relationship to be created between disks. The differencing disk contains only changes from the parent VHD. Typically, the VDI virtual machines have a very lean environment with no productivity or business applications installed; rather it is just the OS, configured for a VDI environment, with a few agent components. The actual client OS is basic (meaning easy to manage), and if you have 100 client VMs, most of the VM content will be exactly the same, with differences related only to domain membership, machine name, and some general "chatter" changes made by Windows 7 and Windows 8.

The question therefore becomes "Why can't I create one master Windows 7 VHD file and then create 100 client VMs in the form of differencing disks (or differences from the master), thus reducing my disk space needs?" A differencing disks–based solution is completely possible, and, if done correctly, it's a good idea. Basically all of the main reads for VMs created with a differencing disk come from the master VHD, while any changes/writes are written to the differencing disk; because the amount of change should be minimal, the differencing disks will remain fairly small, probably only a couple of GBs each.

WARNING It is very important to ensure the volume containing the master VHD has very good input/output operations per second (IOPS) capabilities to handle reads coming from hundreds of virtual machines.

Another great VM configuration technology that should definitely be used is the Hyper-V Dynamic Memory feature. *Dynamic Memory* can really help increase the density of virtual machines on a single host by giving the VMs only the amount of memory they need in real time rather than setting aside a large static allocation to cover the rare times it is actually needed.

Understanding High-Availability Needs for the VDI Architecture

In a normal environment, where the desktop OS resides on the end user's device, only one user is affected if that device crashes. On the other hand, when a component in a VDI environment is unavailable, hundreds if not thousands of users cannot get to their desktops, which could destroy the productivity of the company. It is therefore vital to ensure that there is no single point of failure in the VDI architecture by using high-availability solutions that make each component resilient to failure.

As the heart of your VDI architecture, the RD Connection Broker is made fault tolerant using *failover clustering*; in other words, the RD Connection Broker is a cluster-aware service that will survive the loss of any node. As a best practice you would normally co-locate the RD Session Host in redirection mode with the Connection Broker. Consequently, make sure you install the RD Session Host and configure it in redirection mode on all nodes in the cluster. Create a DNS resource record that has the IP address of each session host configured. This means when clients connect they get all the IP addresses sent to them in varying order, and if one server is not available, the clients will just try the next IP address.

The Hyper-V servers should also be made part of a failover cluster. This can be done by placing the virtual machines on the Hyper-V hosts with the most available resources. The question of virtual machine resilience often comes up; however, the actual OS environments should be considered "state free" because the user data and applications do not actually reside permanently on the guest OS. So if a guest VM is lost, another should just be created in its place.

The *Network Load Balancing (NLB)* service is used to load balance between multiple RD Gateway instances that are installed. You can use the NLB service that is part of Windows, or you can use a hardware load balancer. The same NLB technologies are used to make RD Web Access highly available.

Improving User Experience by Leveraging Virtualization

While the Remote Desktop Services components of the Windows Server operating system provide a huge part of the VDI solution, other technologies and configurations must be applied to complete the solution.

LEVERAGING OTHER TYPES OF VIRTUALIZATION TO OFFER A COMPLETE USER EXPERIENCE

In the "Reviewing the Components of a Successful VDI Implementation" section, I focused on the components needed for the actual VDI architecture. But to be useful, the actual desktop environment needs to be composited when a user logs on. This requires the other virtualization technologies I discussed earlier in the book, namely application virtualization and user/data virtualization.

> **CROSSREF**   For additional information see Chapter 4, Virtualizing Desktop Applications, and Chapter 5, Virtualizing User Data.

Consider what needs to happen when a user logs on to a VDI environment and receives a clean OS image with nothing on it other than the App-V client:

1. The user logs on to the OS using his or her AD account.

2. Once the user is authenticated, the parts of the profile that have not been abstracted using folder redirection are pulled down. This requires a minimal amount of information and is very fast. All the customizations are now present in the user's session in addition to the folder redirection settings; in other words, all the user's data, favorites, and so on are present.

3. The App-V client then communicates with the App-V management server to ascertain which applications apply to the logged-on user. It then populates shortcuts on the desktop and Start menu and configures the relevant file type associations.

4. The user now has a fully functional desktop and can launch applications and access data with no delays.

Windows Server 2012 RDS adds a new feature for VDI environments that helps with the handling of the user profile and avoids the use of Roaming Profiles. In Windows Server 2012, a separate User Profile disk can be used to store user personalization for both virtual desktops and session-based desktops, including settings that are not normally stored in the user profile.

UNDERSTANDING PERSONAL AND POOLED DESKTOPS

All the VDI discussions thus far in this chapter have been focused on VDI client pools, or configurations in which a number of virtual machines running the client OS are grouped together. As users connect, they are automatically assigned to one of the

VMs in their pool that is not currently in use. Once the user has finished and logged off, the VM is placed back into the pool and is ready for the next user. Because users potentially (and probably) get a different VM each time they connect, it is essential that you have desktop virtualization solutions in place to ensure a consistent desktop experience (such as Roaming Profiles, folder redirection, and application virtualization).

Pooled desktops should be the default for all users; however, there may be certain users who need the same client OS instance every time they connect. Maybe they are modifying the OS in some way, or perhaps they have an application that needs to be installed because it can't be virtualized. Whatever the reason, you do have the capability to statically assign a VM to a particular user so he or she always gets the same client OS. A dedicated VM is known as a *personal desktop* and is configured through the Active Directory Users and Computers MMC snap-in. Figure 11-4 shows a virtual desktop being assigned to a user.

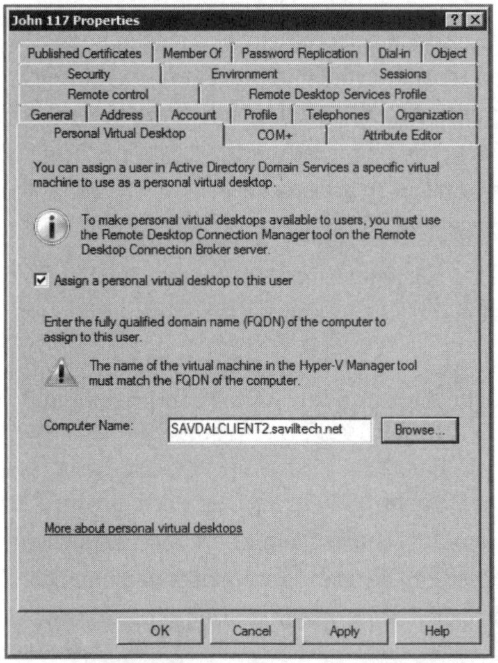

> ▶ Personal desktop users should be screened very carefully because managing personal desktops requires a huge amount of work. They cannot be deleted and re-created in the same way that pooled desktops can, because they have both user state and data.

FIGURE 11-4: Check the Assign a personal virtual desktop to this user option and select the VM to use via the Browse button.

When assigning a VM to a client, it is important to remember that a user can be assigned only one personal desktop, a VM can be assigned to only one user as a personal desktop, and a personal desktop must not be in a VDI pool. Make sure the personal desktop name exactly matches the name of the VM, which needs to be the Fully Qualified Domain Name (FQDN). This means you need to name the VMs with the FQDN of the client OS.

EVALUATING END DEVICE SUPPORT

The RDP has improved greatly over recent Windows releases, and with Windows Server 2012 it works very well over WAN networks, but one challenge that remains is RDP client support for non-Microsoft platforms. This leaves you with a big decision that will likely drive the VDI technology you use. What client end devices are going to be supported, and where will those devices fit into the VDI environment, from the perspective of network connectivity?

> CROSSREF See Chapter 7, Using Presentation Virtualization, for a refresher on the Remote Desktop Protocol.

The good news is that most platforms do actually have an RDP client of some kind, but it's probably not provided by Microsoft. I found numerous RDP clients for iOS and Android, some of which are paid applications with full support, such as those from Wyse, the maker of some of the most popular thin clients on the market.

Also consider the end device experience. I see kids out of high school doing amazing things on mobile devices, and many of my clients frequently access Windows applications through these devices, but my experiences of trying to use a full Windows client remotely on an iPad have been met with limited success. That being said, it's not something I've invested a lot of time in becoming fluent with.

ENHANCING YOUR VDI WITH REMOTEFX

Windows Server 2008 R2 Service Pack 1 introduced two huge technologies. The first is Dynamic Memory and the second is RemoteFX, which is aimed squarely at VDI environments. The goal of RemoteFX is to provide a consistent experience to end devices, no matter what the capabilities of those devices actually are.

Normally, the RDP leverages client-side capabilities for Windows Media playback, such as WMV files, and for desktop composition, such as Aero Glass and Flip 3D. If the client device does not support media redirection, the user experience is very basic.

Additionally, because the remote operating system is in a virtual machine with no graphical hardware, many types of applications cannot run, such as those using DirectX, Silverlight, Flash, and so on.

RemoteFX actually consists of three technologies: Graphical Processor Unit virtualization, enhanced codec, and USB port-level redirection. Together they give a great desktop experience remotely. In Windows Server 2008 R2 SP1, the RemoteFX technology was supported only in LAN environments, but in Windows Server 2012 this has been extended to WAN scenarios as well. I want to look at each capability in a bit more detail.

Graphical Processing Unit (GPU)

The virtualization of the Graphical Processing Unit (GPU) in the server allows virtual GPUs to be made available to the virtual machines running on the Hyper-V server. The virtual GPUs can be leveraged by the Windows 7 SP1 guest operating systems running in those virtual machines. Windows 7 SP1 includes updated integration services, which allow the guest OS to see the virtualized GPU and use it without additional software installation.

Because the virtual Windows 7 SP1 guest can now see a virtualized, full-featured GPU, advanced graphics can now be rendered server-side and the screen output sent to the RDP client for display. This not only includes server-side rendering of Aero effects, multimedia, and other types of media and applications not previously possible (such as the aforementioned Flash, Silverlight, and DirectX applications), but also enhanced capabilities in applications such as PowerPoint 2010 and Internet Explorer 9. Because all the rendering is performed on the Hyper-V server within the VM, the actual client capability does not matter anymore. I can connect from a full, rich client or a basic thin client, and the experience and graphical fidelity will be the same, because all the graphical processing can be done server-side. The only requirement is that the end client must support RDP 7.1, which was introduced in Windows 7 SP1 and includes the RemoteFX support.

Once a RemoteFX-capable client establishes a connection to a RemoteFX-enabled VM, it will appear as if the VM actually has a GPU and an amount of graphical memory based on the RemoteFX configuration for the VM. Running DXDiag on the client will show the presence of a WDDM graphics driver and the Microsoft RemoteFX Graphics Device, along with support for DirectDraw, Direct3D, and AGP Texture acceleration. The actual version of DirectX 3D supported is 9.0c for the initial SP1 release. Although there is OpenGL support in RemoteFX, the version of OpenGL supported is very old and is essentially limited to that provided out of the box in Windows, OpenGL version 1.1.

Because the GPU is virtualized, you don't need a discrete GPU for every RemoteFX-enabled VM. Just like CPU virtualization, where a single logical CPU (such as a core) can be mapped to many virtual CPUs, a GPU can be virtualized to up to 12 virtual GPUs, allowing great scalability.

One key consideration when you virtualize the GPU is the amount of graphical memory each VM will need. With RemoteFX, you can't overcommit GPU memory, so to achieve the 12:1 ratio, you would need to ensure the graphics card has sufficient video RAM for all the VMs. Each RemoteFX-enabled VM has a fixed amount of GPU RAM assigned, which varies depending on the resolution and number of displays defined.

In the Windows Server 2008 R2 SP1 implementation of RemoteFX, the requirement of a GPU in the Hyper-V server was a challenge for many environments that did not have powerful GPUs in their servers. Windows Server 2012 solved that problem by introducing a software rasterizer, which allows RemoteFX capabilities in VDI and session-based environments that do not have physical GPUs. The new graphical capabilities mean a lot more screen update data and, therefore, bandwidth.

Enhanced Codec

The second part of the RemoteFX technology package is a new codec that was designed to efficiently encode and decode the display updates associated with the more intensive RemoteFX-enabled workloads. Before RemoteFX became widely available in Windows Server 2012, this codec was the only part of RemoteFX that was available to Windows Server 2008 R2 Remote Desktop Session Hosts. The new codec is used to automatically improve the graphical fidelity of RDP connections.

RemoteFX USB Redirection

The final piece of the RemoteFX technology is often overlooked; however, it really completes the full-featured remote desktop experience. USB redirection enables the redirection of any USB device from the local client to the remote session.

Some advances in the types of devices that could be redirected to a remote session were available prior to the RemoteFX USB redirection feature. For example, you could redirect a keyboard, mouse, microphone, smart card, disk, and imaging devices with inbox-type functionality. However, these were all redirected by abstracting them into one of the supported basic RDP redirection device types. This meant that you could access these devices on the remote session without needing to install drivers on the remote OS. On the other hand, this also meant that you might

▶ My USB foam missile rocket firing device with camera also did not work before RemoteFX.

miss out on some device-specific functionality, and many USB devices that didn't fall into those high-level types could not be redirected, such as multi-function printers, advanced communication devices, scanners, and barcode readers.

The RemoteFX USB redirection feature solves these problems by actually redirecting at the USB port level in a similar way to how RDP handles redirection of serial and parallel ports. With RemoteFX USB redirection, the actual USB Request Blocks (URBs) are intercepted at the client device and sent to the remote session. This means that any type of USB device can be redirected.

This does not mean that you would no longer want to use RDP high-level device redirection for the devices it supports. RemoteFX USB redirection is designed to supplement the RDP redirection by supporting devices that RDP redirection couldn't, and some good reasons exist for continuing to use RDP redirection.

With RDP high-level supported device redirections, optimized protocols are used for each of the redirection types—such as input (keyboard/mouse), audio, drive, smart card, port, printer (Easy Print), and plug-and-play—to minimize bandwidth usage and ensure the best responsiveness and experience for that type of device. Additionally, RDP redirections don't require extra drivers in the remote session and multiple remote sessions can access the same local device simultaneously. Because of these optimizations, the RDP high-level device redirections can be used in both LAN and WAN environments.

Now consider RemoteFX USB redirection that occurs at the USB port level. Because the port is being redirected, no device/load-specific optimizations can be made. The USB raw data is intercepted by RemoteFX and passed over RDP to the remote session. The driver for the device must be installed in the remote session because that is where it will be plugged into a virtual USB port. Also, because you are redirecting at a port level, only one session can access a device at a time and that includes the local client. If you redirect a device using RemoteFX USB redirection from your local client, neither the local client nor another session can see the device, so just make sure you don't use RemoteFX USB redirection to redirect your keyboard. RemoteFX USB redirection is also optimized for LAN environments and cannot be used on WAN connections like the rest of RemoteFX.

Although RemoteFX USB redirection does not use any GPU resources, it is tied to the RemoteFX experience. And, in Windows Server 2008 R2 SP1 environments, redirection cannot be used with RDSH or a non-RemoteFX-enabled Windows 7 SP1 VDI virtual machine; whereas in Windows Server 2012, these restrictions are all removed, allowing RemoteFX USB redirection and virtual GPUs to be used in Remote Desktop Session Host environments.

RemoteFX was a great feature in Windows Server 2008 R2 SP1 and Windows 7 environments, but the GPU requirement limited its actual usage. With the addition of the software rasterizer in Windows Server 2012, the removal of the GPU requirement and the support of RemoteFX in session-based environments and WAN scenarios make it a technology that should be embraced in most environments.

Understanding Licensing in a VDI Environment

One role I didn't mention in the VDI architecture was the Remote Desktop Licensing Server. The RD Licensing Server is needed because VDI requires a Remote Desktop Services Client Access License for every user or device in the VDI environment. In most cases, if you have a different number of users than devices, you'll license based on the smaller quantity, or what works out cheaper for your organization. It is important to remember that the RDS CAL licenses per device are tracked, but per-user licenses are not because there are too many variables. For example, a user may have many different role-based accounts, so tracking the number of user accounts would not be a valid measure of users. Therefore, the per-user tracking is honor-based.

The other big licensing requirement for VDI is the right to connect to a virtualized Windows Client operating system, which is not a standard right. The good news is that if your client operating systems are covered by Software Assurance (SA), virtual desktop access rights are already included. For non-SA devices, you can subscribe to a Windows Virtual Desktop Access (VDA) per-device per-year license. The VDA would be used for contractor/BYOD computers, thin clients, and other types of devices, such as iPads. It's important to remember that even if you don't use Microsoft's VDI solution, you still have to correctly license the Windows Client operating system to be remotely accessed.

> **NOTE** Microsoft walks you through all the VDI license requirements at http://download.microsoft.com/download/5/0/5/5059CBF7-F736-4D1E-BF90-C28DA-DA181C5/Microsoft%20VDI%20and%20Windows%20VDA%20FAQ%20v2%200.pdf.
>
> If you'd prefer a more portable version, you can download a great fold-up brochure at http://download.microsoft.com/download/7/8/4/78480C7D-DC7E-492E-8567-F5DD5644774D/VDA_Brochure.pdf, which gives examples of use and the licenses required.

EXPLORING THIRD-PARTY VDI SOLUTIONS

The Windows Server 2008 R2 VDI solution worked well for smaller implementations because of the static nature of the virtual machines. Windows Server 2012 takes the in-box VDI solution to the next level with user profile disks and virtual desktop templates. That being said, sometimes another level of technology—such as the need to dynamically stream a single gold image or, most frequently, the need to provide better support for non-Windows client devices—may also be needed.

Two of the main Microsoft partners in the VDI space are Citrix and Quest, both of which offer VDI solutions that leverage some Microsoft virtualization capabilities, such as Hyper-V and App-V, but replace other components, such as the RD Connection Broker, RD Gateway, and RD Web Access. Both of these vendors offer a single solution, Citrix XenDesktop and Quest vWorkspace, that include both VDI and session-based desktop scenarios. XenDesktop replaces RDP with its own Independent Computing Architecture (ICA) protocol, which has other complementary technologies grouped into a solution known as HDX. Citrix has clients for nearly every platform and also works very well in WAN scenarios. On the other hand, vWorkspace leverages RDP but enhances it with its own customizations. Both third-party solutions offer improved image management capabilities, allowing a single gold template image to be used dynamically as new users connect, automatically populating the virtual machine with the latest content from the gold image. These solutions also use less space on the storage subsystems, which can be a huge factor when dealing with potentially thousands of desktops.

My recommendation is to look first at the Microsoft VDI solution. If the Microsoft VDI solution can't handle all of your requirements, then look at the third-party solutions that really offer the ultimate VDI solution, but obviously at additional cost.

SUMMARY

VDI is the hosting of the client operating system in the datacenter, which is then accessed remotely by users from their devices. Architecting an actual VDI solution requires many components to enable and manage the connections to the client virtual machines, but other virtualization technologies are also needed to dynamically create users' desktop environment including their customizations, data, and applications.

At the start of this chapter, I gave you a large number of scenarios where VDI can be a solution, but remember I also said other solutions might be more cost effective while giving the same or better experience. In Chapter 13, I break down all the options and give advice on which is the right technology in the different scenarios.

CHAPTER 12

Accessing the Desktop and Datacenter from Anywhere and Anything

IN THIS CHAPTER

▶ Understanding the habits of today's workforce

▶ Identifying what services users need access to and from what environments

▶ Providing corporate services to the Internet

▶ Enabling secure access to corporate applications and data

▶ Making the most of session virtualization and VDI

With the shift in many organizations to supporting a mobile, distributed workforce that may connect from many different locations and devices over varying types of network, it is important to enable access to corporate services for these mobile workers while maintaining the security needs of the company. This chapter covers some of the main types of service that mobile users need, how these services have traditionally been offered, what new options are available, and what works and what doesn't work for all the different types of user devices you may need to support in your organization.

UNDERSTANDING A CHANGING WORKFORCE— EVERYONE IS MOBILE

The International Data Corporation (IDC) estimates that by the year 2013, in the United States 75.5 percent of the workforce, or nearly 120 million people, will be mobile; and Japan is not far behind. As other countries catch up to this percentage, organizations must ensure that they can offer mobile users the same services provided to on-premise users, a challenge that marks a decided shift in how companies operate.

While mobile users may not have a direct connection to the corporate network, due to improvements to mobile broadband and technologies such as 4G, which offers up to 1 Gbps for low-mobility communications, plus free WiFi available in most restaurants and even stores, most mobile users do have a good connection to the Internet. The goal is to provide users with the services they need from the corporate network to Internet-connected devices. This also includes people using their home computers, adding another dimension to the challenge. Because organizations are providing services not only to machines on the Internet but also to noncorporate-owned devices, some solutions will be disqualified. In this increasingly mobile world, you are dealing not only with Windows PCs, but also iPads, Android slates, smartphones, and many other types of devices. This wide variety affects not only which connectivity solutions are possible, but also the ability to actually run software. For example, I can't run my Windows line-of-business application directly on an iPad, but as a mobile worker I want equivalent functionality. Meeting the needs of this relatively new mobile workforce requires a two-step approach: understanding what services need to be offered, and then exploring the options to provide them.

Looking at the worst-case scenario can often help an organization identify which services need to be offered to mobile workers—and is sometimes the best way to do it. Although I use myself for the example here, the user could just as easily be a member of a sales team or many other roles. In my case, I have a corporate laptop, a home computer, an iPad, and a Windows Phone. (I'm not suggesting a Windows Phone is the worst-case phone scenario, but rather illustrating the various devices you have to accommodate!)

▶ Low mobility refers to stationary users, such as employees sitting in an office, and walking users. High mobility would be driving in a car, for example, which results in slower link speeds (but still around 100 Mbps).

PROVIDING E-MAIL ACCESS

The number one, top-tier application most users identify as being necessary to do their job is e-mail. Without it, many users cannot function, and e-mail must be available on every device used during the day. When I get up in the morning, it is the alarm clock on my phone that wakes me, and I quickly check whether I have any new e-mail messages. I also want to see my e-mail on my iPad, on my home machine, and obviously on my corporate laptop. Keep in mind that when I say e-mail, I am also referring to my calendar, my contacts, and my tasks, all of which are integrated with my e-mail system—and to which I want "anywhere access."

Providing e-mail access through many devices is a fairly simple process thanks to widespread adoption of ActiveSync, a method for accessing Exchange-based services over the HTTPS protocol, which is available from most locations because it's used for any secure access to a website, such as when shopping on Amazon or viewing your bank account information. It is relatively easy for organizations to set up ActiveSync support on their Exchange implementation, and once it is configured, users can access their work e-mail from any device with ActiveSync support by just entering their e-mail address and password—thanks to the Autodiscover service in Exchange.

If a device does not support ActiveSync or an ActiveSync application is not available, you have two options. The first, and least functional, option is to use legacy protocols for e-mail access such as POP3 and IMAP. These will not provide a rich e-mail experience, but they are available on almost any platform with any mail client. In addition to a poor experience, POP3 and IMAP don't use HTTPS, so alternative ports are used for communication—and these might be blocked at some locations, especially companies you may be visiting, such as a client or vendor.

The second option is to use the Exchange web-based interface, *Outlook Web App (OWA)*, which offers an experience very close to running the native Outlook 2010 application within the web browser. As shown in Figure 12-1, the Outlook Web App has access to all the same information, including mail, calendar, contacts, and tasks; just right-click on objects as you would in the native Windows Outlook 2010 application. The downside is that no information is saved locally; you have to be connected to the web to see your mail. All operations are handled within the web browser, which means Exchange can't interact with other applications on the device. For example, you can't synchronize the calendar on your device. Nonetheless, it's still a great way to get access to e-mail from any device with Internet connectivity.

Accessing e-mail is actually fairly easy, and this same capability to access other services over HTTPS is becoming more widely available, particularly those from Microsoft as the industry tries to shift from traditional corporate access methods, as I'll be discussing soon. Microsoft Lync, the corporate communication solution for voice, meetings, and chat; Microsoft SharePoint for collaboration via team sites; and document management all support communication over HTTPS—enabling easy, secure access from nearly any location. SharePoint is accessed using a web browser, and Lync has a very small client component that, like Exchange, supports

▶ Think of a port as a channel of communication that must be open at the firewall, which typically blocks traffic by default. HTTPS uses port 443, which is normally open to allow access to secure websites, but other ports are typically blocked.

▶ I use the web-based version when I'm using someone else's machine or a kiosk, as it requires no local configuration. Just type in the URL. OWA works on most browsers, including those on Linux.

auto-discovery based on entering the e-mail address and password of the user. Lync has clients available for Windows, iOS (which means iPhone and iPad), and Android. The Lync clients for iOS and Android can be found on the respective marketplaces for those platforms.

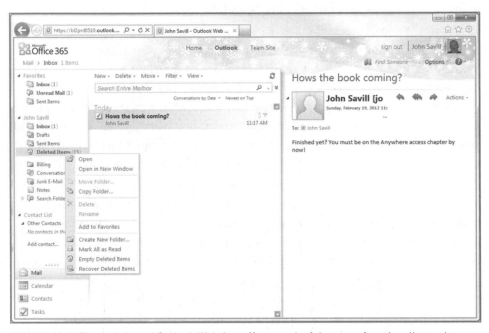

FIGURE 12-1: The web-based Outlook Web App offers much of the same functionality as the Windows application.

In short, users have mail, communication, and collaboration capabilities from basically any device and any location. The only work required by the organization is offering some services out to the Internet, which sounds very easy but can have large security implications. That's why many organizations engage a consulting organization that is well versed in the necessary technologies to ensure a functional but secure Internet-accessible service. It can be even easier, however. As I describe in Chapter 14, Microsoft currently offers numerous public cloud services, which are hosted on Microsoft servers and accessed over the Internet. If your organization uses these public cloud solutions, then there is no hosting of servers to the Internet in your datacenter or worrying about the security of internal servers—everyone accesses the applications externally over the Internet. Office 365 is the public cloud solution offering Exchange, Lync, and SharePoint capabilities to organizations from Microsoft's datacenters. This hosted service provides a very easy way to provide access over the web to users on any device. The more services an organization moves to the public cloud, the easier it becomes for users to be highly mobile, while reducing security and Internet bandwidth concerns.

What else do users want to access? Data is obviously a top item: their spreadsheets, presentations, and much more. If this data is stored in SharePoint, then you already know the solution—it can be accessed externally. However, your organization might not be comfortable offering this service out to the Internet or the data may be on file servers and not SharePoint. In some cases, data should not leave the company premises, so making it available remotely is not desired anyway.

The data may not be a document; it could be data stored on a database that is accessed by a line-of-business application. This means the user requires access to the application, which in turn needs access to the data. Most client-server applications are not designed to operate over the Internet, and most client applications are Windows applications that won't run on devices such as an iPad.

Additionally, many organizations now have intranets, which are websites hosted on the internal network only and typically used for company information, filling out expense reports, completing time reporting, and many other operations. By definition, intranet sites are not intended for publication to the Internet. Clearly, in many cases users will need access to the corporate network facilities.

▶ If an organization hosts a lot of services to Internet-connected clients, then all that traffic must flow over the corporate connection to the Internet, which may be significant and therefore very costly.

PROVIDING REMOTE SERVICES

While there are many great ways to expose some of the more widely utilized services, such as e-mail and other communications, as you saw in the preceding section there are still many types of activity that require access to the corporate network from the Internet.

Using Virtual Private Networks

The traditional solution to providing corporate network access from outside corporate locations is to use a *virtual private network (VPN)*; and while the VPN is still widely in use, its importance is being downgraded for a number of reasons.

First, let me give you a 30,000-foot view of what a VPN does. A VPN provides a secure tunnel between two communication endpoints, typically a computer and a corporate datacenter. Once the secure tunnel is established, any other type of traffic can flow through it—such as web requests to an intranet, access to corporate file servers, or anything else allowed according to the VPN configuration. Numerous

▶ VPNs do have other uses, such as connecting separate datacenters in a secure fashion over the Internet or even over private networks. I am focusing here on the user scenario to access corporate resources.

types of technology are used to enable VPNs, but they all provide essentially the same thing: full access to a corporate network from a remote computer over an Internet connection, as shown in Figure 12-2. One key aspect of a VPN is that it runs on a specific port based on the type of VPN technology used. This reduces the number of ports that need to be opened between an organization and the Internet, since all other traffic is communicated through the single VPN connection. Once the VPN is established, full communication is possible in both directions, enabling users to access corporate resources and enabling corporate IT to manage machines, such as pushing patches, updating malware definitions, and applying policies.

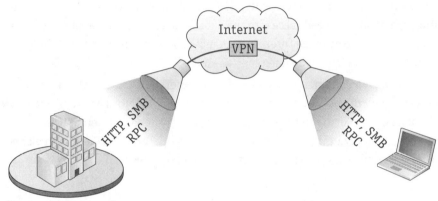

Corporate Datacenter

FIGURE 12-2: A laptop with an Internet connection can connect via VPN to the corporate datacenter and have full access to all services.

Windows Server includes a built-in VPN capability in its Network Policy and Access Services role; and a more enterprise-oriented solution is part of the Forefront Unified Access Gateway (UAG) product, which offers a more full-featured VPN solution that can include the use of smart cards in addition to service publication technologies such as Exchange and SharePoint. Both Microsoft (UAG) and non-Microsoft solutions enable the use of *key fobs*, tokens that provide one-time access codes for enhanced security. One very popular technology I have used in the past is the RSA SecurID, which generates a new passcode every 60 seconds (http://www.rsa.com/node.aspx?id=1156).

To use the VPN, the user typically launches a VPN client and enters any credentials (which might include the use of a smart card or key fob), and then the VPN connection is established. From this point, users can access the resources on the corporate network and their machines can be managed from corporate IT. When users finish what they are doing, they disconnect the VPN connection. One advantage of a VPN is that the VPN client can typically be installed on both corporate and noncorporate machines, enabling users to leverage their home machines to connect to corporate resources.

In the movies, road warriors are tough fighters, trying to survive in a post-apocalyptic world, avenging the loss of their family. Until then, however, road warriors are typically mild-mannered field salespeople fighting to sell whatever it is they sell: toner, paper, software, and so on. These road warriors basically only ever access their e-mail and customer relationship management (CRM) solutions. These CRM solutions, such as Microsoft Dynamics CRM or those from www.salesforce.com, are commonly hosted on the Internet, while e-mail is accessed through a browser or over dedicated connections such as ActiveSync, as already discussed. Such users don't need to connect directly to the corporate network. Therefore, they never launch a VPN client, so they never get updates or new policies. This is a problem.

VPNs can also be difficult and cumbersome to use, depending on the implementation. It requires a manual effort to connect to and disconnect from the corporate resources. As I described in the preceding scenario, if users do not need direct connectivity to corporate resources, then their device will never connect, which means IT cannot manage the asset. Another challenge can exist for non-Windows computers such as iPads or even Linux desktops, for which a VPN client may not be available, thereby preventing the device from being used.

Using DirectAccess

Windows 7 Enterprise Edition introduced a new capability, *DirectAccess*, which enables a transparent experience for the end user, providing access to corporate resources when they are needed without requiring a VPN application or any other manual action. Whenever the device is connected to the Internet, behind the scenes DirectAccess sets up a connection to corporate resources, also giving corporate IT access to the computer, which makes any maintenance, such as patching and policy application, much easier and more consistent.

To enable communication, DirectAccess primarily is based around IPv6 traffic, which is then encrypted with IPsec, ensuring security of the data as it travels over the Internet. However, there is a problem. The Internet is currently IPv4-based, not an IPv6 network, although it will shift to IPv6 at some point in the distant future. In the meantime, other technologies have to be used to enable the IPv6 traffic to flow over the IPv4 Internet. This capability to run IPv6 over an IPv4 network is accomplished using one of three technologies:

> IPv6 is the next generation (version 6) of the Internet Protocol (IP), enabling a much larger address pool and optional header components. IPv6 is enabled by default in Windows Server 2008 and later.

> **Teredo:** Allows IPv6 to be encapsulated in IPv4 traffic where the host is behind a network address translation (NAT) space and has a private address.

This would be the normal scenario for a user at home or in a restaurant, where the Internet connection goes through a gateway router.

▶ **6to4:** Allows IPv6 to be encapsulated in IPv4 traffic where the host has a direct (non-NAT) public IPv4 address.

▶ **IP-HTTPS:** If neither Teredo nor 6to4 can be used (most likely due to a firewall), then IP-HTTPS is used, a new protocol in Windows 7 and Windows 2008 R2 that allows IPv6 to be tunneled using HTTPS (port 443).

Once the traffic gets to the corporate intranet, ISATAP (Intra-site Automatic Tunnel Addressing Protocol) can be used to send the IPv6 packets over an IPv4 network, but the target the user is trying to connect to—such as a file server—still has to be IPv6-capable. If the target is not IPv6-capable, then you need to use a technology like Microsoft's Forefront User Access Gateway (UAG) to act as an IPv6/IPv4 translator (NAT-PT/NAT64). In my experience, organizations that implement DirectAccess nearly always use UAG as well for the best experience and functionality, and in the scheme of things UAG is relatively inexpensive. UAG provides great wizard functionality for DirectAccess configuration, and better scaling when using multiple DirectAccess servers in an array.

What is very useful about DirectAccess is that it does not blindly send every user request over the DirectAccess connection. A Name Resolution Policy Table (NRPT) is used to identify which targets should be accessed via DirectAccess by trapping DNS requests. For example, I would specify the DNS suffix `savilltech.net` in the NRPT on my laptop as requiring DirectAccess. Whenever a DNS query ends with `savilltech .net` (such as when I want to fetch a file from `fileserver1.savilltech.net`), the table entry is triggered and enables the DirectAccess connection. Any noncorporate requests are not handled by the table, but go directly out over the Internet.

You can have very granular control over how you use DirectAccess. While I describe the link as allowing users to connect to corporate resources and corporate IT to manage the device, it doesn't necessarily have to be a two-way permission. You can set up DirectAccess to enable corporate IT to connect to Internet-connected devices but not enable those devices to connect to corporate resources.

While DirectAccess works very well in Windows 7 and Windows Server 2008 R2, it can be very hard to set up; and the IPv6 requirement causes many organizations pain. The good news is that with Windows Server 2012, Direct Access is enabled with a one-click wizard, bringing much of UAG's wizard usefulness straight into Windows Server 2012 and simplifying the certificate and IPv6 requirements. Additionally, Windows Server 2012 adds support for geographically distributed DirectAccess environments, which means a Windows 8 client will try to connect to its closest DirectAccess server. For example, a domestic client would first try the U.S., but in a failure scenario that client will automatically connect via a DirectAccess server in Europe.

However, don't turn off your VPN yet. I don't think of DirectAccess as a VPN killer but rather a technology that may replace the VPN on a subset of machines. DirectAccess requires the clients to be running Windows 7 Enterprise Edition or above and they must be domain-joined. This rules out using it on home machines. It also cannot be used on non-Windows devices, which means there are still plenty of scenarios in which a VPN is required. Nonetheless, for machines that are DirectAccess-capable it offers a much richer experience for the user and IT than a traditional VPN.

Using the Remote Desktop Gateway

All the solutions up to this point enable connectivity to the corporate location from Internet-connected machines, but DirectAccess is only for corporate, domain-joined Windows machines, and VPN may not work on certain types of devices like iPads. Nor do these solutions enable running Windows applications on non-Windows devices—again, that iPad!

There is no viable solution to natively run a Windows application on a non-Windows operating system such as iOS. This is especially true with something like an iPad, as Windows computers are based on an x86 architecture, whereas devices like an iPad are ARM-based—meaning machine virtualization is not an option. Machine virtualization could be a solution if you want to run a Windows application on something like a Macintosh machine. The solution, therefore, is to use session virtualization or VDI, whereby the user device serves as a Remote Desktop Protocol endpoint to communicate with either a Remote Desktop Session Host or VDI environment located in the corporate datacenter. User devices can be sent just the application window bitmap or a complete desktop—whatever works best for the use case scenario and device being used. For example, on a device such as an iPad, use of a full desktop isn't feasible, whereas sending the device the Word application window would be. The use of session virtualization is shown in Figure 12-3.

▶ Even if the user device could run the Windows application natively, it might still be better to use session virtualization to avoid installing applications on the user's machine and to prevent data from leaving the datacenter.

RDP clients are available for most devices, or you can use a solution such as Citrix XenApp or XenDesktop, which has a client application for nearly every type of device and operating system currently available. Additionally, solutions like those from Citrix may provide a better experience than the native Microsoft Remote Desktop Protocol over networks with lower bandwidths and higher latencies through the use of the Citrix ICA/HDX protocol.

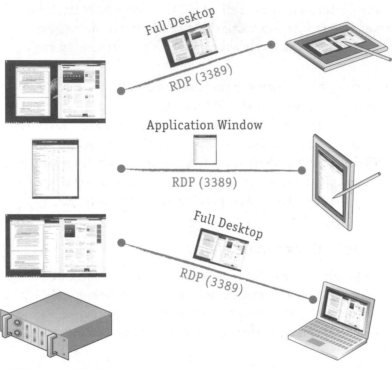

FIGURE 12-3: Using session virtualization, any device with an RDP client can receive a full desktop or an individual application window.

▶ TS Gateway was renamed Remote Desktop Gateway (RD Gateway) in Windows Server 2008 R2.

▶ This is always the best option. Avoid placing services directly in perimeter networks where possible. Use a solution like UAG that is designed to face the Internet and securely publish services.

Remote Desktop Protocol uses TCP port 3389 between the client endpoint and the RDP server, which would typically be blocked by the firewall between a corporate datacenter and the Internet. One solution is to connect via VPN from the user's device and then launch the RDP client; however, as already mentioned, VPN clients can be cumbersome and may not be available on all platforms.

One option, and the focus of this section, is to copy what many other services have done to cure the problem of lacking encryption of information and needing to enable communication through firewalls: encapsulate the traffic inside HTTPS. First introduced in Windows Server 2008, Terminal Services Gateway (TS Gateway) enables a server to be accessible to the Internet either by being placed in the perimeter/DMZ network with direct Internet connectivity or by being published by some other application publishing technology such as UAG, thereby allowing the TS Gateway to act as a gateway for all RDP communications. It's actually very simple. On the RDP client, a configuration is made specifying that a gateway is to be used and will therefore be sent all the RDP traffic. When RDP communication takes place, the client wraps all the RDP traffic inside an HTTPS packet encrypted with the certificate of the TS Gateway server and sends it to the TS Gateway. The TS Gateway then extracts the RDP data from the HTTPS envelope and forwards it to the true target of the RDP communication. The target for the RDP traffic could be an RD Session Host, a physical server with Remote Desktop enabled, a VDI desktop, or anything that supports the server end of RDP. The RDP target's response is sent to the TS Gateway, which then wraps the RDP back into HTTPS and sends it to the RDP client. Because all RDP communication on the Internet is being sent over HTTPS, it's encrypted. This whole process is shown in Figure 12-4.

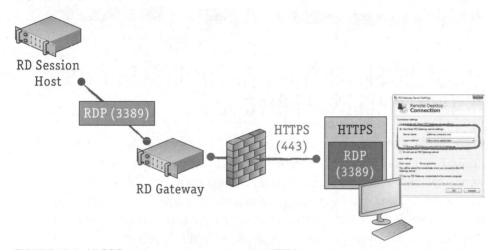

FIGURE 12-4: All RDP packets are encapsulated in HTTPS, providing encrypted communication over the Internet and traversable through most firewalls.

At this point you may be wondering whether this is a huge security risk. Are you not just opening your environment to any machine out on the Internet? Fortunately, you can use very fine controls with TS Gateway, such as permitting only certain users to connect, and/or only certain client machines. For example, you can specify that only client machines with a certain certificate installed can connect, and then connect only to specific RDP targets. Moreover, in addition to the security performed at TS Gateway, the user still has to authenticate to the RDP target, although a single credential can be used for both the gateway and target to simplify the connection process.

What is great about the TS Gateway functionality is that you can configure it within an RDP configuration file that also includes the final target RDP. You can then just send that RDP file along with a certificate to install to any machine, providing instant access to a published desktop or application without any special VPN configuration or hardware. I have often seen this used by retail organizations and

▶ *Important! Just because it's possible, does not mean it's the right solution. Session virtualization and VDI both require significant datacenter infrastructure and licensing investments, so be sure this is really needed.*

help-desk organizations that have people working from home; instead of sending them complete VPN solutions and corporate desktops, they just send the RDP file—enabling employees to use their own computers because all the actual processing is done in the corporate datacenters. The home computer is merely displaying screen updates and sending mouse and keyboard commands.

With TS Gateway, basically any device can connect to the session virtualization or VDI and have access to a desktop or application. As mentioned earlier, Citrix has its own version of TS Gateway that works with the Citrix session virtualization and VDI solutions; but whether you use a purely Microsoft solution or an enhanced solution with Citrix, you can enable any device if that is the goal of your organization.

ENSURING SECURITY AND CLIENT HEALTH WITH NETWORK ACCESS PROTECTION

Great. Using whatever combination of technologies just covered, and maybe some others not covered, you can now enable any machine to connect to your corporate network. Really, great? Terrible is what my first impression would be. I'm now allowing everyone's personal computers to connect to my corporate network via VPN, DirectAccess, or RD Gateway—are you nuts?! What websites has that machine visited? What as yet undiscovered viruses are lurking on the machine just waiting to connect to my corporate network and shut me down? Maybe that machine was last patched three years ago and has never had malware protection.

This is a very valid and sane reaction, and the solution comes in the form of another new Windows Server 2008 capability, *Network Access Protection (NAP)*. NAP allows a machine to be queried for a Statement of Health (SoH), and only if that SoH meets the requirements of the organization is the machine allowed to complete its connectivity. NAP can be used for health checking with DHCP, 802.1x, IPSEC, RD Gateway, a VPN, and DirectAccess. The process works as shown in Figure 12-5 and is outlined at a high level in the following steps:

1. The client attempts communication, which in this example is RD Gateway but could be a VPN connection, requesting an IP from DHCP, DirectAccess, or any other supported service. In addition to requesting a connection, the client sends its SoH.

2. The SoH for the client is sent to the policy server for evaluation and compared to the defined policies.

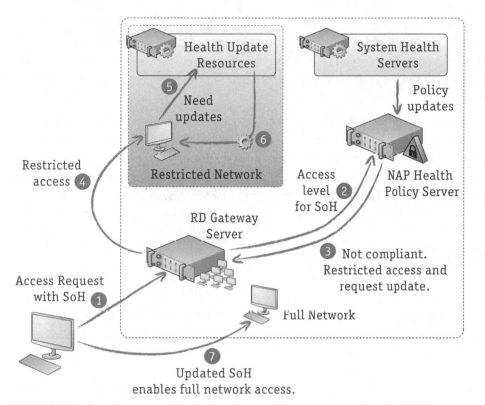

FIGURE 12-5: Example communication flow for an RD Gateway connection using NAP

3. In this case the SoH does not meet requirements, so the client is deemed unhealthy and instructed to be placed in a quarantined, or restricted network where it can be made healthy.

4. The client is placed in a restricted network with access only to resources to help make it healthy.

5. The client requests updates such as Windows Updates, malware definition updates, and policy.

6. Updates and policy are sent to make the client healthy.

7. Now healthy, the client requests access again and this time the policy server deems the client healthy and instructs the communications server to grant the client access to the full network.

Note that this is not just a process to allow or disallow access to the network. Merely rejecting an unhealthy client would protect the network, but it would not help a user gain access, making it very unpopular. Instead, NAP gives the client feedback about why access was not granted, and uses a special quarantined network that enables the client to be made healthy and therefore get full access to the network. This is the best for everyone. The user gets access to corporate resources and the integrity of the corporate network is assured by only allowing connectivity to healthy clients.

Although the Statement of Health can be extended by third parties, three standard health validators are typically used: when the machine was last updated from Windows Update, the most recent date of malware definition files, and the state of the local Windows firewall. With these three items satisfied, an organization can be fairly confident the machine is at least patched and free of viruses.

SUMMARY

CROSSREF When possible, use encryption tools such as BitLocker and BitLocker To Go on drives and USB devices that contain corporate or sensitive data. These tools are discussed in Chapter 5.

This chapter covered the major Microsoft technologies, such as web-based services, traditional VPN-type solutions, DirectAccess, and session-virtualization connections using RD Gateway, to enable access to corporate resources. There are obviously many other third-party solutions to enable different types of connectivity. In addition to connectivity, an organization must decide how to enable access to its applications, a challenge that is predominantly solved with session virtualization and VDI for noncorporate devices. Using session virtualization not only enables access to Windows applications on non-Windows devices, but it also helps keep corporate data on corporate servers, rather than allowing potentially sensitive data to be scattered across user laptops, slates, and home machines.

CHAPTER 13

Optimizing the Desktop and Datacenter Infrastructure

At this point in the book, a large variety of virtualization technologies have been covered; and if it wasn't already apparent, you can now see that virtualization touches basically every aspect of corporate IT. That can also make it seem overwhelming. Which technology should you use and how do the different options affect the user experience? Which workloads should be virtualized and which ones shouldn't? How do you ensure that your virtual and physical systems are highly available, and how do you enable disaster recovery? This chapter examines the key factors to consider when choosing the architecture for your environment, and how to bring virtualization technologies together to create the best infrastructure for your organization.

DESIGNING THE BEST USER ENVIRONMENT

I want to start with the desktop. While your customers' first interactions with your company may be via a website that is hosted from your datacenter or public cloud service, it is the organization's employees (or partners or individual contributors or whatever term is used) who represent the organization. Looking first at the desktop also helps to identify services you need to offer, which will likely be housed in the datacenter.

The user environment is made up of layers, as shown in Figure 13-1. When users connect to their workspace, they see their own customized environment, which consists of desktop shortcuts, the Start menu, libraries of information, their own desktop background, application customizations, and so on. Those shortcuts and customizations give users access to their personal and shared data, which is manipulated with applications. Those applications run on the OS, the layer of least concern to users. This is not to say users don't care about the OS; users certainly appreciate new OS features that make their lives easier, such as improved searching and faster responsiveness. However, the OS is just a vehicle that gets the users where they are going—it enables access to their data, which is what they ultimately care about.

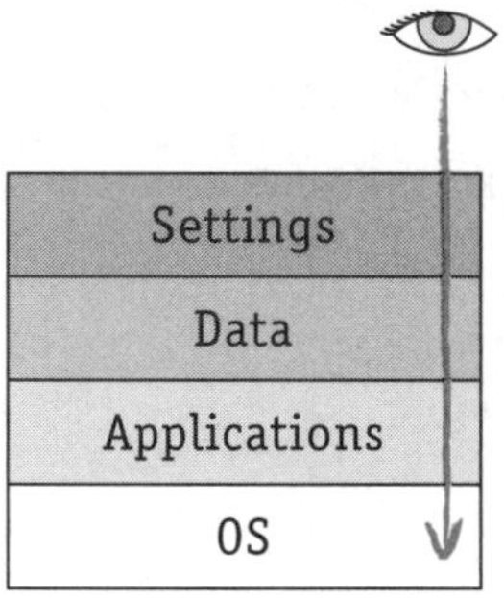

> ▶ The operating system is a huge concern to the IT department because it is the operating system that enables enhanced security, connectivity, and manageability, all of which drive IT efforts.

FIGURE 13-1: Most users view their environment with a top-down approach.

What you are doing today, you will likely continue to do—working with Windows 7, Windows 8, and beyond. That means having user profiles, data, and applications local to users' machines, which means bonded to the operating system installed on those machines. If your users never have problems, never need to use more than one device, and never need to reinstall an application; and if you don't have application-to-application compatibility challenges, you know there will never be a VDI or session virtualization requirement, and you have no desire to simplify your desktop management, then carry on—but there is certainly a better way.

Guidance on User Data and Settings

Unfortunately, hard drives fail, laptops are lost, companies are broken into and machines stolen, and many other scenarios occur in which local data on a machine can be lost. The capability to redirect data from a desktop to be stored in the datacenter and cached locally for offline access is a well-established technology in Windows—namely, Folder Redirection and Offline Files. This is a very mature technology and it should definitely be used for key areas, such as My Documents and Desktop, two common places where users store data. Storing data in the datacenter not only protects against local machine failure but also ensures that the organization has full access to data in the event of auditing or compliance scenarios in which a discovery of data must be performed. It also enhances the end-user experience by exposing previous versions of data through point-in-time copies, with very little additional configuration or resource requirement, through the use of Shadow Copy technologies, which I covered in Chapter 5.

Do not just stop at My Documents and Desktop, though. Remember to look at all the other areas discussed in Chapter 5. Maybe My Pictures is important to your organization, or you need My Music redirected as well. The AppData\Roaming folder provides the capability for application settings to be available across many machines. Configure noncritical areas to not roam, remaining local to each machine.

Data virtualization is a no-brainer. Folder Redirection and Offline Files are great technologies with a trusted reputation of providing efficient functionality that can be relied on. Although many organizations would not dispute the benefits of Folder Redirection and Offline Files, they are not typically implemented; and like many of the desktop items I'm going to talk about, implementing them as part of a desktop or OS refresh is a great time to introduce technologies like settings, data, and application virtualization, because a large amount of testing and re-architecture are already occurring.

In terms of settings, if Folder Redirection is the green pasture of happy places, then Roaming Profiles is often considered the dark swamp of despair. However, as I described in Chapter 6, Roaming Profiles in Windows 7 is a fairly solid solution, provided most of the data from the profile has been removed using Folder Redirection. Unfortunately, many users still bear the scars of Roaming Profiles in Windows XP, which resulted from frequent profile corruptions and large delays in logon and logoff. Keep in mind, however, that user data alone does not complete the user's experience—the user shortcuts and customizations are key to their productivity, so ignoring profiles is not really an option.

That does not mean I suggest using Roaming Profiles. In reality, I find them too restrictive because they cannot handle a mix of Windows XP and Windows 7 machines using a single shared profile, they don't handle using a client OS and a server OS such as with session virtualization, and they don't handle a mix of local and virtualized applications. Instead, as covered in Chapter 6, I recommend using the User Experience Virtualization (UE-V) technology, which allows for the roaming of settings for specific applications the organization cares about rather than the entire profile. In addition, with UE-V those application and user settings can apply between client and

▶ Must-Do #1: Use Folder Redirection for user data areas.

server operating systems and local and virtualized applications. There is a catch, however. UE-V is not designed to support Windows XP.

My advice here is to base the majority of your desktops, and certainly any virtual infrastructure such as VDI or session virtualization, around at least Windows 7 and Windows Server 2008 R2 technologies, which are fully supported with UE-V. Additionally, because you will likely update application versions between Windows XP and Windows 7, many settings will be different because of differences in the operating systems. Windows XP would likely be the user's legacy single desktop that is eventually retired, so definitely use Folder Redirection so that all data is available across all machines; but for XP machines, leave a local profile, and for everything else use UE-V for that consistent settings approach. If there is a requirement to share a profile between Windows XP and Windows 7, then look at third-party solutions such as those from AppSense. If UE-V is not available to you and you cannot buy a third-party solution, then definitely investigate the Windows 7 Roaming Profile solution, as it's better than no settings virtualization. The important thing is to make the user's profile available across different operating systems.

▶ Must-Do #2: Utilize UE-V for user setting virtualization; and for the XP machines, leave a legacy local profile.

Providing Applications and Desktops for the User

Now that you have made the data and user settings available everywhere, you need to make the applications—the tools that enable users to manipulate the data—available as well; and, as I described in Chapter 4, there are many aspects to application management:

1. Initial deployment of applications, including to a fresh machine that may require 20 applications

2. Updating deployed applications

3. Solving compatibility problems between applications

4. Testing any new application to make sure it plays well with existing applications

5. Reducing the amount of time it takes to get an application through IT testing and packaging processes and deployed to desktops

6. Keeping desktops as clean as possible by reducing the "footprint" of numerous installed applications

Those are just some of the application management considerations, but application virtualization solves these challenges; and App-V, the Microsoft application virtualization technology, offers the best set of features for application virtualization—including great integration with Microsoft solutions like System Center Configuration Manager for delivery and third-party products such as Citrix XenApp. When applications are virtualized, the challenges of application-to-application compatibility are eliminated because each application runs in its own bubble. Applications run locally on operating systems without actually having to be installed, which drastically reduces the time it takes for an application to be made available because no installation routine is required, updates are very simple, and the operating system is kept clean because no changes are made with a virtualized application. The virtualization of applications and the isolation of other applications also eliminate the required regression testing for new applications to ensure they don't break existing applications, enabling new applications to go through testing much faster. With all this in mind, my recommendation for organizations is to think virtual first, then install applications locally as the exceptions, which could be because of the following:

▶ The application contains a driver that cannot be separated from the rest of the application.

▶ The application uses system services like agents for systems management or malware protection.

▶ The application provides services to many other applications, or has many snap-ins or plug-ins that are not centrally managed and would make defining the many dependencies between virtualized applications difficult.

▶ The application is part of the operating system—for example, Internet Explorer.

Another option for delivering applications is to host them using session virtualization in a Windows Server 2008 R2 or Windows Server 2012 Remote Desktop Services environment and then publish the applications to the user's desktop. With RDS, the application is not actually running on the user's local operating system; only the application's window is shown on the user's local desktop. No local resources are used on the user's local OS (other than displaying the window) and all the actual resources, such as CPU and memory for running the application, are consumed on the servers in the datacenter. Publishing the application with RDS can be a good option if the application processes highly sensitive data that should not leave the datacenter, or it accesses large amounts of data that is stored in the datacenter, in which case running the application in the datacenter on the same local network as the data provides the best performance. Running applications using session virtualization can also be a good option if the application frequently changes or has complex configurations that don't work well with application virtualization.

▶ Virtualized applications can be linked using Dynamic Suite Composition if direct communication between virtualized applications is required.

▶ Must-Do #3: Use application virtualization as the default, and then use locally installed applications on an exception basis.

▶ Remember that virtualizing the applications using App-V on the RDS host is a great option, even when using session virtualization-published applications, for easy management and to keep the RDS host OS as clean as possible.

Many organizations use a combination of virtualizing applications with App-V and delivering applications with RDS (or an enhanced experience with partner solutions such as Citrix XenApp), using whatever makes the most sense. The key point is that neither scenario requires application installation on the local operating system, enabling new applications to be made available to desktops nearly instantly.

Remember that App-V is not a solution for application-to-operating-system incompatibility, so if you have applications that will not run on Windows 7, such as that legacy Windows XP application or that corporate service that still needs Internet Explorer 6, you'll have to find another solution. To support legacy applications that you are unable to make work on Windows 7 and for which there is no upgrade or replacement, you have two options.

The first option is to use a Windows Server 2003 Terminal Server and run the legacy application or Internet Explorer 6 on the Windows Server 2003 Terminal Server, and publish just that application to the user's desktop using Citrix XenApp or Quest vWorkspace. If the only need for these solutions is to publish IE6, Microsoft has an IE6 Compatibility Offering in partnership with Quest specifically designed for solving Internet Explorer compatibility challenges. This does require keeping some legacy Windows 2003 Terminal Servers around, but it enables an organization to carry on with Windows 7 deployment and minimizes any overhead on the desktops.

The second option, Microsoft Enterprise Desktop Virtualization (MED-V), is used when the use of a Terminal Server running Windows 2003 is not possible, perhaps because the application will only run on a client operating system or more than one instance of the application cannot run on a single OS even in a separate session. MED-V provides a Windows XP virtual machine running silently on the user's local Windows 7 desktop and contains the legacy application and, optionally, Internet Explorer 6. Minimal management is required on the Windows XP image because of its age and the lack of new updates, and the only resource requirement on the local machine is some additional memory and disk space, because the CPU use would have been needed if the application were running on the Windows 7 OS anyway.

Figure 13-2 puts this all together. Here you can see that the user's environment is constructed as needed, with each part handled separately and brought together at logon no matter what machine the user logs on to. The only part that is hard-linked to the OS is MED-V, which would be used for specific legacy applications only—assuming MED-V were used, which would be a temporary remedial use at most. When the user logs on, Folder Redirection immediately takes care of making the data available, and the user's profile is synchronized using UE-V, a third-party solution, or Roaming Profiles. Applications are available straightaway using App-V or published using session virtualization RemoteApp capabilities, and any legacy applications can also be taken care of using RemoteApp or MED-V.

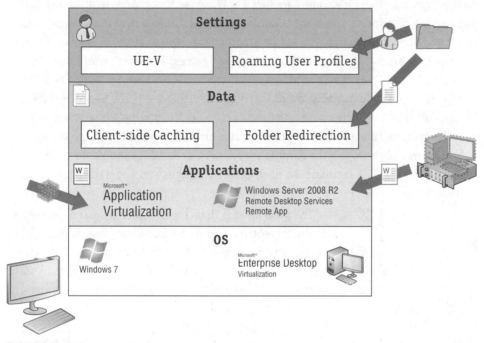

FIGURE 13-2: All the virtualization technologies discussed enable the user's workspace to be dynamically constructed at logon.

With this combination of desktop virtualization technologies in place, users can literally sit down at any desktop and have the same experience. Their data, settings, and applications will always be available.

Supporting Any Device

The preceding scenario is sound and truly reflects the complete story until 2011, when the focus turned to optimizing the user's desktop through the many new desktop virtualization technologies. At this point there was a marked shift in the user population that greatly changed the dynamic of the user workspace. What is notable about this latest shift is that it's embraced by senior management and executives whose titles start with "chief"—meaning IT departments have to take notice and respond. That shift was the consumerization of IT, which includes users bringing their own devices to the office and wanting to use them from multiple locations: at home, at Starbucks, and really anywhere.

▶ The iPad is a good example. It's is a great piece of hardware that efficiently performs the main job for which it is intended: consuming information. However, it's not the best option for creating a PowerPoint presentation.

Notice I say device and not a Windows computer. The device could be a mobile phone running iOS, Android, or Windows Phone. It could be a slate device using an ARM processor, or a user's home Windows 7 or Windows 8 machine. In other words, you need to plan for environments that do not rely on the end device's local capabilities if you are going to support users leveraging their own devices, or even corporate devices that are not the normal Windows-type devices. The user's world now looks more like Figure 13-3. People want to use their own devices because they like them; they are not typically concerned with whether a device is really the best one on which to do their work. In other words, the user's focus is the device's size and design, or its form factor. Once they access their device, users just want to run the various applications they like, and the corporate applications and data should be facilitated in some manner. This introduces a new set of challenges and opportunities for the IT department.

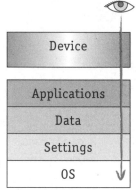

FIGURE 13-3: When the device has the focus, everything else must accommodate it.

The good news is that the architecture just described—using user settings and data virtualization and application virtualization—puts your organization in a great position to enable the various types of new end-user devices. The approach will likely need to be different when users use a noncorporate, personal device.

Because the devices that users bring to the workplace are not part of the corporate domain, you cannot just install applications or even agents, such as those for App-V, on them, and the exact capability of each machine will not be certain. The device could be capable of handling Windows applications but may not have a large amount of memory, or it may be an ARM-based slate such as an iPad that is not compatible with Windows applications. It could even be a Linux laptop! You cannot assume anything can be run natively on the user's own machine; the best that you can aim for is treating the device as a remote desktop client device—that is, a Remote Desktop Protocol (RDP) client is available for it. Fortunately, there is an RDP client for nearly every type of device. The protocol and device support is actually one reason why some organizations use solutions from Citrix, which uses its own ICA protocol and offers ICA clients for literally every device on the market.

▶ These same circumstances apply to contractor laptops and possibly offshore workers, so the bring-your-own-device solution can be used for these scenarios, too.

As covered elsewhere in this book, there are two ways to deliver users a remote desktop: session virtualization, whereby users connect to a session on a server operating system such as Windows Server 2012, or virtual desktop infrastructure, whereby users connect to a client operating system that is running in a virtual machine. The data, settings, and application virtualization become necessities with either approach because users will likely get a different OS each time they connect, meaning their environment must be created each time using all those desktop virtualization technologies.

Comparing Desktop Infrastructure Solutions: Which Is Right for Your Organization?

This brings us to architecting the right desktop solution for your organization and the main question you need to address: VDI or session virtualization? I want to be very clear up front: There is no right, one-size-fits-all answer. In this section I share my experiences and offer my insights regarding when VDI or session virtualization works best, but these are only guidelines that provide some context for making a decision. In reality, most companies I work with use a mix of session virtualization and VDI. The bottom line is that no matter what approach or combination of approaches is used, the same user settings, data, and application virtualization can be used for all of them and for all the physical desktops in the organization, giving users a consistent experience across every device they will ever use—physical, session, or virtual.

Figure 13-4 provides a high-level overview of both solutions. Here, session virtualization is on the left and VDI is on the right. With session virtualization, users connect to their own session on a shared server operating system, such as Windows Server 2008 R2; and with VDI, users connect to their own desktop operating system, such as Windows 7, running inside a virtual machine running on a machine virtualization platform such as Microsoft Hyper-V.

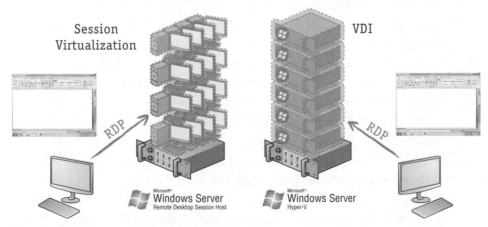

FIGURE 13-4: The two primary virtual desktop solutions: session virtualization and VDI

In order to make the best decision, you need to dive deeper and understand the key differences between the two solutions. However, to provide some context, first I want to describe what these technologies have in common. It's important to explore this from both the user's experience and the infrastructure and management perspective. Both factors must be evaluated to help guide an organization to the most effective solution.

What is the same is the desktop environment. Although with session virtualization the user connects to a server operating system and with VDI the user connects to a client operating system, under the covers both the server and client OS share a huge amount of code. Therefore, the actual desktop experience will look and feel exactly the same: same Start menu or Start screen, same features and capabilities, same ability to run the applications, and each user can still have a unique IP address. The same RDP protocol is used to connect to both environments, which means the same client devices can be used. User settings and data virtualization plus application virtualization can and must be used with both session virtualization and VDI.

▶ This isn't completely true with session virtualization. The operating system is not constantly deleted and re-created, so applications can be installed onto the operating system, but virtualizing the applications is still the best option.

The key difference is that for session virtualization, users have their own session on a shared operating system, whereas with VDI, users have their own operating system instance. In other words, the fundamental difference is the level of isolation a user has from other users. For a crude analogy, you can think of session virtualization as a shared office space: Everyone has their own cubicle but because they share one room they have to behave—no singing loudly, no changing the office, and so on, because that would affect the other users. However, they can customize their own cubicle as desired, such as decorating it or rearranging the furniture. Conversely, you can think of VDI as multiple offices, with everyone having their own heavily padded space; users can run around, bouncing off the walls and screaming, and they won't affect users in other offices.

This means that session virtualization is a good fit for task-based workers who run applications such as Internet Explorer, Office, and line-of-business applications but don't need to customize the operating system. They can still customize their desktop wallpaper and shortcuts, and personalize their applications. Users in session virtualization need to be locked down so they can't install and uninstall applications or reboot the operating system, which would affect everyone else on the server.

VDI is a good fit for power users, developers, or users who run applications that will not run on a server operating system. Basically, if users are required to modify the actual operating system or reboot it, then VDI must be used.

This is why many companies opt to use a combination of session virtualization and VDI: session virtualization for the majority of users and VDI for those power users. At this point you may be wondering why a combination would be used if VDI works for everyone. Why use two solutions? That's a fair question, and one that brings us to the other differences between session virtualization and VDI.

Session virtualization uses a server operating system that hosts large numbers of sessions for many concurrent users—potentially hundreds of users on each session host, depending on the applications being run and the amount of memory needed. Each session may use hundreds of megabytes of memory, assuming a fairly heavy application workload for each user. If you have a server with 64GB of RAM, you can probably accommodate around 300 users on that box. That's one operating system instance with 300 users.

With VDI, using the same piece of hardware, you can run a hypervisor on it, thereby creating many virtual machines, and each virtual machine runs a full client operating system (which has CPU and memory requirements) on which you can run the applications. Hypervisors make use of some great memory technologies to get the most from the box, only assigning memory as the OS needs it. Typically, a client OS needs around 700MB of memory just to log on, and then additional memory as applications run. For example, imagine a very low 1GB of memory per virtual machine, but keep in mind that realistically, the actual memory needed could be as high as 2GB. On that same server, discounting the memory required for the base OS and hypervisor, that will only leave memory for up to 62 virtual machines.

Using session virtualization on that server, you get five times more users than you would using VDI, and in some environments it might be 10 times more users. That's a huge difference in bang for the buck for the same hardware. Other differences also make VDI more expensive.

Consider the infrastructure required. Both session virtualization and VDI require methods for users to connect via RDP, and both require a connection broker, but a VDI solution also requires a lot more management infrastructure to handle creating the client virtual machines, refreshing them, and ongoing overall management. The licensing is also different: whereas session virtualization requires an RDS Client Access License, VDI requires numerous licenses, depending on the exact solution.

As I explained in Chapter 11, the issue is not that session virtualization has capabilities beyond VDI, but rather that VDI is more expensive, requires more hardware, and needs more management than session virtualization. For these reasons, use session virtualization when possible and save VDI for when it's truly needed.

I've heard of organizations talking about moving to VDI to save money. I've never found this to be achievable. If an organization has a poorly managed desktop environment, then moving it to the datacenter with VDI will mean a poorly managed VDI and a bigger mess. Although moving to VDI normally introduces a new infrastructure

▶ Session virtualization actually offers a very rich application publishing capability rather than providing an entire desktop, which can be a reason to use session virtualization over VDI. Think of small devices where a desktop doesn't display well.

that makes the environment more manageable, in such cases the investment could have been used to clean up the physical desktop environment, eliminating the need to purchase all the hardware for the VDI servers!

Interestingly, when I talk to clients who need to enable Bring Your Own Device (BYOD) scenarios or off-site employees or contractors, most of them talk VDI; they never consider session virtualization. That's because many companies have purely VDI solutions. Because they don't have any session virtualization in place, they assume VDI is the solution for everything. If you only have a hammer, then a hammer is the right tool for everything! Take time to understand your requirements and identify the right solution based on the factors I've discussed. Your starting point should be a normal desktop operating system that is well managed. If that is not an option for any of the reasons already covered (e.g., BYOD, disaster recovery, off-site contractors, highly secure environments containing data that should not leave the datacenter), then think session virtualization. If session virtualization is not an option because the users are power users or developers, or the applications will not run on a server OS or run multiple instances on one OS, then use VDI. Keep in mind that you don't have to pick one solution. Use a well-managed desktop environment for corporate assets that can run a modern desktop OS, and use session virtualization and VDI where they are appropriate. You will likely have all three.

Notice how many times I have mentioned a well-managed desktop environment. Most companies have good desktops and laptops that can run Windows 7 and Windows 8, so adopting session virtualization or VDI to reduce management of the machines is a huge waste of all the resources available on those desktops and laptops. Ensure that you have the right management infrastructure in place to patch the client operating systems, good processes to deploy new operating systems, and use the user settings and data virtualization and application virtualization to simplify the environment. That, in itself, will prevent the desktops in your environment from becoming a help-desk headache.

This does not mean you should never consider using session virtualization or VDI for your desktops. For example, suppose your organization has not done a desktop refresh for six years and the machines are running Windows XP on 128MB of memory and a Pentium II processor. That hardware will not run Windows 7; in fact, it's probably barely running Windows XP! I had an experience with a company in just this position. They wanted to move to a modern OS but had nowhere near enough budget to refresh 5,000 desktop machines. Their solution was to set up a farm of Remote Desktop Session Hosts, replace Windows XP with a Windows Fundamentals for Legacy PCs system, which enables a machine to basically act as an RDP client, and configure that local client OS to connect to the new farm of Remote Desktop Session Hosts. Each

▶ Must-Do #4: Use session virtualization as the default for providing remote desktops or applications and use VDI for specific use case scenarios.

▶ Must-Do #5: Implement the desktop virtualization technologies discussed and get a good desktop management infrastructure in place.

desktop got a new widescreen monitor, keyboard, and mouse; and when the users logged on, they got a Windows 7 desktop experience (even though it's actually Windows Server 2008 R2, they can't tell) and assumed they had new PCs. They had no idea they were using session virtualization and RDP! This is one scenario in which session virtualization can rescue a small hardware budget, and is a twist on the methodology used by organizations that don't buy desktops in favor of buying thin clients that can only be RDP clients. The older desktop machine still acts as an RDP client, but there are more options if the organization's strategy for desktop environments changes in the future.

I want to reiterate that whenever I talk about session virtualization, VDI, and RDP, there are great partners, such as Citrix and Quest, that build on the Microsoft solutions to provide their own session virtualization and VDI solutions. Therefore, if what Microsoft provides in Windows Server 2008 R2 and Windows Server 2012 doesn't meet your needs, consider these partner offerings.

LEVERAGING THE LATEST TECHNOLOGIES TO DESIGN THE OPTIMAL DATACENTER

Once the desktop architecture is taken care of, some services will have to be enabled through the datacenter, such as File Services for storing all that user data and settings, ways to deliver the virtualized applications, Group Policy to configure all the settings, VDI and session virtualization environments, and patching services. It's a long list, but fortunately all those services can be virtualized using a machine virtualization solution such as Hyper-V. This section provides a detailed look at how that virtualization will change your datacenter.

> CROSSREF   The public cloud is discussed in detail in Chapter 14.

Considering the Public Cloud

Many organizations spend huge amounts of time, effort, and expense on applications and services that consume much more than they should. Looking at the public cloud services available, a new company would be smart to consider using such services if possible. E-mail, collaboration, application platforms, and customer relationship management are all critical capabilities that require large initial investments to get up and running, whereas using a public cloud Software as a Service or Platform as a

Service enables a "pay as you go" solution; you pay a small amount when your company is started and an increasingly larger amount as it grows. This is perfect for a growing startup.

Conversely, an established company is always looking for ways to reduce its IT expenditure or re-allocate the spending between different buckets; in this case, moving some services off-premise and to the cloud may make a lot of sense, particularly if you are looking for new features or site disaster recovery. Using a cloud service like Office 365 instantly gives an organization enterprise e-mail, communication, and collaboration that are replicated across multiple sites for a per-user, per-month fee.

▶ Must-Do #6:
Always consider
the public cloud
for new services,
especially when the
need is limited in
duration or has an
unknown resource
requirement.

If a need arises for a new application that is short-term, has high availability needs, or has huge burst scenarios, then hosting that application on Windows Azure would be a great choice. Familiarize yourself with the public cloud solutions available and use them to your advantage. That is, use them where it makes sense, not to sidestep internal processes or address the shortcomings of internal provisioning processes. The example described in Chapter 14 notes that some organizations take six weeks to provision a new VM after it is requested. Because of this long delay, business units often decide to just use the public cloud instead. That is a poor reason. Instead, fix the internal process using self-service and the private cloud described throughout this book.

Deciding Whether a Server Workload Should Be Virtualized

While the public cloud is great, you will undoubtedly want to keep many workloads internally on your company's systems. Presently, your company is probably using some kind of server virtualization, whether it's VMware ESX, Microsoft Hyper-V, Citrix XenServer, or something else. In addition, your organization is probably using multiple hypervisors; the most common scenario I see is ESX organizations evaluating Hyper-V, so both are used in their datacenter.

▶ Must-Do #7:
Think virtual first
for new operating
system instances
and physical only
when virtual is not
possible.

The default for most organizations is virtual first for any new server workload, except for servers with very high resource requirements and some specialty services, such as domain controllers that provide the Active Directory domain services for the environment. Most of these exceptions result from limitations on the previous generation of hypervisors.

As I described in Chapter 8, Windows Server 2012 Hyper-V Beta now supports the capability to run very large virtual machines, each with 32 virtual CPUs and 1TB of memory, a virtual NUMA topology projected onto the VM, direct access to network cards using SR-IOV, and access to both iSCSI and Fibre Channel storage. Very few workloads cannot run in a virtual machine just as if they were on bare metal, which includes high-resource workloads such as SQL Server. Even if you have a physical server that has only one virtual machine running because it needs all the resources, virtualizing is still a good idea because all the other benefits of virtualization would still apply:

- ▶ Abstraction from the underlying hardware, providing complete portability
- ▶ Ability to move the VM between physical hosts for hardware maintenance purposes
- ▶ Leveraging Replica and other high-availability features of Hyper-V where needed
- ▶ Consistent deployment and provisioning

There may still be some applications you cannot virtualize, either because they need more than the resource limits of a virtual machine or, more likely, because of lack of support. Some application vendors do not support their applications running in a virtualized manner, either because they have not had time to test it or they offer their own virtualization solution and will therefore only support their product on their hypervisor. Oracle is a good example; they support virtualization of their products only on their own Oracle VM hypervisor. Remember, applications are unaware that they are running on a virtual operating system. The application running within a virtual machine sees only the guest operating system, which essentially looks the same as if it was running on bare metal. There are a few exceptions, as certain types of device will be different as the virtual device is seen, such as network and storage, so virtualizing an application should not introduce problems with today's hypervisors.

Continuing with the Oracle example, in my experience the Oracle products work just fine on Hyper-V, and Oracle support will even try to assist you on a best-efforts basis if there is a problem with it running on a non-Oracle hypervisor; but if the problem cannot be fixed, you have to be prepared for the application vendor to require you to reproduce the problem on a supported configuration, such as on a bare metal system without virtualization—or, in Oracle's case, on the Oracle VM hypervisor. Technology can help here; there are third-party solutions that normally help with physical-to-virtual conversions when organizations want to move to a virtual environment, but they can also take a virtual machine and deploy it to bare metal. This could be an emergency backup option for organizations that want to standardize on one hypervisor and run all applications on virtual operating systems, even when it is not officially supported.

▶ This is very rare. In fact, I've not heard of this happening with modern hypervisors, but an organization has to be prepared. Most clients I work with accept this very small risk.

Organizations have to make a decision at this point, and it really comes down to their tolerance for some risk, however small, and how critical the application is, should it encounter a problem. If you have a noncritical application, then virtualizing in a nonsupported configuration that has been well tested by the organization is probably OK. Conversely, if it's a critical system that requires instant vendor support when a problem occurs, then running in an officially unsupported configuration is probably not the best option.

As covered in Chapter 8, Windows Server 2012 introduces much better support for virtualized domain controllers, which means an organization can now virtualize its domain controllers on Windows Server 2012 virtual machines hosted on Windows Server 2012 Hyper-V and not have concerns that the cluster won't be able to start, or if a snapshot of a domain controller were applied the sky would fall down on them.

Although I have focused on Windows workloads and how Windows can be virtualized, many organizations have some non-Windows servers as well. As discussed in Chapter 8, Hyper-V has excellent support for a number of Linux distributions, and many Linux distributions that are not officially supported will still work and can use the Hyper-V Integration Services to get a great experience; just because it's not a Windows server does not mean it cannot be virtualized. Some Linux/Unix workloads cannot be virtualized on any x86 hypervisor because they are based on a non-x86 architecture. A good example is Solaris running on SPARC, which cannot be virtualized on an x86 hypervisor because SPARC is a different hardware architecture. If you are using the x86 version of Solaris, then it would probably run on Hyper-V, but currently (2012) it's not supported. If you are running this Solaris workload it's probably important, so running it in an unsupported manner would not make sense.

▶ If you are not running your domain controllers on Windows Server 2012 Hyper-V, then at least a couple of domain controllers should not be virtualized, or at least keep them out of clusters. Nor should you ever try to apply a snapshot!

▶ Don't forget about the free Microsoft Hyper-V Server, which is a great option for organizations with non-Windows server workloads, including Linux and Windows desktops.

Using a Private Cloud

I talk to many customers about the private cloud—and while some are open to it, others hate the idea. The latter group feels this way largely because of a misunderstanding about what the private cloud means to the organization. Instead of asking customers whether they want a private cloud, the following questions get a much more positive response:

- ▶ "Do you want easier management and deployment?"
- ▶ "Do you want better insight into networking and storage?"
- ▶ "Do you want to abstract deployment processes from the underlying fabric, enabling deployments to any datacenter without worrying about all the underlying details, such as SANs, VLANs, IP subnets, and so on?"

- ▶ "Do you want to better track usage and even charge back business units based on that usage?"

- ▶ "Do you want to be able to deploy multi-tiered services with a single click instead of focusing on every virtual machine that is needed?"

- ▶ "Do you want to simplify the process of creating new virtual environments?"

After getting yes answers to every question, I could take it a step further:

- ▶ "Do you want to enable users to request their own virtual environments or service instances through a self-service portal, with full approval workflow within quotas you define that are automatically enforced, including virtual machine automatic expiration if required?"

I may start to get some head-shaking on this one. IT teams can have concerns about letting users have self-service—even with quotas, approval workflows, and full tracking. That's OK. Like using public cloud services, after implementing end-user self-service it can take some time for IT to trust the controls and the process and realize that it won't result in VM sprawl and a Wild West of uncontrolled VM mayhem. In reality, the private cloud enables better tracking and more controls than the processes currently used in most organizations.

The key point is that adopting a private cloud provides benefits both to IT department and to the organization as a whole, allowing far greater utilization of the resources the company already has, better insight into those resources, and much better responsiveness to the requirements of the business, such as provisioning new environments and the ability for the business users of the infrastructure to focus on what they really care about, the application.

Going back to the first set of questions, if your answer to any of those is yes, then a move to the private cloud model makes sense. Keep in mind that you don't have to expose all of its capabilities to end users. You can have self-service capabilities but only let the IT teams use them to better enable provisioning processes.

Remember that the private cloud provides a foundation on which you can offer many types of service. You can offer basic virtual machines for an in-house Infrastructure as a Service; you can offer machines preconfigured with certain runtime environments like .NET or J2E to enable Platform as a Service, whereby business units can easily run their applications; and you can even offer complete services that encapsulate an entire multi-tiered application through service templates, providing Software as a Service. The best solution is the one that makes the most sense for your organization, although typically a company will start with basic Infrastructure as a Service, offering virtual machines and then building up from that point on as confidence and experience grow.

▶ Must-Do #8: Don't dismiss the private cloud. Understand its capabilities and the benefits it can bring at many different levels of the organization.

Dealing with Backups, Disaster Recovery, and High-Availability Needs

I want to focus on backup first, as I think it's the easiest operation to manage. Yes, you still have to do it! There is nothing about virtualization that eliminates the need to perform backups of your applications and data. Although virtualization includes efficient features for ensuring high availability and even replication of virtual machines—including a few previous points in time over the preceding few hours—these capabilities cannot prevent a corruption from going unnoticed for a day or so. Many services currently provide the ability to recover information without using a backup. Active Directory has a recycle bin to recover deleted objects; Exchange has a recycle bin to recover deleted mail items; SharePoint has a recycle bin for deleted data; and file servers have shadow copies to enable easy access to previous point-in-time views of the file server, and restore capabilities. In short, although high availability and replication reduce the number of backups required, you should still perform backups—especially for long-term archival and retention purposes.

The next question is where to perform the backup. Now all the operating systems in your environment are virtual machines running on hypervisors. Your first thought may be to just perform the backups on the Hyper-V parent partition that is running Windows Server 2008 R2 or Windows Server 2012, and this may actually be OK. When a backup is performed, Hyper-V notifies each guest operating system, through the Hyper-V Integration Services, that a backup is being performed. Those guest operating systems will in turn call whatever Volume Shadow Copy Service (VSS) writers are registered, ensuring that all information is flushed out to disk and any changes quiesced. This means a backup of the virtual hard disk at the Hyper-V parent partition results in an application-consistent backup—that is, it is fully usable and its integrity is assured if the VM needs to be restored. Great!

There is one caveat, however, and it can be a big one. Focus on the restore, not the backup. We don't perform a backup because we like backing up; we do it in case we need to restore. Many backup solutions provide the capability to perform granular restores, which means you don't need to restore the entire OS. You can restore a file, a certain SQL Server database, a specific SharePoint document. If your backup agent is running only at the Hyper-V parent partition, then your restore granularity for services running in the virtual machines is likely to be very limited. You will likely be able to restore the entire VM only, or perhaps files from within the VM, but it won't be service-aware. If you also run the backup agent within each VM that has a service for which you want granular restoration capabilities, then the backup software will know about the service and can use special backup processes to intelligently protect

▶ Windows Server 2012 Hyper-V Replica enables replication of the virtual hard disks of virtual machines and even includes the capability to perform application-consistent VSS snapshots periodically.

▶ This means that writes to disk are stopped while the snapshot is performed, ensuring the disk data remains consistent during the backup.

▶ Must do number 9: Don't focus on the backup. Focus on how you want to use the backup; this means the restore process.

databases, mailboxes, and so on. This means if a restore is required, the user performing the restore has granular restoration capabilities. This is a very important consideration. If your backup software has granular restoration capabilities for a service, then any virtual machines running those processes should also have the backup agent installed. For the other virtual machines you can choose to just back up at the Hyper-V parent partition level because there would not be any additional benefit to backing up the guest.

Virtualization is extremely helpful in restore situations. When you back up a virtual machine you are backing up a complete unit that is independent of the hardware in the physical server. This means in restoration scenarios, you can restore the VM to any piece of hardware as long as it runs the same hypervisor version—a great benefit, especially in disaster-recovery scenarios.

High availability, like backups, is often misunderstood, and organizations often begin using the high-availability and replication features available in the hypervisor and stop using those features of the applications running inside the virtual machine. The argument seems sound: Why run 10 different high availability and replication solutions for all my different applications when I can just use one at the hypervisor level?

It would be sound if the functionality were the same, but it's not, at all. Consider high availability at a virtual machine level in an unplanned failover scenario. If the guest OS crashes, then as far as the failover cluster is concerned the host is still running and nothing will happen—the service would just be down. Now imagine the Hyper-V host crashes. Failover clustering would determine the host was down and move the virtual machines to other hosts in the cluster. Then the virtual machine would be started, which may take a couple of minutes, and hopefully it starts without issue and the application data is not in a dirty state that requires some manual actions to clean because the OS was just halted due to the node suddenly stopping. This would result in the service being unavailable for minutes and maybe longer.

Now consider using application high-availability features, such as Exchange database availability groups (DAGs) or SQL Server mirroring. If there is a failure of an instance of the application that is part of an application high-availability group, then another instance of the application will automatically take over the service without any downtime and no risk of the application data being in a dirty state. Additionally, the application would be aware of the failure of another instance and be able to take steps to check for any possible lost transactions. In short, application high availability provides a more functional experience with less downtime than using a hypervisor-level high-availability solution. Some applications don't even support the use of hypervisor high-availability solutions, and some that do recommend not using it if the application high-availability capabilities are used.

▶ Run backup agents inside a VM when the backup software has capabilities specific to the application running in the VM.

▶ Windows Server 2012 failover clustering can do some basic virtual-machine-level health checking and perform actions.

▶ Must-Do #10:
Use application
high-availability
features before
using the hypervisor
high-availability
features.

This is not to say you should never use the hypervisor high-availability or replica capabilities. I use these simple rules:

▶ If the application has its own high-availability and/or replica solution, then use it.

▶ If the application does not have its own high-availability and/or replica solution, then use the hypervisor technologies.

▶ If the application has its own high-availability and/or replica solution but also supports the concurrent use of a hypervisor high-availability solution, then use the application high availability as primary but also put the virtual machine in a hypervisor high-availability environment. This enables the virtual machine to easily be moved around using Live Migration for hypervisor host maintenance purposes.

How Virtualization Affects Management

Virtualization does not have to change the way you manage your datacenter. It's possible to continue managing each operating system instance and deploying each instance by booting from an ISO, but you would not be getting the most from the technologies available and management would be far more labor intensive than it needs to be.

One of the biggest changes that virtualization introduces to the datacenter initially is how new servers are provisioned. Instead of installing operating systems via an ISO file, you use virtual machine templates, which can include customizations, automatic joining to the domain, and installing applications and running scripts. Most likely you will have a few virtual hard disks that can be used by many different templates that can be tailored for the exact needs of the organization.

The longer-term goal is to shift from creating virtual machines to deploying instances of services that are made up of many virtual machines and service templates, as explored in Chapter 9. Service templates mark a big change in how services and virtual machines are provisioned, but you should strive to use them for the benefits they offer, including easy deployment, updating of deployed instances by updating the template, server application virtualization, and automated configuration of network hardware. This is not to say normal virtual machines will never be deployed. Service templates are great to enable the deployment of services within an organization, but some applications just need to be deployed once; for these applications, the additional work to create a service template does not make sense.

Whatever you decide in terms of management, don't end up with two completely different management solutions or even potentially three:

- One management solution for virtual machines

- One management solution for physical machines

- One management solution for the virtual infrastructure, such as the hypervisor

The goal is to manage your environment as simply and with as few tools as possible. Look for a solution that enables complete management, one that does not require a lot of exception solutions for different aspects of your datacenter. Patching is a great example. Numerous solutions will just patch virtual machines, others patch hypervisors, and still others patch desktops. A solution such as System Center Configuration Manager 2012, however, provides patching for all servers. These can be physical or virtual, and include your desktops; and because Hyper-V is part of Windows, SCCM can patch the hypervisor itself. One solution patches everything. SCCM can also integrate with many third-party products, enabling you to apply updates to hardware such as firmware and BIOS, and for both Microsoft and non-Microsoft applications.

There is one patch-specific functionality that is very nice for virtual machines. Imagine you have a virtual machine that has been turned off for six months but now you want to turn it on again. Because it has not been patched during those six months, it's not desirable to start it in its unpatched state. Microsoft has a solution accelerator, the *Virtual Machine Servicing Tool (VMST)*, which will patch virtual machines that are not turned on, virtual machines stored in the library, and even virtual machine templates—all with patches defined in SCCM or Windows Software Update Services. The VMST is currently at version 3 and is based on System Center Virtual Machine Manager 2008 R2, not 2012, but by the time you read this there may be a newer version released for SCVMM 2012.

The same principle applies to all aspects of your datacenter: Try to avoid point solutions. System Center Operations Manager can monitor your physical servers, the virtual servers, the operating system, applications, custom .NET and J2E applications, networking equipment, and even non-Windows components, providing you with a comprehensive view of your datacenter. The same applies for backup, for service management, and for orchestration: Keep it simple and minimize the use of separate tools. If you do have a number of different tools, System Center Orchestrator 2012 can provide a single automated process that can perform activities on all the tools in your environment.

▶ Must-Do #11: Find a management infrastructure that can manage your whole environment.

I'd like to close this section with a few words about orchestration, as it brings together all the facets of the datacenter. As your organization uses more and more IT and has more and more operating system instances to manage, technologies like service templates help to shift the focus to the application instead of the operating system; however, a large number of operating systems will still require management. To truly scale, you must look at automation capabilities and working with multiple operating system instances at the same time. In Chapter 15 I cover the new Server Manager in Windows Server 2012 that enables managing multiple servers as if they were a single unit, but in terms of automation it's important to move away from using a GUI.

▶ Must-Do #12:
Learn PowerShell.
It's the future of
everything.

PowerShell is a key part of enabling automation. Especially in Windows Server 2012, nearly everything that can be done with the GUI can be done with PowerShell, enabling actions to be not only scripted but also, and more important, executed on many machines concurrently and in an automated fashion. Building on orchestrating tasks, and beyond just PowerShell, take some time to look at System Center Orchestrator. Clients I talk to are very excited about its capabilities, including connecting to any existing system through various methods and graphically creating runbooks (sets of actions that should be performed in a sequence and based on results from previous actions across all those connected systems). Start with something small, some set of actions you perform manually each day, and automate them in Orchestrator. Another good way to familiarize yourself with Orchestrator is to take a simple PowerShell script you have and model it in Orchestrator instead. Once the clients I've worked with start using Orchestrator, they consider it the greatest thing since sliced bread and use it for everything.

SUMMARY

My primary recommendation is to get your datacenters on the latest version of Hyper-V; the new capabilities make it the best virtualization platform available. It includes support for many more virtual machines, larger clusters, better replication and availability features, better support for direct access to network hardware, network virtualization, full PowerShell management, and guest-level Fibre Channel access—all of which means you can virtualize more workloads and therefore simplify your datacenter and its management. That's just scratching the surface.

On the desktop, implement solutions that give you a well-managed workspace. Take advantage of user settings, data and application virtualization, and solutions like System Center Configuration Manager to deploy and patch your desktop and server operating systems. Use session virtualization and VDI where they solve a real need, not as the default because some great marketing has convinced you it's always the right solution. Otherwise, leverage a well-managed desktop first. Task-based workers can likely use session virtualization, whereas power users need VDI; it's fine to have both in your organization, and you very likely will.

It probably seems daunting. Change is always stressful, especially if you are currently struggling to keep things running by either not patching servers or patching them manually, and always installing servers by running around with a DVD or USB key. However, a huge difference can also mean a huge benefit. Getting these processes and solutions in place requires a large time investment initially, but don't hesitate to hire a reputable consulting company to help get you started; just ensure that they don't work in isolation. Work closely with the consultants, being part of the decision-making and planning. That way, when they leave, you understand why things were done and you can follow any best practices they implemented.

▶ This is very common. Because management is done manually, there is no time to substitute better processes. However, if you bite the bullet now and work extra hours, you will make time going forward for exciting stuff.

▶ Must-Do #12.5: Change the way you do things, even if it means some pain today for a much better tomorrow.

CHAPTER 14

Virtualizing with the Microsoft Public Cloud

IN THIS CHAPTER

- ▶ Understanding Microsoft's history as a public cloud service provider
- ▶ What are Windows Azure and SQL Azure?
- ▶ Developing for the Windows Azure platform
- ▶ Accessing Windows Azure Infrastructure as a Service
- ▶ Using Exchange, SharePoint, and Lync in the cloud with Office 365
- ▶ Managing desktops with Windows Intune
- ▶ Analyzing server best practices with System Center Advisor

This book focuses on Microsoft virtualization solutions that are used internally within organizations, but Microsoft also has a long history of offering public cloud services. In recent years, Microsoft has significantly improved and added to those public cloud capabilities; and all the public cloud lessons learned, such as how to provide huge scalability and resiliency platforms, have been applied to Microsoft's private cloud solutions. This chapter examines the most significant Microsoft public cloud services and their potential place in your organization. As organizations strive to streamline their IT services and meet ever higher expectations, using the public cloud might be the right solution in many scenarios.

TRACING MICROSOFT'S HISTORY AS A PUBLIC CLOUD PROVIDER

Although *public cloud* is a fairly new term, the provision of services on a shared infrastructure on the Internet, for both individuals and organizations, has been in place for many years—and Microsoft has been a major player in many of these cloud services. As far back as 1995, Microsoft launched MSN as a dial-up portal; then, in 1997, it acquired Hotmail, one of the first web-based e-mail services. Currently, Windows Live Hotmail has more than 450 million users, and MSN has more than 550 million users. That's an impressive cloud service, and one that has given Microsoft a lot of experience in providing a heavily used Software as a Service (SaaS) offering.

Consider Microsoft Update, the online support service that has been running for 12 years, which enables the Windows operating system and many Microsoft applications to be updated online. With an estimated half billion clients, Microsoft Update is clearly a huge deployment service, which also provides Microsoft with many opportunities to improve and create services.

In 2002, Microsoft introduced Xbox LIVE, which provides users of the Xbox console, and now other platforms such as PC and Windows Phone, with the capability to play online games with other users, to access entertainment services, and even to communicate using recent add-ons such as Avatar Kinect. Xbox LIVE recently introduced a new cloud storage capability that enables game saves to be stored on Xbox LIVE servers and continued from any console a user accesses. Currently, Xbox LIVE has over 40 million members. Similarly, the search engine Bing, also a Microsoft offering, responds to more than 500 million queries per month. And now, Microsoft is applying all that they have learned over the years to providing public cloud services to enterprises, which is the primary focus of this chapter.

USING PLATFORM AS A SERVICE WITH WINDOWS AZURE

In Chapter 1, I talked about the main types of cloud service, with Platform as a Service (PaaS) falling between Infrastructure as a Service (IaaS) solutions, which require organizations to manage the operating system and other functions such as networking, and Software as a Service (SaaS) solutions, which require basically no maintenance effort from organizations other than configuring which users can use a service and which capabilities should be available. A PaaS solution takes care of everything—from the development and runtime environment, database, security, and availability through the storage, virtualization, and operating systems, down to the very infrastructure fabric such as network, storage, and computer. The only component an organization needs to focus on with a PaaS solution is the application itself; everything else related to maintenance, scalability, and availability is handled by the service. This frees developers to focus on making the best application to meet the requirements as long as they adhere to certain rules required by the PaaS.

The Microsoft PaaS solution is *Windows Azure*, which, despite being a Microsoft product, actually provides support for both Microsoft and third-party development environments and languages. These include .NET with Microsoft Visual Studio, Ruby, Python, Java, and PHP. Windows Azure is built with a number of components that make the environment both feature-rich and flexible, enabling it to be used in multiple ways.

An application written for Windows Azure must comply with certain guidelines to ensure that, once deployed, it will be highly available and easily scalable without requiring any changes to the application itself.

Fundamentally, Windows Azure defines three different PaaS roles: a Web role, a Worker role, and a Virtual Machine (VM) role. These roles represent the top-level functional blocks of your custom application. Not surprisingly, these various roles are actually expressed as VMs running in a Hyper-V–based environment. When you deploy your custom application, you specify at least one instance for each of its roles; but to ensure high availability for any production workload, you must specify at least two instances of each.

Many organizations have certain tasks that run only once or twice a month but require huge amounts of computation or storage when they do run. Similarly, some businesses get very busy only on a particular day of the year or seasonally. Only at those times does such a business require thousands of instances of its Web and Worker roles, while the rest of the year it may only need a hundredth of those instances or perhaps run on-premise during that time. Clearly, it is wasteful to have all that computer and storage fabric idle for most of the month. This would be a great type of application to run on a PaaS like Windows Azure, as it could be deployed and scaled during those critical few days each month. This scalability has a direct effect on costs, which is one of the things that makes PaaS solutions so appealing to organizations: that is, you only pay for what you use.

The cost of using Windows Azure is based on several factors, starting with computer hours, which vary in price (at the time of writing, 4–96 cents an hour) depending on instance size. You also pay for storage, for SQL Azure storage, and for

▶ Recall from Chapter 1 that on-premise refers to anything not in the public cloud, such as your datacenters.

▶ Extra Small is a shared 1 GHz CPU core with 768MB of RAM. Extra Large is 8 1.6 GHz CPU cores and 14GB of RAM. There are also intermediate levels of Small, Medium, and Large. You choose the computer size that is needed.

the bandwidth used in and out of the Windows Azure datacenters. On the compute side, you pay for the amount of time the VM is deployed, regardless of whether it is idle or running at full capacity. That is why it's important not to create instances and forget to stop them; you may get a surprising bill!

SUPER BOWL SUNDAY, PIZZA, AND WINDOWS AZURE

I'll be up front: I'm English and I don't understand American football. However, I do understand that it's very popular in America; and when Americans watch the Super Bowl they like to eat pizza. The connection between Super Bowl Sunday and pizza is a great way to illustrate the use of Windows Azure.

This one Sunday, out of the entire year, represents a perfect storm for the pizza delivery business. During the Super Bowl, the entire United States, across all four time zones, is in sync—with people ordering at the same time during the three half-hour breaks. These three spikes require 50 percent more compute power to handle order processing than a typical Friday evening, which is the normal high point for pizza ordering.

Normally, systems have to be built to handle the busiest time, so a pizza company would have to provision a capacity of 50 percent more than they would ever typically need just to be prepared for that one day. Remember, also, that the calculated increase is based on the Friday dinnertime usage, which is already higher than needed any other time of the week. Supporting this capacity on-premise would be a hugely expensive and wasteful exercise. Instead, Windows Azure is used.

During normal times there might be 10 instances of each role handling the website and processing orders. On Fridays between 2 PM and midnight, this increases to 20 instances of each role, and on Super Bowl Sunday between 12 PM and 5 PM, this would increase to 30 instances of each role. The actual numbers needed might vary, but the point here is that the additional instances exist only when needed; therefore, the customer is charged extra only when additional resources are needed and not at other times. This elasticity is the major advantage of public cloud services.

The pizza scenario is a case of *Predictable Bursting,* one of the four key scaling patterns shown in Figure 14-1 and one for which cloud computing provides the obvious solution. Software applications in many other scenarios can benefit from deployment in the cloud, but these four are efficiently solved through the use of a public cloud. *Growing Fast* is typical of a start-up company that doesn't want to invest heavily in infrastructure, as the organization does not know how successful they will ultimately be, but is an instant hit and has to scale up very quickly. Doing my annual tax return was something new to me in America—there is no annual tax return in England—but this is a great example of a service that is only needed for a couple of months per year, so tax return preparation companies such as H&R Block could use cloud services in the *On and Off* usage pattern. *Unpredictable Bursting* is any kind of use that cannot be planned. A news website could get huge spikes when something happens, so the organization has to be able to scale up very quickly then back down once the event has passed.

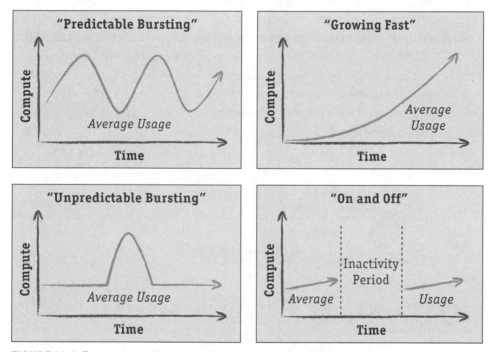

FIGURE 14-1: Four main application-scaling scenarios in which you can best exploit the elastic, highly scalable nature of Windows Azure

If you are part of an organization that needs a highly available application but lacks the infrastructure to support the level of resilience required, then Windows Azure is a great fit. If you have an application with a fairly short life span—for example, one related to a specific promotion or advertising campaign—Windows Azure is a great fit. For any service offering there are choices pertaining to design and hosting. The hosting choice, such as the use of Windows Azure, can affect the actual design based on requirements of the hosting platform chosen. When building new applications, you should consider all the infrastructure requirements before deciding whether Windows Azure could provide the right solution.

Understanding Azure Fundamentals

I previously mentioned the Web role and the Worker role. In this section, I want to dive into more of the components that make up the Windows Azure service and how and when they are used.

As Figure 14-2 shows, there are three main building blocks to the Windows Azure platform. First, there is the Windows Azure component, which provides the primary compute capabilities of the Windows Azure platform, basic types of storage, and the Fabric Controller that actually manages all the virtual machines and hosts that comprise the Windows Azure platform. Second, as the name suggests, SQL Azure provides a relational database management system for Windows Azure, compatible with SQL Server. The Windows Azure AppFabric provides various services for communication between applications in the cloud and on-premise, such as Access Control, Service Bus for messaging between components, and caching capabilities. There is also a Windows Azure Marketplace that enables users to buy and sell Windows Azure applications, components, and data sets.

> ▶ This can get confusing. There is the Windows Azure platform itself, and then one of its components is called Windows Azure, which is where the platform actually got its name.

> ▶ I recommend looking at http://www.windowsazure.com/en-us/home/tour/overview/ for a nice tour of all the Windows Azure functionality.

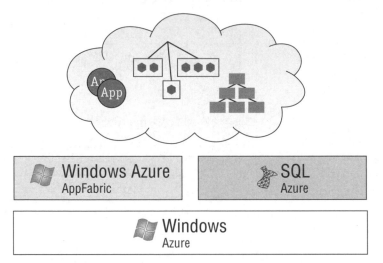

FIGURE 14-2: The three main building blocks of the Windows Azure platform: Windows Azure, SQL Azure, and Windows Azure AppFabric

While the Windows Azure platform is comprised of a number of components, the following sections describe the elements needed to actually run applications on Windows Azure, including servers, storage, load balancing, and more. Microsoft has many datacenters distributed throughout the world where Windows Azure applications can run. The United States, Europe, and Asia have two datacenters each, so customers can select and deploy to the closest location geographically to get the best performance.

WINDOWS AZURE

The main building block of the Windows Azure platform is the *Windows Azure service* itself, which provides the key capabilities to enable the cloud-based hosting of applications and data. This section focuses on the five key parts of Windows Azure, as shown in Figure 14-3.

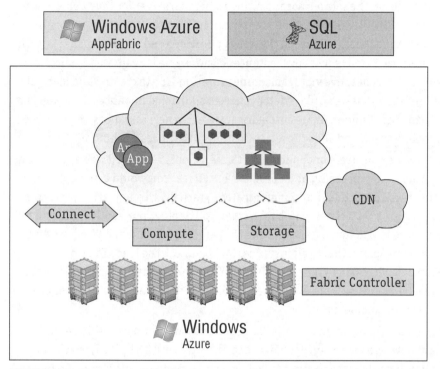

FIGURE 14-3: Five main building blocks make up the core Windows Azure service: Compute, Storage, Fabric Controller, CDN, and Connect. Virtual machines, shown as orange servers, host all the services.

COMPUTE

The Compute component is the most fundamental building block. This is the part that actually runs the application, whether it is a website, custom middleware code, or some legacy application. All the Compute capabilities are enabled through VMs (remember the virtual machine instance sizes from Extra Small to Extra Large). Three types of virtual machine, known as *roles*, are available and each has its specific use cases.

To be very clear, just because virtual machines are used as the Compute units, it does not mean that you, as a Windows Azure customer, are dealing explicitly with virtual machines. The creation and configuration of virtual machines that host your application, the virtual infrastructure, and the operating system management and maintenance are all done for you. That is the point of the Windows Azure PaaS—it's a platform that you leverage to run your applications without having to worry about what's going on behind the scenes, where a virtual machine exists for each instance of a role you request.

The Web role has the sole purpose of acting as the web server for your web applications, such as ASP.NET, PHP, and Node.js applications. The Web role incorporates Internet Information Services (IIS) to run the web applications and automates the setup of the web interface. If you request five instances of a Web role for your web application, then behind the scenes, five virtual machines running IIS are created and load balanced, all running your web code. If later you need additional instances, then you just request them and Windows Azure automatically creates new instances, deploys your custom code to them, and adds those new instances to the load balancing.

▶ Load balancing of HTTP, HTTPS, and TCP is also part of the Windows Azure Compute building block.

The Worker role is used for applications that are not IIS-enabled web applications, typically back-end processing and database activities. You would also deploy an application in a Worker role that communicates externally through other protocols, such as messaging. Just like the Web role, when you deploy your application, you tell Windows Azure how many instances of the Worker role you want and Windows Azure distributes your application to all instances and balances the load. You would deploy applications, such as Java Virtual Machines or Apache Tomcat, in the Worker role, which is really where the Windows Azure flexibility can be seen supporting more than just Microsoft technologies.

I have been talking about how the Windows Azure platform uses VMs behind the scenes and how, as a customer, you never deal directly with a VM. Well, that's not strictly true! If you want to deal with a VM, you can by using a third type of role: the VM role. When you do, a custom Windows Server 2008 R2 VHD image is deployed to Windows Azure. This is particularly useful if you need a highly customized environment that you could not achieve using the Worker role. For example, it allows the potential migration of existing applications to the cloud. I say "potential" because there are some caveats with the VM role. This role is not like an IaaS VM on which you can just run anything you want. In Windows Azure, the VM role is designed to allow customization of the environment or deployment of applications that require complex, interactive installation routines not possible using the automatically provisioned Web and Worker roles.

The key point is that a VM role application is delivered as an image, and the platform automatically creates and deletes instances of that image. The applications within the VM role must be stateless because, if the VM role instance is stopped, its state is reset back to the state of the customer-delivered image. This means the application cannot depend on any data stored locally within the VM; it must be stored in Windows Azure or SQL Azure storage. Because the VM role is stateless, the actual number of scenarios for which it is suitable is fairly limited.

You can have any combination of Web, Worker, and VM roles you want for your application. Some applications may only have Web roles, some may have Web and Worker roles, some could have just VM roles; the flexibility is available to create role instances that meet the needs of the application you are deploying.

Windows Azure does not automatically scale instances of a role; that is, if the instances are running at full capacity, the platform does not automatically add more. This behavior is deliberate; because you are charged for each instance, uncontrolled scaling could be a problem. Instead, through the Windows Azure website, you can easily request additional instances of a role, which are then instantly deployed. Alternatively, you can take advantage of the features of System Center App Controller, which I cover in Chapter 10, or you can programmatically request new instances, enabling you to write your own auto-scaling functionality. There are also third-party solutions such as AzureWatch (http://www.paraleap.com) that will automatically scale your application based on defined thresholds.

> ► This is the most common type of deployment. Imagine customer interaction through the Web roles, which pass information to Worker roles for processing and storage.

STORAGE

All the roles are based around a stateless model because instances are created and deleted as needed, and requests in Windows Azure can go to any instance of a role; there is no guaranteed persistence. This means that while the various roles perform processing and actions, they need to perform these actions on data that must be stored. Windows Azure provides three primary types of available storage.

- ► **Binary Large Objects (BLOBs):** A BLOB is an unstructured collection of bytes that can be used to store nearly anything, including large media files. Windows Azure Drive is a special case of a BLOB. It's a relatively new feature that allows a BLOB to be used as a virtual hard disk (VHD) and formatted as an NTFS volume. This enables applications to interact with it as though it was a disk volume, but it is not storage.

- ► **Tables:** Many people find Windows Azure Tables confusing. They are not like tables in a relational database. Windows Azure Tables simply provide structured storage based on key-value pairs. They are designed to store large

> ► Windows Azure Tables can be thought of as a NoSQL implementation, which is a growing class of database management systems that don't use SQL as their language or implement relational table capabilities.

amounts of data when you require efficient searching but don't need relationships between data items (if you need a relational DB you must use SQL Azure).

▶ **Queues:** You can use queues for a number of purposes, but they are primarily for reliable and persistent messaging between applications within Windows Azure. A common use for queues is for the communication between Web roles and Worker roles. Because queues have only a basic functionality, they are quite fast. They don't have frequently desired characteristics, such as FIFO (first in, first out); instead, developers must implement their own features that build upon the Windows Azure Queue feature.

Windows Azure replicates any stored data three times within the same datacenter to provide maximum protection against any kind of local datacenter storage or system failure. Three times ensures that even if one copy of the data fails, there is still redundancy as two copies remain. To provide resiliency against major site-level disasters, Windows Azure geo-replicates BLOB and table content to another datacenter hundreds of miles away. This geo-replication is not synchronous but it is performed very quickly, which means there is minimal lag between the data content at the primary location and the geo-replicated location. Applications interact with storage using HTTP or HTTPS, and for the tables the Open Data (OData) protocol is used, which builds on web technologies to provide very flexible ways to interact with data.

FABRIC CONTROLLER

Any sufficiently advanced technology is indistinguishable from magic.

—Arthur C. Clarke

Windows Azure seems like magic. As a customer, when you deploy your application, Windows Azure just spins up as many instances as you need. You can scale up or scale down at any time. Your service is always available per the Windows Azure 99.95 percent monthly service-level agreement (SLA), and the operating systems and dependent services are continuously patched and tuned. The *Windows Azure Fabric Controller* enables this magic. It requires a Fabric Agent running on all the VMs and hosts that make up the Windows Azure Compute fabric. The Fabric Controller monitors the agents 24/7, and if it detects a problem, it can spin up new instances of a role. If a user requests more instances of a role, the Fabric Controller creates the new instances and adds them to the load balancer configuration.

▶ This is why you must deploy at least two instances of any role to be covered by the 99.95 percent SLA. The Fabric Controller takes down one instance for patching while leaving the other instance working.

The Fabric Controller also handles all patching and updates. As you deploy more instances, it becomes possible to patch several instances simultaneously. This is configured by creating groupings of role instances called *upgrade domains*. When patching occurs, all instances within an upgrade domain are brought down and updated at the same time; when completed, the next upgrade domain is updated, and so on.

CONTENT DELIVERY NETWORK (CDN)

Although there are Windows Azure datacenters worldwide, for optimal performance, you may want to store high-bandwidth content even closer to the consumer. The *Content Delivery Network (CDN)* enables Windows Azure to cache BLOB data at Microsoft managed Points of Presence (PoPs) that far outnumber the Windows Azure datacenters.

Figure 14-4 demonstrates how the CDN works. The first person in a region to download the content—for example, the latest blockbuster movie from a movie streaming company—would pull down the content via the CDN from the Windows Azure Storage BLOB at one of the major datacenters (step 1). This content is cached at a CDN PoP (step 2), and then the data is sent to the first user (step 3). The second person to request the data in that location pulls the data directly from the PoP cache, getting a fast response (step 4).

Using the CDN is optional. It has its own 99.9% SLA and a pay-as-you-go pricing structure based on transactions and amount of data. Many organizations exploit the CDN for delivering their high-bandwidth data, even if it's separate from an actual Windows Azure application and is easy to enable through a basic CDN request process.

> ▶ As of March 2011, there are 24 locations with CDN PoPs, including eight in each region, listed at http:// msdn.microsoft .com/en-us/library/ windowsazure/ gg680302.aspx.

> ▶ Not necessarily the closest PoP, since Microsoft dynamically optimizes the CDN routing depending on traffic and capacity.

CONNECT

In many scenarios, an organization using Windows Azure to store data or run processes still needs connectivity to their on-premise infrastructure, such as servers or computers. Many organizations want to augment their on-premise capabilities with the public cloud, so communication between the two is critical.

Windows Azure Connect provides a secure communication method between an organization's on-premise infrastructure and Windows Azure Compute using IPSec. You must install a Windows Azure Endpoint Agent on the local

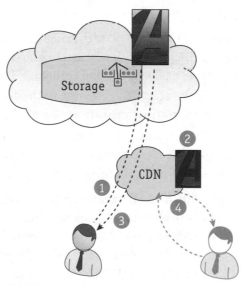

FIGURE 14-4: The caching process when using the CDN

infrastructure host or VM to configure and maintain the IPSec connection. This is not a site-wide VPN connection, but rather a per-operating-system connection on-premise to Windows Azure. This means that if multiple on-premise systems need connectivity to Windows Azure, then the Endpoint Agent needs to be running on each of them. There are numerous uses for this type of connection, such as maintaining a local (on-premise) SQL database to which cloud applications in Windows Azure could connect for certain operations.

TRAFFIC MANAGER

The preceding sections cover the main building blocks of Windows Azure, but a few others are important to cater to the many different ways in which Windows Azure may be used. One such component is *Windows Azure Traffic Manager (WATM)*, which enables an organization to deploy service applications over multiple Windows Azure datacenters and define how user queries are distributed between them (load balanced, closest, or failover) and if this distribution should change at different times of the day. WATM monitors the state of each hosted service and automatically excludes offline instances.

SQL AZURE

Earlier, in the "Storage" section, I explained that despite its name, the Tables feature has nothing to do with relational databases but is rather a key-value store that you can use to hold huge amounts of data. If I wanted to build the next Facebook, I would probably leverage Tables to store all the data. There are many types of data storage that need relationships between data to be defined.

SQL Azure provides relational data through a subset of SQL Server, in the cloud. This gives Windows Azure applications full access to a relational database where needed. SQL Azure includes three primary technologies:

▶ **SQL Azure Database:** An SQL Server service providing a full relational database management system, which applications access via the familiar Tabular Data Stream (TDS) protocol. Behind the scenes, SQL Azure creates three replicas of your database and distributes them among many SQL Server instances. Like the rest of Windows Azure, all patching and maintenance of the SQL Server environment is automatic, requiring no user intervention.

► **SQL Azure Reporting:** This reporting solution enables users to run reports and perform online analytical processing using familiar tools that are used for SQL Server deployments.

► **SQL Azure Data Sync:** This is an SQL Azure–specific technology that is used to synchronize SQL Azure databases, whether they are stored in the cloud or on an on-premise SQL Server. The SQL Azure Data Sync technology is not an atomic synchronization, but one that synchronizes very quickly based on your configuration. A synchronization that requires any actions to be performed on the local and remote SQL instances would be too slow for most use cases.

SQL Azure has a separate pricing model from the Compute and Storage components of Windows Azure; consequently, you can purchase it independently of the other Windows Azure components. It is priced much higher than normal storage because you are actually paying for the SQL Server service, rather than raw disk storage. Two database types are available: Web Edition, which has a 5GB maximum database size; and Business Edition, which has a 150GB maximum database size. Billing is monthly, based on the peak database size in use each day.

WINDOWS AZURE APPFABRIC

Windows Azure AppFabric is not the same component as the Windows Azure Fabric Controller, rather it is more of a technology family that encompasses various technologies that can be used to augment the Windows Azure applications. At the time of writing, three technologies make up the Windows Azure AppFabric:

► **Access Control System (ACS):** When offering services, particularly on the Internet, you may want to control access by using credentials. While these credentials could be application-specific, there are many pain points associated with managing credentials for an application. A better option than maintaining application-specific usernames and passwords where possible is to use other Identity Providers (IdPs), such as Microsoft Live ID, Active Directory Federation Services (ADFS), Facebook, OpenID, Yahoo!, and Google. Different IdPs use different formats for the token, so your application must be able to handle many different types of token. The Windows Azure ACS solves this by first validating the IdP token and then applying configurable rules defined by the application owner to translate the IdP-specific token to a generic ACS token that your application can handle in a uniform way.

▶ **Caching:** Although many applications cache data to improve performance, Windows Azure does not support persistent sessions. Having one application instance cache data related to a user request would be pointless, as the next user request may go to a different instance of the role. The Windows Azure AppFabric Caching service provides a temporary data store in the cloud that is available to all instances of a role. The Caching service is commonly used to cache read-only data from a back-end database, user session data, and application resource data.

▶ **Service Bus:** This managed service supports multiple messaging protocols and provides reliable message delivery between loosely coupled applications in the cloud, as well as hybrid applications distributed across on-premise and cloud systems. The Service Bus provides a secure channel between Web Azure applications and on-premise applications, avoiding the need to create a connection for each call, and getting around difficulties caused by firewall and IP address translation. Service Bus queues reliably store messages in transit, so if an application is down or a mobile device loses signal, the message will still get through eventually.

Infrastructure as a Service with Windows Azure

Previously I talked about the VM role, saying that it was stateless and not the same as Infrastructure as a Service (IaaS). In 2012 Microsoft is extending the Windows Azure platform to support a stateful VM capability to enable an Infrastructure as a Service offering. The IaaS service will enable customers to manage all aspects of the software stack, which includes the OS and application monitoring, management, and servicing. Essentially, the customer manages all aspects of the virtual machine, but it also provides great flexibility in terms of VM usage; basically any application should be able to run without modification.

The big change in the Windows Azure IaaS persistent VM is related to the virtual hard disk. With the Windows Azure IaaS, the virtual hard disks are actually stored in Windows Azure Storage, not locally on the hypervisors. The use of Windows Azure Storage means the disks are replicated three times within the datacenter and then replicated to another site using geo-replication, providing great resiliency against failure. The use of Windows Azure Storage also means that all the capabilities of Windows Azure Storage are available to the virtual hard disks, including very fast copies, which is great for a quick backup or a clone operation.

For the initial wave, key applications will be supported on the Windows Azure IaaS, including the following:

- ► SQL Server 2008, 2008 R2, and 2012
- ► SharePoint Server 2010
- ► Active Directory (Windows Server 2008 R2 and Windows Server 2012)
- ► Linux (and has great support!)

Other products, including MSDTC, IIS, BizTalk 2010, System Center AppController 2012, and SC Operations Manager 2012, are also on the supported road map. Solutions such as Remote Desktop Services will not be supported because of licensing restrictions; Microsoft will provide details when it's released. This support means these products will be fully tested on the Windows Azure IaaS, which means a problem requires only a single call to Microsoft for a fully supported implementation.

From a licensing perspective, customers do not use their on-premise Windows licenses. Instead, the Windows Server operating system is licensed in the cloud on a per-hour basis. Other products will vary depending on the product and the vendor.

The Windows Azure management website is extended to support the creation and management of virtual machines. Additionally, a number of supplied images will be provided for easy VM deployment. From the Windows Azure website, remote desktop connections can be initiated to the virtual machines.

► The difference between an image and a disk is that the image is Sysprepped, which means it's ready for duplication. This is known as a Windows Azure image. Non-Sysprepped would be Windows Azure disks.

One really nice feature of IaaS is an internal DNS feature that allows DNS resolution for the virtual machines for a particular tenant (by tenant I mean a customer using the cloud service). This means all the virtual machines from your organization will be able to resolve each other, but another organization would not be able to query on your VMs. The DNS solution is secure and will not share your information. Likewise, network connectivity such as PING will work between VMs for a particular tenant, which also means multi-server management solutions like Windows Server 2012 Server Manager will work for all the VMs for a single tenant.

The Windows Azure IaaS will have cross-premise connectivity solutions. This means the virtual machines running on the Windows Azure IaaS will be able to connect to your on-premise operating systems using a VPN tunnel. The most common use of this cross-premise technology will be to enable the virtual machines on the Windows Azure IaaS to be part of your on-premise Active Directory.

This does not mean the Windows Azure Platform as a Service should not be used; in fact the PaaS is a richer service, eliminating the need for customers to manage the OS or do any other servicing. What IaaS provides is a first step into the cloud; customers can now easily deploy their existing applications to the cloud using Windows Azure IaaS, and then over time they can transition to the PaaS alternatives. Instead of running SQL Server in a persistent VM as part of Windows Azure, IaaS customers will move to SQL Azure incrementally. Likewise, instead of running SharePoint 2010 in IaaS, over time customers will likely move to Office 365, which has a managed SharePoint solution.

USING SOFTWARE AS A SERVICE WITH MICROSOFT SOLUTIONS

Windows Azure provides an amazingly rich, flexible, and scalable platform to run your custom applications, but sometimes you don't need to develop a custom application. Instead, you might want to use off-the-shelf software in the cloud, or *Software as a Service (SaaS)*. Microsoft offers a number of SaaS solutions, which have been designed based on experience and feedback from users of other public cloud solutions and on-premise solutions. In this section I explore the Microsoft collaboration and management of public cloud solutions.

Collaborative Working with Office 365

Formally known as Business Productivity Online Suite (BPOS), *Office 365* provides an SaaS version of Microsoft's premium communication and collaboration technologies. Office 365 gives organizations access to highly available, Internet-based implementations of Exchange, Lync, and SharePoint, in addition to the browser-based Office Web Apps. This means an organization with no local infrastructure can have full access to all the capabilities of these main back-office technologies. If you have followed the evolution of Exchange, Lync, and SharePoint, you'll have noticed that all three of these products have improved access to their services by using web protocols, such as HTTPS. It is because of the web protocol interface that these services can be hosted on the Internet and accessed using standard Office client tools, such as Outlook, without modification.

Microsoft markets the Office 365 service as a range of plans; there are four main types of plan available, some of which have sub-options that provide different levels of functionality:

- ▶ **P Plans:** For individuals and small businesses with up to 50 people. Each user gets a 25GB mailbox, online Office Web App access, SharePoint Online for internal and public site sharing, and Lync Online for communication, meetings, desktop sharing, and PC-to-PC audio and video calls.

- ▶ **E Plans:** For enterprise customers who need access to powerful, enterprise-level feature sets. Four levels of plan are available, with feature sets that extend those in the P plan to unlimited mail storage, access to local versions of Office and Microsoft server services like Exchange, full enterprise voice capabilities, and more.

- ▶ **K Plans:** Also for enterprise customers but targeted for kiosk workers who are typically deskless and require a smaller subset of functionality. Two levels of plan are available, which differ only in their ability to carry out basic editing of documents with Office Web Apps as opposed to read-only viewing. Also included is a 500MB mailbox, calendar, contacts, and so on, plus access to SharePoint online; but no Lync.

- ▶ A special plan for educational institutions is available that provides various feature options for both staff and students.

Organizations select a plan or choose different plans for different users based on their needs; the service is charged on a per-user per-month subscription basis. I have seen organizations use a form of the E plan for the primary workers in the main office, and the K plan for people out in the field or in manufacturing plants who only need basic functionality. The P plan is great for small businesses or individuals, as it provides the full back-office suite functionality for $6 per month per user.

I'm not going to describe the specific functionality of Office 365; simply put, it offers web versions of Office, Exchange, Lync, and SharePoint hosted for you. All the normal connectivity methods are available, such as web access and ActiveSync access to your mail, SharePoint access through the browser, Windows Phone and Office applications, and Lync using the normal client. Even though Office 365 is a shared infrastructure, your organization has its own address book, calendar sharing, and data security. The environment completely segregates different organizations so it seems as if you have your very own complete Exchange, Lync, and SharePoint

▶ I have a two-user subscription for myself and my wife as part of a new business venture.

▶ Even advanced usage scenarios, such as integration with Exchange from System Center Service Manager, work with Office 365 using the version 2 Exchange connector for System Center Service Manager.

implementation. Figure 14-5 shows the base SharePoint site on which I've not yet done any configuration. Notice that I have full use of all SharePoint features available for my organization to collaborate with.

IDENTITY MANAGEMENT WITH OFFICE 365

Office 365 is run on a shared infrastructure that is not part of your Active Directory (AD) environment. This means users potentially have to maintain multiple identities. There are ways to avoid requiring users to remember separate credentials for the Office 365 services and on-premise services.

The most seamless option is to implement Active Directory Federated Services (ADFS) 2.0 to create an identity federation between your organization and Office 365, along with the Office 365 AD Synchronization tool, which enables users to log on to Office 365 using their local AD credentials. While this requires a bit more work during the initial setup, the ease of use will pay off with fewer help-desk tickets and password reset requests.

If federation via ADFS to Office 365 is not possible, you can still use the AD Synchronization tool to populate the Global Address List in Office 365 with your users' identities. However, in this case, the password from a user's local AD account will not be synchronized to Office 365, which requires a separate password, although this can be made almost transparent to the user with one of the following methods.

▶ You can deploy the Microsoft Online Services Sign-In Assistant to each Office 365 user's desktop; the Assistant will "remember" the credentials needed to sign in to Office 365, avoiding the need for the user to sign in separately for each service or to maintain an additional identity specifically for Office 365. The tool also configures any local Office products to work properly with Office 365.

▶ Another option is to export user credentials from the local environment to a CSV file, then perform a bulk import into Office 365. This has the disadvantage of being a manual process, but it still may be suitable in organizations where users are not frequently provisioned and de-provisioned and you just need to perform an initial population of the Office 365 environment with your employee credentials.

▶ Finally, you can just manually add and remove users one at a time via the Office 365 administration interface, but this option is practical only for very small environments.

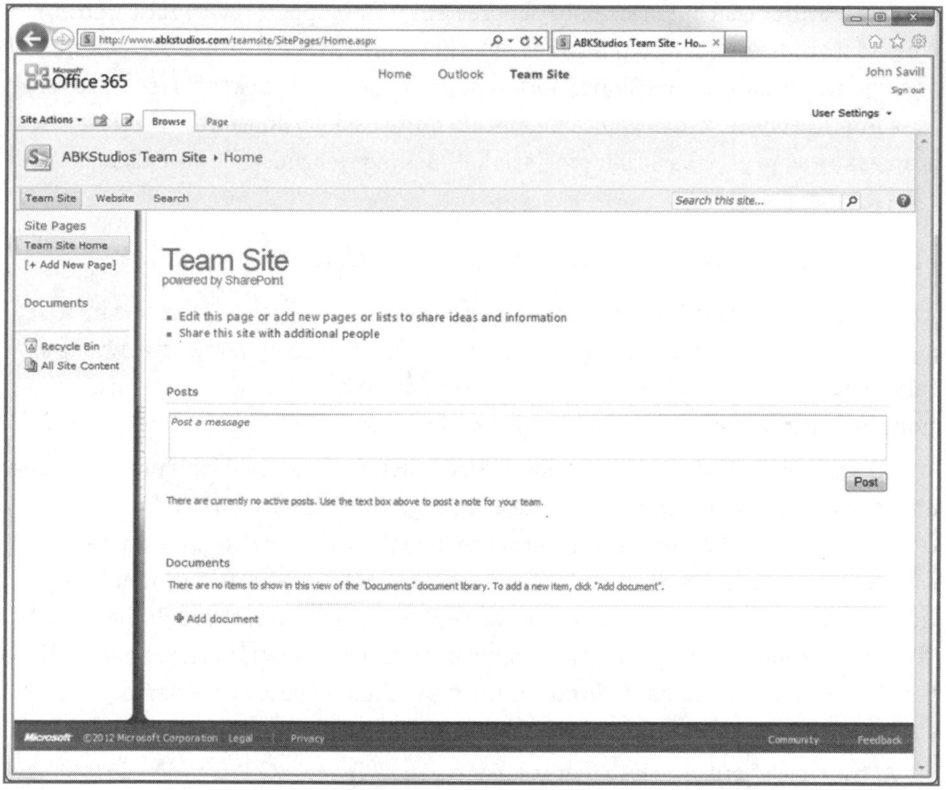

FIGURE 14-5: The basic Office 365 SharePoint home page, which you can customize. You can even manage your public website via the Website option.

Although understanding which products are hosted by Office 365 is simple—that is, Office, Exchange, Lync, and SharePoint—it is important to realize what a huge advantage this can be. Most organizations struggle with managing enterprise-class Exchange, Lync, and SharePoint implementations, in particular. It is extremely challenging and expensive to keep up with maintenance and patching, upgrading to the latest versions, performing regular backups and tuning exercises, and ensuring site-level resiliency. With Office 365, all that is done for you; you just configure the users who should have the services and you are done.

Some organizations use a hybrid approach. Corporate users might use an on-premise Exchange infrastructure while other workers could be provisioned in Office 365; and it is possible to connect the on-premise and off-premise Office 365 to give the appearance of a single infrastructure through a number of Exchange to Office 365 connectors.

One feature small businesses may appreciate is the support for a public website. While only those users in your business who have subscribed to Office 365 can share documents online through SharePoint, that component includes tools for you to create a public website, which you can maintain quite easily using a web interface. This is an easy way to get a basic but professional-looking web presence quickly.

Managing Desktops with Windows Intune

Windows Intune is a fairly new offering, first introduced early in 2011; it had its first major update in October 2011 and is targeting a six-month update cycle. Windows Intune can be thought of as desktop management in the cloud, an off-premise solution similar to System Center Configuration Manager (SCCM).

Like any other SaaS solution, no local infrastructure is required for Windows Intune and it carries a per-machine per-month cost. Organizations access Windows Intune through a website that displays full desktop inventory information (hardware and software), patch deployment status, and malware definition information. In addition, you can initiate operations, such as deploying software, through the website. The only change required locally is deployment of the Windows Intune client to all desktops you plan to manage. Windows Intune includes a customer-specific certificate to ensure that communications between the client and service are secure.

At the time of writing, the client is supported on Windows XP Professional SP2 and Windows XP SP3; Windows Vista Enterprise, Ultimate, or Business; and Windows 7 Enterprise, Ultimate, or Professional. Windows Intune capabilities include the following:

▶ Supporting both 32-bit and 64-bit systems

▶ Managing and deploying updates, including both Microsoft and non-Microsoft updates

▶ Monitoring desktops, registering alerts, and generating notifications based on alert filters—for example, five machines generating an alert within a configured amount of time

▶ Deploying software after uploading applications to Windows Intune

▶ Providing remote assistance

▶ Reporting hardware and software inventory

▶ Managing both Microsoft and non-Microsoft licenses

▶ Providing malware protection using technology based on Forefront Endpoint Protection

▶ Managing security policies, including policy conflict notification

▶ Remember Windows Azure's CDN component? Windows Intune uses the Windows Azure CDN for storage and delivery of software being deployed.

- ▶ Executing remote tasks focused on malware actions and machine restarts, as shown in Figure 14-6

- ▶ Enabling management from "anywhere" using Silverlight web-based administration console to provide a rich user experience

- ▶ Providing read-only administrator access to the web interface, which is useful for training purposes and help-desk users

- ▶ Windows Enterprise Edition rights, included with an additional step-up price, and access to Microsoft Desktop Optimization Pack

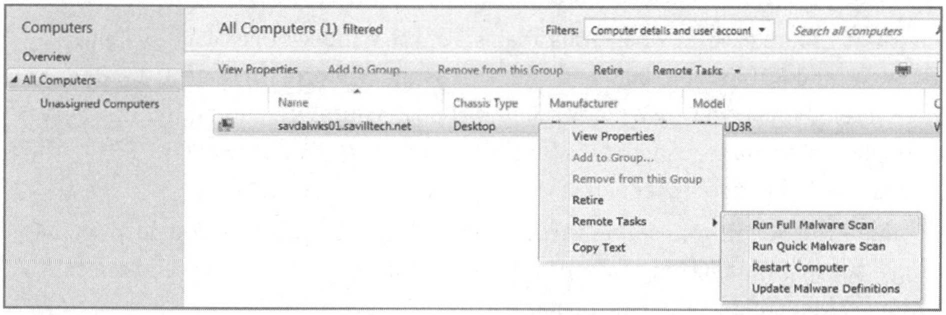

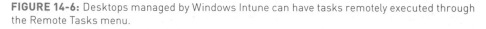

FIGURE 14-6: Desktops managed by Windows Intune can have tasks remotely executed through the Remote Tasks menu.

Windows Intune does not support server operating systems, nor can it perform operating system deployments. On-premise solutions, such as SCCM, provide a much richer set of capabilities, although Windows Intune certainly gains great functionality with each update. What I have seen in the industry is that system administrators are using on-premise solutions, such as SCCM, for corporate machines but employing Windows Intune for remote users, contract employees, and lightly managed or non-domain-joined machines, including machines that are acquired through a merger or acquisition.

> ▶ Although it isn't there yet, the end goal is for Windows Intune to have feature parity with an on-premise SCCM solution, and even surpass it.

> ▶ Windows Intune would be a great option on the CEO's home machine that you are frequently asked to fix!

> **TIP** When I talk about deployment from Windows Intune, I often get asked, "Won't every client download the same piece of software from the Internet every time I set up a software deployment?" This is a valid concern. If you are using Windows Intune to deploy Office to 1,000 machines in your corporate headquarters, you don't want Office downloaded 1,000 times.
>
> The key here is to exploit the caching capabilities of network acceleration solutions that can cache the content downloaded by the first user, making it available to all the other users. If you plan to use Windows Intune to deploy software to a lot of users at a number of different locations, consider installing an on-premise web-caching solution, such as Microsoft Forefront Threat Management Gateway (TMG).

Analyzing Server Usage with System Center Advisor

System Center Advisor (SCA) is another cloud-based solution that helps you monitor your servers and alerts you to problems. It does not patch or resolve problems; rather it collects information from servers in your environment through its agent, which is installed on each SCA-monitored server.

You designate one or more servers that have Internet connectivity as SCA gateways, which gather the data and send it daily to Microsoft's SCA cloud service. The service analyzes the uploaded information, using a knowledge base maintained by Microsoft, and issues alerts and recommendations back to your customer portal.

In its first release, SCA performs analysis of the Windows operating system, AD, Hyper-V, and SQL Server 2008/2008 R2; this scope will grow in the future. Operating systems supported are Windows Server 2008 and later (including Hyper-V Server 2008 R2). The only requirement is for the Microsoft .NET Framework 3.5 SP1 feature to be installed on the server before the agent can be installed.

Enabling SCA in your server infrastructure is a basic process. You download a single setup program that contains the gateway and agent plus a certificate that uniquely identifies your organization.

To deploy, first install the gateway and optionally the agent on a server to enable communication with the System Center Advisor cloud service, and then deploy the agent to the additional servers that should be monitored. Within 24 hours the servers will be visible in the System Center Advisor web portal (http://www.systemcenteradvisor.com), which uses Silverlight to give a rich graphical interface but requires a web browser that supports Silverlight.

Once System Center Advisor is deployed, any issues—such as missing patches and configuration problems—for which best practices are not being adhered to are displayed in your web interface, along with potential solutions. The Advisor also tracks the history of configuration changes on monitored servers.

A basic view of a limited test environment I deployed is shown in Figure 14-7, which depicts the overview screen that provides information about the general health of your environment.

Whereas Windows Intune can be seen as a cloud version of SCCM, SCA is not a cloud version of System Center Operations Manager (SCOM). Although SCA does some very basic monitoring, its main purpose is to identify any configuration issues in your environment and offer guidance on how to adhere to best practices. Despite its name, SCA is not actually part of System Center, but rather a benefit included as part of Software Assurance (SA) for the supported products to help customers validate their installations.

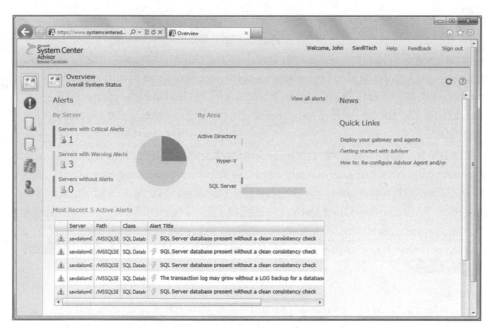

FIGURE 14-7: The System Center Advisor web interface offers a good view of the health of the monitored servers.

SUMMARY

This chapter described some of the main public cloud solutions that Microsoft offers, in particular those related to the infrastructure stack. However, many other high-profile offerings are available. For example, in the Customer Relationship Management arena, there is Microsoft Dynamics CRM Online, an SaaS version of Microsoft's Dynamics solution, which is a power tool to help manage sales, marketing, and customer service operations.

The use of public cloud solutions is a very interesting shift. When you look at the evolution of the computing platform, you can see the shift from traditional data-centers using physical servers for each operating system to virtualized operating systems. Today another shift is under way—from virtualized systems to the private cloud, which focuses more on the application and service than the operating system. The vision for tomorrow is the public cloud, and I hope this chapter has demonstrated that the functionality is certainly available right now. However, one more step is required to complete a move to the public cloud: trust!

When I talk to organizations about the shift to the public cloud, the objections are generally not about technology or capability. Most organizations acknowledge that public solutions have more capability, resiliency, and scalability than anything they could implement on-premise. Additionally, because of economies of scale, using a cloud service is likely to be cheaper than hosting an on-premise solution. So why isn't everything in the cloud? To quote many of my clients, "You want me to store my customer data and emails on a server Microsoft owns? No thanks." Many people just don't trust the public cloud. These concerns are fundamentally about privacy and security.

In reality, however, Microsoft has security, backed up by extensive audits performed by external companies, that surpasses anything most companies could hope to implement. It is just going to take time for organizations to get comfortable with the idea of storing their data in the cloud, but I think we will get there eventually. David Chappell, a well-known expert in public cloud technologies, made a great point about trust that I think sums up why we will see more workloads on the public cloud in the future:

> If you had told me 30 years ago that most of our products would be manufactured in communist China, I would have laughed at you, but we have grown to trust in the quality of that manufacturer (forgiving the odd lead paint incident).
>
> —David Chappell

▶ I don't believe everything will end up in the cloud. Due to regulatory or other factors, some workloads or data will always be on-premise, but certainly more will shift to the cloud in the future.

CHAPTER 15

The Best of the Rest of Windows Server 2012

Windows Server 2012 entered the beta phase as I was writing this book, and I have included as much information as possible regarding changes to Remote Desktop Services and Hyper-V to ensure readers have the latest information. Windows Server 2012 also features numerous other changes around core areas such as Active Directory, storage, high availability, manageability, and installation options, which affect an organization's entire infrastructure and virtualization initiatives. This bonus chapter looks at the key Windows Server 2012 features that will likely make a big difference to your organization and bring new benefits and capabilities. After reading through these features and considering the strong capabilities added to Hyper-V and Remote Desktop Services, it should become clear why Windows Server 2012 is considered to be the definitive *platform* for the cloud, rather than just an operating system or hypervisor. Windows Server 2012 can be used for clouds both public and private.

THE POWER OF MANY SERVERS, THE SIMPLICITY OF ONE—THE NEW TAO OF WINDOWS SERVER MANAGEMENT

I have stressed throughout this book that the private cloud represents a shift in focus from the operating system to the application, with the management infrastructure taking care of creating, maintaining, and retiring operating system instances as required. That said, there are still many situations in which management will be required for certain types of server—and that management has always been handled one server at a time. While system management tools like System Center do enable management of groups of servers, the native Windows tools have always focused on managing one server at a time. Most administrators today will connect to a server via RDP, launch Server Manager or Event Viewer, and perform management tasks remotely. Some will launch Server Manager locally and then remotely connect to another server, but the management is still one server operating system at a time because this is the only option possible with the tools. However, even when using Windows Server 2008 R2, which was the first version to support remote management of a server, some remote management actions were not possible.

Windows Server 2012 changes this old management model with a completely remodeled Server Manager tool that enables the management of multiple servers simultaneously in groups that the administrator creates. This management of many servers as if they were one—because one action can be initiated on all servers—has resulted in a mantra for Windows Server 2012:

The Power of Many Servers, The Simplicity of One

—Microsoft

Windows Server 2012 also provides far more flexibility in specifying the configuration level for a server. Windows Server 2008 introduced an installation mode called *Server Core*, which is a minimal installation of the Windows Server operating system with no graphical shell, no management tools, no .NET, and no PowerShell, and was designed to run certain Windows Server roles such as Active Directory Domain Controller, Hyper-V, and File Server. The goal behind Server Core was to have an operating system with fewer components, excluding those not required for many server roles, which in turn reduced the number of patches needed, possible vulnerabilities, and the number of reboots required associated with patches. There was also a small reduction in resource overhead. The problem with Server Core was that it was very hard to manage; it could not be managed remotely with Server Manager, so users largely ignored it. Windows Server 2008 R2 was an improvement, with remote management via Server Manager and PowerShell support, but the irrevocability of the choice at installation time made using Server Core a scary choice, and it is still avoided by most IT organizations. Windows Server 2012 has eliminated this model, making the graphic shell and management tools into options that can be added and removed like any other feature. This makes it easy to switch a server from being at Server Core level to a Full Server with a graphical interface. This flexible "configuration level" is a capability covered in much more detail in this chapter.

Looking at Server Manager

The new Start screen in Windows 8 client is also in Windows Server 2012. However, when you first log on to a new Windows Server 2012 server, you are logged on to the desktop, not the Start screen, and the new Server Manager will launch. Server Manager is also pinned to the taskbar by default, making it easy to access without having to go to the Start screen.

▶ You can pin the top tools you use to the taskbar of a server by starting the application, right-clicking on its taskbar icon, and selecting "Pin this program to taskbar."

You will see the use of Server Core stressed again in the next section: The default and recommended configuration mode for a Windows Server 2012 installation is Server Core, which means no local graphical interface or management tools. Since the early days of Windows Server, there has been a way to install and run the management tools on a Windows client and manage Windows servers remotely. First there was the administration tools pack, adminpak.msi, for managing Windows 2000 and Windows 2003 servers from Windows 2000 and Windows XP client computers. For Windows Server 2008 and Windows Server 2008 R2, there was a Remote Server Administration Tools (RSAT) download for managing them from Windows Vista and Windows 7, respectively. Each time a server needed management, the corresponding client OS had to be used—managing Windows Server 2003 required a Windows XP client, managing Windows Server 2008 required a Windows Vista client, and managing Windows Server 2008 R2 required a Windows 7 client. The Windows Server 2008 R2 RSAT included Server Manager for the first time, providing a remote management capability. Although all these tools were available, they were not frequently used. Administrators would primarily connect to a server via RDP and then manage each machine locally. Because Windows Server 2012 shifts to a "Server Core first" mentality, managing locally is no longer an option (unless you want to perform all the management via PowerShell). The preferred approach for managing Windows Server 2012 is to install the Windows Server 2012 RSAT on a Windows 8 client and perform all management remotely.

▶ The Windows Server 2012 Remote Server Administration Tools (RSAT) will only install on a Windows 8 client. If you do not wish to use a Windows 8 client, then configure a Windows Server 2012 instance, enable the RSAT feature, and perform remote management from that box.

▶ I recommend adding Server Manager to the taskbar on your Windows 8 client for easy access, as Server Manager is the tool you'll use 90 percent of the time.

Once the Windows Server 2012 RSAT has been downloaded and installed on a Windows 8 client, the next step is to enable the specific management tools for use on the Windows 8 client. Installing the RSAT only makes the feature available. Open the Programs and Features control panel applet on the Windows 8 client and select the Turn Windows feature on or off link, as shown in Figure 15-1. Scroll down to Remote Server Administration Tools and enable the administration tools for the various roles and features, in addition to Server Manager itself, which appears at the bottom of the figure. Once enabled, the administrative tools are available in the Administrative Tools group on the Start screen.

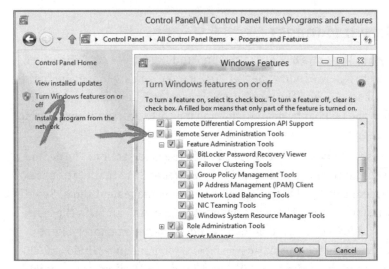

FIGURE 15-1: To enable the Windows Server 2012 administrative tools on a Windows 8 client, use the Programs and Features control panel applet.

▶ For Windows Server 2012, remote management is enabled by default, providing remote management from Server Manager without any configuration being required. Remote desktop connectivity via RDP must still be manually enabled.

Whether you are running Server Manager locally on a server or from a Windows 8 client, the interface is the almost exactly the same, with the same capabilities to add servers and create groups that match the logical grouping you want to manage. There is one difference between Server Manager running locally on Windows Server 2012 and running remotely. Figure 15-2 shows Server Manager running locally on a Windows Server 2012 installation. In the navigation pane, notice the Local Server page, which when selected shows a Properties tile for the local server within the content area, in addition to tiles for Events, Services, Best Practices Analyzer, Performance, and Roles and Features. With the exception of the Properties tile, all the tiles are also available when looking at remote servers. The Properties tile provides easy access to standard configuration items such as server name, domain membership, remote management and access, and IP address configuration.

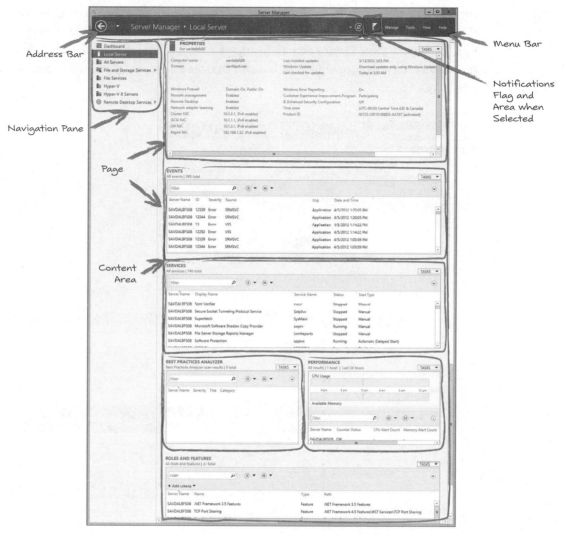

Address Bar

Navigation Pane

Page

Content Area

Menu Bar

Notifications Flag and Area when Selected

FIGURE 15-2: The Local Server page in the navigation pane includes the Properties tile, which enables the configuration of local server settings that cannot be remotely configured through Server Manager.

Figure 15-3 shows the Dashboard view of Server Manager. The Dashboard provides a fast overview of the overall health of all the servers and groups of servers defined within the Server Manager instance. Thumbnails for each group are displayed, with problem areas highlighted in red. In this case, there are issues for the Hyper-V 8 servers, which are also reflected in the All Servers group; the Dashboard thumbnails show a categorization of the issues, such as Services or Manageability. Selecting one of the highlighted areas opens a detailed view of the problem; here the Services Detail shows a stopped service, which can then be resolved across all the affected servers by selecting the Start Service action. In other words, Server Manager not only shows the state of all the managed servers, but also enables management and resolution of problems.

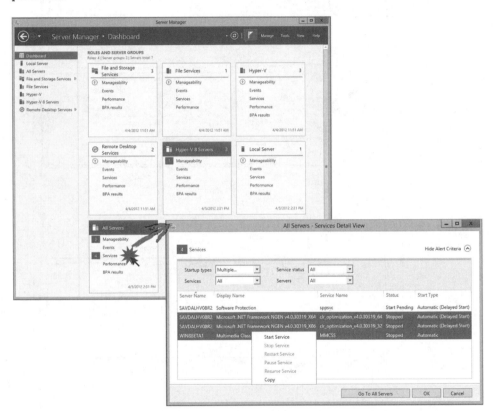

FIGURE 15-3: The Dashboard view, with the Services Detail view for All Servers, which you can open by selecting the red Services area on the thumbnail

> ▶ Server Manager also provides role and feature management of a VHD that has Windows Server 2012 installed. No associated VM is necessary. This is very useful for preparing new operating system environments.

Additional servers are easily added to Server Manager through the Add Servers action from the Manage menu, and through the same Manage menu you can create a Server Group and add or remove roles and features from any server that Server Manager is managing. You can open a server group from the navigation pane, select a particular server, and see details about that server—that is, the Events, Services, Performance, Best Practice Adherence, and Roles and Features tiles shown in Figure 15-2, giving you access to the most important information and basic management actions.

Additionally, management of file services and storage is possible, including full management of volumes and storage spaces, which is covered in more detail later in this chapter. Remote Desktop Services is also fully managed using Server Manager.

Other management tools that are needed for other Windows Server roles and features can be launched from the Tools menu of Server Manager, and these tools can also be used for remote servers and services. Unfortunately, space does not allow complete coverage of all the useful features of Server Manager, which provides an excellent way both to manage many servers as if they were one and to get quick, accessible insight into the health of your environment. For a quick tour of Server Manager, see the video at `http://www.savilltech.com/videos/win8svrmgrpeek/win8svrmgrpeek.wmv`.

USING WINDOWS SERVER 2012 SERVER MANAGER WITH WINDOWS SERVER 2008 AND WINDOWS SERVER 2008 R2

One great capability of the Windows Server 2012 Server Manager tool is that it can be used to manage Windows Server 2008 and Windows Server 2008 R2 operating systems. Enabling remote management by the Windows Server 2012 Server Manager requires installation of the Windows Management Framework (WMF) 3.0 feature, a download from Microsoft that requires you to have .NET Framework 4.0 pre-installed. Once WMF is installed, the server can be added to Windows Server 2012 Server Manager and managed like a Windows Server 2012 OS. The only limitation is that roles and features cannot be remotely managed, which is possible with remote Windows Server 2012 installations.

Understanding Configuration Levels

When Windows Server 2012 is installed, you have the option to install the server as a Server Core installation or a Server with a GUI. However, as explained earlier, this distinction is no longer fixed, although Server Core is now the default installation option for a new Windows Server 2012 installation.

You can easily move a server between Server Core, Server with a GUI, and some additional levels with a single command and a reboot. Figure 15-4 shows the four configuration levels for a Windows Server 2012 installation. Each configuration level is attained by adding a feature component on top of the previous components.

▶ Previous versions of Windows call this a Full installation. The name change reflects Server Core's ability to function as a Full Server platform; it merely lacks a graphical interface and local graphical management tools.

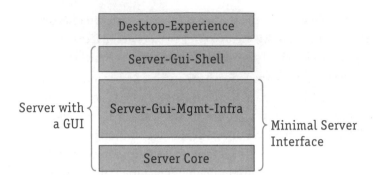

FIGURE 15-4: The four configuration levels for Windows Server 2012 and the features that determine each level

▶ Many Windows Server features also run on Server Core, such as BitLocker, Failover Clustering, Network Load Balancing, WINS, Multipath I/O, and Backup.

At the base of Windows Server 2012 is Server Core, which is the core operating system and services required for the operating system to function. Server Core includes portions of the .NET Framework to enable full PowerShell capabilities. Many roles and features can run on Server Core, and newly added Server Core–compatible features in Windows Server 2012 are Windows Software Update Services (WSUS), Active Directory Rights Management Services (AD RMS), Routing and Remote Access Services (RRAS), Remote Desktop Services Connection Broker, Virtualization Host, and Licensing Server. These are in addition to all the roles that can already run on Server Core, such as Active Directory Certificate Services (AD CS), Active Directory Domain Services (AD DS), Dynamic Host Configuration Protocol (DHCP) server, Domain Name Services (DNS) server, Hyper-V, File and Print Services (including File Server Resource Manager), Streaming Media Services, and Web Server. While originally the Server Core configuration level was targeted only at Windows Server roles, with Windows Server 2012, it is expected that more server applications will run on Server Core, including new versions of SQL Server. A server at the Server Core configuration level uses the command prompt as its shell.

Additional features (under User Interface and Infrastructure) are then added or removed for the other configuration levels, which have different capabilities. The following three configuration levels are available beyond Server Core:

▶ To programmatically check what configuration level a server is using, use WMI or look at the registry key HKLM\SOFTWARE\ Microsoft\Windows NT\CurrentVersion\ Server\ServerLevels, where you can find values for each level.

▶ **Minimal Server Interface:** Enabled with the addition of the Server-GUI-Mgmt-Infra feature. This level provides the Microsoft Management Console and therefore many management tools, Server Manager, and some control panel applets—but no Explorer or Internet Explorer. Of all the levels, this is the largest increment in terms of disk space. This mode allows rich local management without enabling a full graphical shell. Some server applications that might not run on Server Core may run on this configuration level, depending on their dependencies. If an application depends on libraries that are part of the shell or Internet Explorer, they will not be available and the application will fail. The Minimal Server Interface level can be considered a halfway interface stage, offering many of the benefits of Server Core while maintaining ease of use for products or applications not ready for pure Server Core because of the availability of local management tools. Minimal Server Interface still uses the command prompt as its shell.

▶ **Server with a GUI:** Enabled with addition of the feature Server-GUI-Shell on top of Server-GUI-Mgmt-Infra, this includes Explorer and Internet Explorer and associated files. This is a traditional Full Server installation, providing a full graphical shell. All server applications that are supported on Windows Server 2012 should run at this configuration level.

▶ **Desktop Experience:** Adds support for Metro applications, Media Player, and premium graphical features like themes. This would typically not be installed on a server operating system, as it should not be required—although the Exchange Unified Messaging role requires the codecs in the Desktop Experience feature. That's the only valid use I know of unless you want to use the server OS as your desktop operating system.

Moving between the configuration levels is very simple using Server Manager, PowerShell, or the command line. Figure 15-5 shows Server Manager's Remove features wizard. By unselecting features from the User Interfaces and Infrastructure group, you change the configuration level of the server. An example would be unselecting Server Graphical Shell, which is the Server-GUI-Shell feature; doing so would change the server to the Minimal Server Interface level after a reboot.

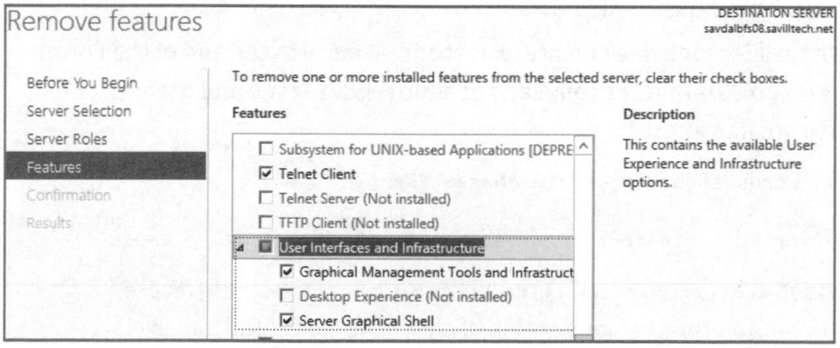

FIGURE 15-5: Unselect User Interface and Infrastructure features to change the configuration level of a server.

To change the configuration with PowerShell, use the `Install-WindowsFeature` and `Uninstall-WindowsFeature` PowerShell cmdlets to add or remove the User Interface and Infrastructure features, respectively. For example, to move from Server with a GUI to Server Core, just remove Server-GUI-Mgmt-Infra (which also removes Server-GUI-Shell because Server-GUI-Shell is dependent on Server-GUI-Mgmt-Infra):

```
Uninstall-WindowsFeature Server-Gui-Mgmt-Infra -Restart
```

To make a Server Core a Full Server with a GUI, use the following:

```
Install-WindowsFeature Server-Gui-Mgmt-Infra,Server-Gui-Shell -Restart
```

Likewise, DISM (Deployment Image Servicing and Management) can be used at the command prompt, but the feature names are slightly different, as shown in the following example from Full Server with GUI to Server Core:

```
Dism /online /disable-feature /featurename:ServerCore-FullServer
```

From Server Core to Full Server with GUI:

```
Dism /online /enable-feature /featurename:ServerCore-FullServer
        /featurename:Server-Gui-Shell /featurename:Server-Gui-Mgmt
```

When Windows Server is installed, all the role and feature files are stored in the winsxs folder. This is generally fine, because consuming a couple of gigabytes of disk space makes sense for the convenience of being able to easily add roles and features that are fully patched without having to insert installation media. However, Windows Server 2012 lets you remove components from the file system, thereby shrinking the disk footprint of Windows Server 2012. If a previously removed role or feature is later needed but the binaries no longer exist on the file system, the server can download the required files from the Microsoft Windows Update service or be pointed to another Windows Server 2012 server or the Windows Server 2012 installation media.

To remove the files for a role or feature, just add `-Remove` to the end of the PowerShell `Uninstall-WindowsFeature` command or add `/remove` at the end of the DISM `/disable-feature` command:

```
Uninstall-WindowsFeature <FeatureName> -Remove
```

```
Dism /online /disable-feature /featurename:<FeatureName> /remove
```

See the video at `http://www.savilltech.com/videos/win8configlevels/win8configlevels.wmv` for a demonstration of changing configuration levels.

▶ Remember: This should only be performed if you are trying to reduce the disk footprint for a server. Don't use it as a default, as it causes more work and network traffic when roles and features are added later.

EXPLORING THE CORE INFRASTRUCTURE SERVICE ENHANCEMENTS

For many organizations, Windows Server 2012 means a hugely improved version of Hyper-V, but it offers much more than that, and in this section you learn about some of the other features that make it a great cloud platform for many different use cases, including multi-tenant environments. The material presented here is by no means exhaustive, but rather an overview of the best parts at a very high level.

Active Directory

Active Directory has become the directory service standard for many of today's organizations and is a requirement for almost every Microsoft service and many third-party services. First introduced in Windows 2000, the now renamed *Active Directory Domain Services (ADDS)* has evolved from strength to strength, providing robust authentication and authorization capabilities in addition to a very powerful directory service. One of its weaknesses has been its complexity in terms of implementation, upgrade, and using some features. For example, upgrading ADDS prior to Windows Server 2012 meant running multiple domain and forest preparations on different domain controllers with different accounts. Great features were added to ADDS—such as fine-grained password policies that enabled defining and assigning different account settings, like password requirements and lockout settings, at a user-group level instead of the whole domain, and the recycle bin, which allowed deleted objects to easily be restored—but no graphical interface was provided to use these features. Windows Server 2012 fixes this deficiency.

For one thing, upgrade and implementation of ADDS is now much simpler. The entire domain controller promotion process, dcpromo, was essentially scrapped and rewritten as a deployment wizard, removing the need to manually run various preparation processes on different domain controllers with different accounts. Providing your account has the right privileges, you can now run a domain upgrade from one machine, accessing the domain controllers remotely.

Active Directory Administrative Center (ADAC) has been a useful addition since Windows Server 2008 R2, adding a graphical management interface for fine-grained password policies and the recycle bin, as shown in Figure 15-6. Notice at the bottom that ADAC implements everything via PowerShell commands; the graphical interface just fronts the PowerShell. As each command is performed, the PowerShell is listed in

▶ Fine-grained password policies required the use of the very unfriendly ADSIEdit tool to create and use policies, and PowerShell had to be used to restore a deleted object from the recycle bin. Not popular!

▶ When running the dcpromo command, the default now is to create a new domain controller in an existing domain, which is a lot more logical, rather than create a new forest.

▶ This is very
useful to help
determine the
PowerShell needed
to perform Active
Directory actions.
Perform tasks
once in the GUI
and then reuse
the PowerShell in
your own scripts.

the PowerShell history window. It's possible to start a task, perform your configurations (such as creating a user, setting properties, adding to groups), and then select End Task. Once you do that, all the PowerShell commands needed to do that task are available in the PowerShell history window and can be copied as a single block of script.

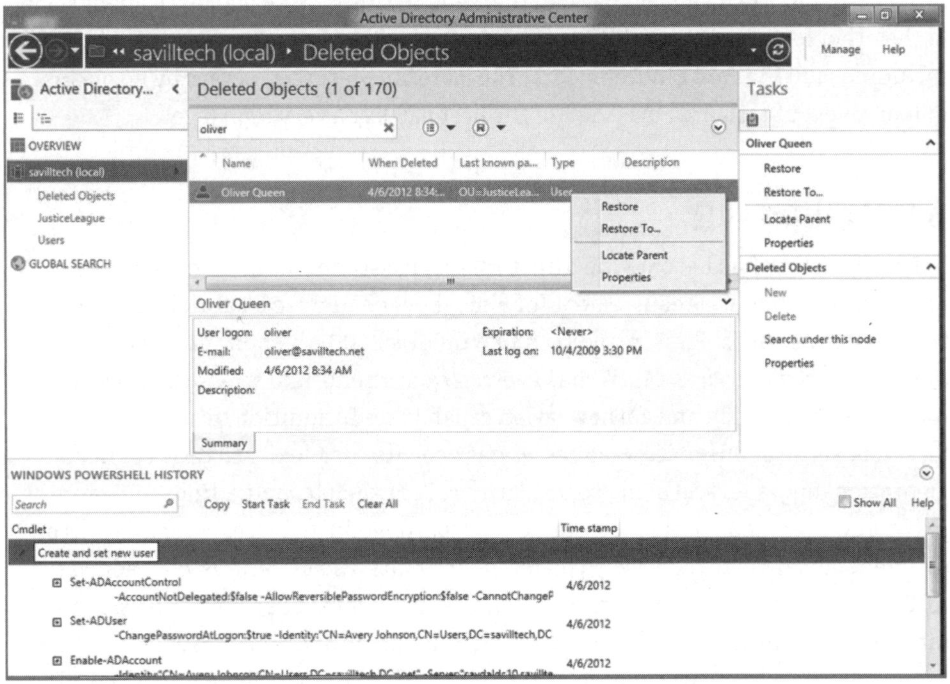

FIGURE 15-6: To perform an easy recovery, navigate to the Deleted Objects node and right-click on the deleted object.

▶ Remember
that a snapshot
is a point-in-time
capture of a
virtual machine's
state, including
disk, memory, and
device.

Another big change in ADDS is that AD is now virtualization-safe. Prior to Active Directory running on Windows Server 2012 Hyper-V, there was a huge problem using snapshots with domain controllers. Active Directory is a multi-master distributed database whose integrity depends on reliable replication of changes. Accordingly, transactions are labeled with a timestamp from a logical clock, whose value must monotonically increase. Active Directory uses an Update Sequence Number (USN), which is incremented locally for each transaction on the Directory; updates are applied in order of the USN. In addition, each time a new object is created, AD assigns it a globally unique identifier (Security ID) by incrementing a Relative ID (RID) value and appending to the domain's ID. If a snapshot is restored on a controller, its database will roll back, along with its values of USN and RID. Subsequent changes will reuse USN values, creating apparently duplicate transactions. The original server will have lost some updates in the restore, while remote servers may reject some subsequent fresh updates because they have already processed those USNs. For example, look at Figure 15-7. Imagine you have a domain controller and that at USN 2 a snapshot is created, and then the DC continues using USNs and the corresponding RIDs up to number 6 for created users. Then, an administrator applies the snapshot created, which puts the domain controller back to USN number 2. The domain controller has no clue its IDs have been put back in time, so it carries on back at USN number 2, creating objects with the same Security IDs, causing problems with security, and the domain controller will no longer replicate correctly with the rest of the domain. Known as *divergence*, this is a serious problem for organizations and one of the biggest causes of Active Directory issues for Microsoft customers. Even though many articles caution against using snapshots with domain controllers, it still happens.

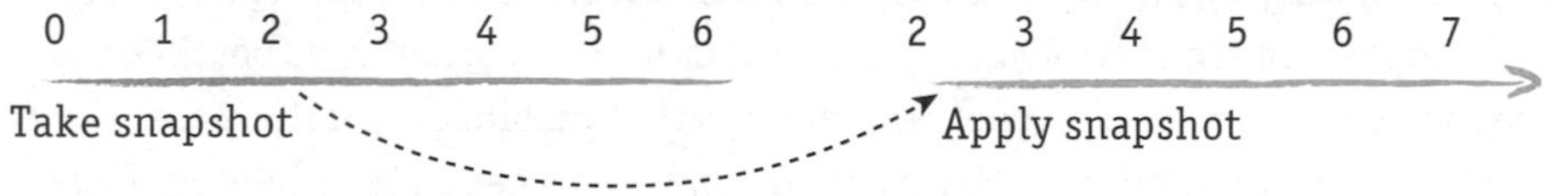

```
0   1   2   3   4   5   6       2   3   4   5   6   7
```

Take snapshot   Apply snapshot

FIGURE 15-7. Update Sequence Number problems when applying a snapshot to a domain controller because of USN reuse

Windows Server 2012 eliminates this issue through the use of a VM-GenerationID, which is provided by the Hyper-V hypervisor. This VM-GenerationID is changed whenever something happens to a virtual machine that affects its point in time, such as applying a snapshot or duplicating a virtual machine. Active Directory stores the VM-GenerationID in the AD database, and each time an operation is performed, such as creating or changing an object, the VM-GenerationID stored in the AD database is compared against the VM-GenerationID provided by the hypervisor. If the VM-GenerationIDs do not match, it means something has happened to the VM in logical time, and at this point the Active Directory service suspends all database transactions to protect the Directory and performs the following actions:

▸ Discards the RID pool (RIDs are allocated in batches to each DC by the RID master server, so this will force the DC to request a new pool).

▸ Resets the invocationID, which identifies the database instance on that DC. Transactions are actually identified by the invocationID with USN appended, so if the invocationID is reset, subsequent transactions will be uniquely identified irrespective of the USN value, ensuring there are no replication problems with other domain controllers.

▸ Reasserts the initial synchronization (INITSYNC) requirement for Flexible Single Master of Operations (FSMO), which are special domain controller roles, which, if the domain controller is an operations master, forces it to update itself from any other domain controller that holds a copy of the partition in which the FSMO role is maintained. This reapplies any master database changes that were lost in applying the snapshot.

These actions enable the domain controller to continue functioning without any risk to ongoing replication or security ID duplication. Today VM-GenerationID is generated only by Windows Server 2012 Hyper-V, but Microsoft has shared the specification with vendors such as VMware and Citrix, so hopefully in the future this virtualization-safe technology for Windows Server 2012 domain controllers will be available on other hypervisors.

Windows Server 2012 introduced another capability that uses VM-GenerationID, and that is cloning a Windows Server 2012 domain controller. By creating a special XML file on the domain controller to be cloned, DCCloneConfig.xml, it is possible to create copies of a domain controller; and through the combination of the presence of a DCCloneConfig.xml file and the new VM-GenerationID generated when the VM is duplicated, the domain controller will initiate a cloning process. Like the AD-safe process, it resets the invocationID, invalidates its RID pool, and then dumps any FSMO roles it may have.

Group Policy

Windows Server 2012 introduces many new capabilities, and new capabilities mean new requirements to manage and configure them. As expected, Group Policy includes many new settings to manage all the Windows Server 2012 capabilities, but there are other changes to Group Policy that, like Active Directory, make Group Policy management, troubleshooting, and reporting much easier. The biggest change is the consolidation of tools. Previously, Group Policy required many different tools and locations for management and troubleshooting: gpupdate, Group Policy Management Console (GPMC), Event Viewer, Trace files, GPLogView, and GPOTool. In Windows Server 2012, tools are now consolidated into the GPMC, and the overall capabilities of the GPMC have been extended.

Using the GPMC, you can now check the overall health of Group Policy on a per-domain basis. This is not a health check of Active Directory; it is a check for problems related to synchronicity between the Group Policy information stored in Active Directory and the information stored in the file system and replicated by SYSVOL. The console displays any potential problems that might require attention.

▶ Although snapshots are now supported for domain controllers, they are *not* a replacement for regular backups, which are still recommended.

▶ This is a very powerful technology that can completely change how organizations think about new domain controllers. With one good DC for each domain, an entire environment can be created quickly in disaster recovery situations.

▶ An identified issue does not always indicate a problem, only that the situation should be checked. Active Directory and SYSVOL use different replication technologies and schedules, so they may become out of sync.

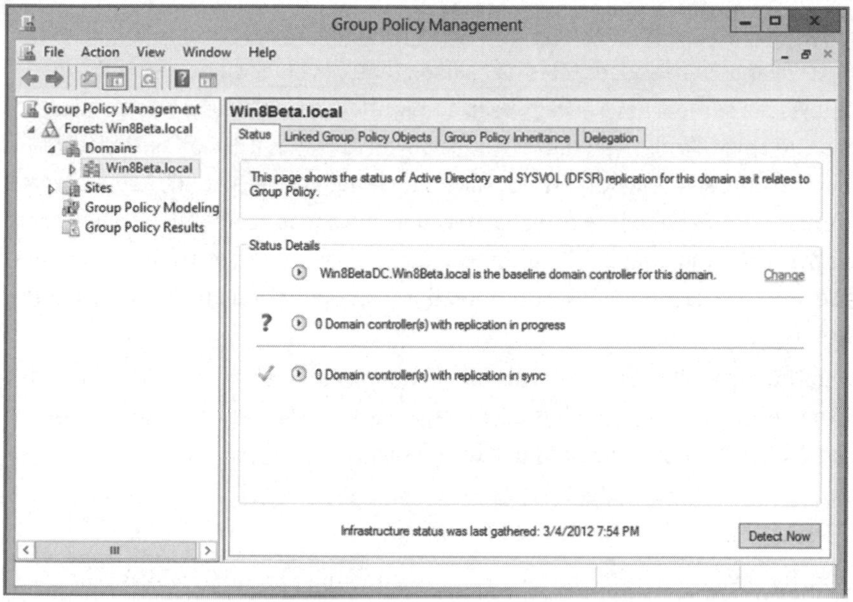

FIGURE 15-8: The basic Group Policy health view in the new GPMC

Another new feature in the GPMC is the capability to select an organizational unit and force a Group Policy update to all included machines. This is accomplished through a remote scheduled task. For more granularity, such as only updating specific machines, use the PowerShell Invoke-GPUpdate cmdlet.

Networking

As described in Chapter 8, network virtualization is a major addition to Windows Server 2012, enabling virtual networks to be defined that are abstracted from the physical network fabric. This enables virtual machines running on Hyper-V servers in different datacenters, and even spread between on-premise and hosted cloud solutions, to behave as though they are on a single subnet.

Another networking improvement is a new failover architecture for Dynamic Host Configuration Protocol (DHCP), which provides a critical service for most infrastructures, allocating IP addresses to hosts. Previously, making DHCP a highly available service has always been troublesome and involved using a cluster or splitting a DHCP scope across multiple servers. The new architecture enables failover partner relationships to be defined between Windows Server 2012 servers, enabling servers to act as hot standbys for each other. If one DHCP server is unavailable, clients can renew their leases through the other DHCP server.

Using New File System Capabilities

The File System and File Services roles have also greatly evolved in Windows Server 2012. Windows file servers have always been thought of as somewhere to store Word documents and PowerPoint files, rather than a powerful capability for use by other services such as Hyper-V and SQL Server; that is no longer the case in Windows Server 2102. The entire approach to how directly attached storage is used is also completely changed, now providing a capability akin to a mini storage area network using pure Windows Server 2012 technologies, including data deduplication and thin provisioning of volumes.

In the following sections, I cover the major changes in File Services. This includes new ways to use locally attached physical storage, new File System options, and optimizations to security management and maintenance.

STORAGE SPACES

Storage is fairly static and has to be micro-managed using normal Windows storage techniques. Dynamic disks can be used to create various RAID configurations, such as disk striping (RAID 0), disk mirroring (RAID 1), and striping with parity (RAID 5); and volumes can be shrunk and grown in newer versions of Windows Server. However, the administrator has to manually specify which physical disks are used for various volumes, and when problems occur the administrator must manually resolve them.

Storage Spaces, a new feature available in both the Windows Server 2012 and Windows 8 client SKUs, enables a completely new way to think about and administer storage. With Storage Spaces, the physical disks that provide the underlying storage of data are completely abstracted from the process of requesting new volumes, now known as spaces; and any actions required to restore data redundancy in the event of a disk failure are performed automatically by the Storage Spaces technology, provided that sufficient physical disks are available.

The first step is to create a *storage pool*, which is a selection of one or more physical disks that are combined for use by the Storage Spaces technology. Supported disk types in a storage pool are USB, SATA, and SAS-connected disks. These disks, often referred to as just a bunch of disks (JBOD), are standard disks with no hardware high availability such as RAID behind the scenes. Using USB-connected drives is a very useful capability for desktop systems, while servers focus on SATA and SAS-connected drives. In addition, shared SAS is fully supported, which means you could use a disk enclosure that is then connected to a number of hosts in a cluster, and the Storage Spaces created on those shared SAS drives would be available to all nodes in the cluster and could be used as part of Cluster Shared Volumes.

If an external disk enclosure is used, Storage Spaces supports the SES protocol, which enables failure indications on the external storage, such as a bad disk LED if Storage Spaces detects a problem with a physical disk. You can also use other technologies, such as BitLocker, with Storage Spaces. When a new storage pool is created, the disks added to it will disappear from the Disk Management tool, as they are now virtualized and used exclusively by Storage Spaces technology. The disks' state can be viewed through the Storage Pools view within File and Storage Services in Server Manager (on servers), or using the Storage Spaces control panel applet (on Windows 8 clients). PowerShell can also be used to query the state of Storage Spaces. This section focuses on using Storage Spaces on the server with Server Manager and PowerShell.

To create a storage pool, perform the following steps:

1. Start Server Manager and open File and Storage Services. Select the target server from the Servers tab and then select the Storage Pools tab, which shows information about existing storage pools, and disks on the system that could be used in a storage pool but are not currently hosting any volumes. These unused disks are shown in a primordial storage pool, as they are the building blocks from which storage pools and spaces can be created.

2. From the Storage Pools Tasks menu, select New Storage Pool..., which launches the New Storage Pool wizard.

3. Enter a name for the new storage pool and an optional description and click Next.

4. On the next screen, select which available physical disks should be added to the new pool and their allocation. By default, this is Data Store, to be used as part of virtual disks created, but it can also be reserved for Hot Spare purposes for use when a disk fails. Click Next when you are done.

5. When the confirmation is displayed, click Create to complete creation of the new storage pool.

Now that a storage pool is available, the next step is to create a storage space within it, which can contain volumes for use by the operating system. Storage Spaces introduces a feature that was previously only available using external storage solutions such as SANs and NAS devices: the capability to thinly provision storage. When creating a storage space, you have two options: fixed, which means all the storage space is allocated at creation time; or thin, which means space is taken from the pool as needed. Using a thinly provisioned disk enables the creation of a storage space much larger than the actual storage available. This does not mean you can store more data in the thinly provisioned disk than is allocated to the pool, but typically volumes fill up gradually over time.

▶ If disk deduplication is enabled, you can store more data on the disk than indicated, depending on the number of duplicate blocks.

For example, you might create an 8TB thin disk that initially has only 2TB of physical storage allocated, but as the amount of data increases and approaches 2TB, you would add another 1TB of physical storage to the pool by adding more disks. As it approaches 3TB, you add another 1TB of storage by adding more disks, and so on. As long as you add physical disks before the current physical pool is filled, there is no issue. When a storage pool reaches 70 percent of its capacity, an alert is generated, giving you enough time to add the required storage. This notification is handled via Server Manager and an event log. When you create a storage space, you only need to know which storage pool it should be created in—no knowledge of the physical disks is required or even openly available, as the point of Storage Spaces is the abstraction of this detail in order to enable you to just create storage spaces as needed.

▶ You can change the threshold using PowerShell.

Before walking through the process to create a storage space, note that the following set of instructions refers to virtual disks, not storage spaces. That's because the Storage Pools page, shown in Figure 15-9, supports many different storage subsystems, of which Storage Spaces is just one. It is possible for other third-party storage subsystems to register within the Storage Pools page and allocate storage, such as LUNs or RAID disks, which are not storage spaces. Therefore, virtual disk is a generic term for a created disk, whereas storage space is the name of a disk created using the Storage Spaces storage subsystem. Here are the steps to create a storage space . . . I mean virtual disk.

1. Select a storage pool in which to create a new virtual disk. In the Virtual Disks section, select the New Virtual Disk... task.

2. Confirm that the correct server and storage pool are selected in the Storage Pool selection page of the wizard and click Next.

3. Provide a name and optional description for the new virtual disk being created and then click Next.

4. Select the storage layout, which can be simple (no data redundancy and data striped over many disks); mirrored, which has data duplicated to additional disks; or parity, which spreads data over multiple disks like simple, but adds parity data so that no data is lost in the event of a disk loss. Prior to Storage Spaces, these layouts would have been referred to as RAID 0, RAID 1, and RAID 5, respectively, but that nomenclature is not used with Storage Space layouts due to differences in implementation. Click Next when you are done.

5. Select the provisioning type, Thin or Fixed, and then click Next.

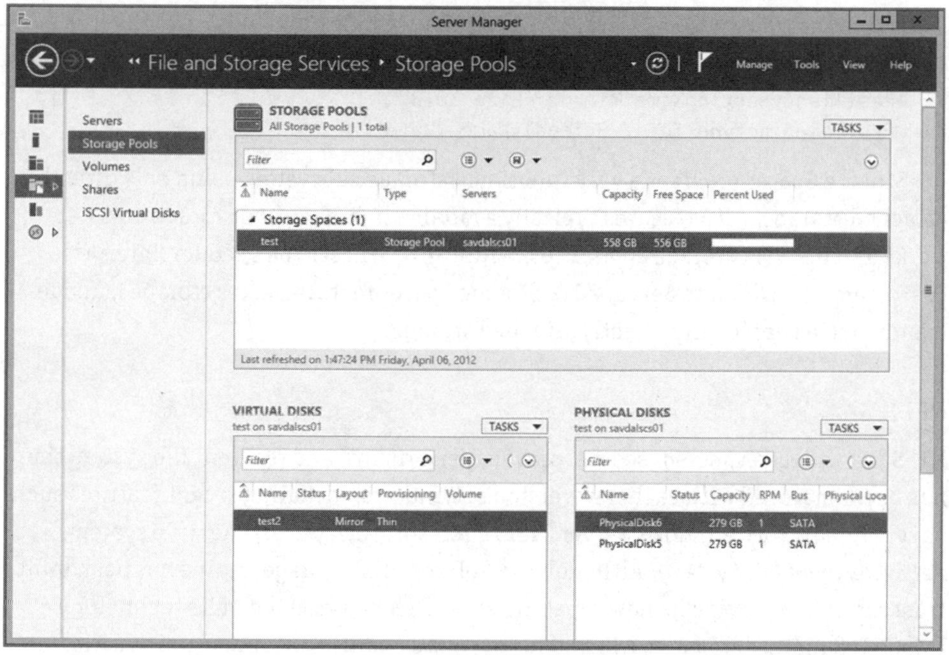

FIGURE 15-9: Storage Spaces configuration is performed through the Storage Pools page within Server Manager.

6. Specify a size. Remember that if Thin is selected, a size larger than the physical free space available can be selected. Click Next.

7. When the confirmation of options is displayed, verify and click Create.

Once the virtual disk is created it will be available within Server Manager and the Disk Management MMC to create volumes and be formatted with a file system. You can see the actual amount of space used from a pool in Server Manager; on a client, you can check the Storage Spaces control panel applet. For a video of this process, see http://www.savilltech.com/videos/StorageSpaces/StorageSpaces5minutedemo.wmv.

Storage Spaces can also be completely managed using PowerShell. For example, to create a new storage pool using three physical disks you could use the following commands:

```
$phyDisks = Get-PhysicalDisk
$storSub = Get-StorageSubSystem
New-StoragePool -FriendlyName "Stuff" -PhysicalDisks $phyDisks[0] , `
$phyDisks[1], $phyDisks[2] -
-StorageSubSystemFriendlyName $storSub.FriendlyName
```

To create a virtual disk in the pool, you could use the following:

```
New-VirtualDisk -StoragePoolFriendlyName "Stuff" `
-ResiliencySettingName Mirror -Size 10TB `
-Provisioningtype Thin -FriendlyName "Data1"
```

Storage Spaces provides a very functional storage subsystem using only directly attached storage, with features typically available in higher-end storage area networks and network storage appliances. While SANs will still be used for Enterprise customers, the Windows Server 2012 Storage Spaces feature makes storage management much easier for any directly attached storage.

REFS

NTFS is a widely respected, secure, proven, performant, and resilient file system that has been improved with each new version of Windows, including recent features such as self-repair. With Windows Server 2102, Microsoft introduces a new file system, *ReFS (Resilient File System)*. Although the ReFS on-disk storage engine has been built from scratch to provide its new capabilities, ReFS borrows much of its technology from NTFS for its file system API and file system semantics, so it maintains a high degree of compatibility with NTFS. Key goals for ReFS are as follows:

- ▶ Maintain a high degree of compatibility with a subset of NTFS features that are widely adopted, while deprecating others that provide limited value at the cost of system complexity and increased footprint.

- ▶ Verify and auto-correct data. Data can become corrupted for a number of reasons and therefore must be verified and, when possible, corrected automatically. Metadata must not be written in place to avoid the possibility of "torn writes." This auto-correction should include detecting bit-level failures on the disk.

- ▶ Optimize for extreme scale.

- ▶ Never take the file system offline. Assume that in the event of corruptions, it is advantageous to isolate the fault while allowing access to the rest of the volume.

- ▶ Provide a full end-to-end resiliency architecture when used in conjunction with the Storage Spaces feature.

▶ *ReFS cannot be used as a boot or system drive.*

Because ReFS is new to Windows Server 2012, most installations will use NTFS. The use of ReFS will likely be limited to specific scenarios or tests; however, expect subsequent versions of Windows Server to replace NTFS with ReFS as the default file system.

DYNAMIC ACCESS CONTROL

Typically, users are given access to data by virtue of being included in a group, created in Active Directory, that is given access to that data—usually a file. Whenever a user needs access to certain data, he or she must be added to the right group. Using this approach to data access, most of the time organizations end up with a huge number of groups to manage because a different group has to be created for all the different variations of access. In many cases the information needed to determine file access is located in the user's account detail as an attribute: their department, their level, their role, or their location. For example, a group for HR is created when HR is listed as the user's department attribute—a process that wastes time and slows down resource access.

Dynamic Access Control enables the creation of policies that allow claim definitions and policies to be created. File servers use these policies once data has been classified either manually or using File Classification Infrastructure. When users try to access a file on a file server that has been configured as subject to the defined policies, the policies are checked automatically and users are given access based on the classification of the data, the properties of the user, the properties of the device they are using, and how they authenticated. This approach obviates the need to manually set access on the file server for every file and hundreds of AD groups. A very simplistic example would be classifying some data as "Top Secret" and then allowing access to that data only to users whose AD title attribute starts with "00." This method enables business requirements to map directly to policies.

Dynamic Access Control is initially daunting because it changes the way you think about maintaining access to data, but it provides great benefits in terms of simplifying permissions and flexibility. I had a client whose file resource previously required 100,000 access control entries to control access, which had to be fully auditable and compliant with a standard. With Dynamic Access Control, those 100,000 entries were replaced with a single policy.

▶ File Classification Infrastructure (FCI) allows metadata to be stored with a file that is set by an application, or FCI can perform scans of content and automatically classify files based on the content found.

CHKDSK

When using Windows Server–based File Services, and specifically NTFS with very large volumes containing many files, when something goes wrong the chkdsk utility needs to be run to repair the problem. Chkdsk is very good at its job but it's a long, laborious task, as it must check the entire disk's content looking for problems. The repair operations actually take almost no time at all; we're talking seconds on a very limited number of files. The problem is that chkdsk takes the volume offline, making the content unavailable while it performs the health check and repair. That's why, along with considerations about performing a data restore in a disaster, NTFS volumes are often kept below a certain size.

Windows Server 2012 separates the chkdsk fix process into two parts. The first part scans the disk and data looking for problems. If a problem is found, it is flagged, but not fixed. The volume remains online while the long search and checking process is performed. When the scan is completed, if there are problems that need to be fixed, chkdsk is run again in a spotfix mode, which takes the volume offline as it performs the repairs on the flagged problems. Because the scan process has been separated from the actual repair process, the volume is only offline for seconds instead of hours or days. Using the chkdsk command, the two instructions needed are as follows (note that the first command takes a long time because it's performing the scan, but there is no impact on volume availability, whereas the second command will take the volume offline or trigger at the next reboot):

```
Chkdsk /scan J:
Chkdsk /spotfix J:
```

Using PowerShell, the commands are as follows:

```
Repair-Volume -Scan J
Repair-Volume -SpotFix J
```

If Cluster Shared Volumes are used there is actually zero downtime when running the spotfix action. That's because CSV adds another level of indirection between the disk and how it is accessed, and CSV can actually pause I/O operations for around 20 seconds. This means when the spotfix action is run, CSV just pauses I/O to the volume while it's taken offline and fixed; but as far as users of the CSV volume are concerned, there is just a slight delay in access and no actual offline action or loss of file handles, and so on. You can see a demonstration at http://www.savilltech.com/videos/StorageSpaces/ChkdskSpotfix3minutedemo.wmv.

DATA DEDUPLICATION

▶ Windows Storage Server has offered Single Instance Storage (SIS) for a number of versions. This new technology in Windows Server 2012 is more powerful and is available in all versions of Windows Server.

Many files often have content similar to other files, especially when looking at virtual hard disks, which have a very large percentage of duplicated content vis-à-vis other virtual hard disks that contain the same operating system. Windows Server 2012 data deduplication is a block-level, scheduled data deduplication process that scans for duplicate content between files and then performs an optimization to store the duplicated blocks once on disk, pointing all files (using reparse points) with the duplicate content to a single store of the optimized blocks, known as the *Chunk Store*. This search for duplicate blocks is scheduled to run at specific times; it is not a continuous real-time process.

To enable the data deduplication, first install the Data Deduplication role, which is part of File and Storage Services → File Services. Once installed, use the Volumes view within File and Storage Services in Server Manager to run the Configure Data Deduplication task. As shown in Figure 15-10, in addition to enabling data deduplication, you can also configure which files and folders should be excluded from disk deduplication, and quiet times when the data deduplication optimization scan process can be allowed to run with a normal priority, enabling higher throughput. Once data deduplication is enabled, it is possible to force an optimization pass immediately using the following PowerShell command, replacing D: with your volume:

```
PS C > Start-DedupJob D: -Type Optimization
```

► Although this is block level, it's still possible to exclude certain directories and file types, which is useful to ensure maximum performance for key files— although data deduplication has only a very negligible performance impact on access to the data.

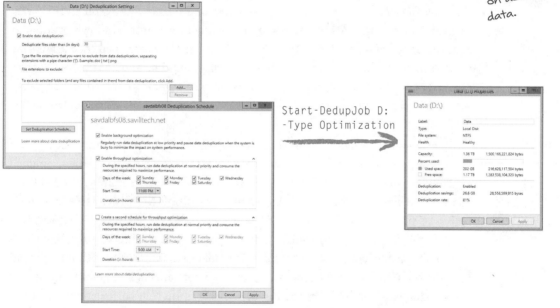

FIGURE 15-10: You enable data deduplication through Server Manager, and you can specify files that should not be optimized.

You can track in-progress data deduplication jobs by running the Get-DedupJob PowerShell cmdlet, which displays details about the jobs and their progress. For an overview of the savings that data deduplication is providing to a system, use the Get-DedupStatus PowerShell cmdlet:

```
PS C:\ > get-dedupstatus

SavedSpace   SavingsRate   OptimizedFiles   InPolicyFiles   Volume
----------   -----------   --------------   -------------   ------
107.63 GB    76 %          23               28              D:
```

If a volume with deduplicated data is connected to a Windows Server 2012 system without the Data Deduplication role installed or to any other operating system, then files that have been optimized with deduplication will not be readable. Files that were not optimized will be readable. Data Deduplication will not run on VHD files that are currently in use by a virtual machine, so it's most useful for VHDs that are being stored. Deduplication is supported only on NTFS, not ReFS, CSV, FAT volumes, or boot and system volumes. It should not be used on running SQL or Exchange servers, as their data is constantly changing; however, their backup volumes are good candidates for deduplication.

SMB 2.2

Server Message Block (SMB), also known as Common Internet File System (CIFS), was first introduced with LAN Manager and then made its way onto Windows, originally running on top of NetBEUI and then TCP/IP. SMB has therefore been the native Windows protocol of choice for remote file access for a long time and has evolved as the needs of remote file access have changed. Windows Server 2012 introduces SMB 2.2, which brings big changes to both the performance and the capabilities of the SMB protocol.

▶ The SMB performance improvements also apply when using the Windows Server 2012 NIC teaming technology.

The overall performance of SMB has been greatly improved, making access to data via SMB essentially equivalent to direct access to the storage. This has been enabled by a number of changes, including SMB Multichannel, which enables bandwidth aggregation across multiple TCP connections over multiple NICs if available for a single SMB session. Using multiple NICs and the new Receive Side Scaling (RSS) features enables multiple CPUs to be used for network processing. While a single processor core can typically handle the inbound traffic from a single 1GB NIC without any problems, when 10GB is used the processor becomes a bottleneck. RSS helps by spreading the workload over multiple processors. SMB Direct is another performance feature, aimed at top-end hardware. It uses a special type of network adapter that has remote direct memory access (RDMA) capability, and it can function at full speed with very low latency while using very little CPU. For server roles or applications such as Hyper-V or SQL Server, this enables a remote file server's performance to equal that of local storage.

High availability to file shares with Failover Clustering has also dramatically improved, with a new transparent failover capability that brings an active-active mode. Cluster Shared Volumes (CSV) were introduced in Windows Server 2008 R2 for the exclusive use of storing Hyper-V virtual machines. The benefit of CSV over traditional volumes is that a CSV volume can be concurrently accessed by all nodes in a cluster, whereas a normal volume can only be mounted on one node at a time. In

Windows Server 2012, CSV use has been extended to certain other types of file server workload, such as hosting SQL Server databases and virtual machines, which are accessed via a SMB share. By combining CSV with the new transparent failover file sharing server, applications using the transparent file share experience zero downtime if one of the cluster nodes fails, with only a very small I/O delay because handles are auto-recovered to the new node used by the server application. The same technology enables file shares to be moved between nodes in a cluster with no downtime to server applications. Beyond failover, the new SMB Scale-Out enables up to four file servers in a cluster to serve as a single logical file server namespace, all available for use at the same time for access to a single file share, which when combined with SMB Multichannel increases the bandwidth available between an SMB client and SMB server.

Increased use of SMB means more backup capabilities are needed, and Volume Shadow Copy Server (VSS) is now supported on remote file shares, enabling the creation of application-consistent shadow copies for server application data stored on a Windows Server 2012 file share. This is important if SQL Server has its database on a Windows Server 2012 file share, as an application-consistent backup is still critical.

ISCSI

While SMB is moving beyond document storage, with server applications leveraging its capabilities, many servers still want block-level access to data. iSCSI is a very widely used SAN connectivity protocol that is natively supported in both Windows Server 2012 and Windows 8 client. Because it runs over TCP/IP, no additional networking hardware is needed. An iSCSI software target, which is an optional component that turns a Windows Server 2008 R2 installation into an iSCSI server, is now available from http://www.microsoft.com/download/en/details.aspx?id=19867. Previously this feature was exclusively part of Windows Storage Server.

With Windows Server 2012, iSCSI is a built-in component of the operating system. The iSCSI Target Server must be installed through Server Manager and is part of the File and Storage Services → File Services role, as shown in Figure 15-11. Once the role is enabled, iSCSI virtual disks are configured through Server Manager. iSCSI targets in Windows Server 2012 are virtual hard disk (VHD) files, which by default are stored in the iSCSIVirtualDisk folder, but this path can be changed. A wizard walks you through the entire process of creating the VHD and creating a new iSCSI target that maps to the created VHD. The wizard also enables you to select a list of iSCSI initiators (clients) that are allowed to connect to the created iSCSI target. You can enter these manually or select them based on existing entries in the server's initiator cache. The Windows Server 2012 iSCSI target supports the RFC 3720 protocol level.

▶ When specifying the iSCSI target name, just put in a friendly name, such as busdisk5. The wizard takes care of creating the proper iSCSI format name, e.g., iqn.1991-05.com.microsoft:server-busdisk5-target. You can change it if you wish.

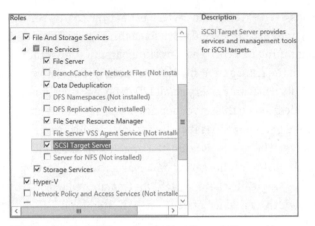

FIGURE 15-11: iSCSI can be enabled through Server Manager and is part of the File Services role.

SUMMARY

Ever since the release of Windows 2000 I have offered half-day seminars covering new features of the latest Microsoft operating system. When the Windows Server 2012 beta was released, I provided a four-hour online overview of its new features. However, I could only cover a fraction of what has been added because of the sheer scale of change and new functionality, all of which propels Windows Server to a true cloud platform. This chapter has touched on some of the features that are related to virtualization or have the biggest impact on it, but take some time to look at Windows Server 2012 and understand that in order to truly get the most out of its features, you may need to rethink how some management actions are performed. Taking that time up front will result in staggering benefits to long-term productivity.

This chapter covered some of the major areas that will affect your virtualization endeavors. Perhaps the biggest changes are around the new Storage Spaces feature, File System changes, and the new SMB capabilities that will be used heavily as your environment starts to use SMB file shares to store Hyper-V virtual machines without having to compromise performance or features. The new flexibility in the use of Server Core will enable servers to be easily configured initially and then reduced to the Server Core configuration level to reduce maintenance and patching specifically. This is especially useful for Hyper-V servers, but should be considered for all Windows Server 2012 installations.

Index

SAS (Secure Attention Sequence), 24

saved state backups, 273

SCA (System Center Advisor), 488–489

scalability

Client Hyper-V, 86

private cloud, 373–374

Windows Server 2012 Hyper-V, 282–284

SCCM. *See* System Center Configuration Manager

SCOM. *See* System Center Operations Manager

SCSM. *See* System Center Service Manager

SCVMM. *See* System Center Virtual Machine Manager

Search charm, 49, 54

Secondary Level Address Translation (SLAT), 88–89

Secure Attention Sequence (SAS), 24

security

NAP (Network Access Protection), 440–442

RSA SecurID, 434

Secure Attention Sequence (SAS), 24

sequencing, 101–103, 104–119

clean environment, creating, 105–107

customizing application components, 115–119

editing applications, 121–125

monitoring phase, 113–114

operating system versions, selecting, 116–118

Package Accelerators, 126–128

Q: drive, 101–102, 107–108, 111–114, 123, 137–140

updating applications, 126

sequencing engineer, 110–111

Server App-V, 361–365

Server Core, 492–493, 497–500

Server Management Licenses (Server ML), 380

Server Manager, Windows Server 2012, 492–500

Server Message Block (SMB), 87

Server ML (Server Management Licenses), 380

server sprawl, 9

Server Virtualization Validation Program (SVVP), 305

Server with a GUI level, 497–500

server-side infrastructure, App-V

full mode, 142–150

lightweight mode, 150–151

standalone mode, 141–142

Service Bus service, Windows Azure AppFabric, 480

Service Catalog, 385, 404–405

Service Manager. *See* System Center Service Manager

service packs, 26–27

Service Template Designer, 368–369

service templates, 365–369

System Center Virtual Machine Manager, 372–373, 400–401

System Center App Controller, 400–401

Service Template Designer, 368–369

services, creating, 366–369

session virtualization

RDP (Remote Desktop Protocol), 210–215

capabilities, 215–218

client uses, 212

RDC (Remote Desktop Client), 215–217

server uses, 211

session interactions, 211

RDS (Remote Desktop Services), 218–219

best practices, 233–234

components, 220–226

end-user experience, 231–232

management tools, 226–228

scenarios for, 229–231

sessions overview, 208–210

third-party solutions, 2, 236–238

VDI (Virtual Desktop infrastructure) and, 17–18, 208, 451–455

Settings charm, 49, 54, 56

SFT files, 120, 126

sftmime command, 140, 142, 145

sfttray.exe, 140